GLOBAL EDUCATION MONITORING REPORT 2019

Migration, displacement and education:

BUILDING BRIDGES, NOT WALLS

UNESCO Publishing

United Nations
Educational, Scientific and
Cultural Organization

The Education 2030 Incheon Declaration and Framework for Action specifies that the mandate of the *Global Education Monitoring Report* is to be 'the mechanism for monitoring and reporting on SDG 4 and on education in the other SDGs' with the responsibility to 'report on the implementation of national and international strategies to help hold all relevant partners to account for their commitments as part of the overall SDG follow-up and review'. It is prepared by an independent team hosted by UNESCO.

This publication can be referenced as: UNESCO. 2018. *Global Education Monitoring Report 2019: Migration, Displacement and Education – Building Bridges, not Walls*. Paris, UNESCO.

Second edition
Published in 2018 by the United Nations Educational, Scientific and Cultural Organization
7, Place de Fontenoy, 75352 Paris 07 SP, France

Graphic design by FHI 360
Layout by FHI 360

Cover photo: Rushdi Sarraj/UNRWA
Infographics by Housatonic Design Network

Cover photo caption: Palestine refugee students on their first day in UNRWA schools in the second semester, in Gaza.

Typeset by UNESCO
Printed on recycled, PEFC certified paper, with vegetable inks.

ISBN: 978-92-3-100283-0

This report and all related materials are available for download here: http://bit.ly/2019gemreport

Foreword

People have always moved from one place to another, some seeking better opportunities, some fleeing danger. These movements can have a great impact on education systems. The 2019 edition of the *Global Education Monitoring Report* is the first of its kind to explore these issues in-depth across all parts of the world.

The Report is timely, as the international community finalizes two important international pacts: the Global Compact for Safe, Orderly and Regular Migration, and the Global Compact on Refugees. These unprecedented agreements – coupled with the international education commitments encapsulated in the fourth United Nations Sustainable Development Goal (SDG) – highlight the need to address education for migrants and the displaced. This GEM Report is an essential reference for policy-makers responsible for fulfilling our ambitions.

Currently, laws and policies are failing migrant and refugee children by negating their rights and ignoring their needs. Migrants, refugees and internally displaced people are some of the most vulnerable people in the world, and include those living in slums, those moving with the seasons to eke out a living and children in detention. Yet they are often outright denied entry into the schools that provide them with a safe haven and the promise of a better future.

Ignoring the education of migrants squanders a great deal of human potential. Sometimes simple paperwork, lack of data or bureaucratic and uncoordinated systems mean many people fall through administrative cracks. Yet investing in the education of the highly talented and driven migrants and refugees can boost development and economic growth not only in host countries but also countries of origin.

Provision of education in itself is not sufficient. The school environment needs to adapt to and support the specific needs of those on the move. Placing immigrants and refugees in the same schools with host populations is an important starting point to building social cohesion. However, the way and the language in which lessons are taught, as well as discrimination, can drive them away.

Well-trained teachers are vital for ensuring the inclusion of immigrant and refugee pupils but they too need support in order to manage multilingual, multicultural classes, often including students with psychosocial needs.

A well-designed curriculum that promotes diversity, that provides critical skills and that challenges prejudices is also vital, and can have a positive ripple effect beyond the classroom walls. Sometimes textbooks include outdated depictions of migrations and undermine efforts towards inclusion. Many curricula are also not flexible enough to work around the lifestyles of those perpetually on the move.

Expanding provision and ensuring inclusion require investment, which many host countries cannot meet alone. Humanitarian aid is currently not meeting children's needs, as it is often limited and unpredictable. The new Education Cannot Wait fund is an important mechanism for reaching some of the most vulnerable.

The message of this Report is clear: Investing in the education of those on the move is the difference between laying a path to frustration and unrest, and laying a path to cohesion and peace.

Audrey Azoulay
Director-General of UNESCO

Foreword

The 2019 *Global Education Monitoring Report* has been brought together by a team of international migrants. Four of its members are children of refugees. They don't deny that people look at migration – and migrants – from different viewpoints. Their research demonstrates the extent to which education can help open up those perspectives and bring greater opportunities for all.

For migrants, refugees and host communities, there is the known and the unknown. All that some people know, however, is deprivation and the need to escape from it; they don't know whether there will be opportunity at the other end. In recipient communities, people may not know whether and how their new neighbours, wearing different clothes, having different customs, and speaking with a different accent, will change their lives.

Migration is characterized by both order and disorder. Societies often strive to manage population movements but nonetheless may face unpredictable inflows. Such movements may create new divisions, while others have demonstrably benefited both source and destination countries.

In migration flows, we see both will and coercion. Some people move proactively to work and study while others are forced to flee persecution and threats to their livelihoods. Recipient communities and politicians may argue interminably whether those who arrive are pushed or pushing, legal or illegal, a boon or a threat, or an asset or a burden.

There is both welcoming and rejection. Some people adjust to their new environment while others cannot. There are those who want to help and those who want to exclude.

Thus, around the world, we see migration and displacement stirring great passions. Yet there are decisions to make. Migration requires responses. We can raise barriers, or we can reach out to the other side – to build trust, to include, to reassure.

At the global level, the United Nations has worked to bring nations together around durable solutions to migration and displacement challenges. During the UN Summit on Refugees and Migrants in 2016, I called for investing in conflict prevention, mediation, good governance, the rule of law and inclusive economic growth. I also drew attention to the need for expanding access to basic services to migrants to tackle inequalities.

This Report takes that last point further by reminding us that providing education is not only a moral obligation of those in charge of it, but also is a practical solution to many of the ripples caused by moving populations. It must be, and should always have been, a key part of the response to migration and displacement – an idea whose time has come, as the texts of the two global compacts for migrants and refugees show.

For those denied education, marginalization and frustration may be the result. When taught wrongly, education may distort history and lead to misunderstanding.

But, as the Report shows us in the form of so many uplifting examples from Canada, Chad, Colombia, Ireland, Lebanon, the Philippines, Turkey and Uganda, education can also be a bridge. It can bring out the best in people, and lead to stereotypes, prejudices and discrimination being discarded for critical thinking, solidarity and openness. It can offer a helping hand to those who have suffered and a springboard to those who desperately need opportunity.

This Report points directly to a major challenge: How can teachers be supported to practise inclusion? It offers us fascinating insights into humanity and the age-old phenomenon of migration. I invite you to consider its recommendations and to act on them.

The Right Honourable Helen Clark
Chair of the GEM Report Advisory Board

Helen Clark

Acknowledgements

This report would not have been possible without the valuable contributions of numerous people and institutions. The *Global Education Monitoring Report* (GEM Report) team would like to acknowledge their support and thank them for their time and effort.

Invaluable input was provided by the GEM Report Advisory Board and its chairperson, Helen Clark. Special thanks also go to our engaged and committed funders, without whose financial support the GEM Report would not be possible.

We would like to acknowledge the role of UNESCO and its leadership. We are very grateful to many individuals, divisions and units at UNESCO headquarters, notably in the Education Sector and the Bureau for the Management of Support Services, for facilitating our daily work. The UNESCO Institute for Statistics (UIS) played a key role by providing access to its data through the UIS Data API and by ensuring methodological support. We would like to thank its director, Silvia Montoya, and her dedicated staff. Additional thanks go to colleagues at the International Institute for Educational Planning, UNESCO-UNEVOC and the UNESCO field office network.

The GEM Report team would like to thank the researchers who produced background papers informing the GEM Report's analyses: Benta Abuya, Mona Amer, Batjargal Batkhuyag, Kolleen Bouchane, Subramaniam Chandrasekhar, Sebastian Cherng, Mary Crock, Frédéric Docquier, Tungalag Dondogdulam, Sarah Dryden-Peterson, Galen Englund, Philippe Fargues, Martha Ferede, Ameena Ghaffar-Kucher, Sonia Gomez, Ulrike Hanemann, Mathieu Ichou, Daniel Owusu Kyereko, Mary Mendenhall, Renato Moreira Hadad, Hervé Nicolle, José Irineu Rangel Rigotti, Andrés Sandoval Hernández, Laura Allison Smith-Khan and Massimiliano Tani. Special thanks also to UNESCO's Charaf Ahmimed, Tina Magazzini, Debra Mwase and Akemi Yonemura for the research they provided.

We are grateful to several institutions and their research staff who also produced background papers: Deakin University (Zohid Askarov and Chris Doucouliagos), Demographics Australia (Aude Bernard, Martin Bell and Jim Cooper), Education Reform Initiative (Burcu Meltem Arık Akyuz, Didem Aksoy, Aysel Madra and Ertugrul Polat), Institute of International Education (Rajika Bhandari and Chelsea Robles), International Bureau of Education (Renato Opertti, Heidi Scherz, Giorgia Magni, Hyekyung Kang and Sumayyah Abuhamdieh), International Institute for Applied Systems Analysis (Guy Abel, Stephanie Bengtsson, Keri Hartman, Samir KC and Dilek Yildiz), International Organization for Migration (Sophie Nonnenmacher), Macquarie University (Salut Muhidin), Plan International (Kelsey Dalrymple), Right to Education Initiative, Shenzhen 21st Century Education Research Institute, UNICEF Innocenti Centre (Despina Karamperidou, Dominic Richardson and Juliana Zapata) and the University of Pennsylvania (Emily Hannum, Li-Chung Hu and Wensong Shen). Special thanks also to the Japan International Cooperation Agency, which coordinated the research work of Kazuo Kuroda, Miki Sugimura, Yuto Kitamura and Sarah Asada, Rie Mori, Mariko Shiohata, Tomoko Tokunaga and Hideki Maruyama.

Additional thanks go to numerous institutions that hosted consultations on the GEM Report's concept note, as well as the many individuals and organizations that provided input during the international consultation process. Thanks also to Francesca Borgonovi, Lucie Cerna and the team at the Organisation for Economic Co-operation and Development who co-organized and hosted the forum on data for research in education, migration and displacement as part of the Strength through Diversity project, and to its participants for their valuable contributions.

The following individuals provided valuable inputs and feedback at various stages of report development: Margherita Bacigalupo, Judit Barna, Ed Barnett, Nicole Comforto, Veronica De Nisi, Christoph Deuster, Monika Eicke, Md. Sajidul Islam, Tamara Keating, Ifigeneia Kokkali, Joan Lombardi, Katie Maeve Murphy, Joseph Nhan-O'Reilly, Susan Nicolai, Sylke Schnepf, Ann Scowcroft, Tom Slaymaker, Mari Ullmann and Hirokazu Yoshikawa.

A group of independent experts reviewed the draft of the GEM Report's thematic part and provided valuable feedback. For their input we thank Philippe De Vreyer, Sarah Dryden-Peterson, Martin Henry, Marie McAuliffe, Patricia Pol and Ita Sheehy.

The report was edited by Jessica Hutchings, whom we thank for her tireless work. Our thanks also go to Justine Doody for writing the summary.

We also wish to acknowledge those who worked tirelessly to support the production of the report, including Rebecca Brite, Erin Crum, Shannon Dyson, FHI 360, Kristen Garcia, Whitney Jackson, Aziza Mukhamedkhanova and Katherine Warminsky.

Many colleagues within and outside UNESCO were involved in the translation, design and production of the 2019 GEM Report and we would like to extend to them our deep appreciation for their support. Specific thanks go to Rooftop and Housatonic Design Network for their support to the development of the GEM Report's communication and outreach materials. Additional acknowledgements must be made to, among many others, Human Rights Watch, the International Labour Organization, the International Organization for Migration, the Refugee Trauma Initiative, Save the Children, Shutterstock, the Office of the United Nations High Commissioner for Refugees and the United Nations Relief and Works Agency for Palestine Refugees in the Near East for the use of their photos.

Finally, we would like to thank the short-term interns and consultants who provided much input to the GEM Report team: Sarah Barden, Huacong Liu, Clare O'Hagan, Amy Oloo, Benedetta Ruffini, Julieta Vera and Hajar Yassine.

The *Global Education Monitoring Report* team

Director: Manos Antoninis

Daniel April, Bilal Barakat, Madeleine Barry, Nicole Bella, Anna Cristina D'Addio, Glen Hertelendy, Sébastien Hine, Priyadarshani Joshi, Katarzyna Kubacka, Kate Linkins, Leila Loupis, Kassiani Lythrangomitis, Alasdair McWilliam, Anissa Mechtar, Claudine Mukizwa, Yuki Murakami, Carlos Alfonso Obregón Melgar, Judith Randrianatoavina, Kate Redman, Maria Rojnov, Anna Ewa Ruszkiewicz, Will Smith, Rosa Vidarte and Lema Zekrya.

The *Global Education Monitoring Report* is an independent annual publication. It is funded by a group of governments, multilateral agencies and private foundations, and facilitated and supported by UNESCO.

Australian Aid
Canada
Ministry for Foreign Affairs of Finland
République Française – Ministère de l'Europe et des Affaires Étrangères
Federal Ministry for Economic Cooperation and Development
William + Flora Hewlett Foundation
Irish Aid – Rialtas na hÉireann – Government of Ireland
mastercard foundation
Open Society Foundations
Norwegian Ministry of Foreign Affairs
Sida – Swedish International Development Cooperation Agency
Swiss Agency for Development and Cooperation SDC
UKaid from the British people
UNGEI United Nations Girls' Education Initiative
UNESCO – United Nations Educational, Scientific and Cultural Organization

For more information, please contact:
Global Education Monitoring Report team
UNESCO, 7, place de Fontenoy
75352 Paris 07 SP, France
Email: gemreport@unesco.org
Tel.: +33 1 45 68 07 41
www.unesco.org/gemreport

Any errors or omissions found subsequent to printing will be corrected in the online version at www.unesco.org/gemreport.

***Global Education Monitoring Report* series**

2019	*Migration, displacement and education: Building bridges, not walls*
2017/8	*Accountability in education: Meeting our commitments*
2016	*Education for people and planet: Creating sustainable futures for all*

***EFA Global Monitoring Report* series**

2015	*Education for All 2000–2015: Achievements and challenges*
2013/4	*Teaching and learning: Achieving quality for all*
2012	*Youth and skills: Putting education to work*
2011	*The hidden crisis: Armed conflict and education*
2010	*Reaching the marginalized*
2009	*Overcoming inequality: Why governance matters*
2008	*Education for All by 2015: Will we make it?*
2007	*Strong foundations: Early childhood care and education*
2006	*Literacy for life*
2005	*Education for All: The quality imperative*
2003/4	*Gender and Education for All: The leap to equality*
2002	*Education for All: Is the world on track?*

Contents

The references for the 2019 *Global Education Monitoring Report* can be downloaded at the following link: https://en.unesco.org/gem-report/sites/gem-report/files/2019_Report_References.pdf

List of figures, tables, and text boxes

FIGURES

TABLES

TEXT BOXES

#EducationOnTheMove
DISPLACEMENT
INTERNATIONAL MIGRATION
HIGHLY SKILLED PEOPLE
INTERNAL MIGRATION
FROM VILLAGES TO CITIES

Executive summary

Leave no one behind. This is among the most aspirational global commitments of the United Nations 2030 Agenda for Sustainable Development. Migration and displacement are two global challenges the agenda needs to address in achieving the 17 Sustainable Development Goals (SDGs), including SDG 4: 'Ensure inclusive and equitable quality education and promote lifelong learning opportunities for all'.

Migration and displacement interact with education in many ways. These links affect those who move, those who stay and those who host immigrants, refugees or other displaced populations. Internal migration mainly affects many rapidly urbanizing middle income countries, such as China, where more than one in three rural children are left behind by migrating parents. International migration mainly affects high income countries, where immigrants make up at least 15% of the student population in half of schools. It also affects sending countries: More than one in four witness at least one-fifth of their skilled nationals emigrating. Displacement mainly affects low income countries, which host 10% of the global population but 20% of the global refugee population, often in their most educationally deprived areas. More than half of those forcibly displaced are under age 18.

Migration and displacement affect education. They require systems to accommodate those who move and those left behind. Countries are challenged to fulfil the international commitment to respect the right to education for all. They must often act quickly, under severe constraints or even opposition from some constituencies. They need to address the needs of those cramming into slums, living nomadically or awaiting refugee status. Teachers have to deal with multilingual classrooms and traumas affecting displaced students. Qualifications and prior learning need to be recognized to make the most of migrants' and refugees' skills.

Education also affects migration and displacement. It is a major driver in the decision to migrate. Domestically, those with tertiary education are twice as likely to migrate as those with primary education; internationally, they are five times as likely. Education affects not only migrants' attitudes, aspirations and beliefs but also those of their hosts. Increased classroom diversity brings both challenges and opportunities to learn from other cultures and experiences. Appropriate education content can help citizens critically process information and promote cohesive societies; inappropriate content can spread negative, partial, exclusive or dismissive notions of immigrants and refugees.

COUNTRIES ARE INCLUDING IMMIGRANTS AND REFUGEES IN NATIONAL EDUCATION SYSTEMS

Governments have taken increasingly bold steps to assume education responsibilities previously provided for only in international agreements. In recent years, the world has moved towards including immigrants and refugees in national education systems. Exclusionary practices are being abandoned as a result of forward-looking decisions, political pragmatism and international solidarity. Countries party to the 2018 Global Compact for Safe, Orderly and Regular Migration and the Global Compact on Refugees, which extensively refer to education, recognize education as an opportunity.

Historically, assimilation was the norm in most high income countries hosting foreign workers in the post-war period. Among 21 high income countries, Australia and Canada had adopted multiculturalism in their curricula by 1980. By 2010, it had been adopted in Finland, Ireland, New Zealand and Sweden as well, and partly adopted in over two-thirds of the countries.

Historically, most governments also provided parallel education to refugees, but such systems usually lacked qualified teachers, examinations were not certifiable, and funding risked being cut at short notice. Rather than keeping the hope of return alive, parallel education during protracted displacement diminished the chance of a meaningful life in first countries of asylum. Today, however, countries such as Chad, the Islamic Republic of Iran and Turkey shoulder substantial costs to ensure that Sudanese, Afghan, Syrian and other refugees attend school alongside nationals. In the

2017 Djibouti Declaration on Regional Refugee Education, seven education ministers from eastern Africa committed to the inclusion of education for refugees and returnees into sector plans by 2020. Uganda has already fulfilled the promise.

Education for the internally displaced is vulnerable to intractable conflicts. Colombia, with the world's second-largest internally displaced population, suffers the continued operation of armed groups. Yet, for the past 15 years, it has taken measures to ensure displaced children are treated preferentially in terms of access to education.

Internal migration is also challenging inclusion in education. Rural migrant workers constitute 21% of the Chinese population following the largest wave of internal migration in recent history. Residence permit restrictions introduced in an attempt to control the flows led the majority of migrant children in cities including Beijing to attend unauthorized migrant schools of lower quality. Since 2006, the government has progressively revised the system, requiring local authorities to provide education to migrant children, abolishing public school fees for them and decoupling registered residence from access to education for migrants. In India, the 2009 Right to Education Act legally obliged local authorities to admit migrant children, while national guidelines recommend flexible admission, seasonal hostels, transport support, mobile education volunteers and improved coordination between states and districts.

MAJOR BARRIERS TO EDUCATION FOR IMMIGRANTS AND REFUGEES PERSIST

Immigrants may be nominally included but practically excluded. They may be kept in preparatory classes too long, for instance. In Austria's Styria state, children above age 15 not deemed ready for secondary school are not entitled to attend and, after assessment, are transferred to special courses. Some countries separate students with lower academic ability, often those with immigrant backgrounds, into less demanding tracks, which compromises subsequent opportunities. Moroccan and Turkish second-generation immigrant students in Amsterdam were five time as likely as natives to enter lower secondary vocational tracks at age 12. Tracking starts as young as age 10 in Germany. In addition, immigrants tend to be concentrated in specific neighbourhoods and in schools with lower academic standards and performance levels, which negatively affects their education achievement. Segregation is exacerbated when native students move to wealthier neighbourhoods or their families evade policies to maintain a diverse student body.

Barriers to immigrant education may persist despite efforts towards inclusion. In South Africa, education legislation guarantees the right to education for all children irrespective of migration or legal status, but immigration legislation prevents undocumented migrants from enrolling. School gatekeepers may insist on complete documentation, believing the law requires it, as with Central Asian immigrants in the Russian Federation. In the United States, anti-immigration raids led to surges in dropout among children of undocumented immigrants wary of deportation, whereas an earlier policy providing deportation protection had increased secondary school completion.

Immigrant children may advance relative to peers in home countries but lag behind peers in host countries. In the United States, children of immigrants from eight Latin American and Caribbean countries had 1.4 more years of education, on average, than those who had not emigrated. Yet their attainment and achievement often lagged behind those of host country peers. In the European Union, twice as many foreign-born youth as natives left school early in 2017. In 2015, in Organisation for Economic Co-operation and Development countries, first-generation immigrants were 32% less likely and second-generation immigrants 15% less likely than natives to attain basic proficiency in reading, mathematics and science. The point in the life cycle at which people ponder or undertake migration is a key determinant of their education investment, interruption, experience and outcomes. In the United States, 40% of Mexican immigrants who arrived at age 7 did not complete secondary school, compared with 70% of those who arrived at age 14.

Asylum-seeking children and youth are detained in many countries, often with limited or no access to education, including in Australia, Indonesia, Malaysia, Mexico, Nauru and Thailand. In Hungary, asylum-seeking families with children, and unaccompanied children above age 14, stay in one of two transit zones without access to education, except that provided by civil society organizations (CSOs), while their applications are processed.

The degree and evolution of refugee inclusion in national education vary across displacement contexts, affected by geography, history, resources and capacity. Concentration of refugees in remote camps, as in Kenya, may result in only partial inclusion and geographical separation. Resources can be a key constraint: Lebanon and Jordan, with the most refugees per capita, have adopted double-shift education, producing temporal separation. In several contexts, refugees continue to be educated in separate, non-formal community-based or private schools, the largest recent displacement of Rohingya fleeing Myanmar for Bangladesh being a prominent case. Such schools may be initiated and supported by international organizations or refugees and local communities themselves, and may or may not be certified. In Pakistan, the primary net enrolment rate of Afghan refugee girls was half that of boys and less than half the primary attendance rate for girls in Afghanistan.

Refugee education remains underfunded. Although the two main databases are inconclusive, this report estimates that US$800 million was spent on refugee education in 2016, split roughly equally between humanitarian and development aid. That is only about one-third of the most recently estimated funding gap. If the international community employed humanitarian aid only, the share to education would have to increase tenfold to meet refugees' education needs.

Improving refugee education funding requires bridging humanitarian and development aid in line with commitments in the New York Declaration for Refugees and Migrants. Implementation of the Comprehensive Refugee Response Framework since 2016 to operationalize these commitments in 15 countries is generating useful lessons, although the withdrawal of the United Republic of Tanzania has drawn attention to improvements still required. The Education Cannot Wait fund for emergencies, and its potential to mobilize new, predictable, multiyear funds, should support closer cooperation between humanitarian and development actors and the inclusion of refugees in national education systems.

EDUCATION IMPROVEMENTS CAN HELP MIGRANTS AND REFUGEES FULLY REALIZE THEIR POTENTIAL

Curricula and textbooks often include outdated depictions of migration and displacement, despite broad public support for change in some contexts: 81% of respondents in EU countries agreed school materials should cover ethnic diversity. By not addressing diversity in education, countries ignore its power to promote social inclusion and cohesion. A global analysis showed that social science textbook coverage of conflict prevention and resolution – e.g. discussion of domestic or international trials, truth commissions and economic reparations – was low at around 10% of texts in 2000–2011.

Teachers affected by migration and displacement are inadequately prepared to carry out the more complex tasks this entails, such as managing multilingual classrooms and helping children needing psychosocial support. In six European countries, half of teachers felt there was insufficient support to manage diversity in the classroom; in the Syrian Arab Republic, 73% of teachers surveyed had no training on providing children with psychosocial support. Teacher recruitment and management policies often react too slowly to emerging needs. Germany needs an additional 42,000 teachers and educators, Turkey needs 80,000 teachers and Uganda needs 7,000 primary teachers to teach all current refugees.

Schools with high immigrant and refugee populations need targeted resources to support struggling learners. Only a handful of high income countries explicitly consider migration status in school budgets. Other dimensions of disadvantage, including the neighbourhood deprivation and limited language proficiency often associated with these students, typically trigger higher per-student funding in schools with higher concentrations.

Adult migrant and refugee education needs are often neglected. Non-formal education programmes can be critical for strengthening a sense of belonging, and much rests on municipal initiatives. Literacy skills support social and intercultural communication and physical, social and economic well-being, but significant barriers limit access to and success in adult language programmes in some countries. A 2016 survey of asylum-seekers in Germany showed that 34% were literate in a Latin script, 51% were literate in another script and 15% were illiterate. Yet the latter were the least likely to attend a literacy or language course.

Financial literacy can protect migrants and help households make the most of remittances. Remittances increased education spending by over 35% in 18 countries in Africa and Asia and by over 50% in Latin America.

Reducing transaction costs to 3%, from the current global average of 7.1%, could provide an additional US$1 billion for education every year.

Recognition of qualifications and prior learning can ease entry into labour markets, especially concerning professional qualifications. If migrants and refugees lack access to employment that uses their skills, they are unlikely to develop them further. Existing mechanisms are often fragmented or too complex to meet immigrants' and refugees' needs and end up underutilized. Countries also must harmonize tertiary education standards and quality assurance mechanisms to recognize academic qualifications at the bilateral, regional or global level. Adopting the Global Convention on the Recognition of Higher Education Qualifications, expected in 2019, will be key.

The two new compacts on migrants and refugees recognize education's role and set objectives aligned with the global commitment to leave no one behind. This report makes seven **recommendations** that support implementation of the compacts:

- Protect the right to education of migrants and displaced people
- Include migrants and displaced people in national education systems
- Understand and plan for the education needs of migrants and displaced people
- Represent migration and displacement histories in education accurately to challenge prejudices
- Prepare teachers of migrants and refugees to address diversity and hardship
- Harness the potential of migrants and displaced people
- Support education needs of migrants and displaced people in humanitarian and development aid.

THE INTERNATIONAL COMMUNITY IS HONING ITS SDG 4 MONITORING TOOLS

SDG 4 not only sets an ambitious education agenda but also poses the challenge of monitoring targets that include multiple learning outcomes, inequality dimensions and curricular content. While some criticize the monitoring framework as too ambitious, its key role is to be formative, drawing countries' attention to core issues absent before 2015. It should trigger investment in robust national monitoring mechanisms of education equity, inclusion and quality. Several initiatives by countries, CSOs and multilateral institutions ensure the education sector is well placed to report at the first formal review of SDG 4 at the 2019 High-Level Political Forum. The following are a few highlights based on the most recent available data.

- **TARGET 4.1:**
  Primary and secondary education. Completion rates in 2013–2017, which can serve as a baseline for the SDG period, were 85% for primary, 73% for lower secondary and 49% for upper secondary education. This report proposes a new method to synthesize completion rate estimates from multiple sources. Progress has been made towards defining minimum proficiency in reading and mathematics. Regardless of the form this definition takes, results from selected middle income countries taking part in the Progress in International Reading Literacy Study in 2001–2016 show that progress will be slow. While the percentage of grade 4 students who met the low benchmark in 2015 varied from 22% in South Africa to 86% in Georgia, the average progress has been about one percentage point per year.

- **TARGET 4.2:**
  Early childhood. In 2017, about 70% of children participated in organized learning one year before the official primary school entry age. While consensus on a common measure of early childhood development may prove hard to reach, it is important for countries to invest in strong national systems for monitoring cognitive, linguistic, physical and social-emotional development.

- **TARGET 4.3:**
Technical, vocational, tertiary and adult education. The tertiary gross enrolment ratio reached 38% in 2017. There is growing consensus on ensuring that the global indicator captures all adult education opportunities, work or non-work related, formal or non-formal.

- **TARGET 4.4:**
Skills for work. Only a handful of upper middle income countries report on information and communications technology skills, but the available data indicate just one in three adults employs elementary skills, such as copying and pasting or attaching files to emails.

- **TARGET 4.5:**
Equity. In many low and middle income countries, rural students have half the chance – and often much less – of completing upper secondary school, compared with urban peers. Estimates may need to be reassessed in view of new definitions of urban areas being developed by the international community.

- **TARGET 4.6:**
Literacy and numeracy. The latest global literacy rate estimate, 86%, indicates 750 million adults are illiterate. There are almost 40% more illiterates aged 65 and above than illiterate youth. In relative terms, the elderly are more likely to be isolated illiterates, living in households with no literate members, in richer than in poorer countries.

- **TARGET 4.7:**
Sustainable development and global citizenship. Between the fifth and sixth consultations on the 1974 UNESCO Recommendation, the percentage of countries adopting its principles in student assessment rose from just under 50% to almost 85%. Yet only 21% of countries reported that teaching hours dedicated to the principles were 'fully sufficient'.

- **TARGET 4.a:**
Education facilities and learning environments. In 2016, two-thirds of schools had basic drinking water, two-thirds had basic sanitation and half had basic hygiene services. In 2013–2017, there were over 12,700 attacks on education, harming over 21,000 students and education personnel.

- **TARGET 4.b:**
Scholarships. The volume of scholarships funded by aid programmes has been stagnant since 2010 at US$1.2 billion. In 2017, there were 5.1 million mobile students, corresponding to an estimated outbound mobility ratio of 2.3%, up from 2% in 2012.

- **TARGET 4.c:**
Teachers. Using national definitions, 85% of primary school teachers globally were trained in 2017, a decline of 1.5 percentage points since 2013. The rate is lowest in sub-Saharan Africa, where the pupil/trained teacher ratio is 60:1.

- **EDUCATION IN THE OTHER SDGS:**
Decent work, cities, police and justice. Education affects other SDGs, notably through professional capacity development. Lack of trained social workers, urban planners, law enforcement officers, judges and other legal professionals jeopardizes progress towards the respective goals and targets.

- **FINANCE:**
An estimated US$4.7 trillion is spent on education worldwide annually: US$3 trillion (65%) in high income countries and US$22 billion (0.5%) in low income countries. Governments account for 79% of total spending and households for 20%. Aid to education, despite reaching a high in 2016, accounts for 12% of total education spending in low income countries and 2% in lower middle income countries.

To meet even the most basic education needs of children in crises would require the share of education in humanitarian aid to...

Burundian refugee, Nigirabarya, 31, is head teacher at Hope Secondary School in Nduta refugee camp, Tanzania. Hope is the only secondary school in the camp. Its walls are crumbling and there is a shortage of teachers. 'We don't have a lab for the science students or any textbooks. One good thing is that we have qualified teachers but we need at least 15 more.'

CREDIT: Georgina Goodwin/UNHCR

CHAPTER

1

Introduction

The 2019 Global Education Monitoring Report*'s specific findings and practical recommendations on education and migration will make an important contribution to the implementation of the Global Compact for Safe, Orderly and Regular Migration, which will be formally adopted by member states at an intergovernmental conference in Marrakesh on 10 December 2018. The report brings the agenda of the Global Compact and that of SDG 4 closer together and creates clarity for countries now tasked with transforming words into policy and policy into reality.*

The objectives of the Global Compact for Migration echo many of the targets in the fourth Sustainable Development Goal and give renewed emphasis to the principles of non-discrimination and inclusion, recognizing that effective access to education for migrant children is a fundamental human right. Education is also a critical path to integration into society and the best investment in sustainable development. It provides migrant children with opportunities for their own advancement as well as a chance to contribute both to their country of residence and, in many cases, eventually also to their country of origin.

Louise Arbour, Special Representative of the United Nations Secretary-General for International Migration

Education is a human right and a transformational force for poverty eradication, sustainability and peace. People on the move, whether for work or education, and whether voluntarily or forced, do not leave their right to education behind. The 2019 Global Education Monitoring Report *underscores the huge potential and opportunities of ensuring that migrants and displaced persons have access to quality education.*

António Guterres, Secretary-General of the United Nations

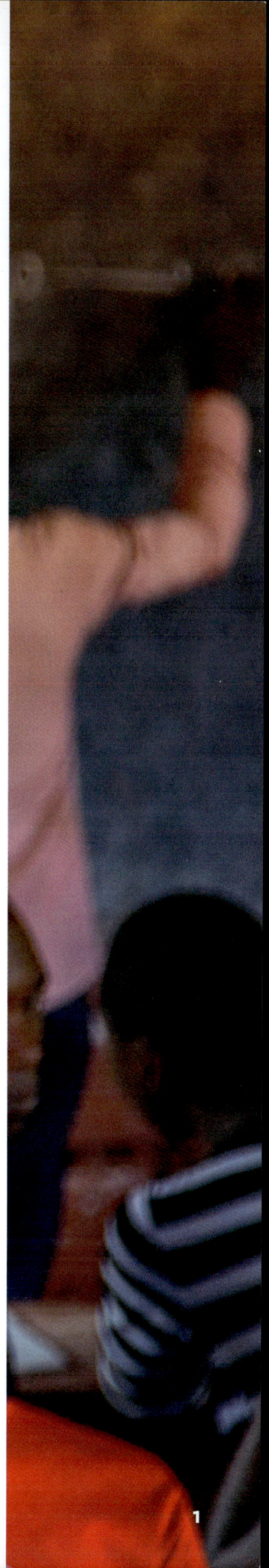

KEY MESSAGES

Migration is 'an expression of the human aspiration for safety, dignity and a better future' but also 'a source of divisions within and between States and societies'.

Migration and displacement can affect education, requiring systems to accommodate those who move and those left behind – but also those with migrant backgrounds who do not speak the language of instruction at home.

Education can also affect migration and displacement. It is a major driver in the decision to migrate. It is also key to providing citizens with critical understanding, promoting cohesive societies and fighting prejudice, stereotypes and discrimination.

About 1 in 8 people are internal migrants, living outside the region where they were born. About 1 in 30 are international migrants, almost two-thirds of them in high income countries. And about 1 in 80 are displaced by conflict or natural disaster, 9 in 10 of whom live in low and middle income countries.

To address the challenges of migration and displacement, all 193 UN member states signed the New York Declaration for Refugees and Migrants in September 2016 to strengthen and refine responsibility-sharing mechanisms. The declaration set in motion processes for two global compacts.

The Global Compact for Safe, Orderly and Regular Migration conveys a generally positive message of education as an opportunity to make the most of migratory flows and addresses a wide range of issues related to access to education, education beyond schooling and skills recognition.

The Global Compact on Refugees renews the commitments made in the 1951 United Nations Convention Relating to the Status of Refugees but goes further to promote inclusion of refugees in national education systems, calling for more coherent planning in crises and protracted displacement.

This report looks at migration and displacement through the eyes of teachers and education administrators faced with the reality of diverse classrooms, schoolyards, communities, labour markets and societies. It aims to answer two questions:

- How do population movements affect education access and quality? What are the implications for individual migrants and refugees?
- How can education make a difference in the lives of people who move and in the communities receiving them?

Powerful, moving stories of migration and displacement occur around the world. People wave goodbye to families in train stations, setting off for factory or mine jobs in faraway cities and countries with a promise to return. Caravans of people flee persecution, leaving burned homes behind. People sell their precious few possessions for a boat ticket to a new place, determined to succeed. People watch their children grow up speaking a different language; wait anxiously for news of loved ones attempting risky passage over mountains and seas; save to send children to study in the city or overseas; gratefully receive a wire transfer from a cousin or a friend; are detained with no information on what will happen to them next; sleep roughly for months, moving from one odd job to another; find a warm, welcoming place, or suffer discrimination and humiliation, in foreign communities. Some migrating people never had it so good and never look back; others find themselves unable to adapt to a different culture and feel nostalgic the rest of their lives.

These stories of ambition, hope, fear, anticipation, ingenuity, fulfilment, sacrifice, courage, perseverance and distress remind us that '[m]igration is an expression of the human aspiration for dignity, safety and a better future. It is part of the social fabric, part of our very make-up as a human family' (United Nations, 2013). Yet migration and displacement are 'also a source of divisions within and between States and societies ... In recent years, large movements of desperate people, including both migrants and refugees, have cast a shadow over the broader benefits of migration' (United Nations, 2017, p. 2).

While there is shared responsibility for the common destiny formally endorsed in the 2030 Agenda for Sustainable Development, migration and displacement continue to elicit some negative responses in modern societies. These are exploited by opportunists who see benefit in building walls, not bridges. It is here that education's role to 'promote understanding, tolerance and friendship among all nations, racial or religious groups', a key commitment in the Universal Declaration of Human Rights, takes centre stage, and it is the focus of this report.

The report looks at migration and displacement through the eyes of teachers and education administrators faced with the reality of diverse classrooms, schoolyards, communities, labour markets and societies. Education systems around the world are united in the commitment to achieve the fourth Sustainable Development Goal (SDG) – 'Ensure inclusive and equitable quality education and promote lifelong learning opportunities for all' – and to leave no one behind. For all students to fulfil their promise, systems need to adjust to their needs irrespective of their backgrounds. Education systems also need to respond to societies' need to be resilient and adapt to migration and displacement – a challenge affecting countries with large or small migrant and refugee populations.

> Education's role to 'promote understanding, tolerance and friendship among all nations, racial or religious groups' is the focus of this report

THE FRAMEWORK: MIGRATION AND DISPLACEMENT INTERACT WITH EDUCATION IN MULTIPLE, OFTEN MUTUAL WAYS

Migration and displacement interact with education through intricate two-way relationships that affect those who move, those who stay, those who host migrants and refugees and those who may do so (**Table 1.1**). The point in the life cycle at which people ponder or undertake migration is a key determinant of education investment, interruption, experience and outcome. Children migrating from areas with lower levels of education development may gain access to opportunities otherwise unavailable. Yet migrant students' attainment and achievement often lag behind those of their host country peers (**Box 1.1**).

Migration and displacement can profoundly affect education, requiring systems to accommodate those who move and those left behind. Countries need to recognize migrants' and refugees' right to education in law and fulfil this right in practice. They need to tailor education for those cramming into slums, living nomadically or awaiting refugee status. Education systems need to be inclusive and fulfil the commitment to equity, which cuts across the 2030 Agenda. Teachers need to be prepared to deal with diversity and the trauma associated with migration and, especially, displacement. Recognition of qualifications and prior learning should be modernized to make the most of migrants' and refugees' skills, which contribute greatly to long-term prosperity.

“Migration and displacement can profoundly affect education, requiring systems to accommodate those who move and those left behind”

Education also profoundly affects migration and displacement – both their volume and how they are perceived. Education is a major driver in the decision to migrate, fuelling the search for a better life. It affects migrants' attitudes, aspirations and beliefs, and the extent to which they develop a sense of belonging in

BOX 1.1:

Education is both a strength and a vulnerability for populations on the move

This report covers all types of population movement (**Figure 1.1**). The largest but most neglected is internal migration. On average, 1 out of 8 people lives outside the region or province where they were born. While many internal movements have innocuous consequences, some – particularly in rapidly urbanizing low and middle income countries – have serious effects on the educational opportunities of those moving and those left behind. Access to education at destination may be constrained due to deliberate administrative rules or simple neglect.

On average, about 1 out of 30 people lives in a country other than the one where they were born. Almost two-thirds are in high income countries, which explains the political prominence of the issue in those countries. International migrants are more likely to be of working age and, therefore, older than the population in destination countries. While most move to work, the extent to which their skills are recognized, utilized and rewarded is a key factor in the extent to which they succeed. But many move for education, which several measures can facilitate. Their migration also affects descendants, in the next generation if not beyond.

Some 1 out of 80 people are displaced within or across borders by conflict or natural disasters, with the number having risen rapidly in recent years. Nine out of ten of the displaced live in low and middle income countries. Delivering education for displaced people is part of restoring their sense of normalcy, structure and hope, but it can be challenging, conditioned by the unique social, economic and political contexts of displacement. Education needs to help these populations cope with protracted displacement and prepare them for a variety of futures.

Definitions for various categories of people on the move are meant to establish clear criteria that ensure respect for their rights. Yet even apparently clear-cut categories are less so in practice. In defining international migrants, for instance, some countries and organizations base nationality on descent, others on place of birth. Some categories provoke considerable controversy; fierce political arguments erupt over whether people migrate willingly to seek a better future or are forcibly displaced by human-caused or natural disasters. Host communities may interrogate migrants' and refugees' motivation (e.g. whether for work or education), legality (e.g. whether documented) or responsibility (e.g. whether victims of a crisis). Such arguments can divert focus from migrants' and refugees' well-being.

Note: See glossary for definitions of concepts related to migration and displacement.

FIGURE 1.1:
People move for a variety of reasons

Internal migrants move within a country, usually in one direction, from village to town, but also on circular routes, following their livelihoods.

In India, many children, such as Subhdeep, leave school for three to four months each year to help their families pick cotton. It is difficult to keep up when they return, and many children drop out.

International migrants move across country borders to work, either with authorization from the host country ...

Sofia's parents migrated from Morocco. She grew up in France but also feels strong links to Morocco. Both countries feel like home to her.

... or without the documents required under immigration laws and rules to enter, reside or work abroad.

Aide stands outside her wooden house in the Camilo Daza barrio of Cúcuta, Colombia, with her four children, who came with her from Venezuela. She has no access to health care or education for them, as they are undocumented.

Some young people move across borders to pursue further studies in a foreign university.

Khadidja, an Algerian medical school graduate, went to France to fine-tune her skills because of the country's reputation for medical education.

Internally displaced people are forced to move within their country, remaining under the protection of their government.

Mbuyu, from Tanganyika province, Democratic Republic of the Congo, has not been to school for two years. He is among those displaced by ethnic conflict that has entailed fierce clashes, extortion, plundering, property destruction, torture, murder, arbitrary arrest, forced labour, forced marriage and rape.

Asylum-seekers are those whose requests to seek refuge from persecution in another country need to be processed.

These young men are among the many asylum-seekers from Afghanistan, Iraq and the Syrian Arab Republic who sleep rough around Budapest's railway stations.

If successful in their requests, asylum-seekers obtain **refugee** status, which protects them and provides rights under international conventions.

Vinda sits with her mother Hamrin and two sisters in their home in a camp in Iraq. Originally from Qamishli, Syrian Arab Republic, the family fled the war four years ago. Her father works outside the camp. Vinda hopes to become a teacher.

Note: See glossary for definitions of concepts related to migration and displacement.
Photo credits (top to bottom): Oskar Kollberg/Save the Children, Dominic Egan, Paul Smith/UNHCR, Roméo Balancourt/IOM, Colin Delfosse/UNHCR, Andras Hajdu/UNHCR and Claire Thomas/UNHCR.

TABLE 1.1:
Selected examples of the relationship between education and migration/displacement

		Effects of migration/displacement on education	Effects of education on migration/displacement
Origin	Migrants	• Migration leads to education provision challenges in slums. • Education systems need to adjust to the needs of populations moving in seasonal or circular patterns.	• The more educated are more likely to migrate.
	Left behind	• Migration depopulates rural areas and challenges education provision. • Remittances affect education in origin communities. • Parent absence affects children left behind. • Emigration prospects disincentivize investment in education. • New programmes prepare aspiring migrants.	• Emigration of the educated has consequences for development of affected areas, e.g. through brain drain.
Destination	Immigrants and refugees	• Educational attainment and achievement of immigrants and their children usually lag behind natives. • Refugees need to be included in national education systems. • Refugees' right to education needs to be ensured.	• Migrants tend to be overqualified, their skills not fully recognized or utilized, and their livelihoods altered. • Internationalization of tertiary education prompts student mobility.
	Natives	• Diversity in classrooms requires better-prepared teachers, targeted programmes to support new arrivals and prevent segregation, and disaggregated data.	• Formal and non-formal education can build resilient societies and reduce prejudices and discrimination.

Source: GEM Report team based on Fargues (2017).

their destination. Increased diversity in classrooms brings challenges, including for natives (especially the poor and marginalized), but it also offers opportunities to learn from other cultures and experiences. Curricula sensitive to addressing negative attitudes towards immigrants and refugees are needed more than ever.

With migration and displacement becoming hot political topics, education is key to providing citizens with a critical understanding of the issues involved. It can support the processing of information and promote cohesive societies, which are especially important in a globalized world. Yet education should go well beyond tolerance, which can mask indifference; it is a critical tool in fighting prejudice, stereotypes and discrimination. If poorly designed, education systems can promulgate negative, partial, exclusive or dismissive portrayals of immigrants and refugees.

THE CONTEXT: THE WORLD IS STARTING TO ADDRESS THE EDUCATION NEEDS OF MOVING AND HOSTING POPULATIONS

Migration is one of the key positive mobilizing forces in human history and development, and the principle that refugees should not be sent back to places where their lives or freedoms are threatened is a foundation of international law. Yet migration and displacement also pose challenges at the local, national and international levels. To address them requires mobilizing resources and coordinating actions. In September 2016, all 193 UN member states signed the New York Declaration for Refugees and Migrants to strengthen and refine responsibility-sharing mechanisms (United Nations, 2016).

The declaration set in motion processes for two global compacts: one on migrants, the other on refugees. The country-led Global Compact for Safe, Orderly and Regular Migration has been heavily contested and is at constant risk of derailment by threats of withdrawal, including by the United States. The Global Compact on Refugees, led by the office of the United Nations High Commissioner for Refugees (UNHCR), faced fewer challenges but also saw withdrawals from its operational component, the Comprehensive Refugee Response Framework. The final drafts of both compacts, released in mid-2018, outline key commitments on education.

EDUCATION IN THE GLOBAL COMPACT FOR SAFE, ORDERLY AND REGULAR MIGRATION

Including education in the migration agenda is novel, despite education being a core aspect of migrants' realities. For instance, the International Organization for Migration, which became a UN agency in 2016 following the New York Declaration, has not had an education strategy or specialized expertise. Instead, it has responded over six decades to a large variety of project-related intervention requests, ranging from covering school transport costs and supporting vocational education programmes in sending countries to training border officials (Sanz, 2018).

It may not be surprising that a systematic approach is lacking on such complex, diverse and contested terrain. However, the migration compact's final draft text puts most issues addressed in this report on the agenda (**Table 1.2**). It conveys a generally positive message of education as an opportunity to make the most of migratory flows. A paragraph under objective 15 on access to basic services captures education; paragraphs under objectives 16 and 17 refer to education beyond schooling. Emphasis is given to skills recognition, outlined in detail under objective 18.

What the compact's commitments on education will accomplish is unknown, since it is non-binding. This report aims to support countries in implementing the commitments.

> “This report aims to support countries in implementing the education commitments in the Global Compact for Safe, Orderly and Regular Migration”

Implementation success also depends on the mechanisms set up to assess progress. Starting in 2022, an International Migration Review Forum, to take place every four years, will be aligned with the High-Level Political Forum, the apex mechanism for global SDG follow-up and review.

EDUCATION IN THE GLOBAL COMPACT ON REFUGEES

While the right to education is guaranteed by a series of human rights treaties, including the Convention on the Rights of the Child, refugees' right to education in host countries was already guaranteed in the 1951 United Nations Convention Relating to the Status of Refugees, later expanded with a 1967 protocol that removed time and geographical restrictions.

The 145 parties to the convention and 146 parties to the protocol have committed to refugees receiving 'the same treatment as is accorded to nationals with respect to elementary education'. They should also receive 'treatment as favourable as possible, and, in any event, not less favourable than that accorded to aliens generally in the same circumstances with respect to education other than elementary education and, in particular, as regards access to studies, the recognition of foreign school certificates, diplomas and degrees, the remission of fees and charges and the award of scholarships' (Art. 22).

In addition, UN General Assembly Resolution No. 302 (IV) of 8 December 1949 addressed Palestinian refugees' right to education. UNHCR and the United Nations Relief and Works Agency for Palestine Refugees in the Near East are responsible, with host governments, for ensuring this right is fulfilled.

While the 1951 convention has protected refugees and provided access to services, including education, for nearly 70 years, its core principle of shared responsibility has not been sufficiently respected (Türk and Garlick, 2016). The need to renew the commitment with a clearer support framework led to the Global Compact on Refugees, whose final draft dedicates two paragraphs to education, focusing on financing to support specific policies (**Table 1.3**). It makes clear the duty of countries to improve access to education and develop policies on refugees' inclusion in national education systems, which is considered best practice in the UNHCR Education Strategy 2012–2016.

TABLE 1.2:
Selected education-related excerpts from the Global Compact for Safe, Orderly and Regular Migration

Objectives and commitments	Actions
OBJECTIVE 2. Minimize the adverse drivers and structural factors that compel people to leave their country of origin 18. We commit to create conducive ... conditions for people to lead peaceful, productive and sustainable lives in their own country.	e) Invest in human capital development by promoting entrepreneurship, education, vocational training and skills development programmes and partnerships ... with a view to reducing youth unemployment, avoiding brain drain and optimizing brain gain in countries of origin.
OBJECTIVE 15. Provide access to basic services for migrants 31. We commit to ensure that all migrants, regardless of their migration status, can exercise their human rights through safe access to basic services.	f) Provide inclusive and equitable quality education to migrant children and youth, as well as facilitate access to lifelong learning opportunities, including by strengthening the capacities of education systems and by facilitating non-discriminatory access to early childhood development, formal schooling, non-formal education programmes for children for whom the formal system is inaccessible, on-the-job and vocational training, technical education, and language training, as well as by fostering partnerships with all stakeholders that can support this endeavour.
OBJECTIVE 16. Empower migrants and societies to realize full inclusion and social cohesion 32. We commit to foster inclusive and cohesive societies by empowering migrants to become active members of society and promoting the reciprocal engagement of receiving communities and migrants in the exercise of their rights and obligations towards each other.	i) Promote school environments that are welcoming and safe, and support the aspirations of migrant children by enhancing relationships within the school community, incorporating evidence-based information about migration in education curricula, and dedicating targeted resources to schools with a high concentration of migrant children for integration activities in order to promote respect for diversity and inclusion, and to prevent all forms discrimination, including racism, xenophobia and intolerance.
OBJECTIVE 17. Eliminate all forms of discrimination and promote evidence-based public discourse to shape perceptions of migration 33. We commit to eliminate all forms of discrimination, condemn and counter expressions, acts and manifestations of racism, racial discrimination, violence, xenophobia and related intolerance against all migrants.	c) Promote independent, objective and quality reporting of media outlets ... including by sensitizing and educating media professionals on migration-related issues and terminology. g) Engage migrants, political, religious and community leaders, as well as educators and service providers to detect and prevent incidences of intolerance, racism, xenophobia, and other forms of discrimination against migrants and diasporas and support activities in local communities to promote mutual respect.
OBJECTIVE 18. Invest in skills development and facilitate mutual recognition of skills, qualifications and competences 34. We commit to invest in innovative solutions that facilitate mutual recognition of skills, qualifications and competences of migrant workers at all skills levels.	a) Develop standards and guidelines for the mutual recognition of foreign qualifications and non-formally acquired skills. b) Promote transparency of certifications and compatibility of National Qualifications Frameworks. c) Conclude ... mutual recognition agreements. e) Build global skills partnerships amongst countries that strengthen training capacities of national authorities ... with a view to preparing trainees for employability. g) Engage in bilateral partnerships ... that promote skills development, mobility and circulation, such as student exchange programmes, scholarships, professional exchange programmes and trainee- or apprenticeships. j) Develop and promote innovative ways to mutually recognize and assess formally and informally acquired skills.
OBJECTIVE 20. Promote faster, safer and cheaper transfer of remittances and foster financial inclusion of migrants 36. We commit to promote faster, safer and cheaper remittances by further developing existing conducive policy and regulatory environments.	f) Provide accessible information on remittance transfer costs by provider and channel, such as comparison websites, in order to increase the transparency and competition on the remittance transfer market, and promote financial literacy and inclusion of migrants and their families through education and training.

Source: United Nations (2018a).

TABLE 1.3:
Education-related excerpts from the Global Compact on Refugees

68. In line with national education laws, policies and planning, and in support of host countries, States and relevant stakeholders will contribute resources and expertise to expand and enhance the quality and inclusiveness of national education systems to facilitate access by refugee and host community children (both boys and girls), adolescents and youth to primary, secondary and tertiary education. More direct financial support and special efforts will be mobilized to minimize the time refugee boys and girls spend out of education, ideally a maximum of three months after arrival.

69. Depending on the context, additional support could be contributed to expand educational facilities (including for early childhood development, and technical or vocational training) and teaching capacities (including support for, as appropriate, refugees and members of host communities who are or could be engaged as teachers, in line with national laws and policies). Additional areas for support include efforts to meet the specific education needs of refugees (including through "safe schools" and innovative methods such as online education) and overcome obstacles to their enrolment and attendance, including through flexible certified learning programmes, especially for girls, as well persons with disabilities and psychosocial trauma. Support will be provided for the development and implementation of national education sector plans that include refugees. Support will also be provided where needed to facilitate recognition of equivalency of academic, professional and vocational qualifications.

Source: United Nations (2018b).

> The Global Compact on Refugees makes clear the duty of countries to develop policies on refugees' inclusion in national education systems

The Comprehensive Refugee Response Framework process, originally Annex I to the New York Declaration, further provides a practical approach to fulfilling obligations and sharing costs. Its pilot implementation has focused on more coherent planning in crises and protracted displacements in selected countries hosting refugees.

THE CONTENTS: GUIDE TO THE REPORT

The 2019 *Global Education Monitoring Report* reviews global evidence on migration, displacement and education and aims to answer the following questions:

- How do population movements affect access to and quality of education? What are the implications for individual migrants and refugees?
- How can education make a difference in the lives of people who move and in the communities receiving them?

TABLE 1.4:
Guide to migration and displacement themes throughout the report

	Thematic part	Monitoring part
Internal migration	Chapter 2	Data focus 12.1: Education in slums Data focus 15.2: Boarding schools
International migration	Chapter 3	Policy focus 8.1: Right to education Policy focus 11.1: Financial education for migrants Policy focus 13.1: Adult literacy programmes for migrants Policy focus 17.1: Teacher migration Data focus 19.1: Immigrant taxes and education budgets Policy focus 19.1: Targeting of schools with immigrant students Policy focus 19.2: Use of aid to control migration Policy focus 19.4: Remittances
Displacement	Chapter 4	Policy focus 9.1: Early childhood education for refugees Policy focus 10.1: Higher education for refugees Policy focus 12.1: Education for refugees with disabilities Policy focus 15.1: Technology for refugee education Policy focus 19.3: Humanitarian aid
Diversity	Chapter 5	Data focus 14.1: International Civic and Citizenship Study Policy focus 14.1: Prevention of violent extremism
Mobility of students and professionals	Chapter 6	Policy focus 10.2: Technical/vocational education for migrants Policy focus 16.1: Scholarships for mobility in Europe and Asia

In the thematic part of the report, Chapters 2 to 4 discuss how three types of population movement (internal migration, international migration and displacement) affect education access, quality and inclusiveness. The three chapters ask whether education outcomes of migrants or refugees differ from those of natives, why gaps emerge and what the main barriers to provision of good-quality, inclusive education are. Chapter 5 discusses how education can affect the lives of those who move and those who host. Chapter 6 focuses on mobility of international students and professionals, and the recognition of their skills and qualifications.

The monitoring part of the report, Chapters 7 to 19, serves two purposes. First, it reviews performance on international education targets. Second, most chapters complement the thematic part with targeted data and policy focus sections relating to migration and displacement issues (**Table 1.4**). An introduction (**Chapter 7**) provides three brief reviews: developments in the SDG 4 monitoring framework over the past year, a summary of progress in the Education for All era (2000–2015) and the final information for 2015 on the key indicators, and an overview of challenges in monitoring education for migrants and refugees. Chapters 8 to 17 address the seven targets and three means of implementation. Chapter 18 reviews the role of education in three other SDGs: decent work (SDG 8), cities (SDG 10) and peace and justice (SDG 16). Chapter 19 looks at public, external and household finance. Chapter 20 concludes by synthesizing key evidence and offering recommendations, primarily targeted at governments.

Zie is an 11-year-old boy in grade 5 who has lived at a boarding school in Weishan county, People's Republic of China, since he was 9. He sees his parents, who work in Dali, at least three times per year. If he could change anything about the school, he would improve the equipment in the classrooms and the conditions for eating.

CREDIT: Louise Dyring Mbae/Save the Children

CHAPTER

2

Internal migration

Migration is a complex phenomenon, more complex in large cities. This is why local governments must work permanently to promote citizenship and combat discrimination.

Education is essential to stimulate migrants' sociocultural inclusion, autonomy and access to the formal labour market. In São Paulo, migrants have their citizens' rights recognized, with an equal right to school enrolment and participation in educational projects.

Bruno Covas, Mayor of São Paolo

KEY MESSAGES

Internal migration peaks among those in their 20s, who often migrate to learn new skills or make the most of those already acquired. In Thailand, 21% of youth said they migrated for education.

People with a primary education are twice as likely to migrate as those with no education at all; those with secondary schooling are three times as likely and those with tertiary four times as likely.

Rural migrants can improve their education attainment when they move to cities, but this is not a hard and fast rule. In Brazil's Northeast region, 25% of those who migrated during secondary school went from being regular to irregular students, compared with 11% of those who stayed behind.

To curb rural to urban migration, many countries made it harder for migrants to enter school. In China, residence restrictions led to unauthorized migrant schools. Since 2006, the government has made major reforms to ease these restrictions and provide public education to all migrants, but challenges remain – migrant children have to provide five different certificates to enrol in schools in Beijing.

Children whom migrating parents leave behind may benefit from stability and remittances but their education and well-being often suffer. In Cambodia, children left behind, especially girls, were more likely to drop out of school.

Children of seasonal workers are often denied their right to education. About 80% of temporary migrant children in seven Indian cities lacked access to education near work sites.

The education needs of nomads and pastoralists are not served by traditional school systems whose curricula and schedules do not fit their way of life. School spot checks in remote areas of Somalia indicated high seasonal fluctuation in attendance: 50% more children were in school in May than in November and December at the end of the dry season.

Many countries have closed or consolidated rural schools due to rural to urban migration or reduced fertility rates. The number of rural schools in the Russian Federation fell from 45,000 to fewer than 26,000 between 2000 and 2015. In reducing costs to improve efficiency, governments must also recognize the important social role schools play in communities.

Rural migrants in low and middle income countries often settle in slums, which suffer from a chronic lack of access to school. In Dhaka, Bangladesh, only about one-quarter of slums were estimated to have a government school.

Faced with dramatic headlines on international migrants and refugees, it is easy to forget that internal migration accounts for the majority of population movements. Rural to urban migration is a particularly salient phenomenon in low and middle income countries, leading to higher levels of urbanization. Declining rural populations are also observed, primarily in richer countries (UNDESA, 2014). Among a variety of possible movements, permanent or temporary, between or within urban and rural areas, it is rural to urban flows and seasonal or circular flows that tend to pose the biggest challenges for education systems.

Education is a key factor in all these movements. Higher levels of education increase aspirations for opportunities outside rural areas. Education is also a goal of migration, with young people seeking skills converging on urban centres offering opportunities for secondary education and above. Education provision needs to accommodate the large flows out of rural and into urban areas. Education systems should also respond to the needs of migrant children, who face various adjustment challenges, depending on their background and cultural and social ties with the destination.

This chapter looks at the interrelationship between internal migration and education. It discusses access to different levels of education, the quality and relevance of education provided, and policy efforts and results, including teaching policy and practice. It examines the education status of various groups of migrants, particularly those facing barriers, and considers education planning challenges resulting from population movements, whether in depopulated rural areas or burgeoning slums.

ONE IN EIGHT PEOPLE LIVE OUTSIDE THE REGION WHERE THEY WERE BORN

A dynamic process, internal migration is difficult to quantify with precision, especially in an increasingly mobile world. Determining comparable trends across countries is hindered by deficiencies in data sources and differences in national definitions. Countries define rural administrative boundaries, size of geographic units across which moves are recorded, and reference periods differently. Circular or seasonal movements are least easily captured.

In 2005, according to census data, 763 million people, or 12% of the global population, lived outside the region of their birth (Bell and Charles-Edwards, 2013). In 2011–2012, according to Gallup data, 381 million adults, or 8% of the global adult population, had moved between regions in the previous five years (Esipova et al., 2013). In 61 countries with comparable data, as much as 20% of the population had changed place of residence over the previous five years (Bernard et al., 2018).

Major rural to urban migration accompanied the economic growth of the 19th to mid-20th century in most of today's high income countries. As countries transition to urbanized, ageing societies, these movements have subsided (Champion et al., 2017). Today, the largest internal population movements occur in low and middle income countries, particularly China and India. In 2016, about 77 million Chinese migrant workers moved to find work in another province, 93 million moved within their province, and 112 million short-distance migrants worked in cities close to their regions (Hannum et al.,

> In 2016, about 77 million Chinese migrant workers moved to find work in another province and 93 million moved within their province

2018). In India, inter-state migration rates doubled between 2001 and 2011 (World Economic Forum, 2017). An estimated 9 million migrated between states annually from 2011 to 2016 (India Ministry of Finance, 2017).

Rural to urban migration has played a relatively smaller role in urban population growth in sub-Saharan Africa (De Brauw et al., 2014). Yet it still has major implications for population redistribution in some countries and makes urban development planning challenging (Mberu et al., 2017). In Nigeria, a 2010 survey revealed that 23% of the population had changed area of residence for at least 6 months within the previous 10 years, with about 60% of internal migrants living in urban areas. In 7 out of 36 states, including Abia and Lagos, migrants constituted more than two-fifths of the population (Isiugo-Abanihe and IOM Nigeria, 2016).

New data sources provide more granular information on internal migration patterns. Facebook data have been used to study coordinated migration, defined as at least 20% of the population of one city having moved to another (Hofleitner et al., 2013). An analysis of 1.5 million people's mobile phone records over four years showed high levels of temporary and circular migration in Rwanda undetected by government surveys (Blumenstock, 2012).

Migration rates vary by age and among countries. In 53 countries with data on long-distance migration, the median age at peak migration was 23, the range varied from 19.5 in Belarus to 30 in Spain, and the median migration intensity rate was 3.2% (**Figure 2.1a**). The bulk of Indonesian migrants, for instance, were aged 20 to 24, and 1 out of 10 moved between districts in 2010–2015 (**Figure 2.1b**). From an education perspective, migration affects relatively few primary school-age children and slightly more secondary school-age youth. It mostly affects those who may be migrating for post-secondary education.

FIGURE 2.1:
Most people who migrate internally do so in their 20s

a. Internal migration intensity rate and age at peak, selected countries by region, latest available year

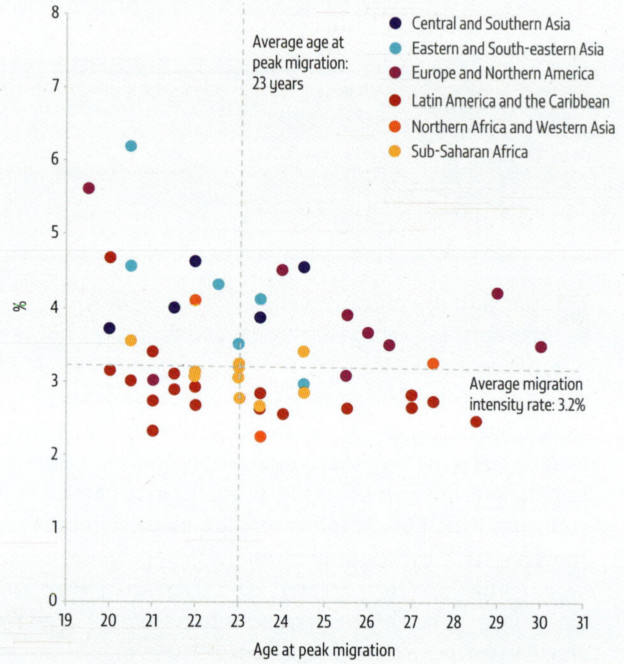

Note: The figure refers to long-distance migration.
Source: Bernard et al. (2018).

b. Internal migration intensity rate by age and destination, Indonesia, 2010–2015

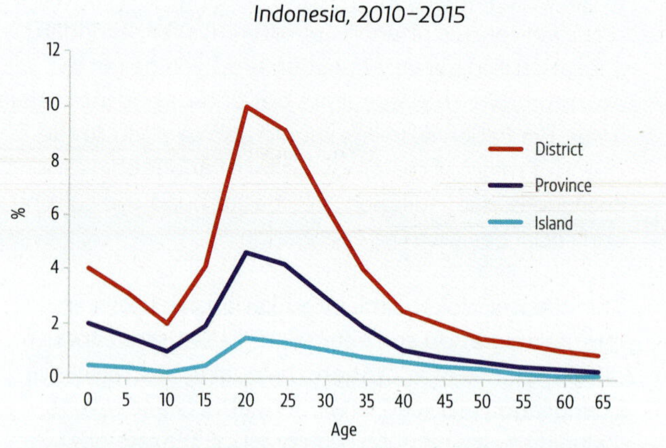

GEM StatLink: http://bit.ly/fig2_1
Source: Muhidin (2018).

EDUCATION PLAYS A KEY ROLE IN THE DECISION TO MIGRATE

Education of better quality in urban areas is a prominent reason for migration among younger people. In Thailand, 21% of youth said they migrated for education (**Figure 2.2a**). Among adults, family and employment motivate migration more than education. Still, 9% of Colombian and 8% of Iranian adults have migrated for education (**Figure 2.2b**).

A longitudinal analysis based on the Young Lives study found that between one-third and one-half of youth aged 15 to 19 in Ethiopia, India, Peru and Viet Nam migrated at least once between 2009 and 2013. The major migration streams were rural to rural in Ethiopia and India, urban to urban in Peru and rural to urban in Viet Nam. Education was the main reason, except for Indian girls, with the more educated more likely to migrate for further education (Gavonel, 2017).

Internal migration for higher education is linked to variations in affordability and quality. In Sweden, analysis of data from 15 cohorts shows that high-performing secondary school students are more likely to attend top universities, which are predominantly located in urban areas (Ahlin et al., 2017). In the United States, almost 400,000 out of 1.5 million recent secondary graduates moved out of state for tertiary education in 2014 (Strayer, 2016; United States DOE, 2015).

The more educated are more likely to relocate on the prospect of higher returns on their education (World Bank, 2009). Preferences and aspirations as a result of education also prompt people to leave rural areas irrespective of the earning potential migration may provide (UNDP, 2009). Across 53 countries, the probability of migration effectively doubled among those with primary education, tripled among those with secondary and quadrupled among those with tertiary, compared with those with no education (Bernard et al., 2018) (**Figure 2.3**).

In most countries, rural to urban migrants are more educated than those who stay in rural areas, especially in countries with low average education levels. In Guinea, Mali and Senegal, rural to urban migrants have four times as many years of schooling as those who stay behind; in Chile and Jamaica, they have 1.6 and 1.2 times as many, respectively (Bernard et al., 2018).

Migration by the highly educated redistributes human capital within countries (Faggian et al., 2017). In Germany and Italy, migration by university graduates increased regional labour market disparities (Fratesi and Percoco, 2014; Granato et al., 2015). In Brazil, patterns of mobility vary by education. Among the less educated, migration itself and the distances travelled have declined since the mid-1980s, while the more educated travel farther, especially to state capitals (**Figure 2.4**).

FIGURE 2.2:

Education is an important reason for internal migration among youth

Reasons for internal migration, selected countries, latest available year

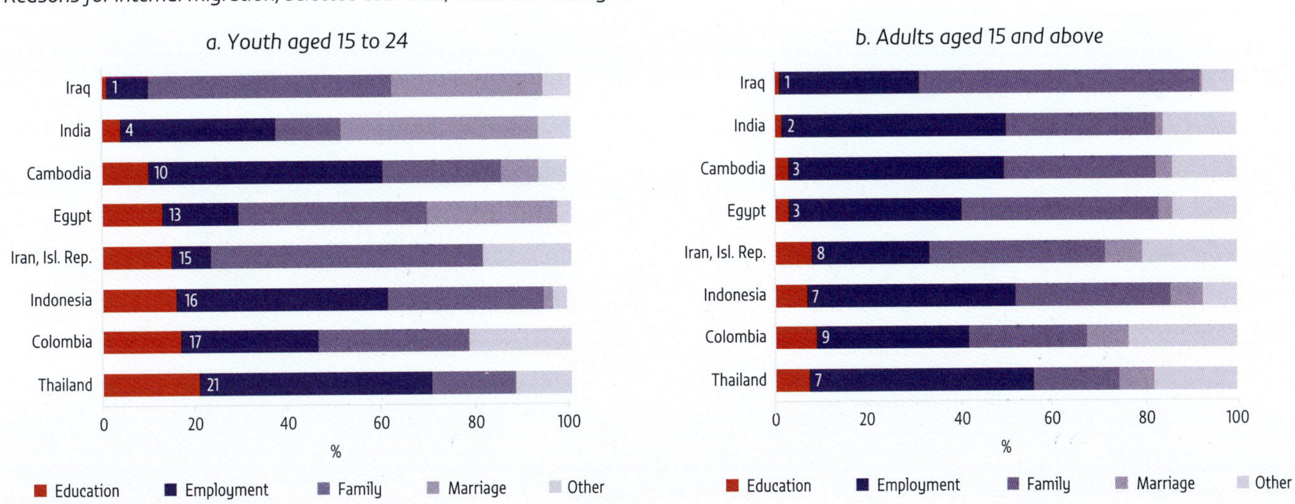

GEM StatLink: http://bit.ly/fig2_2

Sources: Bernard et al. (2018), based on IPUMS database.

FIGURE 2.3:

The more educated are more likely to migrate

Migration intensity rate by education, selected countries, five-year intervals, 1999–2010

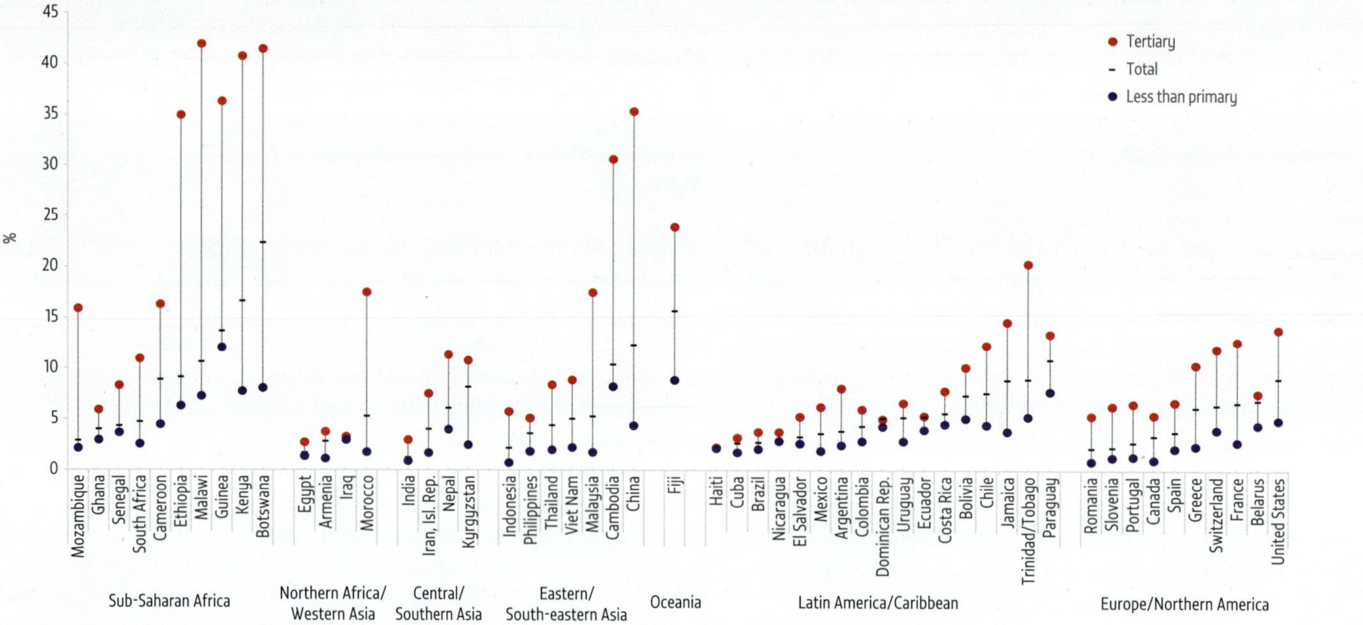

GEM StatLink: http://bit.ly/fig2_3
Source: Bernard et al. (2018).

FIGURE 2.4:

In Brazil, more educated people migrate more and farther

Net migration between pairs of Brazilian microregions, 1986–1991 and 2005–2010

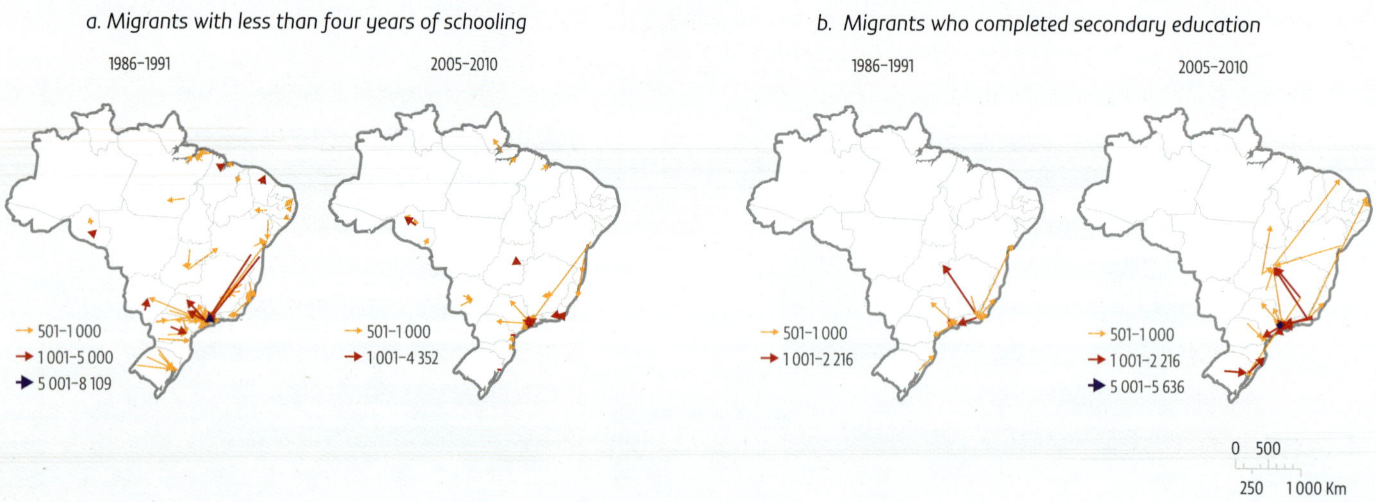

Source: Rigotti and Hadad (2018).

MIGRATION IMPROVES EDUCATION OUTCOMES FOR SOME BUT NOT ALL

Rural to urban migration can increase educational attainment in countries where access to education in rural areas is very low. Among a group born in selected rural districts in Indonesia, those who migrated to a city as children attained three more years of schooling than those who did not (Resosudarmo and Suryadarma, 2014). An analysis in the 2015 *Education for All Global Monitoring Report* showed that, given the large urban–rural gap in primary attainment rates in sub-Saharan Africa, the increase in the percentage of people living in urban areas would alone have raised the average primary attainment rate by 1.5 percentage points between 2000 and 2010 (UNESCO, 2015).

Yet expectations are not always met, and some migrant children may not enjoy the same education outcomes as their peers. An analysis for this report of longitudinal data from 2007 to 2015 in Brazil showed that 15% of students born between 1993 and 2009 had migrated at least once. Among adolescents born in 2000/01 in the Northeast region, those who migrated during secondary school had worse progression rates than those who stayed: 25% went from being regular to irregular students, compared with 11% of non-migrants. For most migrants, moving to locations with better schools, such as Minas Gerais state or São Paulo, did not improve their education progression (Rigotti and Hadad, 2018). In Italy, analysis of internal migration from southern to northern provinces found that migrant children, especially boys, had a higher probability of early dropout (Aina et al., 2015). In Turkey, internal migration between the 1990 and 2000 censuses reduced the lower and upper secondary completion rates of those who were already residing in an area, especially among youth of low socio-economic status (Berker, 2009).

Educational opportunities of children affected by internal migration – whether migrant or left behind – may be compromised for several reasons, from precarious legal status to poverty. Unaccompanied children may work in situations of extreme vulnerability. Governments may not uphold the right to education. Biases and stereotypes may reduce the quality of education and overall well-being of migrant children.

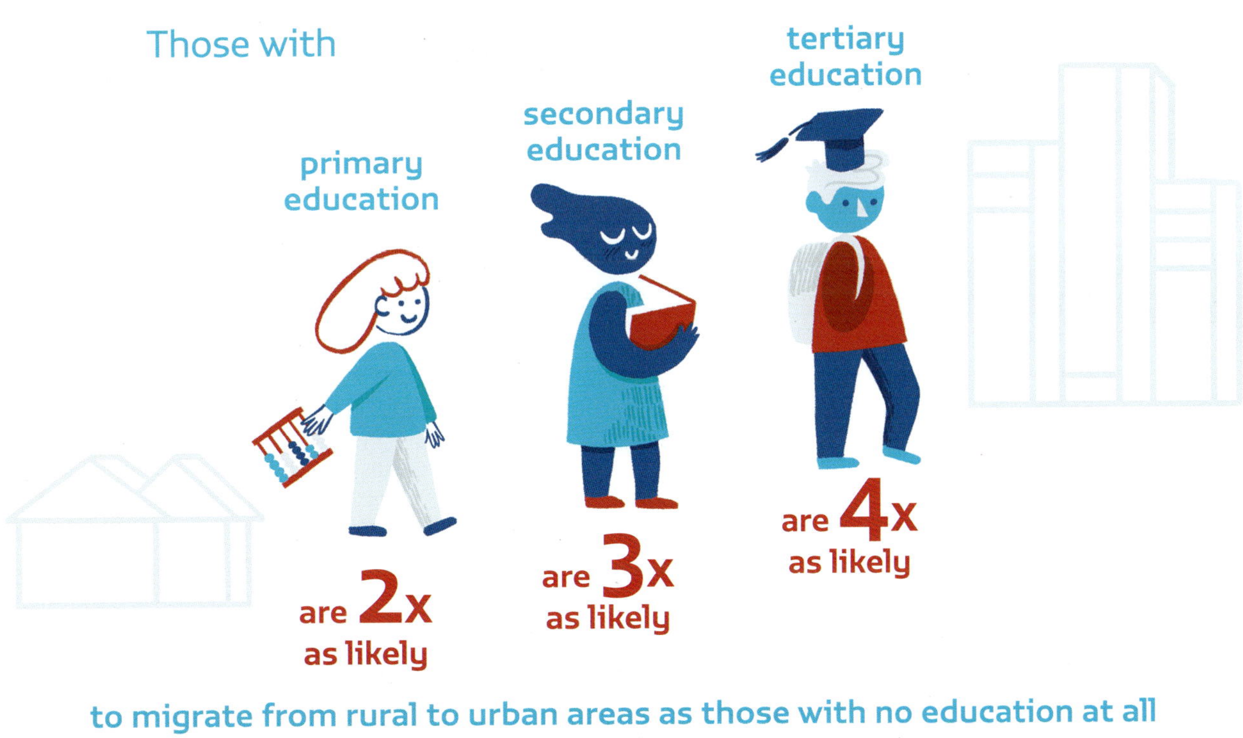

INTERNAL MIGRATION CONTROLS AFFECT EDUCATION ACCESS

In many countries, fears of unsustainable urbanization and rural–urban imbalances have prompted policies to curb such migration. In 2015, 79% of the 190 countries with data responded that, over the previous five years, they had instituted population policies to reduce rural to urban migration or to decentralize large urban centres (UNDESA, 2017). While the tendency is to provide incentives, in the strictest cases where explicit controls are imposed and public service provision is linked to residence and legal status, migrants' access to education can be affected.

China's *hukou* registration system, established in the 1950s to limit population mobility, classified residents as rural or urban and linked access to services to the registered place of birth. Many reforms have since weakened these barriers; however, education access and quality disadvantages for migrants persist (Hannum et al., 2018).

Viet Nam's *ho-khau* system similarly restricted migrants' access to public education, and poor rural to urban migrants moved to areas underserved by public schools (Cameron, 2012). Recent reforms aim to abolish restrictions (Huy, 2017), but the legacy of past policies still disadvantages migrants with temporary status. Data from the 2015 Household Registration Survey showed that 89% of youth aged 15 to 17 with permanent status were enrolled in upper secondary school, compared with 30% of those with temporary status (World Bank and Viet Nam Academy of Social Sciences, 2016).

Migration controls in China have eased, but their effects persist

Urbanization in China started in the 1980s, and rural migrant workers now constitute 21% of the population. Census and mid-censal survey data from 1990, 2000 and 2005 showed that migrant children were significantly less likely to be enrolled in school than non-migrant children or those left behind (Wu and Zhang, 2015). In the early 2000s, due to residence permit restrictions, more than half of migrant children attended unauthorized migrant schools in Beijing that were considered of lower quality and lacking in qualified teachers and infrastructure (Han, 2004).

Since then, the *hukou* has undergone significant revision. The government required local authorities to provide education to migrant children in 2006 and abolished public school fees for rural migrant children in 2008 (UNESCO, 2015). A major 2014 reform sought to establish a national resident registration system and decouple registered residence and access to services. The State Council approved a document in 2016 asking all but the largest cities to ease restrictions and allow college graduates, skilled workers and overseas returnees to obtain urban *hukou* (*China Daily*, 2016).

However, barriers to education persist for migrants. Public schools can use paperwork to limit access. In Beijing, migrants must provide five certificates to be eligible for schooling: temporary resident permit, proof of Beijing residence, proof of Beijing employment, all household members' *hukou* certificates and attestation of the lack of a qualified guardian in the home town (Zhou and Cheung, 2017). Some education bureaux impose additional requirements for public school admission (Tsang, 2018). In Shanghai, schools may reject migrant children through admission tests and other strategies to maintain their academic reputation, or segregate migrants in lower-status classrooms (Yiu, 2018). Migrant youth have also tended to be relegated to vocational schools (Ling, 2015).

“In Beijing, migrants must provide five certificates to be eligible for schooling”

The legacy of past restrictions on migrants remains. Until recently, strict *hukou* rules meant all students had to take secondary and tertiary entrance examinations where they were registered. Rural migrants thus were ineligible to sit examinations in their cities of residence, and curricular differences made it harder to do well in their *hukou* areas (Zhou and Cheung, 2017).

Parents frequently complain about teacher quality in migrant schools (Goodburn, 2015; Ye, 2016). Teachers' views of migrant youth, moreover, may affect education quality. Analysis for this report based on the 2014 Child Well-Being Survey in Shanghai showed that teachers were more likely to perceive migrant youth as struggling in language class, even after controlling for academic performance. They also had less favourable perceptions of migrant youth behaviour and of migrant parents (Cherng, 2018). Discriminatory attitudes could be attributed partly to policy. Some teachers felt that investing in migrant children's learning was not worthwhile, since they used to be barred from public high school in Shanghai (Yiu, 2014).

Policies vary among cities, affecting teachers' working conditions. In Beijing, interviews with civil society experts suggested that only one-third of the estimated 140 migrant schools were legal in 2012. Teachers suffer lower pay and lack of job security due to schools' illegal status. In Guangzhou, the number of working hours of migrant school teachers is monitored, but teachers have to collect various fees, and some are expected to meet student recruitment quotas (Friedman, 2017).

CHILDREN LEFT BEHIND FACE PARTICULAR EDUCATION CHALLENGES

Migration also affects the millions of children left behind with one parent or other family members. They may benefit from stability and remittances, but their education, psychological development and well-being often suffer. The effects have been most studied in Asian countries, especially China.

An analysis of 600 households in Cambodia showed that children left behind, especially girls, were more likely to drop out (Vutha et al., 2014). In India and Viet Nam, cognitive ability test scores were lower among children aged 5 to 8 whose parents had migrated, especially long term, when parent communication was scarce (Nguyen, 2016). A separate survey found that Vietnamese labour migrant children left behind had significantly more mental health challenges, negative emotional symptoms and peer relationship problems than other children (Van Luot and Dat, 2017).

Educational opportunities of children left behind in China are often at risk

The number of Chinese migrant workers who left their families behind increased by 20 million to 132 million between 2008 and 2014 (**Figure 2.5a**). Between 2005 and 2010, the number of children left behind grew from 59 million to 61 million, of whom 23 million were under age 5 (**Figure 2.5b**). The *China Family Development Report 2015* estimated the percentage of left-behind rural children at 35% (Yan, 2015). Another estimate suggested that 9 million rural children under age 16 lived without both parents in 2016; of these, 8 million lived with grandparents (Hannum et al., 2018). A non-government organization (NGO) survey in rural areas of six provinces found that over 9 million children had not met with their parents once in a year (Hong'e, 2015). A migrant population survey found that 44% of children lived without one parent in 2016 in Anhui, Henan and Sichuan provinces, key sources of migrant workers (Hannum et al., 2018).

Evidence on migration's effect on the education and well-being of children left behind is mixed. A study of 13,000 students in 130 rural primary schools in ethnic minority areas of north-western China found that it had a positive impact on academic performance, especially among underperforming students (Bai et al., 2018). Another study found that left-behind adolescents performed on a par with their peers, motivated by a belief that their parents migrated primarily to benefit their education (Hu, 2017).

FIGURE 2.5:
Chinese migrant workers are leaving their younger children behind

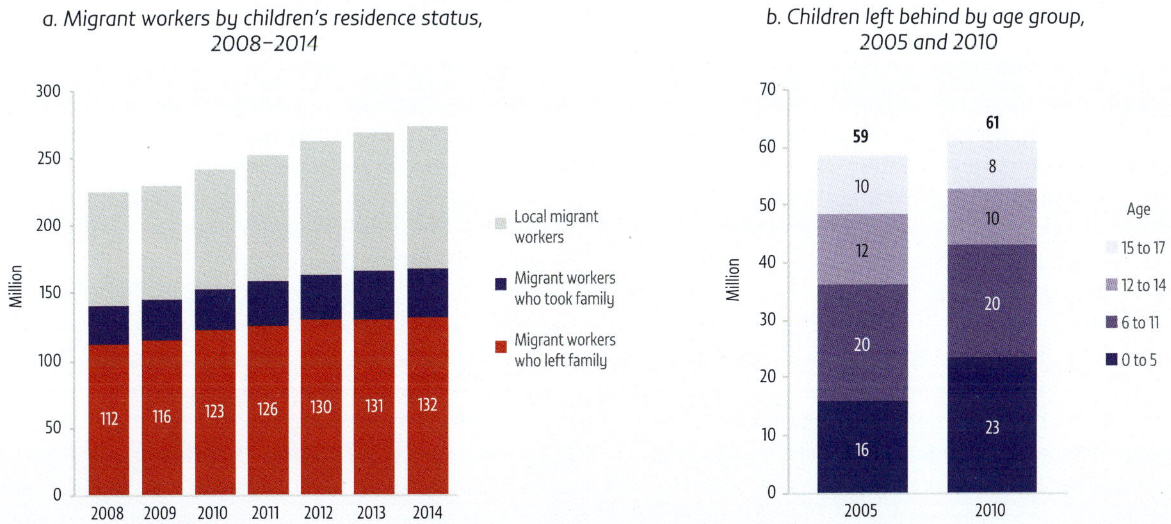

GEM StatLink: http://bit.ly/fig2_5
Source: All China Women's Federation and National Bureau of Statistics of China (2016).

Yet a rural household survey showed that parent migration had a significant negative impact on education outcomes, which was somewhat alleviated by parents' return, especially among secondary students and girls (Liu et al., 2018). New analysis for this report based on the China Education Panel Survey found that children with absent mothers had lower grades in mathematics, Chinese and English. Children with one or both parents absent exhibited more symptoms of depression than those with present parents. Longitudinal data analysis from rural Gansu province (2000 and 2015) found that children with absent fathers had 0.4 fewer years of education (Hannum et al., 2018).

> “In China, children with absent mothers had lower grades in mathematics, Chinese and English”

A systematic review of studies among left-behind children in China found that they had lower self-concept and more mental health problems than children overall (Wang et al., 2015). Teachers of left-behind children often lack the resources, understanding or opportunity to communicate to family or guardians the need for them to provide adequate support and attention (Jingzhong and Lu, 2011). The scale of the issue garners significant media attention, focused on major issues such as boarding school abuses and a rise in numbers of rural juvenile offenders (*The Economist*, 2015).

To address the challenge, in February 2016, the State Council issued a directive on a policy, involving 27 ministries and departments, regarding provision of care for left-behind children. The ministries of civil affairs, education and public security led an investigation into the situation of the left-behind children, and 26 provinces had implemented the new policy by the end of 2016. Yunnan province determined that, by 2017, 80% of primary and 100% of lower secondary students left behind should be enrolled in boarding schools, and all schools should have at least one psychological counsellor (Hannum et al., 2018).

In November 2016, eight ministries issued a special action, which, among other directives, called on local governments to urge parents to appoint a guardian accepting responsibility for left-behind children and help prevent dropout by requiring primary and secondary schools to track attendance vigilantly. Children without parents or guardians receive care from relevant aid administration and welfare agencies. In October 2017, the Ministry of Civil Affairs announced the official launch of a National Left-Behind Children Information Management System (Hannum et al., 2018).

Boarding schools have been a key part of the strategy in dealing with children left behind (**Data focus 15.2**). This approach can work. A longitudinal study of junior secondary schools in five provinces in western China compared the mathematics and Chinese test scores of students who began to board at school between 2006 and 2008 with those of students who were not boarding. Students who started to board had lower scores in the beginning of the period but two years later were performing better than their non-boarding peers (Beijing Normal University, 2009). But often, boarding schools tend to be understaffed and underequipped. A recent analysis showed that boarding school students in 59 rural counties in 5 provinces had worse nutrition, health and education outcomes than non-boarding students (Wang et al., 2016). Management training for administrative staff needs to be strengthened to improve child welfare.

Community centres and clubs could be an alternative strategy since these are run with the support of highly dedicated volunteers, even in resource-poor communities. The limited evidence suggests that they benefit the psychosocial well-being of left-behind children (Hannum et al., 2018).

SEASONAL LABOUR MIGRATION AFFECTS EDUCATIONAL OPPORTUNITIES

Seasonal labour migration is a survival strategy for poor rural populations around the world. In Bangladesh, more than 2.6 million rural migrant workers are employed in construction outside the agricultural seasons in 2010 (Reza, 2016). Seasonal migration can disrupt education and expose children to child labour and workplace hazards. They are often treated as an additional workforce and may have to leave school to work (Bengtsson and Dyer, 2017).

On some commercial farms in South Africa, children had to work in order to live with their migrant parents. A lack of accessible, affordable day care in rural areas meant younger children were brought to the fields and exposed to the same workplace hazards as their older siblings and parents (Van de Glind, 2010). In Turkey, a study of children aged 6 to 14 participating in seasonal agricultural migration

> Boarding schools for migrant children need to be well staffed and equipped, with adequate emphasis on psychosocial support and engagement with the community

in 2010/11 found that, while 97% were in school, 73% started school at a late age, and they were absent 59 out of 180 school days (Development Workshop, 2012).

In Thailand, partnerships among NGOs, civil society organizations (CSOs) and real estate or construction companies aim to support migrant children in construction site camps. Narai Property Co. Ltd partnered with the Foundation for the Better Life of Children to ensure non-formal education in its camps. Since 2016, the company has provided a mobile school and team of teachers who rotate among seven camps (UNICEF and Baan Dek Foundation, 2017).

In Cambodia, women working in the garment industry have low levels of literacy. In collaboration with the factories, NGOs and UNESCO, the government developed a factory literacy programme which delivered textbooks, teachers' guides and teacher training for literacy classes. The programme was rolled out to 11 factories in 2017, with a planned expansion to 14 additional factories in 2018 (No et al., 2016).

India has made numerous attempts at educating children of seasonal workers

In India, 10.7 million children aged 6 to 14 lived in rural households with a seasonal migrant in 2013. About 28% of youth aged 15 to 19 in these households were illiterate or had not completed primary school, compared with 18% of the cohort overall (Chandrasekhar and Bhattacharya, 2018). About 80% of seasonal migrant children in seven Indian cities lacked access to education near work sites, and 40% worked, experiencing abuse and exploitation (Aide et Action et al., 2015).

The construction sector absorbs the majority of short-term migrants. A survey in Punjab state of 3,000 brick kiln workers in 2015/16 found that 60% were inter-state migrants. Between 65% and 80% of all children aged 5 to 14 living at the kilns worked there seven to nine hours per day. About 77% of kiln workers reported lack of access to early childhood or primary education for their children (Anti-Slavery International and Volunteers for Social Justice, 2017).

For over 40 years, NGOs have helped establish mobile crèches in various cities, targeting construction workers' children and trying to engage governments and companies in the process (Bajaj and Gupta, 2013). An NGO reported using the 1996 Building and Other Construction Workers Act to advocate for crèches on construction sites. Some integrated programmes include nutrition, health and hygiene, education, and community engagement and advocacy supports (UNESCO, 2013).

> In India, NGOs have helped establish mobile crèches for over 40 years in various cities, targeting construction workers' children

Recent national government initiatives recognize seasonal migrant issues. Under the 2009 Right to Education Act, local authorities are legally obliged to admit migrant children. National-level guidelines include recommendations to allow flexible admission, develop seasonal hostels, provide transport and mobile education volunteers, and improve coordination between sending and receiving states and districts (Chandrasekhar and Bhattacharya, 2018).

However, there are many implementation challenges. A pilot programme run at brick kiln work sites in three areas of Rajasthan state in 2010–2011 assigned out-of-school children unique identification numbers to track their progress. The programme did not improve learning substantially. Teachers on the sites cited culture, language, lifestyle, cleanliness and clothing as major barriers between them and the kiln labour community. Teacher and student absenteeism was rampant due to the poor teaching and learning conditions and the need for students to work at the kilns (Reed, 2012).

Most proactive state interventions focus on keeping children in home communities rather than addressing the challenges seasonal migrant children face. Gujarat state established seasonal boarding schools for migrant children, provided education for out-of-school children and collaborated with CSOs to enhance online tracking of migrant children. In Maharashtra state, seasonal migrants were unwilling to leave children in boarding schools. The state government then developed alternative community-based arrangements. Village authorities (*gram panchayats*) engaged local volunteers to provide after-school psychosocial support to left-behind children. Odisha state assumed responsibility for seasonal hostels set up by the Learning and Migration Program of the American India Foundation, an NGO. It also signed a memorandum of understanding with Andhra Pradesh state in 2012 to encourage collaboration and improve migrant well-being. Tamil Nadu state provided textbooks in other languages to migrant children (Chandrasekhar and Bhattacharya, 2018).

CHILD DOMESTIC WORKERS ARE AMONG THE MOST VULNERABLE TO EXCLUSION FROM EDUCATION

Many rural children work as domestic help in urban households. They are among the most vulnerable to non-attendance at school, although estimates are scarce. In 2012, around 17.2 million children aged 5 to 17 were in paid or unpaid domestic work in an employer's home; two-thirds were girls (ILO, 2017b).

In Indonesia, about 59% of child domestic workers in Jakarta and other metropolitan areas were girls from rural areas. More than half had primary education only; a further 26% dropped out at grade 7 or 8 (Patunru and Kusumaningrum, 2013). In Peru, over 95% of domestic workers were women, and most were rural to urban migrants who migrated at a young age. Ethnographic research from Lima noted that young girls viewed domestic work as a way to leave rural areas and continue education. However, workload often prevents the latter, limiting future employment prospects (Alaluusua, 2017). In Ethiopia, a study of nearly 5,300 out-of-school girls from six regions found that on average, they migrated unaccompanied at age 14. Few attended school after moving; most entered paid employment, domestic work being the most accessible (Erulkar et al., 2017).

Fostering is a common strategy in many African countries. Parent migration is one reason for fostering children out; education is a common reason for fostering children in (Beck et al., 2015; Marazyan, 2015). Nearly 10% of Senegalese children were foster children, with a clear gender disparity. Boys were more likely to be sent to households placing greater emphasis on education, ending up more educated than their siblings. Girls were almost four times more likely to help with host household chores and were less likely to be hosted for education reasons (Beck et al., 2015).

Protecting these children calls for free, high-quality public education and social protection, along with early interventions to curb child labour or prevent entry into hazardous work (ILO, 2015, 2017a). Trained teachers can also help protect child domestic workers' education rights. Anti-Slavery International, an NGO, developed focused teacher education programmes in Peru and India, and in the Philippines, established regular school visits to raise teacher awareness and school-based liaison officers for child domestic workers (Anti-Slavery International, 2013). In collaboration with the International Labour Organization, a trade union in the United Republic of Tanzania set up child labour committees in villages as watchdogs for children recruited into domestic labour (ILO, 2013, 2017b).

NOMAD AND PASTORALIST EDUCATION NEEDS ARE NOT ADDRESSED

Mobility is an intrinsic part of life for many nomads and pastoralists, who depend on livestock. Interventions should recognize their needs and improve education's relevance to nomadic lifestyles and new realities. It is difficult to determine the number of people practising pastoralism, as they tend to be undercounted in household surveys and censuses (Randall, 2015). One estimate claims that there are at least 200 million pastoralists globally (Davies and Hagelberg, 2014). Their education situation is dire. In 2015 in Somalia, only 16% of nomadic and pastoralist children over age 6 were enrolled – less than half the national average – and only 12% of adult nomads were literate, compared with the national average of 40% (**Figure 2.6**).

About 1,000 households were tracked in remote rural areas of the Somali autonomous regions of Galmudug and Puntland and federal member state of Somaliland between 2013 and 2016. School spot checks indicated

> "In 2015, only 16% of nomadic and pastoralist children over age 6 were enrolled in Somalia, less than half the national average"

high seasonal fluctuation in student numbers: 50% more children were in school in May than in November-December at the end of the dry season (JBS International, 2017).

Migrating students struggle to develop literacy and numeracy skills at the same pace as their peers. To help pastoralist children catch up after long absences, a project in Somalia worked with teachers and local education officials on specific skills gaps, connecting numeracy to financial literacy and business development and developing leadership skills. It has rolled out in 150 primary schools in Galmudug, Puntland and Somaliland (CARE International, 2016).

There were 108 mobile schools in South Sudan in 2013, serving between 4,000 and 12,000 students. In addition, the South Sudan Interactive Radio Instruction programme, implemented between 2004 and 2012, produced 480 30-minute lessons for students in grades 1 to 4 and reached over 400,000 children (Forcier Consulting, 2016). For nomadic herder families in Mongolia, which represent 30% of the total population, children benefited from a system of boarding schools that has come under pressure in recent years (**Box 2.1**).

FIGURE 2.6:

Pastoralist populations in Somalia have very low enrolment and literacy rates

Enrolment rate (aged 6 to 17) and adult literacy rate, national average and pastoralists, 2015

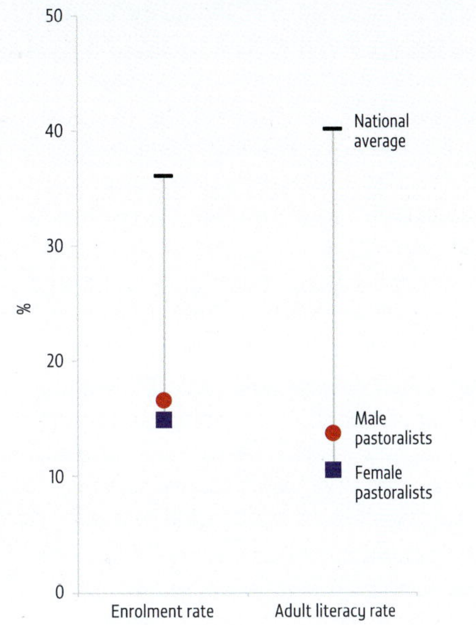

GEM StatLink: http://bit.ly/fig2_6
Source: Somalia Ministry of Education, Culture and Higher Education (2017a).

BOX 2.1:

Nomadic pastoralists are adjusting to changing conditions in Mongolia

Until 1990, Mongolia had a well-functioning system of boarding schools that catered to the highly scattered nomadic population (Steiner-Khamsi and Stolpe, 2005). In recent years, drought, overgrazing, natural resource degradation, livestock privatization and job opportunities in the mining sector have affected nomadic life, prompting migration to cities. Between 2012 and 2016, enrolment declined by 14% in *soum* schools, which serve sparsely populated administrative units with an average population between 1,500 and 3,000 people. By contrast, it increased by 25% in schools in the capital city, Ulaanbaatar, some of which introduced a third shift.

Approximately 10,000 6-year-olds from herder families entered grade 1, out of which 2,000 stayed in dormitories. Among pastoralist families, there is a growing tendency for mothers to stay with their children in the *soum* centres, away from fathers and the rest of the family who herd. A recent policy is to provide free access to school dormitories for herder children. In 2016/17, 72% of the 35,000 children in dormitories were herder children. However, some dormitories have poor heating, water and sanitation.

In 2013, the average mathematics score at the end of grade 5 was 64% in Ulaanbaatar schools and 50% in *soum* schools. Apart from basic skills, nomadic knowledge does not receive significant attention in curricula. While the curricula have flexibility to introduce locally relevant content and skills, in practice, there is little effort to make the curriculum relevant for nomadic lifestyles and political support may be favouring farming over herding (Batkhuyag and Dondogdulam, 2018).

Efforts focus on adjusting education to seasonality and mobility

Many countries with significant nomadic or pastoralist populations have dedicated government departments, commissions or councils, such as the federal Special Directorate in Ethiopia, the National Council for Nomadic Education in Kenya, the Nomadic Education Commission in Nigeria and the Department of Education for Nomads in Sudan. Afghanistan's 2004 Constitution recognizes nomads' right to education (Bengtsson and Dyer, 2017). In Somalia and its federal member state of Somaliland, pastoralist education features prominently in the latest Education Sector Strategy Plans (Somalia Ministry of Education Culture and Higher Education, 2017b; Somaliland Ministry of Education and Higher Studies, 2017).

Among strategies to deal with seasonality, boarding schools have been successful in retaining pastoralist learners, including girls, in Ethiopia, western India and Oman (Bengtsson and Dyer, 2017). Mobile schools, for the most part, are limited in scale due to their costs. In Turkana county, Kenya, mobile schools were highly dependent on availability of water and food, with attendance dropping significantly when these could not be ensured (Ngugi, 2016).

Most education systems are not adapted to seasonal movements. Rigid school calendars are a barrier for pastoralist children who cannot adjust their mobility needs. Pastoralist learners also challenge traditional teaching. Teachers may be reluctant to re-enrol temporarily absent children or feel that taking extra measures goes beyond their responsibility (Coffey, 2013).

A network of schools, any of which could be exited and entered at any time, might be a viable solution but would require an efficient and effective tracking system to share progression information among schools. In Ethiopia, migrant communities shared information about their moves via a network card. A migration register, combined with a learning register or card that travels with the child and tracks progression until completion of lower secondary, could help pass information among schools (Bengtsson and Dyer, 2017).

> "The Africa Educational Trust operates in 42 pastoralist communities in Somalia and helps train community educators to accompany learners"

Some countries have made teachers more mobile. A teacher from the community moves with pastoralists to deliver Koranic education in the *duksi* school serving pastoralists in Ethiopia, Kenya and Somalia (Bengtsson and Dyer, 2017). The Africa Educational Trust helps train community educators to accompany learners in 42 pastoralist communities of Somalia, although the training does not necessarily lead to official teacher qualifications (Africa Education Trust, 2017). In Ethiopia's mobile camel library system, a teacher guides learners in reading, and a herder supervises the programme (Bengtsson and Dyer, 2017).

Nomad and pastoralist education should be more relevant

Education for nomadic populations should recognize and value their way of life. Uganda's alternative basic education system runs mobile schools for children in cattle camps. Taught in the local language, classes focus on numeracy, literacy, and livestock production and health (Forcier Consulting, 2016). But even alternative basic education, often considered a solution to nomadic education, is not universally accepted. A study in Samburu county, Kenya, found that 80% of respondents did not think available alternatives appropriately accommodated mobility (Lanyasunya et al., 2012).

Analysis from three semi-arid counties in Kenya found that schools did not teach subjects relevant to pastoralist livelihoods. Curricula were often incompatible with children's languages and experiences and did not include community traditions. In Wajir county, among pastoralists, only 27% of primary school-age children and 9% of secondary school-age adolescents were enrolled in 2014. Instead, they attended pastoralist or religious schools, which parents deemed more relevant and accessible (Scott-Villiers et al., 2015). The issue of secular vs religious schools is key to the challenge of the *almajiri*, a large group of itinerant children in northern Nigeria (**Box 2.2**).

Limited employment prospects factor into decisions to continue schooling. Fishing provides income-generating opportunities for a migrant community in Ghana, which increases the risk that children drop out of school (Ananga, 2013). In the United Republic of Tanzania, pastoralists perceived formal education as entailing lower benefits and higher costs than did other wealthier households. Children of farmers were over twice as likely as pastoralist children to progress to fee-charging secondary schools, and children of business owners almost six times as likely (Hedges et al., 2016).

Vocational education can be particularly relevant to pastoralists, especially agricultural skills for a nomadic lifestyle. The Food and Agriculture Organization of the United Nations (FAO) has worked with nomadic communities on pastoralist field schools in Djibouti, Ethiopia, Kenya, South Sudan and Uganda since 2012. Courses focus on farming-related skills aimed at increasing livestock management efficiency and mitigating climate change effects such as drought, which plague the region and greatly affect pastoralists (FAO, 2013). In South Sudan, the FAO is collaborating with UNESCO to help the government provide mobile learning opportunities for pastoralist communities, including formal curriculum which includes livestock management and livelihoods diversification training (FAO, 2018).

INDIGENOUS GROUPS STRUGGLE TO PRESERVE THEIR IDENTITIES IN CITIES

In much of the world, education systems not only failed to provide relevant education to indigenous populations but focused instead on forcing assimilation through schooling. Australia, Canada, New Zealand, the Russian Federation and the United States, among other countries, separated indigenous children from their communities and placed them in boarding schools, where they were often subject to mental and physical abuse, prohibited from learning or speaking their native languages, and prepared for manual or domestic work (ECOSOC, 2010).

Today, this legacy is compounded by poverty and migration to urban areas, which often implies further cultural erosion, language loss and discrimination. Urban indigenous populations encounter a policy bias that associates indigeneity with rurality or remoteness. Regulatory frameworks on indigenous rights make little or no reference to indigenous people living in cities, increasing their chances of being politically invisible (Brand et al., 2016).

In New Zealand, the 1950s and 1960s Māori internal migration to cities was rapid, encouraged by the government to boost the workforce (Kukutai, 2011). The share of Māori living in urban areas, which in 1926 was 16%, grew to 62% in 1966 and 85% in 2006. Only

“Vocational education can be particularly relevant to pastoralists, especially agricultural skills for a nomadic lifestyle”

BOX 2.2:

Integrating religious and secular education for *almajiri* children in northern Nigeria

As part of its nomadic education policy, the federal and state governments in northern Nigeria have introduced several initiatives over the years to improve access for mobile populations, such as mobile schools and collapsible classrooms, canoes and boats for migrant fishing communities, and improved infrastructure and technology aids (Okonkwo and Ibrahim, 2014). However, the main challenge remains tackling the socio-economic challenges that sustain the *almajiri* system.

The *almajiri* are migrant 'pupils of Islamic knowledge' (Taiwo, 2013, p. 67) who migrate from their rural homes to urban areas in northern Nigeria and follow an itinerant religious teacher who delivers Koranic education. In the *almajiri* system, a teacher can be responsible for up to 100 students, predominantly poor boys who often end up on the street begging for alms (Hoechner, 2018). Nomadic pastoralists, in particular, favour the *almajiri* Koranic system over formal education as more relevant to the needs of their society.

A federal task force identified the integration of Koranic education into basic education programmes as key to revitalizing *almajiri* education. Between 2010 and 2013, the government invested in 117 model *almajiri* schools in 26 out of 36 states (Olaniran, 2018). However, integration may not be achieved if parents have concerns about the quality of formal secular schools (Antoninis, 2014). This is a common problem across western Africa (d'Aiglepierre and Bauer, 2018). It requires efforts to increase the demand and gain the trust of students, parents and teachers who prefer the existing non-formal education system.

In Kano state, an intervention that targeted 700 traditional teachers focused on collaborating with them to select those teachers who would teach non-religious subjects. In addition, to engage the community, the intervention also offered school meals, farm inputs and cash transfers at a small scale. About 70% of the original cohort passed the junior secondary transition exam (ESSPIN, 2014).

26% of Māori could speak the Māori language by 1960, prompting a call for culturally relevant and bilingual Māori education, which was included in a 1988 Royal Commission report (ECOSOC, 2010; Ryks et al., 2014). Yet the 2013 census showed that only 21% of Māori could hold a conversation about everyday things in Māori (New Zealand Ministry of Social Development, 2016).

In some countries, schools have incorporated indigenous culture. In Australia, parents appreciated an urban primary school, with almost 25% indigenous students, embedding indigenous knowledge and introducing indigenous symbols, such as flags, artwork and maps (Baxter and Meyers, 2016). Over 50% of Canada's indigenous people live in cities. Analyses of urban aboriginal populations showed the importance of education in improving their quality of life and found that incorporating culturally appropriate curricula and practices, including aboriginal languages, ceremonies and elder participation, mattered for early childhood education outcomes (Beaton and McDonell, 2014; Findlay et al., 2014).

While urban indigenous students in Latin America typically outperform their rural peers, completing secondary at a rate 3.6 times higher, they lag behind urban non-indigenous students. In Mexico, 54% of indigenous people live in cities (World Bank, 2016). Intercultural, bilingual education is a major initiative to reduce exclusion but is not systematically implemented. Indigenous parents perceive primary schools as viewing their identity negatively. Younger generations in cities are significantly less likely to speak indigenous languages in Ecuador, Mexico and Peru (Del Popolo et al., 2007).

Chile's Mapuche have pushed for education rights, especially during school protests in 2006. In 2010, indigenous languages were incorporated into the official curricula in schools with over 50% indigenous enrolment, which were more likely to be found in rural than in urban areas. In 2013, this was extended to schools with at least 20% indigenous enrolment but as a voluntary initiative (Webb and Radcliffe, 2013). Teachers in an intercultural and bilingual pre-school felt that, in addition to learning the language, they needed more cultural knowledge and first-hand experience with indigenous communities (Becerra-Lubies and Fones, 2016).

MIGRATION CHALLENGES EDUCATION PLANNERS IN VILLAGES AND CITIES

Migration affects education planning, with both rural depopulation and unplanned urban and peri-urban growth posing challenges. Ingenuity, local initiative and flexibility are needed to address the negative consequences of such demographic pressures on children, parents and communities.

DEPOPULATION PROMPTS CONSOLIDATION OF SMALL RURAL SCHOOLS

Rural depopulation has implications for small rural schools. Education planners must balance efficient resource allocation with the welfare of small communities. England (United Kingdom) had more than 2,000 schools with fewer than 100 students in 2018 (United Kingdom Department of Education, 2018), while 9% of primary and 17% of secondary government-funded spaces were unfilled in 2017 (United Kingdom Education and Skills Funding Agency, 2017). In France, the number of kindergartens and elementary schools fell by about 17,500, or 25%, between 1980 and 2016 (France Ministry of Education, 2017).

Between one-quarter and one-third of primary and lower secondary schools in Norway and Sweden with fewer than 100 students closed between 2006 and 2017; even so, about 30% of public schools still have fewer than 100 students (**Figure 2.7**) (OECD, 2015). Finland closed or consolidated almost 80% of schools with fewer than 50 students – more than 1,600 schools in all – between 1990 and 2015 (Autti and Hyry-Beihammer, 2014; Statistics Finland, 2017).

> “Rural schools in the Russian Federation fell from 45,000 to fewer than 26,000 between 2000 and 2015”

Urbanization and reduced fertility present similar challenges in many middle income countries. The number of rural schools in the Russian Federation fell from 45,000 to fewer than 26,000 between 2000 and 2015 (Goble, 2017). In China, the number of rural primary schools decreased by 52% between 2000 and 2010. On average, 63 primary,

FIGURE 2.7:

Nordic countries have consolidated schools substantially

Number of schools and small schools, Norway and Sweden, 2006–2017

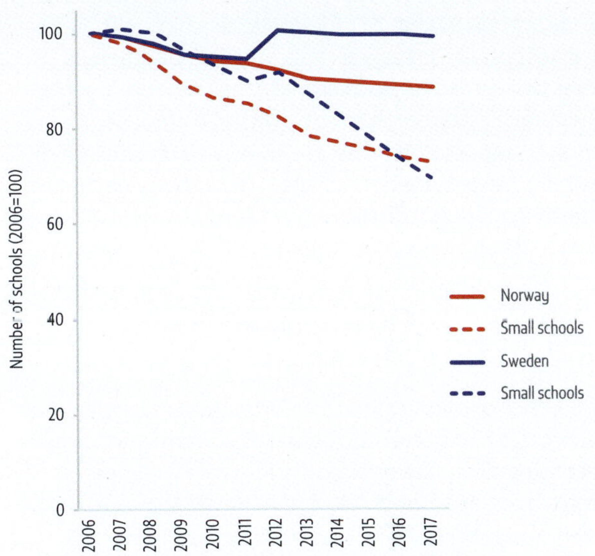

GEM StatLink: http://bit.ly/fig2_7

Notes: Statistics on Norway are based on primary, lower secondary, and combined primary and lower secondary schools. Statistics on Sweden are based on comprehensive schools.

Sources: Statistics Norway (2018); Swedish National Agency for Education (2018).

30 teaching and 3 junior high schools close daily (Rao and Jingzhong, 2016). In India, school-age population forecasts will push governments to reconsider outdated distance-based norms for school construction (Siddhu et al., 2015).

Small-class schools in Kazakhstan constituted half of all schools but enrolled only 11% of students in 2013–2014 (Pons et al., 2015). Almost half of Thailand's 30,000 schools had 120 students or fewer as of 2011 (Buaraphan, 2013), and close to 30% had average class sizes of fewer than 10 students (OECD and UNESCO, 2016).

School consolidation requires consultations and governance reforms

In considering consolidation to reduce costs and improve efficiency, governments must recognize the important social role schools play in communities. Funding staff and maintenance for a handful of students may not be sustainable. Small schools may not attract qualified teachers for adequately diverse learning. Yet small schools offer closer interpersonal interactions among teachers, parents and students. Analysis of 2015 Programme for International Student Assessment data showed that students from smaller schools had fewer discipline, tardiness and absenteeism issues (OECD, 2016b). Consolidations in the United States have disrupted community life without yielding significant cost or performance benefits (Ares Abalde, 2014).

Successful consolidation requires careful consideration. The Scottish Schools Consultation Act introduced a consultation process, before school closures, involving parents, students, parent councils, church and other community bodies, teaching staff and trade unions. A school would close only if there were sufficient explanations and no viable alternative (Education Scotland, 2015). Between 2010 and 2012, about two-thirds of European countries engaged in school consolidation (European Commission et al., 2013). Some countries instead accepted the high cost of sustaining small rural schools delivering education of quality; in others, geographical isolation made further consolidation impossible (Ares Abalde, 2014).

Consolidation costs should also be taken into account. In Austria, municipalities closing schools compensate the regions absorbing them (Nusche et al., 2016). In Estonia, municipalities closing lower secondary schools receive funding for at least a few years, local governments consolidating upper secondary schools are eligible for special grants, and the national government covers student transport (Santiago et al., 2016). Lithuania's new education law made municipalities responsible for optimizing the network of schools. Central authorities provided data, analysis, recommendations and guidelines to support the consolidation process. The government developed priority measures to preserve small rural primary schools and provided safe transport with hundreds of new buses (Shewbridge et al., 2016).

“ The Scottish Schools Consultation Act introduced a consultation process before school closures, involving parents, students, parent councils, church and other community bodies, teaching staff and trade unions ”

Networks help keep rural schools vibrant

One policy that can keep rural schools vibrant is to encourage them to share resources and learn from each other. A district school board in Ontario, Canada, made e-learning widely available to ensure that all students could complete secondary education (Ontario Ministry of Education, 2017). Quebec, Canada, strives to sustain 'last village schools' and create a network to revitalize and professionalize small rural schools (Ares Abalde, 2014). Chile has 374 micro-centres for rural teachers to meet and discuss common challenges (Santiago et al., 2017). Rural schools in Catalonia, Spain, are part of rural education zones and share teachers for some courses, such as foreign language and music (Ares Abalde, 2014).

> "Chile has 374 micro-centres for rural teachers to meet and discuss common challenges"

In the Republic of Korea, population decline in the 1980s and 1990s led to a recommendation that all schools with fewer than 180 students be closed. Those remaining frequently organized into hubs of two to four schools, with one managing education programmes and facilities. Major investments were made to modernize facilities, develop excellent rural high schools, financially support rural schools and facilitate public boarding schools (Ares Abalde, 2014). In China, governments, schools and communities have responded in various ways to support small rural schools (**Box 2.3**).

Some schools switch to multigrade teaching, although teacher preparedness is a challenge. In mountainous areas of Austria and Switzerland, small schools organize multigrade classrooms to cope with low enrolment. Teachers report isolated work environments and lack of training. Nevertheless, teachers in Vorarlberg, Austria, reported support from strong small rural school networks (Raggl, 2015).

MIGRANTS IN SLUMS HAVE FEWER EDUCATIONAL OPPORTUNITIES

The arrival of migrants in cities often leads to residential segregation characterized by gated communities, private security and private transport. Slums are the most visible manifestation in low and middle income countries. Large slums typically include a mix of new arrivals, long-term migrants and non-migrants. In 2006, it was estimated that every day, between 100 and 300 families in search of work arrive in Mumbai, India, often ending up in slums (Agarwal, 2014). Overcrowding can lead to social tensions between new arrivals and long-time migrants

BOX 2.3:

A variety of approaches support small rural schools in China

Rapid consolidation in China has challenged rural schools' ability to provide high-quality education. In 2015, the government equalized rural and urban public funding per student, effectively raising rural school funding. However, an administration system whereby counties allocate funding and staff quotas to school districts, led by central schools in towns (*xiangzhen*), often turns village schools into passive recipients.

Since 2011, the government has engaged in major renovation and upgrading for small rural school facilities, officially recognized as needing special attention. A free lunch programme was launched in 2012 to improve nutrition for poor students.

Policies to raise teaching quality in rural areas include various placement and exchange programmes. The 2006 Special Teaching Post Plan for Rural Schools recruited university graduates to work for three years in rural schools in central and western China, particularly in remote regions with minority populations. In 2015, about 90% of teachers stayed in their posts after the work term (OECD, 2016a).

In some school districts in Gansu and Hunan provinces, small rural schools coordinate class schedules so teachers can teach at different schools on different days.

In some cases, NGOs, local communities and schools themselves have increased resources and established resource sharing networks. In 2014, Lizhou district, Sichuan province, established the first local small school consortium. Other consortiums have emerged since in Puyang, Henan province; in Pingliang, Gansu province; and in Danzhou, Hainan province, sharing teachers, developing courses collectively and providing financial resources.

The Chinese Rural Small School Association, now with more than 800 member schools, was initiated in 2015 to provide teacher education and online courses for small rural schools and to advocate for policies tailored to the most disadvantaged rural schools. The association also increased small rural schools' public media presence (Han et al., 2018).

with distinct networks and backgrounds, as observed in the Philippines (Baker et al., 2017). An analysis of three Indian cities also found that new migrants were the most marginalized, regardless of social or religious background, due to lack of documentation and tensions with older migrants (Sahoo, 2016).

While the share of the urban population in developing countries living in slums decreased from 39% in 2000 to 30% in 2014, the slum population continued to grow and is estimated at at least 800 million (UN Habitat, 2016c). Using data on slum, school-age and urban populations and projections, the GEM Report estimates that there could be 80 million more children in slums in 2030 than in 2015. Slum settlement quality, legal status and basic service provision vary widely among and within countries, but hundreds of millions of slum dwellers lack basic services, including public education (UN Habitat, 2016c) (**Data focus 12.1**). In 2009, the secondary school attendance rate in Bangladeshi slums was 18%, compared with 53% in urban areas. The primary school attendance rate was 55% in the slums of Delhi, India, in 2004–2005 but 90% in the city as a whole (UNICEF, 2012).

Education trajectories for some slum-dwelling migrants nonetheless improve over time, with a positive impact on their lifetime opportunities. Longitudinal analysis in Rio de Janeiro, Brazil, found some movement out of favelas as families' education and employment prospects improved (Perlman, 2010). Longitudinal data from two informal settlements in Nairobi, Kenya, found that 96% of children aged 6 to 14 who migrated for schooling were in school, compared with 60% of those who migrated for better jobs (Abuya, 2018).

Improving education access and quality in slums has not been a priority

Although education is mentioned in inclusive urban development frameworks, it is usually not a priority in urbanism debates, which focus on housing, water and sanitation (United Nations Task Team, 2015). A 'slum household' is one deprived of one or more of the following: improved water source, improved sanitation facilities, sufficient living area, housing durability and tenure security; education does not make the list (UN Habitat, 2003, 2016b). Securing tenure and establishing rights are key steps towards education

> More than 40% of migrants and other residents in two informal settlements in Nairobi were enrolled in private schools between 2003 and 2010

provision, but an explicit focus on education is also needed. The 2016 *India Habitat III National Report* promised an inclusive urban agenda with universal provision of basic services, including education (India Ministry of Housing and Urban Poverty Alleviation, 2016).

Slum property rights questions thwart investment in education

Governments are often reluctant to invest in education infrastructure in slums because their inhabitants settled on land they did not own. Lack of public investment limits the availability of schools. A slum settlement survey in Dhaka, Bangladesh, showed that there were fewer than 300 government primary schools in slums, and only about one-quarter of slums were estimated to have a government school in 2007. About 15% of children aged 6 to 14 were out of school and engaged in full-time work, primarily in the garment sector (Quattri and Watkins, 2016). Informal and densely populated areas of Cairo are underserved in terms of the number of public schools within walking distance (TADAMUN, 2015).

After decades of failed attempts to dismantle slums or relocate them outside the city centre, countries are focusing on upgrading them to integrate their populations into the fabric of the city (UN Habitat, 2016a, 2016c; UNESCO, 2016b). Inclusive housing policies can have a positive impact on education outcomes. In Argentina, access to land titling was associated with long-term education improvement (Galiani and Schargrodsky, 2010). An impact evaluation of the Rio de Janeiro Favela-Bairro II slum upgrade programme found a small but significant positive impact on day care and school attendance (Álvarez et al., 2011).

> In Argentina, access to land titling was associated with long-term education improvement

Upgrade programmes increasingly use participatory approaches. Innovative participatory approaches to count slums and enhance slum dweller visibility to influence policy could improve education access. Johannesburg, South Africa, set up a Migrant Advisory Council, Migrant Advisory Panel and Migration Unit for this purpose (South African Cities Network, 2016). Results of such initiatives for education access and quality are not yet well documented (Shack/Slum Dwellers International, 2018).

Social policies can support slum populations, but registration problems persist

Social protection programmes targeted at the urban poor and slum dwellers can help improve migrant living conditions and, indirectly, access to education. However, rigid registration and documentation requirements often hinder migrant participation (Hopkins et al., 2016). Eligibility for benefits under the Mumbai Slum Areas Act required proof of residence prior to 1 January 1995 and slum recognition by the city government (Subbaraman et al., 2012).

Urban social protection programmes are less common than rural ones but are growing in number. Expanding social protection to urban areas is often cumbersome, as many urban poor are seasonal or temporary migrants. New migrants may be less politically visible and thus less able to improve their access to safety nets. In Kenya, the urban social protection programme required national identification, thus excluding the 5% of preselected slum dwellers who were refugees, unable to prove Kenyan nationality or from child-headed households (Gentilini, 2015).

Private providers fill the gap in education provision in slums

The lack of sufficient government schools in slums has led to provision by NGOs (BRAC, 2017; Jagannathan, 2001) and private actors. School mapping exercises have shown the extent to which slum dwellers use non-government schools in cities such as Kampala, Uganda; Lagos, Nigeria; Lahore, Pakistan; and Nairobi, Kenya (UNESCO, 2015, 2016b). The proportion of private schools in four low income areas of Kampala was 94%, and they accounted for 84% of pre-primary to secondary enrolment (Härmä et al., 2017). More than 40% of migrants and other residents in two informal settlements in Nairobi were enrolled in private schools between 2003 and 2010 (Abuya, 2018).

Although often the only option, these schools may not meet minimum standards and are poorly regulated. Schools in slums tend to employ untrained educators or para-teachers. An initiative to raise teacher quality in Nairobi slums focused on training Teacher Advisory Centre coaches and tutors and providing them with guides and textbooks. An evaluation showed that student literacy outcomes improved, particularly where the coach to teacher ratio was high (Piper and Zuilkowski, 2015).

Technology also bridges the education gap in some slums. Jaago ('wake up'), an award-winning initiative operating in 13 schools and an orphanage in Bangladesh, provides online learning to refugees and children in slums, including internal migrants. It started delivering lessons over messaging and video services but now connects teachers in Dhaka with learners through an interactive tool (UNESCO, 2016a).

CONCLUSION

Governments, particularly in middle income countries, must improve the education situation of internal migrants, who account for a significant proportion of hard-to-reach, out-of-school children. Data on migrant numbers and education status are lacking. Addressing undercounting will improve the visibility of slum populations, seasonal migrants, and nomads and pastoralists so as to ensure that eventually all individuals of all ages enjoy the right to education.

Planning needs to integrate internal migration patterns and challenges, with a focus on reducing legal, administrative and financial barriers to education provision. Innovative approaches, such as flexible calendars and migrant tracking, and development of teacher capacity should be prioritized. While boarding schools often facilitate mobility, their conditions need adequate attention. Inclusive education requires ensuring that migrants receive relevant skills and education from qualified teachers in non-discriminatory environments. More broadly, social protection, urban inclusion and livelihood programmes need to integrate education needs and demands into their efforts to support the most marginalized.

Children at a protest against a proposed federal crackdown on illegal immigration in Los Angeles, California, United States.

CREDIT: Krista Kennell/Shutterstock.com

CHAPTER

3

International migration

Many of us realize there is a strong link between international migration and education. At times, however, we have been forced to rely on scant and scattered evidence of this complex relationship. The contribution set out in this report brings together the existing evidence on migration and education to paint a picture of incredible opportunity as well as point to where and why educational disadvantage can occur. It provides the analytical cornerstone to help guide our decisions on education in a range of migration contexts – and this at a time in which the international community is striving to meet the SDGs and maximize the significant benefits of migration globally.

William Lacy Swing,[1] Director General of the International Organization for Migration

[1] IOM Director General from 1 October 2008 to 30 September 2018

KEY MESSAGES

The number of international migrants increased from 93 million in 1960 to 258 million in 2017. Their share of the population fell from 3.1% in 1960 to 2.7% in 1990 before reaching 3.4% in 2017.

In OECD countries, the share of first- and second-generation immigrant students increased from 9.4% to 12.5% between 2006 and 2015. In addition, 8.9% of the population were natives of mixed heritage and 1.8% were returning students born abroad.

The more educated are more likely to emigrate. Global emigration rates were 5.4% for those with tertiary education, 1.8% for those with secondary and 1.1% for those with primary.

Immigrants tend to be more educated than their hosts. In Brazil and Canada, there is at least a 20 percentage point gap between immigrants and natives with tertiary education.

Migrants often find their education constrained by legal, administrative or linguistic barriers. In 2017, twice as many foreign-born youth as natives left school early in the European Union.

Age at migration is a major determinant of education needs, opportunities, trajectories and outcomes. In the United States, 40% of Mexican immigrants who arrived at age 7 did not complete secondary school, compared with 70% of those who arrived at age 14.

Educational gaps between immigrants and natives tend to persist across generations. In Belgium, there is a 17 percentage point gap between second-generation immigrants and natives who stopped education at the lower secondary level.

Migrants' education attainment and learning improve faster than those of people left behind. In the United States, children of emigrants from Colombia had 2.3 more years of education, on average, than children of those who did not emigrate.

In many countries, including Australia and Malaysia, undocumented immigrants and unaccompanied children in detention often have limited or no access to education.

Lack of language proficiency is an education disadvantage. In 2012, an average of about 53% of low-literacy first-generation immigrant students in 23 high income countries received remedial courses, from 13% in Slovenia to almost 80% in Finland.

Separating low achievers from the most talented disadvantages immigrant students. In Linz, Austria, where tracking starts at age 10, students with immigrant backgrounds were 16 percentage points less likely than natives to choose an academic track in grade 5.

Movements of people across borders have become more diverse and complex in recent years, with an increasing impact on educational opportunities and education systems.

Even when people move for better work and life opportunities, as distinct from being forcibly displaced (**Chapter 4**), they also almost always face adjustment costs, which bear on their ability to invest in education or use their skills. Access to and benefit from education may be constrained for legal or administrative reasons or compromised by linguistic barriers or discrimination. Lack of robust and transparent mechanisms to recognize prior learning and credentials can obstruct use of skills. Even in more advanced receiving education systems, immigrants and, to a lesser extent, people with immigrant backgrounds often lag behind their peers, although they may attain more education and skills than they would have at home.

Education systems also bear adjustment costs in accommodating new arrivals. As the main opportunity to get to know and respect immigrants and people with immigrant backgrounds, schools play a lead role in an inclusive society, but increasing diversity presents challenges for teachers, students and parents. While the Global Compact for Safe and Regular Migration positions international migration as a shared responsibility, education is not prominent on the agenda (United Nations, 2018). The role of teachers and the fight against school segregation deserve wider recognition.

This chapter describes the scale and diversity of international migration and illustrates how it interacts with educational opportunities, attainment and achievement. The chapter highlights disadvantages faced by immigrants and reflects on policies and practices that can expand access to education. Subsequent chapters address other aspects of the migration–education nexus, in particular how improving the quality of education can help societies become more resilient to migratory flows (**Chapter 5**) and what actions facilitate the mobility of the highly skilled (**Chapter 6**).

INTERNATIONAL MIGRATION AFFECTS ALL REGIONS

The number of international migrants increased by more than two and a half times, from 93 million in 1960 to 241 million in 2015 (**Figure 3.1a**). However, contrary to popular perceptions, the percentage of international migrants in the population has remained fairly constant. It fell from 3.1% in 1960 to 2.7% in 1990 and has been increasing since 2000 to reach 3.3% in 2015 (World Bank, 2018) (**Figure 3.1b**).

The United Nations estimates that the number of international migrants increased to 258 million in 2017, or 3.4% of the global population. Of those, 64% reside in high income countries. Unlike low and middle income

> “People with immigrant backgrounds often lag behind their peers, although they may attain more education and skills than they would have at home”

FIGURE 3.1:

The intensity of international migration has increased slightly since 2000

International migrants, 1960–2015

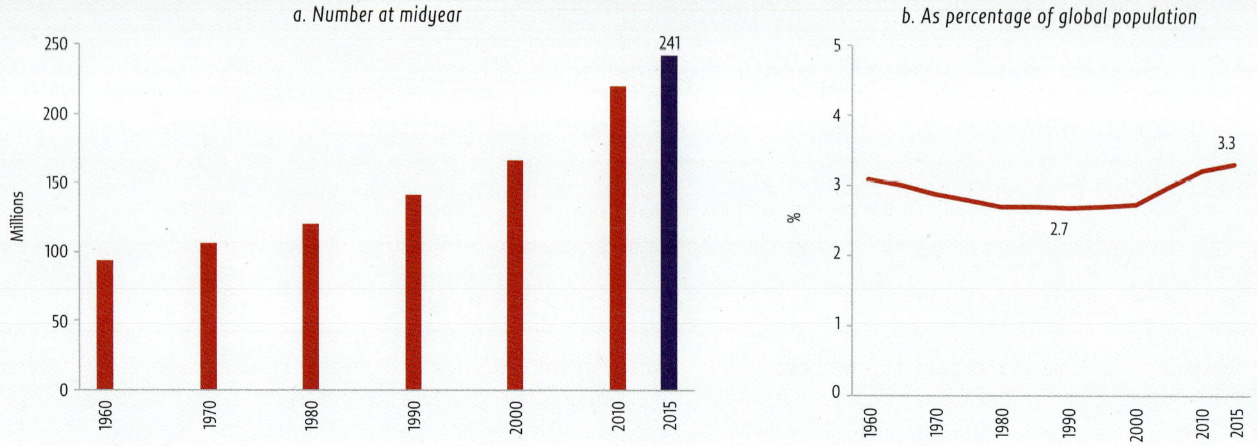

GEM StatLink: http://bit.ly/fig3_1
Source: World Bank (2018).

countries, where the share of migrants in the population has remained constant and low at about 1.5%, the share in high income countries increased from 10% in 2000 to 14% in 2017. In Gulf states, such as Kuwait, Qatar and the United Arab Emirates, migrants are the majority group (United Nations Department for Economic and Social Affairs, 2017b).

Immigration rates are two to three times above the global average in countries as diverse as Costa Rica, Côte d'Ivoire, Malaysia and South Africa (IOM, 2017; United Nations Department for Economic and Social Affairs, 2017b). About 40,000 out of 470,000 primary school children in Costa Rica are immigrants, mainly from Nicaragua (IOM, 2018). Immigrants as a share of the total population fell in Côte d'Ivoire, from 12% in 2000 to 9% in 2017, which was still the highest in sub-Saharan Africa outside oil-rich and small states. More than half were from Burkina Faso in 2012 (Teye et al., 2015). Immigrants, chiefly from Bangladesh, Indonesia, Myanmar and the Philippines, make up 15% of Malaysia's labour force. Their remittances increased fivefold between 2006 and 2015 (Endo et al., 2017). As of 2015, 4 million people in South Africa, or 7% of the population, were born abroad: three out of four came from neighbouring countries, especially Lesotho, Mozambique and Zimbabwe (Crush et al., 2015).

Conversely, countries with emigration rates exceeding 5% of the population are located in the Balkans (Albania and Bosnia and Herzegovina), the Caribbean (Guyana and Jamaica), the Caucasus (Armenia and Georgia), Central Asia (Kyrgyzstan and Tajikistan) and Central America (El Salvador and Nicaragua). Countries with lower emigration rates but high absolute numbers of emigrants include Nepal, the Philippines and Sri Lanka (IOM, 2017).

Important migration corridors are eastern Europe to western Europe; northern Africa to southern Europe; and southern Asia to the Gulf. Mexico to the United States is the largest corridor in absolute terms, with 12.7 million migrants in 2017 (**Figure 3.2**).

There are also lesser known flows for which current, accurate estimates are difficult. In some cases, social media offers innovative and alternative data sources (Zagheni et al., 2017). An increasing number of sub-Saharan African migrants aiming to settle in Europe remain in transit countries, such as Morocco (Mourji et al., 2016). Haitians have emigrated to Chile (Pavez-Soto and Chan, 2018). Venezuelans have emigrated to neighbouring non-Spanish-speaking countries, as well as Brazil (Mahlke and Yamamoto, 2017) and Trinidad and Tobago (Nakhid and Welch, 2017).

FIGURE 3.2:
Large migration corridors exist throughout the world
Number of international migrants from a single origin country living in a single destination country, selected migration corridors, 2017

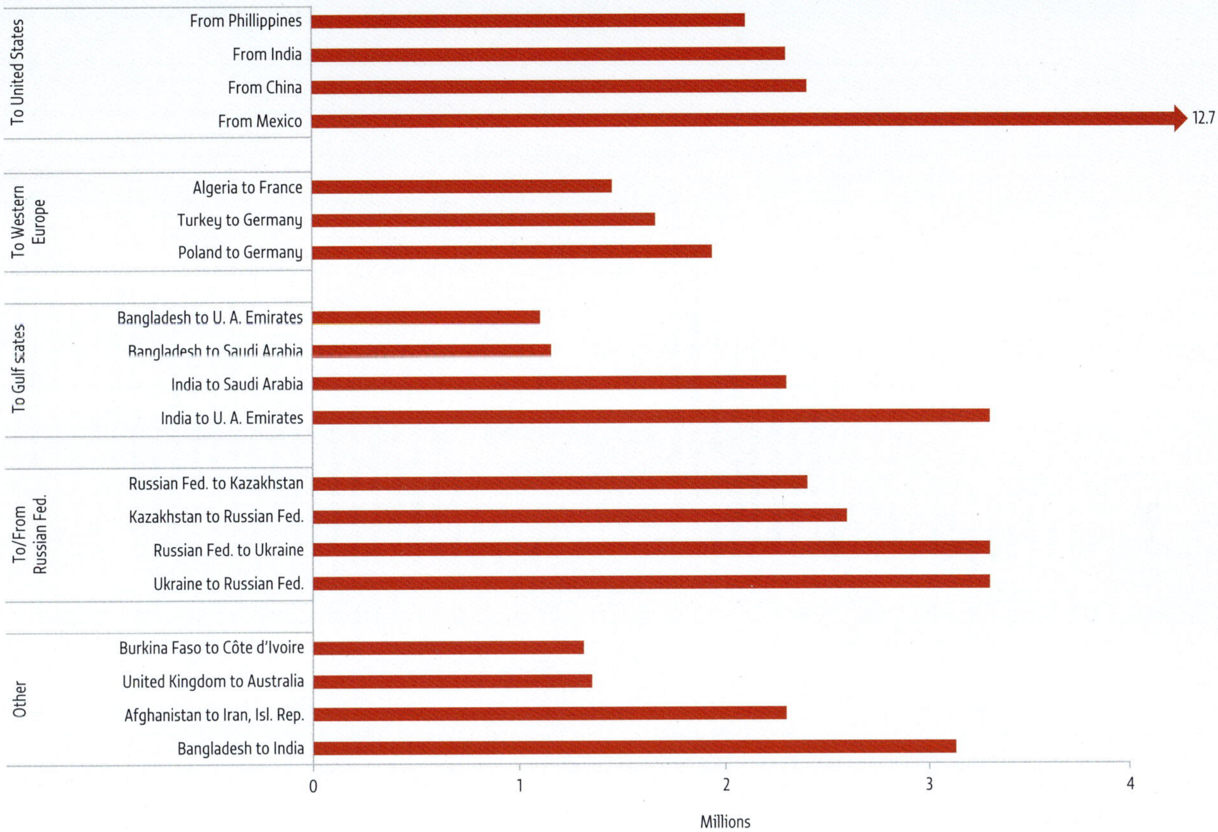

GEM StatLink: http://bit.ly/fig3_2
Source: United Nations Department for Economic and Social Affairs (2017b).

Overall, migrants are older than the general population. In 2017, 14% of international migrants were under age 20, a much lower percentage than the general population (**Figure 3.3**) or among those forcibly displaced (**Chapter 4**).

Migration affects the educational opportunities of both migrants and their children. Analysis of Programme for International Student Assessment (PISA) data suggested that, in the majority of Organisation for Economic Co-operation and Development (OECD) countries, at least one out of five 15-year-old students were immigrants or had immigrant backgrounds in 2015 (OECD, 2016) (**Figure 3.4**). On average, 5.4% were first-generation immigrants, 7.1% were second-generation immigrants, 8.9% were natives of mixed heritage and 1.8% were returning students born abroad. The share of first- and

FIGURE 3.3:
Migrants tend to be older than the general population
Distribution of international migrant and global population by age, 2017

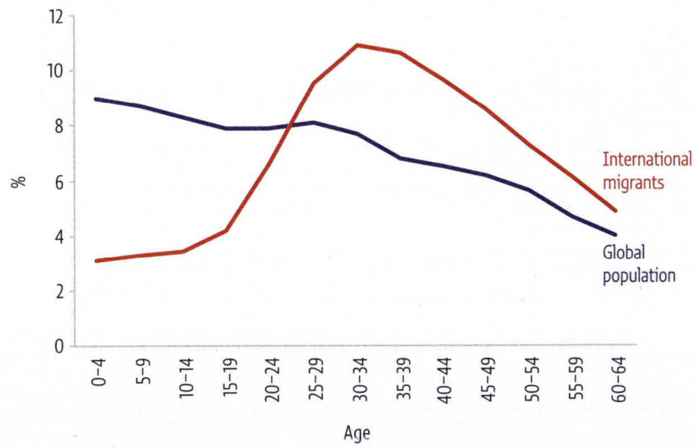

GEM StatLink: http://bit.ly/fig3_3
Source: United Nations Department for Economic and Social Affairs (2017a).

FIGURE 3.4:

In most OECD countries, at least one out of five 15-year-old students were immigrants or had immigrant backgrounds

Distribution of 15-year-old students by type of immigrant background, selected countries, 2015

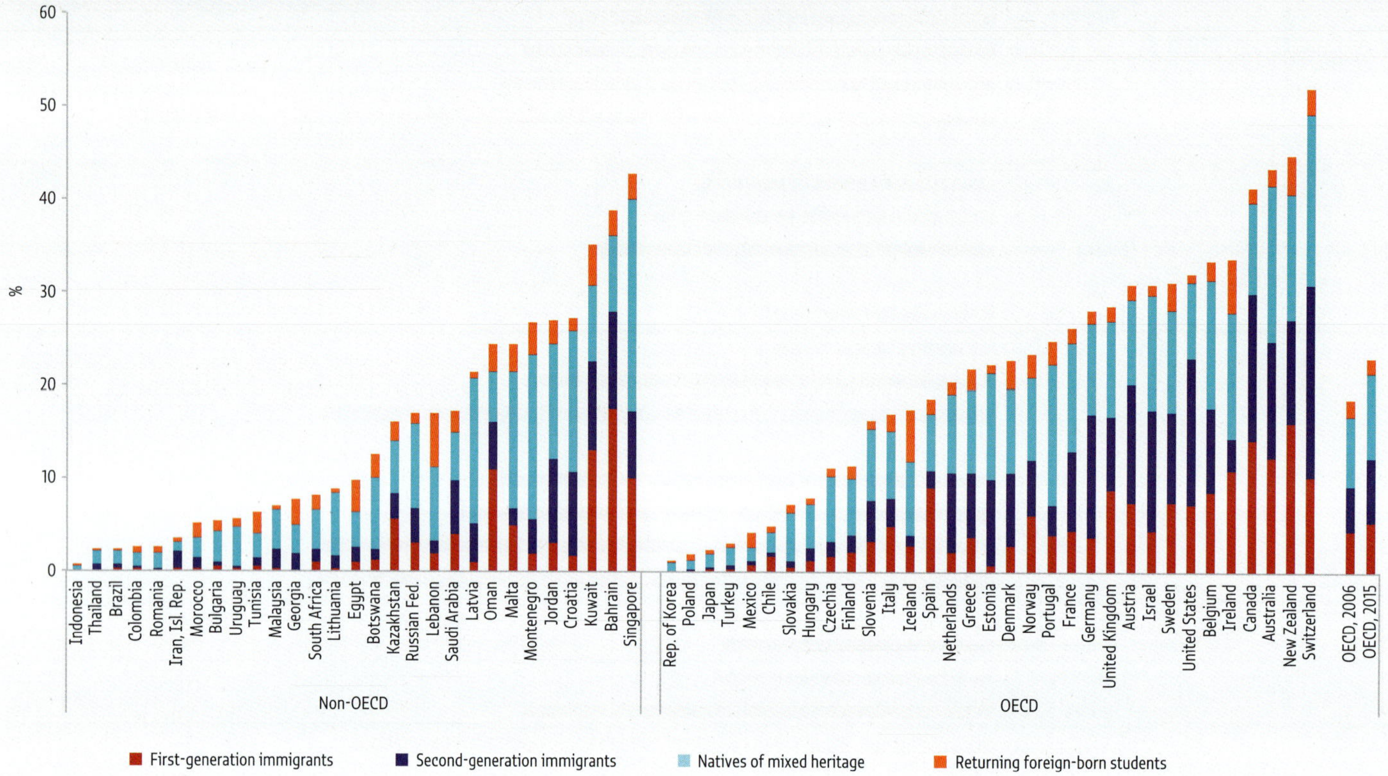

GEM StatLink: http://bit.ly/fig3_4

Note: The figure excludes five countries and territories with even higher rates of students with immigrant backgrounds: Hong Kong, China; Luxembourg; Macao, China; Qatar; and the United Arab Emirates.

Source: GEM Report team analysis based on the 2006 and 2015 PISA and 2015 TIMSS.

second-generation immigrant students increased from 9.4% to 12.5% between 2006 and 2015. It exceeds 30% in Canada and Switzerland. An estimate for this report shows that, in high income countries, in 52% of secondary schools at least 15% of students have immigrant backgrounds.

MIGRATION INFLUENCES – AND IS INFLUENCED BY – EDUCATION

In terms of educational attainment and achievement, understanding migration's impact involves comparing those who do and do not migrate, while acknowledging they differ in more than the decision to migrate. The other key comparison is between immigrants and natives, who similarly differ in more than migration status. For instance, immigrants tend to live in poorer areas served by lower-quality schools, contributing to their lower education attainment and skills acquisition.

EDUCATION INCREASES THE PROBABILITY OF MIGRATING

Migrants are not a random population. They differ from the general population in characteristics both easily observed (e.g. education) and harder to observe (e.g. motivation), both of which influence migration. The more educated are more likely to emigrate, being better able to gather information, respond to economic opportunities, utilize transferable skills and finance emigration. In 2000, global emigration rates were 5.4% among those with tertiary education, 1.8% for secondary and 1.1% for primary (Docquier and Marfouk,

> In 2000, global emigration rates were 5.4% among those with tertiary education, 1.8% for secondary and 1.1% for primary

2006). US immigrants' educational attainment was higher than the average for 31 of 32 sending countries (Feliciano, 2005).

Selective immigration policies in some countries produce notable differences in education status between immigrants and native populations. In 2008–2012, 41% of US immigrants from Africa had at least a bachelor's degree, compared to 28% of other immigrants. Those from Nigeria (61%), South Africa (57%), Kenya (47%) and Ghana (35%) were among the most educated (Gambino et al., 2014).

Where immigrants are less educated than natives, it is because they come from poorer neighbouring countries with lower average educational attainment, e.g. Albania to Greece, Haiti to the Dominican Republic and Nicaragua to Costa Rica (**Figure 3.5**). Immigrant populations can also be heterogeneous in this respect. In South Africa, more immigrants than natives have completed tertiary (a gap of seven percentage points) but also more have no formal education at all (a gap of three percentage points) (Fauvelle-Aymar, 2014).

Immigrants' educational attainment at time of emigration also varies by the conditions under which they cross borders. For instance, US immigrants from El Salvador, Haiti, Mexico and Nicaragua without proper documentation had more education, on average, than those who came on temporary contracts. Both had less education than those who became legal residents (**Figure 3.6**).

The relationship between education and migration also depends on what job opportunities exist and how low, middle and high skills are rewarded in the country of origin and the country of destination (Docquier and Deuster, 2018; Tani, 2018).

MIGRATION AFFECTS THE EDUCATION OF THOSE LEFT BEHIND

Migrants often leave children behind. In some Caribbean countries, between 10% and 20% of all children are left behind (Dillon and Walsh, 2012). An estimated 12% to 17% of the Kyrgyz population are migrant workers, with many parents unwilling or unable to take their children with

FIGURE 3.5:

Immigrants tend to be more educated than natives

Gap between immigrants and natives in share of people with tertiary education, selected countries, 2009–2015

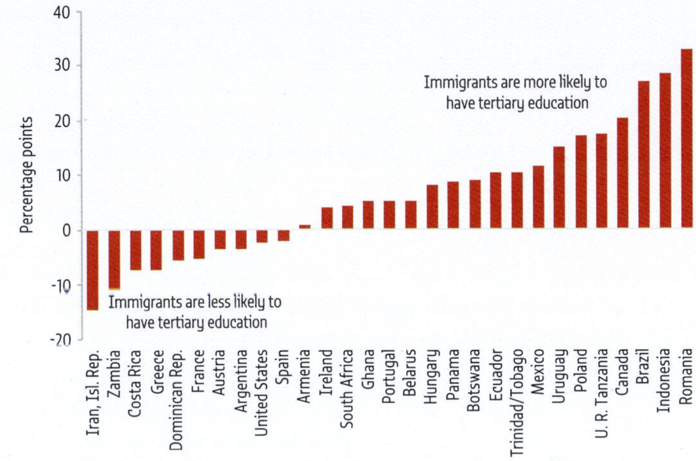

GEM StatLink: http://bit.ly/fig3_5
Source: GEM Report team analysis based on IPUMS data.

FIGURE 3.6:

US immigrants from Latin America and the Caribbean who lacked documents had more education than those who came on temporary contracts

Years of education, by documentation used during last visit to the United States, immigrants from selected Latin American and Caribbean countries

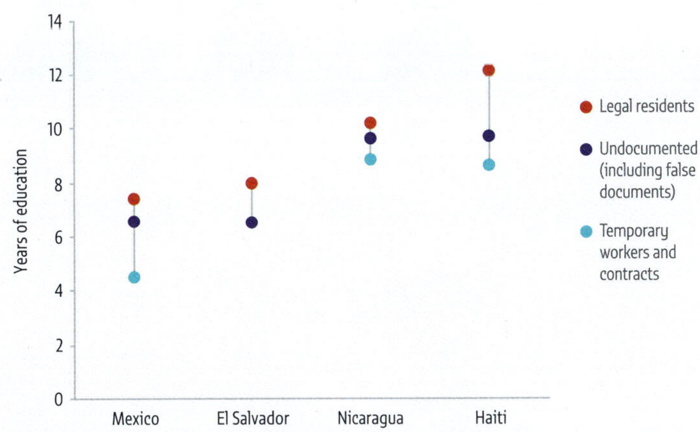

GEM StatLink: http://bit.ly/fig3_6
Source: GEM Report team analysis based on Latin American Migration Project and Mexican Migration Project data.

them (FIDH, 2016). An estimated 1.5 million to 3 million children in the Philippines, one of the largest sources of international migrant workers, have a parent living abroad (Cortes, 2015).

The effect of migration on left-behind children's education depends on context. Remittances may relax financial constraints that impede access to education (**Policy focus 19.4**). Yet effects may be nil or negative if (a) remittances are small and children must work, (b) absences reduce parent supervision and monitoring of school performance or (c) prospects of lucrative work for less educated migrants reduce the incentive to stay in school.

Given these different contexts, studies have shown a range of results. In the Philippines, school attendance increased and child labour decreased in households with international migrants (Yang, 2008). In Tajikistan, effects on school attendance were negative (Dietz et al., 2015). In Mexico, the likelihood of left-behind children completing secondary increased by 12 percentage points if mothers had migrated (Miranda, 2011). Mexican girls also completed more years of school if fathers migrated to the United States, but not if they migrated within Mexico (Antman, 2012). By contrast, in Guatemala, enrolment was 37 percentage points lower if fathers migrated internationally (Davis and Brazil, 2016).

MIGRANTS PAY AN EDUCATION PRICE IN DESTINATION COUNTRIES

Immigrants often leave education early. In 2017, 19% of foreign-born people aged 18 to 24 in the European Union had left school early, compared to 10% of natives (Eurostat, 2017). The early school leaver rate in Spain was 32% among the foreign-born and 16% among natives (**Figure 3.7**). Only Ireland, the Netherlands and the United Kingdom had lower rates among the foreign-born.

Age at migration is a major determinant of education needs, opportunities, trajectories and outcomes (OECD, 2018; van Ours and Veenman, 2006). Whether one enters the host system at the beginning, middle or end of compulsory education greatly affects outcomes. For instance, 26% of boys who emigrated from the former Soviet Union to Israel at age 16 to 18 dropped out before completing secondary school, compared to 13% of those who emigrated at age 6 to 9 (Cohen Goldner and Epstein, 2014). In the United States, 40% of Mexican immigrants who arrived at age 7 did not complete secondary school, compared to 70% of those who arrived at age 14 (Beck et al., 2012).

Immigrant students in OECD countries are nearly twice as likely as natives to repeat a grade (OECD, 2015, 2018). Analysis for this report based on the 2007–2013 *Panels*

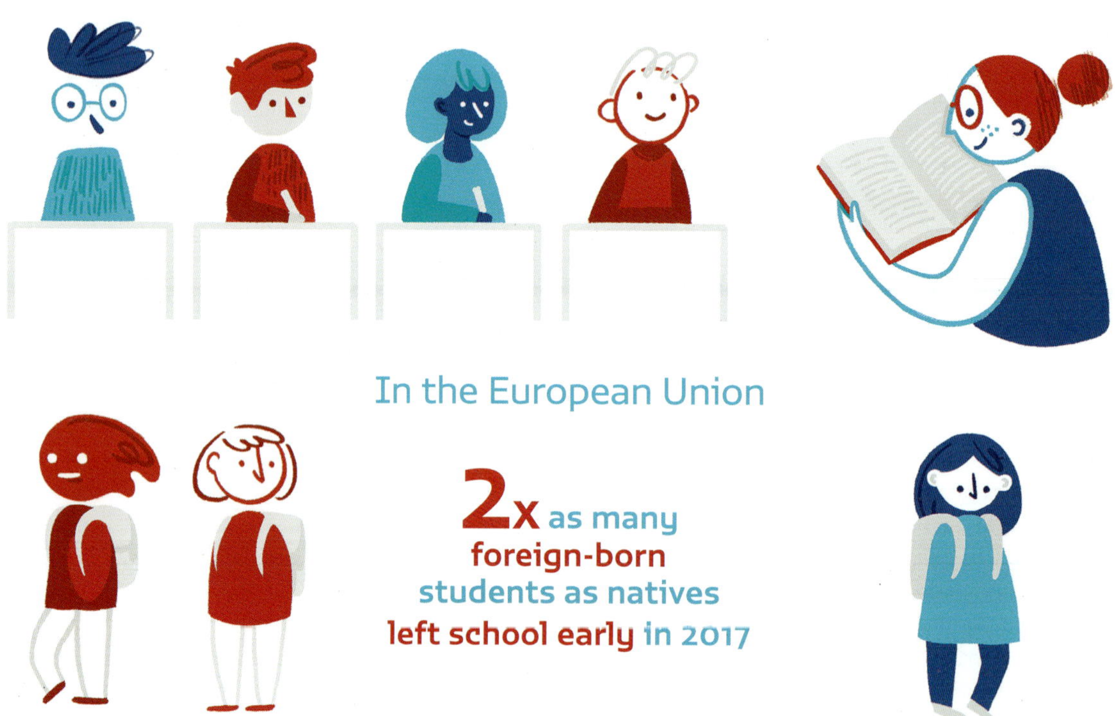

FIGURE 3.7:

Immigrants are more likely than natives to leave school early

Early leaver rate from education and training among youth aged 18 to 24, selected European countries, 2017

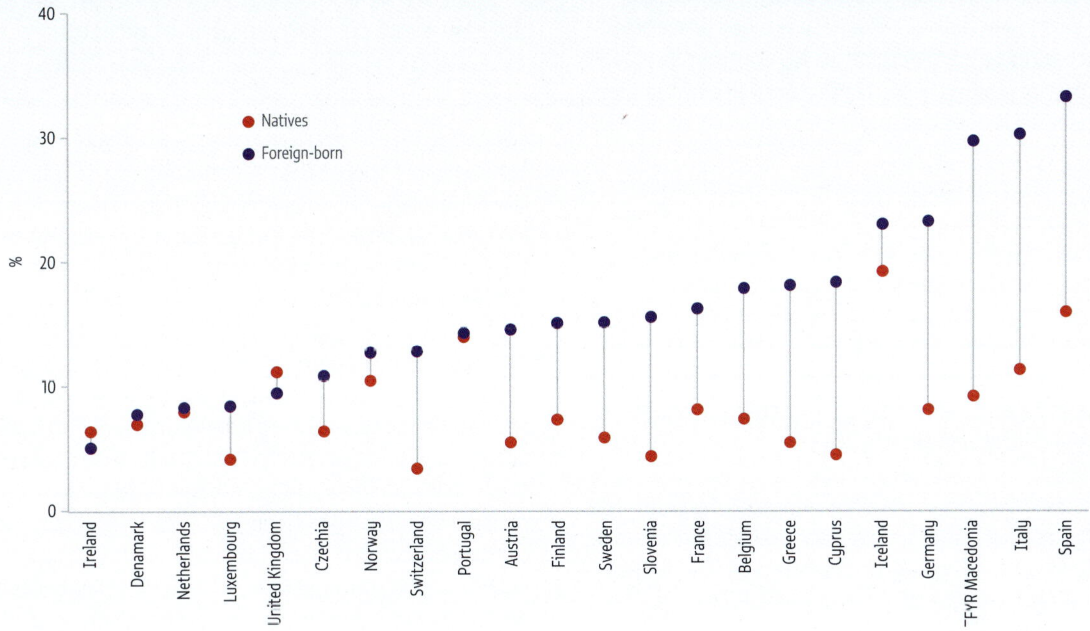

GEM StatLink: http://bit.ly/fig3_7
Source: Eurostat (2017).

d'élèves (Student Panel Survey) in France showed that 15% of children of French parents repeated at least one secondary grade, compared to 32% of children of immigrants from Turkey and 33% of children of immigrants from Mali. The probability of children of Vietnamese immigrants repeating was just 6% (Ichou, 2018) (**Figure 3.8**). First-generation immigrant students in Spain were almost twice as likely to repeat a primary grade as natives (Gonzalez-Betancor and Lopez-Puig, 2016).

Educational attainment gaps can span generations

Education gaps between natives and those with immigrant backgrounds persist in most countries, but there are significant exceptions, factors accounting for the gap and evidence of catching up. Overall, second-generation immigrants are more likely than natives to stop their education at the lower secondary level. There is a 17 percentage point gap in Belgium, falling to 4 percentage points after accounting for parental education (OECD, 2017).

A comparison of second-generation Turkish immigrants across six countries showed the compounding effect

FIGURE 3.8:

In France, students with immigrant backgrounds were more likely than natives to repeat a secondary grade

Share of children who repeated at least one secondary grade, by parents' place of birth, France, 2007–2013

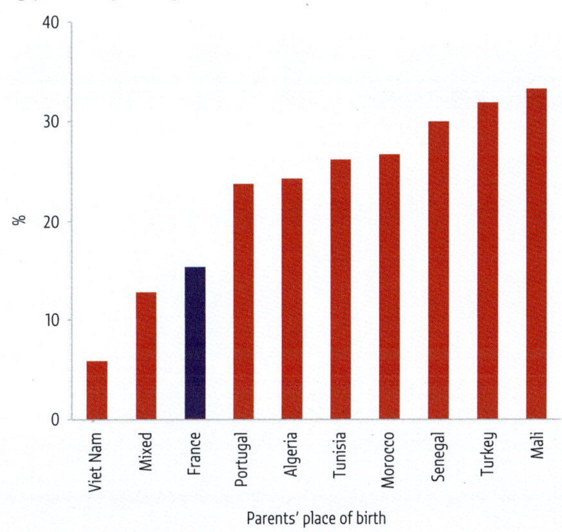

GEM StatLink: http://bit.ly/fig3_8
Source: Ichou (2018).

of institutional factors on the probability of accessing tertiary education. In France and Sweden, 37% and 32% attended tertiary education because they accessed pre-primary education early, were tracked into ability streams late in secondary education and, even when tracked into lower ability streams, were not prevented from accessing tertiary education. By contrast, in Austria and Germany, where the above factors were not in place, only 15% and 5% accessed higher education (Crul, 2013).

One explanation of smaller gaps in some outcomes – the probability of an academic track, for instance – is that migrants were positively selected, i.e. they had higher education levels than their peers in origin countries. This is possibly, but not exclusively, the result of selective immigration policies in destination countries. In England (United Kingdom), immigrants from countries such as China, India and Pakistan were positively selected (van de Werfhorst and Heath, 2018).

Immigrants' educational attainment improves over time relative to that of natives. One measure of progress is the percentage of immigrants who achieve a higher education level than their parents. An analysis of 11 countries showed that second-generation immigrants were more educationally mobile than natives, although, for most countries, the low education of immigrant parents explained this effect (Oberdabernig and Schneebaum, 2017).

> In the United States, the secondary graduation rate among third-generation Mexican Americans was only slightly below that of non-Hispanic whites

FIGURE 3.9:
Children of Latin American migrants attained more education than children of those who stayed
Gap in years of education between children in migrating and non-migrating households, selected Latin American countries

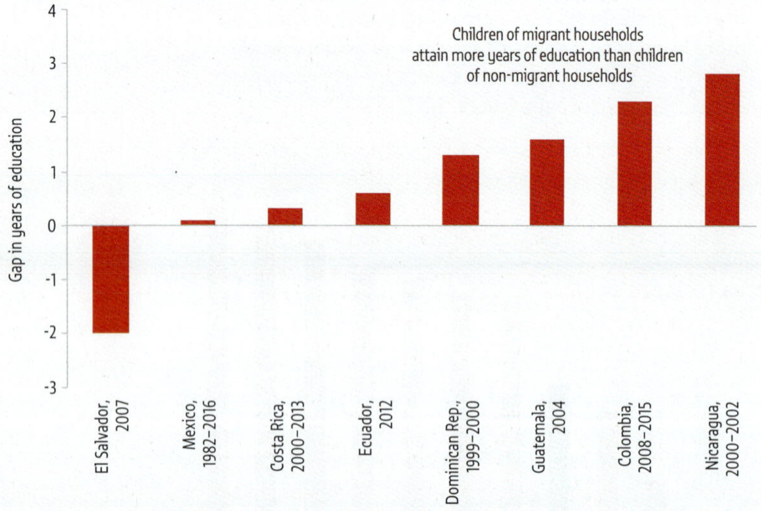

GEM StatLink: http://bit.ly/fig3_9
Source: GEM Report team analysis based on Latin American Migration Project and Mexican Migration Project data.

Estimating the speed with which immigrants beyond the second generation catch up with natives encounters the problem of measuring immigrant background with accuracy. A study in the United States that addressed this challenge showed that the secondary graduation rate among third-generation Mexican Americans was only slightly below that of non-Hispanic whites. There were significant gains in years of schooling, college attendance and bachelor's degree completion between second- and third-generation Mexican Americans (Duncan et al., 2017).

Migrants' education status improves faster than that of those left behind

Assessing migrants' trajectories relative to those left behind requires specialized, high-quality data. Since 1982, the Mexican Migration Project has covered Mexico–United States migration in 161 communities and about 27,000 households, 4% of which are in the United States. The Latin American Migration Project has collected information on migration to the United States from 10 countries in Latin America and the Caribbean since 1998. Children of emigrants had 1.4 more years of education, on average, than children of those who had not emigrated, except in El Salvador and Mexico (**Figure 3.9**).

While the education attainment effect for individual migrants may be large as they move from countries with lower average schooling levels to countries with higher levels, the global effect is much smaller than might be expected. New research for this report shows that the share of post-secondary attainment will increase by less than 0.1 percentage points among adults and by about 0.2 percentage points among youth by 2050. This small effect is a reminder that migration rates are low and that few migrants arrive young enough for their education trajectory to change a lot. Moreover, migrants tend to come from households with education attainment that is higher than average in the origin country (IIASA, 2018).

Academic proficiency rates are lower for immigrants than for natives

Attainment is not the only outcome of interest. Among 15-year-old students, 49% of first-generation and 61% of second-generation immigrants attained at least level 2 proficiency in reading, mathematics and science on the 2015 PISA, compared to 72% of native students (OECD, 2018). Among the OECD countries for which 2006 and 2015 PISA results can be compared, level 2 proficiency increased by seven percentage points among second-generation immigrants but decreased by three percentage points among first-generation immigrants (**Figure 3.10**).

Lower socio-economic status explains about 20% of the immigrant learning gap in the OECD – up to 50% in some countries. The difference in the percentage of students who achieved minimum proficiency in reading, mathematics and science in the 2015 PISA falls from 24 to 13 percentage points in France and from 22 to 12 points in Greece after accounting for socio-economic status (OECD, 2018).

IMMIGRATION AND CITIZENSHIP POLICIES HAMPER ACCESS TO SCHOOL

The right to education is enshrined in the Universal Declaration of Human Rights (Article 26) and the United Nations Convention on the Rights of the Child (Article 28). The International Convention on the Protection of the Rights of All Migrant Workers and Members of Their Families also recognizes the right to education for immigrant children irrespective of their official migrant status (Article 30), although only one out of four countries, almost all of which are immigrant-sending, have ratified it to date (OHCHR, 2018). In practice, restrictive immigration policies, inconsistencies among laws and heavy host country documentation requirements may prevent fulfilment of this right (**Policy focus 8.1**).

FIGURE 3.10:

Second-generation academic proficiency has improved over time in OECD countries

Percentage of first- and second-generation immigrant students aged 15 achieving PISA level 2 proficiency, selected countries, 2006 and 2015

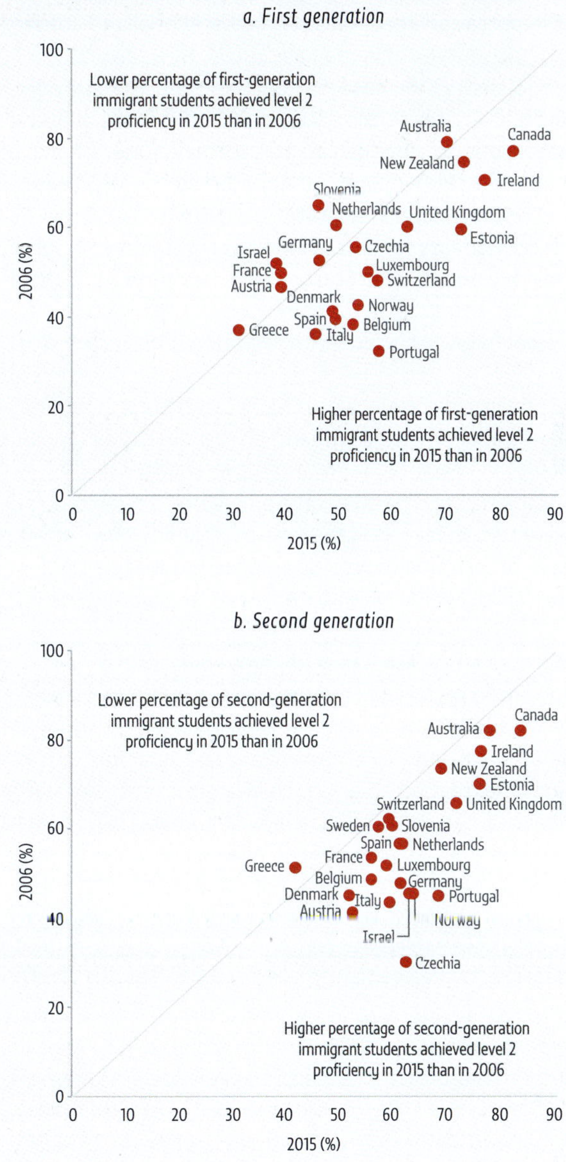

GEM StatLink: http://bit.ly/fig3_10
Source: GEM Report team analysis using PISA data.

UNDOCUMENTED IMMIGRANTS FACE OBSTACLES IN ACCESS TO EDUCATION

Of the 11 million unauthorized immigrants in the United States, two-thirds had lived there for at least 10 years (Krogstad et al., 2017). It is estimated that 7% of all children in the country are born to unauthorized immigrants (Capps et al., 2016). In some cases, the threat of deportation keeps children out of school. In February 2017, absenteeism in the Las Cruces, New Mexico, school district increased by 60% after an immigration raid (Las Cruces Public Schools, 2017). The school board subsequently amended its policy, mandating schools to stop collecting student immigration status information and reject federal Immigration and Customs Enforcement agent requests for access to school grounds without judicial warrant (Alba Soular, 2017). In April 2018, 20% of Hispanic students in Hamblen County, Tennessee, missed school following another immigration raid (Scown, 2018).

All states except Alabama, Georgia and South Carolina allow undocumented students to enrol in higher education. However, in such cases many public colleges and universities charge even long-time state residents out-of-state tuition fees (Golash-Boza and Merlin, 2016). Attempts have been made to provide residency under certain conditions which have an impact on education (**Box 3.1**).

Morocco's Law No. 4 of 2000 limited access to education exclusively to Moroccan children, but the 2011 Constitution recognized the right to education of all children, and a 2013 Ministry of Education circular extended access to children from sub-Saharan African countries but no others. Still, some document requirements may be difficult to meet (Caritas Maroc, 2015; Qassemy et al., 2014). For instance, the Casablanca Regional Academy of Education and Training requires medical certificates, especially from Ebola-affected countries, for enrolment (Caritas Maroc, 2015; Qassemy et al., 2014). About 7,500 migrant children were enrolled in public schools in 2015–2016 (*Le Matin*, 2015). However, a non-government organization estimated that less than half of the 8- to 17-year-olds received in its Casablanca, Rabat and Tangier centres attended school in 2014 (Caritas Maroc, 2015).

Undocumented immigrants are vulnerable to frequent changes in policies towards them, which affect the education of their children. In Thailand, although a 'person' in the 1999 Education Act was defined as someone with state-issued documents, undocumented migrants could attend Thai schools after a 2005 Cabinet resolution granted equal per capita funding for both native and immigrant students and all students were entitled to a certificate on completing their studies, regardless of identity documents. But as monitoring of school decisions is weak, many school leaders have resisted admitting immigrant students citing the cost of providing them with education and their higher rate of dropout (Nawarat, 2017). Moreover, frequent crackdowns on undocumented workers have negative consequences. In the Tak province, which neighbours Myanmar, most immigrant teachers lacked residency documents. Undocumented immigrant parents were less likely to send their children to schools for fear of being arrested (*The Nation*, 2017).

BOX 3.1:

The United States has yet to address obstacles to undocumented immigrants and their education

The Development, Relief, and Education for Alien Minors (DREAM) Act refers to successive legislative proposals to grant residency to undocumented young people who arrived before age 18. The first was introduced in 2001; none have passed (American Immigration Council, 2018).

In 2012, the Obama administration introduced the Deferred Action for Childhood Arrivals (DACA) programme. Targeting those undocumented youth who arrived as children, it provided renewable two year protection from deportation and eligibility for a work permit, under conditions including current school attendance or a secondary certificate. About 700,000 out of the 1.3 million people eligible had applied by May 2018. Almost 80% were Mexican; overall, 92% were Latin American (MPI, 2018).

Immigration policies that offer young undocumented migrants a long-term perspective can encourage investment in education. DACA increased secondary graduation rates by an estimated 15% as eligible immigrants sought to meet the conditions (Kuka et al., 2018). However, given that the programme provided an incentive not only to complete secondary school but also to work, the effects on post-secondary attendance and completion were more nuanced. Undocumented students must choose between full-time post-secondary education or dropping out to work. One study found that DACA recipient dropout rates at four year colleges may have increased by over 14 percentage points. No such effect was observed at community colleges, where flexible courses can accommodate working students (Hsin and Ortega, 2018).

In Chile, the number of Haitian immigrants increased from less than 5,000 in 2010 to 105,000 in 2017, as laws allowed immigrants from the region to get visas on the border and then apply for work permits (Charles, 2018b). Haitians have been subject to racist remarks in public and through social media according to the National Institute for Human Rights (INDH, 2018). With 68% of Chileans wanting stricter immigration controls, a new immigration law was introduced in April 2018 to regularize existing immigrants but also tighten work permit criteria (Charles, 2018a; The Economist, 2018). While the 2008 Presidential Directive No. 9 defined Chile as a welcoming country that would provide public education to all children, regardless of migration status, the provision of education has been at the discretion of local government officials (Reveco, 2018).

UNACCOMPANIED MIGRANT MINORS ARE PARTICULARLY VULNERABLE

Globally, the number of unaccompanied minors increased nearly fivefold from 66,000 in 2010–2011 to 300,000 in 2015–2016 (UNICEF, 2017). They are particularly mobile, difficult to count and vulnerable to exploitation and abuse, while their education needs are frequently unmet. In France, unaccompanied minors cannot attend school until they receive child protection care, a process which can take a very long time (France Human Rights Defender, 2016).

Unaccompanied minors are increasingly held in detention centres, where they often lack access to education. About 50,000 children from El Salvador, Guatemala, Honduras and Mexico were stopped at the US border on average every year between 2013 and 2017 (United States Customs and Border Protection, 2018). In the United States, paediatric and mental health professionals visiting family detention centres reported that education services were inadequate (Linton et al., 2017). In Mexico, 35,000 minors, more than half unaccompanied, were held in detention centres without organized education besides ad hoc activities with a limited education component, such as craft sessions and religious discussions (HRW, 2016).

A general problem is keeping unaccompanied minors in school, even with legislation and policies to move them out of detention swiftly and protect their right to education, as in Italy (**Box 3.2**). Older children tend to be placed in special programmes, which may increase the risk of dropout. In Germany, more than 60% of unaccompanied minors under age 16 attended a regular school in 2017, while about 30% attended special classes for newly arrived students. By contrast, almost 85% of those over age 16 attended special classes (Tangermann and Hoffmeyer-Zlotnik, 2018).

BOX 3.2:

Italy takes measures to provide education to unaccompanied and undocumented migrant minors

About 73% of 86,000 minors who arrived in Italy in 2011–2016 were unaccompanied. Of those who arrived in 2016, most (92%) were boys, of whom 82% were aged 16 or 17 (Ruffini and D'Addio, 2018). Since 2015, reception of unaccompanied children has been organized in Primary and Secondary Reception Centres. Only the latter provide education, and they depend largely on regional funds. Large inflows into Primary Reception Centres may prolong constraint on access to education for many (Grigt, 2017).

Law No. 47 of 2017 enhanced support and protection for unaccompanied and separated minors and strengthened some of their rights, including the right to education at all levels. It halved the maximum time unaccompanied minors could spend in Primary Reception Centres, from 60 days to 30, and sped up the identification procedure to no more than 10 days. Law No. 142 of 2015 aimed to integrate all children in schools and granted unaccompanied or undocumented minors access to Italian language classes. Those without residence or identification documents could enrol with a self-declaration. However, only a minority of unaccompanied minors regularly attend school and appear in the official statistics (Italy MIUR, 2017b).

STATELESS PEOPLE FACE EDUCATION BARRIERS

It is estimated that 10 million people worldwide are stateless, lacking a recognized nationality. For some, this is due to past or current migration. About 700,000 live in Côte d'Ivoire, brought as labourers from neighbouring countries in colonial times. Access to primary school requires proof of nationality, although schools' goodwill may overcome this barrier in practice (UNHCR, 2015). Secondary and tertiary enrolment requires birth certificates, identity cards and residence permits (Nonnenmacher and Yonemura, 2018).

In Malaysia's Sabah state, children of Filipino and Indonesian migrants are identified as *orang asing* (foreigner) on birth certificates and cannot attend public school (Lynch, 2008). Haitians in the

BOX 3.3:

Stateless Haitians do not fully enjoy the right to education in the Dominican Republic

Immigrants make up 5.6% of the Dominican Republic population, 88.5% being Haitians (Dominican Republic National Statistical Office, 2018). Administrative and judicial means have been used to denationalize them and deport them to Haiti. In particular, Law No. 285 of 2004 and Constitutional Court decision 168 of 2013 stripped nationality from thousands, many of whom had been registered properly at birth and possessed national identity cards (*cédula*), voter cards or passports. Central Electoral Board decisions had similar consequences (IACHR, 2015). Law No. 169 of 2014 attempted to address international criticism, which promised to restore citizenship to certain groups, but has yet to resolve the issue (Mordecai et al., 2017).

Faced with documentation barriers, many children are excluded from education. A 2012 national immigrant survey showed that the primary net attendance rate of children aged 6 to 13 was 52% among those born in Haiti, 79% among those born in the Dominican Republic to immigrant parents and 82% among those born in other countries (Dominican Republic National Statistical Office, 2013). Even when they manage to get enrolled, progression is difficult. Haitian immigrants require proof of nationality to register in the national database and sit national examinations for secondary admission. Even if they overcome those barriers, schools may ask students who have reached age 18 for a copy of their national identity card, which in practice often means they cannot graduate. Knowing they may be unable to obtain a diploma, many children disengage from education (Georgetown Law Human Rights Institute, 2014).

Dominican Republic (**Box 3.3**), Nubians in Kenya and the *bidoon* (without nationality) in Bahrain, Kuwait, Saudi Arabia and the United Arab Emirates also face difficulty accessing education services due to uncertainty surrounding their nationality (Institute on Statelessness and Inclusion, 2017).

EDUCATION POLICIES CAN SUPPORT MIGRANTS' ACCESS TO SCHOOL

In addition to immigration policies, governments have a wide range of education policy tools to promote access to schooling for immigrants. The Migrant Integration Policy Index, a research project that assesses the extent to which policies in 38 mostly high income countries meet international standards for promoting socio-economic and civic integration, has included education as one of its policy areas of focus since its third edition in 2011. It examines whether governments sufficiently encourage children of immigrants to achieve and develop on a par with children of natives. One of its four dimensions assesses whether immigrant children and their teachers are 'entitled to have their specific needs addressed in school' (Huddleston et al., 2015). In 2015, eastern and southern European countries ranked lowest on this dimension; Nordic countries and the United States ranked highest (**Figure 3.11**).

The remainder of this section assesses three education policy areas that are key for access: early childhood education; language support programmes for children; and policies related to streaming, selection and segregation. Subsequent chapters cover other education policies, notably those focused on education quality (curricula, teaching and learning materials, and teacher preparedness: **Chapter 5**), technical and vocational education (**Policy focus 10.2**), financial education (**Policy focus 11.1**), language support programmes for adults (**Policy focus 13.1**) and school fund to address immigrant needs (**Policy focus 19.1**).

IMMIGRANT PARTICIPATION IN EARLY CHILDHOOD PROGRAMMES MUST BE PRIORITIZED

Providing early childhood care and education to immigrant children is an essential foundation. On average, 15-year-old immigrants who attended pre-primary education scored 49 points higher in reading on the 2012 PISA than those who did not, a gap corresponding to more than one year of school (OECD, 2015). In Austria and Germany, immigrants' pre-school attendance increased the probability of an academic track in secondary school (Crul et al., 2012).

> “Providing early childhood care and education to immigrant children is an essential foundation”

Yet immigrant children tend to have lower access to preschool than native children. In Hessen state, Germany, 27% of children under age 3 with immigrant backgrounds attended child care centres, compared with 44% of natives (Hessen Ministry of Justice for Integration and Europe, 2013). In Basel, Switzerland, children with immigrant backgrounds, who stood to benefit most from contact with German-speaking children, were least likely to access early childhood care and education outside the family (Keller and Grob, 2010). In the United States, pre-school enrolment of undocumented 3- and 4-year-olds lagged behind that of both documented immigrants and natives (Capps et al., 2016).

Various interventions have sought to expand access. In Italy, municipalities often prioritize legal residents over undocumented ones for access to nursery school, although many cities, including Milan and Turin, have opened the door to undocumented migrants' children. Family-run nursery schools set up by immigrants provide affordable day care irrespective of documentation status (Ruffini and D'Addio, 2018). Serbia's pre-school education law allows even undocumented foreign-born children to enrol in pre-school, or schools delivering the preparatory pre-school programme, under the same conditions and rules as nationals (Right to Education Initiative, 2018). Municipal authorities in Sweden have to inform newly arrived families of their pre-school and school education rights. Pre-school curricula should also provide opportunities for non-Swedish-speaking children to develop their first language (Skolverket, 2018).

Other countries are more prescriptive. A 2017 Danish law requires 3-year-old children of immigrants not attending pre-school to take a language test. Those insufficiently proficient in Danish are required to attend pre-school and receive additional language training. Social benefits are withheld from parents who do not participate (CPH Post, 2017).

FIGURE 3.11:

Countries vary in targeting the needs of immigrant children, parents and teachers

Migrant Integration Policy Index: targeting in education dimension, 2015

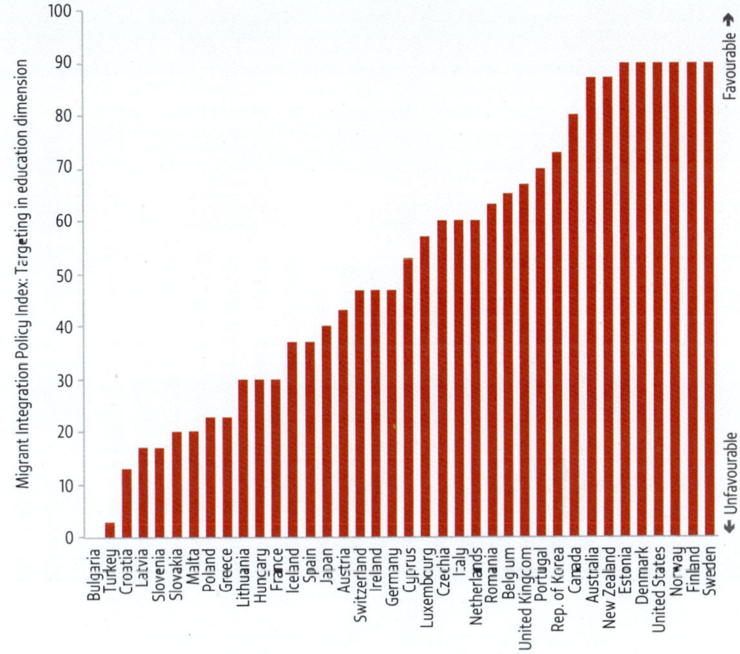

GEM StatLink: http://bit.ly/fig3_11

Note: The targeting dimension consists of five indicators: (a) access to advice and guidance on the education system (information in immigrant origin languages; resource persons and centres; interpretation services); (b) support to learn language of instruction (in pre-primary and compulsory education using second-language learning standards); (c) monitoring of immigrant students; (d) targeting of immigrant students (through guidance, such as teaching assistance or homework support, and financial resources); and (e) teacher education programmes (pre- and in-service) that address immigrant learning needs and teacher expectations of immigrant students.

Source: Huddleston et al. (2015).

LANGUAGE SUPPORT PROGRAMMES ARE KEY IN IMMIGRANT EDUCATION

Lack of language proficiency is an education disadvantage. Proficiency facilitates socialization, relationship-building and a sense of belonging. Lack of proficiency increases the risk of discrimination, bullying and low self-esteem (OECD, 2018).

About 60% of first-generation and 41% of second-generation immigrant students in OECD countries in the 2015 PISA did not speak the assessment language at home. In these countries, non-native speakers were 1.5 times more at risk of not reaching PISA proficiency level two in mathematics, reading and science than native speakers. Above-average gaps between native and non-native speakers emerged in reading in Finland and Italy and in mathematics in Germany and Switzerland (OECD, 2015, 2018).

> "About 60% of first-generation and 41% of second-generation immigrant students in the 2015 PISA did not speak the assessment language at home"

In OECD countries, new arrivals are often mainstreamed into classes matching their age and are offered language support, although only one-third of countries assess language skills on arrival. In 2012, an estimated 53%, on average, of low-literacy first-generation immigrant students were in extra out-of-school literacy courses in 23 countries, from 13% in Slovenia to almost 80% in Finland and Sweden (**Figure 3.12**).

FIGURE 3.12:

Half of immigrants receive language support in OECD countries, on average

Percentage of low-literacy first-generation students in remedial courses, selected high income countries, 2012

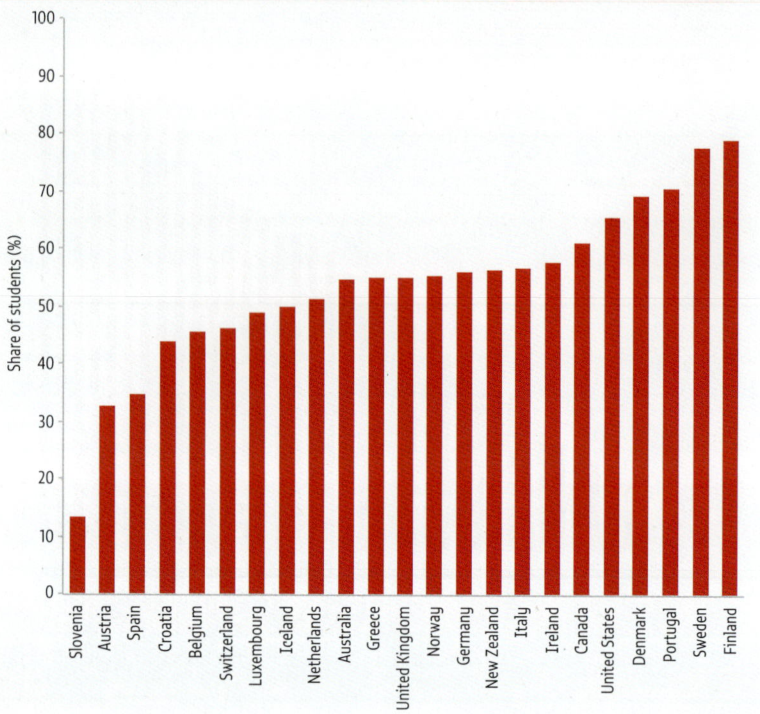

GEM StatLink: http://bit.ly/fig3_12
Source: Huddleston et al. (2015).

In Europe, the duration of language preparatory classes for newly arrived migrants for primary and lower secondary education varies, from one year or one school year in Belgium, France and Lithuania to two years in Cyprus, Denmark and Norway, three years in Latvia and four years in Greece (European Commission/ EACEA/Eurydice, 2017). Classes also vary by mode of delivery, as examples from four European countries suggest.

> “Countries should provide remedial language and other facilitating programmes for immigrants”

Germany has several models of the Willkommensklasse ('Welcome class'). Apart from state-level variation, schools also adjust overall models to their circumstances. Classes differ by their focus on language vs subject learning and by the phasing of transfer to a regular class. But the principal difference is between segregation or inclusion of newly arrived immigrants in regular classes (Ahrenholz et al., 2016). In the case of unaccompanied minors, Saarland has special language classes for unaccompanied minors (Tangermann, 2018). The quality of language support programmes is affected by heterogeneity of skills in the classroom, different arrival times of students during the school year, the existence of whole-day schools (where such language support activities are best provided) and inequalities between urban and rural areas.

In the Netherlands, in primary education, municipalities request school boards to set up reception classes in regular schools to prepare immigrants for participation in regular classes within one year, although some students may begin attending regular classes part time. There are almost 200 such classes. In some cases, especially in rural areas, immigrants are enrolled in regular schools from the beginning. In secondary education, reception classes are organized at the national level, although schools vary in the maximum age they accept (16 or 18) and the duration of the classes (one to three years) (Le Pichon et al., 2016).

Spain has three main models. In temporary classrooms, students attend during part of the school day, the time decreasing as language skills progress. In language immersion classrooms, students stay for a great part if not the entire day before they can join a regular classroom, where they can receive additional support. Madrid's Aulas de Enlace ('Link classrooms') is an example of this model. The financial crisis decreased immigration rates and cut budgets, which led to a reduction in the number of these classes by 70% between 2006 and 2015 (Silió, 2015). Intercultural classrooms extend the focus beyond language, establishing links between families and schools (Rodríguez-Izquierdo and Darmody, 2017). While regions tend to follow one of the three models, there is considerable flexibility. In the autonomous community of Andalusia, in addition to temporary classrooms during school hours, there are language support programmes for immigrants during extracurricular activities and a distance training programme (Junta de Andalucìa, 2018).

Sweden has a Language Introduction Programme for newly arrived immigrant students over age 15 attending upper secondary school. Only about 9% of those who started the programme in 2011 completed upper secondary school with a diploma or certificate (Skoverket, 2016). These preparatory classes have since been regulated. They cannot exceed two years, and placement is partial, with some activities provided in mainstream classes. Sweden has developed materials to help map students' experience and knowledge in both home language and Swedish. In 2016, 36,000 students were attending the programme (Bunar, 2017).

Outside Europe, the government of Canada provides continuous support in language of instruction. Courses use established second-language learning standards with specialized and certified teachers. A public body monitors curricular standards. Some provinces, including Alberta, Nova Scotia, and Ontario, have similar requirements (Huddleston et al., 2015). The number of immigrants requiring language support in Japan increased by 18% between 2014 and 2016 but there is still a shortage of teachers who are trained in Japanese language education and related fields. Of 60 cities and prefectures designated to foster the progression of immigrant students to secondary education, 30 provided special measures for entrance examinations allowing extended examination time, reading aids to help with the pronunciation of Chinese characters, use of a dictionary or fewer examination subjects (Tokunaga, 2018).

STREAMING, SELECTION AND SEGREGATION COMPOUND IMMIGRANT EDUCATION CHALLENGES

> "Do not separate immigrant students from others, either in different education tracks or different schools"

The tendency for immigrants to attend lower-quality classrooms and schools has a critical effect on their progress. Low achievers may be streamed away from academic courses and into technical or vocational tracks at key transition points, or immigrant communities may be concentrated in poorer neighbourhoods with disadvantaged schools.

Early ability-based selection mechanisms disadvantage immigrant students

Many countries separate low achievers into less demanding tracks. Ability sorting leads to inequality and a stronger association between social background and student results. While vocational training can motivate disadvantaged students put off by more academic tracks, it may compromise subsequent opportunities for students with immigrant backgrounds. In Italy, 59% of immigrant graduates from general secondary school transitioned to university, compared to 33% of professional school and 13% of technical school graduates (Italy MIUR, 2018).

Tracking starts as young as age 10 in Austria and Germany (**Box 3.4**). In Linz, Austria, students with immigrant backgrounds are 16 percentage points less likely than natives to choose an academic track in grade 5 (Schneeweis,

BOX 3.4:

Parents and schools have resisted school desegregation in Berlin

Before the large refugee influx in 2015–2016, Germany experienced several waves of immigration, notably the arrival of guest workers in the 1960s and 1970s. In 2014/15, 31% of students had immigrant backgrounds (Gönsch et al., 2016).

German states' secondary school admission policies vary but include early selection. Historically, and currently in the five largest states, students are channelled into three school types: *Hauptschule*, *Realschule* and *Gymnasium*, the latter being the most selective. Gradually, several states have been introducing a comprehensive school, the *Gesamtschule*. This reform is thought to have contributed to the decline in the immigrant–native learning achievement gap between 2000 and 2015, which still remains above the OECD average (Davoli and Entorf, 2018). As of 2014, immigrants were still under-represented in *Gymnasien* (26%) and over-represented in *Hauptschulen* (48%), while half of all children of immigrants in *Hauptschulen* left school without a certificate or apprenticeship (Gönsch et al., 2016).

In Berlin, the share of students with an immigrant background was 37% in 2014/15, higher than the national average. Already in 1982, the Berlin state parliament had recommended that the share of foreign students in classrooms should not exceed 50%. At that time, classes entirely of foreign students were common. By 1989, 55% of immigrant students in *Hauptschulen* were in such classes, which were formally abolished in 1995 (Glenn and de Jong, 1996).

However, segregation continues in both primary and secondary education. An analysis of 108 primary school catchment areas in four districts showed that one out of five schools enrolled twice as many students with immigrant backgrounds than lived in the area. This is a consequence of parents circumventing official primary school assignment, and schools offering ways, such as separate classes based on parent choice of religious or foreign language instruction, to attract native students and better teachers (Fincke and Lange, 2012; Open Society Justice Initiative, 2013).

Following other states, Berlin introduced *Sekundarschule* in 2010/11, integrating *Hauptschule*, *Realschule* and *Gesamtschule*, to promote ethnic diversity in secondary education (Morris-Lange et al., 2013). It maintained the *Gymnasien*, which selected 60% of their students, with an extra 10% reserved for siblings, leaving 30% selected by lottery (Basteck et al., 2015). Yet other constraints – e.g. only one-third of all *Sekundarschulen* offered classes needed to prepare for the final *Abitur* university entrance examination – limited the effectiveness of the reform. In 2017/18, some *Sekundarschulen* student bodies were still 100% non-German mother tongue (Sekundarschulen Berlin, 2018).

2015). In Amsterdam, the Netherlands, 9% of Moroccan and 11% of Turkish second-generation immigrant students entered vocational tracks in lower secondary at age 12 in 2007/08, compared to 2% of natives (Crul et al., 2012).

Early tracking in the transition to secondary school particularly disadvantages male students with immigrant backgrounds. In Germany, they were seven percentage points more likely than their native peers to receive a recommendation for the lowest track and seven percentage points less likely to receive a recommendation for the highest track, after controlling for test scores in reading and mathematics (Lüdemann and Schwerdt, 2013).

Some countries keep immigrant and native students separate, e.g. by extending the duration of preparatory classes. This occurs above a certain age, usually the compulsory schooling age limit. In Austria's Styria state, children above age 15 who are deemed not ready for secondary are not entitled to attend school and, after assessment, are transferred to special courses (FRA, 2017).

Segregation compounds migrant education challenges

Immigrants tend to be concentrated in specific neighbourhoods, usually suburban. Immigrant students often end up segregated from natives in schools with lower academic standards and performance levels, which negatively affects their educational achievement (Entorf and Lauk, 2008; Rangvid, 2007). Immigrants attending schools with a majority of native students also have higher education aspirations, even if these effects are often mediated by their socio-economic status or the socio-economic context of the school (Minello and Barban, 2012; Van Houtte and Stevens, 2010).

Most European countries exhibit segregation. In France, analysis of the 2007 Student Panel Survey found that immigrants were more likely to be in classes of over 15% immigrant composition. In particular, this was the case for 17% of first-generation immigrants, 12% of second-generation immigrants, 5% of children of mixed heritage and 2% of natives (Fougère et al., 2017). In Germany's Hessen state, about 41% of children who did not speak German at home attended child care centres where at least half the children did not speak German at home (Hessen Ministry of Justice for Integration and Europe, 2013). Non-native speakers in the United Kingdom were more likely to attend school with disadvantaged native speakers (Geay et al., 2013).

Segregation is exacerbated by native students moving to wealthier neighbourhoods, for instance in Denmark (Rangvid, 2007) and the Netherlands (Ohinata and van Ours, 2013). In the United States, for every four new non-English speakers in public secondary education, one native student switched to private school (Betts and Fairlie, 2003). School choice has increased ethnic polarization of schools in Australia (Al-deen and Windle, 2017).

In some cases, there is a negative correlation between share of immigrants and education outcomes of natives, usually the most disadvantaged. In Denmark, there was a negative but small effect of immigrant concentration on the reading and mathematics performance of natives (Jensen and Rasmussen, 2011). In Israel, having immigrant classmates in primary decreased the probability of the most disadvantaged native students passing the upper secondary matriculation examination (Gould et al., 2009). In Italy, immigrant student concentration in the classroom was found to lower natives' test scores in reading and mathematics by 2% (Ballatore et al., 2015). In Norway, a 10 percentage point increase in the share of immigrants in a school was associated with a 3 percentage point increase in native dropout (Hardoy and Schøne, 2013). In the Netherlands, there was no effect on natives' achievement when immigrant classmates had been in the country for some years, but higher shares of recent immigrants were associated with lower natives' language test scores, especially among natives with low parental education (Bossavie, 2017a, 2017b).

Countries use different tools to combat segregation, with mixed success

Countries have tried different ways to mitigate the effects of residential segregation (Brunello and De Paola, 2017). In Wallonia, Belgium, three laws were enacted between 2007 and 2010, the short-lived second of which favoured a lottery system for school assignment. With the current law primarily based on proximity, the only tools to limit residential segregation effects are partnerships between more and less disadvantaged schools and a quota for students with low socio-economic backgrounds (Ryelandt, 2013). France reformed the *carte scolaire* system of school assignment in 2007 to increase diversity by improving management of catchment area boundaries and derogations. However, in Marseille, the percentage of first grade lower secondary students enrolled in other than their neighbourhood public school increased from 43% in 2006 to 46% in 2013, reaching up to 67% in certain

> Italy set a classroom maximum of 30% first-generation 'foreign-born' students to limit segregation

neighbourhoods, in part as middle-class parents switched their children to private schools (Audren et al., 2016).

In Italy, a 2010 circular set a classroom maximum of 30% first-generation, 'foreign-born' students (Santerini, 2010). Derogations were granted if, for instance, they spoke Italian or if the classroom composition was already above the limit. In the Emilia Romagna region, 13% of schools and 25% of pre-schools applied for derogations in 2017. In practice, 17% of primary classrooms exceeded the limit (Italy MIUR, 2017a).

CONCLUSION

International migration is a global phenomenon, with major economic, social and cultural implications. Education is a driver of migratory flows but is also significantly affected by movement of people. Depending on the context, migration can be a bridge to improve the education status of children and youth from low and middle income countries. While they may struggle and fall behind native peers, most eventually catch up, fulfilling the dream of a better life.

Nevertheless, many immigrant children and youth face several serious obstacles that exclude them from national education systems and prevent them from making the most of opportunities in their new environment. Some countries do not offer all children and youth the same rights to education, especially if they do not possess the necessary documents. Governments need to remove barriers related to access (especially to early childhood education and education past the compulsory school age), language proficiency, grouping by ability and segregation.

Schools in many countries have reception protocols for new arrivals and may vary teaching materials and make them more accessible from a linguistic point of view. However, they often adopt an emergency response perspective in compensating for immigrant students' deficits. Separate schooling for long periods, for instance, may accentuate deficits and disadvantage. Governments should replace such approaches with structural interventions that make inclusion effective. Such interventions concern not only immigrant children but also school organization, families and institutional actors responsible for education. Chapter 5 explores these interventions further, as well as those outside schools involving children, young people and adults.

Refugee children from Ethiopia and Somalia attend schools in a refugee camp close to the Djibouti-Somalia border.

CREDIT: Petterik Wiggers/UNHCR

CHAPTER

4

Displacement

This report provides a compelling rationale for the emphasis on education in the Global Compact on Refugees and the imperative of including refugees in national education systems and Education Sector Plans.

The New York Declaration calls for urgent collaboration among a range of actors to support the work of governments to include refugees in national education systems, and ensure that communities hosting refugees receive adequate and sustained development funding – essential to achieving the SDGs.

Young people who stay in school have vital opportunities to develop their minds and their capacities for community-building, civic participation and leadership.

Together we can make this a reality. The time to act is now.

Filippo Grandi, UN High Commissioner for Refugees

KEY MESSAGES

There are 87 million displaced people in the world: 25 million refugees, 3 million asylum-seekers, 40 million internally displaced due to conflict and 19 million displaced due to natural disasters. Their vulnerability is exacerbated when they are deprived of education.

More than half of all refugees are under the age of 18. At least 4 million refugee children and youth aged 5 to 17 were out of school in 2017.

In many conflict-affected countries, refugees and internally displaced people strain already struggling education systems. Refugees from South Sudan in Uganda settle in the poor West Nile subregion, where the secondary net attendance rate was 9% in 2016 – less than half the national rate.

Natural disasters can also cause displacement that disrupts education, even if the consequences are relatively short-lived. In Bangladesh, disasters such as storms and floods damage 900 schools each year, on average.

Consensus has gradually emerged that refugee education should not be provided in parallel systems that lack qualified teachers, do not offer certified examinations and risk having their funding cut at short notice. But geography, history, resources and capacity affect the degree of refugees' inclusion in national systems.

The Ethiopia Refugee Proclamation gives refugees access to national schools and host children access to refugee schools. The Islamic Republic of Iran decreed in 2015 that schools should accept all Afghan children, regardless of documentation. Turkey plans to move all Syrian refugee children to public schools by 2020.

Despite a commitment to inclusion, some countries' refugees are geographically separated because they settle in remote areas, as in Kenya, or temporally separated because resource constraints make a second shift necessary, as in Lebanon.

Chad included refugees in its temporary education plan in 2013 to address issues such as language of instruction, recognition of diplomas and the threat of loss of culture and national identity. It converted 108 refugee schools into regular public schools in 2018.

Alternative education programmes help children whose education was interrupted by displacement. An accelerated learning programme in Dadaab camp, Kenya, which condensed the national eight-year curriculum into four years, increased access for refugee boys.

Major displacement poses challenges for teacher recruitment, retention and training. If all refugees enrolled, Turkey would need 80,000 additional teachers, Germany would need 42,000 teachers and educators, and Uganda would need 7,000 additional primary teachers.

The Education 2030 Framework for Action recognized that 'Natural disasters, pandemics and conflicts, and the resulting internal and cross-border displacement, can leave entire generations traumatized, uneducated and unprepared to contribute to the social and economic recovery of their country or region' (UNESCO, 2015).

The number of displaced people was estimated at 87.3 million in late 2017 – the highest level since the end of the Second World War. It consists of two broad categories: those who crossed an international border seeking protection from conflict and persecution (25.4 million refugees and 3.1 million asylum-seekers) and internally displaced people (IDPs; about 58.8 million people). Of the latter, 40 million were displaced due to conflict and violence, while 18.8 million were forced to move, albeit for shorter durations, as a result of natural disasters (IDMC, 2018c; UNHCR, 2018d). The estimate does not include those forced to move due to slow-onset disasters related to climate change pressure on livelihoods or displacement due to large-scale development projects (Behrman and Kent, 2018; Ionesco et al., 2016).

Displaced people tend to come from some of the world's poorest and least served areas, and their vulnerability is further exacerbated when displacement deprives them of education. The Education 2030 Framework for Action summed up the purposes education should serve in such contexts when it emphasized that education should be 'immediately protective, providing life-saving knowledge and skills and psychosocial support to those affected by crisis'. It called upon countries to 'develop inclusive, responsive and resilient education systems' to meet their needs (UNESCO, 2015). But the position of refugees who rely on host countries to extend international rights to education is not identical to those of people displaced within their home countries and whose governments bear specific responsibilities to fulfil their citizens' rights.

> "The vulnerability of forcibly displaced people is further exacerbated when they are deprived of an education"

In the case of refugees, as part of the September 2016 New York Declaration, all United Nations (UN) member states committed 'to provide quality primary and secondary education in safe learning environments ... within a few months of the initial displacement'. Countries have since worked out responsibility-sharing arrangements in refugee responses as part of the Global Compact on Refugees, which further commits them to 'contribute resources and expertise to expand and enhance the quality and inclusiveness of national education systems' for both refugee and host populations. These arrangements are being piloted among the 15 countries where the Comprehensive Refugee Response Framework (CRRF) is being rolled out.

Following a review of displacement situations and the effects on education, this chapter turns to the core issue of providing inclusive education for refugees: the extent to which they are included in national education systems, together with the challenges and opportunities in policy and practice for ensuring that this education is relevant and responsive. Selected additional important issues related to refugee education are addressed in the monitoring part of the report, including early childhood care and education (**Policy focus 9.1**), tertiary education (**Policy focus 10.1**), displaced people with disabilities (**Policy focus 12.1**), the role of technology (**Policy focus 15.1**) and the effectiveness of humanitarian aid (**Policy focus 19.3**). The chapter concludes with discussions of education for the internally displaced and those displaced by natural disasters.

DISPLACED POPULATIONS ARE CONCENTRATED IN A FEW COUNTRIES

At the end of 2017, seven countries hosted 51% of the world's 19.9 million refugees, excluding Palestinian refugees. Turkey hosted the most (3.5 million). In addition, 5.4 million Palestinian refugees lived in four countries. In total, low and middle income countries hosted about 89% of refugees (UNHCR, 2018c; UNRWA, 2017b) (**Figure 4.1a**).

Two aspects of the global refugee population composition are particularly important. First, about 52% are under age 18. Second, about 39% of refugees with available

> "At the end of 2017, six countries hosted 61% of the world's 40 million people internally displaced due to conflict"

FIGURE 4.1:
Refugees and internally displaced people are concentrated in a few countries

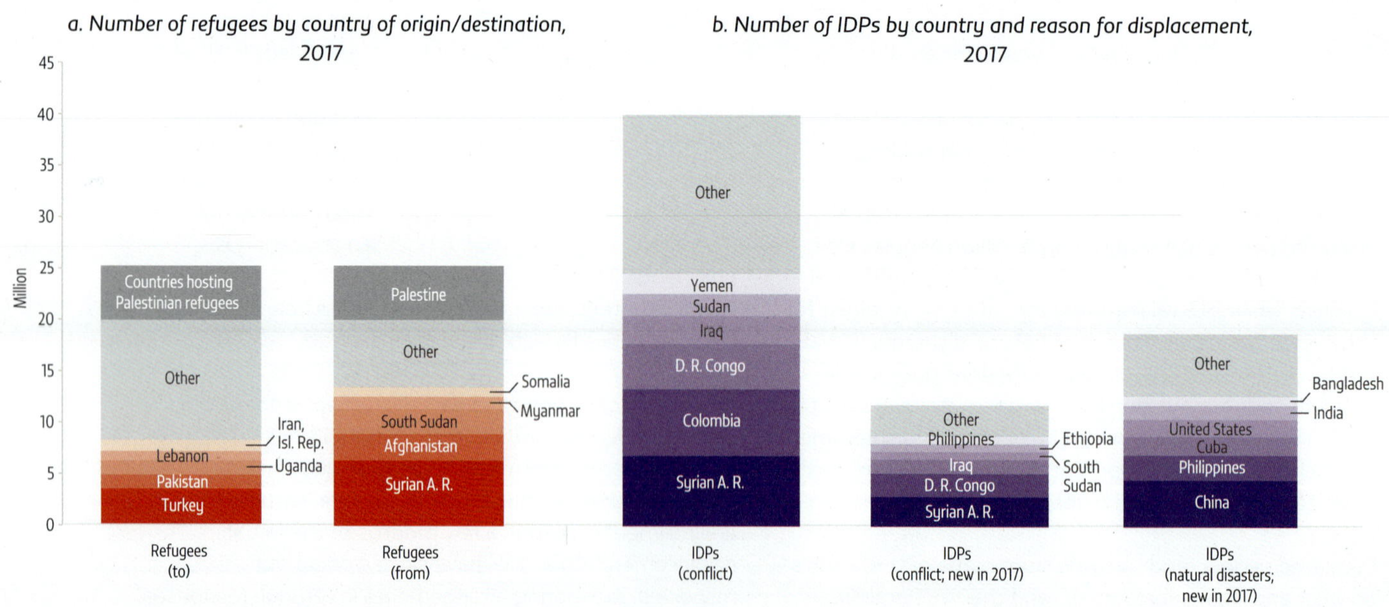

GEM StatLink: http://bit.ly/fig4_1
Sources: IDMC (2018b); UNHCR (2018c); UNRWA (2017b).

accommodation data live in managed, self-settled, or transit camps or collective centres (UNHCR, 2018c), mostly in sub-Saharan Africa in places such as Bidibidi in Uganda (about 285,000 refugees from South Sudan), Dadaab in Kenya (about 235,000, mainly from Somalia), Dollo Ado in Ethiopia (about 209,000, mainly from Somalia) and Kakuma in Kenya (about 148,000, mainly from Somalia and South Sudan), as well as in Kutupalong in Bangladesh (about 600,000 refugees from Myanmar) (UNHCR, 2017b, 2017c, 2018b, 2018e). Most refugees live in individual accommodation in urban areas (UNHCR, 2018c) where they seek security, anonymity, job opportunities and better access to services.

The numbers given above do not include people who have fled to countries that are not party to the 1951 Refugee Convention and its 1967 protocol or that do not consider that certain conditions constitute persecution. In May 2015, Lebanon instructed the Office of the UN High Commissioner for Refugees (UNHCR) to stop the registration of Syrian refugees, who had reached 1.2 million by that point. Around 500,000 Syrians who were never registered by UNHCR are excluded from the new residency policy in March 2017 that waived residency fees for refugees registered by UNHCR (Janmyr, 2018). In 2015, Tunisia officially hosted fewer than 1,000 refugees (UNHCR, 2016a), even though some 1 million Libyans had fled there from the civil war (Karasapan, 2015).

At the end of 2017, six countries hosted 61% of the world's 40 million people internally displaced due to conflict. The Syrian Arab Republic leads the list with 6.8 million, including 2.9 million newly displaced in 2017. Numbers of new IDPs also surged in 2017 in the Democratic Republic of the Congo, Iraq and South Sudan. In addition, of the 18.8 million people internally displaced due to natural disasters, 68% lived in six countries, led by China with 4.5 million. Such displacement tends to be temporary (IDMC, 2018c) (**Figure 4.1b**).

The Internal Displacement Monitoring Centre (IDMC) of the Norwegian Refugee Council has a comprehensive monitoring platform displaying information about reports of conflict or natural disasters, which aid in estimating numbers of IDPs. A machine learning tool reads, filters and analyses news and UN or non-government reports and extracts information, which is then validated (IDMC, 2018d). While many of the sources are familiar, non-traditional data sources, such as satellite imagery and social media data, are also used (IDMC, 2018c). Non-traditional sources can circumvent security concerns and registration systems that hamper easy identification of the displaced in many contexts. Self-identification may be very biased, as many of the displaced do not want to be identified for fear of persecution (Baal and Ronkainen, 2017).

DISPLACEMENT REDUCES ACCESS TO EDUCATION

Estimating the number of displaced people is complex, as their movement is unpredictable and takes place in challenging circumstances. Estimating their education status is even more complex due to missing information. In the case of asylum-seekers, it is very difficult to track whether children, some of whom end up detained, have access to education (**Box 4.1**). In the case of refugees, while it is easier to report on school enrolment of refugees in camps, enrolment data of registered refugees in urban areas are also frequently available.

> "It is very difficult to track whether asylum-seeking children, some of whom end up being detained, have access to education"

It is difficult to collect information on the education status of the 58% of refugees living in urban areas. Few countries identify refugee status in school censuses explicitly. Turkey, where 93% of Syrian refugees live outside camps (UNHCR, 2018c), is an exception. The government supplemented its education management information system (EMIS) in public schools with a parallel system for 'foreign students', which monitors temporary education centres. After a policy was introduced to include these centres in the national education system, the primary net enrolment ratio of Syrian students increased from 25% in 2014 to 83% in 2017. However, their secondary net enrolment rate rose much less, from 16% to 22% (Arik Akyuz, 2018; UNHCR, 2018i).

Overall, UNHCR estimates that 61% of refugee children were enrolled in primary school and 23% of refugee adolescents in secondary school in 2017. In low income countries, the ratio was below 50% in primary and just 11% in secondary education (**Figure 4.2**). About 4 million 5- to 17-year-old refugees were out of school in 2017 (UNHCR, 2018g).

BOX 4.1:

Regulations around asylum can also impact access to education

Asylum-seeking children and youth are detained in many countries, including Australia, Indonesia, Malaysia, Mexico, Nauru and Thailand, often with limited or no access to education. Thailand's immigration laws permit unlimited detention for asylum-seekers from Myanmar, Pakistan and Somalia, impairing access to education (Save the Children, 2017).

The EU Reception Conditions Directive obliges EU countries to grant asylum-seekers access to the education systems 'under similar conditions as nationals' no more than three months after their application (Art. 14). In practice, children and youth often wait months or years to attend school. When border checkpoints closed on the so-called Balkan route in March 2016, thousands of families were detained in transit centres without basic services, including education.

While the Netherlands, Poland and Slovakia provide education irrespective of length of stay, in Austria, Bulgaria, Denmark, Finland, France, parts of Germany, Greece and Hungary, children in immigration detention had no access to any form of education, on the grounds of short length or exceptional nature of stay (FRA, 2017). In Hungary, all asylum-seeking families with children, and unaccompanied children above age 14, have to stay in one of two transit zones on the border with Serbia while their applications are processed. Children in these transit zones have no access to education except that provided by civil society organizations (Bakonyi et al., 2017).

Asylum-seeking children's entitlements are not fully enshrined in law in all five Nordic countries. In Iceland, the process is not determined in the Compulsory School Act but is instead subject to negotiation between the Directorate of Immigration and municipalities. Generally, across these countries, municipalities can have varying time-frames and interpretations of their obligations (UNICEF, 2018).

FIGURE 4.2:

Only 11% of refugee adolescents in low income countries are enrolled in secondary school

Percentage of 5- to 17-year-old refugees enrolled by level of education, 2017

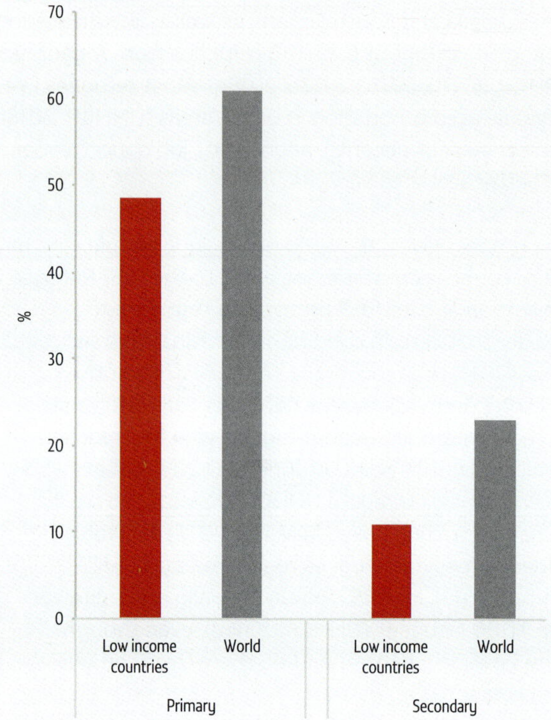

GEM StatLink: http://bit.ly/fig4_2
Source: UNHCR (2018g).

> About 4 million 5- to 17-year-old refugees were out of school in 2017

Differences in refugee enrolment rates can be considerable within countries. In 2016, the secondary gross enrolment ratio for refugees in Ethiopia varied among districts from 1% in Samara to 47% in Jijiga (UNHCR, 2016b). Gender gaps, for instance among Afghan refugees in Pakistan, can be very wide (**Box 4.2**).

Refugees are often from very vulnerable communities that lacked education prior to displacement. A study of 2,400 people granted permanent humanitarian visas between May and November 2013 in Australia showed that 23% of females and 17% of males were illiterate in their language on arrival (Marshall, 2015). In Chad, among 6- to 14-year-old refugees from the Central African Republic, Nigeria and Sudan, 3 out of 10 were illiterate (UNHCR and WFP, 2017).

Refugees often arrive in underserved areas of host countries, stretching already limited resources. For instance, refugees from South Sudan in Uganda, who represent over 70% of the total, settle in the poor West Nile subregion (UNHCR, 2018h), where the secondary net attendance rate was 9% in 2016 – less than half the national rate (UBOS and ICF, 2018).

BOX 4.2:

Forty years on, Afghan refugees do not receive adequate education in Pakistan

The first wave of Afghan refugees arrived in Pakistan with the Soviet invasion in 1979. The number peaked at 3.3 million in 1989, but 1.4 million were still registered in 2017, of whom 0.5 million were aged 5 to 18 (UNHCR, 2018c, 2018f). An estimated 1 million other Afghans living in Pakistan are unregistered (HRW, 2017).

Pakistan is not a signatory of the 1951 Refugee Convention, but its constitution, as amended in 2010, guarantees the right to free, compulsory education for all children aged 5 to 16, with no discrimination between citizens and foreigners. In practice, Afghan refugees have access to a range of schools, largely outside the public domain: private (from low-cost to elite); *madrasas*, which are free and provide food and boarding; community-based schools; and non-formal schools. In addition, UNHCR-managed refugee schools cater to 57,000 Afghan students in 52 refugee villages in Khyber Pakhtunkhwa province but have limited funding and struggle to hire and retain qualified teachers (Nicolle, 2018; NRC and UNHCR, 2015). Refugee schools use the Afghan curriculum in preparation for return and reintegration into the Afghan education system, despite protracted displacement having led to a second generation of Afghan refugees in Pakistan (UNHCR, 2018j).

Yet access to education for refugees, especially girls, is extremely low. A 2011 survey identifying refugee status put the Afghan refugee primary net enrolment rate at 29%, less than half the national rate in Pakistan of 71%. The primary net enrolment rate for refugee girls (18%) was not only half the rate for boys (39%) (**Figure 4.3**) but even less than half the primary attendance rate for girls in Afghanistan in the same year. Only 5% of Afghan refugees attended secondary school (UNHCR, 2016c).

FIGURE 4.3:

Fewer than one out of five Afghan refugee girls were enrolled in primary school in Pakistan

Net primary enrolment rate, Afghan refugees and national average, by gender, Pakistan, 2011

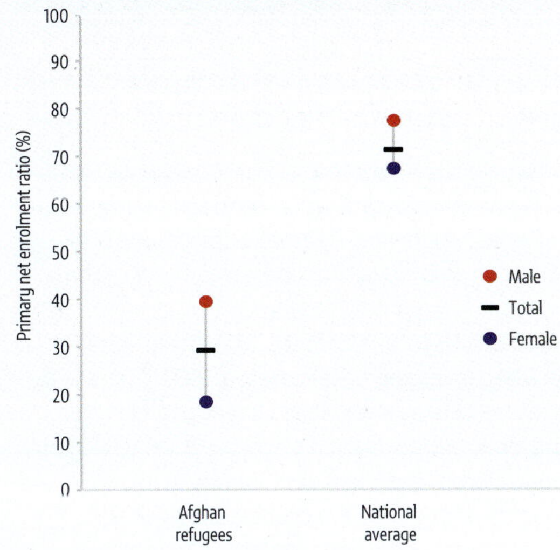

GEM StatLink: http://bit.ly/fig4_3
Source: Nicolle (2018).

A legacy of girls' low education access is an 8% literacy rate among female refugees (UNHCR, 2016c), compared with 33% among Afghan refugees overall in Pakistan and Pakistan's national average of 57% (Nicolle, 2018). A vicious circle arises: sociocultural traditions demand that adolescent girls can be taught only by women, but there are very few female teachers (NRC and UNHCR, 2015).

Data on the quality of refugee education are scarce

The very few data sources that assess quality and learning outcomes often paint a bleak picture of refugee education. In Kenyan refugee camps, schools must comply with Ministry of Education minimum standards and registration guidelines for alternative provision of basic education and training. Yet average pupil/teacher ratios were very high in Dadaab refugee camp, especially in pre-primary (120:1) and primary (56:1). Only 8% of primary teachers were certified national teachers, and 6 out of 10 refugee teachers were untrained. On average, six students shared a desk, and four shared a textbook in English, mathematics, science and social studies (Women Educational Researchers of Kenya, 2017).

> In Dadaab refugee camp, only 8% of primary teachers were certified national teachers, and 6 out of 10 refugee teachers were untrained

A citizen-led assessment in the four Ugandan districts with the largest numbers of refugees in 2016 showed that they faced worse school and living conditions than natives. The average pupil/teacher ratio was twice as high in schools inside refugee settlements (113:1) as in those outside (57:1), as was the share of families living on one meal per day (28% vs 13%). Despite these conditions, learning outcomes, albeit very low, did not vary much among grade 5 students: in Yumbe district, which hosted the largest number of refugees, 30% of refugees and 32% of natives had grade 2 reading skills (Uwezo, 2018).

TRACKING EDUCATION TRAJECTORIES OF THE INTERNALLY DISPLACED IS DIFFICULT

Internal displacement, whether due to conflict or natural disasters, has a negative impact on education. In many conflict-affected countries, internal displacement has put a huge strain on already struggling education systems.

In north-eastern Nigeria, as of late 2017, there were 1.6 million IDPs, including an estimated 700,000 school-age children, as a result of violent attacks on civilians by Boko Haram, which began in 2009 (UNOCHA, 2017b). Boko Haram has destroyed nearly 1,000 schools and displaced 19,000 teachers (HRW, 2016). Reports indicated it had killed almost 2,300 teachers by 2017 (UNOCHA, 2017a). The latest education needs assessment found that out of 260 school sites, 28% had been damaged by bullets, shells or shrapnel, 20% had been deliberately set on fire, 32% had been looted and 29% had armed groups or military in close proximity. Ongoing safety concerns, coupled with teacher salaries that do not cover even basic expenses and delays in payment, perpetuate a shortage of qualified teachers. Most of those who remain work on a voluntary basis (Igbinedion et al., 2017).

The IDMC estimated that there are 2.6 million IDPs in Iraq as of late 2017 (IDMC, 2018a). About one-third are registered as living in formal camps. In July 2017, formal education attendance rates were 68%, 73% and 76% in Ninewa, Anbar and Erbil governorates, respectively. However, in some IDP camps, the rate was as low as 5%. Attendance rates increased with age: 54% for ages 6 to 11, 57% for ages 12 to 14 and 70% for ages 15 to 17 (CCCM Cluster and REACH, 2017).

In Yemen, as of December 2017, 5% of school-age children are internally displaced (GCPEA, 2018). The impact of extensive internal displacement on education has been compounded by schools being the public buildings most frequently used to shelter IDPs (Al-Sabahi and Motahar, 2017). In general, internal displacement places education systems under strain, as in Ukraine (**Box 4.3**).

Natural disasters can also cause displacement that disrupts education, even if the consequences are short-lived compared with conflict-related displacement. In Bangladesh, earthquakes, storms, floods and rising sea level damage 900 schools each year, on average (Save the Children, 2015). A household and school survey around the time of the 2004 flood collected detailed information on its effects. Singling out the effects of a particular flood,

BOX 4.3:

Conflict has displaced millions in Ukraine, affecting their education

According to UNHCR, there are 1.8 million IDPs in Ukraine as of January 2018 (UNHCR, 2018d). Conflict has heavily affected education infrastructure: 280 education institutions in Donetsk and Luhansk regions had been damaged by October 2015 (UNICEF, 2016). In the cities of Dnipro, Kharkiv, Kiev and Zaporizhzhia, which host the most IDPs, education institutions faced challenges such as shortage of classroom space and lack of resources to provide food and transport. While grass-roots volunteer organizations, civil society and host communities responded to IDPs' immediate needs, poverty reduced the likelihood of youth attending upper secondary and tertiary education. IDP households earned 30% below the subsistence level set by the Ministry of Social Policy (IOM, 2017).

Government responses included creating additional pre-school and secondary places, moving 18 state universities from the east of the country and Crimea, and simplifying IDP admission and transfer procedures (Right to Protection et al., 2017). Under legislation passed in May 2015, the government partly or fully covered tuition for registered IDPs below age 23 and provided other incentives, such as long-term education loans and free textbooks and internet access (COE, 2016). A 2016 circular of the Cabinet of Ministers approved a unified IDP information database under the Ministry of Social Policy to shed light on the needs of displaced populations (Right to Protection et al., 2017).

The 2018 Humanitarian Response Plan focuses on actions to address the effects of trauma, stress and violence through psychosocial services, after-school sessions, life skills learning and conflict-sensitive education. It also involves strengthening the Ministry of Education's capacity to recognize the certification of all students whose education was interrupted (UNOCHA, 2017c).

> In Bangladesh, earthquakes, storms, floods and rising sea level damage 900 schools each year

compared with floods in an average year, is difficult. About 19% of households were flooded for an average of seven days. While 30% of schools closed at some point because of flooding, about 15% closed for two weeks or more. Affected schools were closed an average of seven days more than in the previous year. On days affected schools were open, attendance was one-third lower (FMRP, 2005).

On average, the Philippines suffers 20 typhoons each year and is at high risk for volcanic eruptions, earthquakes and landslides (Save the Children, 2015). After typhoon Haiyan in November 2013, 12,400 classrooms and 2,000 day care centres needed repair, and 4,400 classrooms and 500 day care centres needed replacement. Tents and tarpaulins were distributed for more than 2,000 temporary learning spaces, and learning materials were provided to 435,000 children aged 3 to 17 (Education Cluster, 2014). Investment in robust infrastructure can make a difference. Typhoon-resistant schools equipped with teaching and learning materials led to an estimated average increase of 0.3 years of education (Cas, 2016).

REFUGEES NEED TO BE INCLUDED IN NATIONAL EDUCATION SYSTEMS

Faced with crises, most governments did not provide education for refugees. This was left to the international humanitarian sector, which reflexively set up parallel systems for refugees. Provision reflected the home country system. However, consensus has gradually emerged that this is not a sustainable solution. Displacement is often protracted, parallel systems usually lack qualified teachers, examinations are not certifiable, and funding risks being cut at short notice. Parallel education, therefore, diminishes the chance refugees are included and lead meaningful lives in their first countries of asylum, where their protection has been guaranteed.[1]

The 2012–2016 UNHCR Global Education Strategy urged countries for the first time to offer refugee children access to accredited and certified learning opportunities to enable continuity in education (UNHCR, 2012). The long-term benefits of such a move can be considerable for both host governments and refugees. The objective is to include refugees fully in the national education system, studying in the same classroom with natives after a short period of accelerated classes, depending on prior access, literacy and language, to prepare them for entry at appropriate age-for-grade levels. The degree of refugee inclusion varies across displacement contexts. Geography, history, resource availability and system capacity all affect the evolving nature of inclusion.

In some cases, the move towards inclusion has been gradual, following developments on the ground and an increasing understanding of the potential benefits. Turkey (with an affected population of 3.8 million – the largest in the world – mainly from the Syrian Arab Republic[2]) decided to include all Syrian refugee children in the national education system over the next three years and phase out separate provision (**Box 4.4**). This response provides useful insights into the education policy choices governments make in response to large-scale refugee movements and transitioning from short-term, immediate solutions to more institutionalized, systemic and sustainable approaches in protracted refugee situations. In other cases, government commitment has been intermittent, as in the Islamic Republic of Iran (with an affected population of 1 million, mainly from Afghanistan), where a policy of inclusion has experienced occasional setbacks over a period of four decades (**Box 4.5**).

Ethiopia (with an affected population of 900,000, mostly from Somalia and South Sudan) runs primarily parallel refugee schools. However, these follow the national curriculum, at least from grade 5 and up (UNHCR, 2015c), and the Ethiopia Refugee Proclamation allows refugees to access national schools and host children to access refugee schools. The government is working to formalize refugee inclusion in the national education system further. Responding to a request from the Administration for Refugee and Returnee Affairs, which is responsible for refugee education, the State Minister for General Education issued a circular to all Regional Education Board directors identifying areas for collaboration on refugee education, including curricula and textbooks, student assessment, teacher education and school

1. This section draws on Dryden-Peterson et al. (2018).

2. Statistics in parentheses are based on UNHCR (2018c). They refer to end 2017 and include refugees, people in refugee-like situations and asylum-seekers whose cases are pending.

BOX 4.4:

Turkey has committed to including Syrian children in its education system

As of 2018, Turkey hosts 3.5 million refugees, 1 million of whom are school-age (UNHCR, 2018c). The first Syrian refugees crossed into Turkey in April 2011. Between 2013 and 2018, the share of Syrians living outside camps increased from 64% to 93% (AFAD, 2013; 3RP, 2018). As the refugee population increased and spread beyond camps, philanthropists, non-government organizations (NGOs) and faith-based organizations established informal schools, staffed by volunteer teachers, which offered instruction in Arabic and used a modified Syrian curriculum. They were largely unregulated, operated outside the national system and had very limited quality assurance and standardization of certification at the end of grades 9 and 12.

In late 2014, the Ministry of National Education established a regulatory framework for these temporary education centres (TECs). Syrian families could choose enrolment in TECs or public schools (Turkey Ministry of National Education, 2014). Education provision, data management and regulation of organizations supporting TECs were further standardized in the following two years, and TECs not meeting regulations were closed. In August 2016, the government announced that all Syrian children would be integrated into the national education system. It is estimated that, of Syrian children attending school, the share of those enrolled in TECs fell from 83% in 2014/15 to 37% in 2017/18. It is expected that the remaining 318 TECs will close by 2020 (**Figure 4.4**).

The government mandated all TECs offer 15 hours of Turkish language instruction per week to prepare students for transition to Turkish schools. Inclusion also has serious implications for school infrastructure and teacher preparation. The process has been supported by Promoting Integration of Syrian Children to the Turkish Education System, a project that received EUR 300 million as part of the European Union's EUR 3 billion Facility for Refugees in Turkey (Delegation of the European Union in Turkey, 2017). Two-fifths financed school construction; the rest was allocated to Turkish and Arabic language courses, catch-up education and remedial classes, free school transport, education materials, an examination system, guidance and counselling, training of 15,000 teachers and hiring of administrative personnel (Arik Akyuz, 2018).

Part of the resources also funded a communication strategy, including a website, TV spots, short films and other tools to raise awareness about educational opportunities open to Syrian children (Arik Akyuz, 2018). Parents need to understand what their rights are and how to enrol their children. However, even if they are aware of their rights, some refugee communities may resist inclusion in national education systems, not consenting to their children being educated in a language they themselves do not understand (Dallal, 2016).

FIGURE 4.4:

No Syrian refugee children will attend temporary education centres in Turkey by 2020

Distribution of enrolled Syrian refugee children in Turkey by school type

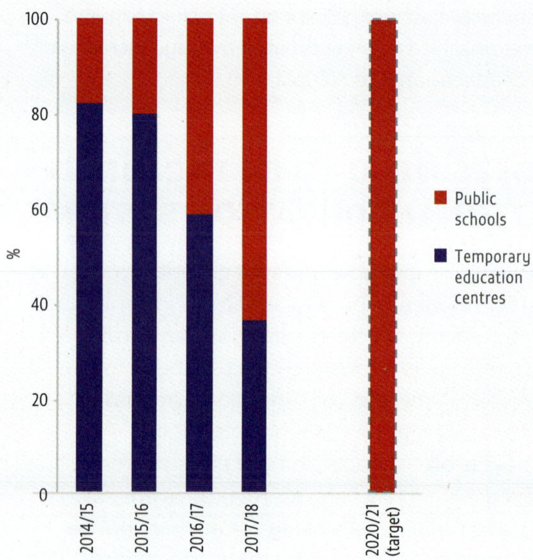

GEM StatLink: http://bit.ly/fig4_4
Source: Arik Ayuz (2018).

BOX 4.5:

Attitudes towards including Afghan refugees in the Iranian education system have been variable

Data on the enrolment of registered and undocumented Afghan refugees in the Islamic Republic of Iran are scant. However, the little evidence that exists suggests that they have had better access to education than Afghan refugees who fled to Pakistan (**Box 4.2**), with primary enrolment more than twice as high (Nicolle, 2018).

When Afghan refugees first arrived in the 1980s, the government targeted awareness-raising campaigns, featuring education as a right and an obligation for all children. While refugees who settled in camps (less than 10% at the time) attended schools there (WFP et al., 2016), those who settled in urban areas attended public schools alongside Iranian peers free of charge (Hoodfar, 2010).

The continued influx of Afghans seeking protection from the civil war and the Taliban in the 1990s resulted in a decision to halt provision of indefinite legal residence permits (HRW, 2013). Moreover, a regulation instructed Afghan refugees to enrol only in schools in the city where their residency documentation had been issued, affecting those who had since moved within the country (Hoodfar, 2007). Undocumented Afghans were unable to use public services legally, although many schools still allowed them to enrol. A temporary easing occurred in 2001–2004, when another regulation allowed undocumented Afghans to return to school (Tousi and Kiamanesh, 2010). In response to their intermittent exclusion, some Afghan communities formed informal schools, which the government initially condoned. Later, many of these unregistered schools were shut down (Squire, 2000).

In 2004, a new directive banned enrolment of undocumented Afghan children and instructed the Ministry of Education to collect fees from Afghan refugee students. The directive also banned Afghan students from enrolling in pre-university centre courses, a prerequisite for applying to the university entrance examination, effectively blocking access to Iranian tertiary institutions (Nicolle, 2018). Regulations issued in 2012 requiring Afghan students to renounce refugee status and obtain an Afghan passport and visa further complicated access to university education (HRW, 2013).

In May 2015, the Supreme Leader decreed that schools should accept all Afghan children, regardless of documentation. In April 2016, a government directive created an educational support card for undocumented Afghan children, protecting them from deportation during their studies and permitting all Afghan students to enrol up to the secondary diploma, although school fees are still charged (Nicolle, 2018). The directive was linked to an increase in public school enrolment of undocumented children by 51,000 in 2016 (Zolfaghari, 2016).

---

inspection. Joint efforts are under way to programme humanitarian and development aid interventions (UNHCR, 2017d). An Education Cannot Wait fund grant supports refugee education planning and management in selected districts at the regional and school levels (ECW, 2018).

> “In Ethiopia, the government is working to formalize refugee inclusion in the national education system further”

Rwanda (with an affected population of 170,000 people, mostly from Burundi and the Democratic Republic of the Congo) pledged in 2016 to include 18,000 refugee children in primary schools and 35,000 adolescents in secondary schools, eliminating the need for parallel camp-based provision (United Nations, 2016). Between 2016 and 2017, the refugee enrolment rate increased from 54% to 80% in primary and from 34% to 73% in secondary schools. Rwanda joined the CRRF in February 2018 (CRRF, 2018b).

There are several cases where, despite a commitment to inclusion, this is not fully achieved. Refugees may be included in the national system, sharing host curriculum, assessment and language of instruction, but with some degree of segregation. Partial inclusion may result from concentration of refugees in distinct locations, such as camps, producing geographical separation. In Kenya (with an affected population of 490,000, mainly from Somalia and South Sudan), schools in the two largest refugee camps are registered with the Ministry of Education. Students study the national curriculum and take national qualifying examinations, but distance from local schools means there are few if any local students.

Resources can be a key constraint. Lebanon and Jordan (with affected populations of 1 million and 730,000, respectively) have the highest number of refugees per

BOX 4.6:

Multiple challenges have affected inclusion of refugees in the Greek education system

In 2015–2016, over 1 million people entered and transited through Greece. Following an agreement between the European Union and Turkey in March 2016 and the closure of borders to other European countries, an estimated 20,000 children remained in the country. Three-quarters live on the mainland, either in camps, urban accommodations or unaccompanied children shelters; the remaining quarter lives on five islands, often exceeding the maximum stay in overcrowded camps.

In August 2016, a government-sponsored committee proposed a refugee education action plan and the establishment of an implementation unit at the Ministry of Education, Research and Religious Affairs. There have been two main types of formal education provision since 2016/17 on the mainland. First, some children attend regular schools – most of them located in zones of education priority – with existing reception classes serving immigrant children. Second, new reception classes for refugee children living in open accommodation sites were established in nearby schools. Children attend an afternoon shift and follow a special programme of Greek, English, information technology, mathematics, music and physical education. Refugee education coordinators serve as liaisons between the refugee and school communities (Greece Ministry of Education Research and Religious Affairs, 2017).

An evaluation of the first year of implementation noted that the goal of introducing normalcy was achieved but also recognized weaknesses. Not having been selected on the basis of prior experience in intercultural education or teaching Greek as a second language, teachers were often unprepared, and few undertook available training programmes. Parent participation and provision of information to families were also limited. There was also active opposition from some local communities, although municipalities played a positive role in diffusing tensions (Anagnostou and Nikolova, 2017).

As of the end of the 2017/18 school year, an estimated 62% of children aged 5 to 17 living in urban accommodations and unaccompanied children shelters were registered in formal education, ranging from 76% of 5- to 6-year-olds to 42% of 16- to 17-year-olds, although no dropout rate estimates are available (UNHCR, 2018a). The government introduced legislation in June 2018 that formalizes the refugee education structures and introduces stricter criteria for teacher recruitment (Greece Government Official Gazette, 2018).

However, insufficient provision on the five islands remains a problem. A recent report found that, while camps are identification sites conceived for very provisional stays, the prolonged stay meant the lack of will to establish the same structures as on the mainland was no longer justifiable. It noted that lack of vaccinations had been used to justify exclusion from the few reception classes. The government opened pre-schools in all but the biggest site in early 2018 and announced it would open reception classes to serve children from all sites for the first time in 2018/19 (Human Rights Watch, 2018).

capita in the world. They have adopted double-shift systems, with one group attending in the morning and another in the afternoon, producing temporal separation. In 2016, 160 of Lebanon's 1,350 public schools operated a morning shift largely attended by Lebanese children and an afternoon shift mostly attended by Syrian refugees. The same teachers often teach both shifts and report being overworked (Dryden-Peterson and Adelman, 2016). Jordan also sought to accommodate the growing Syrian refugee population with double-shift schools. Children in these schools receive fewer hours of instruction than those in public schools on a regular schedule (Culbertson and Constant, 2015; HRW, 2016).

Even countries with more resources can face practical challenges in delivering education to refugees through the national system. It requires effective planning and coordination, as has been well documented in Greece (with an affected population of 80,000, mainly from Afghanistan, Iraq and the Syrian Arab Republic) (**Box 4.6**).

In several contexts, education for refugees continues to be in separate, non-formal community-based or

BOX 4.7:

Burundian refugees are not included in the Tanzanian education system

Most Burundian refugees in the United Republic of Tanzania live in three camps in the Kigoma region that are governed by the Ministry of Home Affairs. UNHCR coordinates their education, funding two international NGOs, the International Rescue Committee and Caritas, to deliver formal schooling. National policy separates refugee education from the national system, and refugee education is not funded by the government or development partners (Dalrymple, 2018).

In 2017, with the support of UNHCR and UNICEF, the Ministry of Education, Science and Technology developed a National Strategy on Inclusive Education 2018–2021, which included objectives and targets for refugee students, seemingly putting aside the previous parallel approach. This followed the government's decision to be one of the first countries to implement the CRRF (Dalrymple, 2018). However, the United Republic of Tanzania's withdrawal from the CRRF process in January 2018 makes it unclear whether a shift to include refugees will proceed (ReliefWeb, 2018). Lack of financial support from international donors is a key reason for the withdrawal, highlighting the importance of global responsibility-sharing in the face of an issue largely affecting the poorest parts of the world (Betts, 2018).

private schools, as with Burundian refugees in the United Republic of Tanzania (with an affected population of 350,000) (**Box 4.7**) or Karen refugees from Myanmar in Thailand (with an affected population of 110,000) (**Box 4.8**). Such schools may be initiated and supported by international organizations or by refugees and local communities themselves. They may or may not be certified. The parallel education system for Palestinian refugees is a unique case (**Box 4.9**).

BOX 4.8:

Karen refugee education in Thailand is mostly delivered in separate schools

The Myanmar government and the Karen National Union (KNU), an organization of the country's third-largest ethnic group, were in conflict since Myanmar's independence in 1948 over ethnic rights and identity, self-governance and natural resources. Democratization began in 2011, and a ceasefire agreement was signed in 2012, although sporadic clashes continue. An estimated 100,000 people still live in nine refugee camps just across the Thai border (Zaw, 2018). Refugee children attend 64 schools, which follow the curriculum of the Karen Education Department affiliated with the KNU (Shiohata, 2018). Thai public schools are not an option for refugees. The Karen generally lack a Thai identity card, and their prior education is not recognized (Dare, 2015).

The democratization process in Myanmar has had a strong education reform component. Following a Comprehensive Education Sector Review, an Education Promotion Implementation Committee drafted a National Education Bill in 2014, which encourages instruction in ethnic languages alongside Burmese and could help address one of the factors behind the conflict (Shiohata, 2018). Teaching Karen as a subject will extend to grade 4 in Bago Region in 2018/19 (Karen News, 2018) and continues to expand in Ayeyarwady Region (Khalain, 2018), both of which have Karen populations. The government is gradually recruiting minority-language teaching assistants, offering volunteers a small salary in December 2017 and considering promoting those with bachelor's degrees to permanent positions (Phyu, 2018).

Using minority languages in public schools could encourage refugees to return to Myanmar, but the challenge remains ensuring returnees benefit. According to the 2015 Demographic and Health Survey, the primary completion rate in Myanmar was 81%. However, in Kayin State, where the Karen constitute the majority, it was 68%, with 60% of boys completing. The secondary completion rate was 15% nationwide but 13% in Kayin State, with just 8% of boys completing.

BOX 4.9:

An established parallel system – the UNRWA approach to education for Palestinian refugees

The United Nations Relief and Works Agency for Palestine Refugees in the Near East (UNRWA) has provided accredited basic education for Palestinian refugees for close to 70 years, in partnership with UNESCO. It currently provides free basic education to some 526,000 refugee children in 711 schools across the West Bank and Gaza, Jordan, Lebanon and the Syrian Arab Republic (UNRWA, 2018b). The agency also operates eight vocational training centres for over 7,000 refugee youth and two education-science faculties providing degree-level teacher education for over 1,800 refugees (UNRWA, 2017b). This comprehensive parallel education system encompasses all aspects of education, from curriculum to inclusive education practices and teacher professional development. UNRWA students have outperformed those in public schools in Jordan, the West Bank and Gaza by an entire year's worth of schooling (Abdul-Hamid et al., 2016).

A parallel refugee education system requires alignment and close cooperation with host governments to ensure the smooth transition of students into the national system, including recognition and accreditation of their qualifications. While UNRWA, as a UN agency, has operational independence, it aligns with many aspects of host government education systems, such as curricula, examinations and timetabling. This is in line with good practice for refugee education (UNHCR, 2015b).

In a protracted refugee context, with multiple crises in the past seven decades, this system has built resilience, allowing it to adapt in times of emergency. In 2011, UNRWA embarked on a systemic, agency-wide education reform with an innovative programme, Education in Emergencies, which emphasizes continuously strengthening education staff capacity to deliver quality education, building a community of practice in the school and fostering close links with parents and the community (UNRWA, 2017a).

The average cost of the UNRWA education programme is US$826 per child per year. The primary source of funding is voluntary contributions from UN member states. For the past 10 years, however, these have not kept pace with needs stemming from an increasingly unstable context. Between 2011 and 2016, 44% of all UNRWA schools were 'directly impacted by armed conflict and violence, either causing physical damage to the schools or significantly disrupting education services' (UNRWA, 2016). In 2017, the United States contributed the equivalent of 25% of the programme and 32% of the total budget of UNRWA (UNRWA, 2018a). In August 2018, the United States announced it would cease its support to UNRWA (BBC, 2018). While other donors have either brought forward or pledged to increase their contributions, this financial instability poses a threat to the continuous delivery of education and other services.

SEVERAL OBSTACLES TO INCLUSION NEED TO BE OVERCOME

Faced with the pressures of displacement but united by a commitment to include displaced students in national education systems, governments and their partners need to develop flexible plans to ensure coordination and coherence. Effective planning can promote safety, resilience and social cohesion. Planning challenges emerge at the domestic and, especially, the international levels, where there is an acute need to bridge the international humanitarian and development aid budgets (**Policy focus 19.3**). Concerns include varying planning horizons, with development donors able to provide multi-year funding, and varying planning architectures, with humanitarian donors often invisible in education sector plans. Plans need to recognize issues related to displacement, including lack of documents, limited language proficiency, education interruptions and poverty.

THE PRESSURES OF DISPLACEMENT ON EDUCATION CALL FOR DATA AND PLANNING

The difficulties related to inclusion are most acutely felt in contexts where education systems are already weak. The UNESCO International Institute for Educational Planning has developed guidance on transitional education plans (TEPs) until a full education sector plan is developed. Whereas a full plan takes years to develop, a TEP generally takes less than 12 months and focuses on immediate needs (GPE and UNESCO-IIEP, 2016). Between 2011 and 2017, Global Partnership for Education supported 11 TEPs (GPE, 2016).

Chad (with an affected population of 410,000, mainly from the Central African Republic and Sudan) became the first country to include refugees in its TEP in 2013. A participatory assessment, conducted in 12 camps, raised three concerns from Sudanese refugees with respect to the transition to the Chadian national education system: the change of language of instruction, recognition of diplomas issued in Chad upon return to Sudan, and the threat of loss of nationality, culture, religion and national identity (UNHCR, 2015a). These concerns were taken into account in the plan. Chad subsequently accessed US$7 million of its agreed Global Partnership for Education allocation in 2015 for an emergency programme covering school lunches, school construction and pedagogical materials (GPE, 2016). In 2018, the government converted 108 schools in 19 camps and refugee sites into regular public schools (CRRF, 2018a).

The Uganda Education Response Plan for Refugees and Host Communities, announced in 2018, is a unique example that addresses education needs in 34 refugee-hosting sub-counties in 12 districts. It brought together development and humanitarian aid partners and will reach just over 675,000 refugee and host students per year, at a cost of US$395 million over 3.5 years (Uganda Ministry of Education and Sports, 2018).

In December 2017, in the Djibouti Declaration on Regional Refugee Education, the education ministers of Djibouti, Ethiopia, Kenya, Somalia, South Sudan, Sudan and Uganda committed to 'integrate education for refugees and returnees into National Education Sector Plans by 2020' (IGAD, 2017b). The annex includes examples of possible actions, such as establishing minimum learning standards for refugees and returnees, integrating refugees into the national EMIS and establishing a regional committee for monitoring implementation of plans (IGAD, 2017a).

To plan refugee education, countries need to improve their EMIS. Chad developed an integrated system, which includes data collection forms for each camp, covering pre-primary to tertiary education and non-formal literacy programmes. This has improved the quality of data available, ensuring harmonized data collection, entry, compilation and sharing (UNESCO, 2016). Jordan's Ministry of Education has also integrated the education status of refugee children in an EMIS platform (Jordan Ministry of Planning and International Cooperation, 2018). South Sudan merged UNHCR data collection with the national EMIS to identify schools at risk. The General Education Strategic Plan uses the information to concentrate support in regions most in need (GPE and UNESCO-IIEP, 2016).

"Plans need to recognize issues related to displacement, including lack of documents, limited language proficiency, education interruptions and poverty"

LACK OF IDENTITY DOCUMENTS AND CREDENTIALS IS A KEY FACTOR IN EXCLUSION

Refugees frequently lack documentation, such as birth certificates, school-leaving certificates and diplomas, which makes inclusion in national education systems more difficult. Constraints on education in destination countries vary, as experienced by Syrian refugees.

Until recently, Jordan required refugees living outside camps to register with the Ministry of Interior and obtain 'service cards' for access to schools. Obtaining a service card requires a birth certificate. Refugees who fled without their birth certificates or who had not registered the births of their children during displacement were ineligible (Human Rights Watch, 2016). In a move towards greater flexibility in late 2016, the Ministry of Education began allowing public schools to enrol children without cards.

> “Governments must protect refugees' right to education, no matter their identification documents or residence status”

In Lebanon, Syrian refugees could enter secondary school if they could prove refugee status and had completed primary school in Lebanon or the Syrian Arab Republic. Many students fled without proof of primary certificates, making private school the only education option, if they could afford it. Since UNHCR was instructed to stop registering refugees in May 2015, it has been harder for Syrians without refugee status to access school (Dryden-Peterson et al., 2018).

The government of Turkey relaxed documentation requirements for Syrians wishing to enrol in tertiary education and provided for the recognition of secondary graduation certificates issued by Syrian authorities. The Ministry of National Education also made special dispensation for those who had completed grade 12 in TECs to sit for ministry-administered examinations that conferred certificates recognized in Turkish university applications (Yavcan and El-Ghali, 2017).

MASTERING THE LOCAL LANGUAGE IS NECESSARY FOR REFUGEES TO FEEL INCLUDED

Lack of knowledge of the language of instruction or the classroom language hinders the ability of refugee students to engage, learn and communicate, and is a barrier to being included in national education systems, especially for older children and youth. In Greece, language difficulty was the main reason refugee children stopped attending formal education (REACH and UNICEF, 2017).

In the early 2000s in Uganda, refugees from the Democratic Republic of the Congo were automatically placed in lower grades because they lacked English proficiency. However, those students had higher repetition rates even when they had mastered instructional content. Placing older students in lower grades overcrowds classrooms where basic literacy skills are attained, places pressure on what are usually the least qualified teachers and raises protection risks for younger children (Dryden-Peterson, 2006). Burundian refugees in Rwanda faced the same challenge. International partners have supported a comprehensive orientation course lasting up to six months, which includes English lessons. Students who reach the right level can join public schools. The programme has teacher education and mentorship elements and a community sensitization campaign to explain the transition to public school (UNICEF, 2015; Wachiaya, 2017).

High income countries have more resources to develop language skills. Refugees granted asylum in Germany take a compulsory integration course (600 hours of language and 100 hours on German law, history, culture and society) (Bundeszentrale für Politische Bildung, 2018). In Oslo, children are offered initial welcome classes lasting up to two years before being included in the national education system at age-appropriate levels (Eurocities, 2017).

Too prolonged, such courses can push refugees out of the education system. Moreover, language needs extend to non-verbal practices that enable understanding of host country social norms. These are not explicitly taught but learned through interaction with natives. This aspect of linguistic inclusion is largely ignored in policy development (Dryden-Peterson et al., 2018).

ALTERNATIVE PROGRAMMES HELP THE DISPLACED CATCH UP AND ACCESS OR RE-ENTER SCHOOL

Alternative education programmes help children whose education was interrupted by displacement (Save the Children et al., 2017). According to the Accelerated Education Working Group, which brings together UN agencies and international NGOs, accelerated education is a 'flexible, age-appropriate programme, run in an accelerated timeframe, which aims to provide access to education for disadvantaged, over-age, out-of-school children and youth' and 'equivalent, certified competencies for basic education using effective teaching and learning approaches that match their level of cognitive maturity' (AEWG, 2018).

Accelerated education programmes are targeted at students aged 10 to 18 who have missed at least one year of school, condensing curricula into a shorter period and granting certification at the end. Variations include catch-up programmes for students who have missed less than a year of school to help them re-enter formal education; remedial programmes for students who are in school but behind the expected grade level; and bridging programmes for students whose main barrier to national education is language proficiency (Shah et al., 2017).

The Norwegian Refugee Council implements an accelerated learning programme in Dadaab that condenses Kenya's eight-year curriculum into four years. The programme is responsive to student needs, with multiple entry and exit points. At the end of each cycle, students can re-enter the formal system at a grade-appropriate level using an assessment framework agreed to by the Ministry of Education and alternative education partners. A review showed that the programme had increased access for refugee boys, although less so for girls (Shah, 2015). While international NGOs tend to run these programmes, education ministries should factor standardized flexible programmes, and supporting capacity development and material deployment mechanisms, into their sector plans.

> "The Norwegian Refugee Council runs an accelerated learning programme in Dadaab, which condenses Kenya's eight-year curriculum into four years"

THE COST OF EDUCATION TO THE DISPLACED IS NOT LIMITED TO FEES

Fees and other education costs can be particularly high for refugees, especially when their freedom of movement and right to work are constrained. Humanitarian aid subsidizes school transport: in Jordan, Iraq and Turkey, the International Organization for Migration and UNICEF introduced a school bus service, enabling 35,000 Syrian children to attend (Kompani, 2018).

Public education in Lebanon is nominally fee-free, but registration, uniforms, textbooks, transport and school meals can make it unaffordable for refugee families. The government piloted Min ila ('To from') with UNICEF and the World Food Programme, offering cash to primary school children enrolled in the afternoon shift to cover transport and compensate households for forgone income when children attend school instead of working. While enrolment was unaffected, attendance in pilot areas increased by 0.5 to 0.7 days per week, or about 20% relative to the control group (de Hoop et al., 2018).

In Turkey, the Ministry of Family, Labour and Social Services; the Ministry of National Education; the Turkish Red Crescent Society; and UNICEF are extending the national conditional cash transfer programme for education to Syrian and other refugees with support from the European Commission, Norway and the United States. Public school, TEC and accelerated learning programme students receive US$8 to US$13 per month, depending on gender and grade, conditional on regular attendance. In addition, a one-time payment of US$22 is planned for each child per semester. As of July 2018, the programme had reached 368,000 children and anticipates reaching 450,000 by July 2019 (Arik Akyuz, 2018).

In Costa Rica, an amendment to the law in 2017 ensures refugees enjoy equal access to the Social Development and Family Allowance Trust Fund benefits, which include education support (UNHCR, 2017a).

TEACHERS ARE THE KEY TO SUCCESSFUL INCLUSION

Teachers are sometimes the only resource available to students in displacement settings, when classroom space or learning materials are in short supply. Yet including the displaced in national education systems poses challenges for teacher recruitment and retention. A proliferation of unregulated, substandard and short-term teacher contracts has a negative effect on working conditions. Teachers also need special training to develop teaching strategies to deal with overcrowded, mixed-age or multilingual classrooms, as well as the stress and trauma linked with displacement.[3]

DISPLACEMENT CONTEXTS EXACERBATE TEACHER MANAGEMENT ISSUES

The diversity of teacher profiles and qualifications in displacement settings has important implications for teacher management. Displacement intensifies the usual pressures on teacher management systems in terms of availability, financing and planning. Coordination of teacher recruitment, compensation and development is often further compromised in fragile contexts, where multiple humanitarian and development aid agencies operate under different rules (Kirk and Winthrop, 2013).

Teacher shortages intensify in displacement contexts

Global data on teachers in refugee education are not available. Mass shortages, especially of qualified teachers, exist across displacement settings, both at the onset of crises and in cases of protracted displacement. In Turkey, it is estimated that 80,000 additional teachers would be needed if all school-age Syrians were to enrol (Sirkeci, 2017). Exacerbating the low availability of teachers are low levels of education among affected populations, remoteness and vulnerability of many teaching posts, language of instruction issues, denial of refugees' right to work, and non-recognition of refugee teacher qualifications (Mendenhall et al., 2018).

> "Teachers need special training to develop strategies to deal with overcrowded, mixed-age or multilingual classrooms"

The German education staff union, Gewerkschaft Erziehung und Wissenschaft, estimates that an additional 18,000 educators and 24,000 teachers are needed, at an estimated cost of EUR 3 billion extra per year (Vogel and Stock, 2017). Shortages have led to a proliferation of contract or voluntary teachers, who have variable qualifications, typically work on short-term arrangements with no job security and earn significantly less than their counterparts in the national service. Retired teachers have been recalled, and 'lateral entrants' (teachers with university degrees but without teacher qualifications) have also been used to fill the gaps (Strauss, 2016; Vogel and Stock, 2017).

3. This section is based on Mendenhall et al. (2018).

To fill the teacher gap caused by the large-scale influx of refugees:

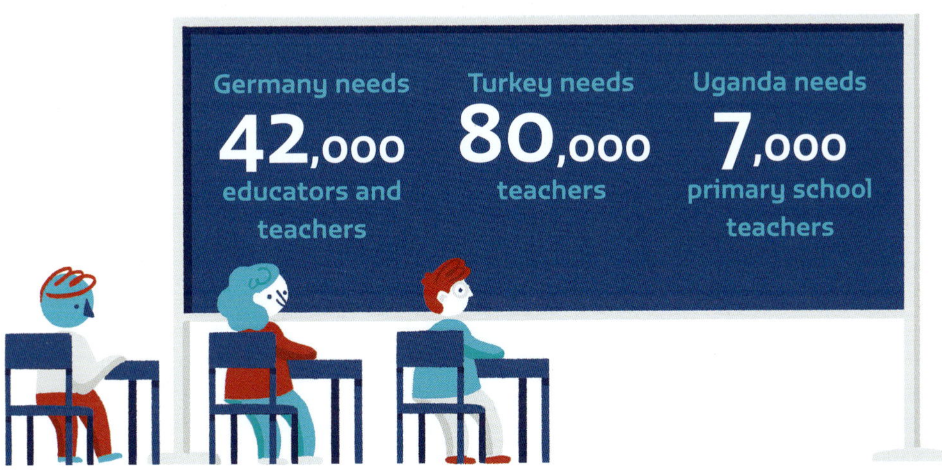

> Female teachers are particularly under-represented in displacement settings, largely due to safety considerations and cultural practices

Uganda will require an extra 7,000 primary school teachers for refugee education, according to its education sector plan (Uganda Ministry of Education and Sports, 2018). Payroll allocations per district would need to be revised to deploy more teachers; according to one estimate, the cost of primary teacher salaries in Uganda's refugee settlements would be US$15 million over the next three years. An additional issue is that South Sudanese refugee teacher qualifications remain unrecognized, even though many serve as classroom assistants (Save the Children, 2017).

Female teachers are particularly under-represented in displacement settings, largely due to safety considerations and cultural practices biased against women (Reeves Ring and West, 2015). The share of female primary teachers was 13% in Dadaab camp, Kenya, in 2016 and 18% at Dollo Ado camp, Ethiopia, in 2014 (UNHCR, 2015c; Women Educational Researchers of Kenya, 2017). The difficulty of recruiting qualified female teachers is compounded by an inability to retain them in areas experiencing violence. In Pakistan, female teachers displaced by violence were hesitant to return to work, fearing for their security where militant groups target schools (Ferris and Winthrop, 2011).

Compensating teachers in displacement situations is challenging

Equitable and predictable teacher compensation underpins sufficient teacher supply, recruitment, retention, motivation and well-being. It poses a critical challenge for national teacher services, whose budgets are already stretched, as well as for humanitarian partners whose short-term, emergency funding cycles are incompatible with the recurring costs of teacher salaries (INEE, 2009). Lack of sufficient resources to pay teachers, weak auditing mechanisms to track teacher pay, destruction of payroll and teacher qualifications records, and poorly maintained teacher management systems are common problems (Dolan et al., 2012).

Volunteer teachers often receive small stipends or incentives because of legal restrictions on employment. Incentive payment scales typically do not account for qualifications, experience and cost of living. In camps, teachers may earn the same as unskilled workers in less demanding jobs (Mendenhall et al., 2018). Teacher salaries often need to be supplemented by monetary or non-monetary community initiatives (Reeves Ring and West, 2015). Sharp disparities between payment of national and refugee teachers can cause tension.

MANY TEACHERS IN DISPLACEMENT SETTINGS LACK FORMAL TRAINING

Teachers in displacement contexts require tailored professional development to address circumstances such as their students' fragmented education histories and the trauma caused by conflict, displacement and resettlement. Instead, they often teach in challenging conditions, with limited, sporadic support. In Lebanon, 55% of teachers and staff had participated in professional development in the previous two years, even though the presence of refugee children affected their daily teaching (EI, 2017).

In many crisis contexts, individuals from the community, with at most a secondary certificate and only their own education experiences to draw on, may be recruited to teach. Their entry into the teaching profession is often sudden and unforeseen, their desire to remain teachers tentative and their confidence to perform their duties low. Yet they may have other valuable traits to contribute, such as shared cultural understanding with their learners (Kirk and Winthrop, 2013). What they need is appropriate training for the circumstances, as seen in Kenya's Kakuma camp, where 73% of primary teachers are uncertified (Mendenhall et al., 2018) (**Box 4.10**).

> 73% of primary teachers in Kenya's Kakuma camp are uncertified

Educators have to manage multilingual classrooms. In Uganda, instructional content is translated within the classroom, slowing the teaching process (Dryden-Peterson, 2015). In Turkey, teachers appointed by the education ministry do not have the training to teach Turkish to foreigners (Coşkun and Emin, 2016). European Union-funded 30-hour orientation training

BOX 4.10:

Alternative approaches prepare underqualified primary teachers in Kakuma camp, Kenya

Multiple approaches are used to support teachers in Kakuma, one of the world's largest refugee camps. A formal approach is the teaching diploma and certificate programmes offered to refugees by Masinde Muliro University of Science and Technology, in partnership with UNHCR and the Lutheran World Federation. One academic programme confers a diploma in primary education, which refugee students (mostly full-time primary teachers) complete over the course of a year. The programme consists of foundational courses (e.g. curriculum studies) and subject-specific courses (e.g. social studies, science, life skills and peace education) (Mendenhall et al., 2018).

The Training Pack for Primary School Teachers in Crisis Contexts, an open-source course developed by the Inter-Agency Network for Education in Emergencies' Teachers in Crisis Contexts Sub-Working Group, is a non-formal approach. It builds basic teaching skills for unqualified or underqualified teachers recruited to teach in emergency settings. The training materials cover the teacher's role and well-being; child protection, well-being and inclusion; pedagogy; and curriculum and planning (INEE, 2017). A complementary coaching pack proposes a peer-to-peer approach through which teachers can seek support from one another, brainstorm solutions, set goals and celebrate their successes (Mendenhall et al., 2018).

A team from Teachers College at Columbia University applied the pack in Kakuma, where over 80% of teachers are refugees. Until recently, newly recruited teachers, who had just finished secondary education, received little if any training. The team added a mobile mentoring component to help camp teachers connect with trained teachers and passionate educators around the world via WhatsApp. Teachers participated in a training workshop, peer coaching support through group discussions and classroom visits, and four to six months of mobile mentoring. Nearly 90% of primary teachers in Kakuma and the new Kalobeyei settlement nearby have been trained, alongside 30 national teachers (Mendenhall et al., 2018).

However, the pack is not yet recognized or certified by the Kenyan education authorities. Moreover, coordination remains a persistent challenge, with multiple organizations working on similar professional development activities, leading to sporadic and discontinuous training experiences (Mendenhall et al., 2018).

> “In response to protracted crises in the region, Chad upscaled refugee teachers' qualifications so that they could be fully certified and work in public schools”

has since been provided to 6,200 contract and 8,800 public school teachers, covering areas including conflict management, teaching methodologies, guidance and counselling skills (Mendenhall et al., 2018).

In high income countries, such as Germany, Italy, Spain and Sweden, teachers may be trained and certified but need new skills to address the needs of refugees (Bunar et al., 2018). Education policy in Germany is decentralized across the 16 states, and refugee-specific responses vary among them, depending on the refugee caseload, experience with migrant students and local policy orientation. States have made definite, if mixed, progress in preparing teachers for language support. Between 2012 and 2015, 10 states began providing explicit content for language support, although only 6 had made language support pedagogy mandatory by 2017 (Baumann, 2017).

SOME COUNTRIES HELP REFUGEE TEACHERS GET CERTIFICATION AND RE-ENTER THE PROFESSION

One solution to address teacher shortages in displacement contexts is to include refugee teachers in national training programmes. Refugee teachers are generally excluded: They may be denied the right to work or strict professional regulations may prevent them from legally joining the national teaching force. Even when retraining is possible, it is often lengthy and costly, requiring full-time study (Mendenhall et al., 2018).

Chad boasts one of the most promising examples of professional pathways for refugee teachers. In response to the protracted crises in the Central African Republic and Sudan, the government, with support from national and international organizations, made refugee schools

> In the Syrian Arab Republic, 73% of teachers had no training in providing psychosocial support for children in their classrooms

use a Chadian curriculum; deployed more Chadian teachers to refugee camps to teach French, civics and geography; and upscaled refugee teachers' qualifications so that they now have opportunities to be fully certified by the Chadian education authorities and work in Chad's public schools (UNHCR, 2015a).

From 2012 to 2014, 98 refugee teachers from the Central African Republic participated in certified training through the Doba Training College. From 2012 to 2016, 341 Sudanese refugee teachers were also certified by the Abéché Bilingual Teacher Training College after a two-year teacher education course offered during the summer months. Additional cohorts of Sudanese teachers are undergoing training, and a few teachers in Djabal camp are working as temporary teachers in Chadian schools. The governments of Chad and Sudan signed a joint agreement with UNESCO, UNICEF and UNHCR to ensure that certification and equivalency are recognized when Sudanese teachers return home (Mendenhall et al., 2018).

There are also initiatives in high income countries. The Refugee Teacher Programme, by the University of Potsdam in Germany, enables Syrian and other refugee teachers to return to the classroom, where they can act as bridge-builders for new arrivals in German schools. The programme supports Germany's efforts to integrate refugees and asylum-seekers into the workforce. The 11-month course consists of several months of intensive German language and teacher education and classroom practice in school. The university received more than 700 applications for 25 places and plans to expand access (Mendenhall et al., 2018; Potsdam University, 2017). In Sweden, teachers' unions created a guide for newly arrived teachers who want to stay in the profession. It explains the teaching standards in the country and provides information about relevant government agencies (Bunar et al., 2018).

TEACHERS NEED SUPPORT TO RESPOND TO LEARNERS WITH TRAUMATIC EXPERIENCES

Displaced learners have often had traumatic experiences of violence and conflict. Studies in high income countries have reported post-traumatic stress disorder prevalence rates ranging from 10% to 25%; in low and middle income countries, rates as high as 75% have been reported (Fazel, 2018). A review of 34 studies on refugee learning found that, in addition to the displacement trauma, learners face several risk factors in their new learning environments, including parental misunderstanding of education expectations, stereotyping and low expectations by teachers, bullying, and discrimination by staff or peers. These experiences can result in mental health problems and disruptive behaviour, which hamper teaching and learning (Graham et al., 2016).

In the absence of accessible mental health services for children, schools may often provide the only access to such services. Reviews of school-based mental health interventions for refugee and asylum-seeking children differentiate between two types of intervention: those based on creative expression through art, music or drama to help students develop social-emotional skills, and cognitive behavioural therapy, which can deal with past experiences, for instance through verbal processing, or with current and future challenges, for instance through self-soothing. Cognitive behavioural therapy techniques appear to have had positive therapeutic effects (Sullivan and Simonson, 2016; Tyrer and Fazel, 2014).

However, the evidence is sparse and mainly comes from high income countries. Moreover, such interventions require specially trained therapists and are beyond teachers' skills and responsibilities (Sullivan and Simonson, 2016). In most cases, teachers lack trauma and mental health training. In the Syrian Arab Republic, 73% of teachers surveyed by the Assistance Coordination Unit, an NGO, had no training in providing psychosocial support for children in their classrooms, let alone self-care (Mendenhall et al., 2018).

The Guidelines on Mental Health and Psychosocial Support in Emergency Settings recommend that teachers can provide psychosocial support by creating a safe and supportive environment through their interactions and specific, structured psychosocial activities (IASC, 2007). Teachers can maintain relationships with students and their families, learn their histories, observe student behaviour for signs of distress and seek help from specialized personnel, such as trauma-trained school psychologists (Sullivan and Simonson, 2016). For that, they need continuous professional development, for instance in constructive classroom management or use of referral mechanisms. They should not, however, attempt to conduct therapy with students (IASC, 2007).

Teachers who work in very challenging and stressful environments need extra support themselves to deal with difficult working conditions. Evidence on these needs remains very limited (Burde et al., 2015).

CONFLICT HAS SEVERE NEGATIVE IMPACTS ON THE EDUCATION OF THE INTERNALLY DISPLACED

The UN Guiding Principles on Internal Displacement state that everyone has the right to education and that 'the authorities concerned shall ensure that such persons, in particular displaced children, receive education which shall be free and compulsory at the primary level. Education should respect their cultural identity, language and religion' (UNHCR, 1998). However, many displacement crises occur in some of the poorest countries, which have limited capacity, and result from conflicts with political dimensions. These factors hamper both recognition of the problem and coordination in delivering education.

The Kampala Convention (formally, the African Union Convention for the Protection and Assistance of Internally Displaced Persons in Africa) has been one of the strongest attempts to recognize IDP rights. Ratified by 27 out of 55 countries as of June 2017 (African Union, 2017), it states that education must be provided to IDPs 'to the fullest extent practicable and with the least possible delay' (Art. 9) (African Union, 2012). However, an analysis of its implementation noted that states often lacked the human and financial capacity to fulfil their protection obligations. As a result, IDPs often relied on international humanitarian assistance (ICRC, 2016).

IDPS AND REFUGEES FACE SIMILAR EDUCATION CHALLENGES

In many cases, the legal, education and administrative responses to IDP education are similar to those affecting refugees.

Colombia has the world's second-largest population of IDPs: 6.5 million in 2017. Displacement continued despite the peace process begun in 2012. In 2015, among the 11% of people who had migrated internally during the previous five years, 6% cited violence as the main reason. The proportion exceeded 10% in the Cauca, Chocó, Putumayo and Valle del Cauca departments (Colombia Ministry of Health and Social Protection and Profamilia, 2017). During the first six months of 2018, about 45,000 students and more than 2,000 teachers were forced to suspend classes following clashes between armed groups in the Norte del Santander department (Norwegian Refugee Council, 2018). The government has focused on the legal framework to protect IDPs. In 2002, the Constitutional Court instructed municipal education authorities to treat displaced children preferentially in terms of access to education. In 2004, after more than 100 petitions, the court further declared that IDPs' fundamental rights, including to education, were being violated (Espinosa, 2009). While the legal framework facilitates identifying IDPs, doing so in practice is difficult in urban areas (IDMC, 2015).

Displacement interrupts the education of many children and adolescents, who need support to re-enter the system. Afghanistan had 1.3 million IDPs in 2017. Children in Crisis, an NGO, has implemented a community-based accelerated education programme to help out-of-school IDPs in informal settlements in and around Kabul to complete grade 6 and transition into the formal education system. However, the programme has been constrained by government requirements for alignment with the community-based education policy, which is quite prescriptive on matters of timetabling, curriculum and rate of acceleration (Ghaffar-Kucher, 2018).

> “Internally displaced teachers face risks and administrative hurdles that make collecting salaries virtually impossible”

Internally displaced teachers also face challenges. They often continue under home district management, leading to risks and administrative hurdles that make collecting salaries virtually impossible. The government of the Syrian Arab Republic requires teachers to return to government-controlled areas to collect their salaries every month; teachers report that colleagues making the journey have been arrested or detained, deterring others from attempting (ACU, 2017).

In Iraq, local authorities in the governorate of origin run IDP schools. Many teachers in IDP schools managed in the Ninewa governorate, for instance, had not received their salaries in months (Dorcas, 2016). In many cases, different education partners offer different stipends, depending on their budgets, causing tension between partners and teachers. In Iraq, 44 partners provide services across 15 governorates and support around 5,200 teachers with stipends or incentives (Education Cluster, 2018). Poor coordination among partners has led to service gaps, pay disparity among teacher categories and tension among partners. The Education Cluster in Erbil recently brought partners together to agree on a coordinated incentive scale, with standard rates for teachers and other types of workers (Mendenhall et al., 2018).

NATURAL DISASTERS AND CLIMATE CHANGE REQUIRE EDUCATION SYSTEMS TO BE PREPARED AND RESPONSIVE

Natural disasters, such as earthquakes or typhoons, place education systems at risk of loss of life, infrastructure damage and displacement, among other threats. Ensuring that education sector plans take such risks into account can reduce potential impacts. Government capacity to do so should be strengthened at all levels so that education services are as little disrupted as possible during all phases, from emergency response to recovery.

In 2017, the United Nations Office for International Strategy for Disaster Reduction and the Global Alliance for Disaster Risk Reduction and Resilience in the Education Sector launched their updated Comprehensive School Safety framework. Its three pillars are safe learning facilities, school disaster management, and risk reduction and resilience education. At the intersection of the three are multihazard risk assessment, education sector analysis, and child-centred assessment and planning (UNISDR and GADRRRES, 2017).

> “The three pillars of the Comprehensive School Safety framework are safe learning facilities, school disaster management, and risk reduction and resilience education”

In Bangladesh, a component of the Third Primary Education Development Program focuses on emergencies, in recognition of the disaster risks facing the country. Its purpose is to carry out a recommendation from the 2011 Local Consultative Group for Disaster Emergency Response: to develop a 'framework to guide integration of Disaster Risk Reduction and Education in Emergencies into sector planning and implementation' (Bangladesh Ministry of Primary and Mass Education, 2015).

Many Pacific island nations recognize climate change as a cause of increasing natural disaster risk and plan education accordingly. In 2011, the Solomon Islands issued its Policy Statement and Guidelines for Disaster Preparedness and Education in Emergency Situations. The objective is for students to continue to access safe learning environments before, during and after an emergency, ensuring that all schools identify temporary learning and teaching spaces. To maintain education quality, all teachers in affected areas should be trained in psychosocial strategies within two months of the disaster, and psychosocial activities should be introduced in all temporary learning spaces and schools within six weeks (Solomon Islands Ministry of Education and Human Resources Division, 2011). The Education Strategic Framework 2016–2030 suggests that the curriculum should introduce 'awareness about climate, environmental, disaster, social cohesion and social protection risk management to promote adaptation, sustainability, resilience and inclusion/equity' (Solomon Islands Ministry of Education and Human Resources Division, 2016).

Within a few decades, climate could be a main reason for displacement. 'Environmental refugee' or 'climate refugee' define any individuals leaving their homes due to climate change effects, such as sea level rise, drought or desertification, although the terms do not yet carry legal implications.

To reduce their vulnerability to climate change, some countries are already considering policy responses. The 'migration with dignity' policy is part of the government of Kiribati's long-term nationwide relocation strategy. It aims to raise the population's qualifications, giving them tools to access decent work opportunities abroad, especially in potential host countries with ageing populations, such as Australia, Japan or New Zealand, where there will be a need for skilled workers. The AUD$21 million Kiribati-Australia Nurses Initiative (2006–2014) offered Kiribati students scholarships to acquire skills and experience at Griffith University in Brisbane, Australia, as well as training opportunities for nurses in Kiribati, and provided programme support for the Kiribati School of Nursing. A review of the programme found low cost-effectiveness and suggested broadening the range of occupations and the countries covered (Shaw, 2014).

CONCLUSION

In recent years, the number of displaced people and the average duration of displacement have increased, reaching the highest levels since the Second World War. These trends have forced a radical rethink of how best to deliver education to affected populations. A key lesson for refugees specifically is abandoning the response of placing them in separate schools, a solution proven unsustainable: It excludes them from both host communities and sustainable livelihood opportunities.

Ensuring inclusion, however, is not straightforward and can be affected by geography, history, resources and capacity. It requires governments exert considerable efforts to coordinate authorities, unify procedures (from data collection to teacher payroll), engage refugee and host communities and design programmes that allow children and youth whose education has been interrupted or who cannot speak the language of instruction to re-enter the education system at an appropriate level. Further complications arise for IDPs and those affected by natural disasters.

Responses are complex to plan and implement, and the role of international partners is, therefore, crucial. They have supported countries in overcoming challenges, from preparing teachers to lowering cost barriers for refugee families. However, they too have a record of inefficiency, especially in bridging short-term emergency responses with long-term, development-oriented planning and support. The New York Declaration, Comprehensive Refugee Response Framework and Global Compact on Refugees commitments move policy in this right direction.

Education for refugee and displaced children and youth is critical to restore a sense of normalcy, but sharing host curricula, textbooks, teachers and infrastructure is only a first step towards inclusion from a social and cultural perspective. Direct contact alone will build neither belonging nor social cohesion. This is only possible through full inclusion in society, starting with education (**Chapter 5**).

'I love school, *efcharisto!*' says 7-year-old Roham from Tehran, moments before taking the bus to the primary school.

CREDIT: IOM Greece

CHAPTER

5

Diversity

It is the inherent duty of a school to challenge students' perceptions through exposure and experience. Education is uniquely positioned to positively impact perception and acceptance of newcomers to our communities. Education equips students with the skills to think critically and to be open to different ways of thinking, being and doing. Communities that embrace culturally responsive education are more welcoming, more connected and, ultimately, safer.

Mandy Manning, English language development educator, 2018 National Teacher of the Year in the United States

Education and tolerance, with a child rights-based approach, go hand in hand. This chapter is an unequivocal and timely push for improved teacher education to prepare them for diversity, currently available in only a few countries. This is critical to ensure that the cultures of refugees, migrants and all marginalized groups are acknowledged and valued.

David Edwards, General Secretary of Education International

KEY MESSAGES

Education shapes attitudes towards immigrants and refugees by providing critical skills to enable engagement with different cultures. It also provides an opportunity for students to engage with immigrants and refugees in school and challenge their own stereotypes.

Immigrants and refugees can suffer from prejudice and discrimination in school, which hampers their learning. In the United States, children from non-English-speaking households are often misdiagnosed as having special education needs.

Public attitudes can affect migrants' and refugees' sense of belonging. Research in the United Kingdom showed that recognition by native peers motivated refugee and asylum-seeking adolescents to study harder.

The more educated have more positive attitudes towards immigration. In countries taking part in the 2017 Migration Acceptance Index survey, 53% of those with tertiary education wanted the level of immigration to stay the same or increase in their country, compared with 46% of those who had completed secondary and 39% of those with primary education or less.

Curricula and textbooks increasingly reflect migration-related issues and recognize other cultures. Among 21 high income countries, only Australia and Canada included multiculturalism in curricula in 1980. By 2010, it was fully integrated in Finland, Ireland, New Zealand and Sweden as well, and somewhat on the agenda in over two-thirds of the countries.

Critical thinking skills and room to explore sensitive issues in an inclusive and non-discriminatory way can help break down cultural barriers. Generation Global, a safe online space for interaction among individuals from different cultures, which reached over 230,000 students in 20 countries, had a positive impact on student open-mindedness to others.

Teachers often feel they lack support and are ill-prepared to teach in diverse, multilingual, multicultural classrooms and to provide psychosocial support. In six European countries, 52% of teachers felt they had insufficient support for managing diversity.

Diversity of teachers is associated with minority students' achievement, self-esteem and sense of safety. Yet in France, only individuals with French, EU or European Economic Area nationality can take teaching examinations.

Awareness-raising about migration and displacement can bridge cultural differences in societies. There Is a Place for Everyone, an awareness campaign in São Paulo, Brazil, promoted the rights of immigrants.

Migration and displacement can challenge education systems. At the same time, education plays a critical role in shaping the experience of both in at least three respects. Good-quality education can help immigrants and refugees adjust to new environments, reducing the psychological toll of change and strengthening their sense of belonging in the host community. An education that includes the historical and contemporary dimensions of migration and displacement can influence native students' perceptions and help them appreciate commonalities and value differences. Formal and non-formal education can increase public understanding, amending discriminatory attitudes and increasing social openness, tolerance and resilience.

> "Re-examine what and how education is being taught to build inclusive societies and help people live together, not just be tolerant"

Education that values diversity is important for all countries, no matter their migration history or present circumstances. Education's role and responsibility go beyond building tolerant societies, which may passively accept but not necessarily embrace differences, to building inclusive societies that appreciate and respect differences and provide high-quality education for all.

Education's transformative functions require change on all levels, from individual students and teachers to national policy frameworks. Curricula and textbooks need to be adapted, and education systems need to invest heavily in preparing teachers to address diversity, both to facilitate individual learning and to foster a welcoming and more understanding community.

This chapter discusses immigrants' and refugees' vulnerability to social bias and exclusion, and education's role in shaping attitudes on migration. Higher levels of educational attainment can promote appreciation of migrants' positive contributions and reduce anxiety about the consequences of migration. Education systems adopt various approaches to inclusion, and their success supports migrants' and refugees' identities, self-confidence and sense of belonging. Education policies should strive to facilitate inclusive, human rights-based pedagogy delivered consistently across education levels and through diverse modalities.

IMMIGRANTS AND REFUGEES ARE SUBJECT TO STEREOTYPES, PREJUDICE AND DISCRIMINATION

Vast differences in historical, cultural and socio-economic contexts make it difficult to compare immigrants' and refugees' situations across countries, but several analyses demonstrate that host populations are not always positively disposed towards immigrants and refugees.

BOX 5.1:

Stereotypes, prejudices and discrimination affect immigrants and refugees

Stereotypes are beliefs about individuals or groups that are often overgeneralized, inaccurate and resistant to change. For instance, teachers might have stereotypical views of how immigrants from certain countries look or behave and expect all individuals with such backgrounds to act and behave the same way, without any knowledge of them.

Prejudice broadly refers to unjustifiable negative evaluations of and feelings towards a group and its individual members. For instance, parents of non-migrant children may feel, without evidence, that immigrant or refugee students are slow to learn and threaten their children's progress.

Discrimination, on the other hand, denotes unjustifiable negative behaviour towards a group or its members. This can happen at the individual level, as when peers never pick immigrant or refugee students as teammates, or the institutional level, when policies block immigrant or refugee access to school by making immigrant registration a condition of enrolment.

These concepts have evolved over time. Some researchers use 'modern' prejudice and discrimination to describe attitudes and behaviours that are biased but can be unexamined, unconscious and relatively ambivalent, as opposed to outright hostile, overt prejudice or discrimination (Cunningham et al., 2004; Lin et al., 2005). Both forms coexist in today's societies (Swim et al., 2003) and are commonly called racism when racially based and xenophobia when based on national origin.

Brain imaging shows that individuals are very quick to classify faces, that they process faces differently to other images, and that they judge social groups (e.g. linked to ethnicity and religion) based on very little information. This can result in classifying immigrants and refugees as 'the other', particularly if they visibly differ from the host population. Such stereotypes or prejudices can lead to discriminatory behaviour (Kawakami et al., 2017; Murray and Marx, 2013). Immigrant and refugee groups, with less social power than the host population, are thus less able to prevent such effects (Major et al., 2002).

In a globalized world, where interacting with people of diverse backgrounds is increasingly the norm, many still evaluate others based on perceptions of group identity rather than on personal qualities. This puts immigrants and refugees at risk of discrimination and exclusion, and of being seen in stereotypical or prejudiced ways (**Box 5.1**).

PREJUDICE AND DISCRIMINATION AT SCHOOL HAMPER IMMIGRANT AND REFUGEE LEARNING

Even where migration and education policies protect the right to education, prejudice and discriminatory practices in schools can keep immigrant and refugee students' needs from being met. Especially during crises, when anxiety and uncertainty are heightened, people may align themselves with those with whom they most closely identify, developing stereotypical and prejudiced perceptions of immigrants or refugees that lead to discrimination (Brader et al., 2008).

> "In the United States, children from non-English-speaking households are often misdiagnosed as having special education needs, based partly on literacy tests biased against them"

In South Africa, schools were trapped between right-to-education policies and the 2002 Immigration Act, which barred schools from admitting anyone without a South African birth certificate. The lack of clear policy was compounded by teachers' prejudice and discrimination against Zimbabwean immigrants. Students taunted immigrants with xenophobic remarks (Crush and Tawodzera, 2014).

In the United States, structural discrimination against students from immigrant families takes several forms. Lack of bilingual programmes puts young children from non-English-speaking households at a disadvantage. They are often misdiagnosed as having special education needs, partly due to literacy tests that are not in their home language (Adair, 2015). Immigrant parents may not feel as welcome to engage with schools as native-born parents and feel they have little influence on how their children are treated or taught in schools. Such discrimination can be intentional or unintentional and stem from factors including lack of connection with immigrant communities, inadequate teacher education and a testing culture focused on narrow learning metrics (Adair et al., 2012).

PUBLIC ATTITUDES CAN SHAPE MIGRANTS' SELF-PERCEPTION AND WELL-BEING

Public attitudes matter because they affect migrants' and refugees' sense of identity and belonging, their well-being and their chances of settling successfully. Migrants and refugees perceive themselves, in part, according to how they are perceived or labelled (Epstein and Heizler, 2015).

Interaction with native perceptions and institutional norms play a major role (Barrett et al., 2013; La Barbera, 2015).

In general, surveys find that refugees tend to be viewed more positively than asylum-seekers or immigrants, especially if the latter are undocumented (Dempster and Hargrave, 2017; Murray and Marx, 2013). The 2016 Refugees Welcome Survey showed that 73% of people in 27 countries strongly or somewhat agreed that people should be able to take refuge in other countries to escape war or persecution. Some 80% would accept refugees into their country or city, 30% into their neighbourhood and 10% into their home (Amnesty International, 2016). However, another survey in 11 countries found that, while most individuals felt compassion for refugees, they were concerned about the impact on security or the economy (TENT, 2016). There was more sympathy and trust towards Syrian refugees in Germany, but it did not result in more willingness to interact with them (Stöhr and Wichardt, 2016).

As for migrants' own perspective, analysis of the 2014 World Values Survey for this report showed that they were less likely than natives to see themselves as belonging to the host country in 34 out of 43 countries. In some, including Bahrain and Kyrgyzstan, more than 10% of migrants felt like outsiders and disconnected from a global, national or local community. Stereotypical or prejudiced media portrayals affect both native perceptions and migrant or refugee self-perceptions (**Box 5.2**).

There is a clear negative relationship between immigrants' and refugees' perception of discrimination and their well-being. In a meta-analysis of 328 studies, perceived discrimination was associated with depression, anxiety and lower self-esteem. The effect was greater for disadvantaged groups and children, and in experimental studies (Schmitt et al., 2014). A study in Greece following more than 500 mostly male 13-year-old students with migrant backgrounds over two years found that native students' attitudes affected immigrant students' well-being. Immigrant students were more likely to perceive little discrimination if they felt liked by natives, even if they perceived discrimination against them as a group (Reitz et al., 2015).

> Adolescent refugees in Uganda found that linguistic differences led to discrimination and meant they were more likely to withdraw from school

Small scale, qualitative research in the United Kingdom showed that refugee and asylum-seeking adolescents found recognition by native peers motivating for building

BOX 5.2:

The media often portray immigrants and refugees negatively

Migration-related media stories often stereotype, using general categories and imprecise terminology and omitting immigrant or refugee voices. Generalizations in the media can reinforce impressions that immigrants will behave consistently in any situation. German undergraduates exposed to news articles using general language (e.g. 'an immigrant broke into a house') were more likely to believe immigrants would be involved in criminal behaviour than those exposed to more specific terms (e.g. 'an 18-year-old immigrant from an identified country broke into the home of an identified celebrity and stole a computer') (Geschke et al., 2010). Prejudiced visual representations can also sway attitudes. Canadians exposed to editorial cartoons depicting immigrants as disease spreaders were more likely to perceive them as sources of disease, leading to dehumanization and, ultimately, negative views on open immigration policies (Esses et al., 2013).

Media coverage of issues related to migration and displacement is increasingly negative and polarizing (SOM, 2012). In 2015, the editor of the Czech Republic's largest newspaper instructed reporters to present immigrants and refugees as a threat (Howden, 2016). In Norway, 71% of migration-related media stories in 2009 focused on problems (Islam in Europe, 2010). Media in the United Kingdom often portray immigrants and refugees as a threat to culture, security and the welfare system (Dempster and Hargrave, 2017; Esses et al., 2017). In 2010, media coverage of a ship containing 492 Sri Lankan Tamils that was intercepted off the west coast of Canada was predominately negative, suggesting their refugee claims were bogus. A poll found that 63% of Canadians wanted the ship turned back, and a bill was introduced to make the country's refugee system stricter (Esses et al., 2013).

Education can mediate negative portrayals of immigrants and refugees by teaching political knowledge and critical thinking skills to aid in deciphering fact from fiction. Studies showed that less informed individuals were more likely to draw on media messages in forming their beliefs (Meltzer et al., 2017) and more susceptible to stereotyping messages (Huber and Lapinski, 2006). In the period after the 11 September attacks in New York, the more educated in Germany maintained relatively positive attitudes towards immigrants, while the less educated shifted sharply to more negative views (Schüller, 2012).

The more educated appear better able to identify misrepresentation. In Switzerland, more education was associated with a more critical evaluation of immigrant information on political posters (Matthes and Marquart, 2013). In a survey following the 2016 United States presidential election, the more educated were more likely to distinguish correctly between real and fake social media stories (Allcott and Gentzkow, 2017).

friendships, seeking psychological help and studying harder (Fazel, 2015). By contrast, adolescent Congolese and Somali refugees in Uganda found that linguistic differences made friendships more difficult and led to discrimination that diminished their well-being and self-worth. As a result, they were more likely to withdraw from school, turn towards harmful connections and join gangs (Stark et al., 2015).

EDUCATION INFLUENCES ATTITUDES TOWARDS IMMIGRANTS AND REFUGEES

Stereotypical, narrow portrayals of immigrants and refugees in schools can have detrimental effects on inclusion. Systems open to all learners can help build societies that welcome diversity and in which immigrants and refugees are engaged citizens.

EDUCATIONAL ATTAINMENT IS LINKED TO MORE POSITIVE ATTITUDES TOWARDS IMMIGRATION

In general, educational attainment is associated with more positive attitudes towards immigrants. Interaction with immigrants and refugees in school helps increase familiarity with and trust in people from other cultures (Gundelach, 2014). Students can learn skills to overcome fear of the unknown, engage constructively with different cultures and avoid simplistic overgeneralization. More educated people were less ethnocentric, placed more value on cultural diversity and viewed immigration's economic impact more positively (Hainmueller and Hopkins, 2014). In countries taking part in the 2017 Migration Acceptance Index survey, 53% of individuals with tertiary education wanted the same or increased levels of immigration, compared with 46% of those with secondary and 39% of those with primary education or less (Esipova et al., 2015).

> “Students can learn skills to overcome fear of the unknown, engage constructively with different cultures and avoid simplistic overgeneralization”

In 38 out of 52 countries in the 2014 World Values Survey, when asked to pick from a list of potential neighbours, interviewees with tertiary education were more tolerant towards immigrants and foreign workers than those with primary education. On average, those with tertiary were two percentage points more tolerant than those with secondary (**Figure 5.1a**), who were two percentage points more tolerant than those with primary education (**Figure 5.1b**). In four out of five countries where immigrants were at least 10% of the population, the more educated were more tolerant.

Younger people tend to have more positive attitudes towards immigration (Ford, 2012; Winkler, 2015). Over half of 16- to 34-year-olds in countries participating in the 2014 European Social Survey favoured granting access to migrants from poorer countries, compared with about 35% of those over age 65. Combining age and education revealed even larger gaps. In France and Slovenia, nearly 80% of the highly educated in the youngest cohort approved of granting access, compared with less than 30% of the less educated in the oldest cohort (Heath and Richards, 2016).

The association between education and inclusive attitudes is viewed critically by those who believe that people who are more tolerant by nature tend to pursue more education or that the more educated are in jobs not threatened by immigration. However, two quasi-experimental studies using European Social Survey data suggest that education does produce positive attitudes. The first, which pooled data from 12 countries, found that an extra year of school was associated with an 8 to 10 percentage point increase in the probability of holding more favourable attitudes towards immigrants (d'Hombres and Nunziata, 2016). The second, which focused on Denmark, France, the Netherlands, Sweden and the United Kingdom, found that an additional year of secondary school was causally linked with a

> “Data from 12 European countries found that one extra year of school was associated with an 8 to 10 percentage point increase in the probability of holding more favourable attitudes towards immigrants”

FIGURE 5.1:

More education is associated with more favourable views of immigrants

Percentage of individuals who would like to have immigrants/foreign workers as neighbours, 2014

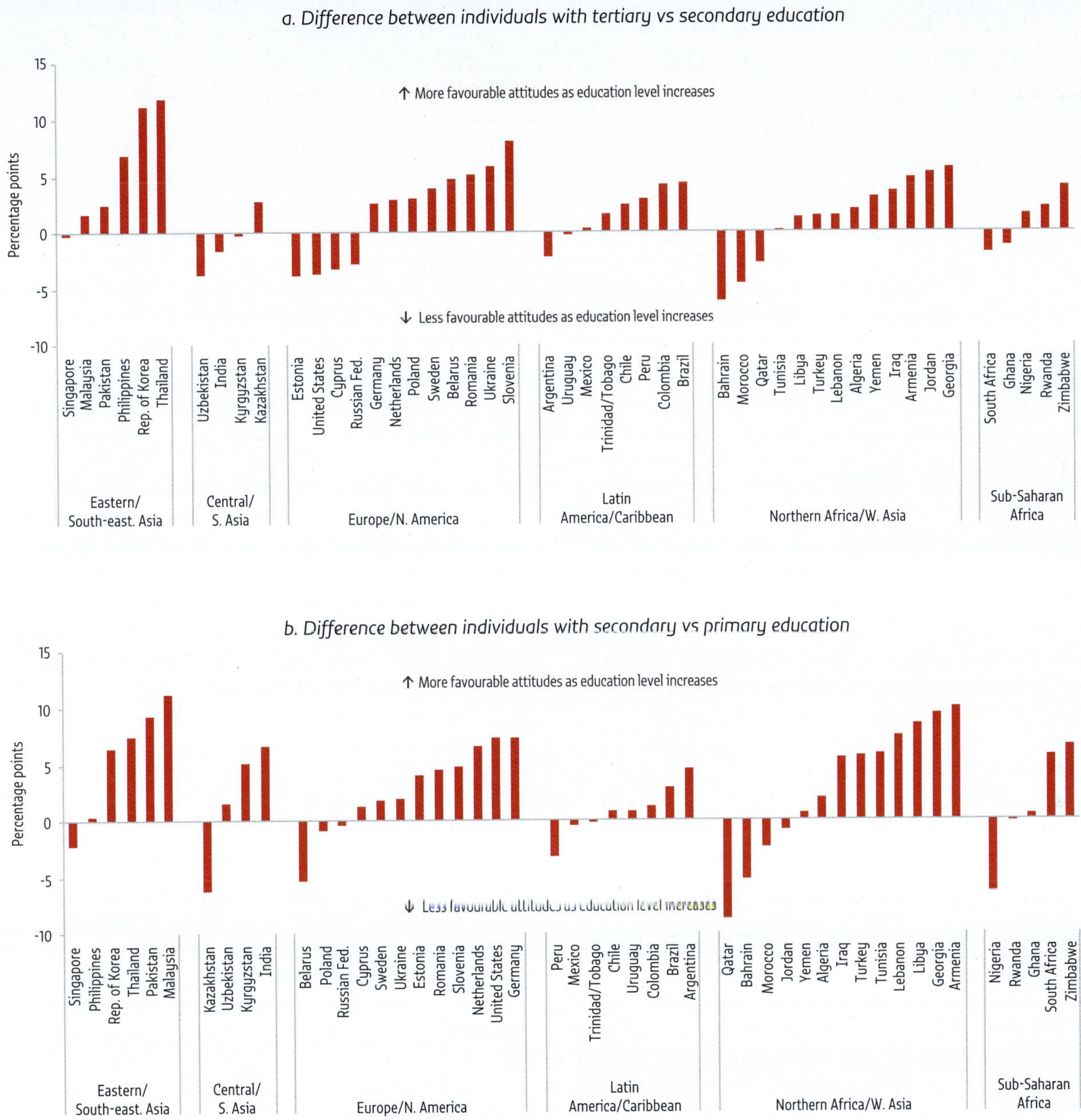

GEM StatLink: http://bit.ly/fig5_1

Source: GEM Report team analysis based on 2014 World Values Survey.

lower probability of opposing immigration, believing that immigration reduces quality of life and identifying with anti-immigration parties (Cavaille and Marshall, 2018).

INCLUSION SHOULD BE AT THE CENTRE OF EDUCATION POLICIES AND SYSTEMS

Addressing diversity is at the heart of the purpose of education but generates contrasting perspectives on which approach to take. Each approach places a different value on migrant and refugee culture, influencing attitudes towards immigrants as well as their self-perception and sense of belonging (**Table 5.1**).

> "Education shapes attitudes towards migrants, as well as their self-perception and sense of belonging"

Proponents of assimilation argue that, rather than nurturing difference, schools should ensure that all students are proficient in the host country's official language and embrace the national culture. Yet assimilation can entail 'complete erosion of difference between immigrants and the host society, and strongly implies the hegemonic role of the host nation', which can be detrimental to immigrants' sense of identity and lead to their cultural confusion and isolation (King and Lulle, 2016).

There is no consensus across countries on use of 'multicultural' and 'intercultural' to describe national education policies, which are therefore seldom differentiated in research literature. However, the *UNESCO Guidelines on Intercultural Education* makes the distinction by arguing that '[m]ulticultural education uses learning about other cultures ... to produce acceptance', while intercultural education strives for a 'way of living together in multicultural societies through ... *understanding* of, *respect* for and *dialogue* between the different cultural groups' (UNESCO, 2006).

TABLE 5.1:
Education system approaches to migrant culture, with degrees of migrant self-perception risk

	Assimilation	Integration (multiculturalism)	Inclusion (interculturalism)
Aim	Migrant culture disappears, and immigrants adopt host norms and values	Parts of migrant culture are accepted or integrated, and migrants are more tolerated or respected	Migrant culture is celebrated, as cultural diversity is valued
Risk	Migrants feel excluded, as their culture is treated as threatening	Migrants feel conflicted, as parts of their culture are valued over others	Migrants feel more welcomed, as their culture is seen to add value

Source: GEM Report team analysis based on King and Lulle (2016) and UNESCO (2006).

Opponents of multiculturalism, thus defined, argue that emphasizing the cultural dimension poses a risk of ignoring the real causes of discrimination against immigrant groups, which may include institutional racism. By contrast, interculturalism helps students learn not only about other cultures but about structural barriers in host countries that perpetuate inequality. With interculturalism, respect and appreciation of differences become part of a larger education project; the paradigm considers diversity the norm and not a special situation.

In the United States, multicultural education policies, such as bilingual or multilingual instruction, have met active pushback (Kim and Slapac, 2015). By contrast, there is increasing focus on inclusion and social cohesion in Europe, especially since the European Commission's *First Annual Report on Migration and Integration* in 2004, which emphasized the skills that education systems need to provide to foster integration (Faas et al., 2014). Still, few countries have specific policies on either multicultural or intercultural education, as does Ireland (**Box 5.3**).

In Italy, a 1994 Ministry of Public Education circular on intercultural dialogue and democratic coexistence defined operational approaches to intercultural education. These highlighted the importance of a climate of openness and dialogue in schools, teacher commitment to interculturalism in subject teaching, integration in curricula and adoption of policies targeting the needs of students with immigrant backgrounds (Santerini, 2010).

Policies in some countries are limited to integration efforts that start by labelling groups, with immigrants expected to integrate into host communities that need not change (Erdal and Oeppen, 2013). The tendency to operate specific intercultural schools may be contrary to inclusion. Although intercultural schools have been part of domestic law in Greece since 1985, they have been parallel to the national system and resisted by parents of native students and by education administrators (Gropas and

BOX 5.3:

Ireland has developed an intercultural education policy

As it transitioned rapidly from a country of emigrants to one of immigrants, Ireland recognized cultural diversity as a permanent reality (Ireland DOJE, 2017). By 2015, immigrant children represented 15% of the population under 15 (Harte et al., 2016).

The Intercultural Education Strategy 2010–2015, released after the first ministerial statement on immigration in 2008, had five goals: (a) a whole-institution approach; (b) capacity development of all education providers; (c) support for language of instruction proficiency (funded by EUR 100 million for language support in schools and EUR 10 million for adult courses), while recognizing the importance of mother tongue in acquiring additional language proficiency; (d) partnerships among schools, parents and communities; and (e) data and monitoring. A portal provided access to intercultural materials for all stakeholders (Ireland DOES, 2010).

The Development and Intercultural Education Project supports pre-service teacher preparedness for intercultural education, specifically incorporating human rights and global citizenship into teaching and recognizing the importance of student attitudes (Ireland DOES, 2014). The 2016 Education (Admission to Schools) Bill removed some access barriers for immigrants, banning fees and wait lists and requiring all schools to publish their admissions policies (Ireland DOES, 2016). Since 2003, Ireland has added additional language options for the secondary leaving certificate examination. In 2018, it will be administered in 18 EU languages, providing greater access to higher education to those with lower proficiency in English or Irish (Ireland State Examinations Commission, 2018).

The 2017 national, cross-departmental Migrant Integration Strategy commits to monitoring school policies to assess impact on immigrant enrolment; encouraging schools to support parent participation; and taking proactive measures to attract immigrants into teaching (Ireland DOJE, 2017). A study for the European Parliament recently recognized that Ireland and Sweden had the strongest monitoring and assessment frameworks for immigrant education in Europe (Essomba et al., 2017). Throughout its transition, among European countries Ireland has maintained one of the lowest native-immigrant gaps in mathematics scores in the Programme for International Student Assessment (Harte et al., 2016). In addition, immigrants and natives aged 13 were indistinguishable in three well-being measures related to happiness, anxiety and self-criticism (Smyth, 2015).

> “Intercultural schools have been part of domestic law in Greece since 1985, but have been parallel to the national system and resisted by parents and education administrators”

Triandafyllidou, 2011; Palaiologou and Faas, 2012). Recent large influxes of immigrants and refugees led the Ministry of Education, Research and Religious Affairs to revise the law in 2016 to strengthen the links of intercultural with mainstream schools.

Education is subject to strong political influences that can support or undermine intercultural education policies at the national or local level. Rising political sentiment against immigration and in favour of tightening border controls decreases the chances of implementing an intercultural education policy. In the Netherlands, deteriorating attitudes towards immigrants have led to an integration policy focused on loyalty to Dutch society. The Ministry of Education has adopted a more assimilationist position, replacing intercultural education with citizenship education, compulsory since 2006 (Leeman and Saharso, 2013).

Another dimension in the development of immigrant students' sense of belonging is the operation of diaspora schools that maintain links with the country of origin. In some cases, such schools may be managed or coordinated by the government of the home country, as in the case of Poland (**Box 5.4**). Challenges include the development of appropriate teaching materials and the provision of trained teachers. Often, communities establish private schools, such as Filipinos in Saudi Arabia, Pakistanis in the United Arab Emirates (Zakharia, 2016), Iranians in the United Kingdom (Gholami, 2017) and Brazilians in Japan (Watanabe, 2010). These may be teaching curricula from the home country, the host country or hybrids. Finally, there are non-formal schools, whose aim is to transmit the linguistic and cultural heritage of the home country to the children

BOX 5.4:

Poland maintains an extensive network of schools for its diaspora

A combination of historic Polish minorities living in neighbouring countries and recent emigration means that more than 1,000 education institutions across almost 60 countries were registered in the database of Polish diaspora organizations in 2018. Germany, Lithuania, Ukraine, United Kingdom and the United States were among countries with the highest number of such institutions.

These schools can be divided into three categories: those which follow the Polish education system and are financed by the Polish Ministry of Education, in cities such as Athens, Moscow and Prague; those which are part of the education systems of other countries and where Polish might be offered for some subjects; and Saturday schools run by civil society groups or religious organizations (Lipińska and Seretny, 2011).

The Polish Ministry of Education has also created the Centre for the Development of Polish Education Abroad (ORPEG) whose role is to support and promote the learning of Polish. ORPEG runs schools at Poland's diplomatic missions in 37 countries. It coordinates the assignment of Polish teachers to work abroad, organizes online learning, supports teacher training and supplies textbooks. It distributed teaching materials for about 30,000 students and 6,000 teachers in 48 countries between 2010 and 2016 (ORPEG, 2017). Starting from 2017/18, Polish students attending ORPEG-led programmes are no longer required to take the oral and written exams, which were required for promotion to the next class (Poland Ministry of Education, 2017).

FIGURE 5.2:

An increasing number of countries include multiculturalism in curricula

Inclusion of multiculturalism in curricula in 21 high income countries, 1980–2010

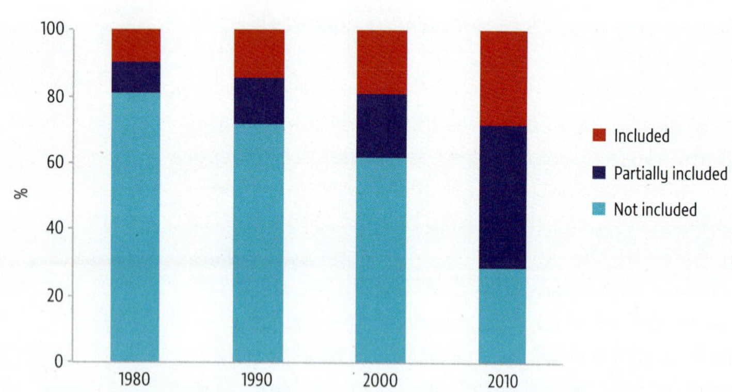

GEM StatLink: http://bit.ly/fig5_2

Note: The definition of multiculturalism used in this figure resembles more closely the definition of interculturalism in Table 5.1.

Source: Westlake (2011).

of immigrants, such as the Latvian community in Melbourne, Australia (Gross, 2015), or the Armenian and Korean communities in Montreal, Canada (Maguire, 2010).

CURRICULA AND TEXTBOOKS ARE BECOMING MORE INCLUSIVE

Curricula and textbooks can counter stereotypes, reduce prejudice, mitigate anxiety towards immigrants and develop immigrants' sense of belonging (Van Briel et al., 2016). They need to reflect diversity to help teachers adopt pedagogical approaches that recognize diverse ways of learning and help schools accommodate multiple perspectives. By contrast, inappropriate textbook images and descriptions can make students from different cultures feel excluded or misrepresented and are more likely to frustrate and alienate them (Hintermann et al., 2014; Weiner, 2018).

In the 22 countries that participated in the 2016 International Civic and Citizenship Education Survey, 54% of grade 8 students endorsed equal rights for all ethnic groups. Analysis for this report showed that endorsing these rights was positively associated with learning about other countries' histories in 12 countries and with open classroom discussions in 18 countries (Sandoval-Hernández and Miranda, 2018).

More countries are modifying curricula to reflect growing social diversity. Among 21 high income countries analysed for a policy index on multiculturalism, only Australia and Canada included multiculturalism in curricula in 1980 (**Figure 5.2**). By 2010, multiculturalism was somewhat on the agenda in over two-thirds of countries and fully integrated in an additional four: Finland, Ireland, New Zealand and Sweden (Westlake, 2011).

A related and extended 2015 study showed that 27 out of 38 predominantly high income countries provided intercultural education as a stand-alone

> "Curricula and textbooks need to help teachers adopt pedagogical approaches that recognize diverse ways of learning and help schools accommodate multiple perspectives"

subject or integrated it into the curriculum. Belgium, Canada, Ireland, Italy, the Netherlands, Sweden and the United Kingdom did both. Denmark, France, Hungary and Poland did not include intercultural education, or, if they did, it did not contain appreciation of cultural diversity (Huddleston et al., 2015).

> In Europe, 81% of people surveyed said that school lessons and materials should include information on ethnic diversity

Curriculum reform depends on political support and consensus among social groups. Increased diversity in curricula has broad public support in Europe: 81% of respondents in the 2015 Eurobarometer agreed that school lessons and materials should include information on ethnic diversity (Van Briel et al., 2016). Including the local community in decisions about curricular content can also influence the implementation of intercultural education policy. In Lisbon, an alternative inclusive curriculum, developed with parents and students, bridged home and school cultures and led to more positive, trusting views of schools among fifth- and sixth-graders (César and Oliveira, 2005).

Recognizing other cultures in individual subjects diversifies education

Multicultural and intercultural values can be incorporated into individual subjects. While history curricula have been found to be ethnocentric, focused on national content with little if any discussion of cultural diversity, other subjects have become more inclusive. In England (United Kingdom), the multicultural history of British identity is included in geography and citizenship. German curricula attempt to address broader diversity issues, especially in geography (Faas, 2011).

An analysis of 12 countries' textbooks for this report found that all countries included migrants and migration discussions in at least some textbooks. In Ontario, Canada, learning about migration concepts starts in grade 2; in the Republic of Korea, notions of multicultural society start in grade 1. However, mentions of migration were commonly limited to historical accounts of settlement and ideas of nation-building and population expansion (Opertti et al., 2018).

In former British colonies, the treatment of migration and colonialization in textbooks evolved over the latter half of the 20th century. In Australia, earlier texts focused on how the 19th-century gold rush drew immigrants from Europe, but more contemporary texts question the impact on Aboriginals and Torres Strait Islanders. In Ontario, Canada, earlier texts focused on benefits of European immigration, while recent texts include the role of First Nations in the development of Canadian identity, and how they were affected by such manifestations of early settlement as displacement and residential schools (Toulouse, 2018). Multiculturalism is not found in earlier Canadian texts but features more prominently in contemporary versions, including in a recurrent chapter section titled 'Identity then and now' (Opertti et al., 2018).

Modern textbooks continue to omit contentious migration-related issues. Mexican textbooks do not discuss undocumented migrants and the relationship with the United States. In South Africa, textbooks overlook xenophobic attitudes and discrimination against immigrants from other African countries. In the United Kingdom, immigration from former Commonwealth countries, often perceived as controversial, is absent.

> Mexican textbooks do not discuss undocumented migrants and the relationship with the United States

By contrast, recent Côte d'Ivoire textbooks discuss refugees and displacement, which were especially prominent after the political crisis in 2002. Curriculum frameworks guide teachers through rights-based education starting in grade 3. The curriculum uses case studies of displaced populations and emphasizes Article 2 of the United Nations Convention on the Rights of the Child, applying the concept of non-discrimination to refugee children. The goal is to develop competences in situations related to child rights and international humanitarian law (Opertti et al., 2018).

Curricula can be adapted locally to embrace diversity

Central governments do not design everything taught in schools; adjustments can be made locally. The Alberta Teachers' Association, in partnership with the Canadian Multicultural Education Foundation, has produced a series of teaching resources to support immigrant and refugee instruction and learning in the province (EI, 2017b). The resources focus on specific groups, such as Karen, Somalis and South Sudanese.

A resource on the Arab community introduces Arab culture and discusses myths and misconceptions about Arabs and Muslims. The series offers suggestions to teachers on how to connect with immigrant and refugee parents and communities and get to know students in an open way. It encourages teachers to understand and include the cultural and linguistic differences in their classrooms and invite students to share their culture. It also offers guidelines and a list of resources for districts and schools (Canadian Multicultural Education Foundation/Alberta Teachers' Association, 2016).

> "Strong school leadership can help promote intercultural competences and culturally responsive approaches"

Strong school leadership can help promote intercultural competences and culturally responsive approaches in terms of curricular content, teaching approaches and school culture (Khalifa et al., 2016). In the United States, in places where school leaders value diversity, students are more likely to engage in intercultural interaction (Pica-Smith and Poynton, 2014). Unfortunately, not all school heads are aware of the issues or motivated or equipped to lead the development of intercultural understanding in their schools. In Malaysia, school leaders who were asked to implement an intercultural programme were hampered by lack of guidance from the government and little autonomy for adaptation (Malakolunthu, 2010).

Teaching that incorporates intercultural competences and pedagogies fosters inclusion

Appropriate, effective and respectful interaction with immigrants and refugees requires cultural competences, which must be taught (Barrett et al., 2013). Activities that promote openness to multiple perspectives need to be embedded in teaching practices. Freedom to explore sensitive issues in an inclusive and non-discriminatory way is essential to developing critical thinking skills and questioning one's own identity and how beliefs are constructed.

One method uses experiential learning through real or imagined interactions. In a quasi-experimental study in the United States, undergraduates who partnered with local immigrant and refugee families developed significantly higher intercultural skills than those who completed the same curriculum without the community component (De Leon, 2014).

Studies show cooperative learning's positive effects on classroom interaction, including improved intercultural relations, acceptance of difference and reduced prejudice. Establishing a common goal is the most important factor in cooperative learning. Students then work together, using specific principles to structure the group's task, ultimately maximizing collective learning (Van Briel et al., 2016). An evaluation of a problem-based learning unit in Germany that had secondary school students reflect on critical incidents involving cultural misconceptions found that participants had improved their intercultural understanding and were better able to grasp multiple viewpoints (Busse and Krause, 2015).

Storytelling and role play or simulations are other ways to encourage open-mindedness. Learners develop their stories or individual biographies then re-create them from another perspective, which requires them to adopt other identities. The process can help students see potential differences (Barrett et al., 2013).

Social media and specialized platforms can be useful tools, allowing students to engage in virtual or face-to-face interactions that facilitate intercultural understanding (O'Dowd and Lewis, 2016). Facebook and Skype are popular platforms used in classrooms for live videoconferencing (Thomé-Williams, 2016). Generation Global, formerly Face to Faith, is a safe online space for dialogue and interaction among individuals from different cultures and faiths. In its first seven years, the programme reached over 230,000 students in 20 countries. A 2017 review found a positive impact on student open-mindedness and attitudes towards people

> "Social media and free apps can encourage interaction among individuals from different cultures and faiths and have positive impacts on student open-mindedness"

from other cultures, compared with non-users (Doney and Wegerif, 2017).

Free apps have also been shown to raise awareness about diversity. Everyday Racism users spend a week role-playing as a Muslim woman or an Indian student and are prompted to respond to encounters with racism. Evaluations found that users had greater confidence in responding to situations of racism, with 60% of students speaking up against racist action after playing (All Together Now, 2018; Van Briel et al., 2016) .

IN MOST COUNTRIES, TRAINING THAT PREPARES TEACHERS FOR DIVERSE CLASSROOMS IS NOT MANDATORY

Teachers need several competences to teach in diverse classrooms with immigrants and refugees. A key one is preparedness to teach students not proficient in the language of instruction (Bunar et al., 2018; PPMI, 2017).

A report on teacher education for diversity in Europe emphasizes improvement in three domains. The first involves knowledge of legal frameworks, dimensions of cultural diversity and methods to address diversity. The second concerns teacher–student and teacher–parent communications, open-mindedness and respect in the school community, motivating student engagement and dealing with conflicts to prevent marginalization. The third concerns management and teaching: addressing sociocultural diversity in classrooms; establishing an inclusive, safe environment; tailoring teaching to student needs; and using diverse approaches for culturally sensitive teaching (PPMI, 2017).

Schools and teachers need to see home cultures as an asset and strive to connect school, home and community cultures (Gichuru et al., 2015; Wells et al., 2016). Teachers should also reflect on their own identity to avoid projecting their culture or reinforcing dominant norms (Kincheloe, 2011).

Teachers often feel ill-prepared or -supported in teaching diverse classrooms (Adair et al., 2012). More than two-thirds of teachers interviewed in France, Ireland, Italy, Latvia, Spain and the United Kingdom agreed slightly, moderately or strongly that adapting to meet the needs of immigrant students increased workload and caused frustration: 52% felt there was insufficient support from management for managing diversity (Fine-Davis and Faas, 2014).

The extent to which teacher education programmes include diversity varies by country. In the Netherlands, New Zealand and Norway, teacher candidates take mandatory courses in supporting students from diverse backgrounds. Courses in the Netherlands include training in intercultural education, expectations about immigrants and their specific learning needs, and knowledge about cultural diversity and its implication for teaching and learning. Similar courses are absent or offered ad hoc in France, Japan and Spain (OECD, 2017). Completing such courses in initial teacher education is usually optional in Europe (Van Briel et al., 2016).

A review of publicly available information on initial and continuing teacher education for diversity across 49 countries for this report found that governments supervised, offered or funded about 30 out of the 105 identified programmes, mainly at the initial stage. The gap in teacher preparedness support was filled by universities, teachers' unions, and non-government and private organizations. About 63% of the government programmes, but hardly any of the others, were mandatory (April et al., 2018).

Moreover, programmes emphasized general knowledge over practical pedagogy (**Figure 5.3**). About 80% of programmes included a focus on cross-cultural knowledge, e.g. overviews of education systems, culture and art around the world. By contrast, student-centred pedagogical approaches included the

FIGURE 5.3:
Few teacher education programmes cover immigrant and refugee students' needs
Percentage of teacher education programmes covering selected diversity competences, 2018

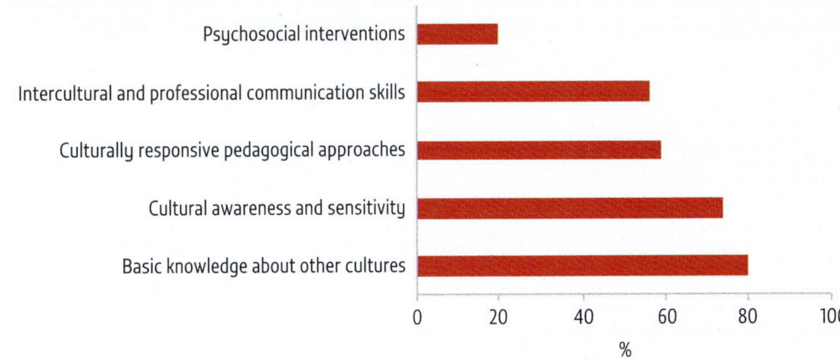

GEM StatLink: http://bit.ly/fig5_3
Note: Based on 105 teacher education programmes from 49 countries.
Source: April et al. (2018).

> In 49 countries, only one out of five programmes prepares teachers to anticipate and resolve intercultural conflicts

theory and practice of teaching in diverse classrooms, bringing in other languages and cultures, and using differentiated instructional strategies to meet the needs of diverse learners.

Some 74% of programmes incorporated cultural awareness and sensitivity training, including self-assessment of cultural bias. Among the more practical pedagogical categories, 59% of programmes had culturally responsive approaches, and 20% included psychosocial interventions, suggesting that only one out of five prepared teachers to anticipate and resolve intercultural conflicts or be familiar with psychological treatment and referral options for students in need (April et al., 2018).

A review of European countries found little evidence that strategic policies on diversity training were in place or that initial teacher education programmes helped teachers develop relevant competences (PPMI, 2017). A review of 45 multicultural teacher education courses in the United States showed that 16% taught conservative approaches, assuming cultural divisions, treating cultures as homogenous groups and encouraging assimilation. Some 58% taught more liberal approaches, focusing on teaching with tolerance and cultural sensitivity, teacher self-reflection, and development of knowledge and necessary pedagogical skills. About 29% taught teachers to develop critical consciousness by explicitly identifying entrenched barriers to equality, with a few courses encouraging them to become agents of change (Gorski, 2009).

> In France, only 4% of teachers had training in multicultural or multilingual education

In-service teachers also need continuing professional development to meet changing education needs in a globalized world. However, the 2013 Teaching and Learning International Survey found that only 16% of lower secondary teachers in 34 education systems had undertaken training in multicultural or multilingual education in the preceding year (OECD, 2014). In France and Israel, 20% of lower secondary teachers worked in schools where more than 10% of students had home languages other than the language of instruction. Yet only 4% of teachers in France had benefited from professional development in multicultural or multilingual education, compared with 20% of teachers in Israel (**Figure 5.4**).

FIGURE 5.4:

Teachers in countries with many non-native speakers of the language of instruction seem inadequately prepared

Prevalence of professional development in multicultural or multilingual education and of schools with medium or high concentration of students learning in a second language, lower secondary school teachers, 2013

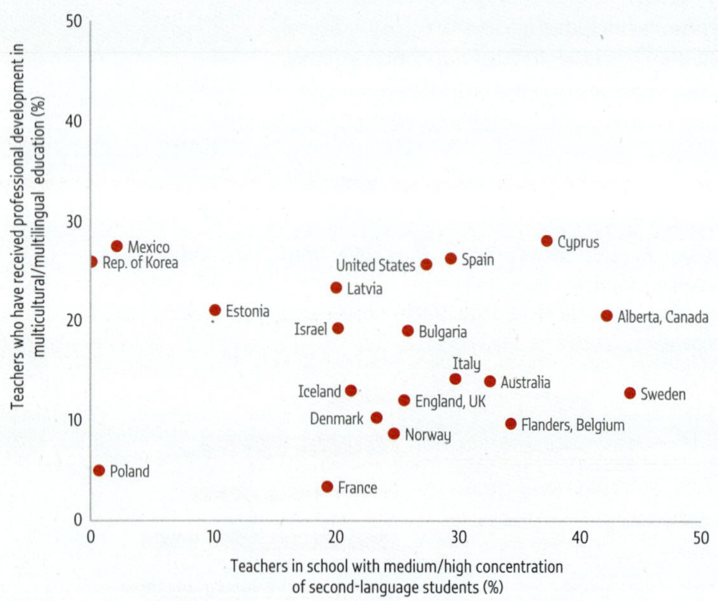

GEM StatLink: http://bit.ly/fig5_4

Note: Medium concentration = 11% to 30% second-language students. High concentration = more than 30% second-language students.

Source: Smith and Persson (2018).

TEACHER DIVERSITY IS LINKED TO IMMIGRANT STUDENTS' LEARNING AND SELF-ESTEEM

Information on diversity in the teaching workforce is limited, and comparisons among countries are challenging as definitions of immigrant background differ. Teachers with immigrant backgrounds in Europe are under-represented relative to the student body composition, particularly in countries with high diversity. This under-representation is fuelled by barriers along the career path, including discriminatory policies on entering the profession. In France, only individuals with French, EU or European Economic Area nationality can take teaching examinations (Donlevy et al., 2016).

> Ireland and Sweden recently accelerated teacher training for migrant and refugee teachers

Those who obtain qualifications may face hiring barriers, including prejudiced evaluators or school selection committees. Research in Dutch schools found that perceptions of language issues or religious differences as risk factors were associated with hiring native candidates over immigrants, even given similar skills and qualifications. Many school management boards also lack diversity, which can further limit immigrant teachers' chances of employment (van den Berg et al., 2011).

One way to increase diversity is to relax requirements. Ireland and Sweden recently accelerated teacher education for immigrant and refugee teachers (EI, 2017a; Marino Institute of Education, 2018).

There are few studies on the impact of teachers with immigrant backgrounds, and those that exist may not distinguish between first- and subsequent-generation immigrants or between immigrant and minority teachers. Some evidence indicates that teacher diversity is associated with immigrant student achievement, self-esteem and sense of safety (King and Lulle, 2016). Immigrant teachers may also demonstrate stronger empathy for immigrant parents' challenges in navigating a new culture and education system, although they are often in a dilemma as their cultural knowledge may be at odds with their pedagogical training (Adair et al., 2012).

An analysis in Sweden found a positive relationship between an ethnically diverse teaching workforce, measured as the share not born in Nordic countries, and the academic achievement of students not born in Nordic countries (Lindahl, 2007).

Immigrant and minority teachers face stigma and stereotyping. A study in England (United Kingdom) found that 31% of minority teachers faced discrimination in schools (NASUWT and Runnymede Trust, 2017). Some Guyanese and South African teachers in the United Kingdom have been subject to racist remarks and discrimination from students (Manik, 2014) and xenophobic attitudes from native teachers (Lashley, 2018). In five US cities, early childhood teachers with migrant backgrounds often felt they had to choose between being culturally responsive to immigrant families and following norms to be seen as professionals. Teachers managed by presenting themselves differently to parents and peers, code switching, changing their demeanour or providing slightly different versions of their beliefs (Adair et al., 2012).

NON-FORMAL EDUCATION IS A CRITICAL BUT NEGLECTED ASPECT OF BUILDING RESILIENT SOCIETIES

Education and awareness-raising about migration and displacement issues do not only take place within school walls. Non-formal education has many forms and purposes. Unfortunately, as governments are rarely the provider, little systematic information is available.

Community centres play a key role. A Turkish non-government organization, Yuva Association, uses community or multipurpose centres for language courses, occupational skills workshops and psychosocial support (Hanemann, 2018). In an emerging immigrant community in the north-eastern United States, a community centre was established to help unite people of different cultures, offering literacy courses, after-school help, sport team activities, community excursions and public event and meeting space. Young immigrant clients and volunteers stated that the centre provided a trusted space where they felt accepted (Brezicha and Hopkins, 2016).

Cultural facilitators or brokers (teachers, instructional aides, school counsellors, community members) can bridge language and culture differences between immigrant and host communities. Those with backgrounds similar to immigrant students are better able to validate the migration experience. Cultural brokers often offer translation services, help navigate the education system, educate school personnel about cultural practices and beliefs, help parents advocate for their children's needs, and provide other practical assistance, such as locating language classes or employment opportunities (Yohani, 2013).

> Cities can take a lead role in inclusion, running awareness campaigns against xenophobia, while promoting immigrant rights

In England (United Kingdom), volunteers at the West End Refugee Service support refugees and asylum-seekers by engaging in everyday activities that provide space for informal conversations and acknowledge the multifaceted lives of those involved (Askins, 2015). In Sweden, the municipality of Linköping trained tutors with knowledge of Somali or Arabic to act as 'link people' for the Learning Together programme. Sharing common language and culture, they act as role models, helping foreign-born parents stay motivated and avoid misunderstandings (Hanemann, 2018).

Cities can take a lead role in inclusion. Education against xenophobia, programmes for employment and social welfare, and immigrant advisory committees are common city-led efforts. São Paulo, Brazil, launched an awareness campaign called There Is a Place for Everyone in São Paulo and, in the autumn of 2017, established the Municipal Council for Migrants, an advisory group that incorporates immigrants into local political life and promotes their rights (WEF, 2017).

To be effective, such initiatives should closely involve immigrant communities. In Saint Petersburg, the Russian Federation, over 130 registered non-government ethnocultural alliances work on interethnic relations and organize activities generally focused on education, enlightenment, culture and the media. However, there are few close interactions with immigrant communities. Tolerance is seen as a goal in itself, rather than a tool for social cohesion, and the emphasis is on demonstrating cultural differences among various ethnic groups (Klimenko, 2014).

Art, community events and sport are powerful avenues of non-formal education. In January 2018, as part of the Lo Que Nos Une (What Unites Us) initiative, the youth group Madiba held a film forum highlighting the everyday reality of immigrants in Costa Rica, including a post-film conversation with the young refugee and immigrant organizers (RET International, 2018a, 2018b). The Migrant World Film Festival, held for more than a decade in Seoul, provides immigrants with an opportunity to showcase their work and discuss cultural differences. The Remapping the Borders festival in 2017 included 17 short and feature films describing experiences of immigrants, followed by a round table with members of immigrant worker associations (Kerry, 2017).

Community festivals in Norway and Spain encourage intercultural exchange. Oslo Extra Large (OXLO) is an integrated campaign that is part of the municipal planning strategy. A 10-point charter recognizes the equality of all inhabitants and commits to tolerance and mutual respect. As part of the annual OXLO week event, municipalities and organizations are encouraged to plan intercultural activities and a US$6,000 prize is awarded to organizations or individuals whose extra effort helped make Oslo an inclusive city (Maytree Foundation, 2012; Oslo Council, 2018). The annual Semana Intercultural Festival in Valladolid, Spain, features reoccurring events, such as a youth concert, activities to introduce newcomers to the local culture and a day devoted to discussions on immigrant issues, as during the You Also Count!-themed festival in 2017 (City Council of Vallodolid, 2017; Maytree Foundation, 2012).

In response to xenophobic attacks on foreigners, the Kaizer Chiefs football team relaunched the #Africa4Life social media campaign during South Africa's 2017 anti-racism week, using its visibility to educate the public about myths that immigrants are a threat and to highlight foreigners' positive contributions (Kaizer Chiefs, 2017).

CONCLUSION

Ensuring that migrants and refugees attend and complete school is only the first step towards inclusion. The main challenge in fully including these students in the host society is to offer an education of high quality that ensures the prevention of prejudices, stereotypes and discrimination. National education systems offer different models but there has been a trend in high income countries to adopt an intercultural education approach, which celebrates migrant and refugee cultures and values cultural diversity.

However, a shift to an inclusive education system has considerable implications. It requires a strategy that covers a large range of interventions from curricula and pedagogic approaches to textbooks and, especially, teacher preparation. A dialogue is needed at the national level over how to open the classroom environment and make migrants and refugees feel welcome, as they juggle different identities and, often, live under the pressure of negative public attitudes and biased media coverage. Inevitably, this means that education needs to extend beyond the school walls to embrace the energy of the host and migrant communities.

A Romanian Erasmus student in Lisbon: 'My time in Lisbon helped me learn to be more tolerant, and to look past stereotypes'.

CREDIT: Fàbio Duque Francisco/GEM Report

CHAPTER

6

Mobility of students and professionals

This chapter on high-skilled migration and the internationalization of higher education tells you the present realities, with opportunities to fuel policy development in Southeast Asia, a crucial chapter to read for national education policy-makers, regional organizations and multilateral agencies.

Gatot Hari Priowirjanto, Director of the Southeast Asian Ministers of Education Organization

KEY MESSAGES

The internationalization of higher education concerns more countries than ever and has major implications for the flow and exchange of ideas and knowledge.

Students base decisions about where to pursue higher education on availability of a university place at home, the costs, and the relative quality of education at home and abroad. Half of all international students move to five English-speaking countries.

Universities recruit international students to diversify the student body and improve their global rankings, but the main driver is income-raising. In 2016, international students brought an estimated US$39.4 billion into the US economy.

The opportunity to gain work experience is a growing driver of student mobility. In 2011–2014, Indian student numbers fell by nearly 50% in the United Kingdom and increased by 70% in Australia after UK policy changes limited post-graduation work visas.

Governments often see student mobility as a way to foster closer ties with other countries. The US Fulbright Scholar Program supports about 8,000 people in over 160 countries each year. Some countries subsidize students' studies abroad in disciplines relevant to national economic growth. The Brazil Scientific Mobility Program funded 101,000 tertiary students to study abroad in 2011–2016.

Internationally mobile university faculty integrate international, intercultural and comparative perspectives into the student experience. In 2016, 90% of US doctorate recipients in computer sciences and mathematics had temporary visas.

Regional qualification frameworks and transferable credits help student mobility, avoid wasting potential and contribute to employment and wage gains. UNESCO has drafted a Global Convention on the Recognition of Higher Education Qualifications for adoption in 2019.

Under the Global Compact for Safe, Orderly and Regular Migration, governments commit to facilitate recognition of skills, qualifications and competences.

Emigration rates of the highly skilled are above 20% in about one-third of 174 countries, including Albania, Eritrea and Grenada. Such mobility can have adverse consequences for poorer countries, but these are tempered by the fact that the very prospect of emigration to prosperous regions spurs education investment in sending countries.

In an increasingly globalized world, young people study abroad and skilled professionals follow employment opportunities across borders. The internationalization of tertiary education requires countries to harmonize their systems. It also brings competition among providers, and a risk of commercial and other interests overshadowing academic mission and values (IAU, 2012). The benefits of education harmonization and professional mobility necessitate recognition of academic and professional qualifications across countries. At the same time, the potential loss of talent remains a concern for poorer countries.

INTERNATIONALIZATION OF TERTIARY EDUCATION TAKES MANY FORMS

Although it affects a minority of students and faculty, the internationalization of tertiary education has major implications for the flow and exchange of ideas and knowledge. Internationalization involves the mobility not only of people but also of courses, programmes and institutions affecting education at home and abroad (Altbach and Knight, 2007).[1]

STUDENT MOBILITY PATTERNS ARE CHANGING

Student migration for full- or part-time study is an increasingly important component of international skilled migration, although international statistics do not capture part-time flows systematically (**Data focus 16.1**).

1 This section is based on the background paper by Bhandari and Robles (2018).

Half of all international students move to five English-speaking countries: Australia, Canada, New Zealand, the United Kingdom and the United States. Over 15% of students in Australia, New Zealand and the United Kingdom are international, and for international doctoral candidates, the share is over 30%. However, recent developments could affect the numbers these countries attract. The United Kingdom's decision to leave the European Union, coupled with student visa restrictions and rising health insurance costs, may diminish the United Kingdom's attractiveness as a destination. Recent uncertainty over the visa regime in the United States may explain increased international enrolment in Canada (Project Atlas, 2017).

> "International tertiary mobility has major implications for the flow and exchange of ideas and knowledge"

The shares of international students in France and Germany have grown to 8% and 6%, respectively, in part because they increasingly offer postgraduate programmes in English (Brenn-White and van Rest, 2012). Other countries have recently entered the market, including China with 10% enrolment in 2017 and the Russian Federation with 6% (Project Atlas, 2017).

Three out of the five largest sending countries in 2016 were in Asia: China, India and the Republic of Korea accounted for 25% of all outbound mobility. While many students travelled to Western countries, 36% of the 1.3 million international students originating in Eastern

> Half of all international students move to five English-speaking countries, while three countries in Asia accounted for 25% of all outbound mobility

Asia and the Pacific stayed in the region in 2016 (Kuroda, 2018). Europe was the second-largest sending region at 23% of the total in 2016, with 76% of the 0.9 million students staying in the region. Intraregional international students accounted for 35% of all international students in the region (Eurostat, 2016; UNESCO, 2017b).

Other notable mobility patterns include sizeable numbers of African students in France and Latin American students in Spain, due to shared language and historical ties. The recent trend of African students in China is owing to growing economic ties. Since 2000, the Forum on China-Africa Cooperation has been providing scholarships for short-term training and long-term university studies in China to African professionals and students. The pledged number of scholarships has increased from 30,000 in 2016–2018 to 50,000 in 2019–2021 (Benabdallah and Robertson, 2018).

Education quality considerations determine individual mobility

Overlapping individual, institutional and government factors drive student mobility. Students base decisions on where to pursue tertiary education on availability of places at the best home universities, ability to pay and relative quality of education at home and abroad.

In some large sending countries, the supply of places in high-quality institutions has not met demand. For instance, to qualify for Chinese tertiary education, students need good scores on the highly competitive university entrance examination, the *gaokao*. Candidates from rich households prepare for study abroad in case they do not pass the examination. In 2016, nearly 170,000 were enrolled in international curriculum secondary schools in China (IEduChina, 2016). Others enrol in secondary school abroad, also with the goal of preparing for foreign universities. In 2015, Chinese students enrolled in secondary school numbered more than 43,000 in the United States, and they have a large presence in Australia, Canada and the United Kingdom (Farrugia, 2014, 2017).

Three-quarters of nearly 16,000 young people in 19 countries rated positively the quality and diversity of tertiary institutions and programmes in the United States (IIE, 2015). Institutional rankings also have a powerful influence, often determining student admission preferences and eligibility for national scholarship programmes (Hazelkorn, 2015; ICEF Monitor, 2017; Redden, 2016; Walcutt, 2016).

Tertiary institutions need foreign students as a revenue source

Some universities recruit international students to diversify the student body, provide exposure to multiple cultures and languages, and improve their global rankings. However, the main driver is revenue. In 2016, international students brought an estimated US$39.4 billion into the US economy – largely in living expenses and tuition – making international education one of the top export industries. Other countries also see a large economic benefit, including Australia (US$24.7 billion), Canada (US$15.5 billion) and the United Kingdom (US$31.9 billion) (Global Affairs Canada, 2017; Maslen, 2018; Universities UK, 2017).

In several Asian countries with declining birth rates and ageing populations, the tertiary education sector is turning to international students to keep institutions open (Farrugia and Bhandari, 2016). Japan aims to mitigate low domestic enrolment by attracting international students from within Asia and farther afield through initiatives such as courses and programmes taught in English (**Box 6.1**). In 2010–2014, the number of international students in the Republic of Korea stagnated at around 85,000. In 2015, it set a goal of 200,000 international students by 2023, or 5% of all places. Scholarships, regulations allowing universities to open international departments or programmes, expansion of English instruction, and increased post-graduation employment opportunities support the goal. In 2017, the number of international students increased to 124,000 (ICEF Monitor, 2018).

> In 2016, international students brought an estimated US$39.4 billion into the US economy

Host-country tertiary education expenditure pays off in incoming international student numbers. A study of 18 European countries showed that a 1% increase in

BOX 6.1:

Japan has intensified efforts to internationalize tertiary education

Tertiary enrolment in Japan is projected to decrease by over 25% between 2018 and 2031 due to low birth rates. Over one-third of private universities operate below capacity, and national or public universities also face financial difficulties. Attracting international students has been one strategy.

After reaching its 100,000 International Students Plan target in 2003, the Japanese government launched a new drive as part of its Asian Gateway strategy, implemented through the Global 30 project (2009–2014). Thirteen universities developed degree programmes in English and enhanced both international student support and inter-university networks, including overseas offices, for sharing education resources. Various ministries coordinated individual stages, from admissions to graduate employment.

Now the Top Global University Project (2014–2023), involving 37 universities split into 2 tiers, has set targets for shares of international full-time faculty; full-time faculty with international degrees; international students; Japanese students who have studied abroad (including those under inter-university agreements); and classes conducted in a foreign language. Amendments to the education law increase university presidents' decision-making autonomy in supporting the objectives.

Other Japanese initiatives include bilateral institutes (e.g. Egypt–Japan University of Science and Technology, Malaysia–Japan International Institute of Technology, Vietnam Japan University), and a new project for collaborative degree programmes with foreign universities (Kuroda, 2018).

expenditure per student led to an average 2% increase in incoming students (Van Bouwel and Veugelers, 2009). An additional institution in the top 200 of the Academic Ranking of World Universities, known as Shanghai Ranking, was associated with a 11% increase in incoming students (Van Bouwel and Veugelers, 2013).

Countries offer work opportunities to attract students

The opportunity to gain work experience is a growing driver of student mobility. Policies governing students' ability to work have affected international student numbers, including in Canada, Germany, New Zealand, the United Kingdom and the United States. In 2011–2014, Indian student numbers in the United Kingdom fell by nearly 50% after policy changes limited post-graduation work visas; meanwhile, their numbers rose by 70% in Australia and 37% in the United States (Project Atlas, 2016).

> "In 18 European countries, a 1% increase in expenditure per student led to an average 2% increase in incoming students"

In the United States, 14% of the more than 1 million international students in 2016/17 benefited from Optional Practical Training (OPT), a temporary post-graduation work visa. Such opportunities are influential drivers of mobility for students from Asian countries, including China, India and Nepal: 31% of Indian students had OPT permits in 2016/17, making them the leading participants. While an OPT extension for science, technology, engineering and mathematics (STEM) graduates from one to three years accounts for some of the recent surge in participation, the growing number willing to stay for longer work periods indicates its importance for many students. Students value the ability to gain practical work experience, earn money and improve their prospects, either for settling in the United States or for a better job at home.

In recent years, with the scale of knowledge-based and innovation-driven economies increasing worldwide, some countries try not only to bolster international students' enrolment but also to retain them in their labour markets. In China, which hosted 443,000 international students in 2015/16, programmes in Beijing, Shanghai and Shenzhen create opportunities for international students in high-tech and e-commerce courses to transition easily into the workforce to address local skills gaps (Sharma, 2017). Germany offers degree programmes with minimal fees and graduate programmes taught in English, and gives its non-EU graduates 18 months to find employment. It reached its enrolment goal – 350,000 by 2020 – three years early (Kennedy, 2017; Nafie, 2017).

> "In China, programmes create opportunities for international students in high-tech and e-commerce courses to transition easily into the workforce to address local skills gaps"

Policies to increase student mobility take various forms

Government involvement in student exchange through bilateral initiatives serves as a form of cultural diplomacy and development aid (Teichler et al., 2011). The Fulbright Scholar Program, launched in 1946 to strengthen ties and build cultural understanding between the United States and the rest of the world, operates through a partnership model: 49 bilateral commissions, along with embassies in 149 countries without such commissions, cooperate with host governments. It supports about 8,000 students, scholars, teachers and professionals in over 160 countries each year (Bettie, 2015).

Under the Bilateral Forum on Higher Education, Innovation, and Research, Mexico established Proyecta 100,000 in 2013, with the goal of 100,000 Mexican students studying in the United States and 50,000 US students studying in Mexico. The United States launched 100,000 Strong in the Americas in 2011, with the goal of 100,000 students moving in both directions between the United States and Latin America (Farrugia and Mahmoud, 2016).

Some government scholarships are a form of development aid. Funded by the European Development Fund, the Intra-ACP Academic Mobility Scheme, implemented by the European Commission in partnership with the Africa, Caribbean and Pacific (ACP) Secretariat, provides access to tertiary education for ACP students (European Commission, 2018).

Some sending countries sponsor study abroad

Countries may subsidize study abroad as a development strategy. The Brazil Scientific Mobility Program, known in Brazil as *Ciência sem Fronteiras* (Science without Borders), operated from 2011 to 2016 and funded 101,000 tertiary students to study abroad in disciplines critical to Brazil's growth. It was designed to enable degree completion in Brazil after a year of academic study and an optional summer internship abroad (Mcmanus and Nobre, 2017).

> “Brazil funded 101,000 tertiary students to study abroad in disciplines critical to its growth”

Saudi Arabia launched the King Abdullah Scholarship Program in 2005 to fund degrees overseas. Saudi students are among the five largest international student groups in the United States. Due to declining crude oil prices, it was reported in 2016 that there would be budget cuts and restrictions on academic eligibility requirements, fields of study and eligible universities (Kottasova, 2016).

Not all governments promote study abroad. In 2009, Algeria sought to restrict scholarships for study abroad for the best baccalaureate graduates (Sawahl, 2009). At one point, Uganda required doctors wishing to pursue studies abroad to make a written commitment to return (Karugaba, 2009).

FACULTY, COURSES, PROGRAMMES AND INSTITUTIONS ARE ALSO MOBILE

Internationally mobile faculty play a key role in internationalizing tertiary education. They can integrate international, intercultural and comparative perspectives into education and boost institutions' international profiles through publications and projects tied to their networks (Knight, 2012). Mobile faculty range from academics sought by elite research universities to those hired to address local shortages, along with 'transient' academics who continue academic careers in the countries where they obtained their doctorates (Rumbley and de Wit, 2017). The Survey of Earned Doctorates in the United States, the country that hosts the most transient academics, suggests that international faculty constitute 25% of new academic positions. In 2016, US doctorate recipients with temporary visas and definite employment commitments varied by subject area, from less than 60% in psychology and other social sciences to almost 90% in mathematics and computer science (NSF, 2018).

> “Almost 90% of US doctorate recipients in mathematics and computer sciences had temporary visas in 2016”

International skilled mobility for education extends to programmes and institutions. Massive open online courses (MOOCs) typically provide an interactive mix of videos, quizzes, discussion forums and, sometimes, peer-graded assignments. Offered through a wide range of education institutions and other providers, they have surged in recent years, with one estimate suggesting that 41 providers had reached 81 million learners in 2017, although the number of new learners had stagnated for the first time at 23 million (Shah, 2018).

Limited only by students' connectivity and hardware (even a mobile phone will do), MOOCs, especially those offered free, can expand access to education, particularly in the developing world. Low course completion is a common critique, although rates vary widely among providers and courses, and also depend on course characteristics. For instance, a review of Harvard and MIT online courses on the learning platform EdX showed that the median certification rate was just 8%, but for learners who paid, it was 60% (Chuang and Ho, 2016). New approaches seek to address the prevalent reasons (e.g. difficulty engaging with instructors, lack of peer support), including providing host country support locally for distance education students (Knight, 2016).

Offshore, cross-border and borderless programmes also enable international education at home (HEGlobal, 2016; Knight, 2016). A study involving Botswana, China, Malaysia, Mexico, Pakistan, the Russian Federation, Singapore, South Africa, the United Arab Emirates and Viet Nam found that the flexibility of transnational education facilitated coursework and degree completion while allowing 59% of students to remain employed (British Council, 2014). Branch campuses and, more recently, regional education hubs (e.g. Malaysia's tertiary education sector; the Knowledge Village in Dubai, the United Arab Emirates; Qatar's Education City; Singapore's Global Schoolhouse) expand international tertiary education. Hubs involve various combinations of domestic institutions, international campuses and foreign partnerships (Dessoff, 2012).

Institutional mobility significantly affects domestic and international tertiary education alike. Traditional student mobility may decline as international students choose home country branches. At the same time, diverse forms of internationalization may continue to grow rapidly, serving more students with varying education needs (Bhandari and Belyavina, 2012).

RECOGNIZING ACADEMIC QUALIFICATIONS MAXIMIZES THE BENEFITS OF STUDENT AND LABOUR MOBILITY

To facilitate student mobility, countries engage in institution-building and complex agreements, such as dual and joint degree programmes, credit transfers and strategic partnerships. Such agreements are but one step towards facilitating greater labour mobility through increased attempts to harmonize standards, deepen quality assurance mechanisms and recognize academic qualifications at the bilateral, regional or global level.

Traditionally, countries have tried to tackle the issues of student mobility and recognition of qualifications independently. While doing so is costly, some countries continue to innovate. Establishing legal rights to recognition can improve uptake and efficiency. In 2016, Austria implemented a comprehensive law on recognition of foreign qualifications, establishing a right to assessment of all levels of education certificates and diplomas (OECD, 2017). The Danish Agency for Universities and Internationalisation, later subsumed in the new Danish Agency for Higher Education, was a one-stop shop for assessing foreign nationals' credentials. Assessments of an advisory or binding nature could be undertaken on demand for both employment and further education. According to a 2010 report, general assessments had an average processing time of 32.5 days, with 89% completed in less than two months. A user satisfaction survey found that assessments had a positive effect on employment and education outcomes (IOM, 2013).

Increasingly, however, countries try to collaborate to maximize synergy. The introduction of common degree standards, quality assurance, qualification recognition mechanisms and academic mobility exchange

> "Countries work on standards, quality assurance mechanisms and qualification recognition at bilateral, regional or global level to facilitate student exchange"

programmes enabled European and partner countries to establish a European Higher Education Area (EHEA) in 2010. This was the culmination of the Bologna Process, begun in 1999, involving the European Commission, the Council of Europe and representatives of tertiary education institutions, quality assurance agencies, students, staff and employers. Currently, 48 countries take part. The latest implementation report recognized that policy development lagged in some areas, including quality assurance of joint programmes, the European Credit Transfer and Accumulation System, and the Diploma Supplement, a document providing a detailed description of study components and learning outcomes achieved (European Commission et al., 2018).

While the Bologna Process and associated reforms made it easier to recognize qualifications among EHEA countries, it did not make it automatic. The Convention on the Recognition of Qualifications concerning Higher Education in the European Region (Lisbon Recognition Convention) of April 1997 legally ensures qualifications recognition among participating countries (Rauhvargers, 2004). As of August 2018, 54 countries have ratified, including 7 outside Europe (Australia, Canada, Israel, Kazakhstan, Kyrgyzstan, New Zealand and Tajikistan) (Council of Europe, 2018).

Good practice and common understanding of recognition require strong country involvement, but also good information systems, to turn international agreements into national law. The European Network of Information Centres in the European Region/National Academic Recognition Information Centres in the European Union is an initiative in 55 countries to improve transparency in international recognition procedures through information on national qualifications.

Following the European experience, the Association of Southeast Asian Nations (ASEAN), which established the ASEAN Economic Community (AEC) in 2015, aims to create a single market and allow the free flow of skilled labour. It receives EU technical assistance in establishing a qualifications reference framework, quality assurance mechanism and credit transfer system. It also aims to introduce an academic mobility initiative based on lessons from the Erasmus+ programme (**Policy focus 16.1**).

In January 2018, Japan and the Republic of Korea ratified the 2011 Asia-Pacific Regional Convention on the Recognition of Qualifications in Higher Education, which came into force as a result. Japan also committed to establishing a national information centre (Mori, 2018). At the third Regional Conference on Higher Education in June 2018, countries in Latin America and the Caribbean agreed to proceed to stronger regional integration in tertiary education (UNESCO IESALC, 2018).

> “In Africa, issues with university management, education quality and credit transfer have hindered students wishing to study in the region”

In Africa, issues with university management, education quality and credit transfer have hindered students wishing to study in the region (Woldegiorgis and Knight, 2017). The five countries of the East African Community established a Common Higher Education Area in 2017 to develop regional standards, guidelines and national commissions and councils. Students will be able to enrol in any of the region's 110 universities without a special examination, and credits will be transferable (Ligami, 2017; Waruru, 2017).

With the aim of building on regional conventions, UNESCO has drafted a Global Convention on the Recognition of Higher Education Qualifications for adoption in 2019. In addition to developing principles for tertiary qualifications recognition across regions, it aims to provide a common quality assurance framework. As with the Lisbon convention, parties will commit to recognizing foreign qualifications (and precursory qualifications), unless a substantial difference can be proved. They will also have to establish recognition authorities, maintain information centres to provide relevant and timely information about national tertiary education systems, and offer qualifications holders the right of assessment (UNESCO, 2015, 2017a).

RECOGNIZING PROFESSIONAL QUALIFICATIONS IS ALSO NEEDED TO MAXIMIZE THE BENEFITS OF MOBILITY

Recognition of professional qualifications, like that of academic qualifications, facilitates and maximizes the benefits of skilled labour migration. Immigrants are often economically excluded because of discrimination, limited social networks, inadequate language skills or visa restrictions (OECD, 2014). Limiting recognition of their qualifications is a further impediment, which immigrants often rate above language skills as a challenge (Eurostat, 2014).

Immigrants whose qualifications are not recognized may not be able to legally practice in regulated professions, such as teaching and nursing, and often occupy jobs that underutilize their skills. Over one-third of immigrants with tertiary education in countries of the Organisation for Economic Co-operation and Development (OECD) are overqualified for their jobs, compared with one-quarter of natives (OECD/European Union, 2015).

Analysis for this report shows that only 30% of those with tertiary degrees gained outside Europe and Northern America work in high-skill occupations. Less than 15% reported their level of education matched their jobs, compared with almost 70% among other immigrants who studied in the host country and nearly 75% among natives.

> "Over one-third of immigrants with tertiary education in OECD countries are overqualified for their jobs, compared with one-quarter of natives"

While labour market outcomes between skilled migrants and natives tend to converge the longer migrants stay, parity can take years (Aleksynska and Tritah, 2013). Skilled African immigrants in Europe who did not upgrade their occupation in the first five to six years tended to persist in low-skill work (Castagnone et al., 2015). In non-STEM jobs, foreign-born workers in the United States took 20 years or more to reach earnings parity with natives (Hanson and Slaughter, 2016).

Harmonized international rules and transparent procedures on qualifications recognition can facilitate international migration. The benefits of functional recognition systems can be substantial. Recognition in Germany increased the probability of immigrant employment by 45 percentage points and the hourly wage by 40% (Brücker et al., 2015; IOM, 2013). In the United States, forgone earnings of underemployed immigrant college graduates could represent US$10.2 billion in lost tax revenue annually (Batalova et al., 2016). The overqualification rate among immigrants in OECD countries whose qualifications are recognized is 10 percentage points lower, on average, than among those whose qualifications are not recognized, after accounting for the field of study and for the country where the qualifications were obtained (Bonfati et al., 2014).

QUALIFICATIONS RECOGNITION NEEDS TO BE SIMPLER AND MORE FLEXIBLE

Governments increasingly acknowledge the importance of recognizing skills and qualifications. Under the Global Compact for Safe, Orderly and Regular Migration, they commit to facilitate recognition of skills, qualifications and competences (United Nations, 2018).

As such agreements require political coordination and common quality assurance standards, they are concentrated in rich, mostly European economies. Even there, a review of EU-funded validation projects found that only six explicitly mentioned immigrants in their overviews (Souto-Otero and Villalba-Garcia, 2015).

Recognition systems are often too underdeveloped or fragmented to meet immigrants' needs (Cangiano, 2015; Lodigiani and Sarli, 2017). In a survey of 13 European countries, only a minority of highly educated migrants had applied for recognition (OECD, 2014). They may be unable or unwilling to invest the resources required by complex, time-consuming and costly processes (CEDEFOP, 2016; Hawthorne, 2013). Recognition systems usually identify competences, then validate them, requiring original certificates or evidence of attainment. Furthermore, the procedures and agencies involved in official recognition and validation vary between regulated and non-regulated professions.

Identifying, documenting, assessing and certifying skills and competences involves multiple government departments and subnational authorities (CEDEFOP, 2016). Recognition bodies are frequently unconnected from bodies responsible for integration and employment (OECD, 2014). Assessment agencies, licensing bodies and academic institutions can harmonize requirements and procedures, such as document verification, to reduce the need to submit documents to multiple agencies. Governments can ensure agencies abide by fair, transparent procedures and adhere to best practices. For example, Ontario (Canada) introduced a 'fairness commissioner' in 2007 to ensure fair access to regulated professions for those with foreign qualifications (Owen and Lowe, 2008).

In 2012, Germany passed a federal law to streamline recognition. Foreign nationals can gain recognition regardless of residence status or citizenship. They can make a legal claim for recognition and receive a decision within three months. Professional qualifications obtained abroad are checked for compatibility with German professional requirements. The law covers around 600 occupational groups (Kovacheva and Grewe, 2015). Among efforts to address lack of transparency and information in recognition procedures, internet portals provide concise, easily accessible information in foreign languages (IOM, 2013). The Recognition in Germany website and app, accessible in nine languages, receive more than 1 million visitors per year (Rietig, 2016).

Still, coordination within a highly decentralized system is challenging. Established in 2005, Germany's IQ Network has evolved into 16 state networks, with over 70 counselling centres, which help applicants through the recognition process but also teach intercultural skills to employment office and job centre staff. The chambers of commerce and industry established a centre for foreign skills approval, IHK FOSA, which processes applications to all its members, making decisions more consistent across states and professions (Rietig, 2016).

Partial recognition is another route into regulated professions with insufficiently harmonized international standards or underdeveloped quality assurance. Applicants may have to pass an examination, work under supervision for a period or refrain from performing certain functions. The Washington Accord is a rare example of a non-regional multilateral initiative that recognizes substantial equivalence in professional engineering qualifications but gives national authorities discretion to mandate extended periods of partial licensure (Hawthorne, 2013).

While immigrants stand to benefit considerably from having their skills validated, they do not make enough use of the available processes. Some countries have developed immigrant-specific validation tools. An Austrian project, Du kannst was ('You have skills'), targets low-qualified immigrants, enabling even those without formal education to sit the same examinations as general vocational students and obtain certification (Souto-Otero and Villalba-Garcia, 2015). Denmark's Competence Card allows immigrants to make their skills more visible to prospective employers and connects them with labour market needs. Professional, linguistic and general skills are assessed and documented electronically, facilitating job search or further education (OECD, 2014).

The European Skills Passport helps EU nationals make their skills and qualifications more easily understood throughout Europe. It consists of an online curriculum vitae, to which official documents can be attached, that details skills and lets authorities, education institutions and partner organizations attest to skills gained during education and work experience. Recently, an alternative version was developed for non-EU nationals, and it has been recommended that a similar version for refugees, developed and piloted in Norway, should be expanded across Europe (CEDEFOP, 2018; European Commission, 2017; NOKUT, 2017) (**Policy focus 10.2**).

Mutual recognition of qualifications in regulated professions is complicated

Legal concerns and public safety issues are obstacles in recognizing professional qualifications. Yet recognition is in the public interest, allowing immigrants to fill vacancies in the health and education sectors instead of working outside their fields (Girard and Smith, 2012). In Canada, only one-quarter of foreign-educated immigrants with relevant qualifications were working in a regulated profession (Sumption et al., 2013).

One of the few examples of multilateral automatic recognition for regulated professions is the European Union's Professional Qualifications Directive. It allows architects, dentists, doctors, midwives, nurses, pharmacists and veterinary surgeons who hold an approved qualification to practise in any member state (Sumption et al., 2013). However, automatic recognition agreements, such as those within the European Union, involved a long process of harmonizing standards and quality assurance mechanisms and an even longer process of economic and political integration. Establishing and maintaining such agreements requires substantial political commitment and resources (IOM, 2013).

> “Establishing and maintaining automatic recognition agreements such as those within the EU requires substantial political commitment and resources”

Countries may reform their education systems and qualification frameworks to conform with those of other countries or regions, which may facilitate mutual recognition in the long term. India is working with Germany to reform the technical and vocational education and training system, modelling curricula and training on the German approach (Desiderio and Hooper, 2015). The Republic of Moldova is introducing a national qualification framework modelled on the European Qualifications Framework (Republic of Moldova Government, 2017).

A few agreements allow intra-regional mobility through regional qualification frameworks. Within the CARICOM Single Market and Economy, qualified people in the Caribbean can move and work freely with a Certificate of Recognition of CARICOM Skills Qualification. While university graduates can obtain the certificate on the basis of their degrees, selected professions, including nurses and teachers, are also eligible if they meet additional requirements (World Bank, 2009) (**Policy focus 17.1**). Since the system came into effect in 1996, 16,000 certificates have been issued (CARICOM, 2017).

Under the Common Market Protocol of the East African Community, partner countries commit to facilitating the free movement of service providers and, where necessary, harmonizing and mutually recognizing academic and professional qualifications. To date, this includes accountants, architects and engineers, and work is under way to recognize lawyers (Kago and Masinde, 2017).

LOSS OF TALENT CAN BE DETRIMENTAL TO POORER COUNTRIES

Student and skilled worker mobility and the associated loss of human capital, a phenomenon known as brain drain, can negatively affect poorer countries. Estimates for this report suggest that emigration rates of the highly skilled are above 20% in just over one-quarter of 174 countries, including Grenada and Guyana in the Caribbean, Albania and Malta in Europe, and Eritrea and Somalia in sub-Saharan Africa (Deuster and Docquier, 2018) (**Figure 6.1**).

Aid in the form of scholarships to donor country universities can exacerbate this trend, as students do not always return. Aid could instead support students or universities in the region, as target 4.b of the Sustainable Development Goals specifies. Public spending can also be biased. A World Bank estimate based on country studies from 2003–2008 found that about 18% of public tertiary education expenditure in sub-Saharan Africa went to scholarships to support study abroad (World Bank, 2010).

Richer countries actively compete for skilled workers. In OECD countries, which have experienced significant growth in skilled worker immigration, there are almost twice as many high-skilled immigrants from outside member countries as from within (Kerr et al., 2016). Fears that emigration could impede development in sending countries due to loss of skills even led to a

FIGURE 6.1:
In several countries, more than one out of five highly skilled people emigrate
Skilled migration rates, selected countries, 2010

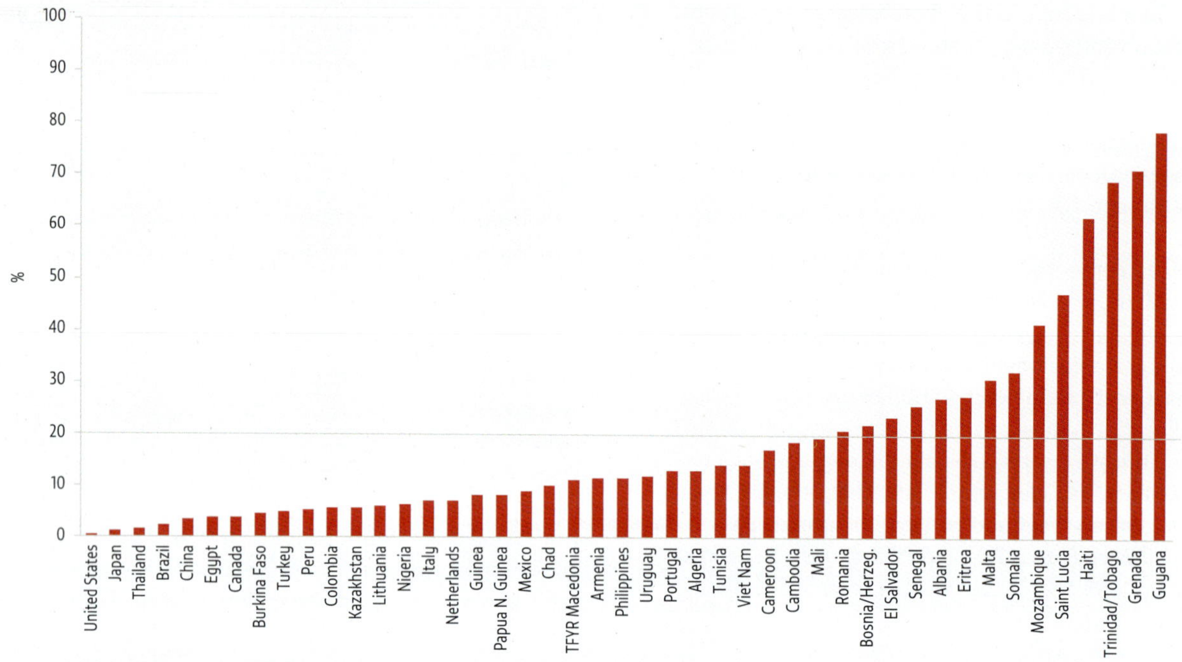

GEM StatLink: http://bit.ly/fig6_1
Source: Deuster and Docquier (2018).

proposal to introduce an emigration tax in the 1970s (Bhagwati and Hamada, 1974).

> "About 18% of public tertiary expenditure in sub-Saharan Africa went to supporting students abroad"

However, skilled migration is also increasingly seen as having more positive effects on education and skills for both origin and destination countries than previously thought. Remittances can benefit sending economies (**Policy focus 19.4**). And the very prospect of skilled emigration to prosperous regions can also spur education investment in sending countries.

Research for this report on the effect of skilled migration on human capital accumulation in sending countries provides updated estimates that account for these opposing forces. It finds that a net high-skilled migration rate of 14% generates the highest positive effects on human capital accumulation and continues to generate positive effects at migration rates as high as 33%. Further generalizing the model to also account for the characteristics of origin and destination countries as well as for low-skilled emigration rates shows that emigration prospects generate net brain gain in 90 countries and net brain loss emerges in 84 countries. On average, the net effect is small in low income and middle income countries (Deuster and Docquier, 2018).

Return migrants can mitigate brain drain effects but need policy support

One of the factors that can mitigate the effects of brain drain is return migration, a phenomenon that is typically neglected because of the perception that migrants leave with no intention to come back. However, migrants may return deliberately as part of their individual migration strategies or following incentives that governments in origin countries provide to attract talent from the diaspora (Agunias and Newland, 2012). Migrants may also return involuntarily, for instance when they are expelled and banned from re-entering or when the economic conditions in the destination countries change, adversely affecting their job opportunities. In either case, return migrants and their families have specific education-related needs, which are often not met.

First, they can face qualifications recognition challenges. Governments can provide advice or offer validation and recognition services to ease their reintegration in the labour market. The Republic of Korea's Happy Return Programme provides skills training and issues career certificates (GFMD, 2013). In the Philippines, under the Technical Education and Skills Development Authority, six agencies oversaw the Permanent Returning Overseas Filipino Workers Network, while Davao province's Skills Registration Database linked returnees to recognition services and prospective employers (ILO, 2010).

Second, return migrants tend to seek self-employment opportunities or to establish a business. However, countries find it challenging to adapt their skills development policies to support returnees' needs (Bardak, 2014) (**Box 6.2**).

BOX 6.2:

Albania's policies need to support entrepreneurship among returnees

Albania has one of the highest emigration rates. In 2015, an estimated 2.9 million Albanians lived in the country and 1.1 million lived abroad (UNDESA, 2015, 2017). The financial crisis in Greece and Italy, host to almost 80% of Albanian migrants, triggered a wave of returns. A survey showed that 70% of male returnees had lost their jobs abroad (IOM and INSTAT, 2013). Between 2008 and 2014, an estimated 150,000 to 180,000 Albanian migrants returned, mostly from Greece (Barjaba and Barjaba, 2015).

As a result, the Albanian labour force expanded by 5% between 2011 and 2014. Analysis of labour force survey data shows that returnees contributed to an increase in employment rates through both self-employment and hiring workers for new businesses. Returnees are more likely than non-migrants to set up businesses and bring non-migrants into the labour force (Hausmann and Nedelkoska, 2017; Piracha and Vadean, 2010).

Vocational centres provide entrepreneurship education options, often with the support of development partners (Nikolovska, 2010). In 2010, the government of Albania developed a five-year reintegration strategy, strengthening 'migration counters' at regional labour offices to refer returnees to public services, including to vocational centres (Albania Government, 2010). The Employment and Skills Strategy 2014–2020 also recognized the challenge of supporting returnees (Albania Ministry of Social Welfare and Youth, 2014). However, in 2011–2015, just 800 returnees accessed migration counters for professional orientation (Vathi and Zajmi, 2017). Expanding this service at the municipality level would improve access, but consistency with the strategy should be increased (Gëdeshi and Xhaferaj, 2016). Moreover, vocational centres may not be the most suitable outlet for entrepreneurship training for returnees.

CONCLUSION

The internationalization of tertiary education, including the movement of students, academics, courses and institutions, has taken various forms in recent years. Countries compete to attract larger numbers of foreign students who are the source of valuable income and reputation for host universities and countries. To facilitate student mobility, universities increasingly embark on dual and joint degree programmes, credit transfers and strategic partnerships. At the same time, countries harmonize standards, deepen quality assurance mechanisms and recognize academic qualifications at the bilateral, regional or global level.

Recognition of professional qualifications also increases the benefits of migration for skilled workers. Those whose qualifications are not recognized are less likely to find skilled work. However, recognition mechanisms are often fragmented or complex to meet immigrants' and refugees' needs and end up being underutilized. They need to be made cheaper and more efficient to overcome a key obstacle to socio-economic integration.

The loss of human capital associated with the migration of students and professionals can negatively affect poorer countries. However, the prospect of emigration can spur individual investment in education and skills in sending countries and mitigate some of the costs of brain drain. Education systems need to adjust to harness the skills of return migrants.

Mina (11 years old), grade 5, Boeung Kachang island, Koh Kong province, Cambodia.

CREDIT: Shallendra Yashwant/Save the Children

CHAPTER

7

Monitoring education in the Sustainable Development Goals

KEY MESSAGES

As of 2018, there are four new indicators for measuring progress towards SDG 4, bringing the total number to 33 out of 43.

2019 will be a key year for reporting on SDG 4, as the High-Level Political Forum on Sustainable Development will review SDG 4 for the first time.

With data now available up until the end of 2015, there are two key findings on the Education for All era:

- Progress stalled in primary education completion after 2008, meaning goal 2 on universal primary completion was missed.
- There was a steady move towards gender parity in primary and secondary education, which was achieved in 2009, four years later than the target date of 2005.

Migrant and displaced populations are heterogeneous in terms of identity, journeys and legal status. Migration and displacement flows can change rapidly and sampling frames may not keep up. Global monitoring of their education status will no doubt remain a patchwork of approaches for some time.

Data on displaced populations tend to be collected in camps, where less than 40% of refugees and even fewer internally displaced people reside.

Flexible approaches to collecting data on migrants and refugees should be considered. Examples include the Latin American Migration Project and the Refugees in the German Educational System study.

The monitoring framework supporting Sustainable Development Goal 4 (SDG 4) on education is ambitious, even if some of the hardest questions of education development remain sidelined. Major efforts are under way to develop indicators, standards and tools to match this ambition, a process requiring close collaboration among international agencies, countries, funders and experts.

In introducing the monitoring part of this report, this chapter first reviews the status of the SDG 4 monitoring and reporting framework, touching on selected developments in its refinement and implementation; subsequent chapters take up specific cases. Second, it takes stock of the Education for All (EFA) era, 2000–2015. While the 2015 *EFA Global Monitoring Report* was dedicated to such an assessment, the full statistical picture across all goals and financial commitments has only just emerged (**Box 7.1**). Third, it introduces education monitoring issues related to migration and displacement, a dimension that the overall SDG monitoring framework has committed to follow closely but that is difficult to realize.

> Major efforts are under way to develop indicators, standards and tools to match the ambition of SDG 4

THE SDG 4 MONITORING FRAMEWORK

In September 2017, the United Nations General Assembly adopted the UN Statistical Commission's list of 232 global indicators for monitoring the SDGs, based on the work of its Inter-agency and Expert Group on SDG Indicators (IAEG-SDGs). The IAEG-SDGs will carry out major reviews of the indicator framework in 2019 and 2024 for approval at commission sessions in 2020 and 2025.

There are 11 global indicators for SDG 4 – one per target, except target 4.2, which has two. The UNESCO Institute for Statistics (UIS) is the sole custodian agency for eight indicators and collaborates with the International Telecommunication Union (ITU) for the target 4.4 indicator on information and communications technology. UNICEF is the custodian agency for target 4.2 on early childhood development and the Organisation for Economic Co-operation and Development (OECD) for target 4.b on scholarship aid.

To complement the 11 global indicators, an annex to the Education 2030 Framework for Action proposed 32 thematic indicators with broader coverage of the education agenda. The SDG 4 monitoring framework thus consists of 43 indicators. While the thematic indicators are optional, countries need to provide reasons for opting out of reporting on them.

A three-tier classification, based on established methodology and data coverage, shows which indicators need further methodological work. Two education indicators are currently identified as tier I ('established methodology ... and data regularly produced by countries'). Five are at tier II ('established methodology ... but data are not regularly produced by countries') and two at tier III ('[n]o ... established methodology'). Disparity indices for target 4.5 depend on the quality of the underlying indicators, resulting in a multi-tier classification, a status shared by 4.1.1 (**Table 7.1**).

There are five other education-related global indicators, focusing on prioritization of education and other social spending in national budgets; access to sexual and reproductive health education for adults; youth not in employment, education or training; mainstreaming of education for global citizenship and sustainable development; and climate change education.

Deliberations and investigation by the IAEG-SDGs since the initial proposal have led to classification revisions. The custodian agencies are responsible for refining tier III indicators. Subcomponents b) and c) of indicator 4.1.1 have been raised to tier II. A process is under way to raise the classification of indicator 4.1.1a on early grades. Methodological concerns have led to the downgrading of indicator 4.2.1 to tier III, although the IAEG-SDGs has set up a group to implement a work plan for its improvement. Following implementation of the work plan for indicator 4.7.1, a methodology was developed, based on country responses to the sixth consultation on implementation of the 1974 Recommendation concerning Education for International Understanding, Co-operation and Peace Education relating to Human Rights and Fundamental Freedoms (**Chapter 14**). It served as the basis for a tier reclassification request to the IAEG-SDGs scheduled for November 2018. Indicators 4.a.1 (previously multi-tier I/II) and 4.c.1 are now tier II, reflecting limited data availability.

The UIS coordinates developments on most of the global indicators for which it is custodian, and on all remaining thematic indicators, through the Technical Cooperation Group on the Indicators for SDG 4 – Education 2030 (TCG), which it convenes with UNESCO. The TCG consists of representatives from the IAEG-SDGs member states and selected international agencies and institutions. Its working groups, especially the one on indicator development, have advanced the definitions of various thematic indicators. Starting with the 2018 data release, the UIS reports on four additional indicators: participation in adult literacy programmes (4.6.3), comprehensive sexuality education (4.7.2), school-based violence (4.a.2) and attacks in schools (4.a.3), bringing the total UIS is reporting on to 33 out of the 43 global and thematic SDG 4 indicators. Work continues or is about to begin on other thematic indicators, including language of instruction, distribution of resources and teacher professional development.

> "The UNESCO Institute for Statistics reports on 33 of the 43 global and thematic SDG 4 indicators"

Two other entities convened by the UIS complement the work of the TCG. The Global Alliance to Monitor Learning works on the technically more sophisticated learning outcome-related indicators, primarily on minimum proficiency in reading and mathematics, adult literacy and digital literacy. It began inviting countries in late 2018, with the prospect of developing into part of the TCG structure. The Inter-agency Group on Education Inequality Indicators works on indicators based on data from household surveys but has not yet included countries.

THE SDG 4 REPORTING FRAMEWORK

The SDG follow-up and review process culminates in the annual High-level Political Forum on Sustainable Development (HLPF). The forum provides political leadership, guidance and recommendations on implementation and follow-up; tracks progress; encourages elaboration of coherent policies informed by evidence, science and country experiences; and addresses new and emerging issues.

The HLPF carries out thematic and goal progress reviews, which focus on a different theme and rotating set of SDGs each year. Education will first be reviewed in 2019. An annual SDG report provides the framework for HLPF reviews. The HLPF also receives voluntary national reviews, submissions from intergovernmental bodies and submissions from various 'major groups and stakeholders' representing civil society.

TABLE 7.1:
SDG 4 and other education-related global indicators by custodian agency and classification tier

Indicator	Custodian agency	Tier
SDG 4		
4.1.1 Proportion of children and young people (a) in grades 2/3; (b) at the end of primary; and (c) at the end of lower secondary achieving at least a minimum proficiency level in (i) reading and (ii) mathematics, by sex	UIS	(a) III; (b), (c) II
4.2.1 Proportion of children under 5 years of age who are developmentally on track in health, learning and psychosocial well-being, by sex	UNICEF	III
4.2.2 Participation rate in organized learning (one year before the official primary entry age), by sex	UIS	I
4.3.1 Participation rate of youth and adults in formal and non-formal education and training in the previous 12 months, by sex	UIS	II
4.4.1 Proportion of youth and adults with information and communications technology (ICT) skills, by type of skill	UIS and ITU	II
4.5.1 Parity indices (female/male, rural/urban, bottom/top wealth quintile and others such as disability status, indigenous peoples and conflict-affected, as data become available) for all education indicators on this list that can be disaggregated	UIS	I/II/III depending on indicator
4.6.1 Proportion of population in a given age group achieving at least a fixed level of proficiency in functional (a) literacy and (b) numeracy skills, by sex	UIS	II
4.7.1 Extent to which (i) global citizenship education and (ii) education for sustainable development, including gender equality and human rights, are mainstreamed at all levels in (a) national education policies; (b) curricula; (c) teacher education; and (d) student assessment	UIS	III
4.a.1 Proportion of schools with access to (a) electricity; (b) the Internet for pedagogical purposes; (c) computers for pedagogical purposes; (d) adapted infrastructure and materials for students with disabilities; (e) basic drinking water; (f) single-sex basic sanitation facilities; and (g) basic handwashing facilities (as per the WASH indicator definitions)	UIS	II
4.b.1 Volume of official development assistance flows for scholarships by sector and type of study	OECD	I
4.c.1 Proportion of teachers in (a) pre-primary; (b) primary; (c) lower secondary; and (d) upper secondary education who have received at least the minimum organized teacher training (e.g. pedagogical training) pre-service or in-service required for teaching at the relevant level in a given country	UIS	II
Other SDGs		
1.a.2 Proportion of total government spending on essential services (education, health and social protection)	ILO, UIS and WHO	II
5.6.2 Number of countries with laws and regulations that guarantee full and equal access to women and men aged 15 years and older to sexual and reproductive health care, information and education	UNFPA	III
8.6.1 Proportion of youth (aged 15–24 years) not in education, employment or training	ILO	I
12.8.1 Extent to which (i) global citizenship education and (ii) education for sustainable development (including climate change education) are mainstreamed in (a) national education policies; (b) curricula; (c) teacher education; and (d) student assessment	UIS	III
13.3.1 Number of countries that have integrated mitigation, adaptation, impact reduction and early warning into primary, secondary and tertiary curricula	UNFCCC and UIS	III

Notes: Tier classifications are defined as follows:
Tier 1: Indicator is conceptually clear, has an internationally established methodology and standards are available, and data are regularly produced by countries for at least 50 per cent of countries and of the population in every region where the indicator is relevant.
Tier 2: Indicator is conceptually clear, has an internationally established methodology and standards are available, but data are not regularly produced by countries.
Tier 3: No internationally established methodology or standards are yet available for the indicator, but methodology/standards are being (or will be) developed or tested.
Source: IAEG-SDGs (2017).

Since SDG-wide reports may pay limited attention to education, the World Education Forum, in its Incheon Declaration, requested 'an independent Global Education Monitoring Report (GEM Report), hosted and published by UNESCO, as the mechanism for monitoring and reporting on the proposed SDG 4 and on education in the other proposed SDGs' (UNESCO, 2015a, para. 18, p. 11). In line with this mandate, Chapters 8 to 17 of this report review progress towards the seven targets (4.1 to 4.7) and three means of implementation (4.a to 4.c), Chapter 18 discusses issues related to education in three other SDGs, and Chapter 19 reviews education financing.

> "Education will be reviewed for the first time in the 2019 High-level Political Forum"

BOX 7.1:

Taking stock of achievements in the Education for All era, 2000–2015

The *EFA Global Monitoring Report* was established in 2001 to inform the international community on progress towards the EFA goals and on the monitoring framework, consisting of 18 indicators (UIS, 2001). The indicators overlapped with those of the Millennium Development Goal (MDG) monitoring framework. The final edition of the report, for 2015, presented at the World Education Forum in Incheon, Republic of Korea, assessed EFA achievements largely on the basis of 2012 data. The UIS, in collaboration with countries, is making a considerable effort to reduce the lag in education data by increasing the efficiency of the survey and data release schedule. The following updated assessment – based on UIS data, unless suggested otherwise – does not change the conclusion that progress during the EFA era, while significant, ultimately fell well short of reaching the targets.

Early childhood care and education

'Goal 1. Expanding and improving comprehensive early childhood care and education, especially for the most vulnerable and disadvantaged children.'

- Insufficient consistent data was collected on participation in 'early childhood development programmes'. But the pre-primary gross enrolment ratio increased from 32% in 2000 to 47% in 2015 (Indicator 1).
- Information on the percentage of new grade 1 entrants who attended 'some form of organized early childhood development programme' was not systematically collected from administrative data, but evidence from 31 low and middle income countries taking part in the UNICEF Multiple Indicator Cluster Survey 5 (2013–2015), which collected this information, suggested that the median ratio was 36% (Indicator 2).

Universal primary education

'Goal 2. Ensuring that by 2015 all children, particularly girls, children in difficult circumstances and those belonging to ethnic minorities, have access to and complete free and compulsory primary education of good quality.'

- The gross intake ratio to grade 1 was constant at 106% in 2000 and 2015 (Indicator 3).
- By contrast, the global average of the net intake rate to grade 1, first reported in 2005, increased from 65% to 69% by 2015 (Indicator 4).
- The primary gross enrolment ratio increased from 99% in 2000 to 103% in 2015 (Indicator 5).
- The primary net enrolment rate increased from 83% in 2000 to 89% in 2015, with the adjusted net enrolment rate – on which the out-of-school children indicator is based – being two percentage points higher (Indicator 6/MDG indicator 2.1).
- The number of out-of-school children decreased from 101 million in 2000 to 62 million in 2015. All the decline had been realized by 2008; progress stalled thereafter.
- The gross intake ratio to the last grade of primary school increased from 82% in 2000 to 90% in 2015. But using household surveys, the report estimated that almost 100 million children had not completed primary school.

Youth and adult skills

'Goal 3. Ensuring that the learning needs of all young people and adults are met through equitable access to appropriate learning and life skills programmes.'

- No indicators were specified for this goal. The report regularly reported on the lower secondary gross enrolment ratio, on the assumption that this level of education was necessary to build foundation skills. The ratio increased from 72% in 2000 to 85% in 2015.

Adult literacy

'Goal 4. Achieving a 50 per cent improvement in levels of adult literacy by 2015, especially for women, and equitable access to basic and continuing education for all adults.'

- The youth literacy rate increased from 87% in 2000 to 91% in 2015. The number of illiterate youths fell from 144 million to 104 million (Indicator 16/MDG indicator 2.3).
- The adult literacy rate increased from 81% in 2000 to 86% in 2015. The number of illiterate adults fell from 786 million to 753 million (Indicator 17).
- The youth literacy gender parity index (GPI) increased from 0.93 in 2000 to 0.97. The adult literacy GPI increased from 0.88 to 0.92 (Indicator 18).

Gender equality

'Goal 5. Eliminating gender disparities in primary and secondary education by 2005, and achieving gender equality in education by 2015, with a focus on ensuring girls' full and equal access to and achievement in basic education of good quality.'

- Using the gross enrolment ratio as the basis, the primary education GPI increased from 0.92 in 2000 to 0.95 in 2005 and 1.00 in 2015; the secondary education GPI increased from 0.92 in 2000 to 0.94 in 2005 and 0.99 in 2015; and the tertiary education GPI increased from 0.99 in 2000 to 1.05 in 2005 and 1.12 in 2015 (MDG indicator 3.1).

Quality of education

'Goal 6. Improving all aspects of the quality of education and ensuring excellence of all so that recognized and measurable learning outcomes are achieved by all, especially in literacy, numeracy and essential life skills.'

- The percentage of primary teachers who had the required academic qualifications was 97% in 2015 in 94 countries with data (Indicator 9).
- The percentage of primary teachers whose training met national standards increased from 85% in 2000 to 93% in 2015. In 21 countries with data, less than 75% of primary school teachers were trained to national standards (Indicator 10).
- The primary pupil/teacher ratio declined from 26.3:1 in 2000 to 23.1:1 in 2015. It declined in 81% out of the 151 countries with data (Indicator 11).
- The primary repetition rate fell from 5% in 2000 to 1.8% in 2015 (Indicator 12).
- The survival rate to the last grade of primary school increased from 76% in 2000 to 80% in 2015 (Indicator 13/MDG indicator 2.2).

BOX 7.1 (CONTINUED):

- No estimates were available for the coefficient of efficiency (intended number of pupil years needed for a cohort to complete the primary cycle as a percentage of the actual number of pupil years spent) (Indicator 14).
- A methodology for monitoring the percentage of children who reached grade 4 having mastered a set of nationally defined basic learning competences was not agreed upon during the EFA period. This indicator is almost identical to the global lead indicator for SDG 4, debated in recent years: a combination of the primary completion rate (SDG thematic indicator 4.1.4) and the proportion of students at the end of primary school reaching a minimum level of proficiency (SDG global indicator 4.1.1b). The 2012 *EFA Global Monitoring Report* suggested that 62% of the cohort of primary school children had reached this level; a subsequent estimate by the UIS lowered the figure to 44% (Indicator 15).

Financing education

- The share of education in gross domestic product increased, from 4.1% in 2000 to 4.8% in 2015 (Indicator 7).
- The share of education in total government expenditure changed little, from 13.6% in 2000 to 14% in 2015 (Indicator 8).

Overall, two key findings stand out. First, with respect to goal 2, after stagnant participation rates until 1997, the primary gross enrolment ratio, net enrolment rate and gross intake rate into the final grade picked up until 2008, after which progress stalled (**Figure 7.1a**). By contrast, with respect to goal 5, although the target of parity by 2005 was not achieved, progress was continuous throughout the 1990s and 2000s, with the result that parity was reached in 2009 in primary and secondary education and had almost been achieved in youth literacy by 2015. However, gender disparity remained in adult literacy, where 63% of illiterates were female, and reversed in tertiary education, where males became less likely to participate (**Figure 7.1b**).

Monitoring the EFA goals showed that a midterm review might be too late to determine whether targets would be reached. Under the 2030 Agenda for Sustainable Development, there is more systematic thinking, not limited to education, on how to address this weakness.

The GEM Report endeavours to highlight cumulative progress against an 'on-track' benchmark for selected indicators. For this purpose, children born between 2010 and 2014 may be considered the SDG generation. These years relate to key education milestones in an approximate but meaningful way. The oldest among this generation turned 5 in 2015, the last year before primary school entry age in many countries; in terms of the 2030 Agenda, they were expected to be in pre-primary education in the academic year at the start of the SDG period (2015–2030). The youngest turn 16 in 2030, potentially the latest age for timely completion of lower secondary schooling.

The SDG generation is thus bracketed by two educationally meaningful birth cohorts. This report largely relies on 2017 data, and the focus on the SDG generation is limited. A key question in the next few years will be how widespread primary school entry is in 2017–2019. If significant numbers of children in those entry cohorts do not start school, universal secondary completion by 2030 will be in grave danger; the world will be playing catch-up with SDG target 4.1 less than one-third of the way into the SDG period.

FIGURE 7.1:

Between 2000 and 2015, the world progressed steadily towards gender parity but not towards universal primary education completion

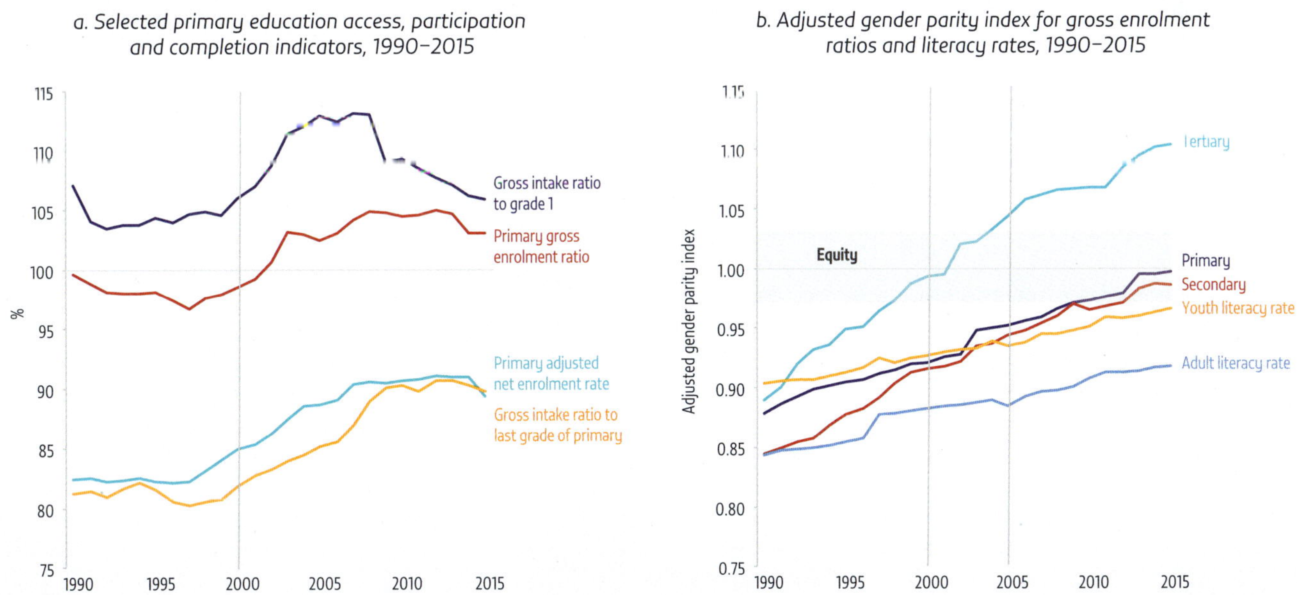

GEM StatLink: http://bit.ly/fig7_1
Source: UIS database.

DATA FOCUS 7.1: MONITORING THE EDUCATION STATUS OF MIGRANTS AND DISPLACED POPULATIONS PRESENTS NUMEROUS CHALLENGES

One overarching principle of the 2030 Agenda is to leave no one behind. Several population groups suffer disadvantages masked by outcome averages. The SDG monitoring framework, therefore, explicitly focuses on disaggregation of indicators by various characteristics historically associated with disadvantage. Target 4.5 and its global indicator do not list migration and displacement status among its examples. However, the 2030 Agenda foundation document recognized their relevance and made it explicit in SDG 17, target 17.18, which calls on donor countries to 'enhance capacity-building support to developing countries ... to increase significantly the availability of high-quality, timely and reliable data disaggregated by ... migratory status ... and other characteristics relevant in national contexts' (United Nations, 2015).

Yet, as evidenced throughout this report, systematic data on the education status of migrants and refugees are patchy, including in otherwise data-rich countries. In the World Bank's Microdata Catalogue, as of mid-2018, over 2,000 out of almost 2,500 household surveys include information on education, but only around one out of seven of those include migration, and only a small fraction of those include information on refugees and/or displacement (World Bank, 2018b).

> "Systematic data on the education status of migrants and refugees are patchy, including in otherwise data-rich countries"

Even where administrative data, household surveys or learning assessments are available, they are frequently limited due to the small number of migrants sampled, responding and asked comparable and meaningful questions concerning their potentially complex migration and education backgrounds. The very education indicators measured may take on a different meaning when applied to migrants. Does 'literacy' refer specifically to host country language(s)? Does literacy in a different script count? How are education qualifications or learning achievements in origin countries mapped on destination country categories?

MIGRANT AND DISPLACED POPULATIONS ARE OFTEN NOT EVEN RECOGNIZED

Central population registers can contain important information on population movements, especially concerning internal migration, but surveys are often necessary. Yet migrant households are mobile and less likely to be present for enumerator visits or interviews due to language barriers or legal concerns. Moreover, increasing the sample of the relatively few international migrants requires oversampling or add-on surveys targeting them. All approaches rely on including the relevant populations in sampling frames.

As migration flows can change rapidly, sampling frames may not keep up. For example, estimates of the number of Venezuelans who have left, in what has been called the 'fastest-escalating displacement of people across borders in Latin American history' can be very imprecise and requires a variety of sources to triangulate information (Freier and Parent, 2018). The United Nations has reported that 1.6 million people left the country since 2015 (ReliefWeb, 2018). In such circumstances, it is very difficult for receiving countries to adapt their data collection tools.

The problem particularly affects displaced populations. Data tend to be collected relatively systematically in refugee camps. However, less than 40% of refugees and even fewer internally displaced people (IDPs) reside in camps or collective centres (UNHCR, 2018). As camps often fall outside standard sampling frames, a key question is how to link their data with population register data. IDPs may be excluded outright from data monitoring systems or not identified. The Internal Displacement Monitoring Centre estimates there are 800,000 IDPs in Ukraine but recognizes that this figure reflects only those in government-controlled areas. Alternative UN estimates put the number at over 1 million (Englund, 2018).

MIGRATION FLOWS TEND TO BE TOO COMPLEX AND HETEROGENEOUS TO MONITOR

Migration and education are treated as statuses rather than processes in data collection. Both migration and education histories need to be queried retrospectively to gain a full understanding. This can be a complex and expensive enterprise, but there have been noteworthy recent initiatives. In 2017, with support from the World Bank, the Euro Asylum Seeker Survey randomly surveyed people in selected reception centres in Greece and Italy in six languages (Arabic, Bambara, English, Farsi, French and Tigrinya). The survey allowed comparisons among

> Data on displaced populations tend to be collected in camps, where less than 40% of refugees reside

asylum-seekers and with origin country populations. It used components of the OECD Programme for the International Assessment of Adult Competencies to assess literacy and numeracy skills (World Bank, 2018a). Among asylum-seekers with primary education, only 50% of those in Greece and 41% of those in Italy achieved the minimum proficiency level in literacy (**Figure 7.2**).

The sample was restricted to asylum-seekers in centres, thus excluding those living outside, earlier waves of arrivals, unaccompanied minors and those who did not complete their journeys. Even so, it found considerable heterogeneity, including significant variation in their journeys. Between 20% and 25% of respondents were 'secondary movers', who had previously settled or were born in other countries, such as the Islamic Republic of Iran or in Libya. Respondents came from countries for which asylum recognition rates ranged from less than 20% (such as Morocco, Lebanon and South Sudan) to more than 90% (Eritrea and the Syrian Arab Republic). Three-quarters of Afghan spouses were together in centres, compared with less than 10% of Eritreans. A significant minority appeared to have prepared for the journey by enrolling in language or other courses. Self-reported skills were found to be consistent with the educational attainment and assessed proficiency of recent migrants to European countries (World Bank, 2018a).

FIGURE 7.2:

Among asylum-seekers in Greece and Italy, about half of primary graduates lack minimum literacy skills

Literacy proficiency levels by education attainment level and country of asylum, 2017

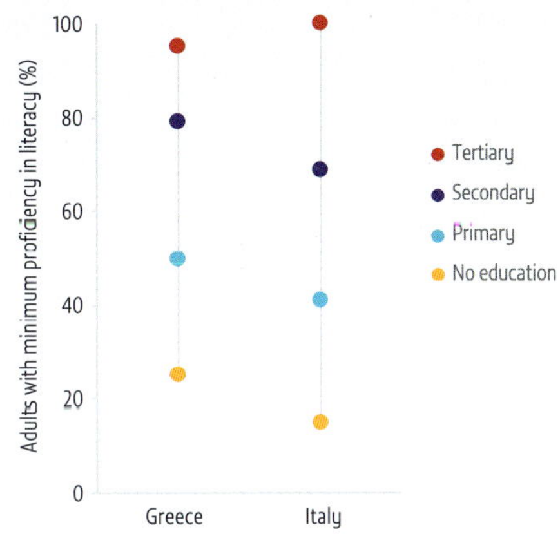

GEM StatLink: http://bit.ly/fig7_2
Source: World Bank (2018a).

FLEXIBLE APPROACHES TO SAMPLING MIGRANTS AND REFUGEES ARE NECESSARY BUT COSTLY

Ensuring inclusion of migrants and refugees in standard, general-purpose surveys is desirable but not always the best solution. In addition to the problem of targeting a sufficiently large sample size, standard surveys do not capture the dynamism of migration.

Research-focused surveys have been used to answer questions linking sending and receiving communities. The Mexican Migration Project has covered Mexico–US migration since 1982 and provides information on years of schooling completed and remittance expenditure on education. As of mid-2017, it included 161 communities and about 27,000 households, of which 4% were in the United States (Mexican Migration Project, 2018). Similarly, the Latin American Migration Project has collected data since 1998 on migration to the United States from Colombia, Costa Rica, the Dominican Republic, Ecuador, El Salvador, Guatemala, Haiti, Nicaragua, Paraguay, Peru and Puerto Rico (United States) (Arp-Nisen and Massey, 2006). The Migrations between Africa and Europe project studies migration between three sub-Saharan African countries (the Democratic Republic of the Congo, Ghana and Senegal) and Europe, including return migration, circulation and transnational practices (Beauchemin, 2012).

General-purpose surveys can also be too infrequent to generate timely information in crisis situations, which affect collection of relevant education data even in countries with high administrative and statistical capacity. Important lessons were learned from rapid data collection using alternative, non-random sampling approaches among recent arrivals in Austria and Germany. Comparisons between the non-random samples, representative samples and official data show that rapid assessments can be sufficiently accurate to provide preliminary policy guidance.

> Germany carries out a longitudinal study, which collects data twice a year in five states and is complemented by a central register of non-national residents

The Displaced Persons in Austria Survey researched emergency accommodation sites that had no resident lists. Comparisons found a good match with official statistics on the age and citizenship of asylum-seekers in Austria. Subsequent data from the national employment service confirmed that respondents' actual skills and qualifications largely matched self-reported academic or vocational education. Requiring school certificates would have underestimated attainment (Buber-Ennser et al., 2016).

Refugees in the German Educational System (ReGES) is a longitudinal study begun in July 2016. It is funded by the Federal Ministry of Education and Research and conducted on behalf of the Leibniz Institute for Educational Trajectories, which is also responsible for the German National Educational Panel Study. ReGES is carried out in five states and collects data twice per year. Focusing on education integration, it surveys teachers, social workers and volunteers, in addition to the 2,400 main participants, aged 4 and up or 14 and up, and their parents (LIfBI, 2016).

Germany also maintains a central register of non-national residents, including recognized refugees and asylum-seekers, which served as the sampling frame for a survey by the Federal Employment Agency, the Federal Office for Migration and Refugees and the German Socio-Economic Panel. Because asylum-seekers enter the register only once their application is officially submitted, staggered samples were drawn up to mid-2016 to capture all arrivals in the three years prior to January 2016. The survey is a panel study, with initial waves in 2016, 2017 and 2018. The first wave covered 4,800 adults in 3,500 households, with a response rate of 50%. An additional refreshment sample of 1,250 households was first surveyed in 2017 (DIW, 2017).

MEASUREMENT TOOLS NEED TO RECOGNIZE THE COMPLEXITY OF MIGRATION TRAJECTORIES

Education at time of survey is insufficient to understand the dynamics of education and migration. At a minimum, information is needed on whether qualifications were obtained before or after arrival. Where respondents have to express education qualifications in terms of host system categories, responses may be invalid and not comparable within or between countries.

One approach to this challenge is to consolidate information on national school systems and credentials. An example that can be embedded into various questionnaires is the Computer-Assisted Measurement and Coding of Educational Qualifications in Surveys (CAMCES) module, developed by GESIS – Leibniz Institute for the Social Sciences. It overcomes manual translation of qualification names by allowing respondents to report educational attainment in their own words and mapping the responses to the 1997 and 2011 International Standard Classification of Education codes. Standardizing and automating data collection, coding and harmonization, together with better coverage of foreign, rare or outdated qualifications, promises more accurate data. As of October 2017, CAMCES contained some 2,100 education qualifications and more than 1,000 alternative expressions, covering nearly all European countries and the origin countries of the largest migrant and refugee groups in Germany (SERISS, 2018).

Existing instruments can also be adapted. Even seemingly small wording changes in migration-related questions can affect responses. After a change to place of birth questions on the OECD Programme of International Student Assessment (PISA) survey from 'inside/outside' the assessment country to a list of countries, non-response to the item jumped from 1.7% to 7.9% in Germany but dropped from 5% to 0.4% in Japan (Richardson and Ali, 2014). While these are outliers, answers to questions that do not account for non-response can affect conclusions about the prevalence of various immigrant backgrounds. The 2018 PISA will ask in detail whether students speak something other than the test language with various members of their families and social circles (OECD and GEMR, 2018).

> The World Bank is supporting adaptation of regular household surveys in Africa and southern Asia to embed questions particularly relevant to non-nationals, including refugees

The World Bank is supporting adaptation of regular household surveys in Africa and southern Asia to embed questions particularly relevant to non-nationals, including refugees, and integrating registers of the office of the United Nations High Commissioner for Refugees (UNHCR) into sampling frames. This initiative builds on a successful adaptation of the 2017/18 Jordanian Household Expenditure and Income Survey (Carletto, 2018).

MIGRATION QUESTIONS ARE BEING FURTHER STANDARDIZED AND MAINSTREAMED

Recent initiatives seek to coordinate collection of data relating to education for migrants and the displaced. The International Organization for Migration (IOM) is collaborating with UNICEF, UNHCR, Eurostat and the OECD to close data gaps that 'leave migrant, refugee and displaced children in danger and without access to basic services' (UNICEF et al., 2018). The IOM's Global Migration Data Analysis Centre does not publish displacement-specific education data, but its Displacement Tracking Matrix, which includes education elements, is being improved and used in an increasing number of countries (Englund, 2018).

In March 2016, the UN Statistical Commission supported the establishment of an Expert Group on Refugee and IDP Statistics. With representation from 50 member states and concerned agencies, it is led by Statistics Norway, Eurostat and UNHCR. Its draft recommendations include (a) collecting demographic data on refugees and persons with refugee backgrounds, (b) including refugees in national statistical systems (civil registration, administrative data, surveys, censuses) and (c) including indicators on living conditions, socio-economic factors and integration measures. It also recommends reporting on education for refugees, including participation in school and pre-school, as well as educational attainment, literacy and numeracy, years spent out of education between ages 5 and 16, host country language proficiency and participation in language courses, and support received for integration into host school systems, in line with recognized best practice (UN Statistical Commission, 2018).

School censuses are rarely designed to cope with large movements of people. Refugee Education Management Information System is a free, open-source, web-based tool being developed by UNESCO and UNHCR to help countries collect, compile, analyse and report refugee education data. It was initially tested and piloted in the United Republic of Tanzania in 2017 and Rwanda in 2018. Rollouts are under way in Kenya, South Sudan, Sudan and Uganda, with at least 10 more countries to follow by early 2019. It is intended not as a parallel system but rather integrated into or at least linked with national systems (UNHCR, 2018).

CONCLUSION

The initiatives and innovative approaches described above are highly welcome and make important contributions to understanding the education of migrants and displaced people around the world. At the same time, they often serve to highlight monitoring complexities. Migrants and refugees are an extremely heterogeneous group in terms of identity, journeys and legal status. There is no one solution to the measurement challenges, and global monitoring of migration and education will no doubt remain a patchwork of approaches for some time.

Teacher and schoolchildren outside of their school centre in Honduras.

CREDIT: Save the Children

KEY MESSAGES

There were 64 million out-of-school children of primary school age in 2017, which means their number stalled for a tenth year in a row.

Using 2013–2017 data, completion rates were 85% for primary education, 73% for lower secondary and 49% for upper secondary.

This GEM Report is proposing a new model to use survey and census data more efficiently to project completion rates to the most recent year.

To achieve universal secondary school completion by 2030, all children need to enrol in primary school by 2018, yet the intake rate in low income countries was 73% in 2016.

In total, 387 million or 56% of children of primary school age and 230 million or 61% of adolescents of lower secondary school age did not reach the minimum proficiency level in reading. A new proposal has been made for the minimum proficiency level for this indicator.

Data over 15 years from a survey of grade 4 students' reading skills, suggest that middle income countries have progressed towards meeting the minimum benchmark by about one percentage point per year, on average, which means they are not likely to meet the target by 2030.

Citizen-led assessments and a new module in the UNICEF Multiple Indicator Cluster Surveys offer valuable insights into the learning achievements of children not in school.

The rights granted by non-discrimination conventions do not guarantee migrant children's right to education in practice. Rigid documentation requirements, whether legally required or arbitrarily imposed by local gatekeepers, can prevent access.

CHAPTER 8

TARGET 4.1

Primary and secondary education

By 2030, ensure that all girls and boys complete free, equitable and quality primary and secondary education leading to relevant and effective learning outcomes

GLOBAL INDICATOR

4.1.1 – *Proportion of children and young people (a) in Grade 2 or 3; (b) at the end of primary education; and (c) at the end of lower secondary education achieving at least a minimum proficiency level in (i) reading and (ii) mathematics, by sex*

THEMATIC INDICATORS

4.1.2 – *Administration of a nationally-representative learning assessment (a) in Grade 2 or 3; (b) at the end of primary education; and (c) at the end of lower secondary education*

4.1.3 – *Gross intake ratio to the last grade (primary education, lower secondary education)*

4.1.4 – *Completion rate (primary education, lower secondary education, upper secondary education)*

4.1.5 – *Out-of-school rate (primary education, lower secondary education, upper secondary education)*

4.1.6 – *Percentage of children over-age for grade (primary education, lower secondary education)*

4.1.7 – *Number of years of (a) free and (b) compulsory primary and secondary education guaranteed in legal frameworks*

Despite the SDG 4's decisive turn to include learning outcome indicators, the international community also set ambitious targets on secondary education participation and completion. Notwithstanding these objectives, the EFA goal to ensure all children attend and complete primary school by 2015 was not attained. Vulnerable populations around the world, including migrants and refugees, continue to be denied the very right to education (**Policy focus 8.1**).

Timely entry can remain below 100% even when primary completion is universal, as in upper middle and high income countries, where the adjusted net intake rate has remained constant at around 90%. The remaining 10% may be enrolled in pre-primary schooling or enter later. But progress in low income countries has stalled in recent years at 72% (**Figure 8.1**). To achieve universal secondary school completion by 2030, the intake rate of the 2018 cohort in all countries needs to at least match the current intake rates of middle and high income countries.

The number of those out-of-school has also stalled since 2008, at 64 million (9%) for children of primary school age, 61 million for adolescents of lower secondary school age (16%), and 138 million (36%) for youth of upper secondary school age (**Table 8.1**). The total out of school population in 2017 was 262 million. These numbers include those who miss out on schooling completely, delay entry or drop out. With the stall in timely entry in low income countries, no decisive drop in the out-of-school rate can be expected in the coming years. Overall, the out-of-school rates remain stubbornly high in sub-Saharan Africa. Since 2000, the region has accounted for an increasing share of out-of-school populations (**Figure 8.2**).

> To achieve universal secondary school completion by 2030, all children need to enrol in primary school by 2018, yet the intake rate in low income countries was 73% in 2016

FIGURE 8.1:

Fewer than three out of four children begin school on time in low income countries

Adjusted net intake rate to the first grade of primary school by country income group, 2000–2016

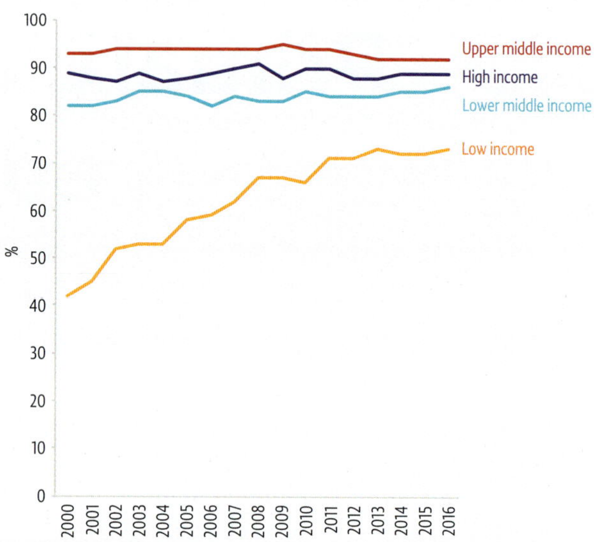

GEM StatLink: http://bit.ly/fig8_1
Source: UIS database.

According to the gross intake ratio to the last grade of each cycle, which relies on administrative data, 90% of children reached the end of primary education in 2017. This figure has not increased since 2008. About 76%

TABLE 8.1:
Selected indicators on school participation, 2017 or most recent year

	Out of school, 2017 (%)			Out of school, 2017 (million)		
	Primary	Lower secondary	Upper secondary	Primary	Lower secondary	Upper secondary
World	**9**	**16**	**36**	**64**	**61**	**138**
Sub-Saharan Africa	21	36	57	34	27	36
Northern Africa and Western Asia	10	14	32	6	4	9
Central and Southern Asia	6	17	47	12	19	67
Eastern and South-eastern Asia	4	9	19	7	8	16
Oceania	9	4	23	0.4	0.1	0.4
Latin America and the Caribbean	5	7	23	3	3	7
Europe and Northern America	3	2	7	2	1	2
Low income countries	20	36	60	24	21	27
Lower middle income countries	10	18	45	31	31	87
Upper middle income countries	4	7	21	7	8	21
High income countries	3	2	6	2	1	3

Source: UIS database.

> Since 2000, sub-Saharan Africa has accounted for an increasing share of out-of-school populations

reached the end of lower secondary education. According to 2013–2017 household survey data, completion rates were 85% for primary, 73% for lower secondary and 49% for upper secondary education (**Table 8.2**). One reason survey-based completion rate estimates may be lower than gross intake ratios is that the survey data were conducted on average a few years before the data collected by school censuses. This report proposes a new method to correct for the issue (**Data focus 8.1**).

The proposed amendments to the completion rate estimates could be combined with global indicator 4.1.1, which monitors the percentage of students who achieve minimum proficiency in learning outcomes at three points in their education trajectory but ignores those who have left school before completing, to describe the achievement of the entire cohort.

FIGURE 8.2:
Sub-Saharan Africa has a growing share of the global out-of-school population
Distribution of out-of-school populations by region, 2000–2015

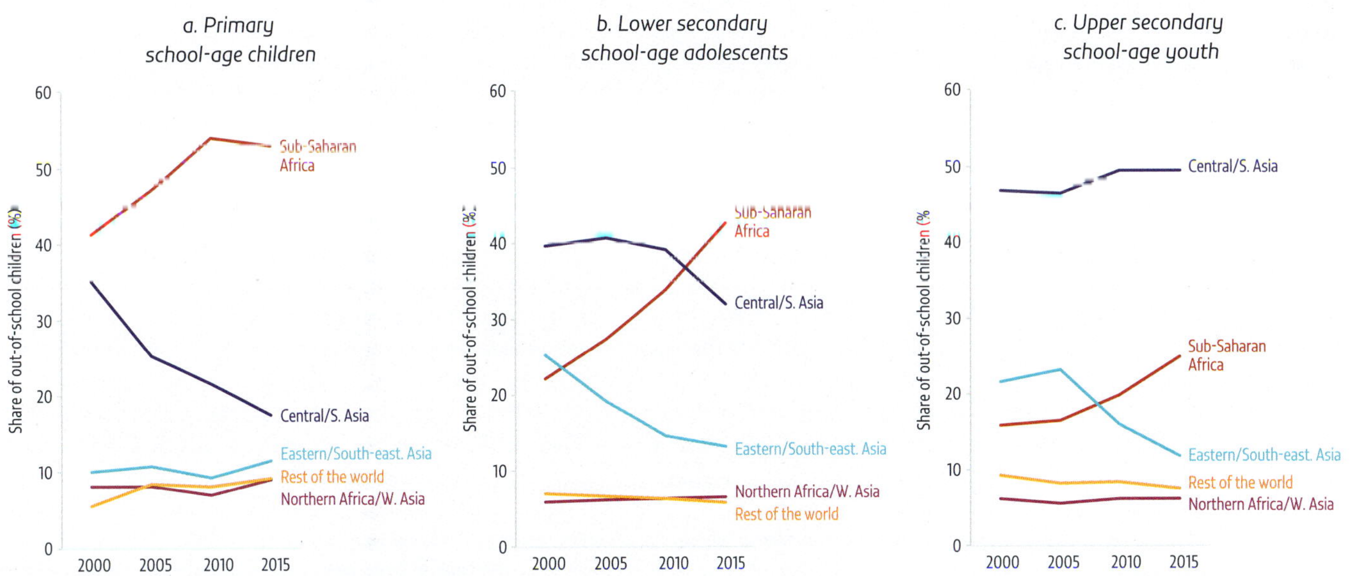

GEM StatLink: http://bit.ly/fig8_2
Source: UIS database.

TABLE 8.2:
Selected indicators related to school completion, 2017 or most recent year

	Completion rate, 2013–2017 (%)			Gross intake ratio to the last grade of cycle, 2017 (%)	
	Primary	Lower secondary	Upper secondary	Primary	Lower secondary
World	**85**	**73**	**49**	**90**	**76**
Sub-Saharan Africa	64	37	27	69	43
Northern Africa and Western Asia	84	74	39	87	73
Central and Southern Asia	89	77	40	96	82
Eastern and South-eastern Asia	95	79	58	97	90
Oceania	…	…	…	94	78
Latin America and the Caribbean	91	81	62	98	79
Europe and Northern America	99	98	87	97	91
Low income countries	59	32	18	66	41
Lower middle income countries	85	71	41	93	77
Upper middle income countries	96	84	60	95	87
High income countries	99	97	86	98	92

Note: (…) means that data are not available.
Sources: UIS database for gross intake ratio to the last grade based on administrative data; UIS and GEM Report team calculations for completion rates based on household survey data.

With respect to indicator 4.1.1, the main new results to be published by a cross-national school-based learning assessment in the past year were those of the Progress in International Reading Literacy Study (PIRLS), which assesses grade 4 students (IEA, 2017). The survey takes place every five years. In the Islamic Republic of Iran, the percentage of grade 4 students who met the low benchmark increased from 56% in 2001 to 65% in 2016, a growth of less than a percentage point per year. Some countries, such as Morocco or Oman, improved at a rate five times faster between 2011 and 2016, which could bring them within reach of the target by 2030. But more data points would be needed to confirm if such progress rates can be sustained. Other countries, such as Azerbaijan and Saudi Arabia, saw the share of students achieving minimum proficiency fall. In South Africa, only 22% of grade 4 students meet the minimum level (**Figure 8.3**).

> “The Progress in International Reading Literacy Study (PIRLS), showed improvements in learning in some countries, but levels fell in others”

Considering that a proposal was put forward for the PIRLS low benchmark to be among those that will form the international benchmark for indicator 4.1.1b, the data are a stark reminder that it would be very hard to meet the target by 2030.

In the past year, the UNESCO Institute for Statistics (UIS), through the work of the Global Alliance to Monitor Learning, has pursued three alternative linking methodologies, both statistical and non-statistical strategies, to improve the comparability of different learning achievement data sources (UIS, 2018).

First, countries that took part in more than one assessment can provide entry points for comparability. However, assessments vary in domains assessed, age range, conditions under which assessments were taken and, not least, students assessed. To address this challenge, a new initiative in 2019 will see students from about three countries each from Latin America (which took part in the Third Regional Comparative and Explanatory Study; TERCE) and West Africa (which took part in the Programme d'Analyse des Systèmes Educatifs de la CONFEMEN; PASEC) sitting both for the new rounds of their respective surveys and for an IEA-administered survey, like PIRLS. This approach, which has become informally known as 'Rosetta stone', will enable more

FIGURE 8.3:

Several countries are not on track to meet minimum learning benchmarks by 2030

Percentage of grade 4 students above the PIRLS low benchmark, selected countries, 2001–2016

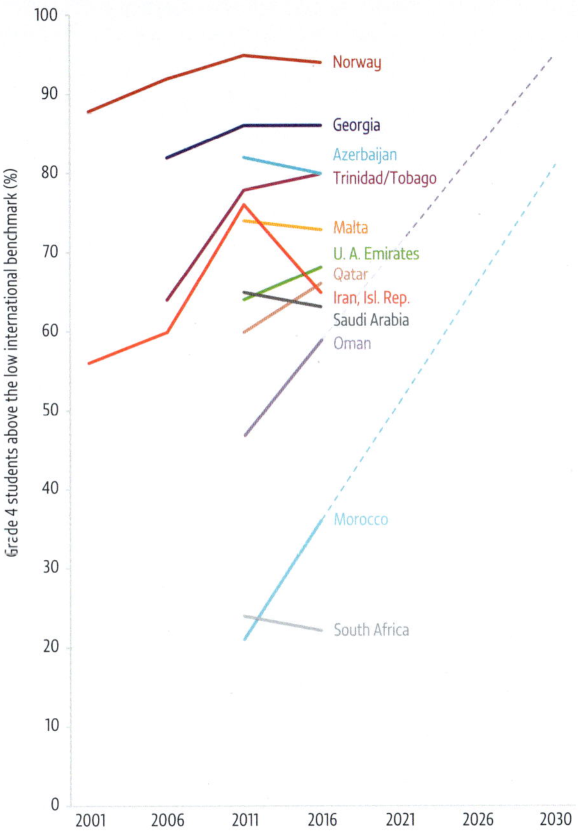

GEM StatLink: http://bit.ly/fig8_3

Note: Selected countries include those where, in any year, fewer than 90% of students were above the low benchmark.

Source: IEA and UNESCO (2017).

robust comparisons across surveys, which cover a large part of the world (IEA, 2018).

Second, linking the main cross-national assessments leaves out countries that do not take part but would like to contribute data from national assessments or other sources to the global indicator (**Box 8.1** and **Box 8.2**). An extensive development programme has seen the UIS, with the support of technical partners, develop a mapping of the content of different assessments and a reporting scale. The next stage is to use expert judgement to moderate items from different surveys and assign them a level of difficulty that would help interpret the proficiency level. This approach is also being used to decide how minimum proficiency levels defined by different cross-national assessments (e.g. the PIRLS low benchmark) can be linked to define an international minimum proficiency level.

Third, in the meantime, efforts continue to link the different proficiency scales into a common standard using statistical techniques. According to the latest estimates, 387 million or 56% of children of primary school age did not reach the minimum proficiency level in reading. This was the case with 81% of children in Central and Southern Asia and 87% of children in sub-Saharan Africa but only 7% of children in Europe and Northern America. In addition, 230 million or 61% of adolescents of lower secondary school age did not reach the minimum proficiency level in reading. Similar estimates apply for minimum learning proficiency in mathematics (UIS, 2017b).

> “387 million or 56% of children of primary school age did not reach the minimum proficiency level in reading”

DATA FOCUS 8.1: ESTIMATING COMPLETION RATES FOR THE EDUCATION 2030 AGENDA

SDG target 4.1 on education completion and target 4.5 on equal access increased interest in using household survey or census data to monitor education indicators. Indeed, there is no alternative for some indicators, such as completion rates for specific population groups, since administrative data on graduates by age or other population characteristics are rarely available.

Survey data bring their own challenges. Most surveys are conducted every three to five years and the results released at least one year later, generating a considerable time lag.

For several indicators, multiple surveys are available and may provide conflicting information. The 2016 *Global Education Monitoring Report* raised the question

BOX 8.1:

Citizen-led assessments continue to evolve

Citizen-led and household-based assessments, as pioneered in India by the non-government organization Pratham almost 15 years ago, have offered valuable insights in measuring the learning achievement of different population groups, including those not in school. A recent longitudinal study in India showed that one out of three children who dropped out between grades 8 and 9 had been able to read a grade 2 level text compared with two-thirds of those who remained enrolled (ASER, 2018; Ramanujan and Deshpande, 2018).

The assessments continue to expand and develop conceptually. For the first time, a pilot citizen-led assessment was conducted in Afghanistan in 2018 (PAL Network, 2018). Under the umbrella of the People's Action for Learning network, such assessments exist in 13 countries and the UIS has recognized citizen-led assessments as a potentially valid data source for indicator 4.1.1a.

While such assessments routinely target children up to age 16, a citizen-led assessment was organized for the first time in India sampling 14- to 18-year-olds (ASER, 2018). The survey aimed to assess the interaction between basic skills and real-life applications. In literacy, while 75% of participants demonstrated basic skills, just over half could correctly interpret instructions on a packet of oral rehydration solution. In numeracy, basic skills are insufficient even for activities involved in simple construction or service jobs. Between one-quarter and one-half of respondents who could divide two numbers could not calculate or tell time, measure lengths or add weights (**Figure 8.4**).

FIGURE 8.4:

In India, even youth with basic numeracy skills cannot perform simple daily tasks needed at work

Percentage of 14- to 18-year-olds who can perform specific tasks, by level of numeracy proficiency, India, 2017

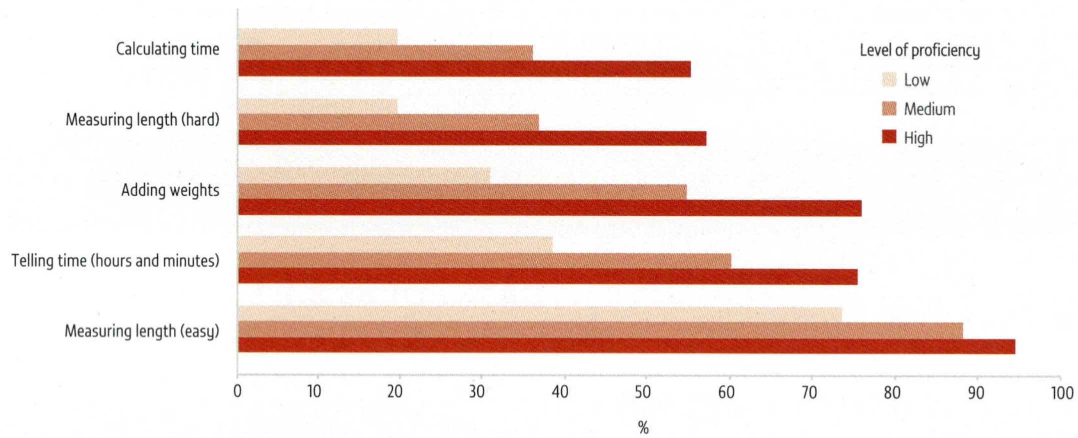

GEM StatLink: http://bit.ly/fig8_4

Note: The level of proficiency is defined as low if the respondent at most recognizes two-digit numbers, medium if the respondent can at most subtract two-digit numbers, and high if the respondent can at most divide a three-digit by a single-digit number. The task of measuring length is described as easy if an object was placed at the '0' mark on the ruler and hard if it was placed elsewhere on the ruler.

Source: ASER (2018).

of reconciling the different sources, for instance the MICS and the Demographic and Health Survey (DHS), two of the main sources of such information (UNESCO, 2016). Averaging estimates or fitting a simple trend to these estimates directly ignores relevant information. Some sources may systematically result in lower or higher estimates relative to others, reflecting differences in sampling frames or how questions are asked. Some sources may show greater variability due to small sample size or other, non-statistical issues that make them less reliable. Some respondents provide information retrospectively and the time that has lapsed increases the risk of errors that need to be corrected.

The international health community faced a similar challenge in measuring indicators based on multiple sources. The UN Inter-agency Group for Child Mortality Estimation adopted a consensus model to generate annual estimates for under 5 (Alkema and New, 2012) and neonatal mortality in each member state (Alexander and

BOX 8.2:

A new source of learning outcomes data – the MICS 6 foundational learning module

The sixth round of the UNICEF Multiple Indicator Cluster Survey (MICS) includes, among other innovations, two relevant new modules, a child functioning module (**Chapter 12**) and a foundational learning module. The learning module aims to capture the literacy and numeracy skills of children aged 7 to 14, in line with global indicator 4.1.1 (UNICEF, 2017). As of mid-2018, about 50 of the surveys under the current MICS 6 round are expected to include the module.

MICS randomly selects and directly assesses one child in each household. The reading assessment includes reading a story, three literal comprehension questions and two inferential comprehension questions. To ensure relevance and cultural appropriateness, the vocabulary presented corresponds to a reading textbook of the country. The numeracy assessment includes number reading, number discrimination, addition, as well as pattern recognition and completion. The numeracy questions are based on the universal skills expected for that level. For both reading and numeracy, children have foundational skills when they can correctly answer all components of the corresponding assessment.

The first two first reports of countries that signed up for the learning module were published in 2018. In the Democratic People's Republic of Korea, about 95% of 7- to 14-year-olds have foundational reading skills, while 82% have foundational numeracy skills (CBS and UNICEF, 2018). In Sierra Leone, the corresponding shares were 16% and 12% respectively. Only 39% of 7- to 14-year olds could read words in a story and just 34% could read numbers (Statistics Sierra Leone, 2018) (**Figure 8.5**).

FIGURE 8.5:

Only one in six children in Sierra Leone had foundational literacy skills

Percentage of 7- to 14-year-olds with foundational reading and numeracy skills, Sierra Leone, 2017

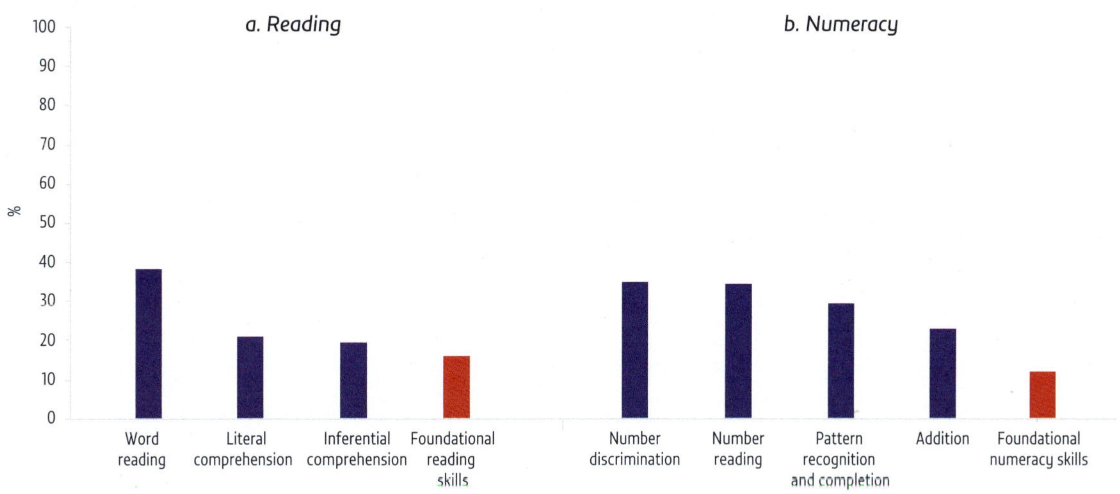

GEM StatLink: http://bit.ly/fig8_5

Source: Statistics Sierra Leone (2018).

Alkema, 2018). The United Nations Maternal Mortality Estimation Inter-agency Group followed a similar process (Alkema et al., 2016).

Although a sophisticated solution, offering valuable guidance for estimating education completion rates, statistical models from one domain should never be applied blindly to another. For instance, even high levels of maternal mortality represent a statistically small proportion of all births. By contrast, completion rates range from near zero to near universal, especially in primary or among specific populations. Likewise, various decisions in developing the health models were based on empirical observations of patterns in mortality, which is not relevant for completion rates. Also important, the availability in some countries of high-quality administrative data registering deaths provided a benchmark against which surveys' statistical bias could be assessed; no equivalent benchmark is available for completion rates.

> The GEM Report is proposing a new approach to estimate completion rates, using a model that reconciles data from multiple surveys

Based on these considerations, the GEM Report team developed a similar model to estimate completion rates, validated the results and provided illustrative estimates (UNESCO, 2018). The approach presents a number of potential advantages. Projecting completion rates of older cohorts backwards can provide a long-term view of the expansion path of primary, lower secondary and upper secondary completion rates. The current level of the indicator can be estimated with a short-term extrapolation from the most recent data using all available information. A plausible current estimate can therefore be reported even if the last survey occurred some years ago, which addresses a key criticism of survey-based estimates. Moreover, there is no need to choose among conflicting figures. The current estimate is more consistent with overall patterns and trends across data sources instead of accepting the latest available estimate at face value.

An example from Mali combines the evidence from five household surveys since 2001, which enables the primary completion rate to be estimated all the way back to the early 1980s but also a current value to be projected although the last survey was carried out in 2015, when the completion rate was estimated at 49%. Two projections are possible. One projects the completion rate indicator, which is defined over the age group of 15–17-year-olds; it estimates that the completion rate in 2018 was 56%. The other accounts for late completion, beyond the age of 15 and 16 years, to estimate the completion rate for the cohort, which is about two to three percentage points higher (**Figure 8.6**).

The results represent a first step towards a consistent series of completion rates using survey data. The next step is recommending the method to the Technical Cooperation Group as the basis to report on the completion rate thematic indicator. With further refinements, it should also be possible to calculate consistent completion rate series disaggregated by some individual characteristics.

FIGURE 8.6:

Primary completion rates have accelerated rapidly in Mali since the late 1990s

Actual, fitted and projected primary completion rate, Mali, 1983–2019

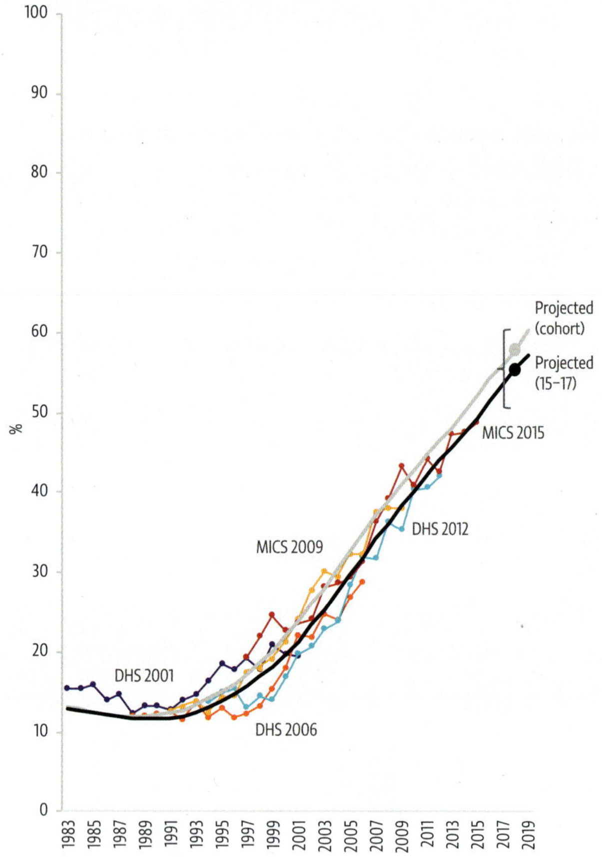

GEM StatLink: http://bit.ly/fig8_6
Source: GEM Report team calculations based on five different household surveys.

The results could also be used to improve calculating the percentage of all children, rather than just students, who meet minimum proficiency in reading and mathematics. Measurement currently combines two components: the percentage of children in school and the percentage of those achieving minimum levels on an assessment (UIS, 2017a). In the new estimate, the completion rate, showing the percentage of children who reach the end of primary or lower secondary, would replace the first component.

> Despite commitments to non-discrimination, the right to education is often conditional on citizenship and/or legal residency status

POLICY FOCUS 8.1: RECOGNIZING THE RIGHT TO EDUCATION OF MIGRANTS, ASYLUM-SEEKERS, REFUGEES AND STATELESS PERSONS

Even countries offering at least nine years of free, compulsory education, in line with the Education 2030 Framework for Action, do not necessarily extend that right to migrants and refugees, either in principle or in practice. Despite treaty commitments to non-discrimination, making the right to education conditional on citizenship and/or legal residency status is perhaps the most common explicit exclusion in constitutions or education legislation. Even in the absence of such conditions, many migrants are prevented from realizing the right through requirements to prove their status in order to enrol. Legal provisions explicitly prohibiting discrimination against migrants in the education sector are the strongest protection against such exclusion.

THE PRINCIPLE OF NON-DISCRIMINATION GUARANTEES THE RIGHT TO EDUCATION

Migrants, internally displaced people, refugees, asylum-seekers and stateless persons are protected through human rights principles of equality and non-discrimination. The general non-discrimination principle is affirmed in legally binding human rights instruments that guarantee the right to education, including the Convention on the Rights of the Child; the International Covenant on Economic, Social and Cultural Rights; the Convention on the Elimination of All Forms of Racial Discrimination; and the UNESCO Convention against Discrimination in Education. Although legal and migration status have not been explicitly included in the language of these treaties, the Committee on Economic, Social and Cultural Rights confirms that 'the principle of non-discrimination extends to all persons of school age residing in the territory of a State party, including non-nationals, and irrespective of their legal status' (CESCR, 1999) and that 'all children within a State, including those with an undocumented status, have a right to receive education' (CESCR, 2009).

Migration-specific international treaties confirm migrants and especially refugees as rights holders, to be treated akin to nationals in education. The 1951 Convention relating to the Status of Refugees states that refugees should have the same benefits as nationals, including recognition of foreign education credentials, and financial support and remission of fees (Art. 22) (UN General Assembly, 1951). The 1954 Convention relating to the Status of Stateless Persons maintains that states 'shall accord to stateless persons the same treatment as is accorded to nationals with respect to elementary education' (UN General Assembly, 1954).

Such references specifically to primary education reflect a time when secondary education was rarely a right even for nationals. However, the committee overseeing the International Convention on the Protection of the Rights of All Migrant Workers and Members of Their Families clarified that 'whenever children who are nationals have access to free secondary education, State parties must ensure equal access by children of migrant workers, irrespective of their migration status' (Art. 75) (CMW, 2013).

> Although all countries have ratified an international treaty that includes a right to education, only 82% of national constitutions contain the provision

The plight of the Rohingya highlights the importance of these treaties. Bangladesh, Malaysia and Thailand have not ratified key treaty commitments to non-discrimination. Without this legal status and protection, Rohingya children are often denied access to education. Due to protracted statelessness, Rohingya children in Malaysia do not satisfy state-funded school registration requirements; those who do cannot sit examinations granting access to secondary (RTEI, 2018).

MIGRANTS ARE INCLUDED AND EXCLUDED IN NATIONAL LEGISLATION

Although all countries have ratified an international treaty that includes a right to education, only 82% of national constitutions contain the provision. Even then, education rights are not always justiciable or legally enforceable (RTE Project, 2017). Moreover, some constitutions limit the right to education to citizens, as in China and Greece, for instance (RTEI, 2018).

In some countries, laws that more explicitly deny rights for undocumented migrants may undermine a constitutional right to education (**Chapter 3**). In Europe, despite constitutional provisions in Bulgaria, Finland, Hungary, Latvia and Lithuania establishing a right to education, other laws exclude undocumented migrants. In South Africa, the constitution and national education legislation guarantee the right to education for all children, irrespective of migration or legal status. However, the 2002 Immigration Act prevents undocumented migrants from enrolling. Provisional registration is allowed without documents, but this rule tends to be ignored (Spreen and Vally, 2012).

In Cyprus and Slovakia, schools are obliged to report families without valid documentation to immigration authorities. In the Netherlands, specific legislation prevents schools checking whether migrants have regular status until they are age 18 (Spencer and Hughes, 2015).

The Australian Benefit Entitlement Act links access to education to legal residency status, contributing 'to a precarious situation for undocumented migrants and rejected asylum seekers' (CESCR, 2017). Barbados' Education Act 'limits the awards of bursaries, grants, awards and scholarships' even when migrant children are legal residents (CMW and CRC, 2017).

Conversely, legislation that expressly affirms the education rights of migrants, refugees or stateless populations increases the likelihood that the right to education will be fulfilled. For instance, according to the Russian Federation's Constitution (§43) and education law (§78), every child has the right to education. Foreign citizens, including recognized refugees, and stateless persons enjoy equal rights to free public pre-school, primary basic and general secondary.

Having said that, stateless children are often unable to obtain primary education because they lack the requested documents to register for school (RTEI, 2018).

In Argentina, many undocumented migrants became regular through the 2004 migration law and subsequent Patria Grande programme of regularization (Cortes, 2017). The migration law states that 'under no circumstances shall the irregular status of an immigrant prevent his or her admission as a student to an educational institution, whether public or private, national, provincial or municipal, primary, secondary, tertiary or university' (RTEI, 2018).

The National Policy for Internally Displaced Persons identifies the right of displaced children to 'the same access to education as children elsewhere in Uganda'. Uganda's policy further requires 'special efforts' to ensure full and equal participation in education by internally displaced women and girls (RTEI, 2018).

FULFILLING MIGRANTS' RIGHT TO EDUCATION FACES IMPLEMENTATION OBSTACLES

While an inclusive legal framework is important, it does not necessarily prevent regional or local discriminatory practices in many countries. School heads are key gatekeepers, deciding who gets through the door. Enrolment may require national identification papers, proof of residency, birth certificates or prior education credentials.

> "Regional or local discriminatory practices in many countries can contradict inclusive legal frameworks"

Many children of migrants, refugees and asylum-seekers lacking documents required for enrolment cannot access education facilities in Egypt, the Islamic Republic of Iran, Iraq, Jordan, Lebanon and Turkey (Equal Rights Trust, 2017).

In Spain, despite constitutional protection and Law No. 2 of 2009 explicitly extending the right to education to all legal and illegal migrants and asylum-seekers, children have been denied access due to lack of a valid passport or identity card. In addition, linking the right to education to participation in the municipal census prevents those without legal residency in the corresponding address from realizing their right to education (RTEI, 2018).

In the Russian Federation, several school head teachers and local authorities interpreted Order No. 32 of the Ministry of Education of 2014 as requiring proof of legal right to residency to enrol (Leech, 2017). While children of regular Kyrgyz migrants have access to education since Kyrgyzstan acceded to the Eurasian Economic Union in 2015, the undocumented majority are not covered (FIDH, 2016). School officials in Uzbekistan also often require proof of residency, a passport or command of the national language before enrolment (RTEI, 2018).

Requiring birth registration or national education credentials has been highlighted as discriminatory practice by the Committee on Migrant Workers and the Committee on the Rights of the Child, which recommend that 'States should put in place adequate measures to recognize the child's former education by acknowledging previously obtained school certificates and/or issuing new certification based on the child's capacities and capabilities' (CMW and CRC, 2017).

School gatekeepers insisting on complete documentation before enrolling migrant children may believe the law requires them to do so. Official clarification and reassurance can be helpful in overcoming such misinterpretations.

In 2014, Italy and Turkey clarified that documentation was not obligatory for enrolment. In Italy, guidelines laid out by the Ministry of Education, University and Research stated that no child should be barred from enrolling due to lack of residency documentation (RTEI, 2018) and that schools are not required to inform immigration authorities (Delvino and Spencer, 2014). A judgement from the Italian Council of State clarified that those without a residency permit may continue their education beyond age 18 to complete secondary school (Italy Council of State, 2014). In Turkey, a new regulation removed restrictions requiring Syrian children to produce a Turkish residency permit prior to enrolment.

A strong national legal framework may further provide formal institutions or avenues to address education rights violations by gatekeepers overstepping their authority, as demonstrated in France (**Box 8.3**).

BOX 8.3:

France provides legal remedies against violation of the right to education

In France, mayors are responsible for pre-primary and primary school registration. Some have refused to register children unable to prove legal residency in the municipality. Doing so is in violation of French law, which clearly states that lack of residency is not grounds for restricted access. In 2016, a circular by the Ministry of Education highlights that enrolment of foreign pupils in a school, whatever their age, cannot be made conditional on the submission of a residence permit. A 2017 addition to the education code further states that the status and housing arrangement of families living in a municipality cannot be valid grounds to refuse admission (RTEI, 2018).

Using this strong legal foundation, parents have various means of challenging discriminatory enrolment decisions. They can refer the case to the ombudsman, a non-jurisdictional, independent authority defending people's rights. The ombudsman has the power of inquiry and intervention respecting discrimination in school registration. In 2017, the ombudsman reprimanded a mayor in the Hauts-de-Seine department for refusing to enrol a student on the basis of origin (France Human Rights Defender, 2017). Judicial appeal is another avenue. The courts have the power to reverse the decision or sanction the violating party. In 2016, a court in Lille ordered a commune a commune to enrol a child, subject to a daily fine of EUR 1,500 (Administrative Tribunal of Lille, 2016). In 2016, the court fined the commune of Ris-Orangis for failing to register foreign Roma students (Administrative Tribunal of Versailles, 2016).

CONCLUSION

Legal, structural and process factors can deny migrant children the right to education. The implicit rights afforded by general non-discrimination provisions do not guarantee their right to education in practice. This is especially true where national legislation explicitly excludes non-citizens or undocumented migrants from education rights. Even absent such explicit discrimination, rigid documentation requirements, whether legally required or arbitrarily imposed by local gatekeepers, can prevent access. Only legislation that mandates the right to education for migrants, including the undocumented and stateless, and their right to non-compulsory education can guarantee these rights. Additionally, formal avenues allowing parents and community members to respond to rights violations and seek remediation need to be in place.

9

Baytna brings children together at NRC community centre, Thessaloniki, Greece, 2018. At Baytna, children develop self-regulation, expression and agency through play, art and movement.

CREDIT: Refugee Trauma Initiative

KEY MESSAGES

Globally, 69% of children attend organized learning one year before the official primary entry age, a rate that is slowly but steadily growing.

The robustness of UNICEF's Early Childhood Development Index is being reviewed. Data from the two latest rounds of surveys in seven countries show that improvement among 3- to 4-year-olds in literacy-numeracy, one of the four domains measured, was generally small.

Relatively few countries show interest in assessing early childhood development in cross-national surveys. But low and middle income countries also struggle to develop national monitoring of school readiness: Only 8 of 34 countries reviewed had collected data on all four domains crucial to this target: cognitive, linguistic, physical and social-emotional.

Globally, over one-sixth of the forcibly displaced are children under age 5, for whom the lack of adequate interventions and protective relationships can lead to long-term mental health, social and economic problems. Best practices for refugee children under the age of five should focus on families and caregivers, and adopt a multi-sectoral approach.

A review of 26 active humanitarian and refugee response plans revealed that nearly half made no mention of learning or education for children under 5 and less than one-third specifically mentioned pre-primary education.

CHAPTER 9

TARGET 4.2

Early childhood

By 2030, ensure that all girls and boys have access to quality early childhood development, care and pre-primary education so that they are ready for primary education

GLOBAL INDICATOR

4.2.1 – *Proportion of children under 5 years of age who are developmentally on track in health, learning and psychosocial well-being, by sex*

4.2.2 – *Participation rate in organized learning (one year before the official primary entry age), by sex*

THEMATIC INDICATORS

4.2.3 – *Percentage of children under 5 years of age experiencing positive and stimulating home learning environments*

4.2.4– *Gross early childhood education enrolment ratio in (a) pre-primary education and (b) early childhood educational development*

4.2.5– *Number of years of (i) free and (ii) compulsory pre-primary education guaranteed in legal frameworks*

Early childhood education and care (ECEC) are crucial for cognitive and emotional development. They also serve an important protective function in traumatic crisis settings (**Policy focus 9.1**). Global indicator 4.2.1 – 'Proportion of children under 5 years of age who are developmentally on track in health, learning and psychosocial well-being, by sex' – reflects the focus on childhood development. By convention, and because UNICEF is the custodian agency, the indicator draws on the UNICEF Early Childhood Development Index (ECDI). The index is based on 10 questions covering 4 domains: literacy-numeracy, physical state, social-emotional development and learning. The questions are included in the UNICEF Multiple Indicators Cluster Survey (MICS) and selected rounds of the Demographic and Health Survey.

> "Early childhood education and care serve an important protective function in traumatic crisis settings"

MICS 4 (2010–2012) first deployed the current version of the ECDI (UNICEF, 2017). Data from both MICS 4 and MICS 5 (2013–2016) are available for several countries, allowing analysis of changes over time. Results suggest that, whereas development is uniformly high with respect to the physical and, to a lesser extent, learning domains, inequality between countries is greatest in social-emotional development and literacy-numeracy. Improvements in the highly unequal literacy-numeracy domain were generally small. They were largest in Belize (from 46% to 52.5%) and Mauritania (from 19% to 27%), but negative in Cameroon and Kazakhstan (**Figure 9.1**).

Concerns about the ECDI's robustness led the Inter-agency and Expert Group on SDG Indicators (IAEG-SDGs) to assign indicator 4.2.1 tier III status, requiring a work plan to improve its methodology. The UN Statistical Commission decided in 2017 to establish an Inter-agency and Expert Group on Early Childhood Development as an advisory and coordination body, which will review UNICEF's efforts to improve the ECDI. UNICEF has reviewed more than 500 items in 10 early childhood development assessment studies (both indirect parent or teacher reports and direct child assessments). It has also carried out cognitive testing of a selected set of items in Bulgaria, India, Jamaica, Mexico, Uganda and the United States and has commissioned background papers on each domain and on methodological and psychometric aspects of the revised index. This work is expected to be completed in early 2019 (IAEG-SDGs, 2018). New items would be introduced from MICS 7 onwards.

But MICS 6 has already introduced one change in early childhood development-related indicators, extending information on adult and parental engagement from children aged 3 to 4 to children aged 2 to 4. These questions inform thematic indicator 4.2.3 – 'Percentage of children under 5 years experiencing positive and stimulating home learning environments'. An expert group led by UNICEF is developing model questions for other surveys, with a focus on ensuring they are globally applicable and account appropriately for cultural diversity.

Other surveys also measure parenting and home environment factors, such as the Programa Regional de Indicadores de Desarrollo Infantil (PRIDI), or Regional

FIGURE 9.1:

With the exception of literacy and numeracy, differences among countries in early childhood development domains are relatively small

Percentage of children aged 36 to 59 months who are developmentally on track, by domain, selected countries, 2010–2012 and 2013–2016

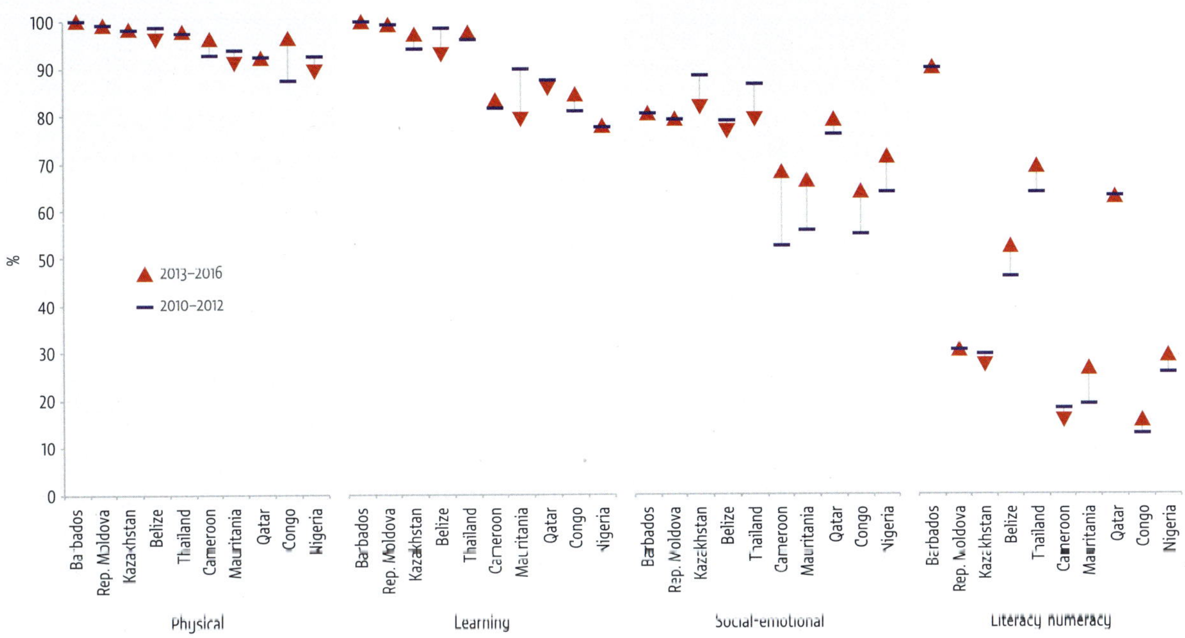

GEM StatLink: http://bit.ly/fig9_1
Note: The figure shows all countries with data in both the MICS 4 and MICS 5 rounds.
Source: MICS country reports.

Project on Child Development Indicators, implemented in four Latin American countries. It showed that the quality of adult–child interactions – whether parents played with, sang to or included children in conversations – had important consequences for development. The gap between children in the top and bottom nurturing environments in social-emotional development (Nicaragua and Peru) and in cognitive development (Costa Rica and Paraguay) grows as children become older. One factor was poverty, which increases parents' stress and can compromise their ability to provide the necessary stimulation (Verdisco et al., 2015).

Results of the Organisation for Economic Co-operation and Development's International Early Learning and Child Well-being Study will appear in 2019. The aim is to assess the cognitive and social-emotional development of 5- and 6-year-olds in institutional settings, such as early childhood education and care centres or schools. The study includes direct assessment of emergent literacy, emergent numeracy, self-regulation and social and emotional skills, together with questionnaires for parents and early childhood educators, as well as study administrator observations (OECD, 2018).

However, relatively few countries are taking part. This is indicative of a general reluctance by high income countries to assess early learning skills in a comparative context. Survey-based measures are unlikely to lead to near-universal country coverage soon. At the same time, several countries do invest in system-wide monitoring of early childhood development and school readiness to identify need for interventions (**Data focus 9.1**). It should be noted that a key purpose of the SDG 4 monitoring framework, especially regarding outcome indicators, is to be formative. It should signal that education outcomes deserve attention and countries should invest in robust monitoring mechanisms. Whether different countries' data on outcomes can be linked is an issue to be tackled at a second stage, especially for complex notions like early childhood development.

Currently, global indicator 4.2.2 – 'Participation rate in organized learning (one year before the official primary entry age), by sex' – ranges from around 42% in low income to 93% in high income countries, with a global average of 69% continuing a slowly but steadily increasing trend. By contrast, the pre-primary education gross enrolment ratio, defined for an education level that lasts as little as one year in some countries and as many as four in others, reached 50% in 2017 (**Figure 9.2**).

> Globally, 70% attend organised learning one year before the official primary entry age, a rate that is slowly but steadily growing

FIGURE 9.2:

Seven out of ten children attend pre-school the year before entering primary education

Participation rate in organized learning (one year before the official primary entry age) and pre-primary gross enrolment ratio, 2000–2016

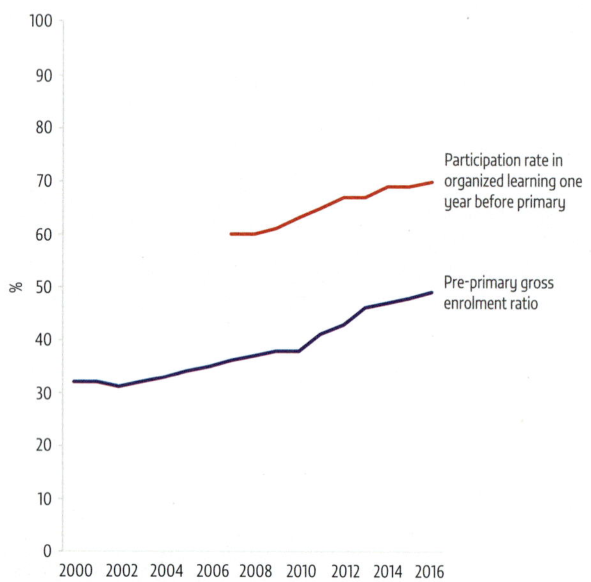

GEM StatLink: http://bit.ly/fig9_2
Source: UIS database.

While global indicator 4.2.1 monitors early childhood development outcomes through age 4, global indicator 4.2.2, which refers to the year before entering primary education, monitors participation in early childhood education for children age 5 for countries with primary entry at age 6. But in one out of five countries, where official primary entry was at age 7 in 2017, no indicator monitors children age 5. This issue affects both developing and developed countries and potentially a significant number of children: a single-year child cohort is almost 5 million in Indonesia and exceeds 1 million in Ethiopia, South Africa and the United Republic of Tanzania.

DATA FOCUS 9.1: FEW COUNTRIES HAVE NATIONAL SYSTEMS TO MONITOR SCHOOL READINESS

The IAEG-SDGs supports diversification of data sources, a notable shift from the Education for All era (2000–2015). Its broader focus, for instance regarding equity and learning, imposes relatively heavy requirements on countries. Arguably, ensuring that countries report to increase coverage may have to be emphasized, in some cases, more than ensuring perfect comparability. While some criticize the SDG 4 monitoring framework as too ambitious, its key role is to be formative, drawing countries' attention to core issues and exploring ways to collect relevant data.

Global indicator 4.2.1 – 'Proportion of children under 5 years of age who are developmentally on track in health, learning and psychosocial well-being, by sex' – is no exception. 'School readiness' and 'developmentally on track' are elusive concepts, viewed differently around the world. Yet sourcing for the indicator has been limited to the MICS and current ECDI. UNICEF is testing a new, expanded set of questions and proposing an updated ECDI through a working group established by the IAEG-SDGs.

Whatever the improvements to ECDI reliability and validity, countries may need more discretion to use existing school readiness measures that serve their needs and are compatible with institutional structures and cultural characteristics. Monitoring early childhood development should identify trends and the potential need for policy interventions and supportive measures, not serve as a high-stakes assessment that may exclude children who are not 'ready' (National Research Council

> 'School readiness' and 'developmentally on track' are elusive concepts, viewed differently around the world

of the National Academies, 2008). School readiness asks not only whether children are ready for school, but also whether schools are ready for children (UNICEF, 2012).

While surveys are crucial for monitoring whether children benefit from ECEC, and for understanding the role of households and families in early childhood development, they are no replacement for national systems collecting comprehensive, annual, large-scale data on individual dimensions of early childhood development. Yet such national systems are rare, including in high income countries (Anderson et al., 2017; Raikes, 2017). In some countries, there are fundamental objections to collecting and using outcomes data for young children (Bertram and Pascal, 2016).

Instead, more commonly, countries have national frameworks and procedures for monitoring provider standards in terms of staffing, training, facilities and curricula, e.g. the 2013 National Early Childhood Care and Education Policy in India (Ministry of Women and Child Development, 2013; Paul, 2017). National early childhood development monitoring should also be distinguished from programme impact evaluations, such as the National Reporting System component of the US Head Start pre-school programme, which aims to reduce education disadvantage among children from low-income families (Wortham, 2012).

The World Bank's Systems Approach for Better Education Results (SABER) has an early childhood development module that has assessed administrative systems' data availability in the domains of cognitive, linguistic, physical and social-emotional development. Only 8 out of 34 countries collected data on all 4 domains (**Figure 9.3**). In addition, the SABER score reflects only the number of domains covered in some form, not how the data were collected or the availability of aggregated data at the national level.

Bulgaria tracks and records child development across the four domains on a systematic schedule and, in pre-school, in relation to expected learning milestones. However, the data are not fully utilized to support

FIGURE 9.3:

Few countries collect data on all four domains of child development

Countries by number of early childhood development domains included in their administrative data system, 2012–2017

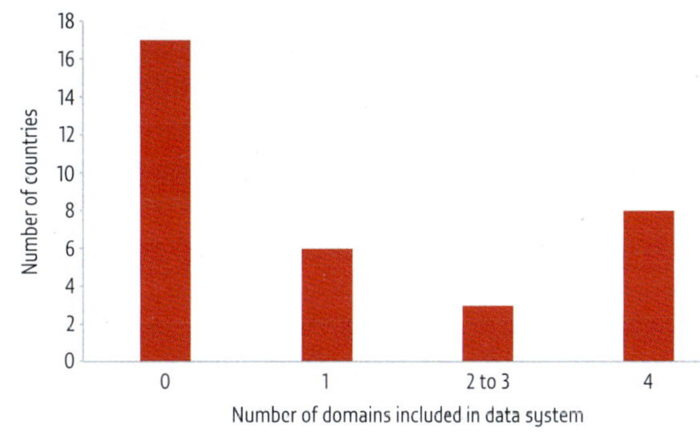

GEM StatLink: http://bit.ly/fig9_3
Note: The analysis is based on 34 low and middle income countries.
Source: Based on SABER national reports.

early childhood development policies (World Bank, 2013a). In Iraq, pre-school teachers record observational assessments of individual development, but the information was not analysed at a higher level (Adams and Denboba, 2017).

The programme Chile Crece Contigo (Chile Grows with You) represents best practice in early childhood development monitoring, tracking children 'comprehensively, with mechanisms to respond to their needs', through multisector services (World Bank, 2013b). In fact, the results are used for strategic planning at the national level, even for children under age 3 (Bertram and Pascal, 2016).

By contrast, the former Yugoslav Republic of Macedonia has maintained a child development portfolio for all children enrolled in early childhood centres since 2014. Teachers document development in relation to the national Early Learning and Development Standards framework. In addition to informing individualized pre-school instruction, the portfolio documents school readiness, smoothing transition to primary education (World Bank, 2015).

South Africa's 2014 National Curriculum Framework similarly mandates informal, observational assessments in six Early Learning and Development Areas (South Africa Department of Basic Education, 2015). Assessments do not assign marks or percentages but do record readiness for primary reception grade. Reports go to parents and schools prior to transition and are used for national monitoring.

Jamaica's approach builds on the 2010 Jamaica Early Childhood Curriculum Guide for 4- and 5-year-olds. Until recently, data collection relied on the Jamaica Survey of Living Conditions, but a new Jamaica School Readiness Assessment, first conducted nationally in 2016, reached almost 86% of 4-year-olds in nearly 88% of early childhood education centres in 2017 (The Early Childhood Commission, 2018). The main purpose is to close gaps in school readiness through individual interventions, but as implementation is centralized, the assessment may also inform national policy.

POLICY FOCUS 9.1: PROVIDING EARLY CHILDHOOD EDUCATION AND CARE FOR THE DISPLACED

Globally, children under age 5 make up 16%, or more than 4 million, of the displaced (UNHCR, 2018a). Such adversity affects young children in the near and long term. Exposure to violence and the stress of dislocation can have devastating effects, particularly in the early years when the brain undergoes its most rapid period of development (Britto et al., 2017). Even children not victimized by physical violence can be traumatized by separation from family and home. Without adequate intervention and protective, caring relationships, displacement and conflict can lead to a generation suffering long-term mental health, social and economic problems (Center on the Developing Child, 2007; International Rescue Committee, 2017).[1]

> "Interventions for refugee children under 5 should focus on families and caregivers and adopt a multisector approach"

Evidence on the positive effects of ECEC on life trajectories is large and growing (*The Lancet*, 2016). Appropriate interventions, including early learning, are crucial for children in violent and unstable contexts who may otherwise lack stable, nurturing and enriching environments. Interventions should focus on families and caregivers, build on existing platforms and adopt a multisector approach. The Nurturing Care Framework, launched in May 2018 by the World Health Organization and partners, is such an approach. It identifies five components, of which one is the opportunity for early learning (WHO et al., 2018).

Among other signs of growing commitment, the 2016 New York Declaration for Refugees and Migrants (Art. 82) called on UN member states to support early childhood education for refugees (United Nations, 2016). In late 2017, the MacArthur Foundation announced a US$100 million grant to the Sesame Workshop and the International Rescue Committee (IRC) for early childhood development intervention in Iraq, Jordan, Lebanon and the Syrian Arab Republic, the largest initiative of its kind in humanitarian response (MacArthur Foundation, 2017). Yet the early learning needs of forcibly displaced young children are largely unmet in many displacement settings.

REFUGEE ACCESS TO EARLY CHILDHOOD EDUCATION AND CARE REMAINS LIMITED

A study of nine upper middle and high income countries suggests that responses to the needs of young children among refugees and asylum-seekers have been 'extraordinarily weak', both in and out of reception centres. This reflects the low priority national policy-makers give to such services and the diffusion of responsibility for planning and delivery across government levels. Canada offers some services for new arrivals, but only as child care for parents enrolled in publicly financed language courses. The Netherlands has no national policy to provide education to refugees below compulsory education age. Even in countries offering services, providers are often ill-equipped to address refugee children's cultural and linguistic diversity and trauma. In Sweden, non-native speakers in pre-school (23% of enrolment) have a legal right to develop their mother tongue, yet just 39% actually receive such support (Park et al., 2018).

Humanitarian and refugee response plans (HRPs and RRPs) evidence little commitment to early childhood development. A review of 26 active plans for this report from the perspective of the five Nurturing

1 This section draws on a paper by Bouchane et al. (2018).

> Nearly half of 26 active humanitarian and refugee response plans showed no mention of early learning needs

Care Framework components revealed significant gaps. On average, the plans included one in six of the recommended elements of the early learning component. Nearly half made no mention of learning or education for children under 5, and less than one-third specifically mentioned pre-primary education or ECEC, including Mali, South Sudan and the Syrian Arab Republic. Only the Ukraine HRP mentioned early childhood recreation kits. Over 40% of plans did not mention intervention components related to responsive caregiving. Slightly over one-third included children under 5 in a strategic objective (Bouchane et al., 2018) (**Figure 9.4**).

NON-GOVERNMENT INITIATIVES DEMONSTRATE THAT DEMAND IS HIGH

Limited public ECEC activity means non-government organizations (NGOs) often fill the gap. ECEC initiatives by the Jesuit Refugee Service (JRS) and Entreculturas reach thousands of refugee children in Chad, the Central African Republic, Lebanon and South Sudan. Little Ripples in Chad is a refugee-led, home-based early childhood programme initiated by iACT, an international NGO. Pilot implementation in 2013 trained teachers, incorporated play-based and social-emotional learning, and offered a daily nutritious meal. The programme expanded to two refugee camps in northern Chad in 2017 and has employed 81 refugee women. It reached almost 3,500 children aged 3 to 5 in 2017 and was expected to reach 6,000 by the end of 2018. An evaluation showed that, after one year, the number of students able to count to five or more went from 43% to 73% and those able to recite correctly at least the first 10 letters of the alphabet grew from 45% to 83% (Bouchane et al., 2018; Dallain and Scott, 2017).

UNICEF and NGO partners deliver a range of services in Kenya's Kakuma and Kalobeyei camps, including early childhood education. Teachers visit each household, picking up almost 900 young children to take part in a programme focused on education and play grounded in the arts. However, classrooms are overcrowded, with an average of 133 children (Steinberg, 2018).

FIGURE 9.4:

Humanitarian and refugee response plans typically cover less than one in five of recommended elements in early learning interventions

Coverage of recommended elements in selected domains in 26 humanitarian and refugee response plans, 2017

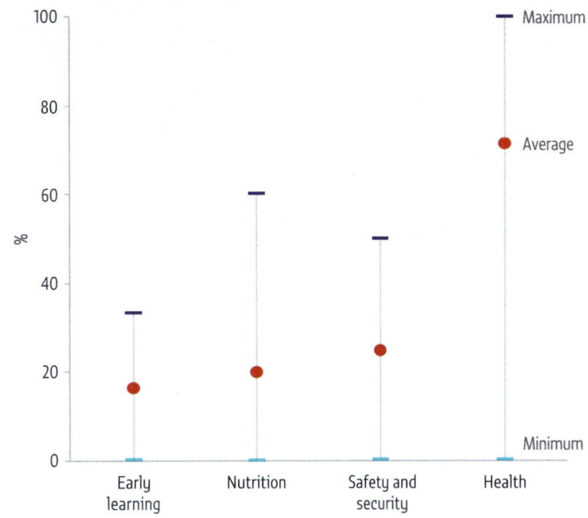

GEM StatLink: http://bit.ly/fig9_4

Note: The elements of the early learning component are: response to children's communication through vocalizations, facial expressions and gestures; language stimulation through talking and singing; encouragement to explore objects with guidance from caregivers; caregiver–child play and reading and storytelling groups; mobile toy and book libraries; and quality day care and pre-primary education.

Source: Bouchane et al. (2018).

The IRC piloted the Healing Classrooms pre-school teacher education programme for Congolese children in camps in Burundi and the United Republic of Tanzania. The programme was adapted in 2014 for Lebanon, where it now serves 3,200 pre-school children and has trained 128 teachers. In each classroom, a Lebanese IRC lead teacher pairs with a Syrian assistant teacher. After a four-month pilot, participating 3-year-olds showed improved motor skills, social-emotional skills, executive function and early literacy and numeracy, with the proportion meeting minimum proficiency doubling from a baseline of about 15% (Bouchane et al., 2018; International Rescue Committee, 2016).

In northern Myanmar, Children on the Edge and the local organizations Kachin Development Group and Kachin Women's Association developed an early childhood development programme whose curriculum attends to the physical and psychosocial needs of more than 500 internally displaced children aged 3 to 6 in 15 learning centres in 8 camps. An impact evaluation suggests that the programme has helped increase their confidence and positivity (Children on the Edge, 2015).

In Turkey, although Syrian children can attend early childhood education in public schools, shortages of places and resources have led many NGOs and international agencies to provide services. In June 2017, UNICEF-led initiatives enrolled 12,800 Syrians aged 3 to 5. Some NGOs (e.g. Mother Child Education Foundation, Support to Life, Mavi Kalem Social Assistance and Solidarity, Yuva Foundation) provide teacher education, education materials, home visits, psychosocial and mental health support, and learning and recreational activities.

GOVERNMENTS NEED TO STEP UP TO COORDINATE AND SCALE PROVISION

With insufficient resources, non-state actors face challenges in scaling up programmes and managing high and increasing demand for pre-school services. Public interventions share some of these challenges, in addition to poor inter-agency coordination and a frequent lack of policy provisions specific to early childhood education for displaced children.

“Non-state actors face challenges in scaling up programmes and managing high and increasing demand for pre-school services”

Some countries have succeeded in establishing partnerships and operating with multiple local and NGO actors. In Belgium, the public ECEC agency for the Flemish community set up centres in the Flanders and Brussels-Capital regions to provide a full range of services for families with children. The agency cooperates with the Belgian Federal Agency for the Reception of Asylum Seekers and the Red Cross, which manage the reception centres (Park et al., 2018).

In the Central African Republic, UNICEF and Plan International, an NGO, initiated a project whose services were later scaled up. Based on needs assessments, interventions targeted children in conflict-affected areas, including internally displaced people. Parenting sessions and teacher education emphasized early learning and child development. The two partners engaged with government to design a long-term support strategy, and early childhood services for children aged 3 to 6 have become an education transition plan priority. An interministerial committee meets regularly to coordinate NGO activities and reach out to other agencies (Consultative Group on Early Childhood Care and Development, 2016).

Ethiopia is expanding refugee education in line with one of nine pledges its government made in New York at the September 2016 Leaders' Summit on Refugees. Three out of five refugee children aged 3 to 6 are supported in 80 early childhood centres in refugee camps and 150 private and public kindergartens in Addis Ababa (UNHCR, 2018b).

Germany adopted a comprehensive plan for refugee and asylum-seeker education, partnering with subnational actors. Sprach-Kitas, launched by the Federal Ministry for Family Affairs, Senior Citizens, Women and Youth, provides ECEC programmes with language-focused support. The ministry plans to invest nearly EUR 400 million in 2017–2020 to expand the programme and staff (Park et al., 2018).

Uganda is working with UNICEF and other partners to improve pre-school access. Less than half of eligible children in refugee hosting districts had access in 2017 (UNICEF, 2018). In line with the Comprehensive Refugee Response Framework, Uganda established policies and strategies to increase the number of certified caregivers and centres providing good-quality integrated early childhood development services (Uganda Ministry of Education and Sports, 2018; UNHCR, 2018b, 2018c). Language of instruction and refugee teacher accreditation remain among the main challenges.

CONCLUSION

A key benefit of high-quality early childhood education is that it acts as a protection mechanism. This makes it all the more important for the displaced to enjoy access, with adequate infrastructure, appropriate materials, qualified and trained teachers, and sufficient funding. A long-term perspective that fosters collaboration among families, communities and teachers is also needed.

Sound ECEC for the forcibly displaced is possible. Despite policy and coordination challenges, public actors must play a central role in scaling up successful local or pilot initiatives. This can be encouraged by closing data collection gaps, monitoring and documenting initiative impact, involving communities in awareness-raising campaigns, and supporting advocacy, central and local capacity development and partnerships with a range of actors, including civil society and humanitarian actors. Countries with ECEC services in their national education plans are moving much faster than others. Government acknowledgement that, for all, 'the first priority is starting early – and staying the course over two decades of childhood' (United Nations, 2018) is an important step in progress on the 2030 Agenda.

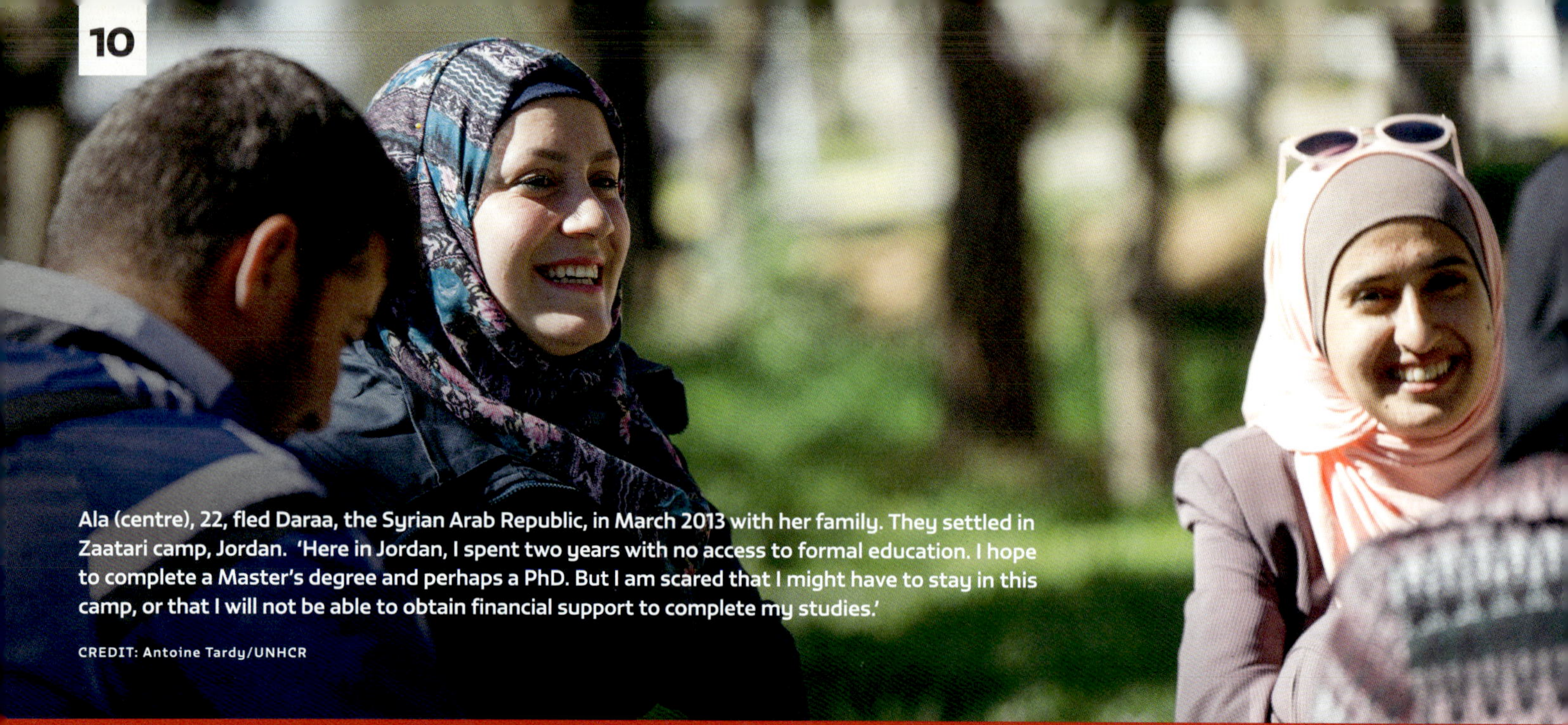

Ala (centre), 22, fled Daraa, the Syrian Arab Republic, in March 2013 with her family. They settled in Zaatari camp, Jordan. 'Here in Jordan, I spent two years with no access to formal education. I hope to complete a Master's degree and perhaps a PhD. But I am scared that I might have to stay in this camp, or that I will not be able to obtain financial support to complete my studies.'

CREDIT: Antoine Tardy/UNHCR

KEY MESSAGES

The new definition on adult participation in education and training covers formal and non-formal provision, as well as work and non-work-related opportunities.

Questions in labour force surveys need to be standardized: addressing all youth and adults, not just the employed; employing a common reference period of the previous 12 months; and extending the scope beyond technical and vocational training.

In middle income countries low annual participation rates in adult work-related education and training may be the norm. In Egypt, annual participation among skilled workers was 4%.

The tertiary education gross enrolment ratio reached 38% in 2017; it exceeded 50% in upper middle countries for the first time in 2016.

Tertiary education is least affordable in sub-Saharan Africa, where it exceeds 60% of average national income in most countries.

In several middle income countries, the richest households are more likely to report receiving a scholarship. Countries that successfully targeted the poor included Colombia, which made loan terms more favourable for poor students, and Viet Nam which provides aid to ethnic minority students.

Higher education for refugees increases their chances of employment and provides motivation to remain in school. A number of laudable initiatives exist, some involving the community, but only 1% of refugees participate in tertiary education.

If migrants and refugees lack access to employment or decent jobs, they are unlikely to invest in developing their technical and vocational skills. Planners can help by recognizing prior non-formal and informal learning and providing career guidance to ease entry into labour markets.

CHAPTER 10

TARGET 4.3

Technical, vocational, tertiary and adult education

By 2030, ensure equal access for all women and men to affordable and quality technical, vocational and tertiary education, including university

GLOBAL INDICATOR

4.3.1 – *Participation rate of youth and adults in formal and non-formal education and training in the previous 12 months, by sex*

THEMATIC INDICATORS

4.3.2 – *Gross enrolment ratio for tertiary education by sex*

4.3.3– *Participation rate in technical-vocational programmes (15- to 24-year-olds) by sex*

Only targets 4.3 and 4.6 focus on the SDG 4 commitment to lifelong learning beyond compulsory education. Target 4.3, to 'ensure equal access for all women and men to affordable quality technical, vocational and tertiary education, including university', covers a wide range of age groups (youth and adults), types of education provision (formal and non-formal) and education purposes (work and non-work). As a result, it is difficult to define a concise monitoring framework that addresses all needs. However, some steps have been taken in the past year to clarify definitions.

Global indicator 4.3.1 – 'Participation rate of youth and adults in formal and non-formal education and training in the previous 12 months, by sex' – aims to consolidate data sources (UNESCO, 2017), but clear guidance on what data to collect has been missing.

In 2018, the Technical Cooperation Group (TCG) on SDG 4 indicators considered a recommendation to adopt a wide and flexible definition for indicator 4.3.1 to encourage countries to collect information on adult education. The proposal would invite countries to add a fixed set of concise questions to existing labour force surveys that (a) would distinguish formal from non-formal education; (b) under non-formal education, would include programmes of any duration and would follow the European Union Adult Education Survey classification, which covers courses, workshops and seminars, guided on-the-job training, and private lessons; and (c) would link global indicator 4.3.1 to thematic indicators 4.3.3 on youth participation in technical and vocational education and training (TVET) and 4.6.3 on participation in literacy programmes.

> In 2018, a wider and more flexible definition was proposed for the global indicator in target 4.3 covering formal and non-formal education

Labour force surveys as the main vehicle for data collection have the advantage of being widely and frequently deployed, but standardizing questions to expand the number of countries with comparable data will not be easy. As previous versions of the *Global Education Monitoring Report* have noted, such standardization remains limited outside Europe. This chapter highlights the difficulties by reviewing three high-quality surveys in Northern Africa and Western Asia (**Data focus 10.1**).

In Europe, two such sources are used routinely. The Adult Education Survey is aligned with the proposed definition but makes data available every five years; 2016 data will be available in late 2018. The Labour Force Survey, focused on formal education, has a four week reference period instead of 12 months and makes data available annually (Eurostat, 2017). It shows that, while adult participation rates remain stable, on average, at about

10% to 11%, trends vary by country, some having been affected more by the financial crisis, such as the United Kingdom (**Figure 10.1**).

Data are much more readily available for formal education, such as secondary-level TVET. The share of technical and vocational-track secondary enrolment is relatively stable. Globally, 22% of upper secondary students are in technical and vocational tracks, compared with 2% of lower secondary students. Students are more likely male, except in Latin America and the Caribbean (**Table 10.1**).

Global participation in tertiary education, measured by the gross enrolment ratio, continued to increase rapidly in many countries, reaching 38% in 2017 (**Table 10.2**). It exceeded 50% in upper middle income countries for the first time in 2016, up from 33% in 2010. Globally, 20% of tertiary students are enrolled in short-degree programmes (International Standard Classification of Education [ISCED] 5), and 68% for bachelor's degrees (ISCED 6). The latter share is highest in low and lower middle income countries, suggesting that part of the expansion of tertiary education in richer countries results from diversification into shorter programmes. Female students are under-represented at the doctoral level (ISCED 8), especially in low income countries.

> The global tertiary education gross enrolment ratio reached 38% in 2017 and exceeded 50% in upper middle countries for the first time in 2016

Social attitudes and education aspirations are one challenge to technical and vocational secondary education in some settings. It is often perceived as less academically oriented and, therefore, a hindrance to entering tertiary education (Clement, 2014). At the aggregate level, however, there is no enrolment trade-off: Since 2000, tertiary participation has grown strongly in almost all countries, but there is no evident relationship with change in share of secondary students in technical and vocational-track education (**Figure 10.2**).

Expanding participation in TVET and tertiary education provides important avenues for youth and adults to advance their employment opportunities.

FIGURE 10.1:

Participation in adult education in Europe has remained stable, but trends vary by country

Adult participation rate in education and training during the previous four weeks, European Union and selected countries, 2008–2017

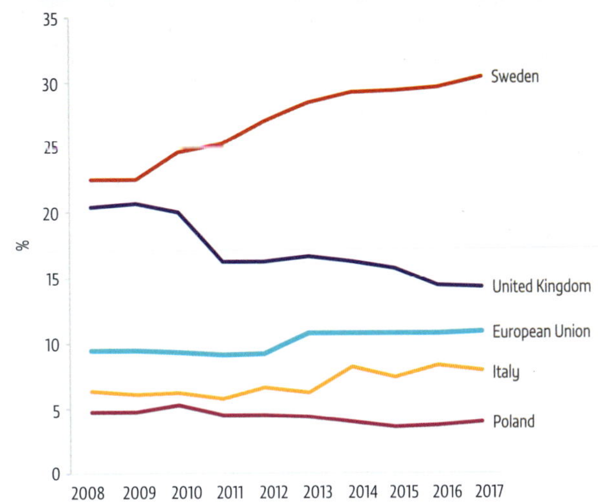

GEM StatLink: http://bit.ly/fig10_1
Source: Eurostat (2018).

TABLE 10.1:

Technical and vocational education participation indicators, 2017

Region	Lower secondary education			Upper secondary education		
	Technical and vocational enrolment (million)	Share of females in TVET enrolment (%)	Share of all lower secondary students (%)	Technical and vocational enrolment (million)	Share of females in TVET enrolment (%)	Share of all lower secondary students (%)
World	6	48	2	57	43	22
Sub-Saharan Africa	0.7	35	2	3	43	13
Northern Africa and Western Asia	0.6	22	2	6	45	30
Central and Southern Asia	0	35	0	5	32	6
Eastern and South-eastern Asia	0	34	0	23	43	36
Oceania	0.3	35	14	0.8	40	45
Latin America and the Caribbean	2	58	6	6	50	23
Europe and Northern America	2	54	4	14	44	34
Low income countries	0.2	33	1	2	41	15
Lower middle income countries	0.9	34	1	13	39	12
Upper middle income countries	2	55	2	29	44	33
High income countries	2	48	4	13	44	28

Source: UIS database.

FIGURE 10.2:

Expanding tertiary education need not have a negative effect on technical and vocational secondary enrolment

Change in the tertiary gross enrolment ratio, by change in the share of technical and vocational enrolment in secondary education, 2005 and 2015

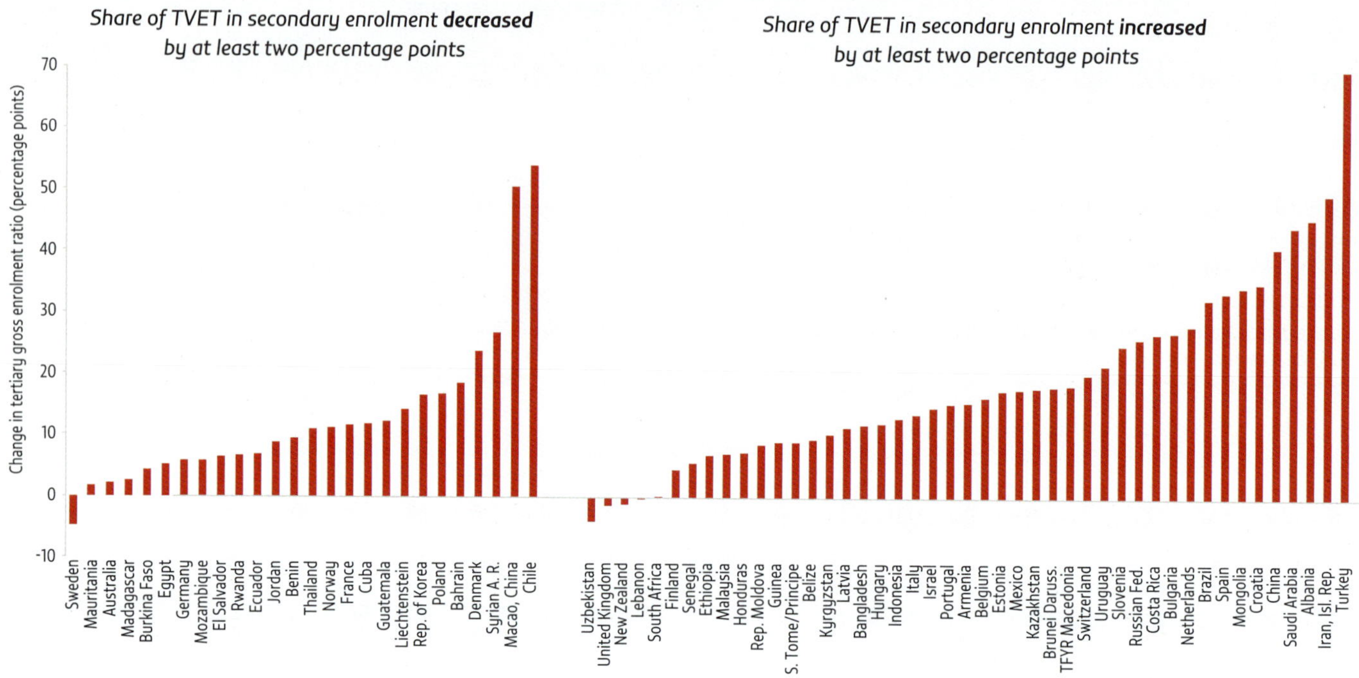

GEM StatLink: http://bit.ly/fig10_2
Source: UIS database.

TABLE 10.2:

Tertiary education participation indicators, 2017

Region	Tertiary enrolment (million)	Gross enrolment ratio (%)	ISCED 5		ISCED 6		ISCED 7		ISCED 8	
			Share of all tertiary students (%)	Share of females (%)	Share of all tertiary students (%)	Share of females (%)	Share of all tertiary students (%)	Share of females (%)	Share of all tertiary students (%)	Share of females (%)
World	**221**	**38**	**20**	**52**	**68**	**51**	**11**	**53**	**1**	**45**
Sub-Saharan Africa	8	9	23	46	68	41	8	37	1	34
Northern Africa and Western Asia	19	44	18	46	72	50	9	49	1	43
Central and Southern Asia	44	25	3	38	83	47	14	50	1	42
Eastern and South-eastern Asia	71	46	32	51	61	52	6	49	1	40
Oceania	2	79	31	60	53	57	13	53	3	51
Latin America and the Caribbean	27	51	12	57	82	56	5	55	1	51
Europe and Northern America	50	77	22	55	56	54	20	57	3	48
Low income countries	6	9	10	40	81	38	8	38	1	27
Lower middle income countries	64	24	6	51	82	48	11	51	1	43
Upper middle income countries	93	52	28	50	63	54	7	51	1	44
High income countries	57	77	23	56	58	53	16	57	3	47

Note: ISCED = International Standard Classification of Education, which includes four levels of tertiary education: short-cycle (ISCED 5), bachelor's degree (ISCED 6), master's degree or equivalent (ISCED 7) and doctorate or equivalent (ISCED 8).
Source: UIS database.

However, challenges remain, especially in terms of cost. How affordability, a key stipulation of target 4.3, should be defined and operationalized needs clarification (**Data focus 10.2**). These challenges, which include recognizing prior learning, are especially important for migrants and refugees, investment in whose skills is key to integration in destination countries (**Policy focus 10.1** and **Policy focus 10.2**).

DATA FOCUS 10.1: ALIGNING LABOUR FORCE SURVEY QUESTIONS ON ADULT EDUCATION AND TRAINING WITH THE GLOBAL INDICATOR

The TCG made concrete recommendations towards defining global indicator 4.3.1, which covers the youth and adult participation rates for formal and non-formal education and training in the previous year. The recommendations, which resemble those proposed in the 2017/8 *Global Education Monitoring Report*, suggest the indicator should capture all education opportunities, whether or not work-related or formal.

The diversity and large number of providers make participant surveys preferable to administrative data to capture such opportunities. The TCG proposed questions in line with the EU Adult Education Survey: During the previous 12 months, had respondents (a) been students or apprentices in formal education or training, and if so at what level most recently; and (b) participated, during leisure or work time, in any of four non-formal activities (course, workshop or seminar, guided on-the-job training, private lesson) with the intention of improving knowledge or skills in any area (including hobbies).

However, the ways surveys ask questions vary considerably, so few are compatible with the requirements of monitoring indicator 4.3.1. Integrated Labour Market Surveys, which have collected high-quality, comparable, nationally representative data in Egypt (four rounds between 1988 and 2012), Jordan (2010) and Tunisia (2014), are a case in point. National statistics offices, in collaboration with the Economic Research Forum, a regional think tank, followed similar methodology. Each round sampled between 5,000 and 12,000 households, and the last two rounds in Egypt (2006 and 2012) followed the same households.[1]

These surveys collected vocational or job-related training programme participation information in two ways. The most recent in Egypt and Tunisia asked all currently employed people whether they had ever taken part in vocational or job-related training programmes outside formal education. Participation proved relatively low: about 10% in both countries.

Second, all surveys asked employed people who reported that their job required a technical skill how they acquired it. Response options were a not-so-clear mix of provider and type: formal education (general or technical), vocational training programmes, enterprise-based training, language courses, computer courses, or other. Participation rates were higher, from 22% in Tunisia to 29% in Jordan (**Figure 10.3**). The question related to lifetime participation, so it is not surprising that the proportion in the general labour force was lower among youth than among all adults. But among those with technical skills, youth reported higher participation, suggesting that pathways to acquisition of these skills have changed.

To relate the data more directly to the indicator, two approaches can be used to estimate annual participation. The first converts the lifetime training participation rate into an annual rate, which would suggest less than 2% participation per year for 15- to 29-year-olds, on average, in Egypt and Tunisia. The second exploits the last two Egyptian labour market surveys' panel structure, allowing an estimation of the proportion of those who changed status over time with respect to lifetime participation.

1 This section is based on a background paper by Amer (2018).

> The diversity and large number of providers make participant surveys preferable to administrative data for the global indicator on adult education

FIGURE 10.3:

Only 1 in 10 employed adults in Egypt and Tunisia had ever participated in training

Youth and adult participation rate in training programmes outside formal education as a percentage of (a) all employed and (b) employed with technical skills, Egypt, Jordan and Tunisia, 2010–2014

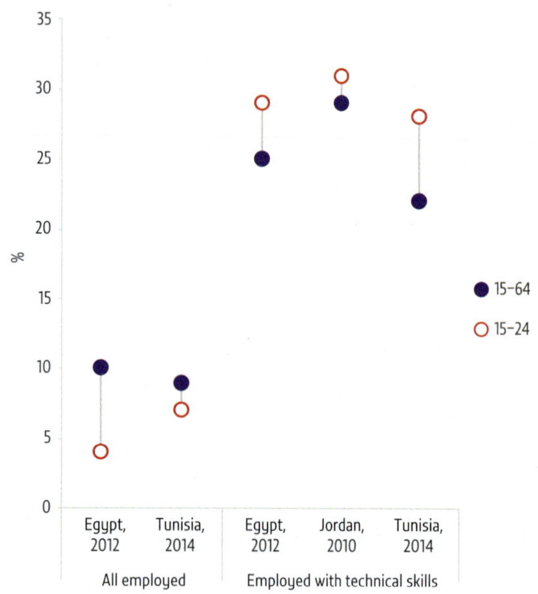

GEM StatLink: http://bit.ly/fig10_3
Source: Amer (2018) based on Integrated Labour Market Survey data.

Among employees aged 15 to 64 with technical skills, 23% of those who had never received training in 2006 had done so by 2012. Ignoring the possibility of repeated participation, this puts annual participation among the skilled in the range of 4%.

Methodological challenges limit the use of this family of surveys for informing the global indicator. First, the training question is directed only to the employed, missing other participants in training (e.g. the unemployed and those outside the labour force). Second, they ask about lifetime participation, not that during a reference period, such as the previous 12 months. Third, they refer only to technical and vocational training, missing the wider range of programmes within the scope of the indicator. Despite these limitations, evidence suggests low annual participation rates in the countries concerned, which are consistent with those of poorer European countries.

The analysis is a reminder that defining the global indicator is only the first step. The next is to detail how different labour force and related surveys ask questions about youth and adult participation in education and training. Where questions diverge considerably from the definition, countries should be encouraged to align questionnaires.

DATA FOCUS 10.2: DEFINING AND MEASURING AFFORDABILITY OF HIGHER EDUCATION

Governments cannot match the growing demand for higher education in many countries, leading to an increasing share of private expenditure, including through fees for enrolment in the growing number of private institutions (Johnstone and Marcucci, 2010). Cost sharing between governments and households can be efficient and equitable if there are no credit constraints. But even if returns on a university degree make private expenditure worthwhile, poorer students must still be able to afford it.

Fees or other charges and financial support must be balanced against both the total cost to the learners and their ability to pay. Direct costs include tuition, other fees, books, materials, transport and living expenses. Student loans, grants, subsidies and scholarships offer financial support. Affordability may be estimated by relating net cost – the difference between private costs and financial assistance – to a measure of households' ability to pay. However, few countries have sufficiently detailed survey data to provide such information (Murakami and Blom, 2008; Usher and Medow, 2010).

An alternative, based on aggregate data, is estimating the ratio of initial household expenditure per tertiary student, provided by the UNESCO Institute for Statistics, to average national income, reported in the World Inequality Database. This affordability index can be calculated for 71 countries across regions and country income groups. By this measure, tertiary education is

> The net private cost per student exceeds 60% of the average national income in most countries with data in sub-Saharan Africa

generally most affordable in Europe and least affordable in sub-Saharan Africa, where the net private cost per student exceeded 60% of the average national income in 7 out of 11 countries with data and reaches around 300% in Guinea and Uganda (**Figure 10.4**). The index hovers at around 100% in Burundi, Cambodia, and Nepal. While it is near 30% in Indonesia, Japan and Viet Nam, that still represents more than 75% of a poor person's income, using a poverty threshold of 40% of the average national income as a benchmark.

Targeted student financial support is a key component of national and international education interventions. For instance, grants, scholarships, loans, and targeted incentive programmes were proposed in 54% of World Bank in 2013 (World Bank, 2014). Yet the effectiveness of targeting in reducing the net cost of tertiary education varies substantially among countries. The World Bank's Skills toward Employment and Productivity (STEP) surveys provide information for 11 low and middle income countries on whether any household member received a government scholarship during the past 12 months (the education level supported is not specified).

Analysis for this report shows that, contrary to expectations, households in the bottom asset quintile in several countries are less likely to report receiving a government scholarship than those in the top quintile (conditional on current tertiary enrolment). The richest households are roughly twice as likely as the poorest to receive a scholarship in China's Yunnan province and

FIGURE 10.4:

Tertiary education is least affordable in sub-Saharan Africa

Ratio of household expenditure per tertiary education student to average national income, selected countries, 2006–2015

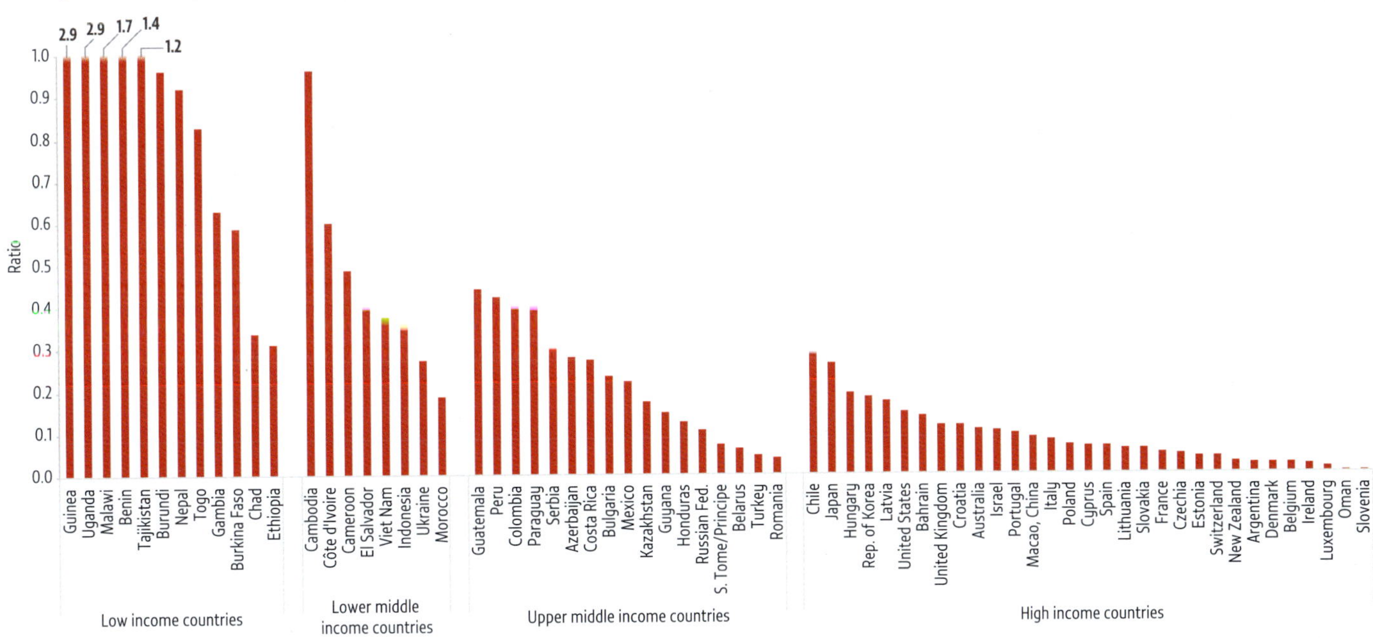

GEM StatLink: http://bit.ly/fig10_4
Source: GEM Report team calculations based on the UIS database and the World Inequality Database.

> Poor households in several middle income countries are less likely than rich households to receive a government scholarship

FIGURE 10.5:

In many countries, scholarships are not targeted to the poorest

Percentage of households with at least one member in higher education that receive public scholarships at any level of schooling, by income quintile, 2011–2013

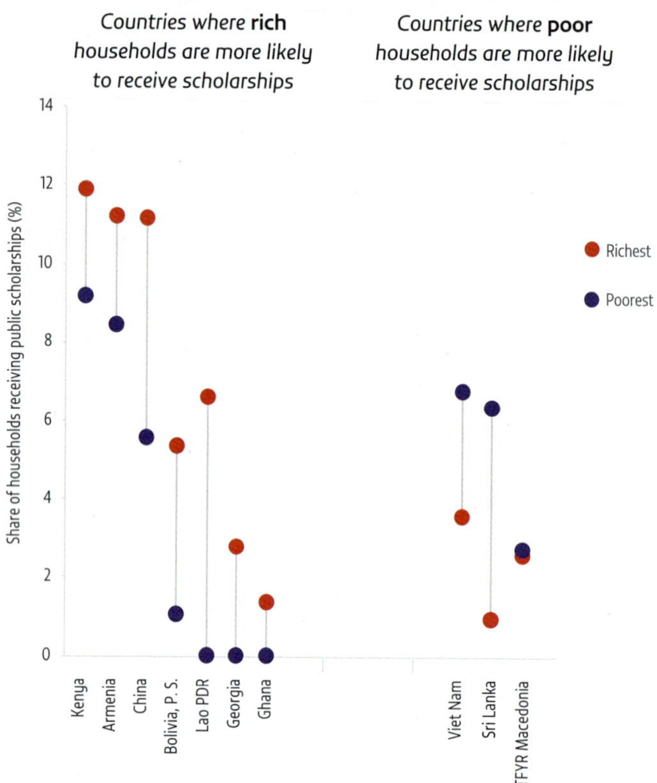

GEM StatLink: http://bit.ly/fig10_5

Note: The surveys sampled urban areas. China refers to the province of Yunnan.

Source: GEM Report team analysis based on World Bank STEP survey data.

six times as likely in the Plurinational State of Bolivia (**Figure 10.5**). Young people from poorer households are less likely to be in higher education at all. Analysis for the World Inequality Database on Education suggests that 1% of the poorest but 15% of the richest attended post-secondary education in lower middle income countries in 2011–2016. Clearly it cannot be assumed that scholarships alone significantly offset the disadvantage revealed by comparing average net private cost to the poverty income level.

Comprehensive policy packages may be more successful, as in Colombia and Viet Nam. Colombia took a multipronged approach to expand access. Partnerships among tertiary institutions, local authorities and enterprises sought to expand tertiary in regions with few or no options. Funding for ICETEX, the main public student loan provider, increased. Loan terms became more favourable, with a zero interest rate for low-income students as of 2011 and easier guarantor requirements (Ferreyra et al., 2017).

Viet Nam introduced policies to encourage fee deductions and student aid programmes benefiting poor and ethnic minority students in the mid-1990s. In 2006, about 22% of disadvantaged university students benefited from fee deductions of up to 50% of tuition. Since 2006, ethnic minority students have received lump-sum assistance amounting to around one-third of overall monthly higher education costs. Scholarships for poor students were raised to cover full tuition as of 2007 (World Bank, 2012).

POLICY FOCUS 10.1: OFFERING TERTIARY EDUCATION OPPORTUNITIES TO REFUGEES

Tertiary education opportunities for refugees are not a luxury. They provide young refugees and their families with an opportunity for increased self-reliance through gainful employment. The prospect of participation in tertiary education contributes to greater primary and secondary enrolment and retention (UNHCR, 2015a). Tertiary education has 'a greater potential than other levels of education to ... enhance the strategic choices that refugees make' (Dryden-Peterson and Giles, 2010, p. 4) and to nurture a generation of change-makers who can take the lead in identifying sustainable solutions to refugee situations. Yet refugee tertiary education participation is estimated at just 1% (UNHCR, 2018) and only receives coordinated attention once displacement becomes protracted (Al-Hawamdeh and El-Ghali, 2017).[2]

2 This section draws on a background paper by Ferede (2018).

> Only 1% of refugees participate in tertiary education

Challenges variously highlighted in this report intersect in tertiary education: recognizing credentials and previous learning, learning host languages, and overcoming prohibitive costs. In protracted refugee contexts, tertiary education comes at the end of cumulative education disadvantages that prevent many from qualifying. Moreover, refugees' tertiary education rights often extend to non-discrimination at most.

The Syrian crisis throws the issue into stark relief. Historically, displacement affects populations with low tertiary education participation, but up to one-fifth of young Syrians had access prior to leaving. The proportion fell precipitously in the aftermath of the war, to an estimated 5% or less, prompting calls for 'no lost generation' (European Commission, 2016). Even in as welcoming and familiar an environment as Jordan, challenges are manifold, from lack of academic and career counselling to lack of financial support (Al-Hawamdeh and El-Ghali, 2017).

SCHOLARSHIPS CAN SUPPORT REFUGEES IN PLACE, IN THE REGION AND IN THE GLOBAL NORTH

Displaced populations have severely limited access to tertiary education. The lack of physical access in or around refugee camps motivated technology-based initiatives. The office of the United Nations High Commissioner for Refugees (UNHCR) and the University of Geneva co-lead the Connected Learning in Crisis Consortium, which provides tertiary education opportunities in conflict, crisis and displacement contexts through face-to-face and online learning. Since 2012, connected learning courses have reached over 7,000 students from refugee and host communities (UNHCR, 2018).

International tertiary education scholarships for refugees emerged long before scholarships became part of the official global development agenda. Among the largest and best-known programmes, the Albert Einstein German Academic Refugee Initiative Fund (DAFI) has supported refugees with scholarships through UNHCR since 1992. In 2016, there were 4,652 DAFI recipients, a substantial expansion from 2,321 in 2015. Around 44% were female. DAFI remains a flexible programme whose geographical coverage is continuously adjusted to reflect refugee movements and education needs. A case in point is the Syrian refugee crisis, reflected in both the overall expansion and shifting geographical coverage. In 2016, Syrians were the single largest group at 38% of all beneficiaries Currently, the largest DAFI programmes are in Turkey, Ethiopia, the Islamic Republic of Iran and Lebanon (UNHCR, 2017).

> The DAFI scholarships run through UNHCR benefited 4,652 recipients in 2016, 38% of which were Syrians

Other scholarship programmes support study in high income countries. Tertiary education is increasingly recognized as an alternative or complementary pathway to a safe host country, not only by individuals (Kirkegaard and Nat-George, 2016), but also by institutions, such as the European Union, which officially recognizes refugee admission through scholarships and study programmes as a protection tool (ERN+, 2017). Canada allows private sponsorship of individual refugees who apply for tertiary education (**Box 10.1**).

ACADEMICS ALSO NEED PROTECTION AND SUPPORT

Academics are as much a part of tertiary education as students. Scholars at Risk (SAR), a programme established in 2000 has in recent years provided sanctuary and assistance to more than 300 academics a year who need protection, arranging temporary research and teaching positions at institutions in its global network. In 2002, it partnered with the Institute of International Education, whose Scholar Rescue Fund supports some beneficiaries. A key advocate of academic freedom, SAR also investigates and speaks out against

BOX 10.1:

Canada adopts a broad-based sponsorship model for admitting refugees to tertiary education

The Student Refugee Program (SRP) of the World University Service of Canada (WUSC) is a sponsorship agreement holder that supports university-based local committees in sponsoring refugees for resettlement and university study. Since 1978, it has allowed more than 1,800 refugees from 39 countries to study at more than 80 colleges and universities across Canada.

A key to its success in integration and mobilization is that the endeavour is driven by students, faculty and staff. They raise awareness and funds, often through student union sponsorship levies; engage other students; and provide day-to-day social and academic support to SRP students. The programme has strict eligibility and selection criteria. Participants must be aged between 17 and 25; be recognized refugees in their country of asylum (except Lebanon); fulfil Canada's eligibility, security and medical immigration criteria; and meet host university entrance requirements. As Canada's Private Sponsorship of Refugees Program is an individual resettlement programme, participants must also be single and without dependents, with a few exceptions made for single mothers.

Participants take language classes and computer training to prepare for entering Canada, and attend pre-departure orientation by the International Organization for Migration. WUSC staff or volunteers deliver additional orientation on life and study in Canada and a welcome pack. Before SRP students arrive, the local committees register them for classes and orientation; arrange housing and meal plans; buy them toiletries, school supplies and calling cards; and fill out applications for the permanent resident card, health card and social insurance number. Since they complete immigration checks before departure, refugee youth arrive as permanent residents, which carries eligibility to work and take out student loans, among many other rights.

Participants typically reap considerable benefits, reflecting the intense investment of time and effort. Reports from refugee camp teachers suggest a potential multiplier effect, in which hopes of post-secondary education and eligibility for the highly competitive SRP are incentives for completing secondary school (WUSC, 2007). At the same time, the amount of personal assistance SRP beneficiaries receive is difficult to scale.

In 2017/18, 160 refugee youth were sponsored, more than half of which originated in the Syrian Arab Republic. In addition, Lifeline Syria, a similar but more narrowly targeted network of Toronto-based universities also operating under the Private Sponsorship of Refugees Program, has sponsored 1,074 Syrians through 248 private sponsor groups as of September 2018 (Lifeline Syria, 2018).

> “The Scholars at Risk programme provides sanctuary and assistance to more than 300 academics a year who need protection”

attacks on tertiary education communities. The UK's Council for At-Risk Academics (CARA) is a SAR partner that provides urgent support to academics forced into exile or, particularly, in immediate danger in home countries, offering multiyear packages instead of short stipends.

France established the Programme national d'aide à l'*Accueil en Urgence des Scientifiques en Exil* ('national programme of urgent aid and hosting of scientists in exile', or PAUSE) in 2017 on the initiative of the scientific and research community and the secretary of state for higher education and research. It supports researchers and lecturers from countries whose political situation prevents them from working and endangers their and their families' lives. It facilitates sufficiently long hosting to enable integration into the French environment and ensure research continuity. Tertiary education institutions and research organizations receive co-funding grants.

INDIVIDUAL SUPPORT NEED NOT CAUSE WIDER BENEFITS TO BE OVERLOOKED

Support for individual students and academics is an end in itself. Yet, since it only reaches a small fraction of those in need – and even then, care must be taken to 'do no harm' (UNHCR, 2015b) – providers of individual support should ensure that the wider community also benefits.

DAFI scholarships, which are not designed as a pathway to high income country residence, recognize origin communities as intended beneficiaries and call on beneficiaries to give back to these communities. Some 70% of Afghan DAFI recipient returnees were employed in sectors relevant to development and reconstruction (Milton and Barakat, 2016). Unfortunately, only 8% of DAFI students overall were enrolled in education science or teacher training in 2015, even though demand for teachers is high and growing in refugee communities.

Networks supporting refugee academics, in addition to offering individual relief, can similarly promote capacity building. In 2006, CARA launched a programme aimed at rebuilding research and teaching capacities in Iraq by connecting Iraqi academics, both in country and in Jordan or elsewhere, with counterparts in the United Kingdom. It launched a second regional programme in 2009 in response to an increase in academics fleeing Zimbabwe, offering grants and fellowships for vital equipment and supplies. In 2012, it established a 'virtual lecture hall' at the University of Zimbabwe, allowing Zimbabwean academics in exile and others to connect in real time.

In 2016, CARA launched a programme for Syrian academics displaced in Lebanon and Turkey, aimed at allowing them to develop an international network to draw on in rebuilding tertiary education once it is safe to return to the Syrian Arab Republic. In a pilot phase, workshops in Turkey on academic skills development and English for academic purposes laid the foundations for further collaboration. UK universities hosted the first fellows on short-term research visits. In late 2017, the programme launched a second phase, funded primarily by an Open Society Foundations grant, which is set to last 18 months. In addition to workshops, it envisages 'research incubation visits', a CARA-commissioned research project and a research funding initiative.

CONCLUSION

Few students and academics take advantage of dedicated tertiary education scholarship and sponsorship programmes. In some initiatives, the tertiary education community supports displacement-afflicted peers, often with a high level of personal engagement. They serve an important role in promoting support for refugee issues among host societies. Nevertheless, tertiary education needs cannot be met one refugee at a time: even successful initiatives' reach remains limited. They cannot substitute for efforts to reduce the structural barriers to tertiary education opportunities that hundreds of thousands of refugee youth face.

POLICY FOCUS 10.2: ADDRESSING THE TECHNICAL AND VOCATIONAL EDUCATION NEEDS OF MIGRANTS AND REFUGEES

TVET programmes can facilitate migrants' and refugees' adjustment to the requirements of the labour market in their destination country. Yet two concerns affect the design of TVET programmes for migrants and refugees. First, they should account for constraints that may lower demand by the displaced for skills development. Second, they should understand and recognize skills migrants and refugees bring to destination countries before matching them with education and training or jobs.[3]

MANY BARRIERS PREVENT MIGRANTS AND REFUGEES FROM FURTHERING THEIR SKILLS

Vulnerability and limited options are defining characteristics of migrants and refugees. Their right to employment may be restricted; only 75 of the 145 parties to the 1951 Refugee Convention grant refugees the right to work as Articles 17–19 stipulate, and it is often subject to restrictions (Zetter and Ruaudel, 2016). Some countries have taken steps to address this problem. Between 2016 and mid-2018, Jordan issued or renewed over 100,000 work permits for Syrian refugees (ILO, 2018). In 2016, Turkey allow 600,000 Syrian refugees to work (Karasapan, 2017). Some high income countries have policies to distribute refugees across their territory but employment prospects may not be one of the criteria of dispersion (OECD, 2016a).

Undocumented migrants and asylum-seekers may not have a legal right to work, discouraging participation especially in employer-based vocational training, as employers are reluctant to hire them (OECD and UNHCR, 2018). In Ireland and Lithuania, the undocumented have no access to the labour market until they are granted asylum and become refugees. In the United Kingdom, asylum-seekers wait 12 months to obtain the right

3 This section is partly based on UNESCO-UNEVOC and University of Nottingham (2018).

> TVET programmes for the displaced should account for constraints that lower their demand for skills development and recognise the skills they already have

to work, while countries including Greece, Norway, Portugal and Sweden grant the right to work when individuals claim asylum (European Employment Policy Observatory, 2016).

Limits on the 'network of contacts and trust that usually help individuals to move proficiently in a social environment' (CEDEFOP, 2011, p. 4) may mean migrants and refugees lack information about employment opportunities, leading to initial unemployment. Even when permitted to work, migrants often end up in low-skill jobs. Initial unemployment and precarious employment in jobs not matching their skills lower the return to migrants on investment in their skills, especially when employers exploit the vulnerable who lack documents. Immigrants in France were half as likely as natives to receive training, and the gap was greater in occupations with high immigrant concentration: In the construction sector, 7% of immigrant workers had been trained, compared with 24% of natives (Safi, 2014).

Language barriers may discourage migrants and refugees from investing in skills once they are established in the labour market. In Sweden, translating learning materials into various languages helped lower vocational training course dropout rates. Beyond general language courses, Sweden also responded to the need for skills development programmes for migrants: TVET institutions developed packages to accelerate vocational language proficiency by integrating language tutoring into vocational education and training specific to a trade or industry (UNESCO-UNEVOC and University of Nottingham, 2018, 2018).

The multitude of providers and entry points can hinder TVET participation. Guidance in navigating unfamiliar education and training environments in the host country labour markets is therefore very important. A programme for refugees in Germany delivers intensive vocational language training and career orientation, aiming to find placements for 10,000 young refugees. The number of youth migration services for 12- to 27-year-olds with migrant backgrounds expanded to 450 nationally, benefitting 110,000 people in 2016. Specific orientation and counselling services were targeted at young people in the asylum process. Jugend Stärken im Quartier ('youth get stronger in the neighbourhood') provides counselling and mentoring to the hardest-to-reach young people in 177 local authorities (Germany Federal Ministry of Education and Research, 2017a). Sweden's Public Employment Service runs an introduction programme to assess refugees' labour market readiness and provide guidance on life in Sweden, language training and specific vocational training, if necessary (OECD, 2016b).

TVET providers and public employment services need to connect migrants with employers to help them gain work experience linked with previous occupations. Internships and volunteering can build the social capital necessary for employment after training (CEDEFOP, 2011). Willkomenslotsen ('welcome mentors') in Germany support small and medium-sized enterprises in recruiting newly arrived skilled workers, including refugees. In 2016, 150 trained mentors provided services in 100 local chambers of commerce and industry and placed 3,441 refugees in training or employment (Germany Federal Ministry of Education and Research, 2017b). The Netherlands' emphasis on lifelong learning and non-linear education trajectories makes TVET responsive to foreigner integration (Desiderio, 2016).

TVET content and teaching quality can increase the chances of migrant and refugee integration. The TVET programme of the UN Relief and Works Agency for Palestine Refugees in the Near East provides practical training to 7,200 Palestinian youth per year through 8 training centres. In Gaza, trainees achieved higher final examination scores than the national average (UNRWA, 2016). The programme in Lebanon has one centre, a career guidance and orientation unit and employment service centres. It is flexible in subjects offered and course duration, is learner centred, ensures strong links with employers and aligns curricula with labour market needs. Several countries in the region offer programmes for Syrian refugees (**Box 10.2**).

> “Undocumented migrants and asylum-seekers may not have a legal right to work, discouraging participation especially in employer-based vocational training”

> Where refugees' informal learning is not recognized, validated and accredited, it compromises their ability to gain access to decent work or further education and training

MANY BARRIERS PREVENT MIGRANTS AND REFUGEES FROM USING THEIR SKILLS

Mechanisms to recognize academic and vocational or professional qualifications exist, but migrants and refugees are unlikely to carry qualifications and certificates with them. Over two-thirds of the parties to the Lisbon Recognition Convention have taken few or no measures to implement Art. VII on recognizing refugee qualifications that cannot be fully documented (UNESCO and Council of Europe, 2016). Little is known about the effectiveness of experiments with technology-based approaches, such as digital credentials, in skills recognition (UNESCO, 2018).

TVET degrees may be less portable than academic degrees because of TVET systems' variability. National qualifications and education quality frameworks to measure prior learning facilitate the process. However, for Syrian refugees in Egypt, Iraq, Jordan, Lebanon and Turkey, no learning and competence assessment exists besides formal national education systems and official, non-formal second-chance programmes accredited by ministries of education (ETF, 2014).

BOX 10.2:

TVET programmes have been set up for Syrian refugees in neighbouring countries

The Syrian crisis led to a number of TVET programmes for refugees. International partner support has been critical. In Turkey, the national employment agency is working with several international organizations to overcome the and administrative obstacles for making jobs accessible to Syrian refugees and to develop vocational training programmes (Kirişci et al., 2018).

In Jordan, the Amaluna ('our hope') project partnered with the private sector to provide vulnerable Jordanian and Syrian 18- to 24-year-olds with employment opportunities. It has so far reached about 2,500 youth, of whom 1,500 have been interviewed and 537 enrolled. Of those, almost four out of five graduated, and one-third were employed. The next step is to scale up the programme to reach more than 30,000 vulnerable youth (UNICEF, 2018). The Norwegian Refugee Council offered courses to Syrian youth in tailoring, hairdressing, welding and computing. The three month courses include life skills, literacy and numeracy. More than 770 youth graduated in 2013–2015 (UNICEF, 2015).

UNICEF, the United Nations Development Programme, the European Union and the multidonor European Regional Development and Protection Programme fund the Makhzoumi Foundation vocational training programme. It works with UNHCR to offer eight week courses to refugees over age 14 in Lebanon, training about 4,500 people, mostly women, annually. Subjects covered include information technology, languages, cosmetology, labour market orientation, entrepreneurial skills and cross-cultural communication. It teaches hands-on, practical knowledge, confers nationally recognized certificates and makes links with employers (ETF, 2017b). Evidence suggests the courses improved beneficiaries' incomes and offered new career pathways.

Since 2009, the Better Work Jordan programme has focused on improving the working and living conditions of immigrant workers in the garment industry, including by providing training, and has reached 65,000 workers in 73 factories. A unified contract agreed in 2015 ensured the same recruitment and employment policies for all migrant workers and clarified their rights. Since 2016, the programme has overseen modifications to the contract to include coverage for refugees, coupled with the issuance of 2,000 work permits for Syrians (Better Work Jordan, 2016a, 2016b).

The German Corporation for International Cooperation has supported the Water Wise Plumbers project in Jordan, which aims to reduce water losses in households, in line with the National Water Strategy, the National Employment Strategy and the Jordan Response Plan for the Syrian Arab Republic Crisis. It trains qualified plumbers, recruiting trainees particularly among Syrian refugees, with an emphasis on women. Graduates have created autonomous cooperatives that promise to make a long term contribution to social objectives (ETF, 2017a).

The main challenge is recognizing prior learning. Where refugees' informal learning is not recognized, validated and accredited, it compromises their ability to gain access to decent work or further education and training (Singh, 2018). An inventory of validation shows that migrants and refugees are under-represented as target groups for validation of non-formal and informal learning (ETF, 2015).

The Council of Europe partnered with Greece, Italy, Norway and the United Kingdom for a European Qualifications Passport for Refugees, which provides an assessment of post-secondary qualifications based on available documentation and a structured interview. It includes information on work experience and language proficiency. In 2017, as part of a pilot exercise in Greece, 92 refugees were interviewed and 73 were issued with a qualifications passport. Partners in Armenia, Canada, France, Germany and the Netherlands are to join a second phase (Council of Europe, 2018).

Under the Federal Recognition Act, Germany offers opportunities to identify and evaluate undocumented professional and occupational competences against the German reference qualifications framework, e.g. via a specialist oral examination or work sample. Sixty assessments took place in 2012, rising to 129 by 2015. Over half the applications by Afghan, Albanian, Iranian, Iraqi, Kosovan and Syrian refugees in this period resulted in full equivalence. Providing information in Arabic and introducing a multilingual recognition app in 2016 made it easier for refugees to take advantage of the service. Between June 2015 and December 2016, around 20,000 refugees took part in recognition consultations (Germany Federal Ministry of Education and Research, 2017a).

In 2013, Norway introduced a national Recognition Procedure for Persons without Verifiable Documentation. Expert committees appointed by the Norwegian Agency for Quality Assurance in Education use academic assessments, take-home assignments and mapping of work history. An applicant survey suggests that over half the refugees whose skills were recognized in 2013 either found a related job or entered further education (OECD, 2016b).

Sweden developed an upper secondary healthcare curriculum for refugees working as healthcare assistants. Prior learning relative to the curriculum is assessed through group discussions and teacher supervision, allowing accelerated access to an upper secondary diploma (Andersson and Fejes, 2010).

Intergovernmental cooperation can also facilitate recognition, validation and accreditation. The Philippines' Technical Education and Skills Development Authority is working with Gulf states and Hong Kong, China, to develop mutual qualification recognition agreements for emigrant workers and has been carrying out testing and certification of expatriates in situ (de la Rama, 2018).

SOME COUNTRIES PREPARE EMIGRANTS TO WORK ABROAD

Some countries with high emigration invest in their nationals' skills to ease adjustment to new environments and make the most of a potentially valuable source of income through remittances. Bangladesh, the Philippines and Sri Lanka combined job-related and pre-departure vocational training with longer compulsory programmes, often involving non-government organizations, private employment agencies and trade unions. On the receiving side, Canada has invested in immigrant support programmes, which are linked to acceptance into the country. A trend of immigration information websites is increasing among destination countries (ETF, 2015).

However, even well-organized pre-departure training may not end up being used abroad. Bangladesh dropped the manufacturing vocational training course from an EU-funded intervention when it was found that Italy, the relevant destination country, was hiring not on pre-departure training or skills assessment but on employer assessment of motivation and adaptation skills. Chosen migrants then received intense on-the-job training (Charpin and Aiolfi, 2011).

> “In the Republic of Moldova, external donors funded numerous pre-departure training initiatives for potential migrants”

In the Republic of Moldova, external donors funded numerous pre-departure training initiatives for potential migrants in recent years. These provided general information on legal migration and employment pathways to the EU, on the one hand, and on the risks of illegal migration and trafficking on the other. In addition to professional training, information regarding language, culture and society is emphasized. However, interest in such pre-departure activities was limited where orientation and training were not linked concretely to actual departure and employment (ETF, 2015).

CONCLUSION

Developing migrants' and refugees' technical and vocational skills concerns more than just education planners. If they lack access to employment or to jobs using and building on their skills, migrants and refugees are unlikely to invest in further development. Planners can help by recognizing prior non-formal and informal learning and providing career guidance to ease entry into labour markets.

Every beneficiary of a Cash for Work programme delivered by the International Organization for Migration has the opportunity to take literacy lessons for three months.

CREDIT: Amanda Nero/IOM

KEY MESSAGES

Monitoring the global indicator on information and communications technology skills involves determining whether adults and youth have carried out any of nine activities. Data are scarce outside high income countries. In 15 upper middle income countries, only two of these activities were carried out by at least one-third of adults: copying and pasting files and attaching files to emails.

But monitoring these basic skills may be insufficiently informative because even simple technology solutions for low-literacy users require intermediate skills. The challenge for monitoring higher-order skills is defining them and finding a cost-effective way to measure them.

DigComp, the Digital Competence Framework for Citizens, first developed in 2013 for EU countries, has been adopted with small adjustments as a global framework for digital literacy skills. Given the huge range of digital literacy assessments, a review is needed to see which would be most relevant and cost-effective.

Monitoring social and emotional skills is challenging. The 2015 OECD Programme for International Student Assessment measured collaborative problem-solving. An interesting result was that native students in schools with more immigrants performed better than those in schools with fewer immigrants in countries including Israel, Italy and Spain.

Financial education can help protect migrants and refugees against scams and enable them to make the most of remittances. Indonesia's national strategy on financial literacy provides prospective and actual migrants with training. Participants were more likely to make a budget and had almost twice the savings as a similar group that did not receive the training.

CHAPTER 11

TARGET 4.4

Skills for work

By 2030, substantially increase the number of youth and adults who have relevant skills, including technical and vocational skills, for employment, decent jobs and entrepreneurship

GLOBAL INDICATOR

4.4.1 – *Percentage of youth/adults with information and communications technology (ICT) skills, by type of skill*

THEMATIC INDICATORS

4.4.2 – *Percentage of youth/adults who have achieved at least a minimum level of proficiency in digital literacy skills*

4.4.3 – *Youth/adult educational attainment rates by age group, economic activity status, levels of education and programme orientation*

Target 4.4 has an impressive scope, as its aim is to encourage investment in the skills youth and adults need for the world of work. Yet its monitoring framework is underwhelming in its relative narrowness. Thematic indicator 4.4.3 on adult attainment is not, strictly speaking, a skills indicator. The other two elements – an indirect measure of skills in information and communications technology (ICT) (global indicator 4.4.1) and a direct measure of digital literacy skills (thematic indicator 4.4.2) – seem a very limited set of measures to monitor such a broad target. For instance, among skills applicable to the world of work, financial literacy skills are key for inclusion, especially for migrants, yet no indicator captures those (**Policy focus 11.1**).

DIGITAL LITERACY SKILLS ARE IMPORTANT BUT DIFFICULT TO MONITOR DIRECTLY

The ICT and digital literacy indicators are nonetheless innovative for an education monitoring framework. First, they aim to capture skills beyond literacy and numeracy. Second, they try to assess skills that are becoming almost universally important for the world of work; not many skills categories can claim to have such worldwide relevance. Third, they challenge governments to think how such skills can be acquired outside school.

The global indicator on youth and adults with ICT skills draws on individuals reporting in household surveys whether they have carried out selected activities in the previous three months. The latest data from the International Telecommunication Union (ITU) show that copying and attaching files to emails are the only skills that more than one in three respondents exercised in typical middle income countries, while the level was between 58% and 70% in the high income group (**Figure 11.1**). Programming remains a minority activity even in high income countries, however.

Measuring the percentage of individuals who have applied a skill in the previous three months may underestimate the percentage who possess the skill but have not used it recently. The Programme for the International Assessment of Adult Competencies (PIAAC) survey of the Organisation for Economic Co-operation and Development (OECD) collects information on the frequency of use of digital skills. While the reference period does not match up perfectly, as there is no category in PIAAC between 'less than once a month' and 'never', these PIAAC figures suggest that the number of rare users is fairly small (**Table 11.1**).

Monitoring actual behaviour is more informative than simply examining diffusion of technology. Mobile phones may be less ubiquitous in poor rural areas than is often assumed, especially after accounting for low utilization and engagement by many groups (Haenssgen, 2018). Engagement with technology may be best understood as a social phenomenon. Third parties are often involved in helping non-users take advantage of mobile technology.

The level of engagement with specific online services, such as Facebook, reflects many factors other than digital skills. A recent study noted, for instance, that the relative gender gap in Facebook use is highly correlated with the gender gap in the ITU's measure of internet access (Fatehkia et al., 2018). Despite their methodological weaknesses, estimates based on online measures may eventually help fill gaps in data coverage across countries or between waves of more robust surveys.

> "Just over one in three in upper middle income countries can copy and attach files to emails, rising to 58% and 70% respectively in high income countries"

A key question is whether the foundational digital skills captured by the global indicator represent a very low threshold. Digital solutions for improved livelihoods can include apps that enable community healthcare workers to register pregnant women with government services, allow people to make payment claims, provide farmers with small-business management tools, and so on. Mapping the skills required to use such tools showed that even solutions aimed at low-skilled and low-literacy users required intermediate rather than foundational digital skills (UNESCO, 2018).

Thematic indicator 4.4.2 – 'Percentage of youth/adults who have achieved at least a minimum level of proficiency in digital literacy skills' – goes well beyond ability to use ICT equipment (Fau and Moreau, 2018). An attempt was made recently, as part of the Global Alliance to Monitor Learning process, to define a global framework for digital literacy based on the Digital Competence Framework for Citizens (DigComp), which was developed by the European Commission. Identifying tools to measure competences in this framework cost-effectively remains the greatest challenge for the target 4.4 monitoring agenda (**Data focus 11.1**).

This initiative, which examined DigComp's relevance outside Europe, identified computational thinking as a skill not covered in the DigComp framework. Understood as the everyday application of the algorithmic, computational nature of problem-solving involving digital technology, this skill is broader than programming and does not necessarily involve specific computer languages (UIS, 2018). The 2018 International Computer and Information Literacy Study includes a new optional assessment strand on computational thinking, defined as 'the ability to identify a problem, break it down into manageable steps, work out the important details or patterns, shape possible solutions, and present these solutions in a way that a computer, a human, or both, can understand' (IEA, 2017, p. 1). Results should help in understanding the relationship between computational thinking and other aspects of computer and information literacy.

FIGURE 11.1:

ICT skills remain unequally distributed

Percentage of adults who performed a computer-related activity in the previous three months, by country income group, 2014–2017

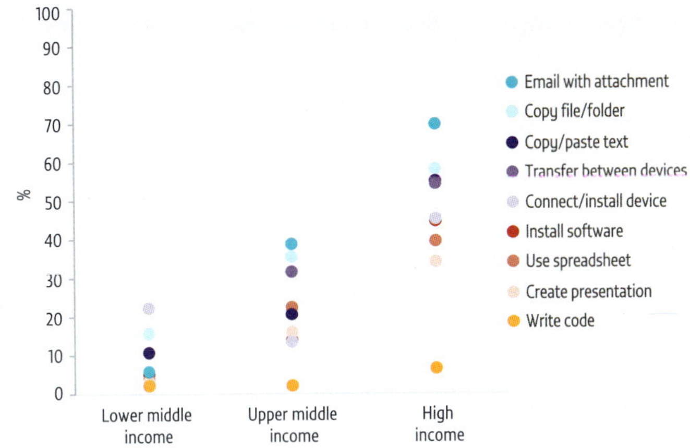

GEM StatLink: http://bit.ly/fig11_1
Note: Medians for middle income countries are based on a small number of countries (5 lower middle income, 15 upper middle income).
Source: ITU database.

TABLE 11.1:

Most people who ever use a digital skill do so frequently, especially at work

Percentage of respondents who perform computer-related activities less than once per month among all those who ever perform them, selected countries, 2011–2015

	At work			Everyday life		
	Use a spreadsheet	Use a word processor	Programme or write code	Use a spreadsheet	Use a word processor	Programme or write code
Chile	9	8	6	17	16	6
Denmark	11	7	6	24	18	6
Japan	10	13	6	23	28	5
New Zealand	9	7	4	22	22	4
Ireland	6	3	9	17	21	3
Russian Fed.	12	8	4	22	20	5
United States	9	7	5	23	21	5

Source: GEM Report team analysis of OECD PIAAC data.

“ A key question is whether the foundational digital skills captured by the global indicator represent a very low threshold given that even solutions for low-literacy users require intermediate skills ”

THERE ARE FEW ATTEMPTS AT CROSS-NATIONAL MONITORING OF SOCIAL-EMOTIONAL SKILLS

In outlining the scope and challenges of measuring progress towards target 4.4, the 2016 *Global Education Monitoring Report* discussed social-emotional skills, including perseverance, self-control and social skills. It described their importance for employment, as well as concerns about the monitoring challenges, such as reaching cross-cultural consensus on definitions and operationalization.

A recent review of Skills toward Employability and Productivity (STEP), a World Bank survey, confirms these concerns. Carried out in mostly urban areas of 15 middle income countries, the survey has included questions on the so-called Big Five personality traits: openness to experience, conscientiousness, emotional stability, extraversion and agreeableness. An analysis of the results called for caution in interpreting measures across cultures and for more research on how to adapt measures to studies in poorer countries (Laajaj et al., 2018).

The OECD is developing an international study to assess the social-emotional skills of 10- and 15-year-olds. The study will use a version of the Big Five model, calling the traits open-mindedness, task performance, emotional regulation, engaging with others and collaboration. It will focus on selected cities and countries and release findings in 2020 (Chernyshenko et al., 2018; OECD, 2017b).

The 2015 OECD Programme for International Student Assessment measured collaborative problem-solving, defined as an individual's capacity to 'effectively engage in a process whereby two or more agents attempt to solve a problem by sharing the understanding and effort required to come to a solution and pooling their knowledge, skills and efforts to reach that solution' (OECD, 2017a, p. 26). Among the 52 education systems that took part, those of Japan, the Republic of Korea and Singapore scored the highest on average. In these countries, at least 10% of 15-year-old students also reached level 4, which means they could solve complex problems while 'maintaining an awareness of group dynamics and ensuring that team members act in accordance with their agreed-upon roles'.

The results also had implications for diversity in schools. Native students in schools with higher proportions of immigrant students performed better on collaborative problem-solving tasks than those in schools with fewer immigrants, controlling for their science performance (OECD, 2017a) (**Figure 11.2**).

DATA FOCUS 11.1: DEFINING AND ASSESSING DIGITAL AND ENTREPRENEURSHIP COMPETENCES

Monitoring SDG target 4.4 on how many youth and adult have 'relevant skills … for employment, decent jobs and entrepreneurship' is likely to entail significant challenges. Few skills, other than literacy and numeracy, are sufficiently relevant across different labour markets to be amenable to global monitoring. Moreover, success in the labour market requires a combination of skills in the right proportions.

As the 2016 *Global Education Monitoring Report* noted, from a global comparison perspective, the focus should be on skills that apply in diverse labour markets, can be acquired through education and can be measured at low cost. Including ICT skills (global indicator 4.4.1) and digital literacy (thematic indicator 4.4.2) in the SDG 4 monitoring framework was appropriate, especially as these become increasingly relevant for employment and participation in social and political life. Yet monitoring digital literacy is difficult and could be costly, and there are no indicators on skills for entrepreneurship. Two recent European Commission initiatives have tried to define and assess digital and entrepreneurship competences.

“From a global comparison perspective, the focus should be on skills that apply in diverse labour markets, can be acquired through education and can be measured at low cost”

FIGURE 11.2:

In most countries, mixed classrooms are better at collaborative problem-solving

Gap in average collaborative problem-solving score between the top and bottom quarter of schools in terms of proportion of immigrant students, 2015

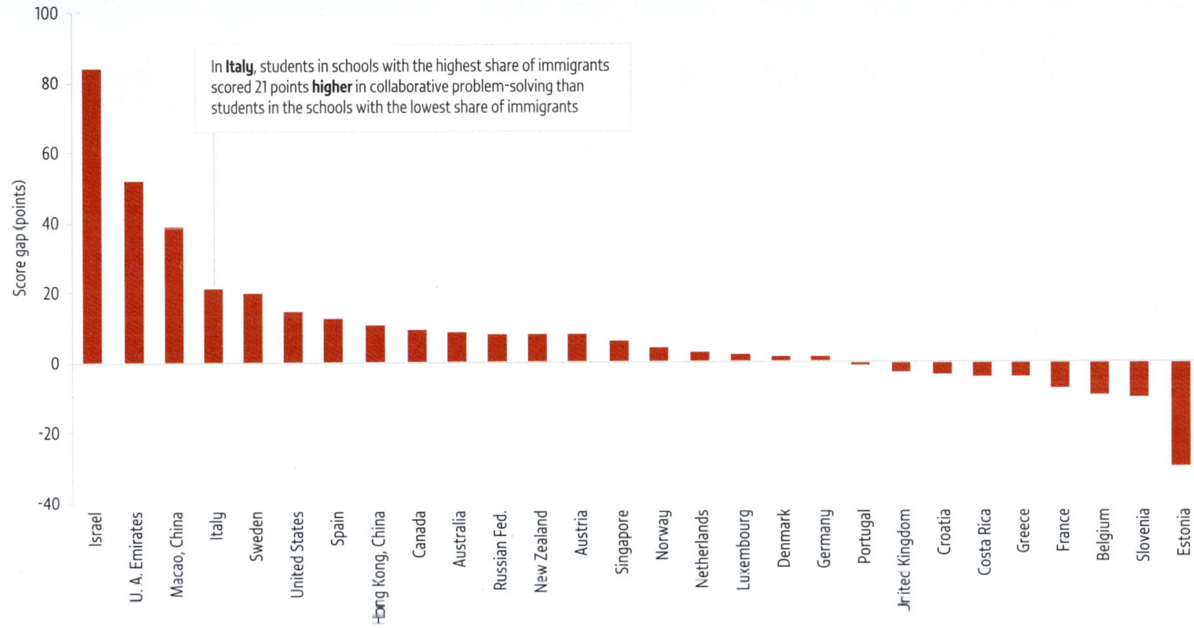

GEM StatLink: http://bit.ly/fig11_2

Note: These values account for students' and schools' socio-economic characteristics.

Source: OECD (2017).

DEFINING A FRAMEWORK AND ASSESSING DIGITAL COMPETENCES

The European Commission's Joint Research Centre (JRC) developed DigComp in 2013. Now in its third edition (2.1), it covers five areas (information and data literacy, communication and collaboration, digital content creation, safety, and problem solving) and 21 competences. Examples illustrate the eight levels of proficiency, e.g. ability to identify portals that would help a job search corresponds to the lowest level of proficiency in the competence of browsing, searching and filtering data, information and digital content (Carretero et al., 2017).

As a comprehensive framework developed over several years in consultation with several countries, DigComp could serve as a global framework for indicator 4.4.2. Under the Global Alliance to Monitor Learning, the Hong Kong University Centre for Information Technology in Education concluded that DigComp was a solid starting point for a digital literacy global framework but would benefit from two extensions: a base level of familiarity with digital devices, usually taken for granted in rich countries, and a wider set of career-related competences reflecting the cultural, economic and technology settings of low and middle income countries, such as examples showing the increasing complexity of skills farmers would need, from making farming and trading decisions using a mobile phone service to buying and selling products using a smartphone app and building a data-driven irrigation system using moisture sensors linked to a laptop (UIS, 2018).

It must also be determined whether an extended DigComp framework could be a solid basis for assessing and monitoring digital literacy skills. A mapping exercise under way within the Global Alliance to Monitor Learning may provide answers. The huge range of digital literacy assessments worldwide vary by focus, purpose (admission, certification, training needs assessment, employment, etc.), target group, uptake, item development, reliability and validity, mode of delivery, cost, scalability and responsible authority (with private providers more closely involved than in literacy and numeracy skills assessments).

> It is a key question which digital literacy assessment could be scaled up in low and middle income countries at realistic cost to serve a global monitoring purpose

Which assessment could realistically be scaled up, used in low and middle income countries and serve a global monitoring purpose is an important issue.

Three potentially interesting models explicitly assess DigComp competences. While their purpose is formative, they could potentially be used for monitoring. Two come from the European Commission. The first is a pilot study of 234 families that looked at digital skills of disadvantaged young people (European Commission, 2018a). The second has been developed with reference to an extension of DigComp for education institutions. It is targeted at school leaders, teachers and students to help schools identify digital literacy strengths and weaknesses and build a school improvement strategy. It has gone through a 2017 pilot phase with 67,000 users, and is to launch formally in late 2018. The aim, included in the European Union's Digital Education Action Plan, is to reach 1 million users by the end of 2019 (European Commission, 2018b).

The third example, Pix, is an online platform for assessment and certification of DigComp skills, managed by the French Ministry of National Education, Higher Education and Research and developed as a state-sponsored and state-managed start-up. Citizens would have free access to a digital skills assessment, diagnosis of strengths and weaknesses and recommendations of learning resources (Vie et al., 2017). In 2019/20, it will be administered to every student in grades 8 to 12 (Pix, 2018).

DEFINING A FRAMEWORK AND ASSESSING ENTREPRENEURSHIP COMPETENCES

Entrepreneurial skills encompass a range of competences, many of which are valuable outside starting a business and are, indeed, only one aspect of successful entrepreneurial activity (ODI, 2012). They involve transversal cognitive and practical skills and require action upon opportunities and ideas to generate financial, cultural or social value for others (Bacigalupo et al., 2016). The JRC developed the Entrepreneurship Competence Framework (EntreComp) in 2016 as a common reference framework in response to the New Skills Agenda for Europe. It includes three areas (ideas and opportunities, resources, and 'into action') and 15 competences. Like DigComp, it defines eight levels of proficiency, explained through examples of learning outcomes, e.g. ability to carry out assigned tasks responsibly corresponds to the lowest level of proficiency in the competence of taking initiative (Bacigalupo et al., 2016).

As with DigComp, the question is whether EntreComp competences can be assessed and monitored through existing surveys. The Global Entrepreneurship Monitor, which surveys adults in 54 countries, includes an indicator on 'fear of failure as a barrier to starting a business' (Global Entrepreneurship Monitor, 2018), which is addressed by three different competences in EntreComp. The World Bank's STEP survey includes questions on grit, a personality trait that EntreComp addresses under 'motivation and perseverance'. However, these surveys are costly to administer, and skills, such as creativity and managing uncertainty, are difficult to measure.

A mapping of a dozen self-assessment tools against the EntreComp competences showed some potential, but respondents would need incentives to take part in a self-assessment for it to yield sufficient data for diagnostic or policy inferences. Completing a test could, for instance, guide respondents to take up specific training opportunities, placement in youth employment programmes, career counselling services or skill certification, according to their strengths and weaknesses. A range of industries, professions and professionals routinely use self-assessment tools for accreditation, including health sector practitioners, managers and teachers. Promoting inclusion of EntreComp-based elements in such tools seems a plausible path to wide adoption. While the data would not represent the general population, they would be relevant for monitoring trends in competences such as 'seeking advice on self-employment' (Bacigalupo et al., 2016).

> It is hard and costly to monitor entrepreneurship skills, which cover a diverse range of competences

POLICY FOCUS 11.1: SUPPORTING MIGRANTS WITH FINANCIAL EDUCATION

Financial literacy helps individuals better manage their economic circumstances and avoid fraud or financial exploitation. Migrants and refugees face particular vulnerabilities. Financial and welfare systems in host communities, as well as abuse reporting mechanisms, may initially be opaque, especially to less educated newcomers. Migrants thus are vulnerable to exploitative contractual agreements, exorbitant recruitment fees, exploitative visa arrangements and outright scams. The consequences range from financial struggles to human trafficking or bonded labour (UNODC, 2015). Low financial literacy is pervasive. Only around one-quarter to one-third of adults are financially literate in the top remittance-receiving countries, a level considerably below those in all but the worst-performing remittance-sending countries (**Figure 11.3**). Among migrants, concepts such as interest compounding, inflation and risk diversification are often not well understood (Lusardi and Mitchell, 2014).

> “Only around one-quarter to one-third of adults are financially literate in the top remittance-receiving countries”

A growing number of government and non-government financial education initiatives target migrants and refugees (Atkinson and Messy, 2013; GPFI, 2015). They aim to educate migrants on efficient approaches to managing remittances (**Policy focus 19.4**) as well as financial products and services beyond remittances. Some also focus on families left behind (OECD, 2016b).

FINANCIAL EDUCATION INITIATIVES CATER TO DIVERSE MIGRANT NEEDS

Like everyone, migrants stand to benefit from a sound understanding of financial products, such as current accounts, savings accounts and electronic payments, as well as from personal money management skills, such as knowing how to budget, track expenses, keep records and understand debt management and credit (interest calculation, principal outstanding, repayment prioritization) (Atkinson and Messy, 2015; OECD, 2016b). In terms of remittances, a financially literate migrant would, at a minimum, need to understand channels and compare cost components,

FIGURE 11.3:

There is a financial literacy gap between remittance-sending and remittance-receiving countries

Percentage of financially literate adults, top remittance-sending and -receiving countries, 2015

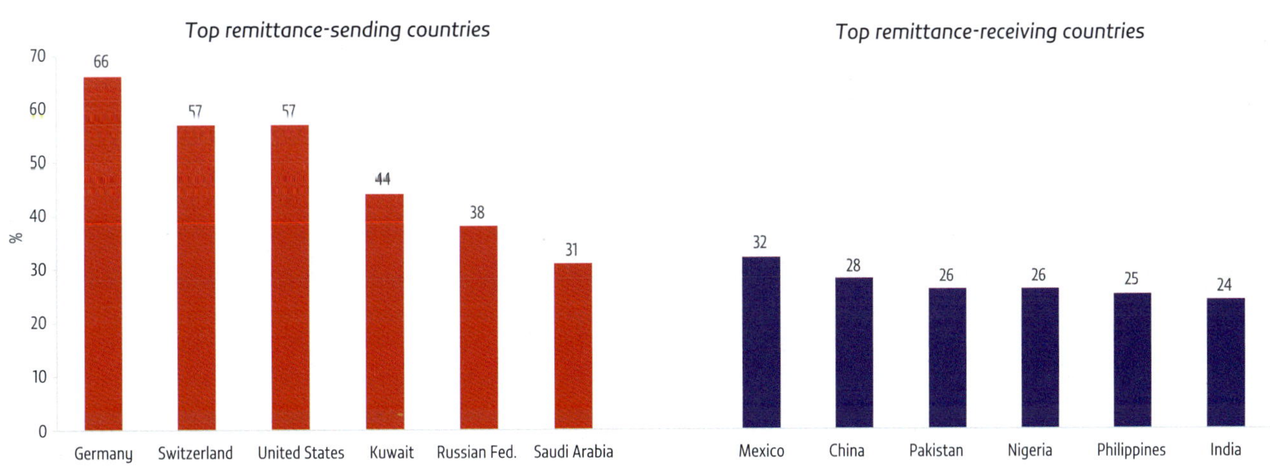

GEM StatLink: http://bit.ly/fig11_3

Note: Adults were defined as financially literate if they answered questions correctly on at least three out of four concepts for financial decision-making: basic numeracy, interest compounding, inflation and risk diversification.

Sources: Klapper et al. (2015) for financial literacy and World Bank (2018) for remittances.

including exchange rates, fees and varying inflation rates. More educated migrants typically exhibit higher than average entrepreneurship rates. Financial literacy provides the foundation for more advanced and specialized skills, such as insurance and retirement planning, accounting and managing business investments and loans.

Numerous global initiatives include a focus on migrants as part of broader agendas promoting financial inclusion, financial literacy and financial education in general. Examples include the OECD International Network on Financial Education and the G20 Global Partnership for Financial Inclusion subgroup on Financial Literacy and Financial Consumer Protection. Several UN agencies and donors offer training and financial literacy materials. For instance, the International Fund for Agricultural Development (IFAD) has a Financing Facility for Remittances. Charitable foundations associated with the financial industry also engage in projects targeting migrants, for instance in Egypt (Attia and Engelhardt, 2016).

Financial education programmes for migrants often involve a combination of international, government, non-government and private-sector stakeholders. In China, a non-government financial education initiative for internal migrants by the Yunnan Institute of Development offers a remittance record product as proof of creditworthiness to help farm families get access to microcredit. The institute also works with the IFAD facility to encourage community-based organizations to share good practice in financial literacy. These initiatives are complemented by door-to-door financial services and financial education in remote areas, where rural credit cooperatives, post offices and other formal remittance channels are scarce (GPFI, 2015).

> “Indonesia adopted the blueprint for a national strategy on financial literacy in 2013, including for prospective migrants”

Indonesia adopted the blueprint for a national strategy on financial literacy in 2013, using evidence from a joint programme with the World Bank (Doi et al., 2012; GPFI, 2015). It provides prospective migrants with training focusing on moments when they may face big financial decisions. The pre-departure stage covers financial planning and basic financial products and services, such as savings and credit. During the migration stage, the focus is on remittances. Participation by not just migrants but also their families proved most effective. Migrants were more likely to make a budget and had almost twice the savings as a similar group that did not receive the training (World Bank, 2017b).

Mexico's Financial Education Committee coordinates members' financial education activities and programmes. The National Savings and Financial Services Bank (BANSEFI), a social development bank focused on promoting financial inclusion, offers financial education courses. The courses contain a module covering remittance types, choosing a financial product, managing use of remittances, and saving and investing money received. They also outline services provided in the United States by the Institute of Mexicans Abroad. BANSEFI reaches out to current migrants through its presence in consulates (OECD, 2018).

Morocco hosts large communities of undocumented immigrants, mainly from sub-Saharan Africa. The Moroccan Foundation for Financial Education partnered with the International Labour Organization to set up financial education programmes for migrants. They conducted qualitative surveys before developing the training to ensure the toolkit met the needs of both migrants and their families (World Bank, 2017a).

The International Organization for Migration launched a joint initiative with MasterCard to support integration of migrants and refugees in Romania. One goal is to help them independently manage their resources through free, weekly financial literacy training at integration centres. Vulnerable groups, including children, women and persons with special needs, are prioritized for personalized assistance (IOM, 2018).

FINANCIAL EDUCATION IS ONLY PART OF FINANCIAL INCLUSION

Even with good literacy levels, migrants may be unfamiliar with financial terms and features of financial products. The Swedish Financial Supervisory Authority, in a programme called *Dina pengar och din ekonomi* ('your money, your finances') provides a film, a brochure and other resources for teachers working with migrants on personal finance. Modules cover Swedish economic terms and the Swedish banking and payment system, and clarify rights and obligations in the financial marketplace in plain language (OECD, 2016a).

> The effectiveness of financial education is constrained by migrants' lack of trust in financial institutions and concerns around risks of deportation from accessing financial services

Migrants may not trust financial institutions, both at home and in host communities. Undocumented migrants and newly arrived refugees often worry that the information requested for access to financial services will be used to identify them and lead to deportation. Tax avoidance and security concerns may also contribute to mistrust. While such mistrust may be justified, in other cases it is based on lack of understanding of immigration rules and the legal implications of providing information to third parties, or on rumours. Indeed, migrants and especially refugees may lack access to a peer network for advice on access to financial services.

Another major barrier concerns the financial industry itself, which may lack relevant or culturally sensitive products for immigrants in host communities and families back home, have insufficient access points (e.g. branches) or offer products with high fees and low flexibility. Few financial products are sensitive to migrant women. Although remittance recipients are women, and they often face economic and social barriers to access to formal financial services, training design in the industry rarely reflects women's needs and constraints (GMG, 2017). Lack of appropriate complaint channels is another key deterrent for migrants unfamiliar with their new settings and for families at home who may simply have no recourse if money is transferred incorrectly.

It is unsurprising, therefore, that financial education initiatives alone are not necessarily effective. Evidence on financial education's impact on migrants' ultimate economic well-being is mixed and context-dependent. Much of it links financial literacy to poor or smart financial decisions, but financial education's causal influence is less clear (Entorf and Hou, 2018). A study of Indian migrants in Qatar found some small impact on financial decisions (Seshan and Yang, 2014). Studies in Australia and New Zealand found that financial literacy programmes did not significantly affect use of formal banking. In Fiji, mobile telephones alone boosted financial literacy (Brown et al., 2014; Gibson et al., 2012). Meta-analyses have produced mixed evidence (Fernandes et al., 2014). The most recent showed a small impact on the financial attitudes and behaviours of disadvantaged groups (Kaiser and Menkhoff, 2017).

A common policy recommendation is to develop more targeted financial education for migrants, since different groups have diverse preferences and economic circumstances. When literacy levels are very low, short exposure to financial training may be insufficient to change behaviour (Lusardi and Mitchell, 2014). Exploring pedagogical approaches may establish whether some elements of financial literacy are better learned by doing (Michaud, 2017). Peer effects within families are important and should be incorporated into financial education programme design (Doi et al., 2012). In Sri Lanka, a financial literacy programme tailors training to migrants, left-behind household members or returnees (Rosenberg, 2017).

CONCLUSION

Migrants and refugees face barriers to financial inclusion that are unrelated to financial literacy. Yet financial education can help protect them against scams and enable households to make the most of remittances. The need for financial education varies by the degree of migrants' skills, by stage of migration and between migrants and dependents left behind. This diversity of needs is met by a wide range of actors engaged in financial education for migrants. Just navigating this supply-driven range of potential training providers may require some sophistication.

National financial education strategies exist in large traditional sending countries in the middle income group. But there is scope in both sending and receiving countries to coordinate financial education for migrants at the national level and integrate it into general migration policy to avoid duplication and to reach all migrants. Successful initiatives involve migrants in their development, actively bring relevant information to households, provide such information at the time financial decisions are made, pay special attention to women and other disadvantaged groups, are integrated with financial and migration service provision, and are well-coordinated among stakeholders.

Masum,* a 12-year-old, came to Dhaka, Bangladesh, on his own two months ago. He attends a centre run by Save the Children's partner organization, INCIDIN and funded by the IKEA Foundation, where children are given a chance to catch up on their education and staff try to connect them to schools. 'I like the centre because I can play here and learn things.'

**Name has been changed.*

CREDIT: Mats Lignell/Save the Children

KEY MESSAGES

While there is gender parity in enrolment globally, on average, up to secondary education, only 49% of countries had achieved parity at the lower secondary education level and only 24% in upper secondary. This is mainly due to enrolment disparities at the expense of boys in many countries.

Considerable disparities exist in completion rates by location and wealth. But cross-categorizing cases by multiple dimensions (e.g. poor rural girls) often results in small sample sizes, which leads to greater imprecision in estimates for these groups.

Rural students have half the chance of their urban peers to complete upper secondary in low and middle income countries. But new data suggesting that more than 80% of the population in Africa and Asia live in urban areas could mean urban-rural education inequalities are even higher.

At least 800 million people live in slums worldwide. The little data that exist tend to show that education indicators in slums are poor. The out-of-school rate of primary school age children and secondary school age adolescents in Bangladesh was twice as high in slums as in other urban areas.

New UNICEF Multiple Indicator Cluster Surveys data on disability showed that among children aged 5 to 17 in Sierra Leone, 0.2% had difficulty seeing and 0.2% had difficulty hearing. Other functional difficulties varied considerably by age, making the data difficult to interpret.

Empowering refugees with disabilities to exercise their voice and including them in mainstream programme design are essential to ensure their inclusion in education.

CHAPTER 12

TARGET 4.5

Equity

By 2030, eliminate gender disparities in education and ensure equal access to all levels of education and vocational training for the vulnerable, including persons with disabilities, indigenous peoples and children in vulnerable situations

GLOBAL INDICATOR

4.5.1 – *Parity indices (female/male, rural/urban, bottom/top wealth quintile and others such as disability status, indigenous peoples and conflict-affected, as data become available) for all education indicators on this list that can be disaggregated*

THEMATIC INDICATORS

4.5.2 – *Percentage of students in primary education whose first or home language is the language of instruction*

4.5.3 – *Extent to which explicit formula-based policies reallocate education resources to disadvantaged populations*

4.5.4 – *Education expenditure per student by level of education and source of funding*

4.5.5 – *Percentage of total aid to education allocated to least developed countries*

Achieving equitable education systems that leave no one behind, which are at the core of SDG 4, require paying attention to disparity in education inputs, processes and outcomes. In terms of enrolment, disparity can be estimated through administrative data for the gender dimension. Globally there is gender parity in enrolment, on average, all the way up to secondary education. Parity has also been achieved on average in all regions in primary and lower secondary education except for primary education in sub-Saharan Africa (0.96). Regional variation is much larger at the upper secondary level, where the adjusted gender parity index ranges from 0.82 in sub-Saharan Africa to 1.12 in Oceania. Even though parity has been achieved on average at the global level, only 24% of countries globally reached parity (**Table 12.1**).

“Globally there is gender parity in enrolment, on average, all the way up to secondary education”

In terms of completion, disparity needs to be estimated through household surveys for the gender (female vs male), location (rural vs urban) and wealth (bottom vs top quintile) dimensions. While school completion by gender is close to parity in the average country, a significant spread remains in many countries, to the disadvantage of either girls or boys, especially in secondary education. With respect to location and wealth, countries are moving

TABLE 12.1:

Adjusted gender parity index of the gross enrolment ratio and percentage of countries that have achieved parity, by education level, 2017

	Pre-primary		Primary		Lower secondary		Upper secondary		Tertiary	
	Adjusted gender parity index	Countries at parity (%)	Adjusted gender parity index	Countries at parity (%)	Adjusted gender parity index	Countries at parity (%)	Adjusted gender parity index	Countries at parity (%)	Adjusted gender parity index	Countries at parity (%)
World	**1.00**	**59**	**0.99**	**62**	**0.99**	**49**	**1.02**	**24**	**1.16**	**6**
Sub-Saharan Africa	1.02	44	0.96	34	0.98	21	0.82	5	0.75	0
Northern Africa and Western Asia	1.00	53	0.99	67	0.99	60	1.02	30	1.19	20
Central and Southern Asia	0.97	38	1.00	57	0.99	50	0.99	46	0.89	7
Eastern and South-eastern Asia	1.00	80	0.99	76	1.00	56	1.03	41	1.15	0
Oceania	1.01	27	0.99	59	1.02	29	1.12	0	...	...
Latin America and the Caribbean	1.02	69	0.97	55	1.01	52	1.10	14	1.27	5
Europe and Northern America	0.99	82	1.00	93	0.99	74	1.01	38	1.23	7
Low income	1.02	30	0.97	35	0.96	10	0.75	10	0.54	0
Lower middle income	1.00	62	0.98	50	1.00	36	0.99	24	1.04	11
Upper middle income	1.01	59	0.99	68	1.01	61	1.06	23	1.20	3
High income	1.00	76	1.00	85	0.99	68	1.03	33	1.27	7

Note: The adjusted parity index is symmetric above and below parity, e.g. if attendance is 80 girls per 100 boys in one country and 80 boys per 100 girls in another country, the two index values are symmetrical around 1.
Sources: UIS database and GEM Report team calculations.

> "In many low and middle income countries, rural students have, at best, around half the chance of their urban peers to complete upper secondary, and often much less than that"

towards minimizing disparity in primary completion, but disparity in secondary completion is considerable. In many low and middle income countries, rural students have, at best, around half the chance of their urban peers to complete upper secondary, and often much less than that (**Figure 12.1**).

While the various types of disparity discussed here are expressed in terms of the parity index, which is singled out in the SDG monitoring framework for monitoring equity, there are numerous ways of measuring and interpreting education differences among groups. As the 2016 *Global Education Monitoring Report* showed, various inequality measures may give seemingly contradictory results. A new *Handbook on Measuring Equity in Education* offers much-needed conceptual and analytic clarity regarding many aspects of equity measurement that go beyond the SDG indicator framework. It distinguishes between analyses focused on whether everyone meets a minimum standard or experiences the same condition and analyses of whether education unfairly depends on some background characteristic, depends only on salient effort or ability, or actively benefits the most disadvantaged (UIS, 2018).

The handbook also illustrates survey limitations in investigating the intersection of various sources of disadvantage. Cross-categorizing cases by multiple dimensions often results in small sample sizes, which leads to greater imprecision in estimates for these groups. Analysis of household surveys over 2013–2017 for this report shows how uncertainty increases, as more dimensions are added. If the estimate of the completion rate for the poorest is 80% (single dimension – wealth), then the actual value will often be as low as 75% or as high as 85% (5 percentage points). But if the estimate of the completion rate for poor rural girls is 50% (three dimensions – sex, location and wealth), then the

FIGURE 12.1:

Many countries remain far from achieving location and wealth parity in school completion, especially in secondary education

Gender, location and wealth adjusted parity index of completion rate, by education level, 2014–2017

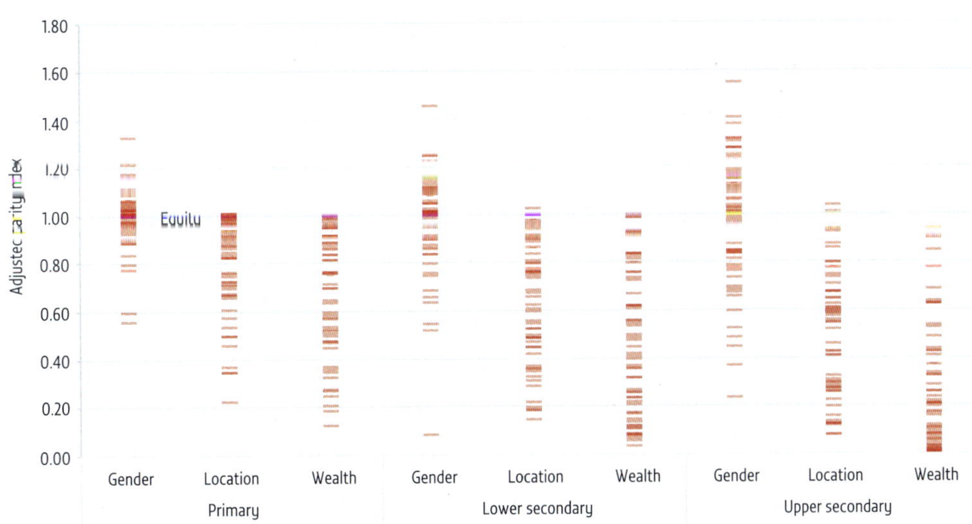

GEM StatLink: http://bit.ly/fig12_1

Sources: UIS and GEM Report team calculations based on household surveys.

FIGURE 12.2:

Completion rate estimates for poor rural girls are less precise than those just for girls

Precision of primary completion rate estimates, by number of intersecting dimensions, 2012–2017

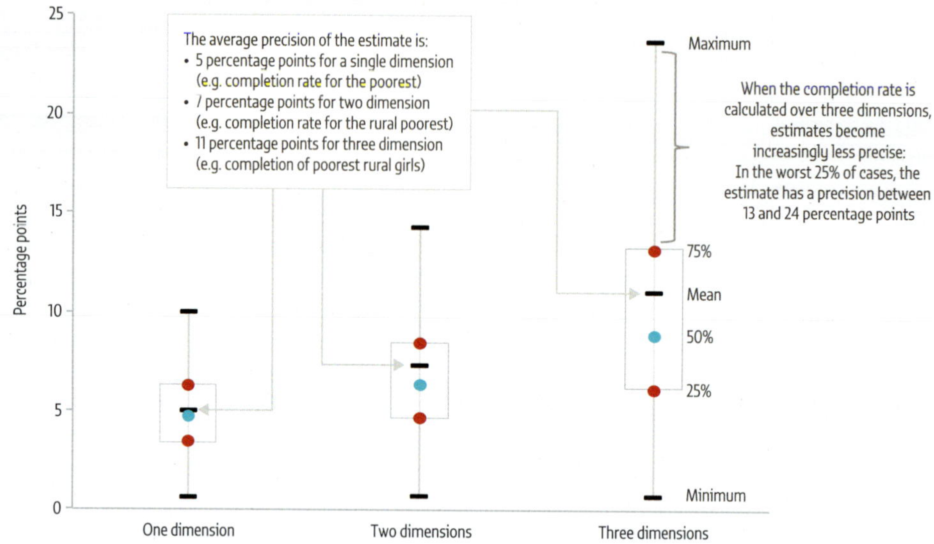

GEM StatLink: http://bit.ly/fig12_2

Note: 'precision' refers to estimated standard errors of the completion rate.

Sources: GEM Report team calculations based on household surveys carried out in 2012–2017.

actual value will often be as low as 39% or as high as 61% (11 percentage points). In the least precise quarter of estimates, the error will often be as large as 13 to 24 percentage points in either direction (**Figure 12.2**).

Another key limitation of disparity measures is that location and wealth are based on national definitions. Moreover, the official definition of an urban area may not reflect the reality in many fast-growing countries (**Box 12.1** and **Data focus 12.1**).

The measurement challenge of intersecting sources of disadvantage arises even before considering other important aspects, such as disability (**Policy focus 12.1**). While global indicator 4.5.1 specifies disability as a disaggregation category, available data do not allow yet for internationally comparable results. It is also not clear that a single disability parity index would be meaningful, given the difference in difficulty associated with various impairments.

The sixth round of the UNICEF Multiple Indicator Cluster Surveys (MICS), scheduled to be conducted in about 60 countries, takes a step towards more comprehensive international data by including a child functioning module. It approaches disability according to functionality and aims to identify children experiencing, or at risk of experiencing, limited participation in an unaccommodating environment (UNICEF, 2017).

Two MICS questionnaires include the child functioning module, with mothers or primary caregivers reporting functional difficulties in a series of domains. The under age 5 questionnaire covers seeing, hearing, walking, fine motor skills, communication, learning, playing and controlling behaviour. The age 5 to 17 questionnaire eliminates fine motor skills and playing and adds self-care, remembering, concentrating, accepting change, making friends, anxiety and depression (UNICEF, 2016).

Results from one of the first MICS 6 surveys indicate that, among children aged 5 to 17 in Sierra Leone, 0.2% had difficulty seeing and 0.2% had difficulty hearing. Other functional difficulties varied considerably by age, making them difficult to interpret. While 1.9% of 5- to 9-year-olds had a functional difficulty in the domain of self-care, the same difficulty was reported for just 0.1% of 15- to 17-year-olds. And 5.1% of 5- to 9-year-olds but only 1.4% of 15- to 17-year-olds had difficulty walking.

BOX 12.1:

The definition of an urban area is much more fluid than commonly thought

Assessing rural disadvantage across countries depends crucially on comparable definitions of 'rural' and 'urban'. Unfortunately, comparability is low. The share of labour engaged in agriculture, population size, population density, idiosyncratic national criteria or any combination of these may determine classification. Moreover, official classification may lag behind structural and population change. This can reflect the rapidity of the change or, in some cases, be deliberate, to avoid the statutory public service investment that comes with urban status.

At the 2016 UN Habitat III conference in Quito, a decision was made to develop a global, people-based definition of cities and settlements to aid in monitoring the SDGs; it will be submitted for endorsement by the UN Statistical Commission in 2019. A collaborative effort between the EU Joint Research Centre, the Food and Agriculture Organization of the United Nations, the Organisation for Economic Co-operation and Development and the World Bank compared administrative classifications of rural/urban status with a combination of remote sensing data on built-up areas and census information on population distribution (JRC, 2018).

One of the alternative definitions tested was the degree of urbanization model, which classifies three categories of 1 km² grid cells: (a) urban centre (contiguous cells of at least 1,500 inhabitants per km² and at least 50,000 inhabitants in total); (b) urban cluster (contiguous cells with at least 300 inhabitants per km² and at least 5,000 inhabitants in total); (c) and rural area (below 300 inhabitants per km² and other cells outside urban clusters and centres. Additional distinctions between municipality types, such as identification of commuting zones, are important for the SDG urban agenda but less salient for SDG 4 inequality measures (JRC, 2018).

Atlas of the Human Planet 2016 set out preliminary results, and the 2018 edition presents updated and refined results in the form of a new global city centre database. Strikingly, whereas national definitions suggest that less than half the population in Africa and Asia lives in urban areas, these new estimates suggest that more than 80% do (JRC, 2018).

This has important implications for monitoring education inequality between urban and rural areas. Current estimates of rural education outcomes may include a large number of locales that are de facto urban, masking the situation of truly rural areas. The population of unrecognized slums on the outskirts of cities in low and lower middle income countries may be even higher than currently estimated, creating still greater urgency around understanding the education situation in slums.

> “In Sierra Leone, children experiencing difficulty walking were three times as likely not to attend school as those without such difficulty”

Still, children experiencing difficulty walking were three times as likely not to attend school as those without such difficulty (Statistics Sierra Leone, 2018).

DATA FOCUS 12.1: ANALYSING EDUCATION IN SLUMS REMAINS CHALLENGING

It is estimated that at least 800 million people live in slums worldwide (UN Habitat, 2016). National definitions or estimation methodologies may result in underestimation. The census may have undercounted the population of Kibera, the largest slum in Nairobi, by at least 18%, a door-to-door household mapping exercise showed (Lucci et al., 2018).

While scarce, data tend to show that education indicators in slums are worse than in other urban areas. Two Nairobi slum surveys showed that the percentage of women with at least secondary education increased from 32% in 2000 to 51% in 2012, but the city average was 68% (APHRC, 2014).

A government census of informal settlements and floating populations in Bangladesh showed that, between 1997 and 2014, the number of slums increased from 3,000 to 14,000, and the share of male slum dwellers with no schooling decreased from 79% to 26% (Bangladesh Bureau of Statistics, 2015). Yet analysis from the 2009 MICS survey showed secondary attendance rates of 18% in slums, compared to 53% in urban areas and 48% in rural areas (UNICEF Bangladesh, 2010). Analysis of the 2016 Child Well-Being Survey of Urban Areas confirmed that the out-of-school rate of primary-age children and secondary-age adolescents was twice as high in slums as in other urban areas (**Figure 12.3**).

Slum dwellers are particularly vulnerable to eviction, resettlement and upgrading, with implications for their education. A study of those displaced by the Sabarmati River Front Project, an urban beautification and infrastructure project in Ahmedabad, India, found

FIGURE 12.3:

In Bangladesh, education access, retention and outcomes are worse for children and young people living in slums

Selected education indicators by urban location, Bangladesh, 2016

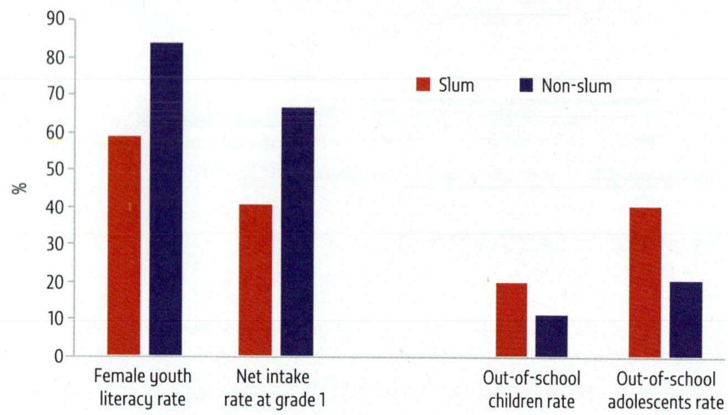

GEM StatLink: http://bit.ly/fig12_3
Note: The figure compares populations living in City Corporations, which are the largest urban areas.
Source: Bangladesh Bureau of Statistics and UNICEF Bangladesh (2017).

> In Bangladesh, the out-of-school rate of primary-age children and secondary-age adolescents was twice as high in slums as in other urban areas

that about 18% of relocated students dropped out, and 11% had lower attendance. Relocated students spent more time and money commuting due to poor transport links (Bhatkal et al., 2015).

Education in slums is still not a data collection priority. National federations of the SDI network, a non-government organization (NGO), formerly called Shack/Slum Dwellers International, conducted community-driven data collection in thousands of slums in over 30 countries (Beukes, 2015; IIED, 2017). Efforts have been under way since 2013 to systematize and standardize data collection, while keeping it flexible enough for community enumerators to update (Shack/Slum Dwellers International, 2018). However, in results of a rapid assessment of 106 informal settlements in Western Cape Province, South Africa, for instance, only about one-fourth provided information on the percentage of children attending school. More commonly, education data were limited to distance from school. One-third of the settlements were more than an hour away from a secondary school (Community Organisation Resource Centre, 2016).

A study of education access in seven slums in Kenya concluded that lack of adequate public schools led to growth in private schools (Ngware et al., 2013). Where such schools are not registered, education activity in slums may be underestimated. School coordinates were collected as part of an open mapping project in Kibera. While the district education officer estimated about 100 schools, the exercise found 330. The data alerted district and other officials to the extent of informal provision and supported advocacy for government funding for more schools (Hagen, 2017). The Nairobi Urban Household Survey also documents growth in private participation. In two informal settlements, the percentage of rural to urban migrant children enrolled in low-fee private schools increased by ten percentage points in seven years, reaching 67% in 2010 (Abuya, 2018).

There is a need to collect data and build advocacy networks to promote good-quality education in slums. As unplanned urban populations grow in poorer countries, a systematic handle on education issues in slums will eventually influence government policy, which so far has tended to ignore informal settlements.

POLICY FOCUS 12.1: REFUGEES WITH DISABILITIES NEED SUPPORT TO OVERCOME MULTIPLE EDUCATION BARRIERS

Access to education is often difficult for children with disabilities in many low and middle income countries, more so if they are forcibly displaced. Their experience can vary enormously, depending first and foremost on the extent to which their needs are identified and addressed. Refugee children with disabilities stand to benefit from international legal instruments that, among other issues, underscore their right to education, whatever the hardships of their situation. The UN Committee on the Rights of the Child adopted a General Comment dealing specifically with children with disabilities, calling for them to be given high priority for special assistance (McCallum and Martin, 2013).[1]

1 This section is based on Smith-Khan and Crock (2018).

> UNHCR now integrates the Washington Group questions into a Vulnerability Assessment Framework, which promises a more nuanced understanding of the risks faced by refugees with disabilities

The Convention on the Rights of Persons with Disabilities recognizes that impairment alone does not create disability but, rather, it is the failure to accommodate and assist that 'disables'. Such failure is more likely in displacement contexts, which are often therefore more 'disabling' (Crock et al., 2017).

EVIDENCE ON REFUGEES WITH DISABILITIES IS LACKING, BUT IMPROVING

The protection model underlying older human rights frameworks encouraged a medicalized approach to disability based on visual identification, medical assessment or volunteered information, with priority given to treatable impairments. The result was, and sometimes still is, a tendency to underestimate dramatically the nature and rate of disabilities.

In Indonesia and Malaysia, identification and recording of disability data by the office of the United Nations High Commissioner for Refugees (UNHCR) and its partners in 2012 tended to be minimal and ad hoc, largely relying on visual identification or self-referral and using basic categories like physical and mental disability. By contrast, a large-scale 2011 survey among 1 million Afghans living in Pakistan asked systematic questions on disability, giving greater insight into variation among people with disabilities, including their access to education. However, accompanying assistance-needs questions were limited. More recent mechanisms that identify and evaluate disability in displacement may provide suitable models for organizations seeking to improve inclusion. Systematic, functionality-based questions, such as those developed by the Washington Group on Disability Statistics, increasingly serve as a global standard.

In Jordan, Humanity and Inclusion, an NGO formerly known as Handicap International, is piloting a modified version of the Washington Group questions and developing related training materials to assist humanitarian actors (Humanity and Inclusion, 2018). Until recently, UNHCR disability-related questions were limited, e.g. combining vision and hearing impairment into one category (Crock et al., 2017). Now UNHCR has adopted the Washington Group short question set and developed, with its partners, the Vulnerability Assessment Framework, which integrates disability discrimination with other types of barriers, stratifying by age and gender (Women's Refugee Commission, 2017). Such initiatives promise a more nuanced understanding of the multifaceted risks and possibilities refugees with disabilities face.

DISPLACED CHILDREN WITH DISABILITIES FACE OVERLAPPING BARRIERS

Disability is not a monolithic concept. Experiences can vary widely according to individual impairment and available accommodation. Context, experiences and personal attributes can lead to very different outcomes (Ben-Moshe and Magaña, 2014). The above-mentioned survey in Pakistan provides insight into access to education and literacy by type of functional difficulty. Those with difficulty seeing were most likely to attend school (52%), while those with self-care difficulties were the least likely (7.5%). In between were those with difficulty speaking (31%) or walking (27%), trauma-originating depression or confusion (23%) and cognitive difficulties (21%) (Smith-Khan et al., 2015) (**Figure 12.4**).

Suitable schools may be distant and appropriate transport limited. Education facilities for refugees often have poor physical accessibility, both in refugee settlements and urban areas. Improvised learning centres especially may be opportunity driven, located in neighbourhoods with poorly maintained roads and footpaths or up multiple flights of stairs with no lift. In Uganda, which grants its large refugee population full access to public education, mainstream schools often lack appropriate facilities and staff training to accommodate children with disabilities (Refugee Law Project, 2014).

Lack of physical accessibility is not the only major barrier for refugee children with disabilities; lack of teacher education also matters (HelpAge International

> Lack of physical accessibility is not the only major barrier for refugee children with disabilities; lack of teacher education also matters

FIGURE 12.4:

The level of school attendance of Afghan refugees in Pakistan depends on the type of impairment

School attendance rate of young Afghan refugees aged 5 to 18, by type of functional difficulty, Pakistan, 2011

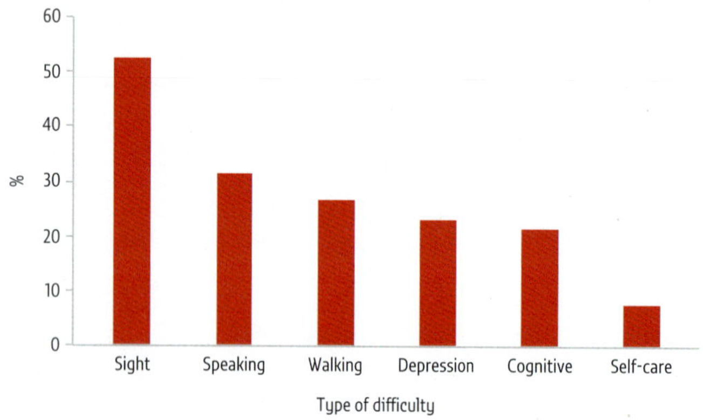

GEM StatLink: http://bit.ly/fig12_4
Source: Smith-Khan and Crock (2018).

and Handicap International, 2014; HRW, 2016). NGO-run classes may likewise lack appropriate training for their (often volunteer) education facilitators to support equal participation, particularly problematic in countries, such as Indonesia and Malaysia, where refugees lack legal status and rely on community learning centres (Smith-Khan and Crock, 2018).

In classrooms, disability among refugees can be hidden or ignored. Impairment can attract social stigma or exacerbate refugees' fear of rejection by immigration or government authorities, leading parents to hide or under-report their children's needs, especially with respect to girls. Children born with disabilities are therefore particularly vulnerable to abuse and abandonment.

The Convention on the Rights of Persons with Disabilities definition of disability also acknowledges compounding difficulties associated with gender, youth and extreme age, language, ethnicity and socio-economic standing.

Syrian refugees who use Syrian Sign Language are less likely to be able to communicate independently and gain access to information in Turkey than in Jordan, whether through (mutually comprehensible) Jordanian Sign Language or written Arabic (Hendriks, 2008). Moreover, there are generally few or no specialized schools in displacement locations. Those that exist have limited places and so typically charge fees. Learning centre teachers in Malaysia observed that some families of limited means kept children with disabilities out of school in favour of sending their siblings.

Lack of access to specialized facilities also means lack of access to assistive technology. Individuals who used assistive technology that facilitated inclusion in education before displacement may not have been able to take it with them. The mother of a young non-verbal refugee explained that fleeing the Syrian Arab Republic for Turkey meant the loss of the computer he used to communicate, entertain himself and engage in education activities, causing him and his family distress and stalling his academic progress (Smith-Khan and Crock, 2018).

ACCOMMODATION IS POSSIBLE AND COMMUNITY ENGAGEMENT CRUCIAL

While education barriers for refugees with disabilities are manifold, they need not be insurmountable. In Uganda, targeted funding for refugees with disabilities in both settlement and urban locations has been allocated specifically to vocational training and income generation. This funding has also helped children with disabilities gain access to education, covering the cost of learning materials, uniforms and boarding fees. While this one-off funding undoubtedly ameliorated beneficiary participation, however, broader environmental and circumstantial barriers persist.

New refugee camps increasingly include accessible infrastructure, as observed in various offices, centres and a new hospital in camps in Jordan, for instance (Smith-Khan and Crock, 2018). In addition, provisions for accessible transport are necessary. An organization providing inclusive theatre workshops in Zaatari camp, Jordan, organizes a minibus to transport children across the large camp to facilitate participation.

Identifying and engaging with host and refugee communities' existing strengths is crucial. Bringing together representatives of Malaysian disabled people's organizations (DPOs) with refugee community leaders showed that DPOs were largely unaware of refugees in their cities. They also had little knowledge of the conflicts and persecution risks in neighbouring countries that drove refugees to flee to Malaysia. This lack of awareness, along with linguistic barriers, may mean missed opportunities to gain practical support and advocacy from local groups, including DPOs.

> "Identifying and engaging with host and refugee communities' existing strengths is crucial"

DPOs in Uganda have a strong presence in civil society and recognition within the government. The DPO umbrella organization, the National Union of Disabled Persons of Uganda, undertakes projects aimed at inclusion of refugees with disabilities in development activities. For example, DPOs engage with and advise a variety of refugee and development agencies, as well as assisting refugees with disabilities to self-organize and self-advocate (NUDIPU, 2018). The Ugandan National Association of the Deaf runs schools in areas bordering two refugee settlements. Two refugee-focused NGOs, the Refugee Law Project and InterAid Uganda, have also been key in building refugees' knowledge about disability rights and facilitating the formation of refugee DPOs (Crock et al., 2017).

CONCLUSION

While research and data on disability in displacement remain limited, examples of good practice demonstrate that collecting high-quality data is a prerequisite to designing appropriate strategies to improve inclusion. Such data need to be sufficiently detailed to recognize the group's significant heterogeneity. Displacement context – whether emergency, transitory or protracted – and disability type affect inclusion challenges. In all cases, failure to accommodate and assist turns impairment into disability. Empowering refugees with disabilities to exercise their voice and including them in mainstream programme design are essential to ensure their inclusion in education. It is likewise crucial to identify existing resources, work with host communities and acknowledge and build on the strengths of refugee communities, including members with disabilities.

Smiles of understanding from Mohammed Abdullah from Iraq (left) and Gholem Reza Ramazani from Afghanistan (right) as they learn media skills in Austria.

CREDIT: Stefanie J. Steindl/UNHCR

KEY MESSAGES

There were 750 million illiterate adults in 2017. The global adult literacy rate was 86% but only 65% in sub-Saharan Africa.

The total number of illiterate young people fell from 144 million in 2000 to 102 million in 2017. But the number of illiterates over age 65 is continuing to rise. In 2016, there were 40% more illiterate elderly than illiterate youth.

Between 15% and 40% of illiterate people are isolated, living in households in which no member can read. In upper middle and high income countries, including Ecuador and Uruguay, isolated illiterates tend to be older and living in one- or two-person households.

Literacy skills support social and intercultural communication and the social, physical and economic well-being of immigrants and refugees.

Illiteracy in a first language makes it more difficult to gain literacy in a second: Those with no or little formal education can take up to eight times longer to acquire basic second language reading skills.

Programmes and approaches vary by country. Since 2005, Norway has made it compulsory for newly arrived adult migrants and refugees to complete 600 hours of instruction in Norwegian and social studies.

Language programmes should include migrant and refugee voices in planning and adapt to a range of populations, including through age- and workplace-specific activities. As part of an evaluation of its first refugee integration strategy, the Scottish government consulted with 700 refugees and asylum-seekers on the design of language and literacy courses.

CHAPTER 13

TARGET 4.6

Literacy and numeracy

By 2030, ensure that all youth and a substantial proportion of adults, both men and women, achieve literacy and numeracy

GLOBAL INDICATOR

4.6.1 – *Percentage of population in a given age group achieving at least a fixed level of proficiency in functional (a) literacy and (b) numeracy skills, by sex*

THEMATIC INDICATORS

4.6.2 – *Youth/adult literacy rate*

4.6.3 – *Participation rate of illiterate youth/adults in literacy programmes*

Adult literacy rates continue their slow increase. In 2017, the global rate was 86%, corresponding to 750 million illiterate adults. Literacy rates range from almost 65% in sub-Saharan Africa to near universal literacy in Europe and Northern America. For low income countries, the average female rate (53%) still trails the male rate (68%) by some 16 percentage points (**Table 13.1**).

Progress in youth literacy has been rapid enough in recent years to lead to an absolute decline in illiterate youth and adults below age 65, largely driven by Asia. The number of illiterate youth aged 15 to 24 has declined in Northern Africa and Western Asia but remains stagnant in sub-Saharan Africa. The number of illiterate elderly, those aged 65 and above, continues to grow in low and lower middle income countries and globally. As a result, there are almost 40% more illiterate elderly than illiterate youth (**Figure 13.1**).

> “The global literacy rate was 86% in 2017, ranging from 65% in sub-Saharan Africa to almost 100% in Europe and North America”

Unlike the case with youth illiteracy, the extent to which improvement in schooling will lower illiteracy among the elderly in the medium term is largely determined by education policies predating adoption of the Education for All programme in 1990. Thus, reducing illiteracy among the elderly and realizing their lifelong right to education will require targeted programming and more research

TABLE 13.1:

Youth and adult literacy indicators, 2000 and 2017

	Youth						Adults					
	Literacy rate		Gender parity index		Number of illiterate (million)		Literacy rate		Gender parity index		Number of illiterate (million)	
	2000	2017	2000	2017	2000	2017	2000	2017	2000	2017	2000	2017
World	**86.6**	**91.4**	**0.93**	**0.97**	**144**	**102**	**81.5**	**86.2**	**0.88**	**0.92**	**786**	**750**
Sub-Saharan Africa	65.9	75.4	0.84	0.90	44	48	56.0	64.6	0.71	0.79	157	200
Western Asia and Northern Africa	85.4	89.6	0.89	0.96	10	9	71.3	80.5	0.76	0.86	65	66
Central and Southern Asia	74.1	89.0	0.81	0.95	77	39	60.1	72.8	0.68	0.8	387	369
Eastern and South-eastern Asia	98.1	98.8	0.99	1.00	6	4	91.4	95.8	0.92	0.97	125	74
Latin America and the Caribbean	95.1	98.4	1.01	1.00	5	2	89.1	93.5	0.98	0.99	39	31
Oceania	…	…	…	…	…	…	…	…	…	…	…	…
Europe and Northern America	99.4	…	1.00	…	0.8	…	98.7	99.2	0.99	1.00	11	7
Low income	58.2	72.9	0.81	0.90	34	36	50.7	60.6	0.69	0.77	115	148
Lower middle income	78.7	89.1	0.86	0.96	97	59	66.7	76.4	0.75	0.84	495	486
Upper middle income	97.3	98.2	0.99	1.00	10	7	90.5	95.0	0.93	0.97	158	104
High income	…	…	…	…	…	…	…	…	…	…	…	…

Source: UIS database.

FIGURE 13.1:
There are almost 40% more illiterate elderly than illiterate youth
Number of illiterate youth and elderly, 2010–2016

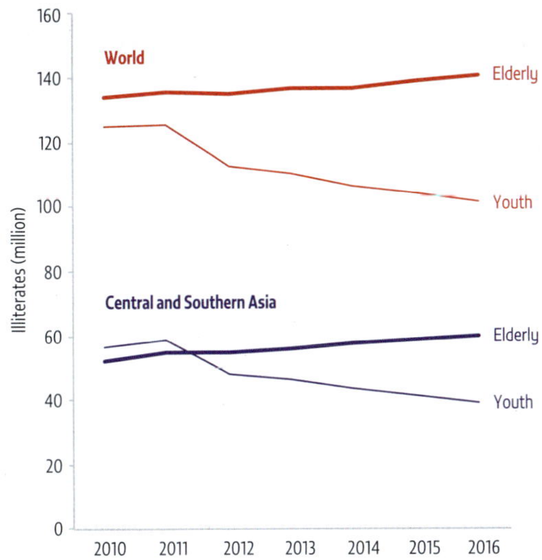

GEM StatLink: http://bit.ly/fig13_1
Source: UIS database.

on their education needs in poorer countries. Perhaps counterintuitively, they are less likely than younger illiterates to live in isolated illiteracy (without at least one literate household member) (**Data focus 13.1**).

> The number of illiterate elderly continues to grow

Estimates largely based on proxy or self-reported literacy, or on the assumption that primary completion entails literacy, suggest near universal literacy in high income countries. Nevertheless, such countries still need literacy programming, for instance to integrate immigrants and refugees who have little or no schooling, or who are literate in other than Latin script, into societies where literacy is a prerequisite for social participation (**Policy focus 13.1**). Even among native populations with universal primary schooling, the number of functionally illiterate adults is often considerable.

The SDG agenda was supposed to usher the international community into a new, more nuanced approach to functional literacy and numeracy skills through global indicator 4.6.1 – 'Percentage of population in a given age group achieving at least a fixed level of proficiency in functional (a) literacy and (b) numeracy skills, by sex'. However, the challenge of collecting such data cannot be underestimated. No new estimates became available in 2016. The three main cross-country comparable surveys that collect data on literacy skills – the Programme for the International Assessment of Adult Competencies (PIAAC) of the Organisation for Economic Co-operation and Development, the World Bank's Skills towards Employability and Productivity surveys and the Literacy Assessment and Monitoring Programme (LAMP) of the UNESCO Institute for Statistics (UIS) – carry high financial, technical and operational costs, especially for poorer countries.

The UNESCO Institute for Lifelong Learning is currently coordinating two expert groups on adult literacy and numeracy in the framework of the Global Alliance to Monitor Learning (GAML). They aim to define the fixed proficiency level countries will use to report on the global indicator and to develop a conceptual model and measurement tools consistent with the PIAAC framework, which was adopted by GAML in 2017 as the framework for the global indicator. A key issue is measurement below the minimum level on the respective PIAAC scales, which are too high to serve as a minimal threshold at the global level. The adaptation or development of new test items in literacy and numeracy for this purpose is estimated to take place in 2019.

Recently, the UIS investigated options for a 'mini-LAMP', a short literacy survey. It considered six approaches: fewer skill domains; purposeful instead of random sampling; the addition of a literacy module to an existing study (e.g. a labour force survey); fully adaptive web-based deployment; focus on a key skills threshold; and decentralized assessment management. The UIS now proposes to adapt the existing LAMP by hosting short modules for literacy and numeracy electronically, to expand the item pool as appropriate for the content framework, and to produce an implementation package countries can take up independently for use in household surveys, subject to quality assurance. The UIS estimates that a mini-LAMP could be set up within 6 months, with implementation periods of 7 months for a computer-based option and 12 months for a paper-and-pencil version (UIS, 2018).

DATA FOCUS 13.1: DIVERSITY IN DISADVANTAGE – THE PHENOMENON OF ISOLATED ILLITERACY

Complex assessments of literacy, such as LAMP and PIAAC, confirm that literacy skills cannot be adequately measured by arbitrarily drawing a line between those who can and cannot read. However, more conventional self-assessed and single-item literacy measures have the advantage of being more likely to be administered in surveys that collect information on every household member. In particular, the approach can help identify the extent of isolated illiteracy: households in which no member can read.

> "About 15–40% of illiterate people come from households in which no member can read"

Isolated illiterate individuals are significantly more disadvantaged than proximate illiterate individuals, in other words those who benefit from one or more literate household members who can explain to them medication instructions or help them fill out official forms. Even with a network outside the family aware someone is illiterate and able to offer support (Riekmann et al., 2016), isolated illiterates tend to have worse labour market and quality of life outcomes than proximate illiterates (Basu et al., 2002; Maddox, 2007; Iversen and Palmer-Jones, 2008).

Census data show the prevalence of isolated illiteracy. The degree of isolation among illiterates is between 15% and 40%. Analysis of census records allowing comparisons over time shows that isolated illiteracy tends to decline as literacy rates increase (Permanyer et al., 2013). However, the relationship may not be linear, as populations age and household composition changes.

Rates of isolated illiteracy tend to be higher among rural residents and females. Yet there are some notable differences across and within countries. In upper middle and high income countries further along their demographic transition, with more older people living on their own, isolated illiterates are relatively older than proximate illiterates. Conversely, in low and lower middle income countries, isolated illiteracy is concentrated among younger people (**Figure 13.2**).

FIGURE 13.2:

Isolated illiterates are older than proximate illiterates in richer countries, but younger in poorer countries

Ratio of isolated/proximate illiterates aged 15–29 to ages 60+, selected countries, 2010–2012

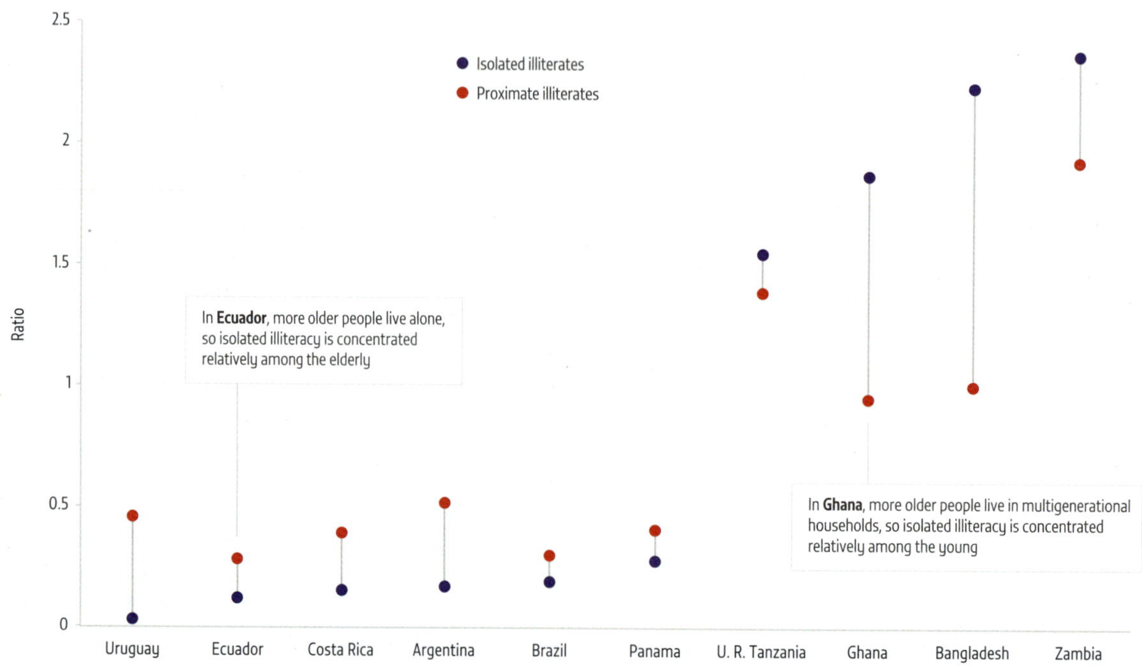

GEM StatLink: http://bit.ly/fig13_2
Source: GEM Report team analysis based on IPUMS data.

One explanation is that younger illiterates are more likely to be from lower socio-economic groups than older illiterates. Household composition is another factor. Older adults tend to have more children aged 10 to 14 with recent schooling. Adult illiterates aged 55 and older tend more in poorer countries to reside in multigenerational extended households and therefore to be likelier to live with younger, more educated family. By contrast, illiterates in richer countries such as Greece and Portugal are less likely to live in such households and more likely to be isolated.

Improved schooling of younger cohorts alone cannot relieve illiteracy isolation. In the medium term, children and youth who do not gain literacy in school tend to be clustered in illiterate households. In the long term, older illiterates are less likely to be living with literate children.

There is no substitute for targeting literacy interventions at isolated illiterates. In richer countries, the target should be old adults living in one- or two-person households. In poorer countries, it should be socio-economically marginalized, often rural young adults, a demographic group that literacy programmes do not sufficiently address, as previous *Global Education Monitoring Reports* have shown. Young, rural adults in Niger are much less likely to have participated in such programmes than older urban dwellers, for instance (UNESCO, 2016).

POLICY FOCUS 13.1: LITERACY AND LANGUAGE PROGRAMMES ARE ONE PILLAR OF INCLUSION FOR ADULT MIGRANTS AND REFUGEES

Migrants' and refugees' literacy varies widely. They may not be able to read any language, having never attended school, attended too few years or been too long out of practice. They may have no knowledge of host country languages. A 2016 survey of asylum-seekers in Germany showed that 34% were literate in a Latin script, 51% were literate in another script and 15% were illiterate (Scheible, 2018). Yet, the latter were the least likely to be attending a literacy course (**Figure 13.3**).

While this report emphasizes the needs of school-age children (**Chapters 3** and **4**), the language challenges of parents, workers, service users and citizens are important. The 2009 Belém Framework for Action on adult learning,

FIGURE 13.3:

In Germany, 15% of refugees are illiterate but are least likely to attend a literacy course

Recent refugee arrivals in Germany, by literacy and participation in language courses, 2016

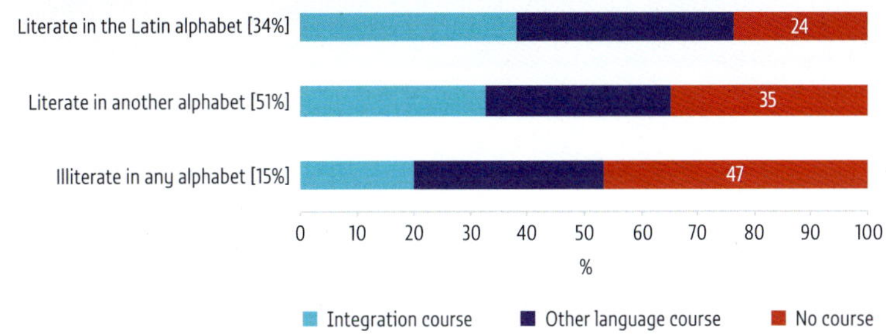

GEM StatLink: http://bit.ly/fig13_3
Source: Scheible (2018).

> The draft Global Compact for Safe, Orderly and Regular Migration does not explicitly mention adult education or literacy

adopted by 144 countries, specified the need to develop education responses for migrants and refugees. In 2015, the UNESCO Recommendation on Adult Learning and Education highlighted the need to enhance access for vulnerable groups, including migrant workers and stateless or displaced people (UNESCO and UIL, 2016).

Germany introduced subsidized language courses for immigrants in 2004 (Isphording, 2015). In Sweden, participants receive monetary incentives for successful course completion (King and Lulle, 2016). Still, large-scale public adult literacy programmes targeted at migrants and refugees are rare, and the draft Global Compact for Safe, Orderly and Regular Migration does not explicitly mention adult education or literacy.[1]

LITERACY HAS MANY BENEFITS FOR MIGRANTS AND REFUGEES

Host language proficiency has multiple individual advantages. Among refugees in Germany, good German

1 This section is based on a background paper by Hannemann (2018).

speaking, reading and writing skills were associated with a 19 percentage point higher probability of employment and 18% higher wages (Hanemann, 2018). Transition into employment is the most important route to well-being and a sense of belonging to the host society for refugees (King and Lulle, 2016). Refugees in South Africa cited lack of confidence in language skills as a reason they hesitated to initiate conversations (Bacishoga and Johnston, 2013).

Conversely, low language proficiency may have negative consequences for health. A longitudinal study of immigrants in Canada found that the odds of those with persistently poor language proficiency self-identifying as in poor health were two to three times higher than for immigrants whose language abilities were persistently good, after controlling for selected pre-migration and post-migration factors (Ng et al., 2011).

Fluency goes both ways in terms of social cohesion. Immigrants and refugees need to know host languages; natives need to appreciate origin languages. In Germany, interest in Arabic language courses reportedly increased following the influx of Syrian and Iraqi refugees (Wierth, 2017).

HIGH INCOME HOST COUNTRIES OFFER DIFFERENTIATED LITERACY PROGRAMMES

Learners illiterate in any language, including their mother tongue, require special consideration, as they are particularly challenged in learning literacy basics and schooling norms. They often need to learn the basics of written text, including the principle that words symbolize spoken language and how words are organized on a page. The mechanics of writing may also be new.

Recognizing migrant and refugee diversity, programmes must be flexible. Intensity, content and timetable should suit individual needs and contexts. More effective literacy programmes include bridging courses that facilitate transition between education levels; integrate language, literacy and numeracy with life skills or job training; and allow learners to progress at their own pace.

> “Those with no or little formal education can take up to eight times longer to reach basic second language reading”

Illiteracy in a first language makes it more difficult and time-consuming to gain literacy in a second (Benseman, 2014). One estimate suggests that those with no or little formal education can take up to eight times as long to acquire basic second-language reading skills (Schellekens, 2011). In Finland, this slow learning pace means the training provided may be too short for illiterate adults (Malessa, 2018). In a longitudinal study following five illiterate female migrants, a 1,400-hour language and literacy course was considered insufficient for achieving functional reading skills (Tammelin-Laine, 2014).

The slow pace can frustrate even experienced full-time teachers. Among identified skills for teachers of migrants are ability to use materials that capture daily challenges migrants encounter and knowledge of methods to teach oral language skills to low-literacy adults. Teachers also need to be aware of how first-language competence affects literacy development in a second language.

As part of a project called European Speakers of Other Languages: Teaching Adult Immigrants and Training Teachers, partner organizations in nine countries are rolling out an online curriculum for teachers. One of the six skills the curriculum aims to build is working with low-literacy learners. Modules are being evaluated through a mix of before and after tests, classroom discussions and self-evaluations (Naeb and Young-Scholten, 2017).

Programmes and approaches, which vary by country, include providing additional learning hours and teaching, and learning in mother tongues to support initial literacy acquisition. Australia's national Adult Migrant Education Program, implemented by state-level providers, offers young migrants, asylum-seekers and refugees 510 hours of English instruction, to be completed within five years. Those with fewer than seven years of schooling are eligible for an additional 400 hours of language courses (Centre for Multicultural Youth, 2013).

The AlfaZentrum for Migrants programme in Vienna offers multiple levels of learner-oriented literacy courses for beginners to more advanced speakers of German. Participants have a voice in the curriculum and day-to-day subjects covered in class, using home or workplace materials they want to understand rather than standardized textbooks. Counselling sessions are used in place of tests for assessment purposes. These help instructors identify the skills, knowledge and experiences migrants have acquired and provide insights to improve the programme (Plutzar and Ritter, 2008).

> Between 2009 and 2015, the UK Skills Funding Agency reduced funding for courses in English as a second language by more than 50%

In Flanders, Belgium, centres for adult basic education for low-educated or low-literacy adults cater mostly for immigrants. One course specifically targets illiterates (Choi and Ziegler, 2015). In 2017, new German legislation broadened adult learning programmes, with different courses for those with and without literacy in their first language. Additional learning hours are provided for those with greater literacy needs (Scheible, 2018). The Netherlands offers separate classes for low-literacy migrants in regional training centres, with the goal of greater independence in everyday life. Curricula are not distinguished by first-language literacy level (Grotlüschen et al., 2016).

Since 2005, Norway has made it compulsory for newly arrived adult migrants, refugees and persons granted humanitarian protection to complete 600 hours of instruction in Norwegian and social studies. New curricula in 2012 included a separate module for illiterate learners. The importance of learning literacy in migrants' most familiar language became apparent. However, few mother-tongue speakers had teacher qualifications. An increasing number of adult learning centres hire the most educated migrant learners as assistants in initial literacy classes to bridge language difficulties between teachers and learners (Sbertoli and Arnesen, 2014).

The Scottish Qualifications Authority added a bridging step, Preparation for Learning, in January 2016. Three literacy units in English for Speakers of Other Language are geared towards refugees and asylum-seekers without English skills or with little literacy in their mother tongue (Scottish Government, 2017).

ADULTS SEEKING TO IMPROVE THEIR LITERACY ALSO FACE BARRIERS

Some countries lack programmes for migrants and refugees to enhance their literacy. Bangladesh has been reluctant to support non-UN agencies providing language services for Rohingya refugees (Hanemann, 2018).

Lack of funding can also limit programme delivery, especially if government resources and support do not align with policy. For instance, while migrants are expected to learn English as soon as they enter the United Kingdom, demand greatly outpaces supply, with some language centres reporting two- and three-year wait lists (McIntyre, 2017). Declining financial support may be driving restrictions in supply. Between 2009 and 2015, the UK Skills Funding Agency reduced funding for courses in English as a second language by more than 50% (Refugee Action, 2016).

Poverty, security concerns and cultural issues may prevent or dissuade individuals, especially women, from attending. Cultural expectations with respect to child care responsibilities, and limited family support, also hamper participation (Hanemann, 2018). Concentration of new arrivals in ethnolinguistic enclaves can reduce language learning by limiting exposure. Negative relationships between enclave density and language acquisition have been found in Australia, Canada, Israel, the United Kingdom and the United States (Isphording, 2015).

The temporary nature of some migration can reduce motivation to learn a new language. Expecting to stay longer in the host country is associated with increased likelihood of language proficiency. Refugee populations may be less likely than immigrants to learn host languages. In the United States, 58% percent of refugees with 20 or more years of residency were still classified at the Limited English Proficiency level (Capps et al., 2015).

Whether immigrants or refugees acquire working proficiency in host languages depends, in part, on the extent to which these languages are different from their mother tongue but also the level of exposure to the language. At the Defense Language Institute Foreign Language Center in the United States, total instructional time for well-resourced courses with isolated immersion aiming for proficiency ranges from 780 to 2,200 hours, depending on the language. However, the conditions are not replicable (Benigno et al., 2017). Reaching oral proficiency takes an estimated three to five years, while academic proficiency can take up to seven (Demie, 2013; Hakuta et al., 2000).

PROGRAMMES NEED TO BE ADAPTED TO MIGRANTS' AND REFUGEES' CONDITIONS

For language programmes to overcome challenges and foster proficiency, they must be adaptable, culturally sensitive and well resourced. To guide organizations providing language support, the Council of Europe published a toolkit in 2017 focused on cultural awareness, approaches to discovering individual learning needs and suggested learning activities, including reflection and scenarios on real-life communication (Council of Europe, 2017).

> "Including migrants and refugees in planning and instruction is one way to support programme adaptation"

Including migrants and refugees in planning and instruction is one way to support programme adaptation. As part of an evaluation of its first refugee integration strategy, Scotland (United Kingdom) consulted with 700 refugees and asylum-seekers on the design of language and literacy courses, with the result that additional attention was paid to those in the very early stages of learning English and with little or no literacy (Scottish Government, 2018).

BOX 13.1:

Cabo Verde has mixed vocational education and adult literacy for African migrants

Over the past two decades, immigration to Cabo Verde, especially from western Africa, tripled. In 2014, two separate studies found that 12.5% of African migrants could not read or write, and 73% of immigrant workers lacked qualifications associated with vocational skills. In response, the departments of education and immigration, in partnership with the Platform of African Communities, immigrant associations and associated NGOs, developed and introduced Promotion of Literacy and Training of Immigrants of the African Communities Living in Cabo Verde in 2016/17. Running until 2020, the programme covers literacy, Portuguese language and vocational training, such as computer skills and carpentry.

Although women's attendance was affected by domestic responsibilities or lack of spousal permission, and learners faced difficulty combining work and studies, 98% of participants successfully completed the first year. Learners were better able to communicate in Portuguese and developed vocational skills, and African women felt more empowered having basic literacy and numeracy skills (Andrade, 2018).

New Zealand adopted a whole-of-government approach to improve refugee resettlement outcomes, with language proficiency identified as one of five outcomes necessary for self-sufficiency, social integration and independence. In 2014/15, the Ministry of Education and the Tertiary Education Commission consulted with former and current refugees on desirable characteristics of and barriers to courses. In 2015, the government funded 47,000 participants in English for Speakers of Other Language courses (New Zealand Ministry of Business, 2017a, 2017b).

Where possible, gaining employment is a priority upon arrival. Technical and vocational education programmes can help newcomers acquire skills and recognized credentials. The Young Adult Migrant English Course at Melbourne Polytechnic in Australia is an example of a sustainable, tailored local programme. It offers three levels of language courses that prepare learners to enter the mainstream technical and further education programme. Funding is key to the programme's sustainability. Being central to the institution's mission, the programme receives recurrent core budget funding, which provides stability and allows the course to take risks and attract highly skilled staff (ACTA, 2017).

In Germany, integration and language acquisition are tied to workforce participation. In an effort to accelerate refugee employment, the government supports a 9-month integration course consisting of 60 hours of cultural orientation and 600 hours of German language instruction. Refugees with at least B1 proficiency, the third of six levels, are eligible for job-related language training courses. In 2016, the government funded 100,000 places, with the aim of enhancing language skills to the level needed to graduate from vocational training programmes. However, courses are often overcrowded and instructors underpaid and underqualified. Pass rates to the B1 level are below 60% (Hanemann, 2018).

In an effort to address irregular attendance among displaced people, the Munich Adult Education Centre piloted Komm Rein ('Come In'), a project providing geographical information and promoting intercultural awareness, ensuring newcomers have first encounters with German as soon as they arrive. Formal and informal interaction time allows participants and instructors to adjust lectures on a near daily basis to accommodate new attendees (Hanemann, 2018). While such programmes often focus on migrant or refugee youth, some, as in Cabo Verde, attend to adults (**Box 13.1**).

Incentives to programme providers must be carefully considered. For instance, the focus on performance-focused outcomes of the Workforce Investment and Opportunity Act in the United States can make some providers risk-averse and more likely to exclude low-literacy immigrants, giving priority to those deemed more likely to make progress. This ultimately slows the economic, linguistic and social integration of the most disadvantaged migrants (Greenberg et al., 2017).

CONCLUSION

Literacy skills support social and intercultural communication and the social, physical and economic well-being of migrants and refugees. However, significant barriers in some countries limit access to and success in adult language programmes. Individuals may not attend if they are unmotivated, do not believe it is relevant or feel insecure attending. Effective programmes are well resourced and culturally sensitive. Language programmes should include migrant and refugee voices in planning and adapt to a range of populations, including through age- and workplace-specific activities.

A young boy holding a globe.

CREDIT: ESB Professional/Shutterstock.com

KEY MESSAGES

The number of countries reporting on the 1974 UNESCO Recommendation, the basis of the global indicator for this target, rose from 57 to 83 between the last two consultations.

The Recommendation's Guiding Principles, including human rights and fundamental freedoms, are only fully reflected in 17% of countries in in-service teacher education but in over 80% of countries in student assessment, up from just under half in the previous consultation.

The IEA International Civic and Citizenship Study shows that 11 of the 18 countries for which a comparison could be made improved students' civic knowledge scores between 2009 and 2016. A special module in 14 European countries showed that 88% of grade 8 students agreed immigrants should have equal rights.

Teaching materials may not fully tap education's potential for peace. Globally, inclusion of conflict prevention and conflict resolution was low at around 10% of social science textbooks over 2000–2011.

Pathways to violent extremism are complex and have multiple causes. High-quality, equitable education that increases respect for diversity can make a positive contribution, albeit only in the long term. An open classroom climate that accepts critical viewpoints needs to be embraced.

Non-formal education in the form of media literacy, safe spaces for discussion, youth clubs and community centres can help people become critical media consumers, increase respect for diversity and ultimately reduce the risk of violent extremism.

CHAPTER 14

TARGET 4.7

Sustainable development and global citizenship

By 2030, ensure that all learners acquire the knowledge and skills needed to promote sustainable development, including, among others, through education for sustainable development and sustainable lifestyles, human rights, gender equality, promotion of a culture of peace and non-violence, global citizenship and appreciation of cultural diversity and of culture's contribution to sustainable development

GLOBAL INDICATOR

4.7.1 – *Extent to which (i) global citizenship education and (ii) education for sustainable development, including gender equality and human rights, are mainstreamed at all levels in: (a) national education policies, (b) curricula, (c) teacher education and (d) student assessment*

THEMATIC INDICATORS

4.7.2 – *Percentage of schools that provide life skills-based HIV and sexuality education*

4.7.3 – *Extent to which the framework on the World Programme on Human Rights Education is implemented nationally (as per the UNGA Resolution 59/113)*

4.7.4 – *Percentage of students by age group (or education level) showing adequate understanding of issues relating to global citizenship and sustainability*

4.7.5 – *Percentage of 15-year-old students showing proficiency in knowledge of environmental science and geoscience*

Monitoring progress on target 4.7, with its unique and novel focus on the content and purpose of education, remains challenging and continues to evolve. Country reporting on the implementation of the 1974 UNESCO Recommendation concerning Education for International Understanding, Co-operation and Peace Education relating to Human Rights and Fundamental Freedoms provides the basis for global indicator 4.7.1. The number of countries that responded increased from 57 in the fifth consultation (2009–2012) to 83 in the sixth consultation (2013–2016). Preliminary results of the sixth consultation are now available at the regional level, while negotiations continue on the possibility of also providing country-level results.

Countries report on the extent to which their education systems reflect the Recommendation's Guiding Principles and associated topics in four domains: education policies, curriculum, teacher education and student assessments. Implementation is weakest for in-service teacher education, which 'fully reflects' the recommendation in 17% of responding countries. The most rapid changes are observed for student assessment, with over four in five countries reporting inclusion of the Guiding Principles in the sixth consultation, up from just under half in the fifth consultation. While reported inclusion of the principles in some form is practically universal, only 21% of countries reported that the teaching hours dedicated to them were 'fully sufficient' (**Figure 14.1**).

The seventh consultation, to be piloted in 2020, will split the curriculum component into content and resources and will bring further improvement to make the case for the Inter-agency and Expert Group for Sustainable Development Goal Indicators to upgrade the global indicator from tier III to tier II.

> The number of countries reporting on the consultation for the global indicator for target 4.7 increased from 57 to 83 in the latest round

The sixth consultation covered prevention of violent extremism, where the role of education is increasingly considered critical. All responding countries in the Arab States, which suffer some of the largest numbers of victims of conflict, included the topic in curricula, compared with between 36% and 74% of countries in other regions. Yet there are limits to what education can be expected to achieve in terms of prevention (**Policy focus 14.1**).

> All countries in the Arab States cover prevention of violent extremism in the curricula

The report on the sixth consultation indicated that assessment relating to the Guiding Principles prioritized knowledge and skills. Hence student-level data from the IEA International Civic and Citizenship Education Study (ICCS) offer an important complementary perspective. Questions in the 2016 ICCS provided interesting insights into students' values and attitudes, especially relating to thematic indicator 4.7.4 – 'Percentage of students by age group (or education level) showing adequate understanding of issues relating to global citizenship and sustainability' (**Data focus 14.1**).

The 2018 Programme for International Student Assessment (PISA) of the Organisation for Economic Co-operation and Development contains a new module on 'global competence', with results to be released in late 2019. It includes questions relating to global citizenship, similar but rarely identical to ICCS questions. The PISA survey also includes assessment of cognitive and social-emotional skills relating to open and intercultural communication, alternative perspectives, conflict resolution and adaptability (OECD, 2018).

FIGURE 14.1:

Only 17% of countries fully reflect human rights and fundamental freedom principles in in-service teacher education

Percentage of countries reflecting principles of the 1974 UNESCO Recommendation in their education policy, teacher education and curricula, 2012–2016

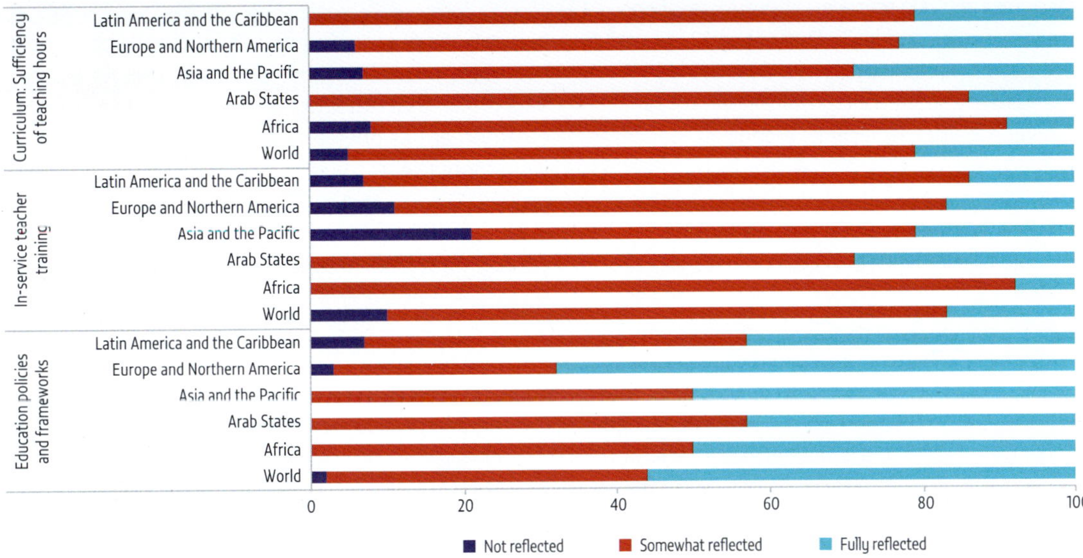

GEM StatLink: http://bit.ly/fig14_1

Source: UNESCO (2018).

Around half the 55 countries expected to take up the global competence module will also take up the cognitive skills assessment.

Before the SDGs were finalized, the UN Major Group for Children and Youth, representing civil society organizations, suggested adding universal access to comprehensive sexuality education for all young people as a standalone SDG 4 target (UN MGCY, 2015). Eventually, thematic indicator 4.7.2 – 'Percentage of schools that provide life skills-based HIV and sexuality education' – was adopted. Countries have been invited to include questions in their education management information systems on whether schools teach (a) generic life skills, (b) sexual and reproductive health and (c) HIV prevention. Data can be gathered through annual school censuses or school-based surveys. Following pilot tests, the UNESCO Institute for Statistics country survey included the sexual and reproductive health question in 2017 and covered generic life skills and HIV prevention in 2018. Reported data will aggregate head teacher responses to a school census form. Questions directed at students as beneficiaries would also be desirable, however.

DATA FOCUS 14.1: ATTITUDES TOWARDS EQUALITY AND DIVERSITY ARE LINKED TO SCHOOL PROCESSES

Contrary to some common perceptions, the SDG 4 agenda not only puts literacy and numeracy indicators at the heart of the education debate but also attempts to introduce indicators on a broader range of learning outcomes. The international community is still working on the operational definitions of these indicators. In practice, the discussions are determined by available comparable information rather than consensus on what should be monitored.

The ICCS, which assesses grade 8 students, is the primary source of data for comparable citizenship-related learning outcomes. Following the first round in 2009, the second round in 24 countries in 2016 aimed to analyse young people's knowledge and understanding of civics and citizenship, and related attitudes, perceptions and activities (Schulz et al., 2017). Although not designed with target 4.7 in mind, it informs measurement and monitoring of thematic indicator 4.7.4.[1]

1 This section draws on a background paper by Sandoval-Hernández and Miranda (2018).

Some 35% of students scored at the highest of five levels, being able to make connections between the processes of social and political organization and influence, and the legal and institutional mechanisms controlling them. Some 13% scored no more than level D, their knowledge limited to recognizing basic features of democracy and simple examples of rules and laws. Out of the 18 countries for which a comparison could be made, 11 countries significantly improved scores between the two rounds, and none showed significant declines (Schulz et al., 2017).

> “Some 35% of students scored at the highest of five levels in the IEA International Civic and Citizenship Study”

Five questions were used to construct an index of the extent to which students endorsed equal rights for all groups defined by ethnicity or race. For instance, 57% of students in 2016 strongly agreed that all ethnic and racial groups 'should have an equal chance to get good jobs', while only 31% strongly agreed that members of these groups 'should be encouraged to run in elections for political office'. Country scores on the index increased significantly between 2009 and 2016. Female students, those with greater interest in civics and political matters and those with greater civics knowledge held more positive attitudes (Schulz et al., 2017).

Endorsing equal rights was positively associated with participation in school activities and perceptions of classroom openness in most countries, and with perceptions of student interaction quality at school in half the countries. An analysis using 2009 ICCS data had shown that students who perceived the classroom environment as open and valued participation in school were more likely to endorse equal rights for all ethnic groups (Treviño et al., 2018). According to 2016 data, in at least half the countries, students who endorsed equal rights for all groups also tended to believe this was good for democracy (**Figure 14.2**).

A special module with questions on immigration was added in 2016 in the 14 European countries taking part. Overall, a large majority (88%) agreed or strongly agreed that immigrants should have equal rights; the rates varied from 76% in Bulgaria (where attitudes had turned more negative since 2009) to 94% in Sweden (where attitudes had turned more positive). Levels of agreement were lowest (on average 68% across countries) on whether immigrants should be able to continue to speak their own language, and were as low as 51% in the Netherlands and 58% in Flanders (Belgium) (Losito et al., 2017).

FIGURE 14.2:

Students who believe in equal rights for all ethnic groups also believe it is good for democracy

Index of endorsement that (a) all ethnic or racial groups should enjoy equal rights and (b) equal rights for all ethnic or racial groups is good for democracy, selected education systems, 2016

GEM StatLink: http://bit.ly/fig14_2

Notes: A score of 50 for the equal rights endorsement index was the ICCS 2009 average. A score of 1 for the equal rights and democracy index meant 'bad for democracy', 2 'neither good nor bad' and 3 'good for democracy'.

Source: Sandoval-Hernández and Miranda (2018).

POLICY FOCUS 14.1: EDUCATION'S ROLE GROWS IN EFFORTS TO PREVENT VIOLENT EXTREMISM

Violent extremism has been defined as 'beliefs and actions of people who support or use violence to achieve ideological, religious or political goals', and radicalization as 'processes by which a person adopts extreme views or practices to the point of legitimizing the use of violence' (UNESCO, 2017a, pp. 19, 20).

Countering violent extremism has diverted huge amounts of resources for intelligence, preparation and investigation to detect and prevent terrorist attacks. In some regions, including Europe, indiscriminate violent attacks are a concern. The diversity of threats has increased but so has the range of responses (Europol, 2018).

Preventing violent extremism is much more challenging precisely because the roots of radicalization are diverse, and its drivers have multiple layers. Prevention is seen nonetheless as a necessary first line of defence against terrorism, and several observers argue that education has a key role in policy and programme design (Bhatia and Ghanem, 2017).

Violent extremism threatens the 2030 Agenda. Extremists tend to turn development challenges, such as poverty, into instruments to achieve their goals or will even exacerbate the challenges as a tactic to create a vicious circle of marginalization, particularly affecting the poorest and most vulnerable (United Nations, 2015). While violent extremism, terrorist attacks and state and non-state civilian targeting undoubtedly directly cause migration and displacement, public opinion in high income countries has come to overemphasize the reverse – that migration is associated with terrorism (Crabtree and Kluch, 2017). This is despite the fact that such a relationship is very tenuous, attacks by foreigners amount to a fraction of those by nationals, and repressive measures in host countries, rather than migration per se, can be a cause of violent extremism (Dreher et al., 2017).

A large body of literature has emerged on the dynamics of radicalization, highlighting both individual and structural drivers (**Table 14.1**). These interact in complicated ways; there is no single or even typical path to radicalization. However, in principle, education can affect both radicalization and reactionary responses.

TABLE 14.1:
Individual and structural drivers of radicalization

Pull factors (individual)	Push factors (structural)
• Individual background (e.g. existential and spiritual search for identity, adolescent crisis, sense of mission, etc.) • Identification with collective grievances and narratives of victimization, provoking powerful emotions • Misuse/distortion of beliefs, political ideologies, polarized and divisive views • Attraction to charismatic leadership, social communities, networks	• Lack of socio-economic opportunities (poverty, corruption, unemployment, etc.) • Marginalization, structural discrimination • Poor governance, violations of human rights, corrupt justice system • Prolonged and unresolved conflicts

Sources: Lelo (2011); UNESCO (2017a); United Nations (2015).

EDUCATION IS KEY TO PREVENTING VIOLENT EXTREMISM, EVEN IF THE RELATIONSHIP IS COMPLEX

Exclusion from education can be a source of grievance that provides fertile ground for radicalization. The collapse of the education system in the Syrian Arab Republic during the war means many young Syrians find it impossible to disengage from armed groups through education. In some cases, armed groups set up schools based on their ideology. Although host countries have taken many steps to include all Syrian refugee children and youth in their education systems, lack of education opportunities due to initial discrimination or lack of documentation has resulted in feelings of helplessness and desperation, increasing young people's vulnerability to exploitation and radicalization (International Alert, 2016).

Research on the causal relationship between education overall and violent extremism or terrorism is inconclusive (Krueger and Maleckova, 2003). This may reflect the complexities of how education interacts with other individual and structural drivers and their effects. A study in eight Arab countries showed that unemployment increased the probability of radicalization only among the more educated; disappointed expectations of improving economic standing through education increased the allure of violent extremism to address grievances (Bhatia and Ghanem, 2017).

Education content also has a bearing. Analysis of extremists' backgrounds found an over-representation of engineers in Islamist and right-wing radicalized circles and of social scientists in left-wing radicalized circles, leading to a theory that academic disciplines may be proxies for individual traits that make some education pathways more likely to lead to selective recruitment (Gambetta and Hertog, 2016). That is, rather than education level, what education means in specific contexts may trigger specific radicalization paths.

Despite such intricacies, the UN Secretary-General's report on the Plan of Action to Prevent Violent Extremism emphasized the mitigating role education can play by promoting respect for diversity, peace and economic advancement as buffers against radicalization (United Nations, 2015). A study of 17 sub-Saharan African countries identified education as one of 4 cornerstones of a strategy against violent extremism (Lelo, 2011). Indeed, violent extremists often see education as a threat and target schools, as in the Boko Haram attacks in Nigeria in April 2014 and the al-Shabaab killing of Kenyan students in April 2015 (United Nations, 2015).

EDUCATION POLICIES CAN EXPLORE MORE OPTIONS FOR PREVENTING VIOLENT EXTREMISM

Results from the sixth consultation on implementation of the UNESCO 1974 Recommendation showed that 60% of participating countries, including all participating Arab states, had given increased emphasis to its Guiding Principles in national curricula in the previous five years. The principles include 'Understanding and respect for all peoples, their cultures, civilizations, values and ways of life' and 'Readiness on the part of the individual to participate in solving the problems of his community, his country and the world at large' (UNESCO, 2018b).

However, teaching materials may not match stated curricular priorities. A global analysis shows that the inclusion of themes on conflict prevention and conflict resolution, such as domestic or international trials, truth commissions and economic reparations, was low at around 10% of social science textbooks over 2000–2011. Coverage was highest in Asia and the Pacific on conflict prevention and in Africa and Latin America and the Caribbean on conflict resolution at around 15% (Bromley et al., 2016).

Teachers have a critical role

Teachers can play an important role in fostering tolerant and critical attitudes. However, preventing radicalization is a sensitive task. Without adequate preparation, teacher efforts may be inefficient or counterproductive (UNESCO, 2016). The principles of democracy, citizenship, human rights and cultural diversity must be consistently applied. Drawing teachers from a particular social group can reinforce social inequality and division (INEE, 2017). Ineffective pedagogical methods, such as rote learning, do not promote social inclusion or build resilience to extremism (UNESCO, 2016).

> "The inclusion of conflict prevention and conflict resolution was low at around 10% of social science textbooks over 2000–2011"

A review of 32 case studies worldwide showed that peer-to-peer learning, experiential learning, teamwork, role playing and approaches stimulating critical thinking, such as open discussions, were most effective at encouraging cognitive, social-emotional and behavioural changes in support of a culture of peace. Selective support for individuals at risk, e.g. home visits to students reported to engage in aggression, also proved effective (UNESCO, 2018a).

Some policies aimed at curtailing violent extremism have been criticized as unduly limiting personal freedoms, such as freedom of speech and expression in education, in the pursuit of security (UNESCO, 2017a). The US Federal Bureau of Investigation's guidance on preventing violent extremism and the United Kingdom's Prevent policy could be interpreted as impinging on schools' role as places for open discussion and inquiry, and increasing law enforcement involvement in education. There is also lack of evidence of their effectiveness (Patel and Koushik, 2017).

Non-formal education offers alternative ways to prevent violent extremism

Schools can be convenient sites for violent extremism prevention initiatives involving stakeholders outside education. An initiative to prevent violent extremism among Moro youth in the southern Philippines aims to empower Christian and Muslim youth by giving them safe spaces in schools and universities to discuss their grievances without fear of repercussions. The private sector provides mentors and resources for youth-led advocacy initiatives (International Alert Philippines Programme/Mindanao Business Council, 2018).

Some programmes use victims' voices to make topics more relevant and salient to students. In Indonesia,

> "The UN Secretary-General's report on the Plan of Action to Prevent Violent Extremism emphasized the mitigating role education can play"

> Without adequate preparation, teachers' efforts to foster tolerant and critical attitudes may be inefficient or counterproductive

the International Centre for Counter-Terrorism has been involved in Victims Voices of the Alliance for a Peaceful Indonesia, which uses bomb attack survivors' stories for advocacy with secondary school students in vulnerable areas. The project also aims to advocate in prisons to raise awareness among prisoners and staff who might underestimate the threat of violent extremism (ICCT, 2018).

The processes of violent extremism are not gender neutral. Violent extremist and terrorist groups often target women and girls for gender-based violence, including abductions, forced marriages, sexual violence and attacks on gender activists (GCTF, 2014). Thus, gender-sensitive strategies for education against violent extremism should engage women and examine their roles. Germany's Expert Center on Gender and Right-Wing Extremism focuses on countering racist, anti-Semitic and radical attitudes. It trains kindergarten teachers, members of youth clubs and community centres, and other civil society actors on using gender-sensitive approaches and democratic principles. It also offers training sessions for journalists, who are key influencers (RAN, 2018) (**Box 14.1**).

Women can lead such education initiatives. For 20 years, the women's organization Pakistan Initiative for Mothers and Newborns in Khyber Pakhtunkhwa province taught mediation and conflict transformation skills to 35,000 youth and 2,000 women (Women Without Borders, 2010). By contrast, approaches that focus on women only as mothers and wives might lead to seeing women as responsible if children or husbands become radicalized (Giscard d'Estaing, 2017).

> Gender-sensitive strategies for education against violent extremism should engage women and examine their roles

CONCLUSION

Pathways to violent extremism are complex and have multiple causes. Only a small minority of people experiencing identified contributing factors actually take the path of violent extremism. High-quality, equitable education can make a positive contribution although it is a long-term process whose effects cannot be immediate (Mirahmadi et al., 2015). While expectations about what formal education can achieve directly should be tempered, its potential contribution to peaceful societies needs to be further pursued along three paths (Davies, 2009). First, education should increase respect for diversity (**Chapter 5**). Second, conflict prevention, resolution without resort to violence and reconciliation need to be systematically introduced in learning materials. Third, an open classroom climate that accepts critical viewpoints needs to be embraced. Nor does education end with schooling. Multiple opportunities exist for preventing violent extremism through non-formal means that actively involve communities.

BOX 14.1:

Building media literacy can offset media and social media's negative influences

When the media channel discriminatory views, it can increase marginalized communities' vulnerability. The media in many European countries disproportionately portray migrants in general and Muslims in particular in relation to social issues, such as rising unemployment and criminality, pandering to racist stereotypes. Extremist right-wing websites spread fabricated sensationalist reports on social media, largely unconstrained by legal or policy measures (ENAR, 2017). Developing journalists' capacities is important for raising awareness about radicalization and the role of the media (UNESCO, 2017b).

Conversely, building media literacy skills allows citizens to be responsible, critical media consumers and producers (Kellner and Share, 2007). This involves teaching people to examine alternative narratives from credible sources, and empowering students to build their own narratives and evidence-based learning. Educational approaches promoting these skills are part of building a culture of democracy and inclusion.

Serbia's School without Violence programme provides web resources on violence, hate speech and discrimination; a platform to share experiences; and teacher training on digital violence prevention and media literacy (European Commission, 2016). In the United Kingdom, a creative design agency, with support from local government funding, created 'digital disruption' workshops aimed at protecting vulnerable youth from violent extremist propaganda online. Teams of experts worked with youth to investigate the ways online misinformation affected them and their peers, and create videos promoting critical thinking when engaging with internet content (Briggs and Feve, 2013).

A fighter from the Central African Republic Patriotic Movement, a Seleka group, who are based next to two schools. All schools in the town are closed because fighters often occupy the buildings.

CREDIT: Edouard Dropsy/HRW

KEY MESSAGES

Globally, 69% of schools have drinking water, 66% sanitation and 53% hygiene on at least a basic service level. A review of 71 national education management information systems showed that only 6% of their questionnaires included soap availability, the key factor of a basic hygiene service level.

The number of countries legally banning corporal punishment in schools increased to 131, up from 122 at the end of 2014.

A review harmonizing data from six international surveys covering 145 countries estimated that almost 39% of boys and 36% of girls aged 11 to 15 reported being victims of bullying.

Too little is known about numbers of boarding students, living conditions in boarding schools or the effects of boarding on student well-being and school success. In Uganda, about 15% of primary and lower secondary school students and 40% in upper secondary school board.

There were over 12,700 attacks on education in 2013–2017, harming over 21,000 students and education personnel and affecting 28 countries. The measure does not include school shootings by lone gunmen or attacks by criminal gangs, which are a scourge in some education systems.

The scalability, speed, mobility and portability of technology make it a suitable option for educating displaced people. But initiatives tend to provide content that is incompatible with national curricula in host countries. International organizations that support such partnerships need to ensure that they serve inclusion of refugees in national education systems.

CHAPTER 15

TARGET 4.a

Education facilities and learning environments

Build and upgrade education facilities that are child, disability and gender sensitive and provide safe, non-violent, inclusive and effective learning environments for all

GLOBAL INDICATOR

4.a.1 – *Proportion of schools with access to: (a) electricity; (b) Internet for pedagogical purposes; (c) computers for pedagogical purposes; (d) adapted infrastructure and materials for students with disabilities; (e) basic drinking water; (f) single-sex basic sanitation facilities; and (g) basic handwashing facilities (as per the WASH indicator definitions)*

THEMATIC INDICATORS

4.a.2 – *Percentage of students experiencing bullying, corporal punishment, harassment, violence, sexual discrimination and abuse*

4.a.3 – *Number of attacks on students, personnel and institutions*

The provision of 'child, disability and gender sensitive' education facilities and 'safe, non-violent, inclusive and effective learning environments for all' is a challenge in many countries. Agenda 2030 includes a range of facility- and environment-related indicators. While they seem straightforward, they highlight challenges in monitoring even basic infrastructure conditions.

MONITORING THE QUALITY OF EDUCATION FACILITIES IS NOT CLEAR-CUT

The World Health Organization/UNICEF Joint Monitoring Programme (JMP) has monitored household access to water, sanitation and hygiene since 1990. It produced consolidated estimates for schools in 2008 and 2013 (UNICEF, 2015), using diverse sources and methodologies. Definitions of adequate sanitation facilities in schools were often inconsistent across countries and data sources. Many data sets were not representative of all school types in a country. Global figures for handwashing facilities could not be estimated at all.

> "Globally, two-thirds of schools had basic water services, two-thirds had basic sanitation services and half had basic hygiene services"

TABLE 15.1:
Descriptors for monitoring water, sanitation and hygiene service quality in schools

Service level	Drinking water	Sanitation	Hygiene
Basic	Drinking water from an improved source, and water available at the school at the time of the survey	Improved sanitation facilities at the school that are single-sex and usable (available, functional and private) at the time of the survey	Handwashing facilities with water and soap available at the school at the time of the survey
Limited	Drinking water from an improved source, but water unavailable at the school at the time of the survey	Improved sanitation facilities at the school that are either not single-sex or not usable at the time of the survey	Handwashing facilities with water but no soap available at the school at the time of the survey
None	Drinking water from an unimproved source or no water source at the school	Unimproved sanitation facilities or no sanitation facilities at the school	No handwashing facilities available or no water available at the school

Source: UNICEF and WHO (2018).

In 2016, the JMP convened an expert group to define harmonized criteria and indicators based on global norms and standards and reflecting information available in existing national and cross-national surveys. In 2018, it published service quality descriptors building on prior classifications (assessed as 'improved' or 'unimproved') and introducing additional criteria (UNICEF and WHO, 2018) (**Table 15.1**).

The report put together sufficient data to provide a comprehensive harmonized global baseline for target 4.a. National information was available in 92 countries for basic drinking water services in schools, 101 countries for sanitation and 81 for hygiene, while 68 countries had baseline estimates for all three. Globally, two-thirds of schools had basic water services, two-thirds had basic sanitation services and half had basic hygiene services (**Figure 15.1**). Although provision of each tends to be correlated at the country level, there is no fixed relationship. In Jordan, 93% of schools have basic drinking water, but only 33% have basic sanitation. In Lebanon, almost 93% have basic sanitation, but only 59% have basic drinking water. In Palestine, both facilities are offered at the basic level in around 80% of schools.

Primary schools tend to have lower service quality than secondary schools. Very few countries had data for pre-schools, and only a minority distinguished between urban and rural schools. Efforts continue to include a core and expanded set of school census questions (UNICEF and WHO, 2018). A review of 71 national education management information systems showed

> Globally, 52% of primary schools and 67% of lower secondary schools had electricity in 2016

that few included these questions. For instance, only 6% of questionnaires included soap availability, the decisive factor between limited and basic handwashing facilities (JMP, 2017).

Electricity, another key aspect of a good-quality learning environment, is also lacking in poorer countries. Globally, 52% of primary schools and 67% of lower secondary schools had electricity in 2016. The respective shares were 17% and 35% in low income countries. One factor making accurate monitoring difficult is the highly unpredictable nature of electricity supply. Access to electricity and the internet can be particularly important in temporary education settings, on which refugees often rely. Its absence can be doubly damaging, as technology, used effectively, can compensate for some disadvantages (**Policy focus 15.1**).

One aspect of infrastructure that existing data do not capture is living conditions in boarding schools. More generally, little is known about the percentage of students who board, although it is particularly high in some countries (**Box 15.1**).

FIGURE 15.1:

Fewer than 7 out of 10 schools have drinking water at a basic service level

Distribution of drinking water, sanitation and hygiene in schools, by service level, 2016

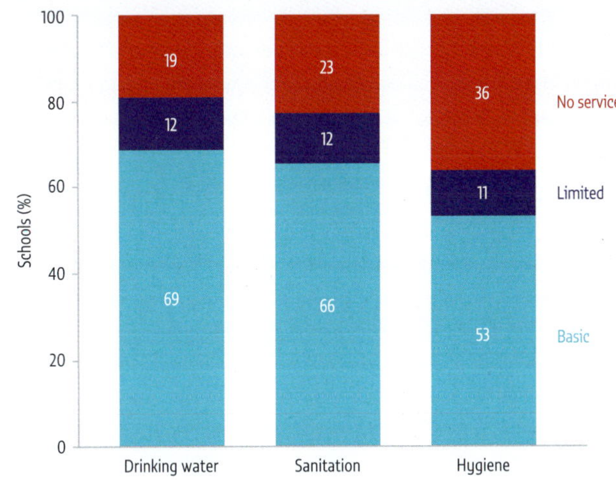

GEM StatLink: http://bit.ly/fig15_1
Note: Numbers are rounded and may not sum to 100%.
Source: UNICEF and WHO (2018).

> The number of countries legally banning corporal punishment in schools has increased to 131, up from 122 at the end of 2014

FEW ASPECTS OF SAFETY AND INCLUSIVENESS IN LEARNING ENVIRONMENTS ARE MONITORED GLOBALLY

There are so many aspects of safety and inclusiveness to monitor that any attempt to be systematic inevitably appears incomplete. Freedom from armed attacks, unfortunately suffered by too many schools, is the very minimum. Monitoring safety and inclusiveness is a feature of the SDG 4 framework, and there are constant efforts to improve methodology (**Data focus 15.2**).

The UNESCO *Global Status Report on School Violence and Bullying* noted significant gaps in available data and evidence (UNESCO, 2017). The number of countries legally banning corporal punishment in schools has increased to 131, up from 122 at the end of 2014 (Global Initiative to End All Corporal Punishment of Children, 2018). Data on prevalence of corporal punishment are infrequent, but in some countries where the practice is illegal, including Cameroon and Trinidad and Tobago, experiences of abuse are nearly universal among students (Gershoff, 2017).

Concepts such as bullying lack standard global definitions, and surveys vary in target age groups, reference periods, phrasing and forms of violence included (UNESCO, 2017). An expert group under the auspices of the Technical Cooperation Group has made recommendations on how to address the methodological challenges to ease reporting on the thematic indicator on bullying (UNESCO, 2018a).

Another study tried to address the methodological differences, and the risk of surveys systematically under- or overestimating the prevalence of bullying, by harmonizing data from six international surveys covering 145 countries. It estimated that almost 39% of boys and 36% of girls aged 11 to 15 reported being victims

BOX 15.1:

Data on boarding students are very limited

There is no international definition of boarding students. Standard household surveys usually cover household members who spend the night under the same roof and eat meals together. Like other institutional settings, such as barracks, hospitals and prisons, boarding schools are typically excluded from household sampling, making it difficult to know whether boarding children are captured.

A 2008 review of 30 surveys had found that only 2 included questions about boarding students (EPDC, 2009). The UNICEF Multiple Indicator Cluster Survey asks respondents to identify children 'living with a relative, staying in a boarding school, been given up for adoption, or may be grown-up children who have left home'. Recent Demographic and Health Surveys in Ghana and Rwanda listed boarding school attendance as a distinct category. But other data that may also be important, such as distance or time travelled to school, are typically not available.

FIGURE 15.2:
In Uganda, 40% of 17-year-old students are boarders
Percentage of students who are boarders, by age, Uganda, 2013

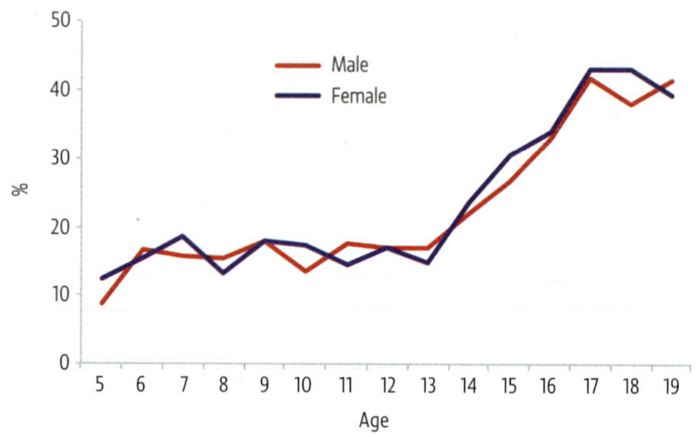

GEM StatLink: http://bit.ly/fig15_2
Source: GEM Report team analysis based on the 2013 Uganda National Panel Survey.

National surveys in the United Republic of Tanzania and Uganda have included more detailed questions on boarding. The Tanzanian survey includes boarding children in the household roster but ascertains only whether the school is a boarding school, not whether the child is boarding (many boarding schools also enrol day students). The Ugandan survey queries both the type of school and the incidence of boarding. The share of enrolled boarding students is between 10% and 20% up to age 13, rising continuously to 40% in the final years of upper secondary education, with little difference between boys and girls (**Figure 15.2**).

Too little is known about living conditions in boarding schools or the effects of boarding school attendance on personal well-being and school success. Conflicting conclusions have been reached in China, where a large school merging programme began in the early 2000s that led to a dramatic increase in number of boarders (**Chapter 2**). But a recent study found a negative impact on academic performance and welfare indicators of boarding students, such as nutrition (Wang et al., 2016). Negative effects can also be observed in rich countries. In France, a policy experiment that randomly allocated disadvantaged students to boarding schools showed that the experience was disruptive and that only a subset of students started doing better academically after two years (Behaghel et al., 2017).

of bullying. After a series of adjustments, the study assigned three levels of risk of bullying in countries (low, medium and high); 28% of countries with data were at the high risk category (Richardson and Fen Hiu, 2018).

The Global Working Group to End School-Related Gender-Based Violence has developed minimum standards and a monitoring framework for an approach to prevention that includes indicators not only on prevalence but also on processes (i.e. whole-school approach) and drivers (UNGEI, 2018). Disaggregation of bullying data is limited by data availability for dimensions other than gender – and even in this case evidence is lacking on bullying related to sexual orientation or gender non-conformity.

DATA FOCUS 15.1: ATTACKS ARE A SCOURGE ON EDUCATION SYSTEMS

Schools are often damaged or targeted during violent conflict. Recognizing this challenge, the international education community added an indicator on attacks to the SDG 4 thematic monitoring framework and approved the Global Coalition to Protect Education from Attack (GCPEA) as the source for information, making it the first non-official source endorsed in an international education monitoring framework.

The GCPEA *Education Under Attack 2018* report is the fourth in a series, following editions in 2007, 2010 and 2014. In response to the 2007 report, produced by UNESCO, the GCPEA was established in 2010 by organizations from the fields of education in emergencies, protection and international human rights concerned about attacks in countries affected by conflict and insecurity. A steering committee of civil society and UN organizations governs the coalition.

> Attacks on schools affected 28 countries in 2013–2017

According to the report, there were over 12,700 attacks on education in 2013–2017, harming over 21,000 students and education personnel. Reported incidents included physical attacks or threats of attacks on schools, students, teachers and other education personnel; military use of schools and universities; child recruitment or sexual violence by armed parties at or in transit to or from school or university; and attacks on higher education. In total, 28 countries were classified into three levels by number of incidents and/or number of students or education personnel harmed (GCPEA, 2018) (**Table 15.2**).

The GCPEA compiles data from three main sources: (a) reports published by UN agencies, development and humanitarian non-government organizations (NGOs), human rights organizations, government bodies and think tanks; (b) a Google-based news media search in multiple languages, supported by the University of Maryland's Global Terrorism Database; and (c) direct outreach to international and national organization staff in the 28 countries affected. Partly because the sources are diverse, access to country data may change over time; the 2014 report criteria would have led to 13 more countries being classified as affected.

Lack of disaggregation by incident type poses additional interpretation challenges. While school shelling is clear-cut, other types – military recruitment of minors at school, for instance – rely on international treaty legalities. In particular, the Optional Protocol to the Convention on the Rights of the Child on the Involvement of Children in Armed Conflict bans under-18 recruitment by armed rebel groups but not by government armies.

TABLE 15.2:

Affected countries by number of incidents of attacks on education, military use of facilities or students and education personnel harmed, 2013–2017

Very heavily affected (1,000 or more)	Heavily affected (500–999)	Affected (20–499)
D. R. Congo	Afghanistan	Bangladesh
Egypt	India	Burundi
Israel and Palestine	Iraq	Cameroon
Nigeria	Pakistan	Central African Republic
Philippines	Somalia	Colombia
South Sudan	Sudan	Ethiopia
Syrian Arab Republic	Ukraine	Kenya
Turkey	Venezuela, B. R.	Libya
Yemen		Mali
		Myanmar
		Thailand

Source: GCPEA (2018).

Yielding to a small number of countries that opposed a categorical ban on under-18 recruitment, the protocol specifies that states will take all feasible measures to prevent children in their armed forces from directly participating in hostilities (OHCHR, 2000).

A more detailed breakdown of incidents by type would support a nuanced interpretation of comparisons, among countries both on and off the list and over time, in terms of whether attacks are becoming more or less severe. Because the GCPEA's mandate is to monitor conflict-affected fragile states and attacks by armed groups, certain types of attack are not captured. Yet any student attacked or killed at school was indisputably not in a 'safe, non-violent' environment in the sense of SDG target 4.a., and the implied monitoring gap is large.

School shootings by lone gunmen, notoriously frequent in the United States, are not included, even if the shooter was ideologically motivated. Although such shooters sometimes have ties to militant organizations, these incidents do not meet criteria for armed conflict at the national and international levels. By conservative estimates, since the 1999 Columbine shooting, at least 187,000 students in 193 schools in the country have experienced a school shooting (Cox and Rich, 2018).

Attacks by criminal gangs similarly fall outside the GCPEA's mandate and are therefore not reported on systematically, although the line between violent organized crime and armed conflict is unclear when on the scale reached in Central America. The 2018 report therefore featured a supplementary account on criminal violence in

El Salvador, Guatemala and Honduras, even though such attacks do not systematically enter its data collection.

POLICY FOCUS 15.1: TECHNOLOGY CAN SUPPORT EDUCATION FOR DISPLACED PEOPLE

Forced displacement often overwhelms education systems that are already weak and unable to absorb large influxes of people rapidly. Even in protracted displacement situations, complex settings limit displaced people's access to formal or non-formal education of good quality. These constraints have motivated a search for alternative solutions for their education needs.

> "Some challenges to refugee education are well met by advantages of technology-based solutions, such as scalability, speed, mobility and portability"

Some challenges are well met by advantages promised by technology-based solutions, namely scalability, speed, mobility (the technology can reach displaced people) and portability (displaced people can carry the technology). Well-designed programmes can be distributed widely to anyone with a connected device, such as a smartphone or tablet (**Figure 15.3**).

Digital solutions can often build on existing infrastructure and be downloaded and disseminated rapidly at minimal marginal cost. Part of the challenge of providing displaced people with education is that they are often on the move, usually because it can take months to reach their intended destinations.

Thus the potential for technology to enhance existing learning environments or create virtual learning environments is gaining increased attention from actors in the technology, humanitarian and education fields. While technology solutions address a range of challenges in education, this section discusses selected examples related to effective learning environments, in line with the intentions of target 4.a. All are characterized by the presence of non-government actors.[1]

1 This section draws on a recent review of technology solutions for refugees by UNESCO (2018c).

FIGURE 15.3:

Four out of ten refugee households have access to smartphones

Mobile network coverage and household mobile phone ownership, by type, global and refugee populations, 2014–2015

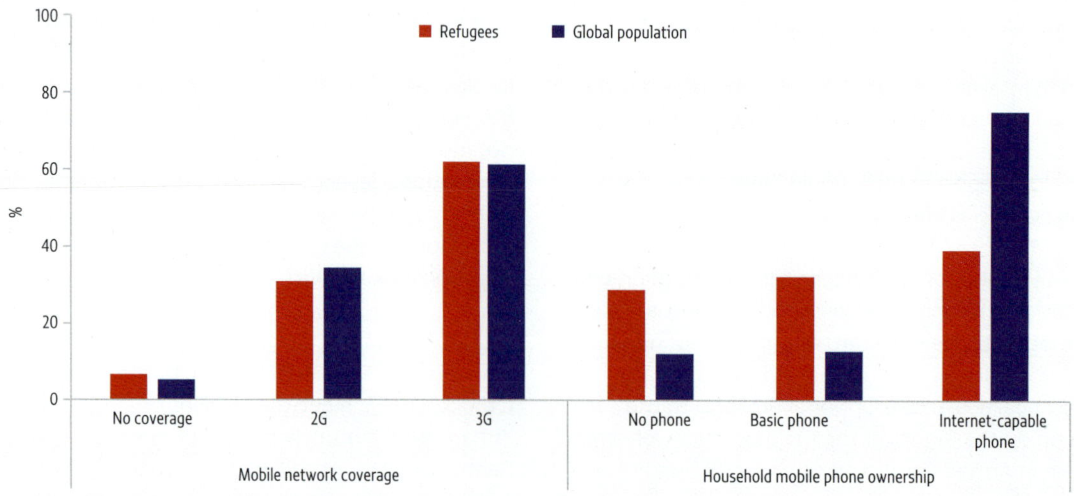

GEM StatLink: http://bit.ly/fig15_3
Source: UNHCR (2018).

> A key question is how content supported by technology can be linked to curricula and the inclusion of refugees in national education systems

TECHNOLOGY AIMS TO SUBSTITUTE FOR TEACHING AND LEARNING MATERIAL AND OTHER RESOURCE GAPS

Education for refugees and internally displaced people has to address the disruptions caused by displacement and the need for tailor-made education systems, at least in the early stages of an emergency. Technology solutions can compensate for lack of standard resources.

The Instant Network Schools programme, a joint initiative of the office of the UN High Commissioner for Refugees (UNHCR) and Vodafone, reaches more than 40,000 students and 600 teachers in 20 primary and secondary schools in the Democratic Republic of the Congo, Kenya, South Sudan and the United Republic of Tanzania; the objective is to reach more than 60,000 students in 2018 (Safaricom, 2017). It equips them with internet through a satellite or mobile network connection, electricity through solar-powered batteries and a backup generator, and dynamic digital content through preloaded and online resources, connecting remote and isolated communities with the rest of the world. Preliminary data from an evaluation in Kenya pointed at a three percentage point increase in attendance rates and a 36% increase in the participation rate for primary school certificate examinations (Vodafone Foundation, 2017).

Despite indications of positive results, a challenge of such interventions is aligning preloaded and online resources with national curricula. As interventions are led by technology firms, there is a tendency to put more emphasis on the technical aspect of installing a platform than on decisions related to content, where actors operate in parallel. A platform available through Instant Network Schools is the Remote Area Community Hotspot for Education and Learning (RACHEL), a portable server developed by the NGO World Possible. It offers access to Wikipedia, Khan Academy modules and health information packages, among other resources, which can be retrieved and loaded onto mobile devices. Khan Academy modules have been used off-line by UNICEF in its Raspberry Pi for Learning initiative for refugees in Lebanon, as well as in the Khan Academy's own KA Lite initiative.

The key question is how these supplementary resources, which appear in several, often overlapping, forms, can be linked effectively to curricula, especially given efforts to include refugees in national education systems. New generations of these platforms, including RACHEL, are introducing learning management system and content alignment options to respond to this criticism.

Two examples of e-learning resources from the Syrian refugee crisis have explicitly attempted to align with national curricula. Tabshoura ('Chalk'), provided jointly by the NGO Lebanese Alternative Learning, two international NGOs and a university education faculty, has developed online resources for pre-schools in Arabic, English and French, building on Moodle, a learning management system. Work focused from the outset on developing resources aligned with the 2015 Lebanese curriculum by grade, subject and project. Teachers created activities suitable for both an interactive platform and meeting the curricular learning objectives. The activities were translated, edited, validated, adapted and digitized, and have been used with Syrian refugees as a supplementary resource (Fahed and Albina, 2016).

Launched in 2012, Nafham ('We Understand') is a free online education website with video content relevant to students from pre-primary to upper secondary. In addition to offering its own original videos, it encourages teachers, students and parents to create videos, which make up one-third of the more than 10,000 videos. These cover over 75% of the Egyptian national curriculum, sorted by grade and subject. The business model is based on online advertising and private-sector partnerships. Originally intended to help families that relied on expensive supplementary private tuition, it expanded to include 1,000 videos covering about 35% of the Syrian curriculum. They have been used as a supplementary resource by the Rumie Initiative's Learn Syria, which provides tablets preloaded with education materials to Syrian refugees in Jordan and Turkey, including e-textbooks from the Syrian Education Commission (GBC, 2016; Rumie, 2018; Wimpenny et al., 2016).

> Technology cannot replace participation in formal schooling and most technology-based interventions work only as complementary or interim solutions

Another potential technology contribution involves important areas not included in curricula, such as psychosocial support. The NGO Libraries Without Borders, with UNHCR, developed the Ideas Box. It has an education component that follows the usual approach of third-party content not aligned with curricula, but also includes additional information and cultural resources. These range from books and films to cameras and graphic design software. The aim is to create a community space that enriches the experience of isolated communities. A qualitative evaluation of its deployment in two Burundi camps hosting Congolese refugees showed a positive impact in measures of resilience (Lachal, 2015).

In Lebanon and Jordan, the International Rescue Committee (IRC), in its Vroom programme, adapted a model developed for low-income families in the United States. It uses videos and animation, delivered through WhatsApp and Facebook, to provide parenting techniques in the form of games and advice. These are combined with parenting skills sessions and home visits to get to the most difficult-to-reach families. An impact assessment suggested that parents who received science-based messages were more likely than those who received the parent-focused text to click on the link and watch the associated video (Wilton et al., 2017).

TECHNOLOGY CAN REACH OUT FASTER TO TEACHERS

Most programmes, such as Instant Network Schools, come with support to teacher professional development programmes. Some technology-based programmes focus directly on teacher professional development, including the teacher mentoring programme in Kakuma, Kenya (**Chapter 4**).

With funding by the US Bureau of Population, Refugees, and Migration, the IRC developed the Connect to Learn initiative, targeting 160 Syrian refugee teachers at Domiz refugee camp schools in Dohuk province, Iraq. Ericsson provided hardware and software, and AsiaCall supported the internet connection. The initiative gave teachers access to custom-made training materials and let them connect with peers to share experiences. The objective was to prepare teachers to implement Healing Classrooms, which focuses on providing psychosocial support to children affected by conflict through a compassionate classroom environment and instructional videos. The professional development programme focused on transforming technology tools into education resources (GIZ, 2016).

In Nigeria, a UNESCO teacher education project, in association with Nokia, showed that teachers valued phone-based practice and professional guidance. Short messages sent every day over a year helped primary teachers plan lessons, ask stimulating questions, prompt reflective responses and assess students in English language and literacy classes. An evaluation showed that the approach, which reached 70,000 teachers, helped develop professional capacities and bring teachers closer together in a network (UNESCO, 2018b).

CONCLUSION

Technology is increasingly used to support student learning and help train teachers in emergency contexts with limited availability of teaching and learning tools. A survey of 144 non-state actors engaged in education for Syrian refugees found that 49% were engaged in developing and distributing technological education innovations (Menashy and Zakharia, 2017). Many general-purpose technology tools, notably mobile phones, are ubiquitous even in refugee camps and prove useful and popular in communities affected by displacement, including for education. Still, technology-based approaches have their challenges. They typically require high upfront investment, and not all groups have access to adequate electricity and connectivity. As with technology interventions in much of the world, impact evaluations often involve implementing organizations, with the result that a robust, objective research basis is lacking (Tauson and Stannard, 2018).

Two issues raise the main questions. A striking feature is that most initiatives provide content prepared for very different learning contexts than those in which refugees generally find themselves. Despite attempts to adapt content, compatibility with host national education systems is the exception. This poses a risk for international organizations that support such initiatives and also adopt the principle of inclusion of refugees in national education systems, as they have a responsibility to work with governments, which are absent from such interventions. It is important to recognize that technology cannot replace participation in formal schooling and that most technology-based interventions can work as complementary or interim solutions.

Second, many initiatives involve private-sector technology firms. Their motivation combines philanthropy and profit considerations, the latter ranging from brand image and innovation testing to, in some cases, entry into new markets. International organizations, which sometimes support such partnerships with few strings attached, are responsible for ensuring that they are well coordinated and serve the ultimate aim of including refugees in national education systems.

Hannah fled the Syrian Arab Republic in 2012. After living in Jordan for five years, she will soon begin studying for a degree at the University Paul Valéry in Montpellier on a scholarship granted by the French local authority.

CREDIT: Benjamin Loyseau/UNHCR

KEY MESSAGES

The volume of scholarships funded by aid programmes has been stagnant since 2010 at US$1.2 billion.

Globally, 2.3% of tertiary education students were internationally mobile in 2017, compared to 2% in 2012, equivalent to 5.1 million mobile students.

EU countries have committed to ensure that by 2020 at least 20% of graduates experience part of their studies abroad, spending 3 months or more or obtaining at least 15 credits in other countries. But non-EU destination countries do not all report back on students' achievements or credits, which hampers monitoring. New estimates for 2016 suggested the outward mobility was 10.7%, well below the target.

After almost 30 years of accumulated experience, evaluations of the flagship Erasmus student exchange programme suggest a positive effect on employment and career opportunities, albeit with some concerns on equity. Credit transfer, qualification framework and quality assurance mechanisms support mobility in Europe; replicating them in aspiring regions, such as South-eastern Asia, will require strong commitment.

CHAPTER 16

TARGET 4.b

Scholarships

By 2020, substantially expand globally the number of scholarships available to developing countries, in particular least developed countries, small island developing States and African countries, for enrolment in higher education, including vocational training and information and communications technology, technical, engineering and scientific programmes, in developed countries and other developing countries

GLOBAL INDICATOR

4.b.1 – *Volume of official development assistance flows for scholarships, by sector and type of study*

THEMATIC INDICATOR

4.b.2 – *Number of higher education scholarships awarded, by beneficiary country*

As the past two *Global Education Monitoring Reports* have noted, there are various interpretations of what target 4.b is trying to achieve, making it difficult if not impossible to clearly identify who is accountable for achieving it. Interpretation aside, the global indicator is insufficiently informative of global progress, relative to achieving the target. Focusing on '[v]olume of official development assistance flows for scholarships' can be misleading. First, volume of aid reveals nothing about recipient numbers. Second, not all countries disburse the bulk of their scholarship programmes through aid; in fact, programmes funded by other sources, especially universities, may dwarf official government scholarships. Third, among countries that do use their aid budgets to fund scholarship programmes, at least one-third of scholarship aid cannot be assigned to recipient countries, even though identifying recipients' origins is a key part of the target.

To the extent that scholarship aid volume illuminates a trend, evidence shows that the trend has been stagnant, with total official flows for scholarships remaining at US$1.2 billion in 2016, the same level as in 2010. Beyond scholarships, donor countries also disbursed US$1.9 billion in imputed costs, i.e. the costs incurred by donor countries' higher education institutions when they receive students from developing countries.

> "The volume of scholarships funded by aid programmes has been stagnant since 2010 at US$1.2 billion"

Even if information on the number of scholarships were available, it would need to be compared with the volume of international student mobility. Globally, the median outbound mobility ratio was 6% in 2017. However, this reflects a relatively large number of small countries with high mobility ratios. Since mobility is lower in large countries, the global outbound mobility ratio was estimated at 2.3%, corresponding to 5.1 million mobile students, up from 2% in 2012. While an increasing share of internationally mobile students move outside their home regions, the share of intra-regional mobility can be large. Most internationally mobile students from Europe stay within the region, their mobility actively promoted through the European Union (EU) Erasmus+ programme, an initiative South-eastern Asia is seeking to emulate (**Policy focus 16.1**).

The target aims not only to make tertiary education more affordable for nationals of 'developing countries, in particular least developed countries, small island developing States and African countries' who are academically prepared but lack financial means to study abroad, but also to provide opportunities not available in home countries. Many students from small countries move to pursue specialized courses that in large countries would only necessitate moving to another city or province, a difference evidenced by the strong negative relationship between country size and outbound mobility ratio (**Figure 16.1**).

Outbound mobility is also negatively related to overall tertiary participation across income groups (**Figure 16.2**). If tertiary students disproportionally come from wealthy households that are also more likely to send their children to study abroad, the mobility ratio will fall as systems expand and less advantaged students gain access to tertiary education. However, the negative slope is steeper than that. Part of the explanation may be that a larger tertiary education system is associated with increased diversification of programmes, which increases the likelihood of students finding what they need at home.

These statistics refer to enrolment. Measuring how many nationals graduate from tertiary education institutions abroad has distinct challenges. Notwithstanding a concerted effort in the European Union, few countries collect such statistics systematically (**Data focus 16.1**).

FIGURE 16.1:

Students from small countries are more likely to study abroad

Relationship between outbound mobility ratio and population, 2016

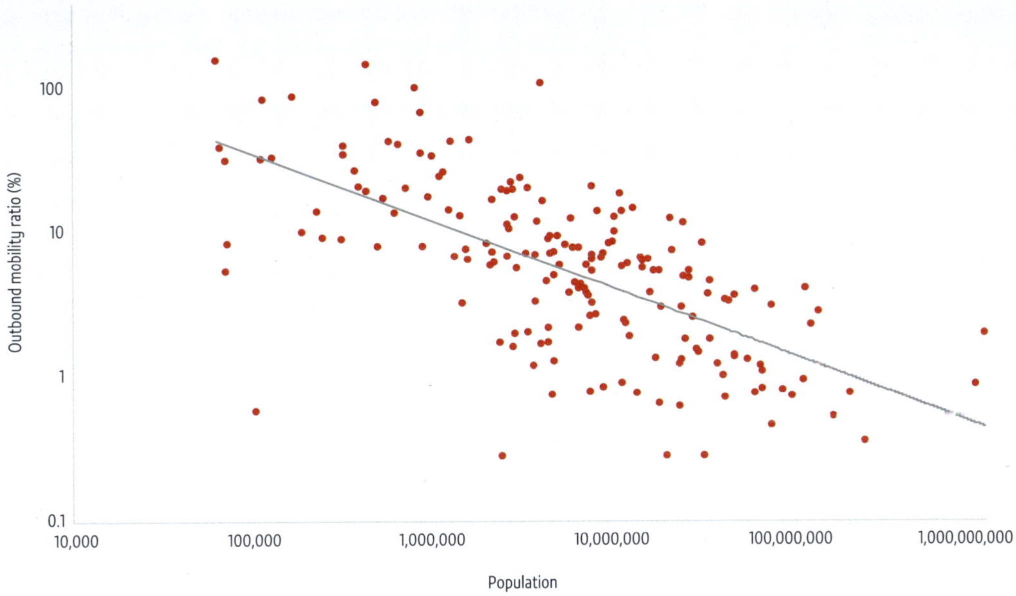

GEM StatLink: http://bit.ly/fig16_1

Source: UIS database.

DATA FOCUS 16.1: MEASURING STUDENT MOBILITY IN EUROPE AND BEYOND

Despite the focus on the internationalization of tertiary education, monitoring developments is hampered by data gaps that stymie even countries with concrete policy objectives in this field. For instance, promoting student mobility is a centrepiece of the EU tertiary education strategy and overall Education and Training 2020 framework. In 2011, the Council of Ministers of Education, Youth, Culture and Sport agreed that on average at least 20% of tertiary graduates in the European Union should have experienced part of their studies and training abroad, including work placements. This Learning Mobility in Higher Education 2020 (LMHE2020) benchmark was to spend at least 3 months abroad or obtain a minimum of 15 credits in the European Credit Transfer and Accumulation System (ECTS). A similar indicator and benchmark were defined for vocational education and training.

The benchmark differs from international student mobility data available at the time. Previously, EU credit mobility data related to the European Union's own programmes, such as Erasmus+, and referred to enrolment. The UNESCO-OECD-Eurostat education data initiative also collected student mobility data in the 1990s exclusively on enrolment. The LMHE2020 benchmark relates to graduation and requires data on both 'credit mobility' and 'degree mobility', which come from different sources, reflecting their different nature.

Credit mobility is temporary by definition, with students completing their degrees at home institutions; therefore, home institutions, typically in graduates' countries of origin, provide data on graduates' credit mobility experience. For the purposes of the benchmark,

> "In 2011, the European Union agreed that on average at least 20% of tertiary graduates should have experienced part of their studies and training abroad"

FIGURE 16.2:

Lower tertiary education opportunities at home are associated with more students seeking opportunities to study abroad

Relationship between outbound mobility ratio and gross enrolment ratio, 2016

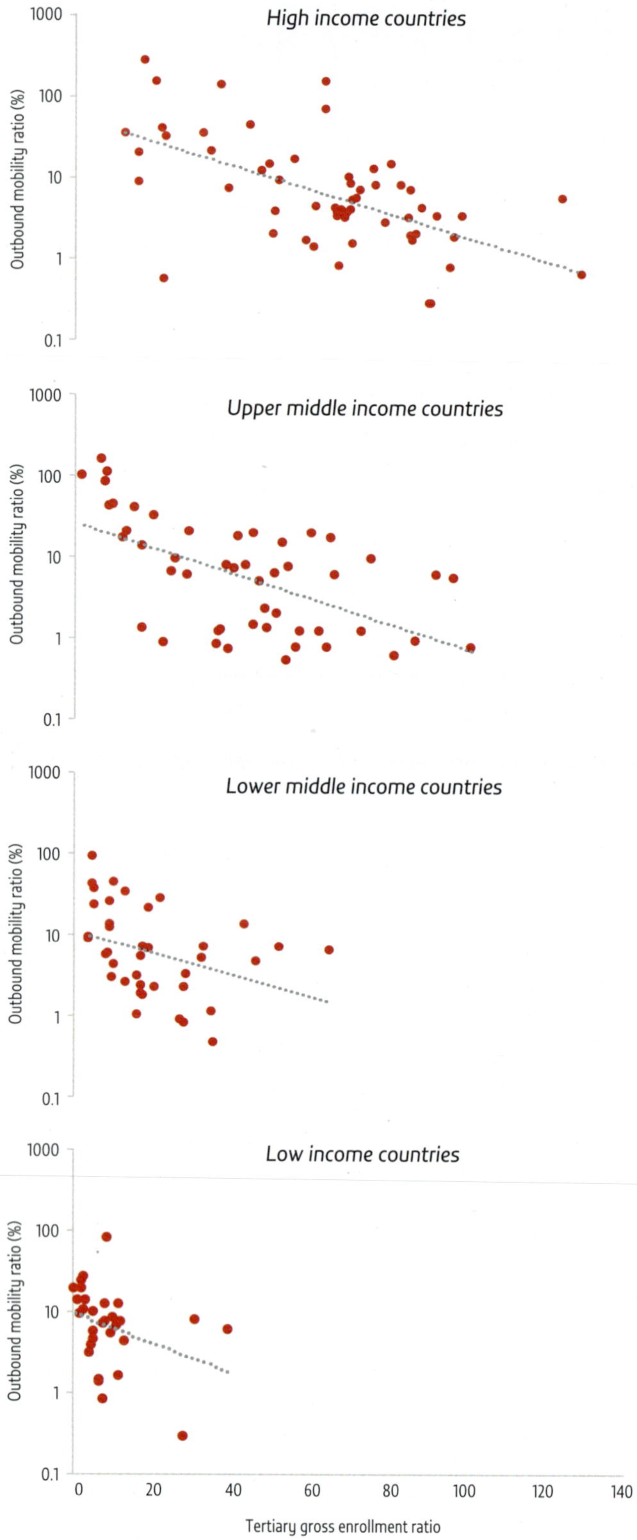

GEM StatLink: http://bit.ly/fig16_2
Source: UIS database.

a graduate's country of origin is defined as the country where he or she completed upper secondary. Until 2016, countries could instead base their reported data on their national definition, even if it used residence or citizenship to define graduates' country of origin. Since 2016, however, countries have reported best available estimates, with country of prior education preferred over residence or citizenship.

In the case of degree mobility, some students leave their countries of origin and enrol in a full degree programme abroad. EU countries generally have no means of knowing who among their upper secondary graduates goes on to graduate from tertiary education in another country. This is especially true for third-country nationals. Hence data on degree-mobile graduates must be collected and reported by the destination countries in which degrees are obtained.

Since EU secondary graduates are potentially globally mobile, the quality of the European Union's LMHE2020 outward mobility benchmark relies on information provided by other countries. For EU member states, reporting for the benchmark became mandatory in 2015. While non-EU countries in the European Higher Education Area are under no obligation, they have an incentive to cooperate so the benchmark can be reported for them, too. For other countries, compliance is voluntary.

Global data collection mechanisms were put in place as part of UNESCO-OECD-Eurostat data collection in 2014. This initiative captures mainly administrative information, using a new methodological manual on learning mobility and data collection. Country coverage need not be truly global to obtain reliable estimates for the benchmark, since EU degree-mobile graduates are highly concentrated in relatively few destinations outside the European Union. The intention is to cover countries accounting for 95% of global EU student degree mobility. So far, Australia, Brazil, Canada, Chile, Colombia, Israel, New Zealand and the Russian Federation have provided the necessary data. Achieving a better coverage would require data from the United States. China, India, Japan, Mexico and the Republic of Korea are other main destinations currently missed.

Degree mobility rates were first estimated for 2013. They were far below the 20% target, although they probably underestimated outward mobility due to the incomplete coverage of destination countries. Even so, it is evident that outward mobility is substantial in many European countries (**Figure 16.3**).

FIGURE 16.3:

In Europe, student mobility increases with the level of study

Outward degree mobility rate by International Standard Classification of Education level, selected European countries, 2013

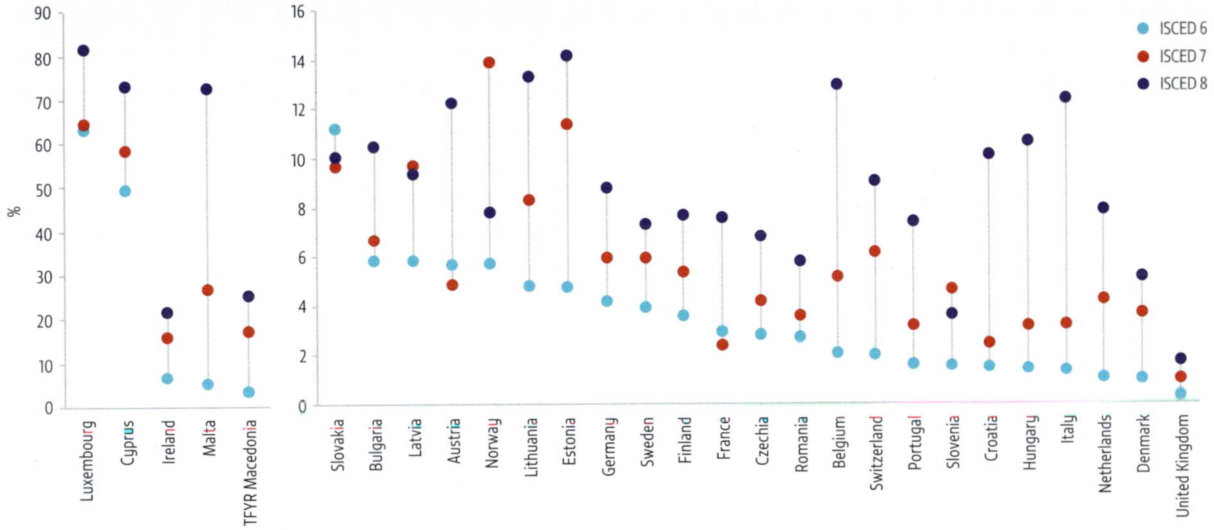

GEM StatLink: http://bit.ly/fig16_3

Note: ISCED = International Standard Classification of Education, including: bachelor's degree (ISCED 6); master's degree or equivalent (ISCED 7); and doctoral degree or equivalent (ISCED 8).

Source: Flisi et al. (2015).

New estimates published for 2016 calculate both degree and credit mobility rates for the first time. They suggest that the outward mobility rate was 10.7%, consisting of a credit mobility rate of 7.6% and a degree mobility rate of 3.1%. The degree mobility progressed from 2.5% at the bachelor's level to 4.3% at the master's level and 8.4% at the doctoral level. By contrast, credit mobility was highest at the master's level (10.4%) (Flisi and Sánchez-Barrioluengo, 2018).

> "In 2016, the outward mobility rate was 10.7%"

The shift in monitoring tertiary mobility by graduation rather than enrolment is a noteworthy experiment. The EU exercise demonstrates data collection challenges. Nevertheless, the wider international community should assume, despite the target 4.b wording, that the ultimate aim of scholarships is to increase opportunities for mobile students from developing countries not only to enrol in tertiary abroad but also to graduate.

POLICY FOCUS 16.1: MOBILE STUDENTS, MOBILE POLICIES? ACADEMIC EXCHANGE PROGRAMMES IN EUROPE AND ASIA

Enrolling in a tertiary education programme abroad can be administratively challenging and may seem difficult to justify for the sake of one or two semesters. Institutionalized programmes can greatly support short-term student mobility. While many institutions maintain bilateral relationships with partners abroad, institutionalizing mobility at the regional level greatly expands opportunities.

The largest and most prominent programme is the European Community Action Scheme for the Mobility of University Students, or Erasmus, introduced in 1987. Participants study for 3 to 12 months in another European country, and home institutions count these courses towards their degrees.

> Erasmus is the largest student exchange programme in the world

Under the Erasmus Charter for Higher Education, receiving institutions provide all necessary student support, including exemption from fees for tuition, registration, examination, and laboratory and library access. Students may receive a travel and subsistence grant of up to EUR 350 per month, depending on living costs (European Commission, 2018b). The programme, known as Erasmus+ since 2014, now covers education and training, youth and sport, academic staff and a student loan guarantee facility. The budget increased from EUR 9 billion for 2007–2013 to EUR 14.8 billion for 2014–2020 (European Commission, 2018a). The most substantial part of the budget is promotion of a 'European dimension' in education and training (78%) and, within this strand, higher education (33% of the total) (European Commission, 2018a). Funding of Erasmus+ is scheduled to double to EUR 30 billion for 2021–2027 (ICEF Monitor, 2018).

During the first three years of Erasmus+, student and staff mobility increased to 1 million participants, mostly undergraduates. Some 3,900 higher education institutions were awarded mobility grants in 2016 alone (European Commission, 2017). The average cost was estimated at EUR 1,500 per participant, or around EUR 15 per participant per day (European Commission, 2018a).

THERE ARE SEVERAL WAYS TO EVALUATE ERASMUS' EFFECTIVENESS

Evaluating the success of Erasmus-supported student mobility needs to take both system outputs and individual outcomes into account.

At the system level, Erasmus triggered the development of what is now called the ECTS, which recognizes workload and achieved learning outcomes based on comparable quality assurance standards (European Commission, 2015). Since its creation in 1989, the ECTS has been applied to all modes of delivery, as well as to non-formal and informal learning contexts outside universities. All Erasmus+ students receive formal recognition of participation. In addition, 80% receive full and 15% partial academic recognition of their learning outcomes. Recognition is also strong in vocational education and training programmes (88% of learning outcomes) (European Commission, 2018a).

At the individual level, Erasmus' aim has been to enhance participants' skills, employability and intercultural awareness, providing opportunities to explore European values and citizen identity with the aim of promoting social cohesion. Around 9 out of 10 participants reported that it increased their resilience, open-mindedness, curiosity, readiness to take on new challenges, tolerance towards others' values and behaviours, and ability to cooperate with diverse people (European Commission, 2014). Although differences between Erasmus alumni and non-mobile students are small, students who studied abroad had more positive attitudes towards immigration and minorities (European Commission, 2018a). The proportion of Erasmus alumni pursuing further education or professional training as their main activity 5 to 10 years after graduation was more than twice as high (9%) as among non-participants (4%) (European Commission, 2016).

However, one should not interpret such findings uncritically. It is important to evaluate the impact of participation on such outcomes, controlling for potentially unobserved differences between participants and non-participants (Hauschildt et al., 2015; Schnepf et al., 2017). For instance, participants may come from more privileged backgrounds, which would improve their future education and employment chances regardless of the mobility experience. In the United Kingdom, about 4.4% of students from high socio-economic backgrounds participated in Erasmus in 2015/16 compared with 2.8% from low socio-economic backgrounds. This gap has increased over time (Schnepf, 2018). Nevertheless, good-quality data from Italy and the United Kingdom indicate that European student mobility positively affected employability (Schnepf and D'Hombres, 2018).

Selectivity reduces the potential of student mobility to develop a European identity. Even before leaving to study abroad, participants are highly educated and display a more positive relationship towards Europe than non-participants (Kuhn, 2012). Some studies have drawn attention to other nuances that limit effectiveness. Erasmus students tend to mingle with other participants, especially those of their nationality, and have limited high-quality interaction with native students (Sigalas,

2010). Driving factors of student mobility, such as language similarity and spatial proximity, mean that many student mobility flows are concentrated in particular countries (Baláž et al., 2018).

EASTERN AND SOUTH-EASTERN ASIA STUDENT MOBILITY PROGRAMMES AIM TO BUILD ON THE EUROPEAN EXPERIENCE

Erasmus' success has inspired recent attempts to adapt European experiences and practices in South-eastern Asia. In 2015, the Association of Southeast Asian Nations (ASEAN) and the European Union launched the EU Support to Higher Education in the ASEAN Region (SHARE) project to harmonize regional tertiary education systems and build an intra-ASEAN student mobility programme funding 400 scholarships across 32 public and private universities (Rasplus, 2018).

Greater harmonization and mobility require coordination among government departments, quality-assurance agencies, regional organizations (including the Southeast Asian Ministers of Education Organization's Regional Center for Higher Education and Development) and the ASEAN University Network. Three credit transfer systems coexisted, and students, academics and administrative staff have had little confidence that studies abroad would be recognized (SHARE, 2016; Yavaprabhas, 2014). Systems needed to identify tools to compare student outcomes effectively, following accumulated practices and experiences of the Bologna Process, instead of simply calculating credit points (Yonezawa et al., 2014).

Despite progress in establishing qualification, mutual recognition, quality assurance and credit transfer frameworks, a regional higher education area is still at a very early stage of implementation. Only 7% of total ASEAN outbound student mobility is within the region and most students prefer to study in Malaysia, Singapore, Thailand and Viet Nam. Cultural and geographic proximity play a role. Indonesians tend to study in Malaysia, for instance (Chao, 2017). Lack of rich student-level data currently hinders better understanding of mobility patterns, so SHARE plans to improve data quality to manage mobility (SHARE, 2017).

The success of student mobility in Europe owes much to close ties and established political cooperation mechanisms between countries. Such mechanisms are still being developed in much of Asia. Inter-institutional agreements may therefore be an alternative driver of integration. Collective Action for Mobility Program of University Students (CAMPUS Asia), an exchange programme funded by the Japanese Ministry of Education, Culture, Sports, Science and Technology, aims to establish a network of universities with China and the Republic of Korea to improve competitiveness in the international academic market and develop leaders (Chun, 2016).

CONCLUSION

After almost 30 years of accumulated experience, stakeholders in EU member states recognize the benefits of mobility and the significance of harmonization to support it. Evaluations of the flagship Erasmus programme suggest a positive effect on employment and career opportunities. Many important structures are in place in the European Higher Education Area to facilitate mobility, including diploma supplements, the European Qualifications Framework, quality-assurance registries and networks, the ECTS and coordination of academic calendars. Replicating these structures in other regions will require strong political will and commitment, but the efforts in South-eastern Asia represent a promising example.

> "Despite progress in establishing qualification, mutual recognition, quality assurance and credit transfer frameworks, a higher education area in South-eastern Asia is still at a very early stage of implementation"

Ekhlas is a refugee who was forced to flee the outbreak of civil war in Sudan with her mother, father and three younger brothers in 2003 and who has become an English Language Learner teacher in Portland, Maine.

CREDIT: Heather Perry/UNHCR

KEY MESSAGES

Internationally comparable data on teacher indicators remain surprisingly scarce. Relatively few countries report even a basic headcount of teachers, and that does not take teaching hours, teachers in administrative positions and other complexities into account.

Using national definitions, 85% of primary teachers globally were trained in 2017, a decline of 1.5 percentage points since 2013. Only 64% of primary teachers were trained in sub-Saharan Africa, where some countries' ability to maintain entry standards while recruiting teachers at high rates is stretched. In Niger, 13% of primary teachers were newly recruited in 2013, one of the highest rates, but only 37% of them were trained.

Only 51% of countries have the minimum data to estimate teacher attrition rates. Moreover, available data are not always straightforward to interpret. They may refer only to public schools, as in Uganda, or may cover regions without accounting for cross-regional mobility, as in Brazil.

Caution is needed in interpreting attrition estimates. Monitoring individual teachers in Australia, revealed that 83% of those who left returned within two years, at least half of them from paid leave.

International teacher migration can improve teacher access to professional development opportunities and host countries' teaching force diversity. But it can also result in sending systems and migrating teachers suffering losses. Regulations and monitoring of recruitment, hiring and working conditions are needed to protect them.

CHAPTER 17

TARGET 4.c

Teachers

By 2030, substantially increase the supply of qualified teachers, including through international cooperation for teacher training in developing countries, especially least developed countries and small island developing States

GLOBAL INDICATOR

4.c.1 – *Proportion of teachers in: (a) pre-primary education; (b) primary education; (c) lower secondary education; and (d) upper secondary education who have received at least the minimum organized teacher training (e.g. pedagogical training) pre-service or in-service required for teaching at the relevant level in a given country*

THEMATIC INDICATORS

4.c.2 – *Pupil-trained teacher ratio by education level*

4.c.3 – *Percentage of teachers qualified according to national standards by level and type of institution*

4.c.4 – *Pupil-qualified teacher ratio by education level*

4.c.5 – *Average teacher salary relative to other professions requiring a comparable level of qualification*

4.c.6 – *Teacher attrition rate by education level*

4.c.7 – *Percentage of teachers who received in-service training in the last 12 months by type of training*

Gathering internationally comparable data on teacher-related indicators for SDG 4 remains surprisingly challenging. Even using the most basic definition of pupil/teacher ratio – a headcount of the number of teachers, which does not account for actual number of teaching hours, teachers in non-teaching administrative positions and numerous other complexities – relatively few countries are able to generate the relevant data, especially for secondary education.

Using national definitions, 85% of primary teachers globally were trained in 2017, a decline of 1.5 percentage points since 2013. The indicator is lowest in sub-Saharan Africa (64%) and Southern Asia (71%). There is no global average of the percentage of trained teachers at the secondary education level, but there are data for some regions, such as sub-Saharan Africa (50%) and Latin America and the Caribbean (80%), where the respective pupil/trained teacher ratios were 43:1 and 21:1 (**Table 17.1**).

TABLE 17.1:
Selected trained and qualified teacher indicators by education level, 2017 or latest available year

Region	Trained teachers (%)		Pupil/trained teacher ratio		Pupil/qualified teacher ratio	
	Primary	Secondary	Primary	Secondary	Primary	Secondary
World	**85**	**…**	**28**	**…**	**26**	**18**
Sub-Saharan Africa	64	50	60	43	53	29
Northern Africa and Western Asia	84	…	23	…	21	15
Northern Africa	84	78	27	21	24	17
Central and Southern Asia	72	…	48	…	38	…
Central Asia	99	96	22	10	22	10
Eastern and South-eastern Asia	…	…	…	…	19	16
South-eastern Asia	97	94	19	19	21	19
Latin America and the Caribbean	89	80	24	21	…	…
Oceania	…	…	…	…	…	…
Europe and Northern America	…	…	…	…	…	…
Low income	74	…	53	…	49	…
Lower middle income	76	…	39	…	34	24
Upper middle income	…	…	…	…	20	15
High income	…	…	…	…	…	…

Note: Ratios calculated on the basis of teacher headcounts.
Source: UIS database.

While available figures on pupil/trained teacher ratios in secondary education appear low in the few regions and subregions for which data are available, except in sub-Saharan Africa, secondary enrolment must grow dramatically in many countries to reach SDG 4. What happens when recruitment of trained teachers fails to keep pace with enrolment is evident at the primary level. In sub-Saharan Africa, while some countries recruit teachers at high rates, doing so can stretch their ability to maintain entry standards as long as teacher education capacity remains limited. In Niger, where 13% of primary teachers were newly recruited in 2013, only 37% of these were trained. Angola, Benin, Malawi and Mali had high expansion rates of the primary teaching force but less than half the new recruits were trained. By contrast, at relatively high rates of expansion, all new recruits were trained in Burkina Faso, Chad, Congo and Côte d'Ivoire (**Figure 17.1**).

“Using national definitions, 85% of primary teachers globally were trained in 2017, a decline of 1.5 percentage points since 2013”

FIGURE 17.1:

Teacher education standards are difficult to maintain with higher recruitment rates

Rate of new teacher recruitment and percentage of trained teachers, primary education, selected sub-Saharan African countries, 2010–2014

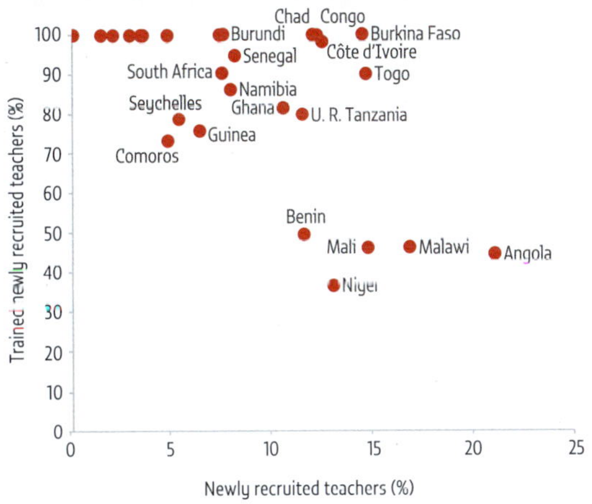

GEM StatLink: http://bit.ly/fig17_1
Source: UIS database.

High recruitment rates do not always indicate education expansion; they may also be necessary to replace teachers who are leaving. Although reliable data on attrition are patchy, some estimates, especially in high income countries, suggest high attrition rates among new teachers. Other evidence implies that most teachers who appear to leave do so for family reasons and return to the profession within two years (**Data focus 17.1**).

Teachers who migrate to take up positions in richer countries are a distinct phenomenon that plagues many smaller and poorer countries. On the other hand, not all demand for trained teachers has to be filled by increasing the number of teachers being trained; trained teachers can be recruited from abroad, although challenges with qualification recognition and exploitation after moving are rife (**Policy focus 17.1**).

There is little comparable evidence on teachers' international experiences and attitudes towards diversity. An expected addition to the SDG 4 knowledge base is a module on equity and diversity in the 2018 Teaching and Learning International Survey (TALIS), which covers 49 education systems. It is run by the Organisation for Economic Co-operation and Development (OECD), which expects to make results available in mid-2019. The module collects information on how much time teachers have spent abroad, whether it was for professional purposes, how the experience shaped their teaching in a culturally diverse environment, how confident they feel teaching students from diverse backgrounds, and what practices they use. A question on teachers' country of birth was made optional; only Alberta (Canada), New Zealand and the United States chose to include it. Although a few countries opted out, TALIS also includes questions on multiculturalism, which offer an opportunity to compare teacher perspectives with those of students, which are collected through the 2018 OECD Programme for International Student Assessment global competence module and the IEA International Civic and Citizenship Study (Le Donné, 2018).

DATA FOCUS 17.1: TEACHER ATTRITION IS HARD TO ESTIMATE ACCURATELY

The recommendation to include the teacher attrition rate as a thematic indicator in the SDG 4 monitoring framework was based on the belief that attrition might reflect low motivation. Reducing avoidable teacher attrition might prove more feasible and cost-effective than attempting to increase teacher education massively.

Only 51% of countries have the minimum data to estimate attrition rates: current-year data on total teachers and new teachers and previous-year data on total teachers. Availability is low even in high income and otherwise data-rich countries (UIS, 2016). Moreover, available data are not always straightforward to interpret.

> “Only 51% of countries have the minimum data to estimate teacher attrition rates”

Accurate estimates require personnel data that assign identification numbers so individuals can be traced as they qualify, enter, exit and re-enter the profession. Data should distinguish among different entrants, including re-entrants, and leavers (**Table 17.2**). Teacher trajectories are often not linear. A five-year tracer study of a small sample of Swedish teachers found that many left temporarily, some motivated by the desire to re-enter with enhanced teaching skills (Lindqvist et al., 2014).

Such personnel data should be integrated at the national level. School districts can typically only estimate turnover from teachers' current location and cannot follow those moving outside a jurisdiction (Macdonald, 1999). Unfortunately, much research on determinants of teacher retention suffers from this limitation, including longitudinal studies from the United States at the state level (Boyd et al., 2008; Plecki et al., 2017) or district level (Nicotera et al., 2017).

In Brazil, teachers are registered at the municipal and state levels, but there is no aggregate information about attrition rates at the federal level. The National Institute for Educational Studies and Research, the research arm of the Ministry of Education, collects information on teacher numbers annually but does not have access to the number of new entrants at the national level. It also collects information on the regularity of the teaching staff, but that indicator is calculated on teacher tenure at the school level, taking five-year periods as the unit of analysis (INEP, 2018).

A similar problem appears in countries with diversified provision. Available data may account for attrition in public schools but not in private or unrecognized schools. A large share of the workforce may consist of contract teachers but attrition data refer only to civil servants. In Uganda, where both issues are present, data from the education management information system (EMIS) capture only public schools and suggest low attrition rates: 4% for primary and 5% for secondary teachers (UNESCO, 2014).

Attrition estimates are also affected by how part-time and multigrade teachers are classified, whether transitions in arrangements are captured as attrition, and how extended maternity leave is categorized. Specific information should be recorded to make results relevant both for understanding potential effects of policies and for planning human resources (e.g. distinguishing types of termination, such as retirement, long-term leave or layoff) (Finster, 2015). In Uganda, among teachers who exited, 25% had died or retired (due to age or illness), 21% had resigned,

TABLE 17.2:
Yearly dynamics of teacher leaving and entry or re-entry

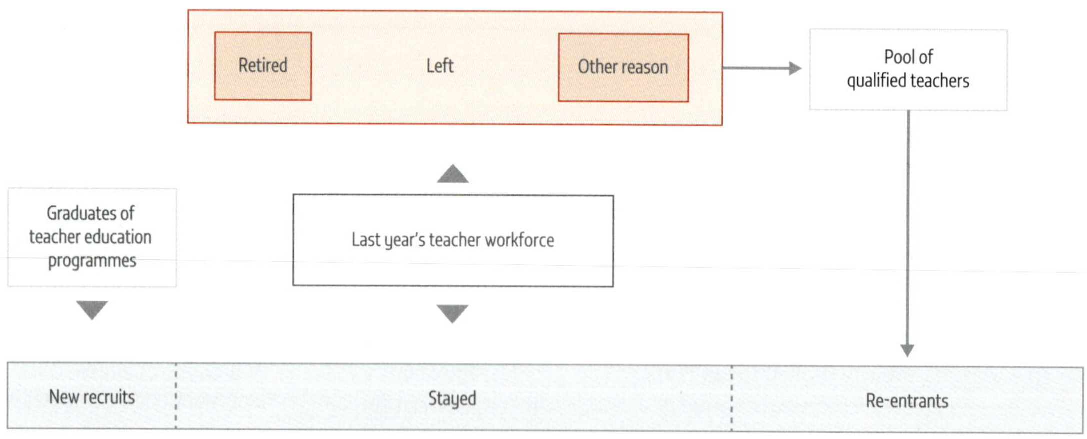

Source: Based on OECD (2005).

15% had been dismissed and 10% had been transferred to non-teaching posts; no cause was established for the rest (UNESCO, 2014).

Some administrative data sources offer good insights into why teachers leave schools or the profession. Research from Chile, Sweden and the United States found higher attrition among teachers who are less experienced; more qualified and, therefore, more employable elsewhere; placed in more challenging or rural schools; inadequately paid; or on short-term contracts (Ávalos and Valenzuela, 2016; Borman and Dowling, 2008; Lindqvist et al., 2014).

Some countries conduct specialized surveys. Chile's Longitudinal Teacher Survey was linked with other data sources to generate valuable insights (Cabezas et al., 2011). Surveys that are not specific to education or teachers can also provide valuable information on attrition and aspects of job satisfaction. Longitudinal data from the Household, Income and Labour Dynamics in Australia survey over 2001–2013 showed that 14% of teachers left the profession each year, on average. Allowing for moves between education levels, attrition was 20% for primary and 18% for secondary teachers. But most teachers who left returned, 83% within two years. At least half of those were on paid leave, suggesting maternity leave (Jha and Ryan, 2017).

Policy-makers are particularly concerned about retaining newly qualified teachers (UNESCO, 2009). Attrition tends to be higher in the first few years than in mid-career (Goldring et al., 2014). However, newly qualified retention estimates vary by information source. In the Netherlands, the estimates differed, for instance, between studies based on samples of university teacher education graduates and those based on government website information on entrants into teacher education. A comparison of these different sources suggested an attrition rate of 12%–13% five years after graduation as the most reliable estimate, which is much lower than that reported in other high income countries (den Brok et al., 2017). But it is consistent with other recent studies arguing that the attrition of newly qualified teachers is not well understood (Weldon, 2018).

Despite the importance of estimating teacher attrition rates, available sources of information tend to be either insufficiently comprehensive in their coverage of the teacher labour market (e.g. across levels or sectors) or insufficiently detailed in monitoring individuals over time. Both factors suggest that reported attrition rates may be overestimated.

> "Available data tend to be insufficiently comprehensive or insufficiently detailed to monitor teacher attrition accurately"

POLICY FOCUS 17.1: TEACHER MIGRATION BRINGS BENEFITS AND RISKS

Teacher migration has drawn considerably less research than the migration of other skilled professionals, such as nurses, doctors and engineers. Like many of these professions, teaching is typically regulated, subject to specific, often rigid, qualification requirements that differ by jurisdiction. Such obstacles have not deterred hundreds of thousands of teachers from migrating between countries. The size of some flows causes teacher shortages for sending countries.

> "Some teacher migratory flows cause shortages for sending countries"

Like other migrants, teachers may be motivated by a mix of economic and other push and pull factors. In South Africa, teachers' perceptions of relative deprivation was a main reason to migrate to the United Kingdom (Manik, 2014). Political instability, discrimination, and poor training facilities and working conditions are other factors that contribute to teacher migration (Ridge et al., 2017). Lack of modern infrastructure, scarcity of teaching materials and inadequate research equipment push Nigerian academics, for instance, to seek work abroad (IOM, 2014).

TEACHING IS A REGULATED PROFESSION IN MANY COUNTRIES

Many countries regulate the teaching profession. Specific authorities assess and recognize competences and qualifications, and gatekeeping mechanisms limit access to teaching positions to those with country-specific

> Many countries limit access to teaching positions to those with country-specific professional qualifications

professional qualifications. In Sweden, teachers, including pre-school teachers, must be registered with the National Agency for Education, which issues a qualified teacher status certification (Skolverket, 2018).

It may not be possible to complete the process to be recognized as a qualified teacher before moving. In Australia, the qualification recognition process must be completed onshore, and English language is mandatory (IOM, 2013). In Quebec, Canada, the French language test required for access to the profession is a barrier to many migrant teachers (Niyubahwe et al., 2013). A review of teachers migrating to Australia, Germany, Israel, New Zealand, South Africa, the United Kingdom and the United States showed that qualification recognition was a major challenge (Bense, 2016).

Immigrants' under-representation among teachers may reflect such barriers. Even in Australia, which actively recruits skilled migrants and where 27% of the population was born overseas, immigrants made up 16% of primary teachers and 19% of secondary teachers in 2013 (McKenzie et al., 2014). Recruitment regulations may mean that uncoordinated or ad hoc teacher migration fails to provide access to the labour market abroad. Only 47% of migrant Zimbabwean teachers in South Africa were working in the sector (Crush et al., 2012).

MANY TEACHERS MIGRATE BETWEEN GLOBAL SOUTH AND NORTH

Migrant teachers may be recruited through bilateral processes or recruitment agencies, or simply be employed as individuals who come to a country independently, often ending up in temporary positions. According to the Database on Immigrants in OECD and non-OECD Countries (DIOC), Canada, Germany, the United Kingdom and the United States have among the largest numbers of immigrant teachers. There were almost 195,000 migrant teachers in Canada, with India, the United Kingdom and the United States as top sending countries. In the United States, there were at least 143,000, an analysis of 2010 DIOC data by the *Global Education Monitoring Report* team showed. Overall, 8% of teachers were born abroad (Startz, 2017).

Teacher qualification regulations often relate to language skills; thus many large flows are between countries with linguistic and cultural commonalities. Teachers from other English-speaking countries, in particular the United Kingdom, are among the largest groups in Australian schools, while Australians are well represented in the UK teaching force. Teachers from Egypt and other Arab countries played a key role in scaling up education systems in the period after the discovery of oil in the Gulf States. This example also illustrates how exposed immigrant teachers are to the vagaries of immigration or education policies (**Box 17.1**).

Migration based on language fluency includes the relatively recent trend of hiring international native English speakers. In Hong Kong, China, the Native-speaking English Teacher Scheme aimed to enhance English language learning through exposure to native anglophone teachers. Similar programmes place native-speaking language instructors in public primary and secondary schools in many European countries (European Commission, 2017a).

International private schools also work to attract teachers from abroad. There were 8,000 private English-language schools worldwide in 2016, and their number is projected to double by 2025 (OFSTED and Wilshaw, 2016). In 2015, 18,000 teachers left the United Kingdom, and about 100,000 British teachers worked abroad in international schools full-time during that school year, making the United Kingdom the world's biggest 'exporter' of teachers (Wilshaw, 2016).

> Teacher qualification regulations often relate to language skills; thus many large flows are between countries with linguistic and cultural commonalities

BOX 17.1:

Arab teacher migration to the Gulf States has evolved over two generations

Education systems in countries of the Gulf Cooperation Council (GCC) expanded dramatically from the mid-20th century with the discovery of oil and gas. Although these countries had no teacher training programmes until the 1960s, they could offer high salaries, attracting teachers from other Arab countries to scale up their systems (Kapiszewski, 2006; Ridge et al., 2017).

Initially, recruitment was via government-to-government circular labour migration programmes. Over time, formal opportunities declined as many GCC education ministries stopped requesting teachers through these programmes. Arab teachers continued to move to GCC countries, however, seeking jobs independently or through employment agencies (Ridge et al., 2017).

Arab teachers in GCC countries faced numerous challenges, both economic and non-economic. Working conditions were often unstable and long-term contracts lacking. Teachers often supplemented their salaries by tutoring. A study of grade 12 students in the United Arab Emirates found that 65% received private tutoring by mostly male tutors, 65% of whom came from Egypt and 29% from other Arab countries (Farah, 2011).

Expatriate Arab teachers maintained a strong presence until relatively recently. In Qatar, they made up about 87% of teachers in government schools in 2013. In the United Arab Emirates, 90% of teachers in government boys' schools and 20% in girls' schools were expatriate Arabs in 2010/11. However, in that academic year the Abu Dhabi Education Council instituted a new curriculum model to introduce English as the language of instruction by 2030 (Ridge et al., 2017). This policy initiative reflected rapid cultural changes. In a survey of Arab youth aged 18 to 24, two-thirds of respondents in GCC countries reported speaking more English than Standard Arabic in their daily lives (Arab Youth Survey, 2017).

Egyptian and Jordanian teachers in Emirati schools are being replaced by English-speaking recruits, largely from high income countries, who are hired under much more favourable terms and afforded generous benefits. By contrast, Jordanian Emirati teachers reported wage discrimination and absence of support (EI, 2016).

TEACHER MIGRATION CAN CREATE SHORTAGES IN SENDING COUNTRIES

Partly as a result of teacher migration, the United Kingdom is experiencing its own shortages. Recruiting teachers from Jamaica and South Africa creates a global domino effect. To alleviate its shortages, South Africa recruits teachers from abroad, especially Zimbabwe (**Figure 17.2**). With 35,000 teachers leaving Zimbabwe for Botswana, South Africa and the United Kingdom during the crisis years in the 2000s, the Zimbabwe education system was seriously affected (de Villiers and Weda, 2017).

Caribbean countries have experienced high teacher emigration in recent decades, not least due to active recruitment efforts from the United Kingdom and the United States. Facing shortages in public schools in the early 2000s, the New York City Board of Education increased international recruitment, attracting hundreds of teachers from the Caribbean, particularly Jamaica

FIGURE 17.2:

Two out of three migrant teachers in South Africa came from Zimbabwe

Migrant teachers by sending country, South Africa, 2010

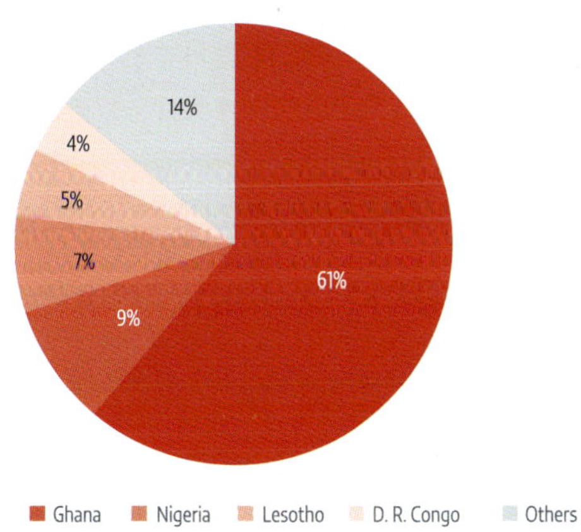

GEM StatLink: http://bit.ly/fig17_2
Note: 'Others' includes India, Eswatini, Uganda, the United Kingdom and Zambia.
Source: Keevy et al. (2014).

and Barbados (Penson and Yonemura, 2012): 350 came from Jamaica in 2001 alone (Hadley Dunn, 2013). For small island states, even relatively few emigrating teachers can create significant shortages (Bense, 2016).

The loss for sending countries can be considerable, both in terms of their investment in the training and education of these professionals and for the education system as a whole. Hard-to-replace mathematics, physics, science and computer science teachers are the most prone to move abroad. These are officially recognized as shortage occupations in many European countries, including the United Kingdom (United Kingdom Government, 2016); as such, they are less constrained by requirements for preferential recruitment of European Economic Area citizens.

INTERNATIONAL AGREEMENTS HELP REGULATE TEACHER MIGRATION

Such developments have led to international initiatives recognizing sending countries' interest in preventing the critical loss of highly skilled teachers. The Commonwealth Teacher Recruitment Protocol (CTRP) responded to small Caribbean countries' concern that they were losing their teaching force to targeted recruitment drives. Commonwealth education ministers adopted the CTRP in 2004 to 'balance the rights of teachers to migrate internationally against the need to protect the integrity of national education systems, and to prevent the exploitation of the scarce human resources of poor countries' (Commonwealth Consortium for Education, 2015).

UNESCO, the International Labour Organization and other international bodies have acknowledged the protocol (UNESCO/Commonwealth Secretariat, 2012). However, as it is a non-binding code of conduct for countries, it does not constrain individual teachers who wish to migrate. Indeed, a survey of 134 final-year teacher students in South Africa found that 91% were not even aware of the CTRP; around one-third of the students wished to teach outside South Africa within five years (de Villiers, 2017).

Other regional agreements on teacher migration may reflect a need for international coordination regarding access to the profession. The European Qualifications Framework was created to help ensure a collective understanding of core competences, including those of teachers, and to regulate which additional qualification requirements could legally be imposed on European nationals who trained as teachers in a member country and wished to exercise their freedom of movement for workers in the European Union. In addition, Erasmus+ programmes support short-term international teacher exchanges (European Commission, 2017b).

PRIVATE AND ONLINE RECRUITMENT AGENCIES ARE NOT WELL MONITORED OR REGULATED

International teacher recruitment is a lucrative business that attracts commercial agencies. In an Education International survey, 64% of respondents with experience as migrant teachers reported using an agency. Nearly one-quarter reported paying a placement fee: less than US$1,000 in most cases, but some paid US$10,000 or more. While a majority would recommend the agency they used, one out of five would not use the same agency again or were unsure they would recommend it due to concerns about harassment, high fees and lack of transparency (EI, 2014).

> “Almost two-thirds of teacher migrants surveyed in 2014 reported using an agency to secure a position abroad”

Indeed, recruitment practices are usually not closely regulated. A review of the websites of 43 United Kingdom-based agencies showed that many did not provide enough or sufficiently relevant information about working conditions (de Villiers and Books, 2009), prompting calls for both sending and receiving countries to register recruiters (EI, 2014).

CONCLUSION

International teacher migration can bring about many positive changes. Like other migrants, teachers may have better lives and gain access to professional development opportunities. Host countries may increase their teaching force diversity. But teacher migration also carries risks for individuals and education systems. Appropriate regulations and agreements are needed to ensure that sending systems do not suffer unsustainable losses that ultimately damage student learning.

Regulations and monitoring of recruitment, hiring and working conditions are needed to ensure that migrant teachers have adequate information to make informed decisions, are hired in the schools and on the conditions promised, and receive targeted support to fulfil their potential and develop professionally. Both national and international regulatory and monitoring systems need to be involved to make the process fair and beneficial to all.

Esther, a nurse at Dispensaire St. Paul de Moulines in Grand'Anse Department of Haiti, counsels women about family planning.

CREDIT: Reginald Louissaint Jr./Save the Children

KEY MESSAGES

To achieve SDG 8 on decent work, many countries need to recruit and train social workers, who are at the forefront of dealing with rights violations. Yet in 2014 there were 116,000 people per government social worker in Nepal. China formalized social work in the late 1980s, and more than 250 universities now offer social work programmes. The national target is 230,000 new social workers by 2020.

To achieve SDG 10 on cities and sustainable urbanization in informal settlements, it is important to address the acute shortage of urban planning professionals in Asia and Africa. There is only one urban planner for every 200,000 people in Kenya and for every 400,000 people in India. United Cities and Local Government, the main global network of local government actors, coordinates peer learning exchanges, engagement with universities and resource materials to support city administrator capacity.

To achieve SDG 16 on peaceful societies, better education and training are needed for (a) law enforcement officers, to help build trust and limit the use of force, and (b) the judiciary, to meet the needs of the estimated 4 billion people globally who lack access to justice. Average police officer training takes 130 weeks in Germany but 19 weeks in the United States – less time than many trade jobs require.

CHAPTER

18

Education in the other SDGs – a focus on decent work, cities, police and justice

(Global indicators from goals other than SDG 4 that are education-related)

GLOBAL INDICATORS

1.a.2 – *Proportion of total government spending on essential services (education, health and social protection)*

5.6.2 – *Number of countries with laws and regulations that guarantee women aged 15–49 years access to sexual and reproductive health care, information and education*

8.6.1 – *Proportion of youth (aged 15–24 years) not in education, employment or training*

12.8.1 – *Extent to which (i) global citizenship education and (ii) education for sustainable development (including climate change education) are mainstreamed in (a) national education policies; (b) curricula; (c) teacher education; and (d) student assessment*

13.3.1 – *Number of countries that have integrated mitigation, adaptation, impact reduction and early warning into primary, secondary and tertiary curricula*

Despite education's role in achieving the other 16 SDGs, there are only five education-related global indicators outside SDG 4. This chapter discusses education components of SDG 8 (decent work and economic growth), SDG 11 (sustainable cities and communities) and SDG 16 (peace, justice and strong institutions), along with education's role in their achievement through the development of national capacity.

EDUCATION IS INTEGRAL TO DECENT WORK, SUSTAINABLE URBAN DEVELOPMENT AND SOCIAL COHESION

Education affects practically all aspects of sustainable development, including the three interconnected goals discussed in this chapter. This section highlights selected recent findings that indicate the rich variety of linkages.

Education has implications for the SDG 8 target to eliminate child labour, although the effect of education interventions is poorly studied and sometimes counterintuitive. In Burkina Faso, boys who did not have a sister increased their workforce participation with greater access to schools, possibly because of shortened school commutes (Dammert et al., 2018). Despite the recognized need to protect children from exploitation, there is continued disagreement about whether all forms of economic activity by minors are harmful and should be banned, and how to exempt apprenticeships and on-the-job training that do not conflict with schooling (Aufseeser et al., 2018).

The impact of employers' education on the supply of decent jobs is rarely researched. In Italy, university graduates are less likely to hire workers on temporary contracts (Ghignoni et al., 2018). Further research is needed, including in low and middle income countries, on how education affects management practices and paying more than minimum wage.

Decent work includes a fair income, which is partly determined by factors including housing affordability, an SDG 11 target. In many cities, unskilled, semi-skilled and poorly paid skilled occupations no longer make it possible to live within a reasonable commute of urban centres. The resulting occupational segregation is exacerbated when real or perceived differences in school quality drive location decisions and wide variation in neighbourhood housing costs. The increase in school choice has increased the probability of gentrification especially in racially isolated communities in the United States (Pearman and Swain, 2017).

While gentrification is generally detrimental to equity, it can under some circumstances create an opportunity for diversity in schools. In high income countries, highly educated, relatively affluent young families moving to city centres rather than suburbs may reduce segregation, as long as long-term lower-income residents are not displaced and new arrivals use public schools (Mordechay and Ayscue, 2018). Socio-economically diverse schools may also influence urban development.

> "One of the SDG 8 targets on decent work that has a clear link with education is the elimination of child labour"

In the United States, students from richer neighbourhoods, and those attending with richer peers, enjoy better education outcomes. Yet a recent study points out that school quality in poorer neighbourhoods does not explain education disadvantage. Rather, poorer neighbourhoods influence school quality. Improving education outcomes requires concentrating efforts on urban development, e.g. environmental health hazards and local violent crime (Wodtke and Parbst, 2017).

Research on education in emergencies highlights the need for safe spaces protected from violence. This dimension of peaceful societies is reflected in three SDG 16 targets and target 4.a. Lower levels of public safety increase the incentive to acquire skills to protect oneself or harm others, and reduce the incentive to invest in education. The benefits of schooling can be fully realized only when accompanied by investment in public safety (Cruz, 2017).

A peaceful society is characterized not only by freedom from violence but also by tolerance of diversity, a dimension in which education has played a key role for centuries. In the United Kingdom, universities have had spillover effects, increasing support for women's and minorities' rights among those who live in proximity to a university, regardless of their education level. The current geographical distribution of universities correlates with exposure to ethnic and religious diversity in medieval times, suggesting education and tolerance co-evolved (Fielding, 2018).

However, there are rising concerns about education's ability to engender liberal attitudes that disseminate throughout society. While education has been one of the strongest predictors of voting against nationalist or populist parties or candidates, the more educated are becoming less immune to populist political messages. In the Netherlands, prejudice against ethnic minorities rose in 1985–2011, especially among the highly educated, offsetting gains from the expansion of education during this period (Thijs et al., 2018).

Globally, education is a preventive factor in corruption, a phenomenon at odds with peaceful and just societies. In a recent systematic analysis of 36 potential determinants of corruption across 123 countries, the lack of primary education emerged as one of the strongest predictors of corruption in developing countries (Jetter and Parmeter, 2018).

EDUCATION HELPS BUILD PROFESSIONAL CAPACITY

Well-educated professionals are crucial to achieving goals in every area of sustainable development. One way of examining education's contribution to other SDGs is to look at how it helps build professional capacity.

... AMONG SOCIAL WORKERS

Achieving ambitious SDG 8 targets related to decent work (target 8.5), forced labour and human trafficking (target 8.7) and labour rights protection for vulnerable groups, such as migrant workers (target 8.8), requires developing the capacity of those who ensure the well-being of individuals and families at risk. Alongside health workers and law and order personnel, social workers are at the forefront of dealing with rights violations among the most vulnerable.

Recent efforts by the Global Social Service Workforce Alliance fill a considerable data gap on social workers in low and middle income countries and highlight wide inequality among countries. In 2014, there were 116,000 people per government social worker in Nepal, compared with 3,000 in the Republic of Moldova (**Figure 18.1**).

Social workers often receive inadequate training. In an assessment of Ethiopia's public social service workforce, 60% of providers reported lacking relevant education, and almost all interviewees expressed a need for more training to perform their jobs (IntraHealth International, 2013). A review of 13 western and central African countries noted the lack of a legal framework and poor adaptation of training to local realities as major shortcomings (Canavera et al., 2014). A review of degree programmes in 13 low and middle income countries in Asia, eastern Europe and sub-Saharan Africa argued that a lack of master's programmes limited the instructor pool and the profession's planning ability at the system level (Global Social Service Workforce Alliance, 2015).

> “Countries need to recruit and train more social workers, who are at the forefront of dealing with rights violations among the most vulnerable”

FIGURE 18.1:

Poorer countries have too few social workers to implement ambitious policies

Population per government social worker, selected low and middle income countries, 2011–2014

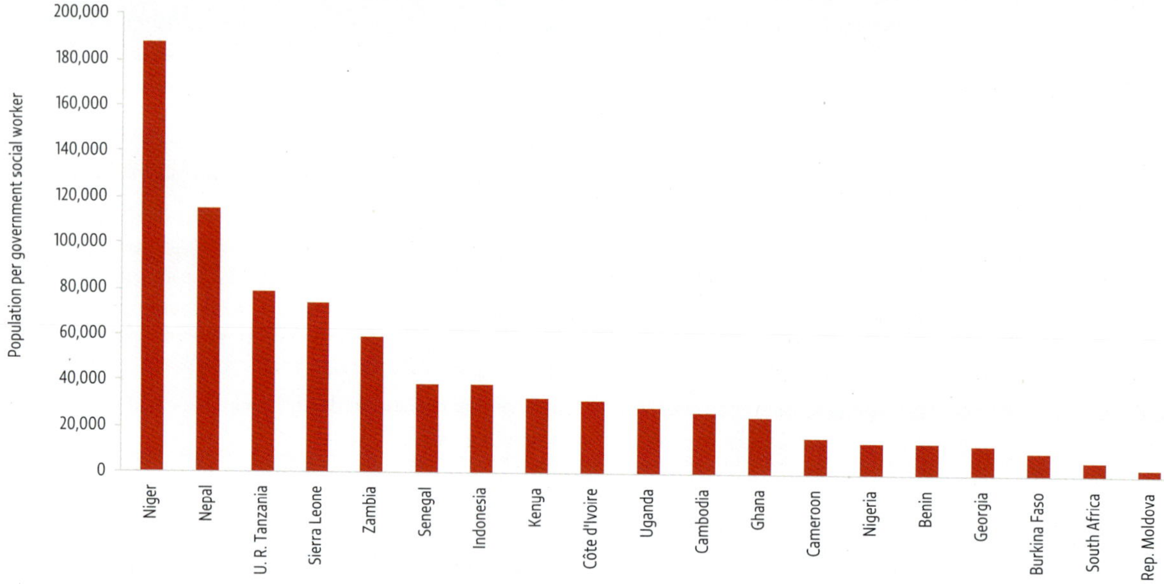

GEM StatLink: http://bit.ly/fig18_1

Notes: Country definitions of social workers vary. Data for Benin, Burkina Faso, Cameroon, Côte d'Ivoire, Ghana, Niger, Nigeria, Senegal and Sierra Leone are from 2011. Data for the other countries are from 2014.

Sources: Canavera et al. (2014); Global Social Service Workforce Alliance (2015).

Many countries have made efforts to strengthen and diversify the profession. China formalized social work in the late 1980s, and more than 250 universities now offer social work programmes. The national target is 230,000 new social workers by 2020 (Roby, 2016).

In South Africa, the number of social workers increased by 70% between 2010 and 2015 (Global Social Service Workforce Alliance, 2016). The Children's Act, which required formalization of kinship-based care arrangements, facilitated this expansion, occasioning the development of norms and standards that gave the Department of Social Development leverage with the National Treasury in budget requests. A special unit of the department uses national data collection, international household surveys and community consultations to identify service needs. Consistent with a plan to increase child and youth care workers from 800 to 10,000 by 2018, more than 5,500 had been trained by May 2016 (Roby, 2016). Between 2010 and 2015, expert respondents in eight sub-Saharan African countries noted an intention to align education and training with workforce planning and expand the workforce overall (Global Social Service Workforce Alliance, 2016).

... AMONG URBAN PLANNERS

More than half the world's people live in cities. Improving city planning and service delivery in line with SDG targets 11.1–11.3 is critical for improving informal settlements and anticipating the projected increase in urbanization. It requires capacity building for strong urban planning institutions and well-trained professionals who can deliver on the new urban agenda (UN Habitat, 2016a).

Many countries face an acute shortage of planning professionals. In India, only 21 universities offer postgraduate town planning programmes; only 5 offer them at the undergraduate level. As a result, the country had only about 4,500 qualified town and country planners, the 2011 census showed. In the same year, the government estimated needing 300,000 town and country planners by 2031 for city development plans

(Meshram and Meshram, 2016). Several African countries, including Ghana and Nigeria, face an even larger gap, intensified by projected high urbanization rates (**Figure 18.2**).

> India estimates needing 300,000 town and country planners by 2031

Academic planning programmes need to integrate physical, social and environmental planning better, including recognizing the importance of planning for education provision. A review of institutions accredited by India's Institute of Town Planners found that many planning students lacked exposure to town and city problems. They were unfamiliar with the functioning of urban development institutions, had limited contact with slums and urban infrastructure projects, and were not up to date on urban development programmes and technical tools, leaving them ill-prepared to take up planning jobs upon graduation (Meshram and Meshram, 2016).

The African Association of Planning Schools collaborated with the University of Zambia to introduce a postgraduate degree in spatial planning in 2013. It emphasizes informality, climate change, access to land and partnerships around urbanization challenges, and is considered the first in Africa to incorporate informality issues fully (Watson and Agbola, 2013). As part of a needs assessments for strategic urban planning in 60 cities, the Mozambique case study noted that municipal professionals' capacity to build their own plans was so limited that the service had to be contracted out. Malawi and Namibia also demonstrated limited local planning skills and coordination with central authorities. The assessment called for academic institutions to improve local officials' planning capacity and to encourage and support networking (UCLG, 2010).

By contrast, China's government invested in over 10 institutions to provide training to city officials. Singapore provides budgets for 100 hours of training per year for all public officers. They also receive individualized guidance and leadership development opportunities (Bouton et al., 2013).

United Cities and Local Government, the main global peer network of local government actors, coordinates peer learning exchanges, localization of the sustainable development agenda, engagement with universities to build capacity, and knowledge management.

FIGURE 18.2:

There are too few urban planners in Africa and Asia

Number of urban planners per 100,000 people and urbanization rates, selected countries, 2011

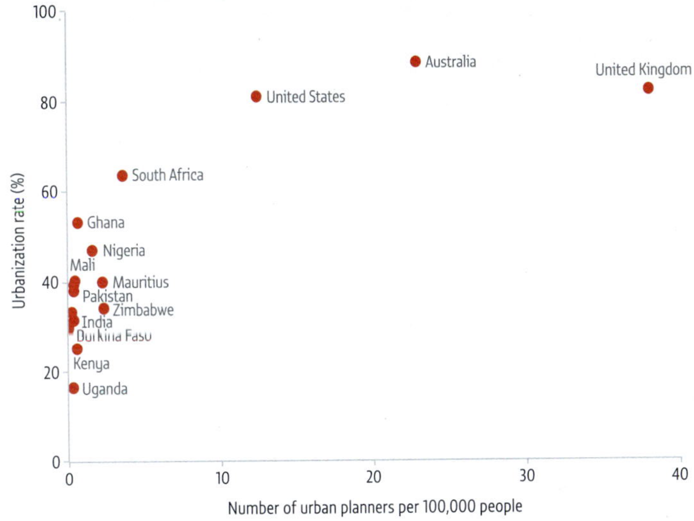

GEM StatLink: http://bit.ly/fig18_2
Note: Data are from 2011 for number of planners and 2014 for urbanization rate.
Sources: UNDESA (2014); UN Habitat (2016b).

Activities, networking opportunities and resource materials support city administrators' capacities (Friedemann, 2016; UCLG and Learning UCLG, 2018).

... AMONG LAW ENFORCEMENT OFFICERS

Law enforcement strongly affects the 'justice for all' and institutional accountability called for by SDG 16 (OECD and Open Society Foundations, 2016). Although police maintain public safety, police brutality and corruption remain major problems that especially affect the most disadvantaged. Improving police education requirements and training to build trust and reduce bias and the use of force are important the world over.

Police violence in the United States has made headline news, notably shootings involving unarmed African American men, leading to the Black Lives Matter movement. The debate highlights dramatic differences in police education and training globally. Average training takes 130 weeks in Germany but 19 weeks in the United States – less time than many trade jobs require. Moreover, in response to reduced applications for police force vacancies, many local police departments in the

United States have decreased education requirements. Only 1% of all police departments require a four-year university degree, and 15% require a two-year degree (Danby, 2017; Yan, 2016).

Yet education can improve police performance. Officers with a university degree in the United States were less likely to use force (Rydberg and Terrill, 2010). Officers with higher education were likelier to have better attitudes in policing in Australia and Europe. But they were less interested in protecting the rights of citizens in India (Paterson, 2011).

Mexico, with the world's fourth-largest police force, has improved police education. In the 1990s, there were 41 academies for over 2,000 departments, and most police received no formal training. Only 14 of the academies required a lower secondary certificate for admission, and most preventive police had primary schooling at most. Successive governments have emphasized the development of federal, state and municipal government capacity and recognized the need to increase law enforcement professionalism through better selection and recruitment, improved training, better remuneration and improved operational procedures (Sabet, 2010).

Many countries collaborate with international agencies or donors to enhance police professional capacity. The International Organization for Migration trained more than 3,000 policewomen across Indonesia on woman and child protection, human trafficking and people smuggling (IOM Indonesia, 2016). In South-eastern Asia, the United Nations has focused on improving enforcement capacity by training trainers to tackle child sexual exploitation in the region (UNODC, 2013).

> "Better education and training is needed for law enforcement officers to achieve SDG 16 on justice for all"

Several countries have made their own efforts to curb police corruption. Singapore has had a very effective Corrupt Practices Investigation Bureau, which is considered a model for other countries. But in 1999, following a corruption scandal involving police officers, the Singapore Police Academy had to take further action. It introduced a value-focused training course, which included a 40-hour programme, based on case studies, to further increase resistance to corruption (Pyman et al., 2012).

Community policing seeks to build trust through a more service-oriented approach. In 2016, Bulgaria began training officers in multi-ethnic communities or neighbourhoods on working with vulnerable groups. Recruiting and training officers to engage respectfully with migrants and refugees have taken on more urgency with the recent influx, spurring new initiatives. The Helsinki Police Department launched a campaign in 2016 to recruit young migrants to the force, which slightly boosted their number (EUFRA, 2017).

... AND THE JUDICIARY

Since 2003, the UN Surveys on Crime Trends and the Operations of Criminal Justice Systems have tracked numbers of judges and magistrates, which vary widely by country. In 2013, Nigeria had 69 professional judges or magistrates for a population of over 170 million, or 0.04 per 100,000 people, compared with 1.2 in Kenya and 4.3 in South Africa (UNODC Statistics, 2017).

Judicial education is a cornerstone of legal systems and of reforms to strengthen particular aspects of them (World Bank, 2003). The UN Office on Drugs and Crime (UNODC) has developed a resource guide on strengthening judicial integrity and capacity. It recommends a focus on practical training in legal education, including social skills, and developing accessible continued professional training for judges. Legal training typically lasts three to five years, but becoming a judge does not always require a law degree, even in high income countries. Some countries provide substantial initial professional training once judges are selected. After passing judicial entrance examinations, new judges in France receive 31 months of training in dedicated schools. Ghana and Jordan are among countries with schools providing continuing education for judges (UNODC, 2011).

> Legal capacity building is needed to meet the needs of the estimated 4 billion people globally who lack access to justice

The UN Development Programme (UNDP) supports a variety of legal and justice reform projects, which often include a capacity-building component. In 2016, 12 judges and prosecutors from remote areas of Guinea-Bissau received training in Brazil on organized crime and human and drug trafficking (UNDP, 2017). A UNESCO programme has provided judicial training on the legal principles and precedents of freedom of information and expression to over 600 judges and legal professionals in African and Latin American countries since 2014, and 10 times as many have undertaken online programmes (Orme, 2018).

Since 2014, UNODC and UNDP have systematically collected data on access to and delivery of legal services. In terms of qualifications, 73% of 68 countries with data require lawyers to show proof of passing a professional examination, and 4% require paralegals to complete a government-accredited training course. But about 20% of responding countries noted major lawyer shortages in rural areas (UNODC, 2016). There is also inequity in legal knowledge by location, including in high income countries. In the US state of New York, all 384 city court judges, but only 39% of town and village justices, were lawyers in 2017 (New York State Commission on Judicial Conduct, 2017).

Overall, it is estimated that 4 billion people lack access to justice. Initiatives to improve the situation often involve civil society organizations (CSOs). A judicial reform in Ecuador, supported by the World Bank, awarded grants to CSOs for a variety of justice-related work, with strong rates of case resolution. Another CSO project, a 240-hour programme to train 150 lawyers in legal assistance, gained Ministry of Education recognition as a professional credential (Maru, 2009).

CSOs providing legal education for grass-roots legal advocates have extended their networks. Namati, a global network of 120 grass-roots justice institutions, provides training and supplies to front-line legal advocates. It builds on early successes in Sierra Leone, where community paralegal services have scaled up rapidly in the past decade through a coalition of national partners. Paralegals trained through Namati have helped thousands of stateless people in Bangladesh and Kenya apply for legal identity documents (Namati, 2014).

CONCLUSION

The *Global Education Monitoring Reports* have elaborated on the interactions between education and other SDGs and the need to review them on a regular basis. The agenda is vast, and these reports can look at only a limited number of goals at a time. This year it focuses on decent work, cities, police and justice, doing so from two angles. First, it reviewed selected examples that showcase the richness of reciprocal effects and serve as a reminder of education's key role or, in some cases, of missed opportunities. Second, it showed multiple ways through which education and training build the professional capacity of those entrusted with the achievement of other goals, in this case social workers, urban planners, police and judicial officers. The message remains clear: Capacity development through education needs to be at the centre of the 2030 Agenda for Sustainable Development.

These Syrian refugee children used International Organization for Migration (IOM) transportation to access this school, which is far away from their camp.

CREDIT: Muse Mohammed/IOM

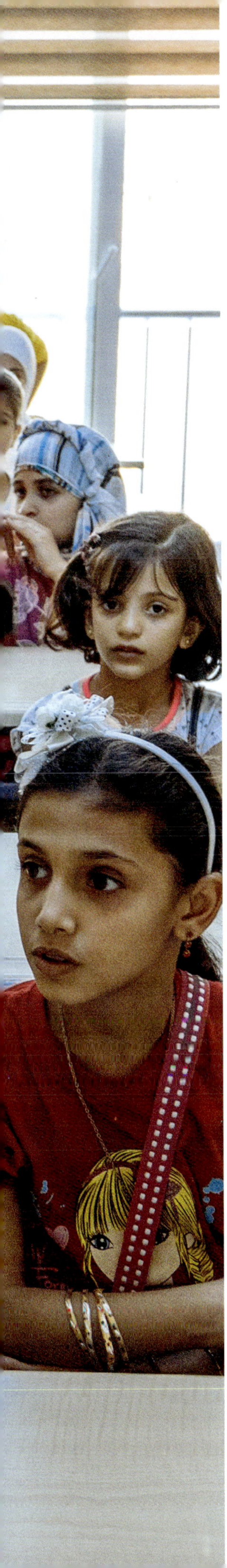

CHAPTER

19

Finance

It is our moral duty to give hope to millions of children affected by crises. Education in emergencies is therefore a top priority for the European Union and for me personally. The European Union's investment has grown sharply in recent years and will reach 10% of the EU humanitarian aid budget in 2019. I encourage all donors to increase their contribution. My wish is to see every child learning, in a safe space under all circumstances, receiving rapid support so that their education is not impacted when crises hit. I can only commend and support UNESCO's and all our education partners' emphasis on this cause.

Christos Stylianides, European Commissioner for Humanitarian Aid and Crisis Management

The 2019 GEM Report lays bare what is at stake if we fail to mobilize humanitarian funding for education in emergencies and protracted crisis. It provides an insightful analysis in support of advocacy, policy and aid reform efforts towards more equitable investment in education in conflicts and disasters. The funding challenge is a chief obstacle to achieving the right to education in crises. The 2019 GEM report reminds us that education must be given priority, as it is the foundation for effective humanitarian assistance and its linkage to sustainable development investments.

Yasmine Sherif, Director of Education Cannot Wait

KEY MESSAGES

Globally, governments account for 79% of total spending, households for 20% and donors for 0.3% (12% in low income countries).

Of all money spent on education, just 0.5% is spent in low income countries.

In 2017, median public education spending was 4.4% of GDP and 14.1% of total public spending.

The fiscal consequences of immigration, including the cost of immigrant education, were modest at ±1% of GDP.

Few countries explicitly recognize migrant status in formula-based allocation of funds to schools. More address their needs indirectly by considering student language or socio-economic status.

In 2016, aid to education reached its highest level since records began at US$13.4 billion.

Multilateral development banks, such as the World Bank, have been reducing the share of education in their loans to middle income countries. A proposal for an International Financing Facility for Education aims to address this issue, but loans would need to be equity-oriented.

Policy-makers should not hold high expectations on the role aid can play in controlling migration.

Humanitarian and development aid provided about US$800 million for refugee education in 2016, but without joint planning.

The Education Cannot Wait fund set up in 2016 is indicative of recent efforts to bridge humanitarian and development aid.

Remittances increased education spending by up to 35% in 18 countries in sub-Saharan Africa, Central and Southern Asia and South-eastern Asia. Lowering the cost of remitting from 7.1% to the SDG 10.c target of 3% would provide households with an extra US$1 billion a year to spend on education.

Achieving the education targets has a price tag. The *Global Education Monitoring Report* estimated that the annual total cost of universal pre-primary, primary and secondary education in low and lower middle income countries would be US$340 billion between 2015 and 2030, or 6.3% of gross domestic product (GDP) (UNESCO, 2015b). Thus, close attention to spending levels is needed, especially in countries (a) whose governments chronically underinvest in education, (b) which do not receive a fair share of external assistance and (c) where households contribute too large a share of the total cost of education.

This chapter is accordingly structured along the lines of the three main sources of education financing: governments, donors and households. Analysis for this report estimates annual spending on education at US$4.7 trillion worldwide. Of that, US$3 trillion (65% of the total) is spent in high income countries and US$22 billion (0.5% of the total) in low income countries, even though the two groups have a roughly equal number of school-age children (**Figure 19.1a**). Governments account for 79.3% of total spending and households for 20.4%. Donors account for 12% of total education expenditure in low income countries and 2% in lower middle income countries (**Figure 19.1b**).

> “Only 0.5% of the global spending on education is in low income countries”

PUBLIC EXPENDITURE

As part of SDG target 1.a, which focuses on ‘mobilization of resources … to end poverty in all its dimensions’, global indicator 1.a.2 calls for monitoring government spending on education, health and social protection, with specific reference to the share of education in public expenditure. However, no explicit education expenditure target is specified, respecting countries’ prerogative to adjust spending priorities according to their needs.

Instead, it is the Education 2030 Framework for Action that endorses two key benchmarks for public financing of education (UNESCO, 2015a):

- Allocating at least 4% to 6% of GDP to education, and/or
- Allocating at least 15% to 20% of public expenditure to education.

Globally, the median public education expenditure was 4.4% of GDP in 2017, with regional averages ranging from 3.4% in Eastern and South-eastern Asia to 5.1% in Latin America and the Caribbean. There is no pattern in expenditure as per capita income rises. High income countries spend 0.9 percentage points of GDP more than low income countries, but lower middle income countries spend 0.3 percentage points more than upper middle income countries. The global median share of total public expenditure dedicated to education was 14.1%, and the regions ranged from 11.6% in Europe and Northern America to 18% in Latin America and the Caribbean (**Table 19.1**).

FIGURE 19.1:

Governments account for four out of five dollars spent on education

a. Total spending on education, by country income group and financing source, 2014 or latest year

b. Distribution of total spending on education, by country income group and financing source, 2014 or latest year

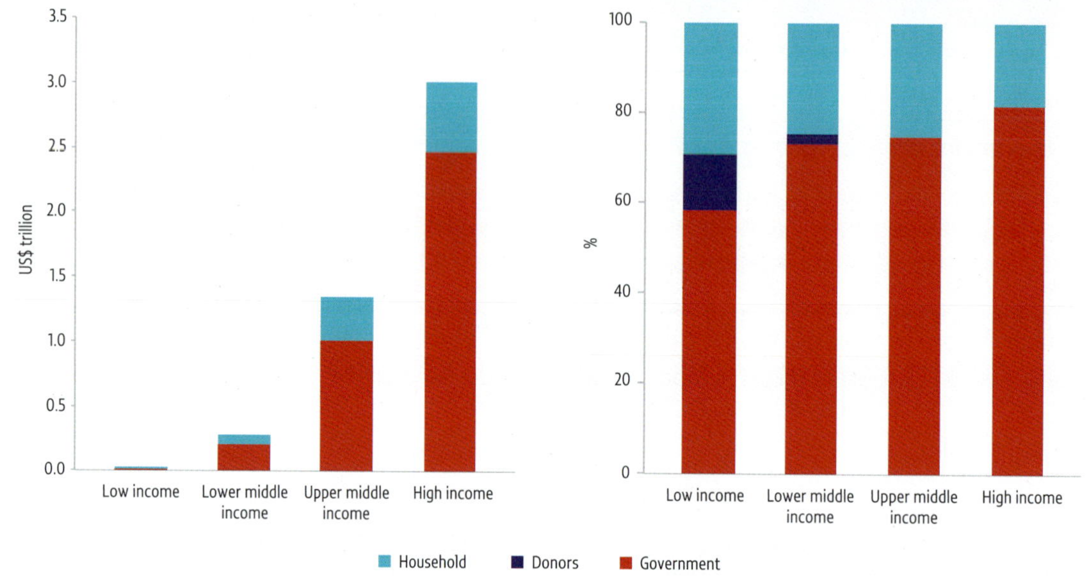

GEM StatLink: http://bit.ly/fig19_1

Note: The analysis rests on three bases: (a) for countries without public expenditure data, amounts were imputed from GDP, public expenditure as a share of GDP and the average share of public expenditure allocated to education in the respective country income group; (b) 60% of aid expenditure is considered reflected in public budgets (therefore subtracted from government expenditure), with the remaining 40% allocated through other channels; and (c) the household share in total education expenditure is estimated at 18% in high income countries, 25% in middle income countries and 33% in low income countries.

Source: GEM Report team analysis based on the UIS (government and household) and CRS (donor) databases.

TABLE 19.1:

Public education expenditure by country income group and region, 2017 or most recent year

			Per student (constant 2015 PPP US$)		
	As share of GDP (%)	As share of total public expenditure (%)	Primary education	Number of illiterate (millions)	Tertiary education
World	**4.4**	**14.1**	**2,028**	**2,716**	**4,322**
Sub-Saharan Africa	4.1	16.5	268	476	2,485
Western Asia and Northern Africa	3.8	12.3	4,392	4,911	5,150
Central and Southern Asia	3.9	15.7	764	1,048	1,951
Eastern and South-eastern Asia	3.4	13.5	2,645	7,700	6,165
Latin America and the Caribbean	5.1	18.0	1,800	2,287	2,517
Oceania	4.7	14.1	…	…	…
Europe and Northern America	4.8	11.6	7,416	7,890	8,621
Low income	4.0	16.1	194	276	1,675
Lower middle income	4.4	16.4	985	1,104	2,029
Upper middle income	4.1	13.9	2,155	2,498	3,185
High income	4.9	12.9	7,990	8,955	10,801

Notes: PPP = purchasing power parity. Estimates are medians, reported if at least 50% of countries in a group have data.

Source: GEM Report team calculations based on UIS data.

In total, 43 out of 148 countries did not meet either benchmark (**Figure 19.2**). They include countries in all income levels (from the poorest, such as Chad, to the richest, such as Qatar) and all regions (e.g. Haiti, Japan, Jordan, Namibia, Pakistan and Romania).

Although education is prioritized more in poorer countries, with the median share of public expenditure dedicated to education consistently in excess of the 15% threshold in low and lower middle income countries, a few have not met this benchmark. Among them, Cambodia, the Democratic Republic of the Congo, Guinea and Uganda pledged to increase their domestic spending at the third Global Partnership for Education financing conference in 2018 (**Figure 19.3**).

In 2016, the average share of public education expenditure dedicated to primary education was 35%, with regional shares ranging from 47% in low income to 26% in high income countries. The global average of total education spending for secondary education was 34%, and regional averages ran from 26% in low income to 38% in lower middle income countries. This pattern is explained by the relatively higher share of adolescents and youth in richer countries who remain in school and complete secondary education (**Figure 19.4**).

There are regional variations in the level of spending per student. Sub-Saharan Africa spent nearly 10 times more per student in tertiary education (US$2,485) than in primary education (US$268) in 2017. The ratio was 2.5 times in Central and Southern Asia. Countries in Europe and Northern America spent almost the same amount per primary, secondary and tertiary student. High income countries spent more than 6 times as much per tertiary student as low income countries, but 32 times as much in secondary education and 41 times as much in primary education.

The calculation of per-student spending is a simple division between total spending and total enrolment at each education level. In practice, many governments often make efforts to distribute spending to schools and students that have more needs so as to promote the principle of equitable education. Formulas are being developed to take into account characteristics that contribute to disadvantage and to allocate resources accordingly. One potential characteristic is the concentration of immigrants in a school or school district; in such cases, more resources to address their needs for preparatory language classes or other support may be called for (**Policy focus 19.1**).

FIGURE 19.2:

At least 43 countries did not meet either education financing benchmark

Public education expenditure as a share of GDP and of total public expenditure, countries below both benchmarks, 2017 or most recent year

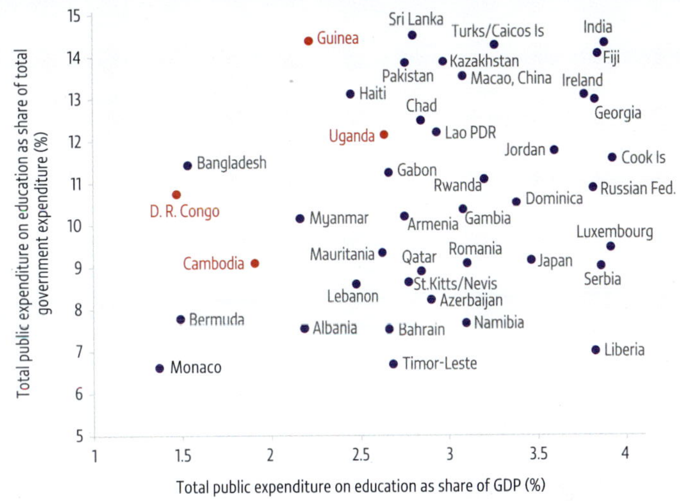

GEM StatLink: http://bit.ly/fig19_2

Note: South Sudan spent less than 1% of GDP and 1% of public expenditure on education.

Source: UIS database.

FIGURE 19.3:

Countries that underspend have committed to increase the share they devote to education

Public education expenditure as a share of total public expenditure, selected countries, before and after the pledge made at the 2018 Global Partnership for Education financing conference

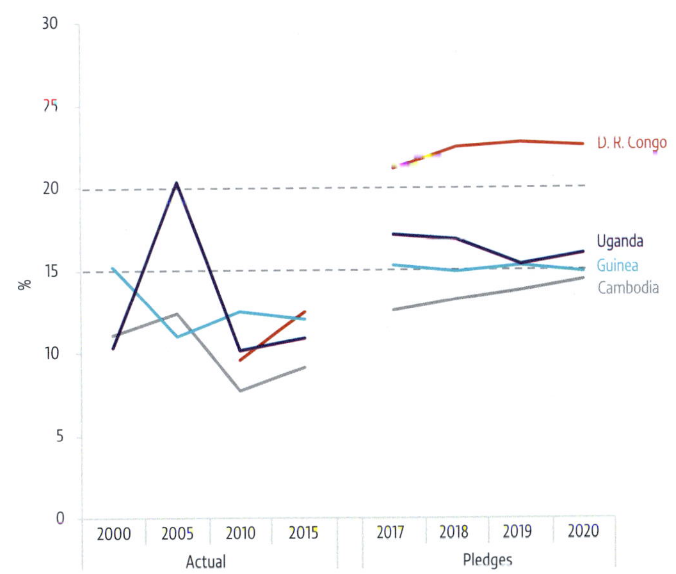

GEM StatLink: http://bit.ly/fig19_3

Sources: UIS database (actual) and 2018 GPE Financing Conference (pledges).

FIGURE 19.4:

The richer a country, the smaller a budget share it devotes to primary education

Distribution of public expenditure on education by level, 2010 and 2016

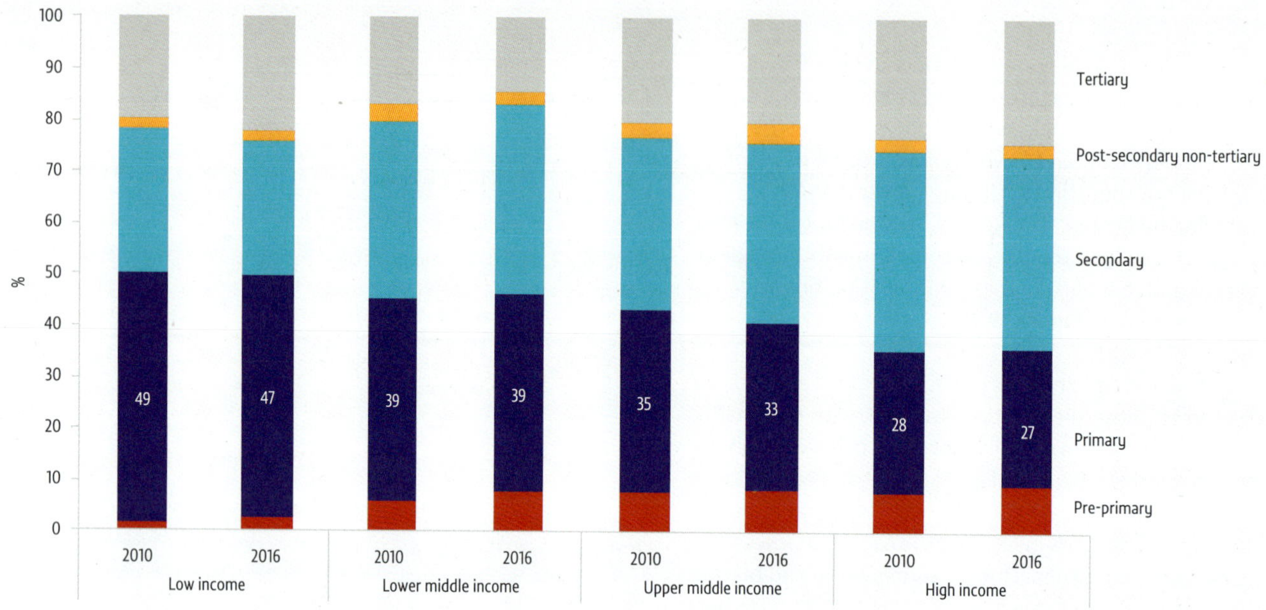

GEM StatLink: http://bit.ly/fig19_4

Note: Shares are defined over the part of the expenditure that could be assigned to an education level.

Source: UIS database.

A high share of immigrants in the school population is considered a potential burden for government budgets and is a subject of considerable debate in many host countries. However, the overall fiscal effects of immigration are relatively small, not least because immigrants also make a contribution to national economies (**Data focus 19.1**).

DATA FOCUS 19.1: THE FISCAL IMPACT OF IMMIGRATION AND IMMIGRANT EDUCATION IS OFTEN EXAGGERATED

Public debate on immigration often focuses on the potentially negative impact on host community welfare. Simple approaches to net economic contribution compare migrant household tax and social security contributions with government spending on migrants in a given year. Education factors into such calculations.

In terms of government revenue, a greater proportion of migrants than natives are of working age and thus expected to contribute to public coffers. Yet immigrants typically generate less revenue because they are disadvantaged in the labour market. Although their likelihood of employment and level of taxable earned income rise with education level, the net contribution increases much less with educational attainment among immigrants than among natives, as those with higher skills are more likely to hold lower-skill, lower-paying jobs. They may also work informally more often (OECD, 2009).

From a government expenditure viewpoint, migrants are more likely to depend on social benefits and use public services, such as education. High income countries often have information on average expenditure per student, but educating immigrants may deviate from the average, e.g. due to additional expenditure for language instruction. On the other hand, immigrants cost less overall, as they are often under-represented in tertiary education, which is more expensive (OECD, 2013).

> From a long-term perspective, immigrants typically have a clearly positive net present value of expected lifetime tax and social security contributions

Fiscal impact varies by government level and time-frame. While income tax and social security contributions often accrue at the national level, a significant component of education funding is local. Immigrant households' net contribution may be positive for the central government and negative for state and local jurisdictions, as in the United States (Kandel, 2011). Additionally, while educating immigrants may appear as a cost in a given year, it is better understood as an investment over their lifetimes. From this long-term perspective, immigrants typically have a clearly positive net present value of expected lifetime tax and social security contributions (National Academies of Sciences, Engineering and Medicine, 2017).

Refugees tend to cost more than immigrants, who are more likely to be working-age adults responding to labour demand. Sizeable refugee inflows may require considerable, if time-limited, expenditure on basic needs, language training and other integration measures. An analysis of the economic impact of the large-scale refugee influx in Germany showed that, after short-term costs of 0.5% to 1.5% of GDP, the positive effects were forecast to outweigh the costs within 3 to 10 years, depending on the scenario. This finding held even under the most pessimistic assumption, that their unemployment would remain above 50% for 10 years and never drop below 35%, and that their productivity would never exceed two-thirds of the average productivity of German workers (Fratzscher and Junker, 2015).

Overall, the fiscal consequences of immigration are relatively modest. A survey of studies that used a wide range of methods to estimate immigrants' net contribution in Organisation of Economic Co-operation and Development (OECD) countries showed that both positive and negative estimates were typically within 1% of GDP (OECD, 2013). This range held across UK migrant categories (e.g. those from inside and outside the European Economic Area) (Vargas-Silva, 2017). The fiscal impact of education for migrants is, surprisingly, minor. Contrary to perceptions, immigrant education's indirect effect on employment outweighs its direct effect on expenditure, at least in most European countries (Boeri, 2010).

Immigrants' net economic impact depends in complex ways on their education profile, their labour participation (conditional on their education) and their children's participation in education. Measuring the impact therefore presents a formidable challenge, subject to different modelling assumptions. However, regardless of approach, immigration's overall fiscal impact is relatively minor, contrary to what lively debate may suggest.

POLICY FOCUS 19.1: FUNDING SCHOOLS WHERE IMMIGRANT STUDENTS ARE CONCENTRATED

In many countries, budgets are tied to number of students enrolled. Although this allocation criterion is simple and transparent, it ignores other measures of need. A thematic indicator under SDG target 4.5 on equity, which tries to capture the extent to which school funding policies explicitly allocate resources to disadvantaged populations, recognizes the need to take other school characteristics into account.

Schools with high numbers of immigrant or refugee students are more likely to have higher funding needs. These students may face language barriers and usually come from a poorer socio-economic background than natives. They also often have lower learning achievement, even after accounting for socio-economic background (OECD, 2012), and are more likely to repeat or drop out. Some financing policies recognize the higher needs of schools supporting migrant and refugee students.

FEW COUNTRIES EXPLICITLY TARGET SCHOOLS WITH IMMIGRANT STUDENTS

Among other aims, formula-based funding allocates additional resources to schools characterized by factors associated with disadvantage to increase equity (Fazekas, 2012). These include school location, local government size and revenue-raising capacity, student ethnic and cultural background, and special education needs. Formula-based funding recognizes the fact that per-student costs to reach given results are higher for disadvantaged children (OECD, 2017).

Additional funding for schools with migrants would support measures addressing language barriers and other challenges in order to improve their academic performance. There are a few examples of programmes that incorporate migrants as an explicit factor in school funding (Sugarman et al., 2016). In Lithuania, schools receive an additional 20% for each national minority student and 30% for each immigrant student in their first school year in the country. The extra funds support integration classes, bilingual education, Lithuanian as a second language and mother tongue instruction (Essomba et al., 2017).

In the United States, the Department of Education has allocated funds to the Migrant Education Program (Title I, Part C) since 1966. States' access to the funds is through a formula based on state migrant student count and state per-student expenditure. In 2015/16, states and local entities provided services to about 310,000 eligible students who are the children of internal migrant workers. About US$374 million is allocated each year, intended for education and support, including teachers trained to address migrants' needs (United States Department of Education, 2018b).

Explicitly including migration status as a factor in school funding formulas is the exception. A review of 11 countries in the Asia-Pacific region did not identify a single example (UNESCO, 2013). Nor does an earlier World Bank publication mention migration in its discussion of formula funding for secondary education in Eastern Asia and Latin America (di Gropello, 2006).

Migrant and refugee students may trigger additional funding indirectly, however. Characteristics that formulas do recognize are often directly or contingently associated with migration. For instance, funding may follow low proficiency in language of instruction or socio-economic deprivation at the neighbourhood level, both common among immigrants.

Some countries have revised their funding formulas to remove immigration status in favour of associated factors. In Flanders, Belgium, the government grants additional funding with reference to low socio-economic status, low education performance, language spoken at home and low education of mothers (OECD, 2015). In 2007, Israel removed immigration status as a funding factor and introduced a new formula that gives a weight of 40% to parent education (Bendavid-Hadar and Ziderman, 2010). The Netherlands has reduced the importance of ethnic background as a criterion and removed the migration factor. The formula focuses instead on parent education in primary and number of students in deprived areas in secondary (OECD, 2017).

England (United Kingdom) is introducing a new national funding formula that will be fully rolled out in the school year 2020/21 (Whittaker, 2018). It abolishes specific funding for migrants and employs 14 factors, grouped in 3 levels, alongside cost adjustment depending on location. One of these levels, which accounts for 18% of allocation, compensates for disadvantages students face.

The formula recognizes three major disadvantages. 'Deprivation' reflects the share of students eligible for school meals and is captured by an index, which measures the proportion of children whose families receive tax credits (9.1% of total spending). 'Low prior attainment' reflects the share of those who do not achieve expected levels in national assessments on entry into primary and

FIGURE 19.5:
About 18% of school funding in England will compensate for disadvantage
Factors in the national funding formula being introduced in England

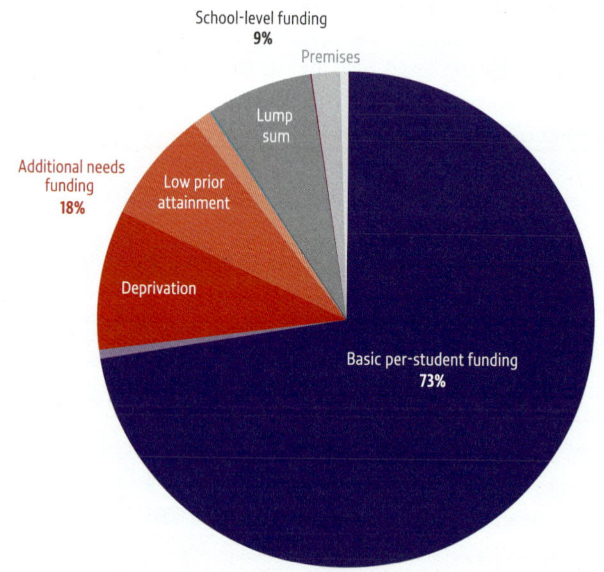

GEM StatLink: http://bit.ly/fig19_5
Source: United Kingdom Department of Education (2017).

at age 10 or 11 (7.4% of total spending). Schools will receive additional funds according to the share of students who speak English as a second language. This information is captured in the school census, which reports individual English language proficiency using a five-point scale, from 'new to English' to 'fluent' (1.2% of total spending) (United Kingdom Department of Education, 2017) (**Figure 19.5**).

Beyond basic funding formulas, additional resources to support migrant and refugee students are often available to schools. In Denmark and Norway, the initial lump sum grant from central government to municipalities accounts for certain demographic characteristics, such as an index of the socio-economic structure of municipalities (Denmark) and the share of immigrant children in municipalities (Norway). However, municipalities have complete discretion in allocation to schools. Denmark's national government introduced school and home counsellors over 2008–2013 to strengthen cooperation between immigrant families and schools (Ravn, 2009). In Switzerland, the Zurich canton government has been targeting schools with high immigrant student populations, devoting funds to language and other support (**Box 19.1**).

Some countries target specific support for language programmes outside funding formulas. In Bulgaria, the 2016 law on schools and pre-schools introduced additional Bulgarian language classes for various groups, including immigrant students. In Italy, any school that wishes to access funding for language support must apply through an annual call for bids. Slovenia's Ministry of Education allocates funds for more than 35 hours of Slovene language classes per school year (Essomba et al., 2017). The US English Language Acquisition programme allocates about US$740 million a year to states in formula grants based on share of learners of English as a second language and recent immigrant students (U. S. Department of Education, 2018a, 2018b).

Additional support targets teachers, who may have trouble connecting with immigrant students and families and respond by lowering education and disciplinary standards, or not respond at all (European Parliament, 2016). Germany funds programmes to recruit and mentor teachers with immigrant backgrounds who can then support immigrant students and be cultural intermediaries with staff (Germany Federal Office for Migrants and Refugees, 2011).

BOX 19.1:

Zurich has legislated targeted funding for schools with high immigrant student populations

Education authorities in the Swiss canton of Zurich first granted permission to conduct Heimatliche Sprache und Kulture (HSK, 'Home Language and Culture') courses on public primary school premises in 1966, initially outside of school hours. In 1972, schools were allowed to integrate them into the regular timetable, and from 1982 grades for the courses could be entered into students' report cards (Zurich Education Department, 2011b). The option to offer such courses was later opened to non-state bodies, and by 2015 there were over 27 recognized providers. These represent major languages, such as Arabic, Chinese, Russian and Spanish, but also smaller ones with sizeable communities in the canton, including Albanian and Kurdish. Around one-quarter of all children in the canton whose home language is not German benefit from the HSK courses each year (Zurich Education Department, 2016).

To gain recognition and access to public schools in the HSK programme, providers must be non-profit, non-partisan and non-denominational, and follow a curriculum aligned with the HSK curricular framework. Initially, curricula reflected an assumption that HSK classes prepared students for an eventual return to and reintegration in their countries of origin. This gave way to a focus on integration into Swiss society, intercultural skills and promotion of bilingualism. HSK teachers must be trained and qualified, and demonstrate intermediate German language proficiency (Zurich Education Department, 2011b). Guidance is provided on best practices in fully integrating HSK classes and teachers into the school community. Regular and HSK teachers are encouraged to discuss individual students' needs and progress, contribute jointly to project learning and promote parental involvement (Zurich Education Department, 2011a).

Schools may receive additional support for such activities in the canton's Quality in Multicultural Schools programme, which provides participating schools with an average of CHF 40,000 per year for activities in the focal areas of language and parental engagement in pre-school, as well as writing at all levels. These activities, known as HSKplus, are intended to further language development, academic outcomes and integration. The programme was first introduced at a pilot stage in 1996 but in 2006 it was adopted in law. It now reaches 120 schools, or one-quarter of all schools in the canton, where at least 40% of students have an immigrant background (Roos, 2017). Schools organize their own activities with support from a team providing coordination, networking, advice, intervention frameworks and best practices. For example, writing support focuses on writing strategies and fundamental skills while taking aspects of writing as a social practice into account (Zurich Education Department, 2014).

Identifying and responding to migrant students' needs, and making budgets, services and supplementary funding available to schools, require a measure of local autonomy. Local school administrators have discretion to allocate supplementary funding for immigrant education in 7 out of the 16 German federal states (OECD, 2017). All US states have school guidelines to determine student eligibility for additional funding and monitor their progress (California Department of Education, 2018; Oregon Department of Education, 2018). However, in some cases, there are concerns about the effectiveness of targeting. In the US state of New Jersey, about half of annual supplementary funding makes up for a lack of local funding rather than targeting identified students (Farrie et al., 2015).

Support linked to migrant and refugee students may overlook structural school and administration challenges. Migrants and refugees with lower education tend to cluster in neighbourhoods with already poorly staffed schools. Increased demand for language teachers and social-emotional support staff is difficult to meet in the short term (Scholten et al., 2017). Attracting teachers to schools in need may require higher salaries and better working conditions (Essomba et al., 2017). Such incentives are difficult to provide outside the regular school budget. Moreover, political decisions can significantly affect ad hoc funding or extrabudgetary support for specific programmes. For instance, discussion of reorganizing the US Office of Elementary and Secondary Education has consequences for migrant-related programmes (Klein, 2018).

CONCLUSION

Formula-based funding is a means of helping schools carry the higher cost of educating students from disadvantaged groups. Only a handful of high income countries explicitly consider migration status a factor for school budgets; other dimensions of disadvantage typically trigger higher per-student funding in schools with concentrations of immigrants and refugees, including neighbourhood deprivation and limited language proficiency, which often characterize migrant status. To what extent schools use these resources to address migrant students' specific challenges, such as need for psychosocial support, is unclear.

AID EXPENDITURE

The SDGs set an ambitious target for the international community. The challenge is daunting even when we consider just one of the targets: By 2030, all young people should be completing a secondary education of good quality. Over 2013–2017, 49% of young people, on average, completed secondary school. More financing is needed but cannot come only from the most challenged countries; international solidarity is called for. In 2015, the *EFA Global Monitoring Report* estimated that an annual funding gap of at least US$39 billion per year between 2015 and 2030 in low and lower middle income countries could be filled if all OECD Development Assistance Committee (DAC) donors and selected non-DAC donors allocated 0.7% of gross national income (GNI) to aid and 10% of their aid portfolios to basic and secondary education (UNESCO, 2015b).

AID TO EDUCATION REACHED A RECORD HIGH IN 2016

Aid to education in 2016 reached its highest level since the establishment of disbursement records in 2002 (**Figure 19.6**). From 2015 to 2016, aid to education grew by US$1.5 billion, or 13% in real terms, to US$13.4 billion. An increase in aid to basic education accounted for two-thirds of this growth. After nearly a decade of stagnation, basic education aid rose by 17%, from US$5.1 billion in 2015 to US$6 billion in 2016, the largest absolute increase since records began. Aid to secondary and post-secondary education also increased, but by a smaller amount, with the result that the share of basic education also reached its highest level at 45%. The share of education in total official development assistance (ODA), excluding debt relief, increased for the first time since 2009, rising from 6.9% in 2015 to 7.6% in 2016.

Aid disbursements to basic education have increased, but they are still not allocated to the countries most in need. Thematic indicator 4.5.5 focuses on the percentage of aid allocated to the poorest countries, which can be defined as those classified by the World Bank as low income countries or by the United Nations as least developed countries. The share of basic education aid to low income countries fell from 36% in 2002 to 22% in 2016. The share allocated to least developed countries exhibits a similar long-term trend. While it increased from 31% in 2015 to 34% in 2016, it is still well below the 2004 peak of 47% (**Figure 19.7**).

FIGURE 19.6:

Aid to education reached a record high in 2016

Total aid to education disbursements, by education level, 2002–2016

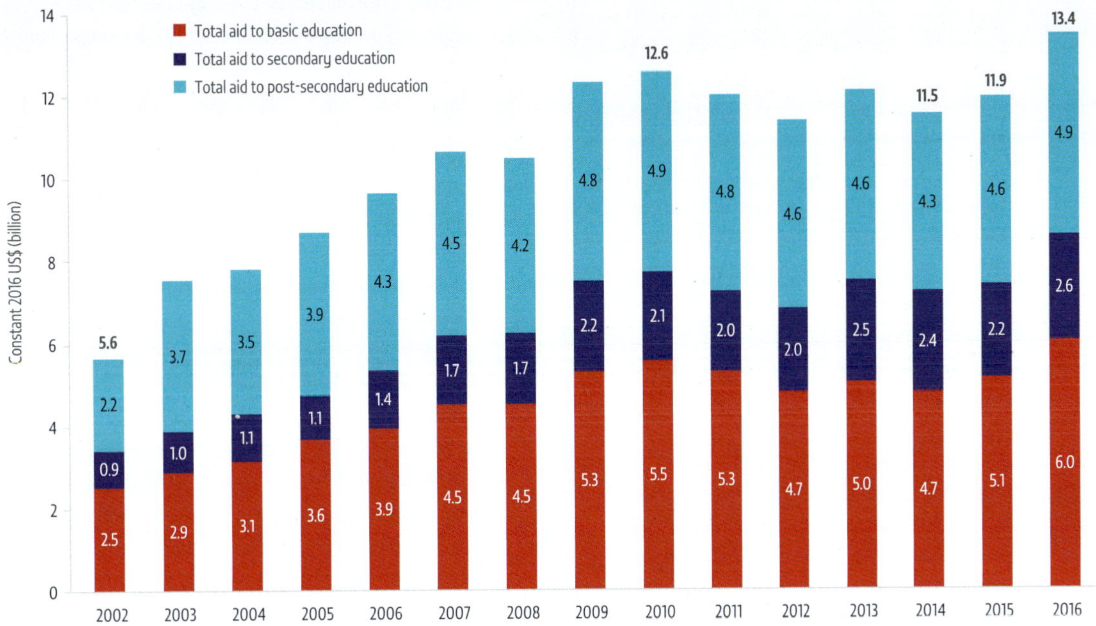

GEM StatLink: http://bit.ly/fig19_6
Source: GEM Report team analysis based on OECD CRS (2018).

FIGURE 19.7:

The share of aid to education going to the poorest countries is trending downward

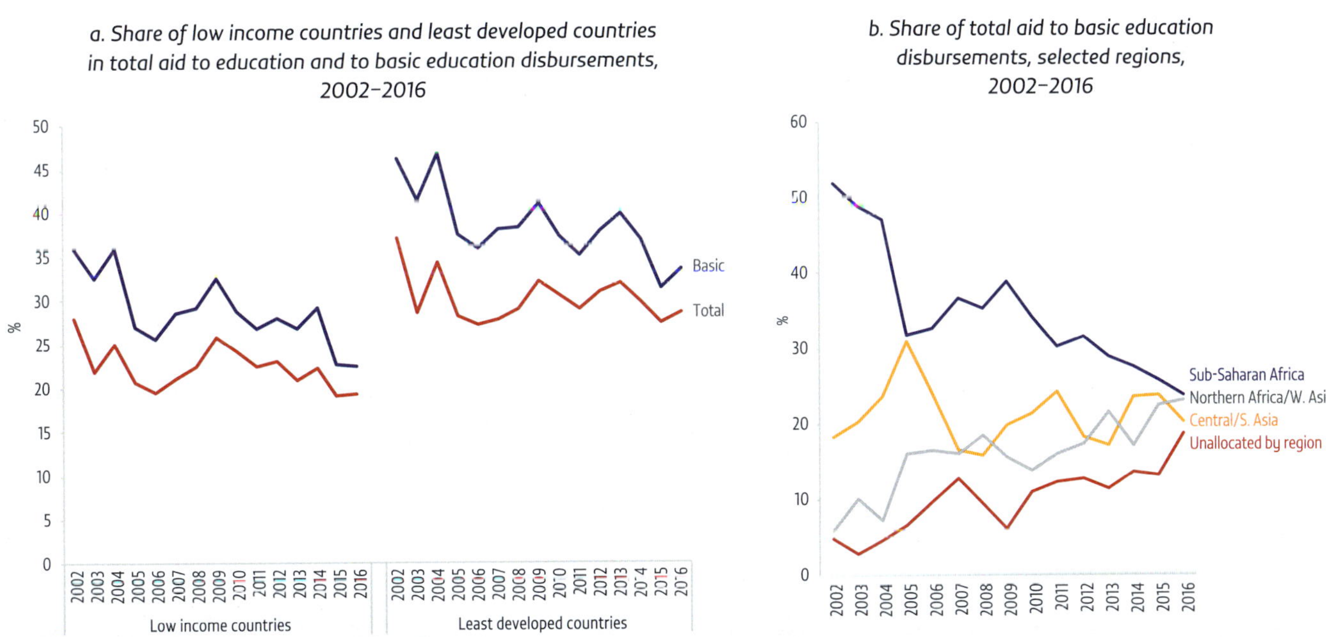

GEM StatLink: http://bit.ly/fig19_7
Source: GEM Report team analysis based on OECD CRS (2018).

THERE HAS BEEN MOMENTUM BEHIND MULTISTAKEHOLDER PARTNERSHIPS IN EDUCATION

The 2015 Addis Ababa Action Agenda recognized the importance of multistakeholder partnerships in external financing. In the case of education, there have been recent developments in the international architecture of three partnerships. In February 2018, the Global Partnership for Education (GPE) secured pledges to replenish its fund for 2018–2020. Education Cannot Wait (ECW) is consolidating its position as a focal point for education financing in emergencies. And the International Commission on Financing Global Education Opportunity (Education Commission) continues building the case for an International Finance Facility for Education (IFFEd). The momentum behind these three mechanisms underlines the resurgence in interest in prioritizing education in international development cooperation.

External financing for education in lower middle income countries needs to increase

Much progress could be made towards bridging the financing gap in low income countries by reforming current aid allocations to (a) redirect more aid to basic and secondary education and (b) target low income countries specifically. However, this would still leave open a large part of the financing gap for achieving SDG 4 targets in lower middle income countries. Aid to these countries tends to fall faster than their tax revenues rise. In 2015, among 10 low income countries with data, the median tax/GDP ratio was 15.2%, while the net ODA/GNI ratio was 9.7%. By contrast, the respective figures in 30 lower middle income countries were 16% and 3.2%. A key question is how to expand external education funding to lower middle income countries.

> “Aid to lower middle income countries tends to fall faster than their tax revenues rise”

The GPE has been effectively targeting the world's poorest countries. In 2016, it disbursed US$351 million to low income countries, out of total disbursements of US$497 million. At its third financing conference in Dakar in February 2018, pledges worth US$2.3 billion were made to replenish the fund for 2018–2020, which will further strengthen its position as the main multilateral financing institution for education in low income countries. It could expand its active portfolio of partner countries from 44 to 65. However, as it fell short of its replenishment target of US$3.1 billion, expanding to more lower middle income countries to reach its declared objective of 89 partners could spread its activities too thinly. Lower middle income countries are eligible to apply for the GPE Multiplier, a tool approved in 2017 that aims to leverage resources: For every US$3 in new external resources a government raises for education, it receives US$1 from the GPE Multiplier to support its plan. The initial US$100 million programme is set to expand to US$300 million by 2020 but this is still well below what is needed.

ECW, the second multilateral financing institution established in recent years, focuses on education in emergencies. It offers a pooled fund for governments, non-government organizations (NGOs) and donors. In addition to ensuring greater and more flexible financing, it aims to improve collaboration and coordination between humanitarian and development actors, encourage national ownership of programmes and foster a cross-sector approach, addressing both immediate and long-term needs. Although it covers middle income countries, its mandate is specific to crises and emergencies and would only partly address needs for system-wide interventions. ECW exceeded its 2017 funding targets by US$20 million and in 2018 received pledges, among others, of US$46 million from Denmark and US$17.5 million from the Netherlands, in its effort to raise US$285 million in 2018–2019.

Deliberations continue on a new education finance facility for middle income countries

It was this need to fund education expansion in lower middle income countries that led the Education Commission to propose forming the IFFEd (Education Commission, 2017). The planned financing mechanism would generate additional resources through multilateral development banks: the African Development Bank, Asian Development Bank, Inter-American Development Bank, European Bank for Reconstruction and Development, and World Bank.

Aid is often seen as a single transfer of resources to developing countries. In practice, it is diverse, using a range of modes, instruments and channels and arriving in two main forms: grants, or loans at concessional terms. Low income countries received 81% of total aid and 79% of total aid to education as grants in 2016. By contrast, lower middle income countries received a larger proportion of education aid as concessional loans, although the share of loans is lower for education (35%) than for total aid (40%) (**Figure 19.8**).

> Low income countries received 79% of total aid to education as grants in 2016

World Bank loans to education, for instance, come through two mechanisms. The International Development Association (IDA) provides loans with concessional terms (i.e. extended terms, long grace periods, below-market interest rates) to 75 countries with limited access to private financial markets. These include all the low income countries, many small island developing states, and selected lower middle income countries, including Nigeria and Pakistan (known as blend countries, because they can also borrow on non-concessional terms). The International Bank for Reconstruction and Development (IBRD) lends mostly to middle income countries on non-concessional terms.

The IFFEd proposal recognizes that multilateral development bank lending for education in lower middle income countries, whether concessional or non-concessional, remains low. For instance, the median share of education between 2002 and 2017 was 10.5% for IDA loans and 6.4% for IBRD loans. Moreover, the share for education in IBRD loans fell from 8.2% in 2012 to 4.7% in 2017, when the total amount of loans for education was just under US$1.1 billion, compared with US$4.4 billion for the energy and extractive industries (**Figure 19.9**).

FIGURE 19.8:

Loans are a considerable part of official development assistance, even in education

Share of ODA disbursements and other official flows by type of aid, 2016

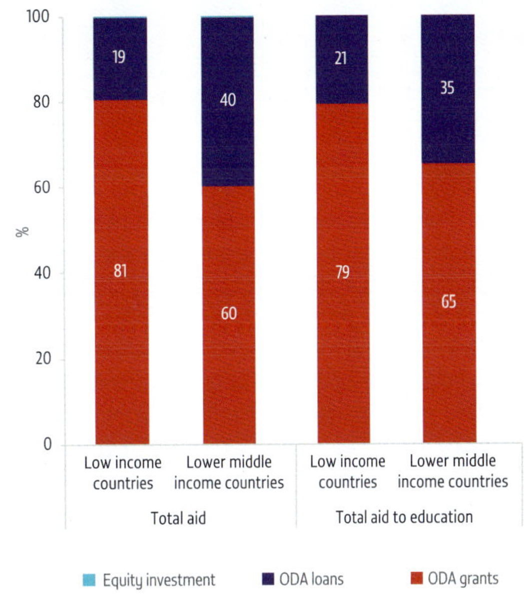

GEM StatLink: http://bit.ly/fig19_8
Source: GEM Report team analysis based on OECD CRS.

FIGURE 19.9:

A low and declining share of World Bank non-concessional loans goes to education

Share of total IDA and IBRD lending, education vs energy and extractives, 2002–2017

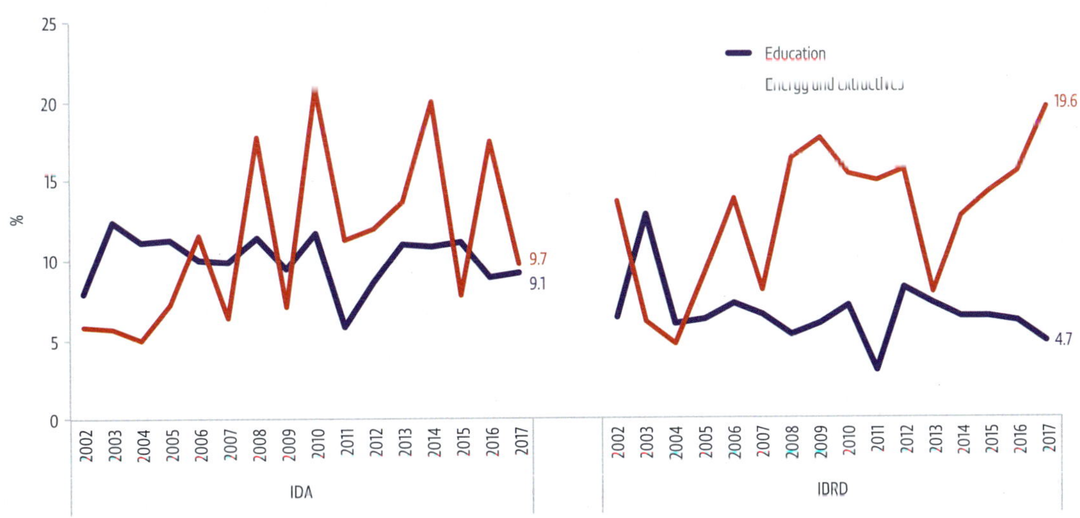

GEM StatLink: http://bit.ly/fig19_9
Source: GEM Report team analysis based on selected World Bank Annual Reports.

> Potential donors to IFFEd and the multilateral development banks have expressed a very wide range of views on issues such as the emphasis on equity or the prominence of results-based allocation mechanisms

Nor is the World Bank unique among multilateral development banks in finding it challenging to provide loans for education.

The key IFFEd objective is to invite donors to provide (a) guarantees (or other forms of contingent commitments) to help insure the portfolio and increase the capacity of multilateral development banks to expand lending to education; and (b) grants to blend with loans to lower their cost and make them more attractive to borrowing countries (Education Commission, 2018). The proposal was noted at the G20 Hamburg Summit in November 2017; the UN Secretary-General made a strong appeal for the international community to support it in May 2018; and multilateral development banks gave their backing at the UN General Assembly in September 2018.

In the coming months, intensive negotiations are expected to clarify the nature of the institutional set-up, level of donor commitment and governance arrangements, which would put the multilateral development banks at the centre. The new entity would need to be rated by credit agencies. In addition, a process would need to be established to demonstrate that IFFEd loans are additional and would not have been granted otherwise. Demonstrating that they are additional and better targeted than current loans may require a larger secretariat than is currently envisaged. Finally, clarity with respect to the potential focus of the loans is needed, as potential donors and the multilateral development banks have expressed a very wide, if not internally inconsistent, range of views on issues such as the emphasis on equity or the prominence of results-based allocation mechanisms.

One pertinent question is whether IFFEd funding would count as ODA. IDA loans, for example, are considered ODA while IBRD loans are classed as 'other official flows'. According to the current OECD definition, to be considered ODA, a loan must have a grant element of at least 25%, be calculated at a discount rate of 10%, and be 'concessional in character'. A new definition of ODA will come into effect in early 2019 by which only loans with a grant element of at least 45% will be reported as ODA for low income and least developed countries. Loans to lower middle income countries will need to have a grant element of at least 15% to be reported as ODA. In addition, only grants and the 'grant portion' of concessional loans will be considered ODA, in contrast to the current definition, whereby the face value of both grants and loans is counted as ODA (OECD, 2015). By these definitions, the grant element of IFFEd funding would be recorded as aid, and the loan element as other official flows.

With increasing interest in different funding mechanisms, one of the challenges going forward will be to ensure coordination to avoid duplication and fragmentation into parallel, vertical structures in different institutions.

POLICY FOCUS 19.2: USING AID AS A TOOL TO MANAGE MIGRATION

Migrant and refugee inflows are a politically sensitive issue in many countries and are often accompanied by calls to control them and to discourage low-skilled migrants or preferentially admit high-skilled ones. Such policies often stimulate irregular migration and discourage circular mobility instead of controlling immigration (de Haas, 2007). Thus there have been calls for a more strategic emphasis on tackling the causes of migration at points of departure.

The idea that external assistance, especially in education, can reduce migration has found some support in academic and policy circles. Evidence on the relationship between aid and controlling migration or preventing displacement is nuanced and context-dependent, but the core idea is that increasing disposable income in origin countries reduces a key incentive for emigration (Lanati and Thiele, 2017).

The surge of migrants crossing the Mediterranean in 2015 prompted EU member states to agree a European Agenda on Migration. One pillar is cooperation with third countries, focusing on 'addressing the root causes behind irregular migration in non-EU countries', as well as on combating smuggling and trafficking. Aligned with this broader strategy, the pooled Emergency Trust Fund for Africa was established in late 2015 to sustain EU migration policies in 26 countries in the Sahel, Lake Chad area, Horn of Africa and Northern Africa. The fund has since grown from an initial EUR 1.8 billion to around EUR 3 billion to finance projects on employment opportunities, food and nutrition, conflict prevention and migration management (Fanjul, 2018).

Some countries' aid policies have explicitly or implicitly related to migration prevention by supporting sending countries' economies. In Spain, a 1% increase in the immigrant population from a particular origin country has been associated with an 18% increase in the probability of its being a Spanish aid recipient and a 0.05% increase in the amount of Spanish aid (Vázquez and Sobrao, 2016). The volume of asylum-seekers and refugees was found to positively affect the aid allocations of Austria, Norway and the United States towards sending countries (Czaika and Mayer, 2011). A study of migration flows from 210 origin countries and territories to 22 donor (and destination) countries showed that the countries sending large numbers of migrants receive the largest amount of foreign aid. For the median origin country in the study, each additional immigrant to an OECD country was associated with US$242 higher foreign aid to the origin country (Bermeo and Leblang, 2015).

There are two arguments countering the logic of using aid to prevent migration. First, higher income relaxes poorer families' budget constraints, allowing them to invest more in migrating. National and cross-national evidence supports this argument. Analysis of Mexico's conditional cash transfer programme Oportunidades showed that availability of a guaranteed stream of extra disposable income made migration more affordable for poor families (Angelucci, 2015). A study of 77 low and middle income countries found a strong positive link between growth in aid and migration levels (Lucas, 2005). Second, bilateral aid may encourage migration because it provides greater access to information about donor countries and lowers migrants' costs (Berthélemy et al., 2009).

Indeed, positive correlation has been established between income and migration at lower levels and negative correlation at higher levels of GDP per capita (Dao et al., 2016). A synthesis of the literature estimated that the total income effect on migration remained positive under per capita income of PPP US$8,000 to US$10,000, a threshold many countries are far from reaching (Clemens and Postel, 2018). Attempts to accelerate the process dramatically through aid are implausible. Raising growth by one percentage point per year in the average recipient country would require aid of the order of 10% of GDP (Clemens et al., 2012).

> "There is positive correlation between income and migration at lower levels and negative correlation at higher levels of GDP per capita"

Some studies suggest that migration depends on specific contexts such as wealth inequality (Bazzi, 2017). Analysis of a 25-year longitudinal data set found that aid supporting better governance or rural over urban development was associated with reduced migration (Gamso and Yuldashev, 2018a, 2018b). Nevertheless, a study of 28 donor (and destination) countries and 136 aid-receiving (and origin) countries over 1995–2014 found a consistently negative effect of aid on migration, which authors attribute to their use of data on migration flows rather than migration stocks (Lanati and Thiele, 2017). However, a study focused on aid's effect specifically on inflows of refugees from 141 origin countries over 1976–2013 found that aid reduced refugee numbers only under exceptional circumstances of high shares of humanitarian aid (Dreher et al., 2018).

Education has a mediating role in the aid–migration relationship

The role of education aid, particularly regarding migration, is very difficult to distinguish due to its relatively small size. To the extent that aid for education helps reduce emigration, it is unlikely to do so quickly. Moreover, the pursuit of short-term impact undermines the long-term intention of external interventions in the education sector (Riddell and Niño-Zarazua, 2016).

Education can nevertheless have an important mediating role in migration for both origin and destination countries. A study of trends in migration from Northern Africa to OECD countries suggested that to the extent aid increased incomes in origin countries it could act as a push factor for migrants with low education. Otherwise, demographic characteristics of the destination country, population density, urban population growth, age dependency ratios and returns to education in destination countries were much more important in determining migration rates (Gubert and Nordman, 2009).

Satisfaction with local public services, including schools, may affect migration intentions more than wealth factors (Dustmann and Okatenko, 2014). An analysis of 187 origin countries suggested that bilateral aid promoted skilled migration. By contrast, total aid increased unskilled migration. Moreover, unskilled migrants are attracted by more redistributive welfare states, while skilled migrants are attracted by those offering better opportunities and greater expected earnings (Berthélemy et al., 2009). A study of 123 countries found that, in poorer origin countries, microeconomic factors explained 25% of the increase in emigration. By contrast, one-third was attributed to changing network sizes, and between one-third and one-half to the changing skills composition of working-age populations (Dao et al., 2016).

CONCLUSION

Arguably, evidence on the relationship between aid and migration is far from conclusive. While the results are sensitive to the choice of estimation method or data, aid policy-makers need to be cautious in placing high expectations on the role aid can play in controlling migration. The volume of migration flows is determined by a myriad of factors aid cannot control. However, investment in education-focused development and humanitarian aid can positively affect both the drivers and the consequences of migration and displacement, as is demonstrated throughout this report.

POLICY FOCUS 19.3: A TURNING POINT IN THE FINANCING OF REFUGEE EDUCATION

Ensuring that refugee children are in school not only restores a much-needed sense of normality but also represents a crucial, if seriously underappreciated, investment. It can address causes of disputes and help rebuild what was lost, sowing the seeds of peace and reconciliation – all the more important in protracted crises. Not attending to education may simply shift the problem to subsequent generations.

As recently as 2015, a review of 13 donors showed that none had a humanitarian, let alone refugee, education strategy or policy (NRC and Save the Children, 2015). However, there has since been stronger support for giving education in emergencies and refugee education greater priority, within a broader effort to improve the efficiency and effectiveness of humanitarian aid.

The first-ever World Humanitarian Summit in May 2016 was a turning point, including for education. Its aim was to find ways to deliver on the five core 'responsibilities' of the Agenda for Humanity put forward in February 2016 by the UN Secretary-General (United Nations, 2016). Under the third responsibility, to 'leave no one behind', which it shares with the 2030 Agenda for Sustainable Development, partners were called upon to ensure that, by 2030, 'all children in crises, whether in conflict zones or displaced, have access to quality education and learning opportunities, because the international community prioritizes and mobilizes resources to support them' (OCHA, 2017, p. 50).

The summit gave rise to or strengthened 20 initiatives. Among them, the establishment of the ECW fund was the clearest sign of a renewed commitment to education in emergencies. Others included the Grand Bargain initiative, which involved a set of efficiency-increasing proposals (Metcalfe-Hough and Poole, 2018), and the New Way of Working initiative, intended to strengthen collaboration in analysis, planning and financing between humanitarian and development aid, including through a Joint Steering Committee on Humanitarian and Development Collaboration (OCHA, 2018).

> “The establishment of the ECW fund gave a clear sign of a renewed commitment to education in emergencies”

Indeed, humanitarian assistance is not even the main, let alone the only, source of funding for fulfilling refugees' education needs. But it is crucial to improve the effectiveness of humanitarian aid to education and link its planning more strongly to the two larger pools of funding: development aid and public expenditure. To prompt a discussion of the broader planning and financing challenges facing refugee education, this section provides an overview of resources the international community has made available to support refugee education.

Estimates of refugee education funding needs vary widely

A study of the cost of education in emergencies for the World Humanitarian Summit by the Overseas

To meet even the most basic education needs of children in crises would require the share of education in humanitarian aid to...

Development Institute estimated that 75 million children aged 3 to 18 in 35 countries would need urgent support. Using assumptions for classroom construction, teacher education and pay, school supplies and student retention, using a markup proposed in the *EFA Global Monitoring Report* costing models, the study estimated an average cost per child of US$156. Accounting for potential government funding left a US$8.5 billion funding gap, or US$113 per child, to be covered by the international community (ODI, 2016).

Two observations can be made. First, US$113 per child is considerably higher than the levels of humanitarian aid currently disbursed on education. The Global Humanitarian Overview 2018 contends that 'humanitarians needed only $232 per person for comprehensive, year-long, multisector humanitarian assistance' in 2017 (OCHA, 2018, p. 13). As education receives only 2% of this comprehensive package, and school-age children represent half the population served, per-student spending would need to increase at least tenfold, and education would take up 20% of total humanitarian aid, assuming refugee education needs were to be covered exclusively by humanitarian aid.

> Save the Children estimated that there was a US$2.4 billion annual funding gap for refugee education

Second, US$156 per student is close to the cost of primary education in low income countries but far below that of secondary education in middle income countries, such as Lebanon (US$894) and Turkey (US$2,618), which host the bulk of Syrian refugee children. A more recent study by Save the Children, an international NGO, estimated the cost of refugee education at US$575 per child, with US$320 to be covered by the international community. This translates into a financing gap of US$2.4 billion per year for 7.5 million refugee children aged 3 to 18 (Save the Children, 2018).

The ECW resource mobilization targets have been informed by these analyses. Within a 15-year horizon, its medium-term target is to raise US$1.8 billion per year by 2021 to reach 8.9 million children (down from an earlier estimate of 13.6 million children) (ECW, 2018a), which translates into US$202 per child, a level that is much higher than, for instance, the US$8 per primary student currently allocated in development aid in sub-Saharan Africa.

It is difficult to track humanitarian and development aid to refugee education

Despite the importance of international financing for refugee education, tracking it is not straightforward. Two international databases provide information: The UN Office for the Coordination of Humanitarian Affairs (OCHA) maintains the Financial Tracking Service (FTS), while the OECD DAC Creditor Reporting System (CRS) provides data on humanitarian as well as development assistance.

The FTS is a voluntary mechanism, used by all humanitarian donors and implementing agencies, that tracks response plans and appeals. Data are continuously updated, providing a snapshot of the current funding situation relative to a given appeal and thus serving the needs of governments, donors and humanitarian actors making timely strategic and operational decisions. The FTS collects information on (a) total humanitarian assistance, (b) the subset that is directed at UN-coordinated appeals and (c) humanitarian assistance by sector.

FTS data reveal three key facts about humanitarian assistance to education. Global humanitarian funding to education has increased rapidly, from US$135 million in 2012 to US$451 million in 2017, of which US$301 million addressed UN-coordinated humanitarian response plans (**Figure 19.10**a). Despite the tripling of humanitarian assistance, the share for education in total humanitarian aid has remained constant, reaching 2.1% in 2017, far below requirements and the indicative target of allocating at least 4% of humanitarian aid to education (**Figure 19.10**b). Furthermore, education continues to be one of the sectors with the lowest percentage of funding requirements met (36% in 2017), well below the average (60%) (**Figure 19.11**).

The data have two key weaknesses for the purpose of monitoring refugee education. First, 42% of total funding for appeals in 2017 was not assigned to specific sectors but was in the multisector category, shared among sectors or unspecified; therefore, the above number could underestimate the amount of humanitarian aid going to education, including for refugees. Second, as the data do not distinguish among interventions, it is not clear which part refers to refugees, so the above number could overestimate the amount disbursed for refugee education.

> “Education has continued to be one of the sectors with the lowest percentage of funding requirements funded (36% in 2017)”

The CRS database has the advantage of putting humanitarian and development aid on the same platform. But it breaks down OECD DAC members' humanitarian aid into just three categories (material relief assistance and services, emergency food aid, and relief coordination) and not by type of humanitarian emergency or by sector, such as education. The latter will change from 2019, with respect to data referring to 2017, when DAC is to update its humanitarian assistance codes and include one for education in emergencies.

For the time being, though, in the absence of project markers, estimating the amount spent on refugee education requires manual analysis of the FTS and CRS databases, project by project. To give an indication of the challenges, the 2016 German-funded projects in the Syrian Arab Republic for 'improvement of access to education for students in Western Aleppo countryside' (US$1.1 million) can be classified as fully education-related, whereas estimating the education share of UNICEF Syria's support for 'strengthening of resilience, education and child protection' (US$12.2 million) requires making assumptions and soliciting further information from implementation agencies that may not use the same classification criteria. In addition, differing definitions of humanitarian assistance and volumes reported mean the FTS and CRS do not match.

An analysis of the CRS database for this report showed that US$425 million was disbursed for refugee education through 225 humanitarian aid projects in 2016. But the CRS database also provides information on official development assistance on education. The analysis showed that a considerable, and less-recognized, amount of development aid also funds refugee education, amounting in 2016 to US$840 million. About US$453 million was disbursed through the United Nations Relief and Works Agency for Palestine Refugees in the Near East (UNRWA) for

> “US$425 million was disbursed through 225 humanitarian aid projects in 2016 on refugee education”

FIGURE 19.10:

Humanitarian aid to education increased for the fourth year in a row

Selected statistics related to humanitarian aid to education, 2000–2017

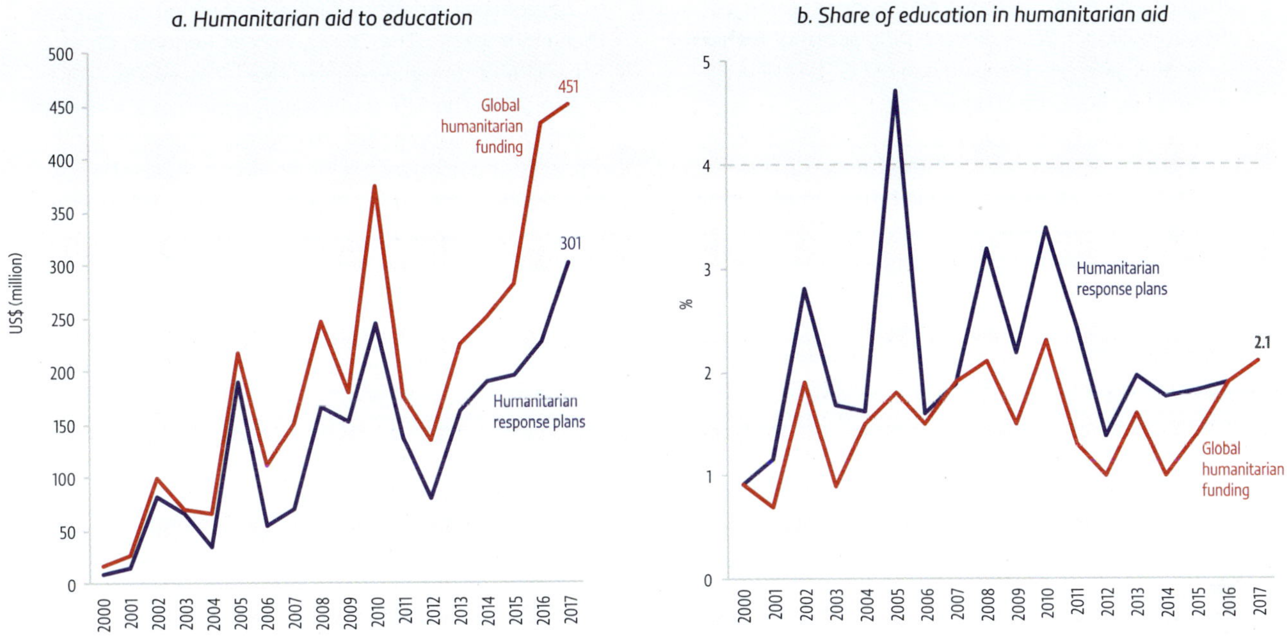

GEM StatLink: http://bit.ly/fig19_10
Source: UN OCHA FTS database.

FIGURE 19.11:

Education has not been receiving the requested humanitarian funding

Share of UN-coordinated appeal requests funded

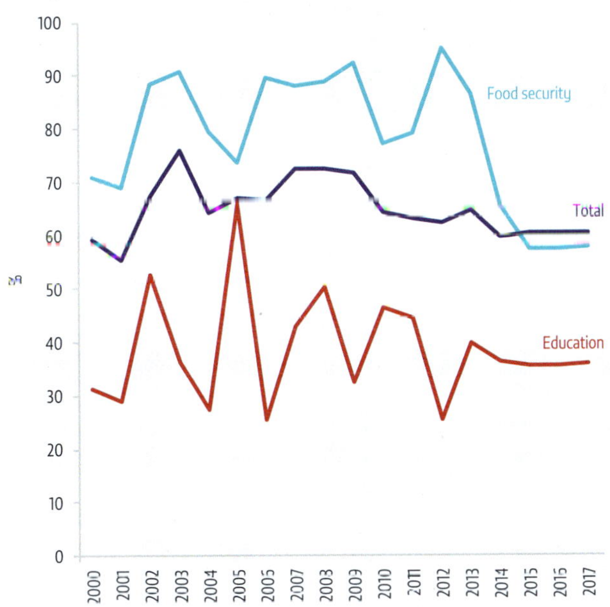

GEM StatLink: http://bit.ly/fig19_11
Note: The FTS database was accessed at the end of May 2018. FTS data may fluctuate slightly depending on the date of access.
Source: UN OCHA FTS database.

FIGURE 19.12:

Refugee education is funded by both humanitarian and development assistance

Aid to refugee education disbursements, by source of aid, 2014–2016

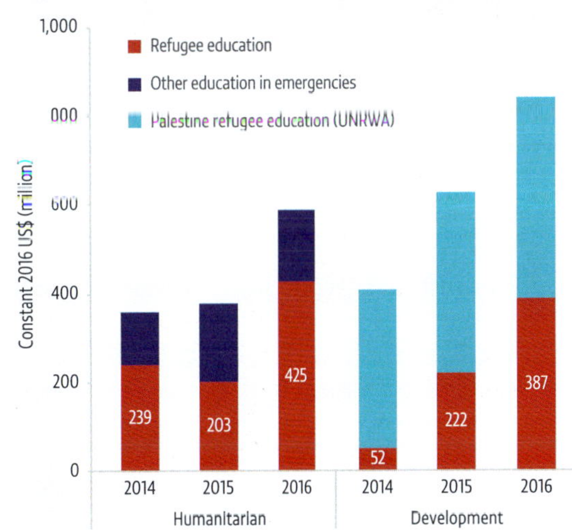

GEM StatLink: http://bit.ly/fig19_12
Source: GEM Report analysis of the CRS database.

Palestine refugees, while US$387 million was targeted at other refugee groups (**Figure 19.12**). Excluding Palestine refugees, this means refugee education received just over US$800 million in 2016, representing about one-third of the annual external financing gap of US$2.4 billion identified by Save the Children.

There are three solutions for filling the gap. Donors could continue to increase their humanitarian aid allocations, holding the share of education constant. This is what has driven the increase in aid to education in emergencies since 2012. CRS data indicate the volume of total humanitarian emergency aid increased from US$9.1 billion in 2012 to US$22.3 billion in 2016. Adding reconstruction, disaster prevention and, particularly, costs for refugees in donor countries, total expenditure almost tripled, from US$14.5 to US$40.9 billion. However, continuing the increase of humanitarian aid is not a sustainable solution, and the rise is more likely to mainly reflect the consequences of the Syrian crisis.

> "The new EU policy framework increased the share of education in emergencies and protracted crises to 10% of its overall humanitarian aid budget in 2019"

Donors could prioritize education within humanitarian aid, given how low education's share has been. In May 2018, a new EU policy framework increased the share of education in emergencies and protracted crises to 10% of the overall humanitarian aid budget in 2019, compared with 1% in 2015. EU institutions collectively allocated US$2.2 billion to humanitarian assistance in 2017 (European Commission, 2018). The FTS database shows that the share of education in the Syria regional refugee and resilience plan also increased, from 2.4% in 2015 to 7.4% in 2016, and remained above the average at 6% in 2017.

By contrast, ECW has set a modest target of raising education's share of humanitarian aid from 4% (excluding the large segment of humanitarian aid not allocated to sectors) to 5.4% by 2021. This suggests there are limits to the potential for increasing education's share of humanitarian aid (ECW, 2018c).

Accordingly, the third solution would be to tap more into development aid budgets for refugee education. For instance, since 2013, the GPE has made its support to countries affected by fragility and conflict more flexible to respond to emergencies. It allows them to develop interim education sector plans and receive up to 20% of their indicative GPE allocation within no more than eight weeks. The Central African Republic, Chad, Somalia and Yemen have used this facility (GPE, 2018). In April 2016, the GPE and UNHCR agreed to strengthen country-level cooperation to improve education for refugees and host communities. This includes the participation of humanitarian actors in Local Education Groups, a coordination mechanism hitherto available for development actors (UNHCR, 2016).

Multilateral development banks play an increasingly important role in financing emergency responses beyond the humanitarian aid architecture. The World Bank established a Global Crisis Risk Management Platform in 2016 to coordinate its diverse financing tools. It created a US$2 billion financing tool, the IDA18 Regional Sub-Window for Refugees and Host Communities, to help the poorest countries manage refugee crises. For middle income countries, it established the Global Concessional Financing Facility, first tested in Jordan and Lebanon in 2016. Each US$1 in grants is leveraged to create about US$4 in concessional financing, and the facility also offers improved coordination. By mid-2017, it had raised US$372 million in pledges and had approved US$193 million for implementation. None had been allocated for education yet, although it is within the facility's scope (World Bank, 2016, 2017a, 2017b).

Joint planning of humanitarian and development aid is key to refugee education

The key to increasing the volume, effectiveness and efficiency of support to refugee education is engagement of development actors to invest in education systems to benefit both refugee and host communities. This is an area of investment that is crucial for the inclusion of refugees in national education systems but in which humanitarian actors had not specialized due to their short-term focus.

Most UN-coordinated humanitarian responses provide short-term relief, lasting a year or less. Multiyear appeals for protracted crises have been underfunded, despite 90% of humanitarian response plans being active for at least three years (UNESCO, 2015c). Lack of continuity and predictability impedes transition from aftermath to recovery and development. Conversely, national education plans have not historically focused on resilience or displacement. They have not engaged with humanitarian agencies, and data collection has not prioritized aspects that would be useful in an immediate crisis response.

> Education is becoming a standard element in humanitarian response plans: 89% of appeals included an education component in 2017

The move towards better articulation between humanitarian and development aid is showcased by ECW's Multi-Year Resilience financing instrument for interventions active up to 3 or 4 years, complementing its more traditional First Emergency Response instrument for interventions active up to 12 months. The Multi-Year Resilience window comes in response to calls for joint planning between humanitarian and development actors, in other words for combining short-term humanitarian education planning with more structural concerns (e.g. financing, decentralization, capacity-building and system-wide reforms), reflected in development-oriented sector planning tools. Uganda is one of the few countries to have put all actors around the table and prioritize such a plan (**Box 19.2**). Its plan is to be supported by a Multi-Year Resilience programme. Similar efforts are under way in Afghanistan, Bangladesh and Palestine (ECW, 2018b).

It is not only multilateral mechanisms that can help bridge the humanitarian-development divide. Individual donors also need to demonstrate their commitment. Australia, Canada, Norway and the United Kingdom report shifts to joint financing through humanitarian and development budgets – but also through peacebuilding cooperation (Aviles, 2017), an example of the so-called triple nexus. Switzerland has brought humanitarian and development assistance strategies under one framework (OCHA and UNDP, 2018). The European Union has developed Joint Humanitarian and Development Frameworks as a basis for planning and programming (European Commission, 2017).

In June 2018, at the G7 Summit in Charlevoix, Canada, four members (Canada, Germany, Japan and the United Kingdom), together with the European Union and World Bank, pledged US$2.9 billion for the following three to five years 'in education for women and girls in crisis and conflict situations' (Canada Office of the Prime Minister, 2018). A test case will be how the commitment will be met while ensuring that the humanitarian and development contributions are linked.

BOX 19.2:

Uganda provides a model multistakeholder approach for humanitarian education response

Uganda hosts the largest number of refugees in Africa: 1.38 million, primarily from Burundi, the Democratic Republic of the Congo and South Sudan (UNHCR, 2017). The 2006 Refugee Act and 2010 Refugee Regulations provide for refugee students to learn alongside nationals. In practice, most refugees attend geographically separate schools, having settled where few nationals reside. National and international processes converged to produce an education sector plan for the 12 districts where most refugees live.

The country's second National Development Plan is committed to promoting socio-economic development of refugees and host communities in refugee-hosting areas. The Office of the Prime Minister is to develop and implement a Refugee Settlement Transformative Agenda enabling districts to provide for refugees. The Education Sector Strategic Plan (2017–2020) includes an objective to develop and implement response programmes for refugees and host communities in the districts concerned.

The government, with the support of development and humanitarian partners, drafted and approved a Refugee and Host Community Education Response Plan in May 2018, allocating US$395 million over three years (to the end of June 2021) to reach about 675,000 refugee and host community students per year. It is a rare example of an in-depth plan that bridges humanitarian and development actors (Uganda Ministry of Education and Sports, 2018).

The Education Response Plan is the type of national response that two processes have tried to catalyse through planning on joint education for refugees that builds on existing initiatives and policies: the Comprehensive Refugee Response Framework, launched with the New York Declaration in September 2016 to support countries embracing a whole-of-society approach to address refugee crises; and ECW, which brought government and non-government partners to the table and supported plan preparation.

Multisector planning of humanitarian aid is also important to strengthen refugee education

Education was long absent from humanitarian needs assessments. Among 27 assessments reviewed a few years ago, none covered education in depth. There was limited focus on data and results, incomplete coverage of different education levels and bias towards access over quality (Winthrop and Matsui, 2013). For instance, 71% of the 2014 Sudan appeal funding for education was for school feeding programmes (UNESCO, 2015c). While a focus on access or school feeding is to be expected, given the pressures under which assessments are carried out, it is insufficient in protracted crises. Plans should be based not on the activities organizations are used to but on those that contribute to inclusive and equitable education of good quality.

The Global Education Cluster, a coordination mechanism set up in 2007 to strengthen preparedness and capacity to respond to emergencies, established guidelines for joint needs assessments (Global Education Cluster, 2010). Following concerns that they were being used too little for planning (ODI, 2016), the cluster is working to improve its guidance on needs assessments and country-level strategies. Education is becoming a standard element in humanitarian response plans: 89% of appeals included an education component in 2017 (ECW, 2018b).

Education should be key in multisector humanitarian intervention plans. For instance, education programmes should collaborate with shelter, because school-to-house proximity determines access, attendance and learning; with child protection, because planning safe spaces is a prerequisite of safe schooling; and with water, sanitation and nutrition, because there are advantages to delivering such services in schools. More generally, schools are important pillars of community infrastructure and catalysts for social progress, as the Rohingya crisis in Bangladesh suggests. That being said, while multisector planning helped ensure greater inclusion of education in the humanitarian response, it did not ensure inclusion of the Rohingya in the Bangladesh education system (**Box 19.3**).

Conclusion

Following years of efforts to improve the level, effectiveness and efficiency of humanitarian aid, the World Humanitarian Summit was a turning point and also helped draw attention to education in emergencies, including for refugees. Education is a test case of the commitment made in the Agenda for Humanity to bridge the humanitarian-development divide, as it straddles sudden-onset emergencies, recovery and development. Humanitarian and development actors need to work together to address the inclusion of refugees in national education systems. Education also needs to be better incorporated in multisector programming, given the great potential for synergy.

For that reason, improving the quality of needs assessments, carrying out joint planning that bridges the humanitarian–development divide and identifying the right financing instruments are issues of high priority. Improving the tracking of humanitarian and development financing for refugee education will also be important to monitor progress in coming years.

HOUSEHOLD EXPENDITURE

Households constitute a significant yet underappreciated source of education spending. Even where primary and secondary education are provided free of charge, families still incur education-related costs. Some costs, such as those for textbooks, supplies and transport, are found in most countries. But others, including informal fees, private school tuition and supplementary private tuition, reflect weaknesses of particular public education systems and can have grave consequences for equitable distribution of educational opportunities. The SDG 4 monitoring framework has helped highlight this threat to equity through thematic indicator 4.5.4: 'Education expenditure per student by level of education and source of funding'.

Lack of data on household contributions had long restricted analysis of education expenditure to that provided by government and aid. The UIS first released household data in 2017, although coverage remains limited. There are 91 countries with any data since 2000, while only 48 have data for 2014–2016, of which 28 are high income, 18 are middle income and 2 are low income (Ethiopia and Uganda). In addition, household budget, income and expenditure surveys do not provide sufficiently detailed questions on spending by individual or by level and type of education attended.

Still, available evidence suggests households may carry a large share of total education expenditure in some low and middle income countries. The contribution of households ranges from 0.1% of GDP in Georgia to 3.9% in Uganda, where they account for 63% of the country's total education spending. In high income countries, for which more data are available, household expenditure

BOX 19.3:

In the Rohingya crisis in Bangladesh, joint sector planning helped deliver education, if not inclusion

Between late August 2017 and early May 2018, about 713,000 Rohingya refugees arrived in Cox's Bazar district, Bangladesh, fleeing targeted violence in Rakhine state, Myanmar. Over 90% live in spontaneous, makeshift settlements or host communities in over 1,600 locations in Cox's Bazar, a district close to the Myanmar border. On the humanitarian side, a Strategic Executive Group guides the Inter-Sectoral Coordination Group. UNICEF and Save the Children lead education sector activities, reflecting cluster architecture, although a national cluster has not been activated. A Ministry of Foreign Affairs national task force leads coordination (Karamperidou et al., 2018).

Unlike in other crises, education was included from the first stage of relief response, and education service delivery began very quickly. From September 2017, UNICEF, in cooperation with three local implementing partners (BRAC, Community Development Centre and Dhaka Ahsania Mission), established temporary learning centres, providing early education to children aged 4 to 6 and non-formal basic education to those aged 6 to 14. There were more than 1,000 such centres in camps and makeshift settlements by the end of April 2018.

Several factors contributed to the quick response. UNICEF was active in the area when the emergency began in October 2016, with 87,000 Rohingya fleeing to Bangladesh. One advantage of its presence was that it had funds for initial education response, although 92% of the education sector's US$26 million requirement was not met in 2017 while the food security sector exceeded its target. Well-established NGOs in Bangladesh meant strong partners were ready to be mobilized on the ground.

Moreover, the Bangladesh government had come a long way in changing its approach. For decades, it refused to recognize most of the Rohingya who had been in the country since 1978 as refugees. It was reluctant to address their education needs, did not accept international assistance and even dismantled centres set up by humanitarian organizations, and was sensitive about language of instruction. But in 2016, it revised its Strategy for Myanmar Refugees and Undocumented Myanmar Nationals, listing education as an intervention area for the first time. This encouraged humanitarian efforts and sensitized local authorities before the massive influx began.

Strong cooperation between education and other sectors on the ground led to multiple examples of integrated service delivery, using learning centres as entry points for non-education interventions. A micronutrient fortification programme and vaccinations were delivered at the centres, which provided health teams with easy access to children in the overcrowded camps. Learning centres also delivered health communications and a curriculum module about open defecation, handwashing and safe drinking water. Later, water, sanitation and hygiene facilities were built at the centres.

However, lack of coordination meant learning centres were sometimes empty, as alternative, non-education interventions competed for children's time. Planners in such instances had lacked sufficient understanding of cultural context and sensitivities. During an action week of interventions to identify and treat acute malnutrition, which mothers had to attend with their youngest children, older siblings brought younger siblings instead because women were expected to stay at home. Inter-agency coordination failures also occurred due to such factors as ineffective communication and high staff turnover (Karamperidou et al., 2018).

accounts for less than 1% of GDP in most cases. The range runs from 0.1% of GDP in Estonia to 1.6% in Japan, where households account for 31% of total education spending (**Figure 19.13**).

> "In El Salvador, households contributed 50% of total education expenditure"

Total education expenditure is the sum of government expenditure and household expenditure on education. Household spending accounts for a significant share in some middle income countries, including El Salvador (50%), Indonesia (49%) and Peru (45%). The situation is again more favourable for households in the 28 high income countries with data, at an average share of 14%.

Tertiary education accounted for 30% of total household education spending, on average, in the 34 countries with data, but the share was over 50% in Chile and the Republic of Korea, almost 70% in Latvia and Lithuania and 74% in the United States. Among middle income countries, tertiary education absorbed over 70% of total expenditure in Mongolia and Ukraine (**Figure 19.14**).

In general, where data are available over time, household expenditure tends not to change drastically from year

FIGURE 19.13:

Household education spending is considerable in some low and middle income countries

Education expenditure as a percentage of GDP by source of funds and country income group, selected countries, 2013–2017

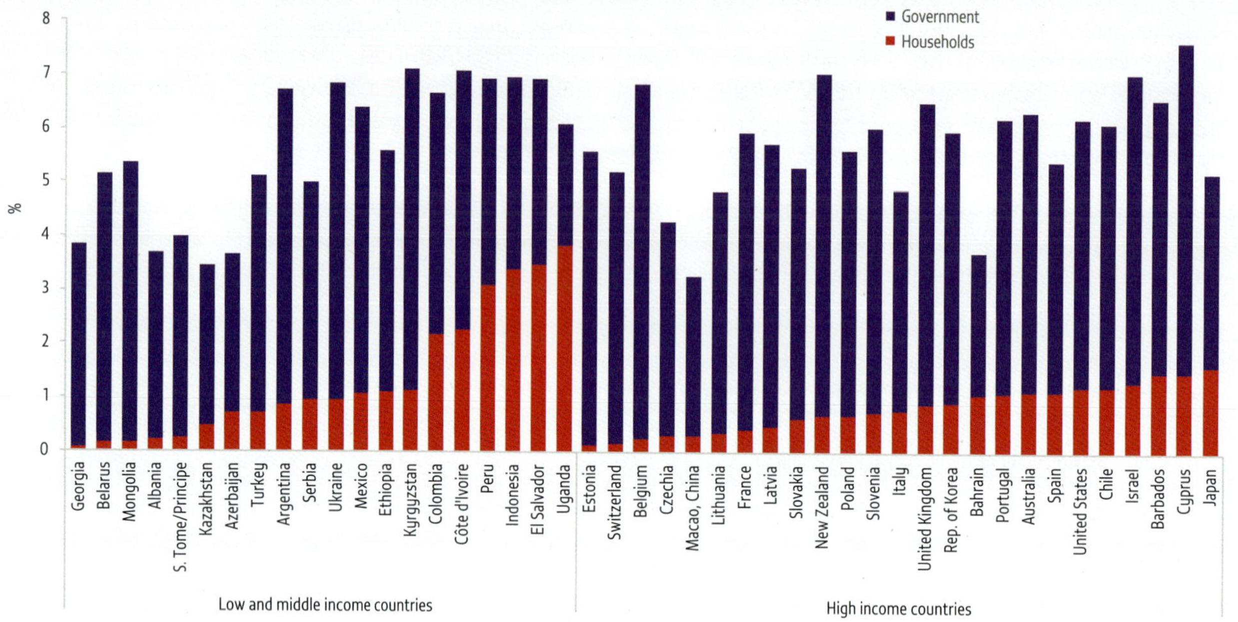

GEM StatLink: http://bit.ly/fig19_13
Source: UIS database.

FIGURE 19.14:

About 30% of household education spending goes to tertiary education

Household education expenditure by level of education, 2016 or most recent year

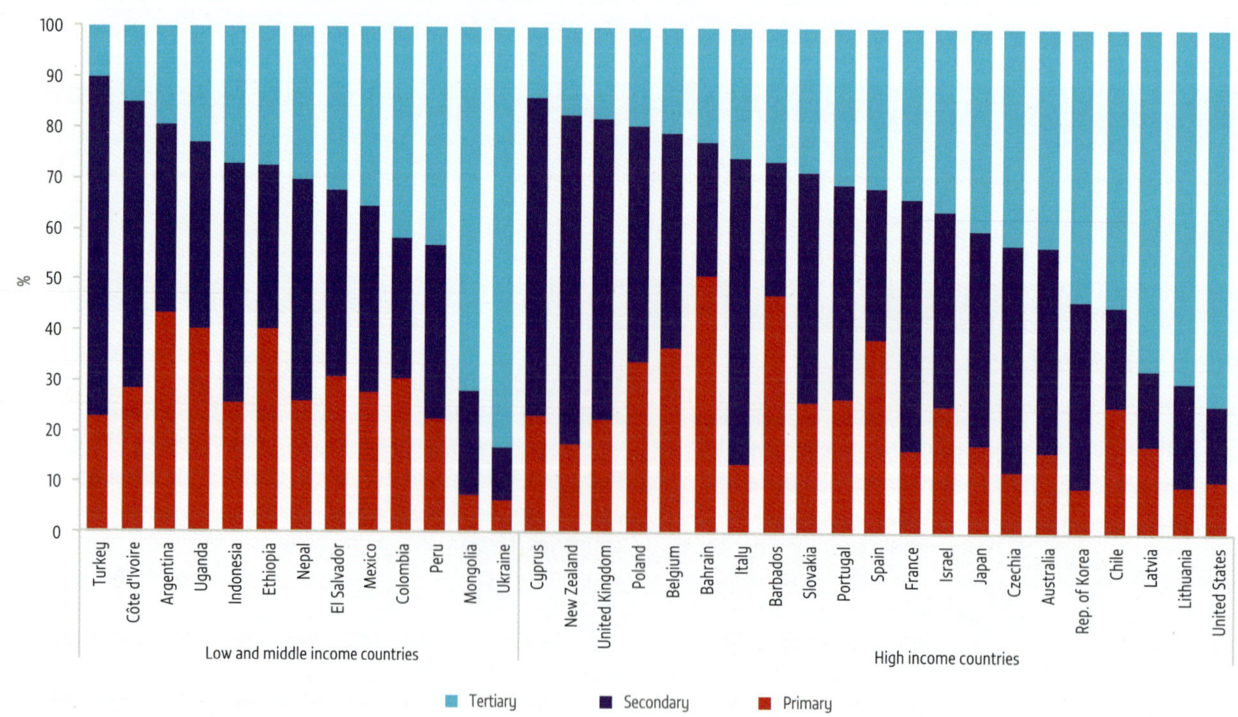

GEM StatLink: http://bit.ly/fig19_14
Source: UIS database.

to year, as patterns of such spending are relatively fixed. However, changes do happen. First, public policy can play a role. In Chile, in the mid-2000s, massive student protests began pressuring the government to resume responsibilities it had abdicated for education financing. Between 2005 and 2015, the household share of total education spending fell from 45% to 20%, converging towards the average global distribution of total costs exemplified by Mexico (**Figure 19.15**).

Second, as disposable incomes increase, households often decide to invest more in education. In some countries, the growth rate of remittances has been rapid, and anticipated decreases in the cost of remitting could have a positive effect on education spending (**Policy focus 19.4**).

Lack of information sources is not limited to low and middle income countries. Lack of data means the level of private spending may also be underestimated in high income countries (OECD, 2011). Some have attempted to diversify sources. Statistics Canada combines information from five surveys to estimate household spending on primary and secondary education: Survey of Uniform Financial System – School Boards, Elementary-Secondary Education Survey, Survey of Federal Government Expenditures in Support of Education, Survey of Financial Statistics of Private Elementary and Secondary Schools, and Provincial Expenditures on Education in Reform and Correctional Institutions. Between surveys, Statistics Canada makes estimates based on previous years. The Financial Information of Universities and Colleges Survey and the Survey of Federal Government Expenditures in Support of Education provide information on the tertiary level (Statistics Canada, 2015, 2017).

POLICY FOCUS 19.4: REMITTANCES BOOST HOUSEHOLD EDUCATION SPENDING

Internal and international migrants support family or community members by remitting earnings. It is a key motivation for migration, and remittances are a substantial income source for many in Africa, Asia and Latin America. Views differ on whether remittances help or hinder household investment in education as well as on what education effects remittances have. Analysis is

FIGURE 19.15:
Distribution of total education costs between government and households changed rapidly in Chile
Education expenditure as a percentage of GDP by source of funds, Chile and Mexico, 2005–2016

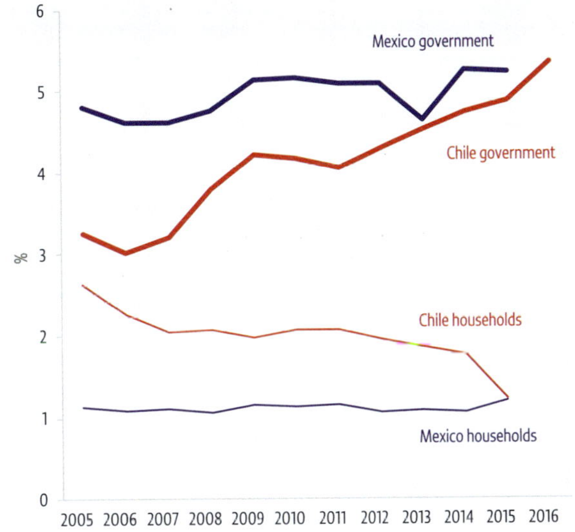

GEM StatLink: http://bit.ly/fig19_15
Source: UIS database.

therefore crucial. To the extent that remittances boost private education spending, current efforts to lower remitting costs could have a substantial effect on the lives of children left behind.

REMITTANCES ARE A CONSIDERABLE PART OF HOUSEHOLD INCOME IN MANY LOW AND MIDDLE INCOME COUNTRIES

Globally, households received US$613 billion in international remittances in 2017, a flow far higher than official development aid. Of this, US$466 billion went to households in low and middle income countries, three times the volume of official development assistance. In absolute terms, India (US$69 billion), China (US$64 billion), the Philippines (US$33 billion), Mexico (US$31 billion) and Nigeria (US$22 billion) received the largest amounts. The countries receiving the most in remittances as a percentage of GDP were Kyrgyzstan (35%), Tonga (33%), Tajikistan (31%), Haiti (29%), Nepal (29%) and Liberia (27%) (World Bank, 2018a).

Internal remittances are more likely to be transferred through informal channels, making robust estimates slightly more difficult (Castaldo et al., 2012). Household surveys supply some estimates. In China, which had some 287 million internal migrants in 2017 (Xuequan, 2018), almost half of rural households surveyed in 2007 received remittances, which constituted 21% of household income. For households in the bottom 25% of pre-transfer income, remittances constituted 60% of household income (Démurger and Wang, 2016).

> In China, almost half of rural households received remittances, which constituted 21% of household income

IN THEORY, REMITTANCES MAY INCREASE OR DECREASE HOUSEHOLD EDUCATION SPENDING

Extra income increases household spending across the board. But whether it increases education spending depends on context. Education competes with other categories, e.g. increased consumption and investment in land, housing or capital goods. Families differ in perceptions of education as a consumption or investment good. Moreover, economic theory contends households that perceive extra income as temporary spend relatively more on investment than consumption (Adams and Cuecuecha, 2010). In addition to the positive income effect and lifting of budget constraints, more diversified income provides an insurance effect, reducing the risk of cutting education expenditure in response to economic shocks (Yang and Choi, 2007).

Migration is often a collective decision, involving extended family, adding layers to how remittances shape education in origin households (Azam and Gubert, 2006). Migration changes household composition and decision-making, which may negatively affect schooling. Children may be required to replace the migrant's labour, take up household chores or care for siblings. And since migration is costly, remittances may not flow immediately, so an initial loss of income can constrain education expenditure. The absence of one or both parents and their input may also hamper education.

Remittances may foster a 'culture of migration', with adverse effects on children's education. In communities with high international migration, transnational movement becomes a norm (Kandel and Massey, 2002), and remittances signal earning opportunities abroad (Mansour et al., 2011). Where low- or semi-skilled migration is feasible and generates relatively high returns, it may incentivize early school-leaving, especially if destination labour markets do not recognize and reward origin-country educational achievement. By contrast, successful migration that is seen to require higher education levels may raise education aspirations and motivate investment of time and effort.

IN PRACTICE, REMITTANCES POSITIVELY AFFECT EDUCATION SPENDING

Recipient households in Guatemala and in Lima, Peru, almost tripled education spending (Adams and Cuecuecha, 2010; Loveday and Molina, 2006). International remittance recipient households in rural India spent 17% more on education compared with households that do not receive any remittances (Parida et al., 2015). In Morocco, remittances amounted to 17% of both rural and urban household education spending in 2003–2007 (Ibourk and Bensaïd, 2014). Families of Filipino workers in the Republic of Korea tripled their health and education spending (Clemens and Tiongson, 2017). In Jordan, however, low-skilled migration led to lower investment in young people's education (Mansour et al., 2011).

Outcomes can differ by gender. An analysis of overseas Filipino workers showed that, on average, women earned less than men and sent a lower proportion of earnings home (Semyonov and Gorodzeisky, 2006). With respect to remittance use, male-headed households in rural Morocco were less likely to invest in girls' than in boys'

> International remittances increased education spending by 35% in 18 countries in sub-Saharan Africa and Central, Southern and South-eastern Asia and by 53% in 7 countries in Latin America on average

Lowering the cost for migrants to send money home

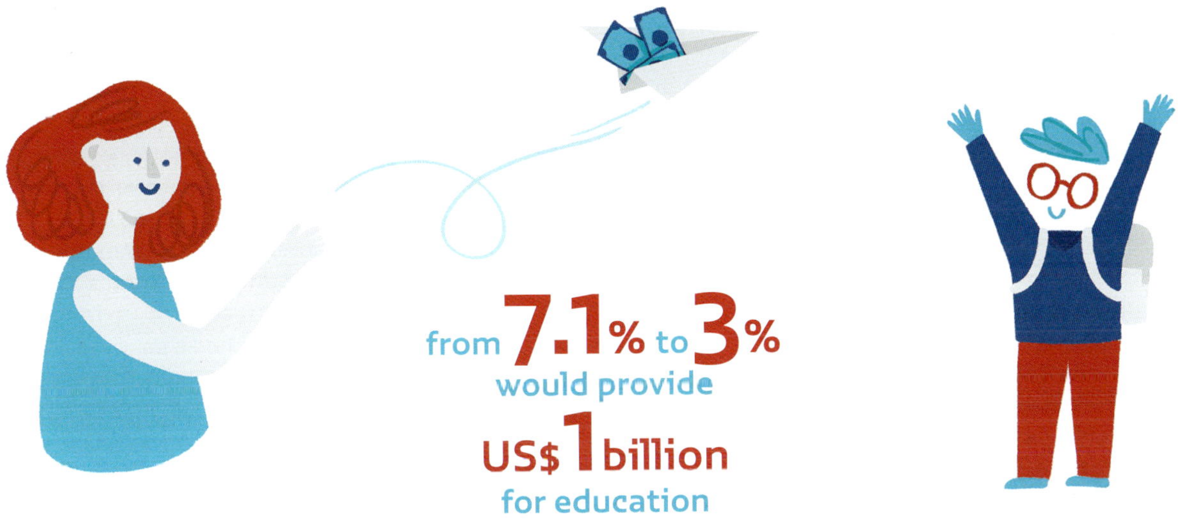

education (Bouoiyour et al., 2016). Remittance-receiving households headed by women tended to spend more on education (Ratha et al., 2011).

A meta-analysis for this report examined 73 high-quality, peer-reviewed articles covering 30 countries. It used the partial correlation coefficient as a measure of remittances' effect on household education expenditure, taking other factors influencing such expenditure into account.

The analysis confirmed the importance of remittances to education spending decisions. International remittances increased education spending by 35%, on average, in a set of studies on 18 countries in sub-Saharan Africa and Central, Southern and South-eastern Asia (**Figure 19.16**). The effect was even larger in Latin America (53%), where household education expenditure tends to be high, but closer to zero in eastern Europe, where household education expenditure tends to be low. The effect of internal remittances was lower but still positive for the majority of countries reviewed. For example, it was 19% in 18 countries in sub-Saharan Africa and Central, Southern and South-eastern Asia (Askarov and Doucouliagos, 2018). Results by gender did not confirm significant differences in remitting behaviour or remittance use, but the number of studies was too small for the effects to be robust.

FIGURE 19.16:

On average, international remittances increase education spending in low and middle income countries

Percentage change in education expenditure arising from remittances

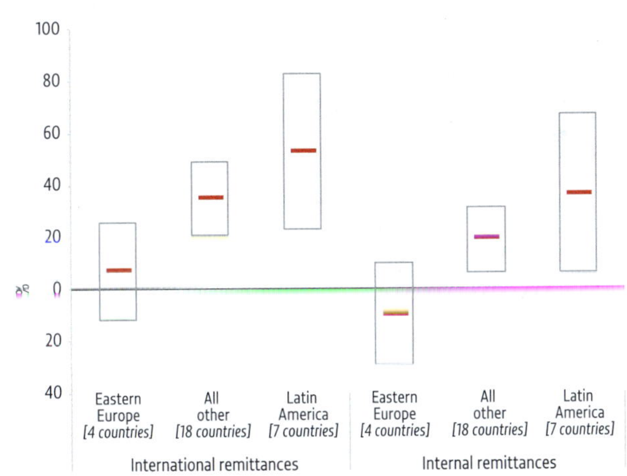

GEM StatLink: http://bit.ly/fig19_16

Notes: The bars show the weighted averages of the effect of the incidence of a household receiving remittances on education spending. The box shows the range of the 95% confidence interval. 'All other' combines countries in sub-Saharan Africa and Central, Southern and South-eastern Asia.

Source: Askarov and Doucouliagos (2018).

Reducing remittance costs can raise education spending

Despite new technology, such as mobile payments and prepaid bank cards, high commissions and other transfer fees along many remittance corridors discourage use of formal channels in favour of more efficient informal and in-kind transfers, as evidence from Fiji and Tonga has shown (Brown et al., 2014). The volume of informal remittances was estimated at between 35% and 75% that of formal remittances (Freund and Spatafora, 2005).

The global average cost of remitting is 7.1%, although averages do not reflect the wide variation by delivery channel and by country. Traditional banks cost the most, averaging 10.6%. Costs vary by destination, from 5.2% (Southern Asia) to 9.4% (sub-Saharan Africa) (World Bank, 2018b). Many corridors in Africa carry fees of over 20% (Watkins and Quattri, 2014). Several organizations, including the African Development Bank, have called for increased competition in the international money transfer market (Bourenane et al., 2011).

The charges far exceed SDG target 10.c, which aims for migrant remittance costs reduced to less than 3% on average and not exceeding 5% for any corridor. Based on the estimated US$613 billion in global remittances in 2017, reducing costs from 7.1% to 3% would translate into savings of more than US$25 billion annually.

Despite recent progress, an accurate global picture of household expenditure on education is yet to emerge. An analysis of 15 sub-Saharan African countries estimated the share of total household spending on education at 4.2% (Foko et al., 2012); a study of 12 Latin American countries found 3.4% (Acerenza and Gandelman, 2017). Taking 4% as a starting point, lowering remittance costs would allow households to spend an additional US$1 billion on education per year. This may be an underestimate, since remittances are more likely to be spent on education, as the previous analysis showed.

This estimate assumes saved transaction fees translate one-to-one into additional remittances. In practice, remittances might adjust more or less strongly. How the reduction in costs is shared between senders and receivers is an open question. Moreover, estimates take into account only the effect of additional remittances that would reach recipients, but remittances might increase with lower costs (Gibson et al., 2007). Lower costs might also appear to increase flows as migrants switched from unrecorded informal transmission channels to formal ones.

EFFECTS OF REMITTANCES ON ENROLMENT, COMPLETION AND LEARNING ARE MIXED

Ultimately, education expenditure is a means to an end. Several studies suggest that remittances' overall effects on education outcomes are positive. In the Dominican Republic, remittances increased the likelihood of attendance among those aged 6 to 17 (Amuedo-Dorantes and Pozo, 2010). In the Philippines, a 10% increase in international remittances reduced unpaid child labour by more than three hours per week (Yang, 2005). In Morocco, children in households that received remittances were 11 percentage points more likely to be attending school than in those that did not (Ibourk and Bensaïd, 2014).

Effects also differ by gender. In Jordan, remittances had a positive impact on post-compulsory education attendance only among young males (Mansour et al., 2011). A study in rural southern Morocco showed that remittances increased school attendance only for boys (Bouoiyour et al., 2016). In Nepal, remittances' effect on retention was three times greater for boys than for girls aged 5 to 10 (Bansak and Chezum, 2009). Conversely, a US$11 increase in monthly remittance led to a one percentage point increase in the enrolment rate of students aged 10 to 17 in Ecuador, although the effect was significant only for girls (Calero et al., 2009). Mexican fathers' migration to the United States was associated with an increase of around 0.7 years in educational attainment for girls but not for boys (Antman, 2012).

Positive findings may reflect particularly selective migration corridors or contexts with low enrolment to start with. Remittances had no effect on enrolment among children aged 11 to 17 in El Salvador (after accounting for household wealth) (Acosta, 2006), younger children in the Dominican Republic (Amuedo-Dorantes and Pozo, 2010) or those aged 6 to 18 in Viet Nam (Nguyen and Nguyen, 2015).

There are also harmful effects concerning well-established low-skill migration corridors. International remittances were associated with a large decrease in enrolment in Guatemala, especially among boys, even though those enrolled performed better as a result of remittances

(Davis and Brazil, 2016). Left-behind students in rural Mexico receiving remittances had poorer education outcomes (McKenzie and Rapoport, 2006), including lower cognitive development in young children (Powers, 2011). Analysis of Latin American Migration Project data in Lima suggested that the risk of education disruption increased with migration. Not accounting for household characteristics that determine the decision to migrate would have led to the opposite conclusion (Robles and Oropesa, 2011).

CONCLUSION

The effects of remittances on private education spending vary widely by migration corridor, the characteristics of senders and receivers, and the measures used. Yet a meta-analysis for this report shows that remittances, especially international, increase education spending at home. The SDG target of lowering remitting costs could increase household education spending in low and middle income countries by US$1 billion per year. However, evidence of a positive relationship between higher education spending due to remittances and improved education outcomes is less robust. More information on how additional income is spent and to what extent it correlates with completion and learning is required.

Displaced Afghan boys form a 'daisy chain' to attend special English classes at the Oinofyta centre, Greece, in 2016.

CREDIT: Achilleas Zavallis/UNHCR

CHAPTER

20

Conclusions and recommendations

The 2030 Agenda for Sustainable Development has placed education at the centre of debates on planet, people, prosperity, peace, partnerships and the future of humanity. This report has noted two areas where progress is under way but where stronger commitment is needed.

First, it has drawn attention to the slow but undeniable progress in monitoring SDG 4. The monitoring framework has the potential to play a formative role that can transform education systems and help them tackle equity, inclusion and quality challenges. But for this potential to be fully realized, the international mechanisms supporting the framework need to be strengthened to help provide clearer guidance to countries.

Second, it has highlighted the role of education in managing migration and displacement challenges, especially in view of two global compacts on migrants and refugees being agreed in late 2018. This concluding chapter summarizes key recommendations that can help get countries on the right track regarding implementation of the education aspects of these compacts.

MONITORING SDG 4 HOLDS GREAT PROMISE FOR EDUCATION SYSTEMS – BUT INTERNATIONAL COORDINATION MECHANISMS NEED SUPPORT

By raising questions on equity, inclusion and quality, the 2030 Agenda has also challenged the education monitoring efforts, which the *Global Education Monitoring Report* is aiming to support. Three years after consensus was reached on the Education 2030 Framework for Action, countries, civil society and international partners are investing in pinning down definitions, improving methodologies and collecting information.

The international agreement around SDG 4 and its monitoring arrangements has succeeded in shifting the debate in education. For instance, this year the report has drawn attention to issues such as the slow annual progress towards universal achievement of a minimum level of proficiency in reading; the low percentage of adults participating in any form of education and training in middle income countries; and the high number of attacks on schools and education personnel, according to information collected by a non-government organization. That these issues, not on the global education agenda just a few years ago, are now being raised is a testament to efforts on all fronts.

This report notes another significant development that has gradually taken place since 2015. The foundations of a cooperation mechanism in international education monitoring are being set. The Technical Cooperation Group (TCG) on SDG 4 – Education 2030 Indicators, co-convened by the UNESCO Institute for Statistics (UIS) and UNESCO, is becoming a forum for countries to voice their experience, preferences and concerns on how progress towards SDG 4 should be measured. It got off to a slow start, as it takes time for countries and international agencies to find a common language that links the national, regional and global levels. Logistical, capacity and resource constraints get in the way. But this is an opportunity that should not be missed.

This report makes five recommendations calling on the SDG – Education 2030 Steering Committee, UNESCO, development partners and countries to make the TCG a stronger forum to support the monitoring of the international education agenda:

- **Strengthen country representation and voice.** So far, not all countries represented in the TCG have been active participants. And yet, as the 2017/8 *Global Education Monitoring Report* noted, to improve accountability, 'countries need to build their capacity for stronger representation' at the level 'where problems are framed, priorities identified and solutions devised'.

- **Ensure each country has two permanent TCG contact points.** The current structure of the TCG reflects the Inter-agency and Expert Group on SDG Indicators rotating membership, with 28 countries being represented. Yet, due to the costs associated with coordination, few countries manage to represent their region well. The risk is that other countries are left without sufficient information to influence the agenda, and precious momentum is lost. Each country, whether a TCG member or not, should have two TCG contact points ex officio, which currently is not the case: one each from the ministry of education (with responsibility for planning or monitoring and evaluation) and the national statistical agency (with responsibility for social statistics), as a step to further institutionalize the process and create a global community of interest.

- **Improve the coherence of the international education monitoring coordination mechanisms.** In addition to the TCG, there are two other related UIS-convened groups. The Global Alliance to Monitor Learning has focused on learning outcome indicators and has recently invited countries to take part in its proceedings in addition to experts. The Inter-Agency Group on Education Inequality Indicators has focused on equity and survey-based indicators. But different groups on closely related topics make it more difficult for countries with fewer resources and weaker capacities to engage. Streamlining the architecture would help keep all eyes focused on the objective of improved monitoring of Education 2030.

- **Engage regional organizations more.** Given the difficulty of bridging national and global levels, regional organizations with education agendas can be important intermediaries to support national policy-makers. A mapping of the regional education monitoring frameworks and their alignment with the SDG 4 framework has been a step in the right direction. But the inclusion of regional organizations in the TCG, which has already begun, could be strengthened.

- **Invest resources.** Setting standards and influencing policy decisions is a core goal of international organizations but is often not high enough on funders' agendas. As the 2017/8 *Global Education Monitoring Report* noted, there is a tendency for allocation decisions to prioritize quick results, a common flaw of results-based approaches. The international community should not underestimate the importance of long-term results. UNESCO should put greater priority on the funding of the international education monitoring coordination mechanisms it convenes. Donor agencies should give greater priority to a global public good such as the TCG, not just in rhetoric but also in practice. They should also refer to the TCG process and its identification of SDG 4 data gaps to target their capacity development and data collection activities accordingly. Some initial guidance on the costing and main gaps of the agenda led by the UIS can inform these resource allocation decisions. The TCG is a key tool for minimizing the scope for fragmentation in data collection and reporting.

Although important methodological developments in measuring key aspects of the Education 2030 agenda are under way, such as completion rates and learning outcomes, important gaps remain. Examples abound. Without an international standard classification of teachers, current measures of qualified and trained teachers are inadequate, as Chapter 17 showed. Despite progress on defining adult education participation, as Chapter 10 showed, the work on data collection is only beginning; lifelong learning opportunities represent half of the SDG 4 formulation but receive only a fraction of global attention. The process of monitoring target 4.7, for some the heart of the agenda, requires a larger mobilization of efforts; to this point, country-specific measures on sustainable development and global citizenship cannot be reported. The list is long. But a good start would be to strengthen the main institutional arrangement set up to develop the SDG 4 monitoring framework.

MIGRATION AND DISPLACEMENT ARE A TEST CASE FOR INTERNATIONAL COOPERATION – AND FOR THE ROLE OF EDUCATION

The 2030 Agenda for Sustainable Development is inextricably linked with the commitment to leave no one behind. *Transforming our World*, the foundation document of the agenda, includes 'refugees and internally displaced persons and migrants' among those 'who are vulnerable [and] must be empowered'. One of the vulnerabilities – but also one of the strengths – of migrant and displaced people is education. As the UN Secretary-General puts it in his endorsement of this report: 'People on the move, whether for work or education, and whether voluntarily or forced, do not leave their right to education behind.'

The report took the broadest definitions of migration and displacement, covering any population movement that had an influence on education. It touched upon the challenges of internal migration, whether rural to urban or circular, whether affecting those leaving or those left behind. It looked at issues as diverse as boarding students' well-being, mobile schools at work sites, restrictions on school access and rural school closures.

International migration has been a growing phenomenon. First-generation immigrants are estimated at 14% of the population in high income countries. Estimates for this report suggest that the combined first and second generations of children with migrant background in these countries increased from 15% in the mid-2000s to 18%, or 36 million, in the mid-2010s, and at current rates could reach 22% by 2030. Their chances are affected by unequal access to early childhood education, large gaps in attainment and achievement compared with students without migrant background, curricula that do not sufficiently support critical thinking, and the intractable issue of school segregation.

Migration of people for education and professional advancement is another growing trend. Student mobility is growing alongside the internationalization of tertiary education. Concerns that poorer countries may lose skilled people to richer countries are somewhat allayed by young people investing more in their education as the prospect of emigration provides them with an incentive. But efforts to make the most of such movements require governments and tertiary education institutions to coordinate on quality assurance and qualification recognition.

The report also looked at the plight of the rapidly growing number of people who are displaced, whether by conflict or natural disaster, inside or across borders. Rates of access to education for the displaced are among the world's lowest, and not only because such crises often occur in some of the poorest places. In the two years since the signing of the New York Declaration on Migrants and Refugees in September 2016, a striking 1.5 billion days of refugee education have been lost. The quality of educational opportunities for these populations is affected by remoteness, language obstacles, unqualified teachers and lack of resources, often combined with sheer lack of experience in responding to sudden influxes of people fleeing their country.

And yet this report has not only listed problems. It has also collected evidence from all over the world about changes of heart. Governments are rapidly embracing the inclusion of refugees in their education systems. Among the top 10 countries hosting refugees, only one, Bangladesh, has so far excluded them from its national education system, while another one, Pakistan, has had an ambivalent stance. But even there, one of the provinces, Balochistan, includes refugees in its education plan.

Lebanon, which hosts the highest number of refugees per capita in the world, doubled its capacity and has opened its schools to 214,000 students, compared with a school cohort of about 750,000 before the crisis. It waived documentation requirements and completion certificates to allow Syrian students to sit national examinations and created non-formal opportunities to help children catch up.

Chad planned for the inclusion of Sudanese refugees in its education system and took steps to recognize the qualifications not only of students but also of teachers, helping them integrate into the national teacher workforce. Uganda, which hosts the largest number of refugees in sub-Saharan Africa, recently completed a three-year plan to include refugees in schools in its 12 most affected districts. Turkey, which hosts the world's largest number of refugees, has committed to include all Syrian refugees in its national education system by 2020 and has already included them in its social protection system, ensuring they benefit from a conditional cash transfer programme that was previously available only to nationals.

The inclusion of immigrants takes a variety of forms. Canada, which has the largest percentage of first- and second-generation immigrants among the seven richest industrialized countries, takes pride in its multicultural heritage, elevating it to a constitutional principle. It has amended its history textbooks, and children can learn about migration from grade 2. Ireland, which transformed in the space of less than a generation from a country of emigrants to the country with the European Union's largest percentage of first-generation immigrants in school, boasts a cross-departmental immigrant strategy where education features prominently. It also ensured that an intercultural education strategy received generous funding in the middle of a deep financial crisis. This is remarkable, given the common tendency during crises to blame immigration for a raft of social and economic problems.

Migration and displacement are charged political issues. This is because they are usually intertwined with multiple layers of cultural, historical, social and economic complications. It is not uncommon to observe policy-makers taking decisions under pressure in response to voices against immigration, sometimes echoed in the media. These tend to ignore the fact that migration has been one of the major drivers of development. In that sense, education for migrants and refugees is not only a matter of appealing to a basic human right. It also has operational and instrumental dimensions. The cost of excluding these populations can be huge in terms of people not fulfilling their potential and increased social tensions.

HOW SHOULD GOVERNMENTS APPROACH THE EDUCATION ASPECTS OF MIGRATION AND DISPLACEMENT?

This report calls on governments to address the education needs of migrant and displaced populations, and those of their children, with the same attention they give to host populations.

Protect the right to education of migrants and displaced people
The principle of non-discrimination in education is recognized in international conventions. Discriminatory barriers, such as birth certificate requirements, should be explicitly prohibited in national law. Existing regulations should have no loopholes or grey areas left open to interpretation by individual local or school-level officers. Governments must protect migrants' and refugees' right to education irrespective of identification documents or residence status and apply laws without exception.

Respecting the right to education must go beyond legislation and administrative process. National authorities should mount awareness-raising campaigns to inform migrant and displaced families of their rights and of school registration processes. Planning authorities should ensure that public schools are within reach of informal settlements and slums and that they are not neglected in urban regeneration plans.

Include migrants and displaced people in the national education system
Some education systems treat immigrants and refugees as temporary or transient populations, different from natives. This is wrong; it impedes their academic progress, socialization and future opportunities, and undermines progress towards diverse, cohesive societies. Public policy must include them in all levels of national education.

Inclusion of immigrants has several dimensions. While a new language of instruction necessitates preparatory classes, students should be separated as little as possible from their native peers. Education systems should not channel students with lower achievement, among whom immigrants are over-represented, into different tracks. Given the geographical concentration of immigrant students in many countries, education planners should use methods such as transport subsidies and random school assignment to ensure residential segregation does not result in education segregation.

Governments need to make sure that refugees' education is interrupted as little as possible. While exceptional circumstances – e.g. physical isolation of refugee communities or host system capacity constraints – may prevent full inclusion, governments need to minimize time spent in schools not following the national curriculum or not progressing towards recognized certificates, as such time compromises education trajectories.

Understand and plan for the education needs of migrants and displaced people
Countries with large immigrant and refugee inflows need to capture data on these populations in management information systems to plan and budget accordingly. Providing school places or work opportunities for migrants and refugees is only the first step to inclusion.

School environments have to adapt to and support students' needs. Those transitioning to a new language of instruction need bridging programmes with qualified teachers. Those whose education was interrupted will benefit from accelerated education programmes enabling them to catch up and re-enter school at the appropriate level. Refugee inclusion in education will be more likely to succeed if it extends to social protection programmes to allow refugees to benefit, for instance, from conditional cash transfers that cover hidden school costs. In the case of internal migrants, notably children of nomads or seasonal workers, governments should consider flexible school calendars, education tracking systems and curricula relevant to their livelihoods.

Adults need support to develop their competences through technical and vocational education and training and to overcome constraints, such as low-skill occupations or high training costs, that discourage their investment in skills. They need financial education programmes so they can manage their economic circumstances, make the most of remittances and avoid fraud or financial exploitation. Non-formal education programmes, which can be offered at the local government level, can supplement efforts to strengthen social cohesion.

Represent migration and displacement histories in education accurately to challenge prejudices
Building inclusive societies and helping people live together requires more than tolerance. Governments must review education content and delivery, adapting curricula and rethinking textbooks to reflect history and current diversity. Education content needs to bring to the fore migration's contribution to wealth and prosperity. It also needs to recognize the causes of tension and conflict, as well as the legacy of migrations that displaced or marginalized populations. Pedagogical approaches should promote openness to multiple perspectives, foster the values of living together, and appreciate the benefits of diversity. They should challenge prejudices and develop critical thinking skills so learners can overcome uncertainties in interacting with other cultures and resist negative media portrayals of immigrants and refugees. Governments need to draw from the positive experiences of intercultural education.

Prepare teachers of migrants and displaced people to address diversity and hardship
Teachers need support to become agents of change in school environments increasingly shaped by migration and displacement.

Current teacher education programmes addressing migration tend to be ad hoc and not part of the main curricula. Governments need to invest in initial and ongoing teacher education that builds core competences and ability to manage diverse, multilingual and multicultural contexts, which also affect native students. Raise awareness of all teachers about migration and displacement, not just those who teach diverse classrooms. Aspiring and practising teachers and school leaders should be given the tools to confront stereotypes, prejudices and discrimination in the classroom, the schoolyard and the community, and to strengthen immigrant and refugee students' self-esteem and sense of belonging.

Teachers in displacement contexts also need to be sensitive to the particular difficulties displaced students and parents face, and reach out to their communities. While teachers are not counsellors, they can be trained to recognize stress and trauma and refer those in need to specialists. If there are no specialists, teachers should be prepared to serve as some families' only access to such services. Teachers of refugees and displaced teachers suffer additional stress themselves. Management policies need to recognize and relieve the extreme hardships under which some teachers work; regulate and ensure equality among types of teaching professionals to maintain morale; and invest in professional development.

Harness the potential of migrants and displaced people
Migrants and refugees possess skills that can help transform not only their and their families' lives but also both host and home economies and societies, whether they return or support from a distance. Using this potential requires simpler, cheaper and more transparent and flexible mechanisms to recognize academic qualifications and professional skills (including those of teachers) and to account for prior learning that was not validated or certified.

Countries need to follow up on Global Compact for Safe, Orderly and Regular Migration commitments regarding mutual qualification recognition, and to conclude negotiations under the Global Convention on the Recognition of Higher Education Qualifications so it can be adopted in 2019. Assessment agencies, licensing bodies and academic institutions should harmonize requirements and procedures at the bilateral, regional and global levels, working with governments and regional and international organizations. Common degree standards, quality assurance mechanisms and academic exchange programmes can support qualification recognition.

Support education needs of migrants and displaced people in humanitarian and development aid
While two-thirds of international migrants are destined for high income countries, 9 out of 10 refugees are hosted by low and middle income countries, which require support from international partners. Meeting needs would require a tenfold increase in the share of education in humanitarian aid. A more sustainable solution is for the international community to fulfil the Global Compact on Refugees and the Comprehensive Refugee Response Framework commitment to link humanitarian and development aid from the early stages of a crisis, supporting inclusive education delivery for refugee and host populations. Education should be included in response design, especially as regards early childhood education and care. It should also be part of a holistic package of solutions involving other sectors, e.g. shelter, nutrition, water, sanitation and social protection. Donors need to reflect these reforms in their humanitarian interventions. Using the momentum of the Education Cannot Wait fund, they need to develop need-assessment capacity and join up planning to bridge the humanitarian-development divide and catalyse predictable multiyear funding.

Thousands of refugees moved before the rains which hit South Sudan. The school is extremely popular with the refugee children and their parents. Many said they had no access to education in their home villages.

CREDIT: T. Irwin/UNHCR

Statistical tables

The statistical tables are organized by each of the seven SDG 4 targets and three means of implementation rather than by education level (from pre-primary to tertiary). In addition, Table I presents basic information on demographic and education system characteristics as well as on domestic education finance, which is a key means of implementation recognized in the Education 2030 Framework for Action.

The SDG 4 monitoring framework consists of 43 internationally comparable indicators. Of these, 11 are considered global indicators and 32 are considered thematic indicators.[1] All are listed in **Table I.1**, which also identifies those indicators reported by the UNESCO Institute for Statistics (UIS) in 2018.[2] While aligned with the SDG 4 monitoring framework, the statistical tables also include other indicators, such as transition from primary to secondary education and student mobility.

METHODOLOGICAL NOTES

Most data in the statistical tables come from the UIS. Where the statistical tables include data from other sources, these are mentioned in footnotes. The most recent UIS data on pupils, students, teachers and education expenditure presented in the tables are from the September 2018 education data release and refer to the school or financial year ending in 2017.[3] They are based on results reported to and processed by the UIS before July 2018. These statistics refer to formal education, both public and private, by level of education. The statistical tables list 209 countries and territories, all of which are UNESCO member states or associate members. Most report their data to the UIS using standard questionnaires issued by the UIS itself. For 49 countries, education data are collected by the UIS via the UIS/OECD/Eurostat (UOE) questionnaires.[4]

POPULATION DATA

The population-related indicators used in the statistical tables, including enrolment ratios, number of out-of-school children, adolescents and youth, and number of youth and adults, are based on the 2017 revision of population estimates produced by the UN Population Division (UNPD). Because of possible differences between national population estimates and those of the United Nations, these indicators may differ from those published by individual countries or by other organizations.[5] In the 2017 revision, the UNPD does not provide population data by single years of age for countries with total population of less than 90,000. For these countries, as well as some special cases, population estimates are derived from Eurostat (Demographic Statistics), the Secretariat of the Pacific Community (Statistics and Demography Programme) or national statistical offices.

ISCED CLASSIFICATION

Education data reported to the UIS are in conformity with the International Standard Classification of Education (ISCED), revised in 2011. Countries may have their own definitions of education levels that do not correspond to ISCED 2011. Differences between nationally and internationally reported education statistics may be due

1 The Inter-agency and Expert Group on SDG Indicators proposed the 11 SDG 4 global indicators. The UN Statistical Commission adopted them at its 48th session in March 2017, and the UN Economic and Social Council adopted them in June 2017.

2 The Technical Advisory Group on post-2015 education indicators originally proposed the 43 indicators. The Technical Cooperation Group (TCG), whose secretariat is at the UIS, endorsed them, with some changes to monitor progress towards the SDG 4 targets. During its meeting in Dubai in January 2018, the TCG agreed UIS would report on 33 indicators in 2018. Several indicators, including some of those for which UIS is currently reporting data, are at varying stages of methodological development.

3 This means 2016/17 for countries with a school year that overlaps two calendar years, and 2017 for those with a calendar school year.

4 The countries concerned are most European countries, non-European OECD members and a changing set of other countries. The most recent reference year for education finance for UOE countries is that ending in 2016.

5 Where obvious inconsistencies exist between enrolment reported by countries and the UN population data, the UIS may decide not to calculate or publish enrolment ratios for some or all levels of education.

to the use of nationally defined education levels rather than the ISCED level, in addition to the population issue raised above.

ESTIMATES AND MISSING DATA

Regarding statistics produced by the UIS, both observed and estimated education data are presented throughout the statistical tables. The latter are marked with subscript (i). Wherever possible, the UIS encourages countries to make their own estimates. Where this does not happen, the UIS may make its own estimates if sufficient supplementary information is available. Gaps in the tables may arise where data submitted by a country are found to be inconsistent. The UIS makes every attempt to resolve such problems with the countries concerned but reserves the final decision on omitting data it regards as problematic. If information for the year ending in 2017 is not available, data for earlier years are used. Such cases are indicated by footnotes.

AGGREGATES

Figures representing regional and other aggregates are either sums, the percentage of countries meeting some condition, medians or weighted averages, as indicated in the tables, depending on the indicator. Weighted averages take into account the relative size of the relevant population of each country, or more generally of the denominator in case of indicators that are ratios.
The aggregates are derived from both published data and imputed values, for countries for which no recent data or reliable publishable data are available. Aggregates marked with (i) in the tables are based on incomplete country coverage of reliable data (between 33% and 60% of the population [or aggregate denominator value] of a given region or country grouping). GEM Report calculated sums are flagged for incomplete coverage if less than 95% of the population of a given region or country income group is represented among the countries for which data are available.

REGIONAL AND COUNTRY INCOME GROUPS

In terms of regional groups, the statistical tables use the SDG regional classification of the UN Statistical Division (UNSD), with some adjustments. The UNSD classification includes all territories, whether independent national entities or parts of bigger entities. However, the list of countries presented in the statistical tables includes only full UNESCO member states and associate members, as well as Bermuda and Turks and Caicos Islands, non-member states that were included in the Education for All statistical tables. The UIS does not collect data for the Faroe Islands, so this territory is not included in the GEM Report despite its status as a UNESCO associate member. In terms of country income groups, the statistical tables use the World Bank groups, which are updated every 1 July.

SYMBOLS USED IN THE STATISTICAL TABLES

±n Reference year differs (e.g. -2: reference year 2015 instead of 2017).

i Estimate and/or partial coverage

- Magnitude nil or negligible

... Data not available or category not applicable

Notes by indicator (**Table I.2**), footnotes to the tables and a glossary provide additional help to interpret the data.

TABLE I.1: SDG 4 monitoring framework indicators

	Indicator	UIS reported in 2018
	Target 4.1	
4.1.1	Proportion of children and young people (a) in Grade 2 or 3; (b) at the end of primary education; and (c) at the end of lower secondary education achieving at least a minimum proficiency level in (i) reading and (ii) mathematics, by sex	Yes
4.1.2	Administration of a nationally-representative learning assessment (a) in Grade 2 or 3; (b) at the end of primary education; and (c) at the end of lower secondary education	Yes
4.1.3	Gross intake ratio to the last grade (primary education, lower secondary education)	Yes
4.1.4	Completion rate (primary education, lower secondary education, upper secondary education)	Yes
4.1.5	Out-of-school rate (primary education, lower secondary education, upper secondary education)	Yes
4.1.6	Percentage of children over-age for grade (primary education, lower secondary education)	Yes
4.1.7	Number of years of (a) free and (b) compulsory primary and secondary education guaranteed in legal frameworks	Yes
	Target 4.2	
4.2.1	Proportion of children under 5 years of age who are developmentally on track in health, learning and psychosocial well-being, by sex	Yes
4.2.2	Participation rate in organized learning (one year before the official primary entry age), by sex	Yes
4.2.3	Percentage of children under 5 years experiencing positive and stimulating home learning environments	No
4.2.4	Gross early childhood education enrolment ratio in (a) pre-primary education and (b) and early childhood educational development	Yes
4.2.5	Number of years of (a) free and (b) compulsory pre-primary education guaranteed in legal frameworks	Yes
	Target 4.3	
4.3.1	Participation rate of youth and adults in formal and non-formal education and training in the previous 12 months, by sex	Yes
4.3.2	Gross enrolment ratio for tertiary education by sex	Yes
4.3.3	Participation rate in technical-vocational programmes (15- to 24-year-olds) by sex	Yes
	Target 4.4	
4.4.1	Proportion of youth and adults with information and communications technology (ICT) skills, by type of skill	Yes
4.4.2	Percentage of youth/adults who have achieved at least a minimum level of proficiency in digital literacy skills	No
4.4.3	Youth/adult educational attainment rates by age group, economic activity status, levels of education and programme orientation	Yes
	Target 4.5	
4.5.1	Parity indices (female/male, rural/urban, bottom/top wealth quintile and others such as disability status, indigenous peoples and conflict-affected, as data become available) for all education indicators on this list that can be disaggregated	Yes
4.5.2	Percentage of students in primary education whose first or home language is the language of instruction	No
4.5.3	Extent to which explicit formula-based policies reallocate education resources to disadvantaged populations	No
4.5.4	Education expenditure per student by level of education and source of funding	Yes
4.5.5	Percentage of total aid to education allocated to least developed countries	Yes
	Target 4.6	
4.6.1	Percentage of population in a given age group achieving at least a fixed level of proficiency in functional (a) literacy and (b) numeracy skills, by sex	Yes
4.6.2	Youth/adult literacy rate	Yes
4.6.3	Participation rate of illiterate youth/adults in literacy programmes	Yes
	Target 4.7	
4.7.1	Extent to which (i) global citizenship education and (ii) education for sustainable development, including gender equality and human rights, are mainstreamed at all levels in: (a) national education policies, (b) curricula, (c) teacher education and (d) student assessment	No
4.7.2	Percentage of schools that provide life skills-based HIV and sexuality education	Yes
4.7.3	Extent to which the framework on the World Programme on Human Rights Education is implemented nationally (as per the UNGA Resolution 59/113)	No
4.7.4	Percentage of students by age group (or education level) showing adequate understanding of issues relating to global citizenship and sustainability	No
4.7.5	Percentage of 15-year-old students showing proficiency in knowledge of environmental science and geoscience	No
	Target 4.a	
4.a.1	Proportion of schools with access to: (a) electricity; (b) Internet for pedagogical purposes; (c) computers for pedagogical purposes; (d) adapted infrastructure and materials for students with disabilities; (e) basic drinking water; (f) single-sex basic sanitation facilities; and (g) basic handwashing facilities (as per the WASH indicator definitions)	Yes
4.a.2	Percentage of students experiencing bullying, corporal punishment, harassment, violence, sexual discrimination and abuse	Yes
4.a.3	Number of attacks on students, personnel and institutions	Yes
	Target 4.b	
4.b.1	Volume of official development assistance flows for scholarships by sector and type of study	Yes
4.b.2	Number of higher education scholarships awarded by beneficiary country	No
	Target 4.c	
4.c.1	Proportion of teachers in: (a) pre-primary education; (b) primary education; (c) lower secondary education; and (d) upper secondary education who have received at least the minimum organized teacher training (e.g., pedagogical training) pre-service or in-service required for teaching at the relevant level in a given country, by sex	Yes
4.c.2	Pupil-trained teacher ratio by education level	Yes
4.c.3	Proportion of teachers qualified according to national standards by education level and type of institution	Yes
4.c.4	Pupil-qualified teacher ratio by education level	Yes
4.c.5	Average teacher salary relative to other professions requiring a comparable level of qualification	No
4.c.6	Teacher attrition rate by education level	Yes
4.c.7	Percentage of teachers who received in-service training in the last 12 months by type of training	No

Notes: Global indicators are highlighted in grey. UNGA = UN General Assembly; WASH = water, sanitation and hygiene.
Source: UIS.

TABLE I.2: Notes on indicators in the statistical tables

	Indicator Notes
	Table 1
A	**Compulsory education by level** Number of years during which children are legally obliged to attend school.
B	**Free years of education, by level** Number of years during which children are legally guaranteed to attend school free of charge.
C	**Official primary school starting age** The official age at which students are expected to enter primary school. This is expressed in whole years, not accounting for cutoff dates other than the beginning of the school year. The official entrance age to a given programme or level is typically, but not always, the most common entrance age.
D	**Duration of each education level** Number of grades or years in a given level of education.
E	**Official school-age population by level** Population of the age group officially corresponding to a given level of education, whether enrolled in school or not.
F	**Total absolute enrolment by level** Individuals officially registered in a given educational programme, or stage or module thereof, regardless of age.
G	**Initial government expenditure on education as percentage of GDP** Total general (local, regional and central, current and capital) initial government funding of education includes transfers paid (such as scholarships to students), but excludes transfers received, in this case international transfers to government for education (when foreign donors provide education sector budget support or other support integrated in the government budget).
H	**Expenditure on education as percentage of total government expenditure** Total general (local, regional and central) government expenditure on education (current, capital and transfers), expressed as a percentage of total general government expenditure on all sectors (including health, education, social services, etc.). It includes expenditure funded by transfers from international sources to government.
I	**Initial government expenditure per pupil by level, in constant 2015 PPP US$ and as percentage of GDP per capita** Total general (local, regional and central, current and capital) initial government funding of education per student, which includes transfers paid (such as scholarships to students), but excludes transfers received, in this case international transfers to government for education (when foreign donors provide education sector budget support or other support integrated in the government budget).
J	**Initial household expenditure on education as percentage of GDP** Total payments by households (pupils, students and their families) for educational institutions (such as tuition fees, exam and registration fees, contribution to parent-teacher associations or other school funds, and fees for canteen, boarding and transport) and purchases outside of educational institutions (such as for uniforms, textbooks, teaching materials or private classes). 'Initial funding' means that government transfers to households, such as scholarships and other financial aid for education, are subtracted from what is spent by households.
	Table 2
A	**Out-of-school children, total number and as percentage of corresponding age group** Children in the official school age range who are not enrolled in either primary or secondary school.
B	**Education completion rate by level** Percentage of children aged three to five years older than the official age of entry into the last grade of an education level who have reached the last grade of that level. For example, the primary completion rate in a country with a six-year cycle where the official age of entry into the last grade is 11 years is the percentage of 14- to 16-year-olds who have reached grade 6.
C	**Percentage of pupils over-age for grade by level** The percentage of pupils in each level of education whose age is two years or more above the intended age for their grade.
D	**Gross enrolment ratio in primary education** Total enrolment in primary education, regardless of age, expressed as a percentage of the population in the official age group. It can exceed 100% because of early or late entry and/or grade repetition.
E	**Primary adjusted net enrolment rate** Enrolment of the official age group for primary education either at that level or the levels above, expressed as a percentage of the population in that age group.
F	**Gross intake ratio to last grade of primary education** Total number of new entrants to the last grade of primary education, regardless of age, expressed as a percentage of the population at the official school entrance age for that grade.
G	**Effective transition from primary to lower secondary general education** Number of new entrants to the first grade of lower secondary education in the following year expressed as a percentage of the students enrolled in the last grade of primary education in the given year who do not repeat that grade the following year.
H	**Lower secondary total net enrolment rate** Number of pupils of the official school age group for lower secondary education who are enrolled in any level of education, expressed as a percentage of the corresponding school age population.
I	**Gross intake ratio to last grade of lower secondary education** Total number of new entrants to the last grade of lower secondary education, regardless of age, expressed as a percentage of the population at the official school entrance age for that grade.
J	**Upper secondary total net enrolment rate** Number of pupils of the official school age group for upper secondary education who are enrolled in any level of education, expressed as a percentage of the corresponding school age population.
K	**Administration of nationally representative learning assessment in early grades (grade 2 or 3), or final grade of primary or lower secondary** The definition includes any nationally representative, national or cross-national formative low-stakes learning assessment.
L	**Percentage of students achieving at least a minimum proficiency level in reading and mathematics** The minimum proficiency level in reading and mathematics is defined by each assessment. Data need to be interpreted with caution since the different assessments are not comparable. In the absence of assessments conducted in the proposed grade, surveys of student learning achievement in the grade below or above the proposed indicator grade are used as placeholders.

Table 3

A **Percentage of children aged 36 to 59 months who are developmentally on track in health, learning and psychosocial well-being**
The UNICEF Early Childhood Development Index (ECDI) is collected through the UNICEF Multiple Indicator Cluster Surveys (MICS) and is a measure of fulfilment of developmental potential that assesses children aged 36 to 59 months in four domains: (a) literacy-numeracy, (b) physical development, (c) social-emotional development and (d) learning (ability to follow simple instructions, ability to occupy themselves independently). The percentage of children who are developmentally on track overall is the percentage of children on track in at least three of the four domains. (*Source:* UNICEF MICS.)

B **Under-5 moderate or severe stunting rate**
Proportion of children in a given age group whose height for their age is below minus two standard deviations from median height for age established by the National Center for Health Statistics and the World Health Organization (WHO). (*Source:* May 2018 UNICEF, WHO and World Bank Joint Child Malnutrition Estimates. Regional aggregates are weighted averages of statistical estimates for the reference year, not of the observed country values in the country table.)

C **Percentage of children aged 36 to 59 months experiencing positive and stimulating home learning environments**
Percentage of children 36 to 59 months old with whom an adult has engaged in four or more of the following activities to promote learning and school readiness in the previous three days: (a) reading books to the child, (b) telling stories to the child, (c) singing songs to the child, (d) taking the child outside the home, (e) playing with the child and (f) spending time with the child naming, counting or drawing things. (*Source:* UNICEF MICS.)

D **Percentage of children under 5 years living in households with three or more children's books**
Percentage of children aged 0 to 59 months who have three or more books or picture books. (*Source:* UNICEF MICS.)

E **Gross early childhood education enrolment ratio in pre-primary education**
Total enrolment in pre-primary education, regardless of age, expressed as a percentage of the population in the official age group. It can exceed 100% because of early or late entry

F **Adjusted net enrolment rate one year before the official primary school entry age**
Enrolment of children one year before official primary school entry age in pre-primary or primary education, expressed as a percentage of the population in that age group.

Table 4

A **Participation rate in adult education and training**
Participation rate of adults (aged 25 to 64) in formal or non-formal education and training in the last 12 months.

B **Percentage of youth enrolled in technical and vocational education**
Youth (aged 15 to 24) enrolled in technical and vocational education at ISCED levels 2 to 5, as a percentage of the total population of that age group.

C **Share of technical and vocational education in total enrolment by level**
Total number of students enrolled in vocational programmes at a given level of education, expressed as a percentage of the total number of students enrolled in all programmes (vocational and general) at that level.

D **Transition from upper secondary to tertiary education (ISCED levels 5, 6 and 7 combined)**
Gross transition ratio from secondary to tertiary education, based on students in all secondary programmes.

E **Gross entry ratio to first tertiary programmes (ISCED levels 5 to 7)**
Students who, during the course of the reference school or academic year, enter a programme at a given level of education for the first time, irrespective of whether the students enter the programme at the beginning or at an advanced stage.

F **Gross enrolment ratio in tertiary education**
Total enrolment in tertiary education, regardless of age, expressed as a percentage of the population in the five-year age group above the official graduation age from upper secondary. It can exceed 100% because of early or late entry and prolonged study.

G **Percentage of adults (15 and over) with specific ICT skills**
Individuals are considered to have such skills if they have undertaken certain computer-related activities in the last three months: copying or moving a file or folder; using copy and paste tools to duplicate or move information within a document; using basic arithmetic formulas in a spreadsheet; writing a computer program using a specialized programming language. (*Sources:* Eurostat database; ITU World Telecommunication/ICT Indicators database.)

H **Percentage of adults (25 and over) who have attained at least a given level of education**
Number of persons aged 25 and above by the highest level of education attained, expressed as a percentage of the total population in that age group. Primary refers to ISCED 1 or higher, lower secondary to ISCED 2 or higher, upper secondary to ISCED 3 or higher and post-secondary to ISCED 4 or higher.

I **Percentage of population of a given age group achieving at least a fixed level of proficiency in functional literacy/numeracy skills**
The threshold level corresponds to level 2 on the Programme for the International Assessment of Adult Competencies scale

J **Youth (15 to 24)/Adult (15 and above) literacy rate**
K **and Number of youth (15 to 24)/adult (15 and above) illiterates**
Number of literate youth (15 to 24) and adults (15 and above), expressed as a percentage of the total population in that age group. Literacy data are for 2010–2016 and include both national observed data from censuses or household surveys and UIS estimates. The latter are based on the most recent national observed data and the Global Age-specific Literacy Projections (GALP) model. As definitions and methodologies used for data collection differ by country, data need to be used with caution.

Table 5

Adjusted gender parity index, by indicator
The gender parity index (GPI) is the ratio of female to male values of a given indicator. If the female value is less than or equal to the male value, adjusted gender parity index (GPIA) = GPI. If the female value is greater than the male value, GPIA = 2 - 1/GPI. This ensures the GPIA is symmetrical around 1 and limited to a range between 0 and 2. A GPIA equal to 1 indicates parity between females and males. (*Sources:* UIS database; GEM Report team calculations based on national and international household surveys.)

A **Completion rate, by level**

B **Percentage of students with minimum level of proficiency at the end of given level**

C **Youth and adult literacy rate**

D **Percentage of adults (16 and over) achieving at least a fixed level of proficiency in functional literacy and numeracy skills**

E **Gross enrolment ratio, by level**

Location and wealth disparity
The location parity index is the ratio of rural to urban values of a given indicator. The wealth parity index is the ratio of the poorest 20% to the richest 20% of values of a given indicator.

F **Completion rate, by level**

G **Percentage of students with minimum level of proficiency at the end of given level**

	Table 6
A	**Inclusion in national curricula frameworks of issues relating to global citizenship and sustainable development** Curricula referred to are for primary education, lower secondary education or both. The degree of inclusion of the issue in curricula is assessed as 'Low' if 1–2 of the 5 items are covered, 'Medium' if 3 are covered and 'High' if 4–5 are covered, while 'None' indicates no inclusion of any items. Aggregates reflect the percentage of countries at 'Medium' or higher. (*Source:* UNESCO-IBE, 2016.) Key terms for 'Gender equality' are: (a) gender equality, (b) gender equity, (c) empowerment of girls/women, (d) gender sensitivity and (e) gender parity. Key terms for 'Human rights' are: (a) human rights, rights and responsibilities (children's rights, cultural rights, indigenous rights, women's rights, disability rights); (b) freedom (of expression, of speech, of press, of association or organization) and civil liberties; (c) social justice; (d) democracy/democratic rule, democratic values/principles; and (e) human rights education. Key terms for 'Sustainable development' are: (a) sustainable, sustainability, sustainable development; (b) economic sustainability, sustainable growth, sustainable production/consumption, green economy; (c) social sustainability (social cohesion and sustainability); (d) environmental sustainability/environmentally sustainable; (e) climate change/variability (global warming, carbon emissions/footprint); (f) renewable energy/fuels, alternative energy sources (solar, tidal, wind, wave, geothermal, biomass); (g) ecosystems, ecology (biodiversity, biosphere, biomes, loss of diversity); (h) waste management, recycling; (i) education for sustainable development, sustainability education, education for sustainability; and (j) environmental education/studies, education for the environment, education for environmental sustainability. Key terms for 'Global citizenship' are: (a) globalization; (b) global citizen(ship)/culture/identity/community; (c) global-local thinking, local-global act); (d) multicultural(ism)/intercultural(ism); (e) migration, immigration, mobility, movement of people; (f) global competition/competitiveness, globally competitive, international competitiveness; (g) global inequality/disparity; (h) national/local citizenship/culture/identity/culture/heritage; global citizenship education; and (i) education for global citizenship.
B	**Percentage of schools providing life skills-based HIV/AIDS education** Percentage of lower secondary schools providing life skills-based HIV/AIDS education (all institutions).
C	**Percentage of 15-year-old students performing at or above level 2 of proficiency in scientific literacy** Scientific literacy is defined as (a) scientific knowledge and its use to identify questions, acquire new knowledge, explain scientific phenomena and draw evidence-based conclusions about science-related issues; (b) understanding of the characteristic features of science as a form of human knowledge and enquiry; (c) awareness of how science and technology shape the material, intellectual and cultural environments; and (d) willingness to engage in science-related issues, and with the ideas of science, as a reflective citizen. (*Source:* OECD PISA, 2015; TIMMS.) **Percentage of students and youth with adequate understanding of HIV/AIDS and sexuality** Youth (aged 15 to 24) who know at least two ways to prevent infection and reject at least three misconceptions. (*Source:* UNAIDS.)
D	**Percentage of schools with basic drinking water, basic (single-sex) sanitation or toilets, and basic handwashing facilities** Basic drinking water means drinking water from an improved source, and water available at the school at the time of the survey. Basic sanitation or toilets means improved sanitation facilities at the school that are single-sex and usable (available, functional and private) at the time of the survey. Basic handwashing facilities means handwashing facilities with water and soap available at the school at the time of the survey. (*Source:* UNICEF WASH in Schools, 2018.)
E	**Percentage of primary schools with:** **Electricity** Regularly and readily available sources of power that enable adequate and sustainable use of ICT infrastructure by pupils and teachers to support course delivery or independent teaching and learning needs. **Internet used for pedagogical purposes** Internet that is available for enhancing teaching and learning and is accessible by pupils irrespective of the device used. Access can be via a fixed narrowband, fixed broadband or mobile network. **Computers** Use of computers to support course delivery or independent teaching and learning needs, including to meet information needs for research purposes, develop presentations, perform hands-on exercises and experiments, share information and participate in online discussion forums for educational purposes. Desktops, laptops and tablets are covered by the definition.
F	**Percentage of public primary schools with access to adapted infrastructure and materials for students with disabilities** Any built environment related to education facilities that are accessible to all users, including those with various types of disability, enabling everyone to gain access to and exit from them. Accessibility includes ease of independent approach, entry, evacuation and/or use of a building and its services and facilities (such as water and sanitation), by all of the building's potential users with an assurance of individual health, safety and welfare during the course of their activities.
G	**Level of bullying** Harmonized classification of overall risk of bullying according to the UNICEF Innocenti Global Bullying Database, combining data from six international surveys on bullying prevalence among 11- to 15-year-olds in 145 countries (*Source:* Richardson and Hiu, 2018; see Chapter 15.)
H	**Level of attacks on students, teachers or institutions** Categorical ranking of the extent to which a country is affected by violent attacks, threats or deliberate use of force in a given period (e.g. the last 12 months, a school year or a calendar year) directed against students, teachers and other personnel or against education buildings, materials and facilities, including transport. The indicator focuses on attacks carried out for political, military, ideological, sectarian, ethnic or religious reasons by armed forces or non-state armed groups. Five levels are captured: No incidents reported: No reports of attacks on education were identified. Sporadic: Fewer than five reported attacks, or fewer than five students and education personnel harmed. Affected: 5–99 reported attacks on education or 5–99 students and education personnel harmed. Heavily affected: 100–199 reported attacks or 100–199 students and education personnel harmed. Very heavily affected: More than 200 reported attacks or more than 200 students and education personnel harmed.
I	**Internationally mobile students, inbound and outbound numbers enrolled and mobility rates** Number of students from abroad studying in a given country, expressed as a percentage of total tertiary enrolment in that country. Number of students from a given country studying abroad, expressed as a percentage of total tertiary enrolment in that country.
J	**Volume of official development assistance for scholarships** Total gross disbursement of official development assistance flows (all sectors) for scholarships (all levels). The sum of the values of regions and country income groups does not add up to the global total because some aid is not allocated by country. **Imputed student costs** Costs incurred by donor countries' higher education institutions when they receive students from developing countries.

	Table 7
A	**Number of classroom teachers** Persons employed full-time or part-time in an official capacity to guide and direct the learning experience of pupils and students, irrespective of their qualifications or the delivery mechanism, i.e. face-to-face and/or at a distance. This definition excludes educational personnel who have no active teaching duties (e.g. headmasters, headmistresses or principals who do not teach) or who work occasionally or in a voluntary capacity in educational institutions.
B	**Pupil/teacher ratio** Average number of pupils per teacher at a given level of education, based on headcounts of both pupils and teachers.
C	**Percentage of trained classroom teachers** Trained teachers are defined as those who have received at least the minimum organized and recognized pre-service and in-service pedagogical training required to teach at a given level of education. Data are not collected for UOE countries.
D	**Percentage of qualified classroom teachers** Qualified teachers are defined as those who have the minimum academic qualification necessary to teach at a specific level of education according to national standards.
E	**Teacher attrition rate** Number of teachers at a given level of education leaving the profession in a given school year, expressed as a percentage of teachers at that level and in that school year.
F	**Relative teacher salary level** Teacher salary relative to other professionals with equivalent academic qualification. Data refer to actual salaries of all teachers relative to earnings for full-time, full-year workers with tertiary education (ISCED 5 to 8). The indicator is defined as a ratio of salary, using annual average salaries (including bonuses and allowances) of teachers in public institutions relative to the wages of workers with similar educational attainment (weighted average) and to the wages of full-time, full-year workers aged 25 to 64 with tertiary education. Values for secondary education are GEM Report team calculations and represent averages of lower and upper secondary values weighted by the number of teachers at each level.

Notes: ITU = International Telecommunication Union; PISA = Programme for International Student Assessment; PPP = purchasing power parity.
Source: GEM Report team drawing on UIS and other definitions.

TABLE 1: Education system characteristics and education expenditure

	EDUCATION SYSTEMS																
	A		B		C	D				E				F			
	Compulsory		Free		Official primary school starting age	Duration (years)				School-age population (000,000)				Enrolment (000,000)			
	1 year of pre-primary	9 years of primary-secondary	1 year of pre-primary	12 years of primary-secondary		Pre-primary	Primary	Lower secondary	Upper secondary	Pre-primary	Primary	Secondary	Tertiary	Pre-primary	Primary	Secondary	Tertiary
SDG indicator	4.2.5	4.1.7	4.2.5	4.1.7													
Reference year	2017																
Region	% of countries				Median					Sum							
World	22	73	45	50	6	3	6	3	3	352	717	771	583 i	177 i	746 i	591 i	221 i
Sub-Saharan Africa	2	44	15	22	6	3	6	3	3	76	168	139	89 i	24 i	165 i	59 i	8 i
Northern Africa and Western Asia	12	88	33	62	6	3	6	3	3	24	54	56	42 i	8 i	55 i	45 i	19 i
Northern Africa	-	83	17	33	6	2	6	3	3	10	27	24	20 i	4 i	27	20 i	7 i
Western Asia	17	89	39	72	6	3	6	3	3	15	27	31	22 i	4 i	27 i	26 i	12 i
Central and Southern Asia	7	64	50	46	6	3	5	4	3	103	189	254	175 i	25 i	210 i	183 i	44 i
Central Asia	20	100	100	40	7	4	4	5	2	6	5	8	6	2	5	8	1
Southern Asia	-	44	22	50	6	2	5	3	4	97	184	246	169 i	23 i	205 i	175 i	42 i
Eastern and South-eastern Asia	22	72	31	31	6	3	6	3	3	81	175	170	154	65	180	149	71
Eastern Asia	29	100	43	43	6	3	6	3	3	57	110	107	99	49	112	96	52
South-eastern Asia	18	55	22	22	6	3	6	3	3	23	65	63	55	16	69	52	19
Oceania	18	59	55 i	64 i	6	2	6	4	3	1	4	4	3 i	1 i	4 i	4 i	2 i
Latin America and the Caribbean	56	83	70	62	6	2	6	3	2	28	60	67	54 i	21 i	65 i	64 i	27 i
Caribbean	27	82	50	61	5	2	6	3	2	2	4 i	4	3	1	3	2	1 i
Central America	100	86	86	43	6	3	6	3	2	10	19	19	16	6	19	17	5
South America	83	83	92	75	6	3	6	3	3	16	35	44	34	11	38	44	18
Europe and Northern America	24	93	57	62	6	3	6	3	3	39	67	81	65 i	33 i	68 i	86 i	50 i
Europe	23	93	54	59	6	3	5	4	3	26	39	53	41 i	24 i	40 i	59 i	29 i
Northern America	33	100	100	100	6	2	6	3	3	13	27	27	24 i	9 i	28 i	27 i	21 i
Low income	3	41	26	19	6	3	6	3	3	59	118	102	65 i	13 i	118 i	42 i	6 i
Middle income	23	69	41	45	6	3	6	3	3	253	518	579	443 i	131 i	545 i	452 i	158 i
Lower middle	17	61	30	36	6	3	6	3	3	149	319	370	264 i	54 i	339 i	258 i	64 i
Upper middle	27	76	51	53	6	3	6	3	3	103	199	210	179	77	206	194 i	93 i
High income	32	91	58	68	6	3	6	3	3	40	81	89	74 i	33 i	83 i	97 i	57 i

A Years of compulsory education, by level.
B Years of free education, by level.
C Official primary school starting age.
D Official duration of education levels in years.
E Official school-age population by level (million) (for tertiary: the five years following upper secondary).
F Total absolute enrolment by level (million).
G Initial government expenditure on education as % of gross domestic product (GDP).
H Government expenditure on education as % of total government expenditure.
I Initial government expenditure per pupil by level, in constant 2015 purchasing power parity US$ and as % of GDP per capita.
J Initial household expenditure on education as % of GDP.

Notes:
Source: UIS unless noted otherwise. Data refer to school year ending in 2017 unless noted otherwise.
Aggregates represent countries listed in the table with available data and may include estimates for countries with no recent data.
(-) Magnitude nil or negligible.
(...) Data not available or category not applicable.
(± n) Reference year differs (e.g. -2: reference year 2015 instead of 2017).
(i) Estimate and/or partial coverage.

FINANCE										
G	H	I								J
		Government education expenditure per pupil								
		2015 PPP US$				% of GDP per capita				
Government education expenditure (% of GDP)	Education share of total government expenditure (%)	Pre-primary	Primary	Secondary	Tertiary	Pre-primary	Primary	Secondary	Tertiary	Household education expenditure (% of GDP)
	1.a.2	4.5.4								
2017										
Median										
4.4	14.1	1,126 i	2,028 i	2,716 i	4,322 i	12 i	16 i	20 i	30 i	...
4.3	16.5	81 i	268 i	476 i	2,485 i	2 i	12	19 i	85 i	...
3.8 i	12.3 i	1,203 i	4,392 i	4,911 i	5,150 i	11 i	15 i	18 i	22 i	...
...	...	- i	1,271 i	3,789 i	3,164 i	- i	15 i	33 i	28 i	...
3.7	11.7 i	3,962 i	6,458 i	5,243 i	5,456 i	13 i	15 i	18 i	22 i	1.0 i
3.9	15.7	338	764 i	1,048	1,951	5	10 i	13	27	...
5.8	17.5	1,019 i	...	3,268 i	557 i	28 i	...	28 i	10 i	0.8 i
3.8	14.5	52	764	696	2,500	1	10	11	30	...
3.4	13.5	1,226 i	2,645	7,700 i	6,165	5 i	13	20 i	21	...
3.6 i	13.5 i	3,730 i	8,675 i	11,155 i	8,499	14 i	15 i	29 i	19 i	0.4 i
3.3	15.4	489 i	1,303	1,996 i	2,859 i	3	9	12 i	21	...
4.7 i	14.1 i	...	...	...	...	...	13 i	...	...	...
5.1	18.0 i	991 i	1,800 i	2,287 i	2,517 i	12 i	16 i	19 i	25 i	...
5.1 i	16.3 i	...	2,005 i	2,769 i	...	5 i	16 i	21 i	...	...
4.8	20.4	791 i	1,221	1,130	1,852	13 i	16	16	38	2.2 i
5.2	16.5	1,619 i	1,582	2,237	3,217 i	15	17	18	20 i	1.2 i
4.8	11.6	5,761	7,416	7,890	8,621	18	21	23	27	0.4 i
4.8	11.6	5,632	6,881	7,858	7,948	18	22	23	27	0.4 i
3.2	10.6	6,522 i	9,447	12,090 i	14,076	15	18	17	21	1.2 i
4.0	16.1	52 i	194 i	276 i	1,675 i	2 i	11 i	17 i	103 i	...
4.3	15.6	631 i	1,433 i	1,774 i	2,714 i	8 i	15 i	17 i	27 i	...
4.5	16.4	434 i	985 i	1,104 i	2,029 i	8 i	13 i	17 i	37 i	...
4.1	13.9	991 i	2,155 i	2,498 i	3,185 i	7 i	16 i	17 i	23 i	...
4.9	12.9	5,311 i	7,990 i	8,955 i	10,801	17	19	23	26	0.6 i

TABLE 1: Continued

	EDUCATION SYSTEMS																
	A		B		C	D				E				F			
	Compulsory		Free			Duration (years)				School-age population (000,000)				Enrolment (000,000)			
	Years of pre-primary	Years of primary-secondary	Years of pre-primary	Years of primary-secondary	Official primary school starting age	Pre-primary	Primary	Lower secondary	Upper secondary	Pre-primary	Primary	Secondary	Tertiary	Pre-primary	Primary	Secondary	Tertiary
SDG indicator	4.2.5	4.1.7	4.2.5	4.1.7													
Reference year	2017																
Sub-Saharan Africa																	
Angola	-	6	-	-	6	1	6	3	3	1	5_{+1}	4_{+1}	3_{-2}	1_{-1}	6_{-2}	2_{-1}	0.2_{-2}
Benin	-	6	-	6	6	2	6	4	3	1	2_{+1}	2_{+1}	1_{-1}	0.2_{-1}	2	1_{-1}	0.1_{-1}
Botswana	-	-	...	...	6	3	7	3	2	0.2	0.3_{+1}	0.2_{+1}	0.2	$-_{-3}$	0.3_{-3}	...	0.1
Burkina Faso	-	11	-	10	6	3	6	4	3	2	3_{+1}	3_{+1}	2	0.1	3	1	0.1
Burundi	$-_{-1}$	$-_{-1}$	...	...	7	2	6	4	3	1	2_{+1}	2_{+1}	1	0.1	2	1	0.1
Cabo Verde	-	10	-	8	6	3	6	3	3	-	0.1_{+1}	0.1_{+1}	0.1	-	0.1	0.1	-
Cameroon	-	6	-	6	6	2	6	4	3	1	4_{+1}	4_{+1}	2_{-1}	1	4	2_{-1}	0.4_{-1}
Central African Republic	-	10	-	13	6	3	6	4	3	0.4	1_{+1}	1_{+1}	0.4_{-3}	-	1_{-1}	0.1	...
Chad	-	10	-	10	6	3	6	4	3	1	3_{+1}	3_{+1}	1_{-3}	$-_{-1}$	2_{-1}	1_{-1}	$-_{-3i}$
Comoros	-	6	-	6	6	3	6	4	3	0.1	0.1_{+1}	0.1_{+1}	0.1	-	0.1	0.1	$-_{-3}$
Congo	-	10	3	13	6	3	6	4	3	0.5	1_{+1}	1_{+1}	0.4_{-3}	...	...	...	$-_{-4}$
Côte d'Ivoire	$-_{-1}$	10_{-1}	$-_{-1}$	10_{-1}	6	3	6	4	3	2	4_{+1}	4_{+1}	2_{-1}	0.2	4	2	0.2_{-1}
D. R. Congo	-	6	-	6	6	3	6	2	4	8	14_{+1}	11_{+1}	7_{-1}	0.3_{-2}	14_{-2}	5_{-2}	0.5_{-1}
Djibouti	-	10	2	12	6	2	5	4	3	-	0.1_{+1}	0.1_{+1}	0.1_{-3}	-	0.1	0.1	...
Equat. Guinea	-	6	-	6	7	3	6	4	2	0.1	0.2_{+1}	0.1_{+1}	0.1_{-3}	$-_{-2}$	0.1_{-2}	...	...
Eritrea	-	8	$-_{-1}$	8_{-1}	6	2	5	3	4	0.3	1_{+1}	1_{+1}	0.4_{-1}	-	0.3	0.2	$-_{-1}$
Eswatini	-	7	-	7	6	3	7	3	2	0.1	0.2_{+1}	0.2_{+1}	0.2_{-2}	...	0.2_{-1}	0.1_{-1}	$-_{-4}$
Ethiopia	-	8	-	8	7	3	6	4	2	9	16_{+1}	15_{+1}	9_{-3}	3_{-2}	16_{-2}	5_{-2}	1_{-3}
Gabon	-	10	-	10	6	3	5	4	3	0.2	0.2_{+1}	0.3_{+1}	0.2_{-3}	...	...	...	...
Gambia	-	9	-	9	7	4	6	3	3	0.3	0.3_{+1}	0.3_{+1}	0.2_{-3}	0.1	0.3	...	...
Ghana	2	9	-	9	6	2	6	3	4	2	4_{+1}	4_{+1}	3	2	4	3	0.4
Guinea	$-_{-1}$	6_{-1}	$-_{-1}$	6_{-1}	7	3	6	4	3	1	2_{+1}	2_{+1}	1_{-3}	...	2_{-1}	1_{-3}	0.1_{-3}
Guinea-Bissau	$-_{-1}$	9_{-1}	...	...	6	3	6	3	3	0.2	0.3_{+1}	0.2_{+1}	0.2_{-3}	...	...	...	...
Kenya	-	12	-	12	6	3	6	2	4	4	8_{+1}	7_{+1}	5_{-1}	3_{-1}	8_{-1}	...	1_{-1}
Lesotho	-	7	-	7	6	3	7	3	2	0.2	0.4_{+1}	0.2_{+1}	0.2_{-1}	0.1_{-1}	0.4	0.1	$-_{-2}$
Liberia	-	6	-	6	6	3	6	3	3	0.4	1_{+1}	1_{+1}	0.4_{-3}	1_{-1}	1_{-1}	0.2_{-1}	...
Madagascar	-	5	3	12	6	3	5	4	3	2	3_{+1}	4_{+1}	3_{-1}	1	5_{-1}	2	0.1_{-1}
Malawi	-	8	$-_{-1}$	8_{-1}	6	3	6	4	2	2	3_{+1}	3_{+1}	2_{-3}	1_{-2}	4	1	...
Mali	-	9	4	12	7	4	6	3	3	2	3_{+1}	3_{+1}	2_{-2}	0.1	3	1	0.1_{-2}
Mauritania	-	9	3	13	6	3	6	4	3	0.4	1_{+1}	1_{+1}	0.4	$-_{-2}$	1	0.2	-
Mauritius	-	11	-	13	5	2	6	3	4	-	0.1_{+1}	0.1_{+1}	0.1	-	0.1	0.1	-
Mozambique	-	-	...	...	6	3	7	3	2	3	6_{+1}	4_{+1}	3	...	6	1	0.2
Namibia	-	7	$-_{-1}$	7_{-1}	7	2	7	3	2	0.1	0.4_{+1}	0.3_{+1}	0.3_{-1}	-	0.5	...	0.1_{-1}
Niger	-	-	...	...	7	3	6	4	3	2	4_{+1}	3_{+1}	2	0.2	3	1	0.1
Nigeria	$-_{-1}$	9_{-1}	-	9	6	1	6	3	3	6	32_{+1}	26_{+1}	16_{-3}	...	26_{-1}	10_{-1}	...
Rwanda	-	6	-	9	7	3	6	3	3	1	2_{+1}	2_{+1}	1	0.2	3	1	0.1
Sao Tome and Principe	-	6	-	6	6	3	6	3	3	-	$-_{+1}$	$-_{+1}$	-	$-_{-1}$	-	-	$-_{-2}$
Senegal	-	11	-	11	6	3	6	4	3	1	3_{+1}	2_{+1}	1	0.2	2	1	0.2
Seychelles	$-_{-1}$	10_{-1}	-	11	6	2	6	3	4	-	$-_{+1}$	$-_{+1}$	$-_{-1}$	$-_{-1}$	$-_{-1}$	$-_{-1}$	$-_{-1}$
Sierra Leone	-	9	-	9	6	3	6	3	4	1	1_{+1}	1_{+1}	1_{-3}	0.1	1	0.5	...
Somalia	$-_{-1}$	$-_{-1}$	...	...	6	3	6	2	4	1	3_{+1}	2_{+1}	1_{-3}	...	...	...	...
South Africa	-	9	-	12	7	4	7	2	3	5	8_{+1}	5_{+1}	5_{-1}	1_{-1}	8_{-1}	5_{-1}	1_{-1}
South Sudan	$-_{-1}$	8_{-1}	-	8	6	3	6	2	4	1	2_{+1}	2_{+1}	1_{-3}	0.1_{-2}	1_{-2}	0.2_{-2}	...
Togo	-	10	-	5	6	3	6	4	3	1	1_{+1}	1_{+1}	1	0.1	2	1	0.1
Uganda	-	7	...	...	6	3	7	4	2	4	9_{+1}	6_{+1}	4_{-3}	1	9	...	0.2_{-3}
United Republic of Tanzania	-	7	2	7	7	2	7	4	2	4	11_{+1}	8_{+1}	5_{-2}	2	9	2	0.2_{-1}
Zambia	$-_{-1}$	7_{-1}	-	7	7	4	7	2	3	2	3_{+1}	2_{+1}	2_{-3}	...	3_{-4}	...	...
Zimbabwe	$-_{-1}$	7_{-1}	...	...	6	2	7	2	4	1	3_{+1}	2_{+1}	2_{-2}	0.4_{-4}	3_{-4}	1_{-4}	0.1_{-2}

G	H	I								J	
FINANCE											
		Government education expenditure per pupil									
		2015 PPP US$				% of GDP per capita					
Government education expenditure (% of GDP)	Education share of total government expenditure (%)	Pre-primary	Primary	Secondary	Tertiary	Pre-primary	Primary	Secondary	Tertiary	Household education expenditure (% of GDP)	COUNTRY CODE
	1.a.2	4.5.4									
2017											
...	...	...	...	...	...	...	...	...	...	...	AGO
4.0$_{-1i}$	18.8$_{-1i}$	252$_{-2}$	194$_{-2}$	229$_{-2}$	1,544$_{-2}$	12$_{-2}$	9$_{-2}$	11$_{-2}$	73$_{-2}$	4.8$_{-4i}$	BEN
...	...	...	...	...	...	...	...	...	...	...	BWA
4.1$_{-2}$	18.0$_{-2}$	13$_{-2}$	271$_{-2}$	293$_{-2}$	2,095$_{-2}$	1$_{-2}$	16$_{-2}$	17$_{-2}$	123$_{-2}$	...	BFA
4.3$_{i}$	19.9$_{i}$	2$_{-4}$	98$_{-4}$	236$_{-4}$	2,363$_{-4}$	0.3$_{-4}$	12$_{-4}$	28$_{-4}$	281$_{-4}$	...	BDI
5.2	16.8	84	1,133	1,338	2,607	1	17	20	39	...	CPV
3.1$_{i}$	16.4$_{i}$	...	...	...	627$_{-4}$	...	...	...	19$_{-4}$	...	CMR
...	...	...	...	...	...	...	...	...	...	...	CAF
2.9$_{-4}$	12.5$_{-4}$	...	...	377$_{-4}$	...	...	...	18$_{-4}$	...	...	TCD
4.3$_{-2}$	15.3$_{-2}$	306$_{-3}$	264$_{-3}$	229$_{-3}$	671$_{-3}$	20$_{-3}$	17$_{-3}$	15$_{-3}$	44$_{-3}$	...	COM
4.6$_{-2i}$	8.6$_{-2i}$	...	...	...	5,124$_{-4}$	...	...	...	91$_{-4}$	...	COG
4.4$_{i}$	18.7$_{i}$	782$_{-2i}$	463$_{-2i}$	811$_{-2i}$	4,268$_{-2i}$	23$_{-2i}$	13$_{-2i}$	23$_{-2i}$	124$_{-2i}$	2.3$_{-2i}$	CIV
1.5$_{i}$	10.8$_{i}$	-$_{-2}$	57$_{-4}$	42$_{-4}$	576$_{-4}$	-$_{-2}$	7$_{-4}$	5$_{-4}$	73$_{-4}$	...	COD
...	...	...	...	...	...	...	38$_{-1}$	1$_{-1}$	...	...	DJI
...	...	...	...	...	...	...	...	...	...	...	GNQ
...	...		...	...	...	...	...	...	...	...	ERI
7.1$_{-3}$	24.9$_{-3}$	...	1,596$_{-3}$	2,736$_{-3}$	12,426$_{-3}$	...	19$_{-3}$	33$_{-3}$	150$_{-3}$	...	SWZ
4.7$_{-2}$	27.1$_{-2}$	53$_{-2}$	117$_{-2}$	250$_{-2}$	3,699$_{-3}$	4$_{-2}$	8$_{-2}$	17$_{-2}$	265$_{-3}$	...	ETH
2.7$_{-3}$	11.2$_{-3}$	...	...	...	...	...	...	...	...	...	GAB
3.1$_{-1i}$	10.4$_{-1i}$	-$_{-3}$	199$_{-3}$	...	...	-$_{-3}$	12$_{-3}$	...	...	...	GMB
4.5$_{i}$	20.2$_{i}$	92$_{-3}$	326$_{-3}$	1,078$_{-3}$	3,082$_{-3}$	2$_{-3}$	8$_{-3}$	26$_{-3}$	75$_{-3}$	...	GHA
2.2	14.4	...	144$_{-1}$	161$_{-3}$	1,754$_{-3}$	...	7$_{-1}$	9$_{-3}$	95$_{-3}$	...	GIN
1.1$_{-4}$	16.2$_{-4}$	...	...	...	...	...	...	...	...	...	GNB
5.2$_{i}$	16.9$_{i}$	40$_{-2}$	313$_{-2}$	...	2,184$_{-2}$	1$_{-2}$	11$_{-2}$	...	75$_{-2}$	...	KEN
6.4$_{+1}$	...	...	649$_{+1}$	940$_{+1}$	...	...	22$_{+1}$	31$_{+1}$	...	...	LSO
3.8$_{i}$	7.0$_{i}$	...	...	...	...	...	...	...	...	...	LBR
2.6$_{-2i}$	17.0$_{-2i}$	...	...	...	564$_{-1}$	...	...	...	38$_{-1}$	...	MDG
4.0$_{i}$	14.3$_{i}$	-$_{-1}$	98$_{-1}$	289$_{-1}$	...	-$_{-1}$	9$_{-1}$	25$_{-1}$	...	...	MWI
3.8$_{-2}$	18.2$_{-2}$	41$_{-2}$	272$_{-2}$	467$_{-2}$	3,373$_{-2}$	2$_{-2}$	13$_{-2}$	23$_{-2}$	165$_{-2}$	...	MLI
2.6$_{-1i}$	9.3$_{-1i}$	-$_{-4}$	400$_{-1}$	557$_{-1}$	3,764$_{-1}$	-$_{-4}$	11$_{-1}$	15$_{-1}$	99$_{-1}$	...	MRT
5.0	19.9	570	3,243	6,588	2,009	3	16	32	10	...	MUS
5.5$_{-4}$	19.0$_{-4}$	...	141$_{-4i}$	484$_{-4i}$	1,597$_{-4}$	...	13$_{-4i}$	44$_{-4i}$	145$_{-4}$		MOZ
3.1$_{-3}$	7.0$_{-3}$	...	...	...	8,119$_{-3}$	...	...	...	79$_{-3}$	-$_{-3}$	NAM
4.5$_{i}$	16.6$_{i}$	574$_{-2}$	214$_{-2}$	621$_{-2}$	2,937$_{-2}$	59$_{-2}$	22$_{-2}$	64$_{-2}$	304$_{-2}$	...	NER
		...		...	...	...	...	...		...	NGA
3.2$_{i}$	11.1$_{i}$	311$_{-1i}$	102$_{-1i}$	693$_{-1i}$	1,897$_{-1i}$	17$_{-1i}$	6$_{-1i}$	38$_{-1i}$	111$_{-2i}$	...	RWA
5.1$_{-1}$	16.0$_{-1}$	379$_{-3}$	359$_{-3}$	258$_{-3}$	1,267$_{-3}$	12$_{-3}$	12$_{-3}$	8$_{-3}$	41$_{-3}$	0.2$_{-3i}$	STP
6.2$_{i}$	21.6$_{i}$	52$_{-1}$	390$_{-1}$	386$_{-1}$	4,831$_{-1}$	2$_{-1}$	16$_{-1}$	15$_{-1}$	191$_{-1}$	...	SEN
4.4$_{-1}$	11.7$_{-1}$	3,305$_{-1}$	3,875$_{-1}$	4,176$_{-1}$	19,298$_{-1}$	12$_{-1}$	14$_{-1}$	15$_{-1}$	71$_{-1}$	-$_{-1}$	SYC
4.6	19.8	-	71	213	...	-	5	14	...	...	SLE
...	...	...	...	...	...	...	...	...	...	...	SOM
6.1	18.7	819	2,281	2,529	6,053	6	18	20	47	...	ZAF
1.0	1.0	...	...	...	...	0.4$_{-1}$	5$_{-1}$	13$_{-1}$	...	...	SSD
5.1$_{-1}$	16.0$_{-1}$	77$_{-2}$	243$_{-1}$	...	1,179	5$_{-2}$	16$_{-1}$	...	77	...	TGO
2.6$_{i}$	12.1$_{i}$	-$_{-3}$	100$_{-3}$	...	...	-$_{-3}$	6$_{-3}$	...	...	3.9$_{-3}$	UGA
3.5$_{-3}$	17.3$_{-3}$	241$_{-3}$	250$_{-3}$	...	...	10$_{-3}$	10$_{-3}$	...	...	...	TZA
...	...	...	...	...	...	...	...	...	...	...	ZMB
7.5$_{-3}$	30.0$_{-3}$	122$_{-4}$	401$_{-4}$	637$_{-4}$	4,621$_{-4}$	6$_{-4}$	20$_{-4}$	31$_{-4}$	225$_{-4}$	...	ZWE

TABLE 1: Continued

	EDUCATION SYSTEMS																
	A		B		C	D				E				F			
	Compulsory		Free		Official primary school starting age	Duration (years)				School-age population (000,000)				Enrolment (000,000)			
	Years of pre-primary	Years of primary-secondary	Years of pre-primary	Years of primary-secondary		Pre-primary	Primary	Lower secondary	Upper secondary	Pre-primary	Primary	Secondary	Tertiary	Pre-primary	Primary	Secondary	Tertiary
SDG indicator	4.2.5	4.1.7	4.2.5	4.1.7													
Reference year	2017																
Northern Africa and Western Asia																	
Algeria	-	10	1	12	6	1	5	4	3	1	4_{+1}	4_{+1}	3	...	4	...	2
Armenia	-	12	3	12	6	3	4	5	3	0.1	0.2_{+1}	0.3_{+1}	0.2	0.1	0.2	0.2_{-2}	0.1
Azerbaijan	1	9	3	11	6	3	4	5	3	1_{i}	1_{i}	1_{i}	1_{i}	0.2	1	1	0.2
Bahrain	-	9	-	12	6	3	6	3	3	0.1	0.1_{+1}	0.1_{+1}	0.1	-	0.1	0.1	-
Cyprus	1	9	1	12	6	3	6	3	3	$-_{i}$	0.1_{i}	0.1_{i}	0.1_{-2i}	$-_{-2}$	0.1_{-2}	0.1_{-2}	$-_{-2}$
Egypt	-	12	-	12	6	2	6	3	3	5	12_{+1}	11_{+1}	8_{-1}	1	12	9	3_{-1}
Georgia	-	9	-	12	6	3	6	3	3	0.2	0.3_{+1}	0.3_{+1}	0.3	...	0.3	0.3	0.1
Iraq	-	9	-	12	6	2	6	3	3	2	6_{+1}	5_{+1}	3_{-2}	...	...	...	...
Israel	1_{-1}	12_{-1}	1_{-1}	12_{-1}	6	3	6	3	3	0.5	1_{+1}	1_{+1}	1_{-1}	1_{-1}	1_{-1}	1_{-1}	0.4_{-1}
Jordan	-	10	-	10	6	2	6	4	2	...	...	1_{+1}	1	0.1	1	1	0.3
Kuwait	-	9	-	12	6	2	5	4	3	0.1	0.3_{+1}	0.3_{+1}	0.2	0.1	0.3	0.3_{-2}	0.1_{-4}
Lebanon	-	10	-	10	6	3	6	3	3	0.3	1_{+1}	1_{+1}	1	0.2	1	0.4	0.2
Libya	$-_{-1}$	9_{-1}	$-_{-2}$	9_{-2}	6	2	6	3	3	0.2	1_{+1}	1_{+1}	1_{-3}	...	...	...	...
Morocco	-	9	-	9	6	2	6	3	3	1	4_{+1}	4_{+1}	3	1	4	3	1
Oman	-	-	-	12	6	2	6	3	3	0.1	0.4_{+1}	0.3_{+1}	0.3_{-1}	0.1	0.4	0.3	0.1_{-1}
Palestine	-	10	1	12	6	2	4	6	2	0.3	1_{+1}	1_{+1}	1	0.1	0.5	1	0.2
Qatar	-	9	-	9	6	3	6	3	3	0.1	0.1_{+1}	0.1_{+1}	0.2	-	0.1	0.1	-
Saudi Arabia	$-_{-1}$	9_{-1}	$-_{-1}$	12_{-1}	6	3	6	3	3	2	3_{+1}	3_{+1}	2_{-1}	0.4_{-1}	4_{-1}	3_{-3i}	2_{-1}
Sudan	$-_{-1}$	8_{-1}	$-_{-3}$	11_{-2}	6	2	6	2	3	2	6_{+1}	5_{+1}	4_{-2}	1_{-1}	5_{-1}	2_{-1}	1_{-2}
Syrian Arab Republic	-	9	3	12	6	3	6	3	3	1	3_{+1}	3_{+1}	2_{-1}	0.1_{-4}	2_{-4}	2_{-4}	1_{-1}
Tunisia	$-_{-1}$	9_{-1}	$-_{-1}$	11_{-1}	6	3	6	3	4	1	1_{+1}	1_{+1}	1	0.3_{-1}	1_{-1}	1_{-1}	0.3
Turkey	-	12	3	12	6	3	4	4	4	4	5_{+1}	11_{+1}	6_{-1}	1_{-1}	5_{-1}	11_{-1}	7_{-1}
United Arab Emirates	$-_{-1}$	6_{-1}	$-_{-1}$	12_{-1}	6	2	5	4	3	0.2	0.5_{+1}	1_{+1}	0.4_{-1}	0.2_{-1}	0.5_{-1}	0.4_{-1}	0.2_{-1}
Yemen	$-_{-1}$	9_{-1}	$-_{-1}$	9_{-1}	6	3	6	3	3	2	4_{+1}	4_{+1}	3_{-3}	$-_{-1}$	4_{-1}	2_{-1}	...
Central and Southern Asia																	
Afghanistan	-	9	1	12	7	1	6	3	3	1	6_{+1}	5_{+1}	3_{-2}	...	6	3	0.3_{-3}
Bangladesh	$-_{+1}$	5_{+1}	1_{+1}	...	6	3	5	3	4	9	16	23	16	4	17	15	3
Bhutan	-	-	-	11	6	2	7	4	2	-	0.1_{+1}	0.1_{+1}	0.1_{-3}	-	0.1	0.1	$-_{-4}$
India	$-_{-1}$	8_{-1}	$-_{-1}$	8_{-1}	6	3	5	3	4	74	126_{+1}	177_{+1}	120_{-1}	10_{-1}	146_{-1}	132_{-1}	32_{-1}
Iran, Islamic Republic of	-	9	-	9	6	1	6	2	4	1	8_{+1}	6_{+1}	6	1_{-2}	8_{-2}	6_{-2}	4_{-1}
Kazakhstan	-	9	4	11	7	4	4	5	2	2	1_{+1}	2_{+1}	1	1	1	2	1
Kyrgyzstan	1	9	4	11	7	4	4	5	2	1	0.5_{+1}	1_{+1}	1	0.2	1	1	0.2
Maldives	-	-	-	12	6	3	7	3	2	-	$-_{+1}$	$-_{+1}$	$-_{-3}$	-	-	...	$-_{-3}$
Nepal	-	-	-	8	5	2	5	3	4	1_{+1}	3_{+1}	5_{+1}	3	1	4	3_{i}	0.4
Pakistan	-	12	-	12	5	2	5	3	4	10	23_{+1}	28_{+1}	19	8	22	13	2
Sri Lanka	-	11	-	13	5	1	5	4	4	0.3	2_{+1}	3_{+1}	2	0.3_{-1}	2	3	0.3
Tajikistan	-	9	4	11	7	4	4	5	2	1	1_{+1}	1_{+1}	1	0.1	1	1_{-4}	0.3
Turkmenistan	$-_{-1}$	12_{-1}	3_{-1}	12_{-1}	6	3	4	6	2	0.4	0.4_{+1}	1_{+1}	1_{-3}	0.2_{-3}	0.4_{-3}	1_{-3}	$-_{-3}$
Uzbekistan	-	12	4	12	7	4	4	5	3	3	2_{+1}	4_{+1}	3	1	2	4	0.3
Eastern and South-eastern Asia																	
Brunei Darussalam	-	9	...	...	6	3	6	2	5	-	$-_{+1}$	$-_{+1}$	-	-	-	-	-
Cambodia	-	-	-	9	6	3	6	3	3	1	2_{+1}	2_{+1}	2	0.2	2	...	0.2
China	-	9	-	9	6	3	6	3	3	51	99_{+1}	94_{+1}	87	44	100	83	44
DPR Korea	1_{+1}	11_{+1}	1_{+1}	11_{+1}	6	2	5	3	3	1_{+1}	2_{+1}	2_{+1}	2_{+1}	...	2_{+1}	2_{-2}	1_{+1}
Hong Kong, China	-	9	-	12	6	3	6	3	3	0.2	0.3_{+1}	0.3_{+1}	0.4	0.2	0.4	0.4	0.3
Indonesia	-	9	-	12	7	2	6	3	3	10	28_{+1}	28_{+1}	22	6	29	24	8
Japan	-	9	-	9	6	3	6	3	3	3	7_{+1}	7_{+1}	6_{-1}	3_{-1}	7_{-1}	7_{-1}	4_{-1}
Lao PDR	-	5	-	5	6	3	5	4	3	0.5	1_{+1}	1_{+1}	1	0.2	1	1	0.1
Macao, China	1	9	3	12	6	3	6	3	3	-	$-_{+1}$	$-_{+1}$	-	-	-	-	-
Malaysia	-	6	-	11	6	2	6	3	3	1_{+1}	3_{+1}	3_{+1}	3_{+1}	1	3	3	1
Mongolia	-	12	-	12	6	4	5	4	3	0.3	0.3_{+1}	0.3_{+1}	0.2	0.2	0.3	...	0.2
Myanmar	-	5	-	5	5	2	5	4	2	2	5_{+1}	6_{+1}	5	0.2	5	4	1
Philippines	1	10	1	10	6	1	6	3	1	2	13_{+1}	8_{+1}	10	2_{-1}	14_{-1}	7_{-1}	4
Republic of Korea	-	9	3	9	6	3	6	3	3	1	3_{+1}	3_{+1}	3_{-1}	1_{-1}	3_{-1}	3_{-1}	3_{-1}
Singapore	-	6	...	...	6	3	6	2	2	0.1_{-1i}	0.2_{-1i}	0.2_{-1i}	0.2_{-1i}	...	0.2_{-1}	0.2_{-1}	0.2_{-1}
Thailand	-	9	-	12	6	3	6	3	3	2	5_{+1}	5_{+1}	5	2	5	6	2_{-1}
Timor-Leste	-	9	-	9	6	3	6	3	3	0.1	0.2_{+1}	0.2_{+1}	0.1_{-3}	-	0.2	0.1	...
Viet Nam	1	9	1	5	6	3	5	4	3	5	7_{+1}	9_{+1}	8	4	8	...	2_{-1}

G	H	I								J	
FINANCE											
Government education expenditure (% of GDP)	Education share of total government expenditure (%)	Government education expenditure per pupil: 2015 PPP US$ – Pre-primary	Primary	Secondary	Tertiary	% of GDP per capita – Pre-primary	Primary	Secondary	Tertiary	Household education expenditure (% of GDP)	COUNTRY CODE
	1.a.2	4.5.4									
2017											
…	…	-	…	…	…	-	…	…	…	…	DZA
2.8$_{-1}$	10.2$_{-1}$	1,289$_{-1}$	979$_{-1}$	1,235$_{-3}$	848$_{-1}$	15$_{-1}$	11$_{-1}$	15$_{-3}$	10$_{-1}$	…	ARM
2.9$_{-1}$	8.2$_{-1}$	4,370$_{-1}$	…	3,765$_{-1}$	3,972$_{-1}$	26$_{-1}$	…	22$_{-1}$	23$_{-1}$	1.0$_{-1}$	AZE
2.7$_{-1}$	7.5$_{-1}$	…	5,222$_{-2}$	8,190$_{-2}$	9,742$_{-4}$	…	11$_{-2}$	18$_{-2}$	21$_{-4}$	1.1$_{-1}$	BHR
6.4$_{-2}$	16.3$_{-2}$	3,962$_{-2}$	10,149$_{-2}$	12,420$_{-2}$	9,229$_{-2}$	13$_{-2}$	32$_{-2}$	39$_{-2}$	29$_{-2}$	1.4$_{-2}$	CYP
…	…	1,117	1,085	1,520	…	10	10	14	…	…	EGY
3.8	13.0	…	…	…	1,032			…	10	0.1	GEO
…	…	…	…	…	…	…	…	…	…	…	IRQ
5.9$_{-2}$	15.0$_{-2}$	4,599$_{-2}$	7,695$_{-2}$	6,721$_{-2}$	6,941$_{-2}$	13$_{-2}$	21$_{-2}$	19$_{-2}$	19$_{-2}$	1.2$_{-2}$	ISR
3.5	11.7	140	1,179	1,506	2,024	2	13	17	23	…	JOR
…	…	13,364$_{-3}$	11,450$_{-3}$	13,773$_{-3i}$	…	17$_{-3}$	15$_{-3}$	18$_{-3i}$	…	…	KWT
2.5$_{-4}$	8.6$_{-4}$	…	…	891$_{-4}$	2,714$_{-4}$	…	…	6$_{-4}$	18$_{-4}$	…	LBN
…	…	…	…	…	…	…	…	…	…	…	LBY
…	…	-$_{+1}$	1,457$_{-4}$	…	-$_{+1}$	-$_{+1}$	20$_{-4}$	…	-$_{+1}$	…	MAR
6.7	16.0	-$_{-1}$	12,361	14,100	18,033$_{-1}$	-$_{-1}$	31	35	42$_{-1}$	-	OMN
4.9	…	…	…	…	…	…	…	…	…	…	PSE
2.9	8.9	…	…	…	…	…	…	…	…	…	QAT
		…	…	…	…	…	…	…	…		SAU
…	…	…	…	…	…	…	…	…	…	…	SDN
…	…	…	…	…	…	…	…	…	…	…	SYR
6.6$_{-2}$	22.9$_{-2}$	…	…	6,057$_{-2}$	6,328$_{-2}$	…	…	53$_{-2}$	55$_{-2}$	…	TUN
4.3$_{-2}$	12.8$_{-2}$	…	3,563$_{-2}$	2,865$_{-2}$	7,991$_{-2}$	…	14$_{-2}$	12$_{-2}$	32$_{-2}$	0.7$_{-2}$	TUR
…	…	…	…	…	…	…	…	…	…	…	ARE
…	…	…	…	…	…	…	…	…	…	…	YEM
3.9$_{i}$	15.7$_{i}$	-	186	205	807$_{-3}$	-	10	11	41$_{-3}$	…	AFG
1.5$_{-1}$	11.4$_{-1}$	-$_{-1}$	…	360$_{-1}$	1,090$_{-1}$	-$_{-1}$	…	10$_{-1}$	31$_{-1}$	…	BGD
7.1$_{i}$	24.0$_{i}$	-$_{-2}$	1,031$_{-3}$	2,489$_{-2}$	4,067$_{-3}$	-$_{-2}$	14$_{-3}$	32$_{-2}$	55$_{-3}$	…	BTN
3.8$_{-4}$	14.1$_{-4}$	533$_{-4}$	497$_{-4}$	855$_{-4}$	2,500$_{-4}$	10$_{-4}$	10$_{-4}$	17$_{-4}$	49$_{-4}$	…	IND
3.8	20.0	143$_{-2}$	1,363$_{-2}$	2,594$_{-2}$	3,185$_{-1}$	1$_{-2}$	8$_{-2}$	15$_{-2}$	18$_{-1}$	…	IRN
3.0$_{-1}$	13.9$_{-1}$	1,778$_{-1}$	…	5,295$_{-1}$	2,471$_{-1}$	7$_{-1}$	…	21$_{-1}$	10$_{-1}$	0.5$_{-1}$	KAZ
7.2$_{i}$	18.5$_{i}$	1,019$_{-1}$	…	1,240$_{-1}$	171$_{-1}$	29$_{-1}$	…	35$_{-1}$	5$_{-1}$	1.1$_{-1}$	KGZ
4.3$_{-1}$	11.1$_{-1}$	1,342$_{-1}$	2,291$_{-1}$	…	4,375$_{-3}$	9$_{-1}$	15$_{-1}$	…	30$_{-3}$	…	MDV
5.1$_{i}$	15.9$_{i}$	52$_{-2}$	311$_{-2}$	263$_{-2i}$	607$_{-2}$	2$_{-2}$	13$_{-2}$	11$_{-2i}$	25$_{-2}$	…	NPL
2.8	13.8	559$_{-1}$	473$_{-1}$	537$_{-1}$	1,431	11$_{-1}$	10$_{-1}$	11$_{-1}$	28	…	PAK
2.5	14.5	-$_{+1}$	1,757	1,707	[illegible]	[illegible]	10	10	[illegible]	…	LKA
5.7 [illegible]	16.4$_{-2}$	783$_{-2}$	…	…	557$_{-2}$	28$_{-2}$	…	…	20$_{-2}$	…	TJK
…	…	…	…		…	…	…	…	…	…	TKM
6.4$_{i}$	19.2$_{i}$	…	…	…	…	…			…	…	UZB
4.4$_{-1}$	11.4$_{-1}$	806$_{-1}$	7,018$_{-1}$	18,700$_{-1}$	25,250$_{-1}$	1$_{-1}$	9$_{-1}$	24$_{-1}$	32$_{-1}$	…	BRN
1.6$_{-3}$	9.1$_{-3}$	99$_{-3}$	177$_{-3}$	…	…	3$_{-3}$	5$_{-3}$	…	…	…	KHM
…	…	…	…	…	…	…	…	…	…	…	CHN
…	…	…	…	…	…	…	…	…	…	…	PRK
3.3	17.8	3,956	8,566	12,726	13,210	7	15	22	23	…	HKG
3.6$_{-2}$	20.5$_{-2}$	293$_{-3}$	1,465$_{-2}$	1,161$_{-2}$	2,081$_{-3}$	3$_{-3}$	13$_{-2}$	11$_{-2}$	20$_{-3}$	3.4$_{-2}$	IDN
…	9.1$_{-1}$	3,505$_{-1}$	8,785$_{-1}$	9,521$_{-1}$	8,499$_{-1}$	…	…	…	…	…	JPN
2.9$_{-3}$	12.2$_{-3}$	489$_{-3}$	522$_{-3}$	719$_{-3}$	1,167$_{-3}$	8$_{-3}$	9$_{-3}$	12$_{-3}$	20$_{-3}$	…	LAO
3.1$_{-1}$	13.5$_{-1}$	…	…	41,504$_{-1}$	24,134$_{-1}$	…	…	40$_{-1}$	23$_{-1}$	0.4$_{-1}$	MAC
4.8$_{-1}$	20.7$_{-1}$	1,482$_{-1}$	4,484$_{-1}$	5,879$_{-1}$	7,202$_{-1}$	5$_{-1}$	16$_{-1}$	22$_{-1}$	26$_{-1}$	…	MYS
3.8	13.5	1,705	1,623	…	393	14	13	…	3	0.2$_{-2}$	MNG
2.2	10.2	…	…	…	…	3	8	11	17	…	MMR
…	…	…	…	…	…	…	…	…	…	…	PHL
5.3$_{-2}$	…	8,804$_{-2}$	10,204$_{-2}$	9,585$_{-2}$	5,128$_{-2}$	26$_{-2}$	30$_{-2}$	29$_{-2}$	15$_{-2}$	0.9$_{-2}$	KOR
2.9$_{-4}$	20.0$_{-4}$	…	…	…	17,094$_{-4}$	…	…	…	21$_{-4}$	…	SGP
4.1$_{-4}$	19.1$_{-4}$	…	3,667$_{-4}$	2,831$_{-4}$	2,859$_{-4}$	…	23$_{-4}$	18$_{-4}$	18$_{-4}$	…	THA
2.7$_{-3}$	6.7$_{-3}$	158$_{-3}$	574$_{-3}$	545$_{-3}$	…	2$_{-3}$	9$_{-3}$	8$_{-3}$	…	…	TLS
5.7$_{-4}$	18.5$_{-4}$	1,226$_{-4}$	1,140$_{-4}$	…	1,846$_{-4}$	23$_{-4}$	21$_{-4}$	…	34$_{-4}$	1.9$_{-4}$	VNM

TABLE 1: Continued

	EDUCATION SYSTEMS																	
	A		B		C	D				E				F				
	Compulsory		Free			Duration (years)				School-age population (000,000)				Enrolment (000,000)				
	Years of pre-primary	Years of primary-secondary	Years of pre-primary	Years of primary-secondary	Official primary school starting age	Pre-primary	Primary	Lower secondary	Upper secondary	Pre-primary	Primary	Secondary	Tertiary	Pre-primary	Primary	Secondary	Tertiary
SDG indicator	4.2.5	4.1.7	4.2.5	4.1.7													
Reference year	2017																
Oceania																	
Australia	-	10	1	13	5	1	7	4	2	0.3	2_{+1}	2_{+1}	2_{-1}	1_{-1}	2_{-1}	3_{-1}	2_{-1}
Cook Islands	-	12	2	13	5	2	6	4	3	$-_{i}$	$-_{+1i}$	$-_{+1i}$	$-_{-1i}$	$-_{-1}$	$-_{-1}$	$-_{-1}$	...
Fiji	-	-	...	...	6	3	6	4	3	0.1	0.1_{+1}	0.1_{+1}	0.1_{-1}	...	0.1_{-1}	...	...
Kiribati	-	9	-	9	6	3	6	3	4	-	$-_{+1}$	$-_{+1}$	$-_{-3}$	...	-	...	...
Marshall Islands	1_{-1}	12_{-1}	1_{-1}	12_{-1}	6	2	6	4	2	-	$-_{+1}$	$-_{+1}$	$-_{-1}$	$-_{-1}$	$-_{-1}$	$-_{-1}$	...
Micronesia, F. S.	$-_{-1}$	$-_{-1}$	$-_{-1}$	8_{-1}	6	3	6	2	4	-	$-_{+1}$	$-_{+1}$	$-_{-3}$	$-_{-2}$	$-_{-2}$	...	...
Nauru	2_{-1}	12_{-1}	2_{-1}	12_{-1}	6	3	6	4	2	$-_{i}$	$-_{+1i}$	$-_{+1i}$	$-_{-3i}$	$-_{-1}$	$-_{-1}$	$-_{-1}$	...
New Zealand	-	10	2	13	5	2	6	4	3	0.1	0.4_{+1}	0.4_{+1}	0.3_{-1}	0.1_{-1}	0.4_{-1}	0.5_{-1}	0.3_{-1}
Niue	$-_{-1}$	11_{-1}	1_{-1}	12_{-1}	5	1	6	4	3	$-_{i}$	$-_{+1i}$	$-_{+1i}$	$-_{-1i}$	$-_{-1}$	$-_{-1}$	$-_{-2}$	...
Palau	$-_{-1}$	12_{-1}	$-_{-1}$	12_{-1}	6	3	6	2	4	$-_{i}$	$-_{+1i}$	$-_{+1i}$	$-_{-3i}$	$-_{-3}$	$-_{-3}$	$-_{-3}$	$-_{-4}$
Papua New Guinea	$-_{-1}$	$-_{-1}$	...	...	7	4	6	2	4	1	1_{+1}	1_{+1}	1_{-3}	0.4_{-1}	1_{-1}	1_{-1}	...
Samoa	-	8	-	8	5	2	6	2	5	-	$-_{+1}$	$-_{+1}$	$-_{-3}$	-	-	$-_{-1}$	...
Solomon Is	$-_{-1}$	$-_{-1}$	...	...	6	3	6	3	4	-	0.1_{+1}	0.1_{+1}	0.1_{-3}	0.1	0.1	...	...
Tokelau	$-_{-1}$	11_{-1}	...	...	5	2	6	4	3	$-_{i}$	$-_{+1i}$	$-_{+1i}$	$-_{-3i}$	$-_{-1}$	$-_{-1}$	$-_{-1}$	...
Tonga	2_{-1}	13_{-1}	$-_{-1}$	8_{-1}	6	2	6	5	2	-	$-_{+1}$	$-_{+1}$	$-_{-3}$	$-_{-2}$	$-_{-2}$	$-_{-2}$	...
Tuvalu	$-_{-1}$	8_{-1}	...	...	6	3	6	4	3	$-_{i}$	$-_{+1i}$	$-_{+1i}$	$-_{-3i}$	$-_{-1}$	$-_{-1}$	$-_{-1}$	...
Vanuatu	-	-	...	...	6	2	6	4	3	-	$-_{+1}$	$-_{+1}$	$-_{-3}$	$-_{-2}$	$-_{-2}$	$-_{-2}$	...
Latin America and the Caribbean																	
Anguilla	-	12	-	12	5	2	7	3	2	...	...	...	...	...	...	...	...
Antigua and Barbuda	-	11	-	11	5	2	7	3	2	-	$-_{+1}$	$-_{+1}$	$-_{-2}$	$-_{-2}$	$-_{-2}$	$-_{-2}$	...
Argentina	2	12	3	12	6	3	6	3	3	2	4_{+1}	4_{+1}	3_{-1}	2_{-1}	5_{-1}	5_{-1}	3_{-1}
Aruba	2	11	1	11	6	2	6	2	3	-	$-_{+1}$	$-_{+1}$	$-_{-2}$	$-_{-3}$	$-_{-3}$	...	$-_{-2}$
Bahamas	-	12	2_{-2}	12	5	2	6	3	3	-	$-_{+1}$	$-_{+1}$	$-_{-2}$	$-_{-1}$	$-_{-1}$	$-_{-1}$	...
Barbados	-	11	2	11	5	2	6	3	2	-	$-_{+1}$	$-_{+1}$	$-_{-2}$	-	-	-	...
Belize	-	8	2	12_{-2}	5	2	6	4	2	-	$-_{+1}$	$-_{+1}$	-	-	0.1	-	-
Bolivia, P. S.	2	12	2	12	6	2	6	2	4	0.5	1_{+1}	1_{+1}	1_{-2}	0.3	1	1	...
Brazil	2	12	2	12	6	2	5	4	3	5_{-1i}	14_{-1i}	23_{-1i}	16_{-1i}	5_{-1}	16_{-1}	24_{-1}	8_{-1}
British Virgin Islands	-	12	-	12	5	2	7	3	2	$-_{-1i}$	$-_{-1i}$	$-_{-1i}$	$-_{-1i}$	-	-	-	$-_{-1}$
Cayman Islands	1	11	2	12	5	2	6	3	3	...	...	...	...	$-_{+1}$	$-_{+1}$	$-_{+1}$	...
Chile	1	12	1	12	6	3	6	2	4	1	1_{+1}	2_{+1}	1_{-1}	1_{-1}	1_{-1}	2_{-1}	1_{-1}
Colombia	1	9	3	11	6	3	5	4	2	2	4_{+1}	5_{+1}	4	...	4	5	2
Costa Rica	2	11	2	11	6	2	6	3	2	0.1	0.4_{+1}	0.4_{+1}	0.4	0.1_{-1}	0.5_{-1}	0.5_{-1}	0.2
Cuba	-	9	3	12	6	3	6	3	3	0.4	1_{+1}	1_{+1}	1_{-1}	0.4	1	1	0.2_{-1}
Curaçao	2	12	...	...	6	2	6	2	4	-	$-_{+1}$	$-_{+1}$	$-_{-3}$	...	$-_{-4}$	$-_{-4}$	$-_{-4}$
Dominica	-	12	-	12	5	2	7	3	2	-	$-_{+1}$	$-_{+1}$	$-_{-2}$	$-_{-1}$	$-_{-1}$	$-_{-2}$	...
Dominican Republic	3	12	3	12	6	3	6	2	4	1	1_{+1}	1_{+1}	1	0.3_{-1}	1_{-1}	1_{-1}	1
Ecuador	3	12	3	12	6	3	6	3	3	1	2_{+1}	2_{+1}	1_{-1}	1	2	2	1_{-2}
El Salvador	3	9	3	12	7	3	6	3	3	0.3	1_{+1}	1_{+1}	1_{-1}	0.2	1	1	0.2_{-1}
Grenada	-	12	2	12	5	2	7	3	2	-	$-_{+1}$	$-_{+1}$	-	-	-	-	-
Guatemala	1	9	3	11	7	3	6	3	2	1	2_{+1}	2_{+1}	2_{-2}	1_{-1}	2_{-1}	1_{-1}	0.4_{-2}
Guyana	-	6	-	6	6	3	6	3	2	-	0.1_{+1}	0.1_{+1}	0.1_{-2}	...	...	...	...
Haiti	-	6	-	6	6	3	6	3	4	1	1_{+1}	2_{+1}	1_{-2}	...	...	...	...
Honduras	1	11	3	11	6	3	6	3	2	1	1_{+1}	1_{+1}	1_{-2}	0.2	1	1	0.2_{-2}
Jamaica	-	6	...	...	6	3	6	3	2	0.1	...	0.2_{+1}	0.3	0.1	0.2	0.2	0.1_{-2}
Mexico	2	12	2	12	6	3	6	3	3	7	14_{+1}	14_{+1}	12_{-1}	5_{-1}	14_{-1}	14_{-1}	4_{-1}
Montserrat	-	12	-	12	5	2	7	3	2	...	...	...	...	-	-	-	...
Nicaragua	1	6	-	9	6	3	6	3	2	0.4	1_{+1}	1_{+1}	1_{-2}	...	...	...	...
Panama	2	9	2	12	6	2	6	3	3	0.2	0.4_{+1}	0.4_{+1}	0.3_{-2}	0.1_{-1}	0.4_{-1}	0.3_{-1}	0.2_{-2}
Paraguay	1	12	3	12	6	3	6	3	3	0.4	1_{+1}	1_{+1}	1_{-2}	0.2_{-1}	1_{-1}	1_{-1}	...
Peru	3	11	3	11	6	3	6	3	2	2	4_{+1}	3_{+1}	3	2	4	3	2_{-1}
Saint Kitts and Nevis	$-_{-1}$	12_{-1}	$-_{-1}$	12_{-2}	5	2	7	3	2	...	...	...	...	$-_{-1}$	$-_{-1}$	$-_{-1}$	$-_{-2}$
Saint Lucia	-	10	-	10	5	2	7	3	2	-	...	$-_{+1}$	-	-	-	-	-
Saint Vincent/Grenadines	-	12	2	12	5	2	7	3	2	-	$-_{+1}$	$-_{+1}$	$-_{-1}$	-	-	-	...
Sint Maarten	2	11	2	11	6	3	6	2	3	...	...	...	...	$-_{-3}$	$-_{-3}$	$-_{-3}$	$-_{-2}$
Suriname	-	6	$-_{-2}$	6_{-2}	6	2	6	4	3	-	0.1_{+1}	0.1_{+1}	$-_{-2}$	-	0.1	0.1_{-2}	...
Trinidad and Tobago	$-_{-1}$	6_{-1}	...	...	5	2	7	3	2	-	0.1_{+1}	0.1_{+1}	0.1_{-2}	...	...	...	...
Turks and Caicos Islands	2_{-1}	11_{-1}	...	...	6	2	6	3	2	...	...	...	...	$-_{-2}$	$-_{-2}$	$-_{-2}$	$-_{-2}$
Uruguay	2	12	2	12	6	3	6	3	3	0.1	0.3_{+1}	0.3_{+1}	0.3_{-2}	0.1_{-1}	0.3_{-1}	0.3_{-1}	0.1_{-2}
Venezuela, B. R.	3	11	3	12	6	3	6	3	2	2	4_{+1}	3_{+1}	3_{-2}	1	3	2	...

FINANCE											
G	H	I								J	
		Government education expenditure per pupil									
		2015 PPP US$				% of GDP per capita					
Government education expenditure (% of GDP)	Education share of total government expenditure (%)	Pre-primary	Primary	Secondary	Tertiary	Pre-primary	Primary	Secondary	Tertiary	Household education expenditure (% of GDP)	COUNTRY CODE
	1.a.2	4.5.4									
2017											
5.3-2	14.1-2	4,861-2	8,711-2	7,947-2	9,954-2	11-2	19-2	17-2	22-2	1.2-2	AUS
4.7-1	11.6-3	...	...	...	...	10-4	10-4	10-4	...	...	COK
3.9-4	14.3-4	...	1,048-4	...	...	...	13-4	...	...	...	FJI
...	...	...	...	...	...	...	...	...	...	...	KIR
...	...	...	...	...	...	...	...	...	...	...	MHL
12.5-2	22.3-2	...	...	...	...	...	...	...	...	...	FSM
...	...	...	...	...	...	...	...	...	...	...	NRU
6.3-1	18.3-1	6,882-1	7,301-1	7,946-1	10,159-1	18-1	19-1	21-1	27-1	0.7-1	NZL
...	...	...	...	...	-	...	...	...	-	-1	NIU
...	...	...	...	...	...	...	...	...	...	...	PLW
...	...	...	...	...	...	...	...	...	...	...	PNG
4.1-1	10.5-1	101-1	525-1	763-1	...	2-1	9-1	13-1	...	...	WSM
...	...	...	...	...	...	...	...	...	...	...	SLB
...	...	...	...	...	...	...	...	...	...	...	TKL
...	...	...	...	...	...	...	...	...	...	...	TON
...	...	...	...	...	...	...	...	...	...	...	TUV
4.0	11.8	3-2	395-2	613-2	...	0.1-2	13-2	21-2	...	...	VUT
...	...	...	...	...	...	...	...	...	...	...	AIA
...	...	...	...	...	...	...	...	...	...	...	ATG
5.6-1	13.5-1	2,504-1	3,045-1	4,319-1	3,217-1	13-1	15-1	22-1	16-1	0.8-1	ARG
6.1-2	22.9-2	...	...	...	...	13-3	17-3	...	143-2	...	ABW
...	...	...	...	...	...	...	...	...	...	...	BHS
4.7	12.9	...	3,584-1	4,842-1	...	...	21-1	28-1	...	1.6	BRB
7.1	21.7	1,345	1,338	2,237	2,517	16	16	27	30	-1	BLZ
7.1-3	16.8-3	794-3	1,582-3	1,219-3	...	12-3	23-3	18-3	...	...	BOL
6.2-2	16.2-2	...	3,163-2	3,395-2	5,211-2	...	20-2	22-2	33-2	...	BRA
6.3-2	...	...	...	...	...	0.1-2	9-2	17-2	49-2	...	VGB
...	...	...	...	...	...	...	...	...	...	...	CYM
5.4-1	21.2-1	4,051-1	4,123-1	4,166-1	4,503-1	18-1	18-1	18-1	20-1	1.2-2	CHL
4.4	15.3	...	2,549	2,466	2,301	...	18	17	16	2.3	COL
7.4	30.2	2,928-1	4,001-1	3,868-1	6,439	18-1	25-1	24-1	39	2.2-4	CRI
...	...	...	...	...	...	...	...	...	...	...	CUB
4.9-4	...	...	...	...	...	...	10-4	23-4	18-4	...	CUW
3.4-2	10.5-2	303-2	1,619-2	2,076-2		3-2	15-2	10-2	...	...	DMA
...	...	1,135-1	2,410-1	2,271-1		8-1	10-1	15-1	...	...	DOM
5.0-1	12.8-2	2,801-1	1,038-1	590-1	6,004-2	25-1	9-1	5-1	52-2	...	ECU
3.8-1	16.1-1	735-1	1,221-1	1,130-1	826-1	10-1	16-1	15-1	11-1	3.9-1	SLV
10.1-1	42.8-1	844-1	6,662-1	3,941-1	1,631-1	6-1	48-1	28-1	12-1	...	GRD
2.8	23.1	846-1	870-1	402-1	1,402-2	11-1	11-1	5-1	18-2	...	GTM
-	-	...	...	...	...	...	...	...	...	...	GUY
2.4-1	13.1-1	...	...	...	...	...	...	...	...	...	HTI
6.0	21.7	692-4	938-4	890-4	1,852-2	16-4	21-4	20-4	40-2	...	HND
5.2	18.4	462	1,981	2,303	3,040-2	5	23	27	36-2	...	JAM
5.2-2	19.0-2	...	2,569-2	2,696-2	6,485-2	...	15-2	16-2	38-2	1.2-2	MEX
...	...	...	...	...	...	...	...	...	...	...	MSR
4.3	17.9-1	...	...	...	...	...	...	...	...	...	NIC
...	...	...	...	...	...	...	...	...	...	...	PAN
4.5-1	18.2-1	1,381-1	1,426-1	1,463-1	...	15-1	15-1	15-1	...	...	PRY
3.9	18.1	1,619	1,542	1,991	1,364-1	12	12	15	11-1	3.1	PER
2.8-2	8.6-2	3,660-2	1,519-2	5,118-1	1,699-2	14-2	6-2	20-1	7-2	...	KNA
5.7-1	22.4-1	445-2	1,440	3,236-1	...	3-2	11	25-1	...	...	LCA
5.8	18.6	356-2	2,028	2,269	...	3-2	18	20	...	...	VCT
...	...	...	...	...	...	...	...	...	...	...	SXM
...	...	...	...	...	...	...	...	...	...	...	SUR
...	...	...	...	...	...	...	...	...	...	...	TTO
3.3-2	14.3-2	...	...	...	...	...	...	...	...	...	TCA
...	...	...	...	...	...	...	...	...	...	...	URY
...	...	...	...	...	...	18-2	19-2	15-2	...	...	VEN

TABLE 1: Continued

	EDUCATION SYSTEMS																
	A		B		C	D				E				F			
	Compulsory		Free		Official primary school starting age	Duration (years)				School-age population (000,000)				Enrolment (000,000)			
	Years of pre-primary	Years of primary-secondary	Years of pre-primary	Years of primary-secondary		Pre-primary	Primary	Lower secondary	Upper secondary	Pre-primary	Primary	Secondary	Tertiary	Pre-primary	Primary	Secondary	Tertiary
SDG indicator	4.2.5	4.1.7	4.2.5	4.1.7													
Reference year	2017																
Europe and Northern America																	
Albania	-	9	3	12	6	3	5	4	3	0.1	0.2_{+1}	0.3_{+1}	0.2	0.1	0.2	0.3	0.1
Andorra	-	11	-	10	6	3	6	4	2	...	...	...	...	-	-	-	-
Austria	1	12	3	12	6	3	4	4	4	0.2	0.3_{+1}	1_{+1}	1_{-1}	0.3_{-1}	0.3_{-1}	1_{-1}	0.4_{-1}
Belarus	-	9	-	11	6	3	4	5	2	0.3	0.4_{+1}	1_{+1}	0.5	0.3	0.4	1	0.4
Belgium	-	12	3	12	6	3	6	2	4	0.4	1_{+1}	1_{+1}	1_{-1}	0.5_{-1}	1_{-1}	1_{-1}	1_{-1}
Bermuda	-	13	1	13	5	1	6	3	4	-	$-_{+1}$	$-_{+1}$	-	$-_{-2}$	$-_{-2}$	$-_{-2}$	$-_{-2}$
Bosnia and Herzegovina	-	9	-	9	6	3	5	4	4	...	...	...	...	-	0.2	0.3	0.1
Bulgaria	2	9	4	12	7	4	4	4	4	0.3	0.3_{+1}	0.5_{+1}	0.4_{-1}	0.2_{-1}	0.3_{-1}	0.5_{-1}	0.3_{-1}
Canada	-	10	1	12	6	2	6	3	3	1	2_{+1}	2_{+1}	2_{-1}	...	2_{-1}	3_{-1}	2_{-1i}
Croatia	-	8	-	8	7	4	4	4	4	0.2	0.2_{+1}	0.3_{+1}	0.2_{-1}	0.1_{-1}	0.2_{-1}	0.3_{-1}	0.2_{-1}
Czechia	-	9	-	13	6	3	5	4	4	0.3	1_{+1}	1_{+1}	1_{-1}	0.4_{-1}	1_{-1}	1_{-1}	0.4_{-1}
Denmark	-	10	-	7	6	3	7	3	3	0.2	0.5_{+1}	0.4_{+1}	0.4_{-1}	0.2_{-1}	0.5_{-1}	1_{-1}	0.3_{-1}
Estonia	-	9	4	12	7	4	6	3	3	0.1	0.1_{+1}	0.1_{+1}	0.1_{-1}	...	0.1_{-1}	0.1_{-1}	0.1_{-1}
Finland	1	9	1	12	7	4	6	3	3	0.2	0.4_{+1}	0.4_{+1}	0.3_{-1}	0.2_{-1}	0.4_{-1}	1_{-1}	0.3_{-1}
France	-	10	3	12	6	3	5	4	3	2_{i}	4_{i}	6_{i}	4_{-1i}	3_{-1}	4_{-1}	6_{-1}	2_{-1}
Germany	-	13	-	13	6	3	4	6	3	2	3_{+1}	7_{+1}	4_{-1}	2_{-1}	3_{-1}	7_{-1}	3_{-1}
Greece	-	9	2	12	6	3	6	3	3	0.3	1_{+1}	1_{+1}	1_{-1}	0.2_{-1}	1_{-1}	1_{-1}	1_{-1}
Hungary	3_{-1}	10_{-1}	3_{-1}	12_{-1}	7	4	4	4	4	0.4	0.4_{+1}	1_{+1}	1_{-1}	0.3_{-1}	0.4_{-1}	1_{-1}	0.3_{-1}
Iceland	-	10	...	...	6	3	7	3	4	-	$-_{+1}$	$-_{+1}$	$-_{-1}$	$-_{-1}$	$-_{-1}$	$-_{-1}$	$-_{-1}$
Ireland	$-_{-1}$	10_{-1}	...	...	5	1	8	3	2	0.1_{i}	1_{i}	0.3_{i}	0.3_{-1i}	0.1_{-1}	1_{-1}	0.4_{-1}	0.2_{-1}
Italy	$-_{-1}$	12_{-1}	$-_{-1}$	8_{-1}	6	3	5	3	5	2	3_{+1}	4_{+1}	3_{-1}	2_{-1}	3_{-1}	5_{-1}	2_{-1}
Latvia	2	9	4	12	7	4	6	3	3	0.1_{i}	0.1_{i}	0.1_{i}	0.1_{-1i}	0.1_{-1}	0.1_{-1}	0.1_{-1}	0.1_{-1}
Liechtenstein	1_{-1}	8_{-1}	...	...	7	2	5	4	3	$-_{i}$	$-_{i}$	$-_{i}$	$-_{-1i}$	$-_{-1}$	$-_{-1}$	$-_{-1}$	$-_{-1}$
Lithuania	$-_{-1}$	9_{-1}	$-_{-1}$	11_{-1}	7	4	4	6	2	0.1_{i}	0.1_{i}	0.2_{i}	0.2_{-1i}	0.1_{-1}	0.1_{-1}	0.3_{-1}	0.1_{-1}
Luxembourg	2	10	2	13	6	3	6	3	4	-	$-_{+1}$	$-_{+1}$	$-_{-1}$	$-_{-1}$	$-_{-1}$	$-_{-1}$	$-_{-1}$
Malta	$-_{-1}$	11_{-1}	2_{-1}	13_{-1}	5	2	6	3	4	-	$-_{+1}$	$-_{+1}$	$-_{-1}$	$-_{-1}$	$-_{-1}$	$-_{-1}$	$-_{-1}$
Monaco	-	11	3	12	6	3	5	4	3	...	...	...	...	-	-	-	-
Montenegro	-	9	-	9	6	3	5	4	4	-	$-_{+1}$	0.1_{+1}	-	-	-	0.1	-
Netherlands	1_{-1}	11_{-1}	...	...	6	3	6	3	3	1	1_{+1}	1_{+1}	1_{-1}	1_{-1}	1_{-1}	2_{-1}	1_{-1}
Norway	-	10	-	10	6	3	7	3	3	0.2	0.4_{+1}	0.4_{+1}	0.3_{-1}	0.2_{-1}	0.4_{-1}	0.4_{-1}	0.3_{-1}
Poland	1	9	4	12	7	4	6	3	3	2	2_{+1}	2_{+1}	2_{-1}	1_{-1}	2_{-1}	2_{-1}	2_{-1}
Portugal	$-_{-1}$	9_{-1}	$-_{-1}$	9_{-1}	6	3	6	3	3	0.3	1_{+1}	1_{+1}	1_{-1}	0.3_{-1}	1_{-1}	1_{-1}	0.3_{-1}
Republic of Moldova	-	11	4	12	7	4	4	5	2	0.2_{i}	0.2_{i}	0.3_{i}	0.2_{i}	0.1	0.1	0.2	0.1
Romania	-	10	3	13	6	3	5	4	4	1	1_{+1}	2_{+1}	1_{-1}	1_{-1}	1_{-1}	2_{-1}	1_{-1}
Russian Federation	$-_{-1}$	11_{-1}	4_{-1}	11_{-1}	7	4	4	5	2	7	6_{+1}	10_{+1}	8_{-1}	6_{-1}	6_{-1}	10_{-1}	6_{-1}
San Marino	$-_{-1}$	10_{-1}	$-_{-1}$	13_{-1}	6	3	5	3	5	$-_{i}$	$-_{i}$	$-_{i}$	$-_{-3i}$	...	...	...	...
Serbia	-	8	-	12	7	4	4	4	4	0.3_{i}	0.3_{i}	1_{i}	0.4_{i}	0.2	0.3	1	0.3
Slovakia	$-_{-1}$	10_{-1}	1_{-1}	13_{-1}	6	3	4	5	4	0.2	0.2_{+1}	0.5_{+1}	0.3_{-1}	0.2_{-1}	0.2_{-1}	0.4_{-1}	0.2_{-1}
Slovenia	-	9	-	9	6	3	6	3	4	0.1	0.1_{+1}	0.1_{+1}	0.1_{-1}	0.1_{-1}	0.1_{-1}	0.1_{-1}	0.1_{-1}
Spain	-	10	3	10	6	3	6	3	3	1	3_{+1}	3_{+1}	2_{-1}	1_{-1}	3_{-1}	3_{-1}	2_{-1}
Sweden	-	9	-	9	7	4	6	3	3	0.5	1_{+1}	1_{+1}	1_{-1}	0.5_{-1}	1_{-1}	1_{-1}	0.4_{-1}
Switzerland	2_{-1}	9_{-1}	2_{-1}	9_{-1}	7	2	6	3	4	0.2	0.5_{+1}	1_{+1}	1_{-1}	0.2_{-1}	0.5_{-1}	1_{-1}	0.3_{-1}
TFYR Macedonia	$-_{-1}$	13_{-1}	$-_{-1}$	13_{-1}	6	3	5	4	4	0.1	0.1_{+1}	0.2_{+1}	0.2_{-2}	$-_{-2}$	0.1_{-2}	0.2_{-2}	0.1_{-2}
Ukraine	$-_{-1}$	11_{-1}	$-_{-1}$	11_{-1}	6	3	4	5	2	1_{-3}	2_{-3}	3_{-3}	3_{-3}	1	2	2	2
United Kingdom	$-_{-1}$	11_{-1}	2_{-1}	13_{-1}	5	2	6	3	4	2	5_{+1}	5_{+1}	4_{-1}	2_{-1}	5_{-1}	8_{-1}	2_{-1}
United States	1	12	1	12	6	3	6	3	3	12_{-1i}	25_{-1i}	25_{-1i}	22_{-1i}	9_{-1}	25_{-1}	25_{-1}	19_{-1}

G	H	I								J	
FINANCE											
		Government education expenditure per pupil									
		2015 PPP US$				% of GDP per capita					
Government education expenditure (% of GDP)	Education share of total government expenditure (%)	Pre-primary	Primary	Secondary	Tertiary	Pre-primary	Primary	Secondary	Tertiary	Household education expenditure (% of GDP)	COUNTRY CODE
	1.a.2	4.5.4									
2017											
2.2	7.5	-	2,643	510	1,074	-	22	4	9	2.1-1	ALB
3.2	19.0	...	...	...	...	13	13	14	24	...	AND
5.5-2	10.7-2	8,671-2	11,567-2	13,605-2	17,938-2	17-2	23-2	27-2	36-2	0.1-2	AUT
4.8	11.1	5,915	...	6,561	3,297	32	...	36	18	0.2	BLR
6.5-2	12.2-2	7,781-2	...	...	14,677-2	17-2	...	...	32-2	0.2-2	BEL
1.5	7.8	...	...	...	...	18-2	8-2	12-2	19-3	...	BMU
...	...	...	...	...	...	...	...	...	...	...	BIH
4.0-4	11.4-4	5,424-4	3,812-4	3,705-4	2,741-4	32-4	22-4	22-4	16-4	-4	BGR
...	...	...	8,019-2	...	16,709-1	...	18-2	...	37-1	...	CAN
4.6-4	9.5-4	...	...	...	5,659-4	...	...	...	26-4	...	HRV
5.8-2	13.9-2	4,942-2	5,003-2	7,921-2	7,025-2	15-2	15-2	24-2	21-2	0.3-2	CZE
7.6-3	13.8-3	16,508-4	12,087-3	15,021-3	20,806-3	35-4	25-3	31-3	43-3	...	DNK
4.7-2	13.0-2	1,680-4	5,138-2	5,195-2	9,642-2	6-4	18-2	18-2	34-2	0.3-2	EST
7.1-2	12.5-2	9,453-2	9,269-2	10,874-2	14,536-2	22-2	22-2	26-2	35-2	...	FIN
5.5-2	9.7-2	7,302-2	7,115-2	10,731-2	13,373-2	18-2	18-2	26-2	33-2	0.4-2	FRA
4.8-2	11.0-2	7,951-2	8,385-2	11,016-2	16,263-2	17-2	18-2	23-2	34-2	...	DEU
...	...	4,472-2	5,247-2	6,029-2	2,456-2	17-2	20-2	23-2	9-2	...	GRC
4.6-2	9.2-2	6,372-2	4,890-2	5,545-2	5,564-2	24-2	19-2	21-2	21-2	...	HUN
7.7-2	18.2-2	10,456-2	11,087-2	9,896-2	12,053-2	22-2	23-2	21-2	25-2	0.3-2	ISL
3.7-2	13.1-2	3,050-2	8,138-2	11,293-2	12,639-2	4-2	12-2	16-2	18-2	...	IRL
4.1-2	8.1-2	6,552-2	7,961-2	8,390-2	9,255-2	18-2	22-2	23-2	25-2	0.7-2	ITA
4.9-2	14.1-2	5,119-2	6,472-2	6,089-2	5,864-2	21-2	26-2	25-2	24-2	0.6-2	LVA
...	...	...	...	...	...	...	...	...	...	...	LIE
3.9-2	12.3-2	4,519-2	5,274-2	4,908-2	5,331-2	16-2	18-2	17-2	19-2	0.4-2	LTU
3.9-2	9.4-2	19,721-2	19,982-2	19,697-2	43,392-2	19-2	19-2	19-2	42-2	0.1-2	LUX
5.3-2	13.2-2	8,819-2	8,261-2	10,695-2	16,081-2	25-2	23-2	30-2	45-2	0.7-2	MLT
1.4-1	7.0	...	...	...	...	...	...	...	...	--3	MCO
...	...	...	...	...	...	...	...	...	...	...	MNE
5.4-2	12.0-2	5,761-2	8,412-2	11,352-2	16,522-2	12-2	17-2	23-2	33-2	--2	NLD
7.6-2	15.7-2	11,443-2	13,275-2	16,271-2	23,037-2	19-2	22-2	26-2	37-2	...	NOR
4.8-2	11.6-2	5,088-2	6,289-2	5,880-2	7,476-2	19-2	24-2	22-2	28-2	0.6-2	POL
4.9-2	10.1-2	4,574-2	6,648-2	8,178-2	7,821-2	15-2	23-2	28-2	26-2	1.0-2	PRT
6.6-1	18.5-1	2,027-1	2,037-1	1,901-1	1,976-1	38-1	39-1	36-1	37-1		MDA
3.1-2	9.1-2	2,535-2	1,000-2	3,492-2	5,167-2	12-2	9-2	16-2	24-2	...	ROU
3.8-1	10.9-1	...	...	...	4,079-2				19-1	0.2-1	RUS
...	...	...	...					...	...	...	SMR
3.9-1	9.0-1	187-2	6,469-2	1,647-2	4,505-1	1-2	47-2	12-2	31-1	0.9-1	SRB
3.9-2	10.3-2	4,850-2	6,130-2	5,668-2	7,908-2	16-2	21-2	19-2	27-2	0.6-3	SVK
4.8-2	11.2-2	5,923-2	7,718-2	7,512-2	7,094-2	19-2	25-2	24-2	23-2	0.7-2	SVN
4.3-2	9.8-2	5,503-2	6,022-2	6,448-2	7,988-2	16-2	17-2	19-2	23-2	1.1-2	ESP
7.6-2	15.5-2	13,459-2	10,222-2	11,301-2	20,658-2	28-2	21-2	24-2	43-2	...	SWE
5.1-2	15.5-2	12,619-2	15,650-2	15,578-2	24,001-2	20-2	25-2	24-2	38-2	0.2-2	CHE
...	...	...	...	...	...	...	...	...	...	...	MKD
5.0-1	12.4-1	2,680-1	2,146-1	2,095-1	3,149-1	33-1	26-1	26-1	39-1	0.8-1	UKR
5.5-1	13.9-1	3,844-1	10,636-1	7,858-1	15,262-1	9-1	26-1	19-1	37-1	0.9-2	GBR
5.0-3	13.5-3	6,522-2	10,875-2	12,090-3	11,442-3	12-2	20-2	23-3	21-3	1.2-3	USA

TABLE 2 : SDG 4, Target 4.1 – Primary and secondary education

By 2030, ensure that all girls and boys complete free, equitable and quality primary and secondary education leading to relevant and effective learning outcomes

	PARTICIPATION / COMPLETION																			
	A						B			C		D	E	F	G	H	I	J
	Out-of-school children (000,000)			Out-of-school rate (%)			Completion rate (%)			Over-age for grade (%)		GER primary (%)	NERA primary (%)	GIR last primary (%)	Transition from primary to lower secondary (%)	NERT lower secondary (%)	GIR last lower secondary grade (%)	NERT upper secondary (%)
	Primary	Lower secondary	Upper secondary	Primary	Lower secondary	Upper secondary	Primary	Lower secondary	Upper secondary	Primary	Lower secondary							
SDG indicator:				4.1.5			4.1.4			4.1.6				4.1.3			4.1.3	
Reference year:	2017											2017						
Region	Sum			Weighted average								Weighted average						
World	64_i	61_i	138_i	9_i	16_i	36_i	85	73	49	9_i	11_i	104_i	91_i	90_i	91_{-1i}	84_i	76_i	64_i
Sub-Saharan Africa	34_i	27_i	36_i	21_i	36_i	57_i	64	37	27	19	26	98_i	79_i	69_i	75_{-1i}	64_i	43_i	43_i
Northern Africa and Western Asia	6_i	4_i	9_i	10_i	14_i	32_i	84_i	74_i	39_i	5_i	10_i	100_i	90_i	87_i	92_{-1i}	86_i	73_i	68_i
Northern Africa	3	1_i	4_i	11	10_i	33_i	84	69	36	5_i	15_i	101	89	89	94_{-1}	90_i	70_i	67_i
Western Asia	3_i	3_i	5_i	10_i	17_i	31_i	83_i	81_i	41_i	4	5	100_i	90_i	86_i	90_{-1i}	83_i	76_i	69_i
Central and Southern Asia	12_i	19_i	67_i	6_i	17_i	47_i	89	77	40	6	...	111_i	94_i	96_i	91_{-1i}	83_i	82_i	53_i
Central Asia	0.1	0.3_i	1	3	5_i	18	100_i	99_i	...	0.1	0.2	103	97	100	99_{-1}	95_i	96	82
Southern Asia	12_i	18_i	67_i	6_i	17_i	48_i	89	76	40	6	...	112_i	94_i	95_i	90_{-1i}	83_i	81_i	52_i
Eastern and South-eastern Asia	7_i	8_i	16_i	4_i	9_i	19_i	95	79	58	5_i	10_i	103	96_i	97_i	97_{-1i}	91_i	90_i	81_i
Eastern Asia	3_i	4_i	9_i	3_i	7_i	16_i	97	83	61	...	...	102	97_i	96_i	100_{-1i}	93_i	93_i	84_i
South-eastern Asia	3	4_i	7	5	12_i	26	90_i	69_i	48_i	5	10	106	95	100	94_{-1}	88_i	84	74
Oceania	0.4_i	0.1_i	0.4_i	9_i	4_i	23_i	...	...	...	17	10	105_i	91_i	94_i	63_{-1i}	96_i	78_i	77_i
Latin America and the Caribbean	3_i	3_i	7_i	5_i	7_i	23_i	91	81	62	7	14	108_i	95_i	98_i	95_{-1i}	93_i	79_i	77_i
Caribbean	0.2_i	0.1_i	0.3_i	9_i	7_i	22_i	93_i	90_i	65_i	10	13	103_i	91_i	93_i	94	93_i	84_i	78_i
Central America	1	1	3	4	12	35	93	79	51	5	7	103	96	97	94	88	84	65
South America	2	1	3	5_i	...	...	90	82	68	7	16	108_i	95_i	98_i	98_i	95_i	83_i	83_i
Europe and Northern America	2_i	1_i	2_i	3_i	2_i	7_i	99_i	98	87	2_i	3	101_i	97_i	97_i	96_{-1i}	98_i	91_i	93_i
Europe	1_i	1_i	2_i	2_i	2_i	7_i	...	97	84	0.5_i	2_i	101_i	98_i	97_i	98_{-1i}	98_i	90_i	93_i
Northern America	1_i	0.1_i	1_i	4_i	1_i	5_i	99	99	92	3	4	101_i	96_i	...	...	99_i	...	95_i
Low income	24_i	21_i	27_i	20_i	36_i	60_i	59	32	18_i	24	28	100_i	80_i	66_i	77_{-1i}	64_i	41_i	40_i
Middle income	38_i	39_i	108_i	7_i	14_i	37_i	89	76	48	6_i	10_i	105_i	93_i	94_i	92_{-1i}	86_i	80_i	63_i
Lower middle	31_i	31_i	87_i	10_i	18_i	45_i	85	71	41	6	9_i	106_i	90_i	93_i	89_{-1i}	82_i	77_i	55_i
Upper middle	7_i	8_i	21_i	4_i	7_i	21_i	96	84	60	6_i	11_i	103	96_i	95_i	98_{-1i}	93_i	87_i	79_i
High income	2_i	1_i	3_i	3_i	2_i	6_i	99_i	97	86	2	4	103_i	97_i	98_i	96_{-1i}	98_i	92_i	94_i

A Out-of-school children, total number (million) and out-of-school rate as percentage of the corresponding age group.
B Education completion rate by level, most recent survey year during 2012–2016 [*Source:* UIS and GEM Report analysis of household surveys].
C Percentage of pupils who are at least two years over-age for their current grade, by level.
D Gross enrolment ratio (GER) in primary education.
E Primary adjusted net enrolment rate (NERA) (%).
F Gross intake ratio (GIR) to last grade of primary education (%).
G Effective transition rate from primary to lower secondary general education (%).
H Lower secondary total net enrolment rate (NERT) (%).
I Gross intake ratio (GIR) to last grade of lower secondary education (%).
J Upper secondary total net enrolment rate (NERT) (%).
K Administration of nationally representative learning assessment in early grades (grade 2 or 3), or final grade of primary or lower secondary.
L Percentage of students achieving at least a minimum proficiency level in reading and mathematics

Notes:
Source: UIS unless noted otherwise. Data refer to school year ending in 2017 unless noted otherwise.
Aggregates represent countries listed in the table with available data and may include estimates for countries with no recent data.
(-) Magnitude nil or negligible.
(...) Data not available or category not applicable.
(± n) Reference year differs (e.g. -2: reference year 2015 instead of 2017).
(i) Estimate and/or partial coverage.

LEARNING											
K Administration of nationally representative learning assessment						L Achieving minimum proficiency (%)					
Early grades		End of primary		End of lower secondary		Early grades		End of primary		End of lower secondary	
Reading	Mathematics	Reading	Mathematics	Reading	Mathematics	Reading	Mathematics	Reading	Mathematics	Reading	Mathematics
4.1.2						4.1.1					
2017											
% of countries						Weighted average					
85	85	93	93	91	91	...	...	...	...	...	...
71	68	93	93	95	95	...	...	...	...	...	...
80i	86i	79i	79i	93i	100	...	...	...	...	...	...
75	67i	50	50	100i	100	...	...	...	...	...	...
83i	91i	90i	90i	91i	100	...	...	...	...	...	...
100i	100i	100	100	88i	89i	...	...	...	...	...	...
...	...	100	100	...	...	...	...	...	...	...	...
100	100	100	100	86	88	...	...	...	...	...	...
100i	100	100i	100i	100i	100i	...	...	...	...	...	...
...	100	100i	100i	100	100	...	...	...	...	...	...
100	100	100	100	100i	100i			...	...	...	...
100	100	94	94	...	...	...	...	...	...	...	...
83	84	95	95	74	74	...	...	...	...	...	...
76	78	94	94	56	56	...	...	...	...	...	...
100	100	100	100	100	100	...	...	...	...	...	...
83	83	92	92	83	83	...	...	...	...	...	...
91i	93i	94	94	98	98	...	...	...	...	...	...
95i	96i	97	97	97	97	...	...	...	...	...	...
50	67	50	50	100	100	...	...	...	...	...	...
76	72	90	90	89	89	...	...	...	...	...	...
87	87	95	96	94	96	...	...	...	...	...	...
89	89	94	94	97i	97i	...	...	...	...	...	...
85	85	95	98	92	95	...	...	...	...	...	...
85i	89	92	90	90	90	...	...	...	...	...	...

TABLE 2: Continued

	PARTICIPATION / COMPLETION																	
	A						B			C		D	E	F	G	H	I	J
	Out-of-school children (000,000)			Out-of-school rate (%)			Completion rate (%)			Over-age for grade (%)		GER primary (%)	NERA primary (%)	GIR last primary (%)	Transition from primary to lower secondary (%)	NERT lower secondary (%)	GIR last lower secondary grade (%)	NERT upper secondary (%)
	Primary	Lower secondary	Upper secondary	Primary	Lower secondary	Upper secondary	Primary	Lower secondary	Upper secondary	Primary	Lower secondary							
SDG indicator:				4.1.5			4.1.4			4.1.6				4.1.3			4.1.3	
Reference year:	2017											2017						
Sub-Saharan Africa																		
Angola	...	...	...	...	...	...	60_{-2}	36_{-2}	19_{-2}	...	...	113_{-2}	...	...	...	...	...	...
Benin	0.1	0.3_{-4}	0.4_{-4}	3	34_{-4}	59_{-4}	54_{-3}	28_{-3}	10_{-3}	13	30_{-2}	127	97	81_{-1}	84_{-2}	66_{-4}	46_{-1}	41_{-4}
Botswana	$-_{-3}$	...	...	10_{-3}	...	...	...	...	...	14_{-3}	33_{-3}	105_{-3}	90_{-3}	69_{-3}	99_{-4}	...	94_{-3}	...
Burkina Faso	1	1_{i}	1_{i}	23	47_{i}	67_{i}	...	...	...	24	61	94	77	64	76_{-1}	53_{i}	37	33_{i}
Burundi	-	0.2	0.4	3	29	59	53	26	12	31_{-1}	65	126	97	70	76_{-1}	71	41	41
Cabo Verde	-	-	-	14	20	34	...	...	...	10	31	96	86	81	99_{-1}	80	74	66
Cameroon	0.2_{i}	1_{-1}	1_{-2}	5_{i}	35_{-1}	53_{-2}	74_{-3}	43_{-3}	16_{-3}	21	28_{-2}	113	95_{i}	70	66_{-2}	65_{-1}	49_{-1}	47_{-2}
Central African Republic	...	...	...	...	...	...	...	...	...	...	...	106_{-1}	...	42_{-1}	...	...	10_{-1}	...
Chad	...	...	...	...	...	...	27_{-2}	14_{-2}	10_{-2}	...	...	88_{-1}	...	38_{-4}	...	...	17_{-4}	...
Comoros	-	-	-	16	30	56	...	...	...	27	48_{-3}	99	84	77	93_{-4}	70	48_{-3}	44
Congo	...	...	...	...	...	...	...	...	...	...	...	...	...	...	...	...	...	...
Côte d'Ivoire	0.4	1	1	11	42	63	57_{-1}	28_{-1}	16_{-1}	15	33	99	89	73	92_{-1}	58	47	37
D. R. Congo	...	...	...	...	...	...	69_{-4}	53_{-4}	26_{-4}	...	...	108_{-2}	...	70_{-2}	95_{-4}	...	50_{-3}	...
Djibouti	-	$-_{-2}$	$-_{-2}$	41	52_{-2}	69_{-2}	...	...	...	9	25	64	59	57	84_{-1}	48_{-2}	44	31_{-2}
Equat. Guinea	0.1_{-2}	...	...	56_{-2}	...	...	...	...	...	39_{-2}	49_{-2}	62_{-2}	44_{-2}	41_{-2}	...	...	24_{-2}	...
Eritrea	0.4	0.2	0.3	62	57	69	...	...	...	32	45	49	38	45	92_{-3}	43	31	31
Eswatini	0.1_{-1}	$-_{-2i}$	$-_{-2i}$	24_{-1}	13_{-2i}	27_{-2i}	70_{-3}	51_{-3}	32_{-3}	45_{-1}	70_{-1}	105_{-1}	76_{-1}	86_{-1}	99_{-2}	87_{-2i}	55_{-1}	73_{-2i}
Ethiopia	2_{-2i}	5_{-2i}	3_{-2i}	14_{-2i}	47_{-2i}	74_{-2i}	52_{-1}	21_{-1}	13_{-1}	22_{-2}	26_{-2}	102_{-2}	86_{-2i}	54_{-2}	91_{-3}	53_{-2i}	30_{-2}	26_{-2i}
Gabon	...	...	...	...	...	...	...	...	...	...	...	...	...	...	...	...	...	...
Gambia	0.1	...	...	21	...	...	62_{-4}	48_{-4}	30_{-4}	27	35	97	79	70_{-1}	94_{-4}	...	63_{-3}	...
Ghana	1	0.2	1	15	11	37	66_{-3}	52_{-3}	20_{-3}	33	43	105	85	95	93_{-1}	89	75	63
Guinea	0.4_{-1}	1_{-3}	0.5_{-3}	21_{-1}	50_{-3}	67_{-3}	...	...	...	16_{-1}	30_{-1}	92_{-1}	79_{-1}	61_{-1}	69_{-4}	50_{-3}	36_{-3}	33_{-3}
Guinea-Bissau	...	...	...	...	...	...	29_{-3}	17_{-3}	7_{-3}	...	...	...	...	...	...	...	...	...
Kenya	...	...	...	...	...	...	84_{-3}	71_{-3}	42_{-3}	...	...	105_{-1}	...	102_{-1}	99_{-2}	...	81_{-1}	...
Lesotho	0.1	$-_{-1}$	$-_{-1}$	18	25_{-1}	43_{-1}	65_{-3}	27_{-3}	11_{-3}	30	50	105	82	79_{-1}	88_{-2}	75_{-1}	43	57_{-1}
Liberia	0.5_{-1}	0.1_{-1}	0.1_{-1}	63_{-1}	32_{-1}	36_{-1}	34_{-4}	26_{-4}	13_{-4}	86_{-3}	82_{-3}	94_{-1}	37_{-1}	59_{-3}	79_{-3}	68_{-1}	37_{-3}	64_{-1}
Madagascar	...	...	...	...	...	...	...	...	...	...	54	144_{-1}	...	68_{-1}	73_{-2}	...	37	...
Malawi	...	0.4_{-1i}	0.5_{-1i}	...	24_{-1i}	62_{-1i}	47_{-2}	22_{-2}	14_{-2}	36_{-2}	44_{-4i}	140	...	77_{-3}	74_{-4}	76_{-1i}	20_{-4}	38_{-1i}
Mali	1	1	1	33	55	72	48_{-2}	28_{-2}	16_{-2}	11	17	80	67	50	78_{-1}	45	30	28
Mauritania	0.2	0.2	0.2	23	44	73	53_{-2}	36_{-2}	16_{-2}	36	48	95	77	68	66_{-1}	56	35	27
Mauritius	-	$-_{i}$	$-_{i}$	4	6_{-1}	18_{i}	...	...	...	1	6	102	96	98	88_{-1}	96_{i}	84	82_{i}
Mozambique	1	1_{-2}	1_{-2}	12	44_{-2}	70_{-2}	...	...	...	40	47	105	88	46	74_{-2}	56_{-2}	23	30_{-2}
Namibia	-	...	...	2	...	...	83_{-4}	56_{-4}	37_{-4}	26	48	119	98	78	92_{-4}	...	70	...
Niger	1	1	1	33	65	86	...	...	...	5	23	75	67	73	55_{-1}	35	18	14
Nigeria	...	...	...	...	...	...	68_{-4}	52_{-4}	50_{-4}	$-_{-3}$	$-_{-3}$	85_{-1}	...	...	90_{-4}	...	...	...
Rwanda	0.1	...	...	6	...	...	54_{-2}	28_{-2}	18_{-2}	40	46	133	94	76	82_{-1}	...	37	...
Sao Tome and Principe	-	$-_{-2}$	$-_{-2i}$	3	9_{-2}	19_{-2i}	83_{-3}	34_{-3}	8_{-3}	15	43	110	97	87	97_{-1}	91_{-2}	74	81_{-2i}
Senegal	1	1	1	25	49	63	50_{-2}	22_{-2}	9_{-2}	7	10	84	75	60	73_{-1}	51	37	37
Seychelles	...	...	$-_{-2}$	...	...	4_{-2}	...	...	...	0.3_{-1}	0.3_{-1}	113_{-1}	...	127_{-1}	97_{-2}	...	125_{-1}	96_{-2}
Sierra Leone	$-_{-1}$	0.2	0.4	1_{-1}	40	62	67_{-4}	40_{-4}	20_{-4}	16	35	121	99_{-1}	68	88_{-1}	60	50	38
Somalia	...	...	...	...	...	...	...	...	...	...	...	...	...	...	...	...	...	...
South Africa	1_{-2i}	...	1_{-2i}	8_{-2i}	...	17_{-2i}	...	...	...	9_{-1i}	22_{-1}	102_{-1}	92_{-2i}	82_{-1i}	96_{-2}	...	75_{-1}	83_{-2i}
South Sudan	1_{-2i}	0.3_{-2i}	1_{-2i}	68_{-2i}	60_{-2i}	68_{-2i}	...	...	...	77_{-2}	91_{-2}	67_{-2}	32_{-2i}	...	...	40_{-2i}	...	32_{-2i}
Togo	0.1	0.2	0.3	8	22	56	61_{-3}	24_{-3}	15_{-3}	23	33	123	92	91	83_{-1}	78	46	44
Uganda	1_{-4}	...	...	9_{-4}	...	...	44_{-1}	26_{-1}	18_{-1}	34	48	99	91_{-4}	51	59_{-1}	...	26	...
United Republic of Tanzania	2_{i}	...	...	20_{i}	...	...	80_{-2}	29_{-2}	8_{-2}	9_{-1}	18_{-1}	85	80_{i}	58_{-1}	...	...	29_{-1}	...
Zambia	0.4_{-4}	...	...	12_{-4}	...	...	75_{-4}	51_{-4}	28_{-4}	28_{-4}	29_{-4}	102_{-4}	88_{-4}	79_{-4}	87_{-4}	...	53_{-4}	...
Zimbabwe	0.4_{-4}	0.1_{-4}	1_{-4}	15_{-4}	10_{-4}	53_{-4}	88_{-2}	73_{-2}	13_{-2}	23_{-4}	26_{-4}	99_{-4}	85_{-4}	89_{-4}	86_{-3}	90_{-4}	65_{-4}	47_{-4}

LEARNING												
K: Administration of nationally representative learning assessment						L: Achieving minimum proficiency (%)						
Early grades		End of primary		End of lower secondary		Early grades		End of primary		End of lower secondary		
Reading	Mathematics	Reading	Mathematics	Reading	Mathematics	Reading	Mathematics	Reading	Mathematics	Reading	Mathematics	COUNTRY CODE
4.1.2						4.1.1						
2017												
Yes	...	...	...	...	...	...	...	...	...	...	...	AGO
Yes	Yes	Yes	Yes	Yes	Yes	10_{-3}	34_{-3}	52_{-3}	40_{-3}	...	...	BEN
Yes	Yes	Yes	Yes	Yes	Yes	...	...	66	66	79	80	BWA
Yes	Yes	Yes	Yes	Yes	Yes	35_{-3}	59_{-3}	57_{-3}	59_{-3}	...	...	BFA
Yes	Yes	Yes	Yes	Yes	Yes	79_{-3}	97_{-3}	56_{-3}	87_{-3}	...	...	BDI
Yes	Yes	Yes	Yes	Yes	Yes	...	...	...	...	...	...	CPV
Yes	Yes	Yes	Yes	Yes	Yes	30_{-3}	55_{-3}	49_{-3}	35_{-3}	...	...	CMR
No	No	Yes	Yes	Yes	Yes	...	...	...	...	...	...	CAF
Yes	Yes	Yes	Yes	Yes	Yes	18_{-3}	48_{-3}	16_{-3}	19_{-3}	...	...	TCD
...	...	...	...	...	...	...	...	...	...	...	...	COM
Yes	Yes	Yes	Yes	Yes	Yes	38_{-3}	71_{-3}	41_{-3}	29_{-3}	...	...	COG
Yes	Yes	Yes	Yes	Yes	Yes	17_{-3}	34_{-3}	48_{-3}	27_{-3}	...	...	CIV
Yes	Yes	Yes	Yes	No	No	...	...	...	...	...	...	COD
No	No	Yes	Yes	Yes	Yes	...	...	...	...			DJI
No	No	Yes	Yes	Yes	Yes	...	...	...	...	...	...	GNQ
No	No	No	No	Yes	Yes	...	...	...	...	...	...	ERI
No	No	Yes	Yes	Yes	Yes	...	...	...	...	...	...	SWZ
Yes	Yes	Yes	Yes	Yes	Yes	...	...	...	...	...	...	ETH
...	...	...	...	...	...	...	...	...	...	...	...	GAB
Yes	Yes	Yes	Yes	Yes	Yes	...	...	...	...	...	...	GMB
Yes	Yes	Yes	Yes	Yes	Yes	71_{-1}	55_{-1}	72_{-1}	61_{-4}	...	...	GHA
No	No	Yes	Yes	Yes	Yes	...	...	...	...	...	...	GIN
Yes	Yes	Yes	Yes	Yes	Yes	...	...	...	...	...	...	GNB
Yes	Yes	Yes	Yes	Yes	Yes	60_{-1}	71_{-1}	80_{-2}	77_{-2}	...	...	KEN
Yes	Yes	Yes	Yes	Yes	Yes	...	...	...	...	...	...	LSO
Yes	Yes	Yes	Yes	Yes	Yes	...	...	...	...	...	...	LBR
No	No	Yes	Yes	Yes	Yes	...	...	...	...	...	...	MDG
No	No	Yes	Yes	No	No	...	...	...	...	...	...	MWI
Yes	Yes	Yes	Yes	Yes	Yes	2_{-1}	3_{-1}	12_{-1}	13_{-1}	...	...	MLI
No	No	Yes	Yes	Yes	Yes	...	...	...	...	...	...	MRT
No	No	Yes	Yes	Yes	Yes	...	...	...	...	...	...	MUS
Yes	Yes	Yes	Yes	Yes	Yes	...	...	...	...	...	...	MOZ
No	No	Yes	Yes	Yes	Yes	...	...	...	...	...	...	NAM
Yes	Yes	Yes	Yes	Yes	Yes	10_{-3}	20_{-3}	8_{-3}	8_{-3}	...	...	NER
Yes	Yes	Yes	Yes	Yes	Yes	...	...	...	...	...	...	NGA
...	...	Yes	Yes		...	...	...		...	...	...	RWA
Yes	Yes	Yes	Yes	Yes	Yes	...	...	...	...	...	...	STP
Yes	Yes	Yes	Yes	Yes	Yes	68	67	61_{-3}	59_{-3}	42_{-1}	16_{-1}	SEN
No	No	Yes	Yes	Yes	Yes	...	...	...	...	...	...	SYC
No	No	Yes	Yes	Yes	Yes	...	...	...	...	...	...	SLE
Yes	No	No	No	Yes	Yes	...	...	...	...	...	...	SOM
Yes	Yes	Yes	Yes	Yes	Yes	84_{-3}	39_{-2}	92_{-3}	71_{-3}	84_{-3}	34_{-2}	ZAF
Yes	Yes	No	No	Yes	Yes	...	...	...	...	...	...	SSD
Yes	Yes	Yes	Yes	Yes	Yes	20_{-3}	41_{-3}	38_{-3}	48_{-3}	...	...	TGO
Yes	Yes	Yes	Yes	Yes	Yes	...	...	52_{-2}	53_{-2}	...	...	UGA
Yes	Yes	Yes	Yes	Yes	Yes	56_{-2}	35_{-2}	...	...	...	...	TZA
Yes	Yes	Yes	Yes	Yes	Yes	1_{-3}	9_{-3}	...	...	...	...	ZMB
Yes	Yes	Yes	Yes	Yes	Yes	...	...	...	...	...	...	ZWE

TABLE 2: Continued

	PARTICIPATION / COMPLETION																	
	A						B			C		D	E	F	G	H	I	J
	Out-of-school children (000,000)			Out-of-school rate (%)			Completion rate (%)			Over-age for grade (%)								
	Primary	Lower secondary	Upper secondary	Primary	Lower secondary	Upper secondary	Primary	Lower secondary	Upper secondary	Primary	Lower secondary	GER primary (%)	NERA primary (%)	GIR last primary (%)	Transition from primary to lower secondary (%)	NERT lower secondary (%)	GIR last lower secondary grade (%)	NERT upper secondary (%)
SDG indicator:				4.1.5			4.1.4			4.1.6				4.1.3			4.1.3	
Reference year:	2017											2017						
Northern Africa and Western Asia																		
Algeria	-	...	...	1	...	...	94_{-4}	57_{-4}	29_{-4}	6	24	112	99	106	99_{-2}	...	79_{-1}	...
Armenia	-	$-_{i}$	...	8	7_{i}	...	99_{-1}	97_{-1}	65_{-1}	0.4	1	94	92	92	98_{-1}	93_{i}	89	...
Azerbaijan	$-_{i}$	$-_{i}$	$-_{i}$	6_{i}	0.4_{i}	2_{i}	...	...	...	4	3	103_{i}	94_{i}	107_{i}	98_{-1}	100_{i}	88_{i}	98_{i}
Bahrain	-	-	-	1	1	6	...	...	...	1	4	101	99	101	99_{-1}	99	97	94
Cyprus	$-_{-2i}$	$-_{-2i}$	$-_{-2i}$	2_{-2i}	2_{-2i}	5_{-2i}	...	99_{-3}	93_{-3}	0.4_{-2}	2_{-2}	99_{-2i}	98_{-2i}	97_{-2i}	99_{-3}	98_{-2i}	98_{-2i}	95_{-2i}
Egypt	0.2	0.4	1	1	8	24	91_{-3}	80_{-3}	42_{-3}	2_{i}	4_{i}	105	99	95	94_{-1}	92	81	76
Georgia	-	$-_{-2}$	-	1	1_{-2}	6	...	99_{-4}	96_{-4}	1	2	103	99	117	100_{-1}	99_{-2}	107	94
Iraq	...	...	...	...	...	...	...	...	...	...	...	...	...	...	...	...	...	...
Israel	$-_{-1}$	$-_{-3}$	$-_{-1}$	3_{-1}	0.2_{-3}	2_{-1}	...	...	...	0.4_{-1}	1_{-1}	104_{-1}	97_{-1}	102_{-1}	100_{-2}	100_{-3}	101_{-1}	98_{-1}
Jordan	...	0.2	0.2	...	28	50	...	...	...	1	3	...	...	...	99_{-1}	72	61	50
Kuwait	-	$-_{-2}$	$-_{-2}$	7	7_{-2}	18_{-2}	...	...	...	2	4	97	93	97	97_{-1}	93_{-2}	90	82_{-2}
Lebanon	0.1	...	...	11	...	...	...	...	...	9	12	93	89	74	98_{-1}	...	52	...
Libya	...	...	...	...	...	...	...	...	...	...	...	...	...	...	...	...	...	...
Morocco	0.1	0.2	1	3	11	29	...	...	...	16	32	112	97	93	90_{-1}	89	65	71
Oman	-	-	-	1	2	12	...	...	...	1	8	107	99	108	98_{-1}	98	100	88
Palestine	-	0.1	0.1	6	10	35	99_{-3}	86_{-3}	62_{-3}	1	2	95	94	96	99_{-1}	90	78	65
Qatar	-	-	-	1	11	32	...	...	...	1	5	104	99	96	99_{-1}	89	83	68
Saudi Arabia	0.1_{-3i}	$-_{-4i}$	0.1_{-3i}	3_{-3i}	3_{-4i}	8_{-3i}	...	...	...	5_{-1}	10_{-1}	116_{-1}	97_{-3i}	114_{-1}	91_{-2}	97_{-4i}	116_{-1}	92_{-3i}
Sudan	3_{-1i}	...	...	40_{-1i}	...	...	65_{-3}	51_{-3}	31_{-3}	...	...	76_{-1}	60_{-1i}	60_{-1}	92_{-2}	...	50_{-1}	...
Syrian Arab Republic	1_{-4}	1_{-4}	1_{-4}	33_{-4}	43_{-4}	67_{-4}	...	...	...	5_{-4}	8_{-4}	76_{-4}	67_{-4}	66_{-4}	...	57_{-4}	50_{-4}	33_{-4}
Tunisia	$-_{-4}$	...	...	0.4_{-4}	...	...	...	...	...	4_{-1}	15_{-1}	115_{-1}	100_{-4}	103_{-2}	89_{-3}	...	71_{-2}	...
Turkey	0.3_{-1}	1_{-1}	1_{-1}	6_{-1}	10_{-1}	16_{-1}	...	...	...	2_{-2}	3_{-1}	101_{-1}	94_{-1}	92_{-2}	100_{-2}	90_{-1}	...	84_{-1}
United Arab Emirates	$-_{-1}$	$-_{-1}$	$-_{-1}$	3_{-1}	1_{-1}	16_{-1}	...	...	...	2_{-2}	4_{-3}	111_{-1}	97_{-1}	105_{-2}	100_{-4}	99_{-1}	82_{-3}	84_{-1}
Yemen	1_{-1}	1_{-1}	1_{-1}	17_{-1}	29_{-1}	57_{-1}	62_{-4}	46_{-4}	31_{-4}	9_{-1}	11_{-1}	92_{-1}	83_{-1}	72_{-1}	84_{-4}	71_{-1}	53_{-1}	43_{-1}
Central and Southern Asia																		
Afghanistan	...	...	...	...	...	...	55_{-2}	37_{-2}	23_{-2}	...	11	104	...	...	...	...	54	...
Bangladesh	1	1	5_{i}	5	10	38_{i}	80_{-3}	55_{-3}	19_{-3}	11	4	111	95	119	88_{-3}	90	78	62_{i}
Bhutan	-	-	-	18	15	31	...	...	...	14	35	93	82	95	100_{-1}	85	80	69
India	3_{-4i}	11_{-4i}	47_{-4i}	2_{-4i}	15_{-4i}	48_{-4i}	92_{-2}	81_{-2}	43_{-2}	5_{-4}	...	115_{-1}	98_{-4i}	96_{-1}	91_{-2}	85_{-4i}	86_{-1}	52_{-4i}
Iran, Islamic Republic of	$-_{-2}$	0.1_{-2}	2_{-2i}	1_{-2}	2_{-2}	35_{-2i}	...	...	...	2_{-2}	3_{-2}	109_{-2}	99_{-2}	102_{-2}	...	98_{-2}	94_{-2}	65_{-2i}
Kazakhstan	-	$-_{-4}$	-	1	0.3_{-4}	2	100_{-2}	100_{-2}	94_{-2}	0.1	0.3	108	99	109	99_{-1}	100_{-4}	110	98
Kyrgyzstan	-	-	0.1	1	0.2	28	99_{-3}	96_{-3}	81_{-3}	0.3	0.5	108	99	104	99_{-1}	100	96	72
Maldives	-	...	...	0.5	...	...	...	...	...	0.3	11	102	100	95	99_{-1}	...	104	...
Nepal	0.2	0.2	1	5	11	26	73_{-1}	63_{-1}	...	37	43	134	95	113	82_{-1}	89	89	74
Pakistan	5_{i}	6	10	24_{i}	46	62	...	...	...	...	-	96	76_{i}	71_{-1}	86_{-2}	54	53	38
Sri Lanka	-	-	0.3	1	2	19	...	...	...	1	1	102	99	102	100_{-1}	98	96	81
Tajikistan	-	...	...	1	...	...	...	...	...	-	-	99	99	92	99_{-1}	...	94	...
Turkmenistan	...	...	...	...	...	...	100_{-1}	100_{-1}	96_{-1}	...	...	88_{-3}	...	...	...	...		...
Uzbekistan	-	0.1	0.3	1	4	16	...	...	...	0.1	0.2	103	99	98	99_{-1}	96	91	84
Eastern and South-eastern Asia																		
Brunei Darussalam	-	$-_{-3}$	-	4	2_{-3}	18	...	...	...	1	3	105	96	107	100_{-1}	98_{-3}	102	82
Cambodia	0.2	0.1_{-2i}	...	9	13_{-2i}	...	72_{-3}	41_{-3}	21_{-3}	20	23	108	91	90	87_{-1}	87_{-2i}	54	...
China	...	...	...	...	...	...	97_{-3}	83_{-3}	61_{-3}	...	...	102	...	100_{-4}	...	...	102_{-4}	...
DPR Korea	...	0.1_{-2}	0.1_{-2}	...	8_{-2}	11_{-2}	...	...	...	...	...	88_{+1}	...	...	...	92_{-2}	...	89_{-2}
Hong Kong, China	...	$-_{i}$	$-_{i}$	...	1_{i}	4_{i}	...	...	...	2_{i}	7_{i}	...	...	...	100_{-1}	99_{i}	104	96_{i}
Indonesia	2	2_{-3i}	2	7	12_{-3i}	15	...	...	...	0.5_{-1}	8_{-2}	103	93	99	91_{-1}	88_{-3i}	90	85
Japan	0.1_{-1}	$-_{-1}$	0.1_{-1}	2_{-1}	0.1_{-1}	3_{-1}	...	...	...	...	...	98_{-1}	98_{-1}	100_{-1}	100_{-2}	100_{-1}	103_{-1}	97_{-1}
Lao PDR	0.1	0.1	0.2	7	22	38	...	...	...	14	29	107	93	102	88_{-1}	78	70	62
Macao, China	-	-	-	1	2	15	...	...	...	2	15	106	99	105	100_{-1}	98	103	85
Malaysia	-	0.2	1	1	12	37	...	...	...	-	-	103	99	99	91_{-1}	88	85	63
Mongolia	$-_{i}$	...	...	1_{i}	...	...	98_{-3}	89_{-3}	63_{-3}	1	...	104	99_{i}	93	99_{-1}	...	...	...
Myanmar	0.1	1	1	2	24	46	83_{-1}	44_{-1}	17_{-1}	11	12	113	98	96	93_{-1}	76	61	54
Philippines	1_{-1}	0.5_{-1}	0.4_{-2}	5_{-1}	7_{-1}	20_{-2}	87_{-4}	71_{-4}	67_{-4}	13_{-1}	23_{-1}	111_{-1}	95_{-1}	104_{-1}	97_{-2}	93_{-1}	86_{-1}	80_{-2}
Republic of Korea	0.1_{-1}	0.1_{-1}	$-_{-1}$	3_{-1}	6_{-1}	0.1_{-1}	...	...	...	0.2_{-1}	0.3_{-1}	97_{-1}	97_{-1}	96_{-1}	100_{-2}	94_{-1}	101_{-1}	100_{-1}
Singapore	$-_{-1i}$	$-_{-1i}$	$-_{-1i}$	0.1_{-1i}	0.1_{-1i}	0.1_{-1i}	...	...	...	0.3_{-1}	4_{-1}	101_{-1i}	100_{-1i}	100_{-1i}	...	100_{-1i}	107_{-1i}	100_{-1i}
Thailand	...	0.3	1_{-2i}	...	11	21_{-2i}	99_{-4}	85_{-4}	56_{-4}	...	7	100	...	93	97_{-1}	89	78	79_{-2i}
Timor-Leste	-	-	-	19	13	28	80_{-1}	66_{-1}	52_{-1}	26_{-1}	43_{-1}	101	81	95_{-1}	94_{-2}	87	80_{-1}	72
Viet Nam	0.1_{-4i}	...	...	2_{-4i}	...	...	97_{-3}	83_{-3}	55_{-3}	1_{-1}	1_{-1}	108	98_{-4i}	105_{-1}	100_{-2}	...	88_{-1}	...

LEARNING												
K: Administration of nationally representative learning assessment						L: Achieving minimum proficiency (%)						
Early grades		End of primary		End of lower secondary		Early grades		End of primary		End of lower secondary		
Reading	Mathematics	Reading	Mathematics	Reading	Mathematics	Reading	Mathematics	Reading	Mathematics	Reading	Mathematics	COUNTRY CODE
4.1.2						4.1.1						
2017												
No	No	No	No	Yes	Yes	…	…	…	…	21_{-2}	19_{-2}	DZA
No	No	No	Yes	No	…	…	…	…	95	…	…	ARM
…	…	Yes	Yes	…	…	…	…	…	…	…	…	AZE
Yes	Yes	Yes	Yes	Yes	Yes	…	72_{-2}	…	…	…	75_{-2}	BHR
Yes	Yes	Yes	No	Yes	Yes	…	93_{-2}	…	…	64_{-2}	…	CYP
Yes	…	No	No	…	Yes	5_{-4}	…	…	…	…	47_{-2}	EGY
…	Yes	…	…	Yes	Yes	…	78_{-2}	…	…	48_{-2}	43_{-2}	GEO
…	…	…	…	…	…	…		…	…	…	…	IRQ
Yes	Yes	Yes	Yes	Yes	Yes	…		…	…	73_{-2}	68_{-2}	ISR
Yes	Yes	…	…	Yes	Yes	…	50_{-2}	…	…	54_{-2}	45_{-2}	JOR
…	Yes	…	…	…	Yes	…	33_{-2}	…	…	…	45_{-2}	KWT
…	…	…	…	Yes	Yes	…	…	…	…	30_{-2}	71_{-2}	LBN
…	…	…	…	…	…	…	…	…	…	…	…	LBY
Yes	Yes	Yes	Yes	Yes	Yes	…	41_{-2}	…	…	…	41_{-2}	MAR
…	Yes	Yes	Yes	Yes	Yes	…	61_{-2}	…	…	…	52_{-2}	OMN
…	…	…	…	…	…	…	…	…	…	…	…	PSE
…	Yes	Yes	Yes	Yes	Yes	…	64_{-2}	…	…	48_{-2}	64_{-2}	QAT
…	Yes	Yes	Yes	…	Yes	…	43_{-2}	…	…	…	34_{-2}	SAU
Yes	Yes	…	…	…	…	…		…	…	…	…	SDN
…		…	…	…	…	…	…	…	…	…	…	SYR
…	…	Yes	Yes	Yes	Yes	…	…	…	…	28_{-2}	25_{-2}	TUN
…	…	Yes	Yes	Yes	Yes	…	…	…	81_{-2}	60_{-2}	70_{-2}	TUR
Yes	Yes	Yes	Yes	Yes	Yes	…	70_{-2}	…	…	60_{-2}	74_{-2}	ARE
…	…	…	…	…	…	…	…	…	…	…	…	YEM
Yes	Yes	Yes	Yes	No	No	…	…	…	…	…	…	AFG
Yes	Yes	Yes	Yes	Yes	Yes	…	…	…	…	…	…	BGD
Yes	Yes	…	…	Yes	Yes	…	…	…	…	33_{-2}	51_{-4}	BTN
Yes	Yes	Yes	Yes	Yes	Yes	25_{-1}	28_{-1}	…	…	…	…	IND
…	Yes	…	…	…	Yes	…	65_{-2}	…	…	…	63_{-2}	IRN
…	…	Yes	Yes	Yes	Yes	…	…	…	96_{-2}	59_{-2}	91_{-2}	KAZ
…	…	Yes	Yes	…	…	…	…	36_{-3}	35_{-3}	…	…	KGZ
…	…	Yes	Yes	…	…	…	…	…	…	…	…	MDV
Yes	Yes	Yes	Yes	Yes	Yes		…	…	…	…	…	NPL
Yes	Yes	Yes	Yes	Yes	Yes	17_{-1}	14_{-1}	52_{-1}	48_{-1}	73_{-3}	68_{-3}	PAK
Yes	Yes	…	…	Yes	Yes	…	…	…	…	…	…	LKA
…	…	Yes	Yes	…	…	…	…	…	…		…	TJK
…	…	…	…		…	…	…	…	…		…	TKM
…	…	Yes	Yes		…		…	…	…	…	…	UZB
Yes	Yes	…	…	…	…	…	…	…	…	…	…	BRN
Yes	Yes	Yes	Yes	Yes	Yes	…	…	…	…	38	17	KHM
Yes	Yes	…	…	Yes	Yes	82_{-1}	85_{-2}	…	…	80_{-1}	79_{-2}	CHN
Yes	Yes	…	…	…	…	94	83	…	…	…	…	PRK
…	Yes	…	…	Yes	Yes	…	100_{-2}	…	…	91_{-2}	91_{-2}	HKG
Yes	Yes	…	…	Yes	Yes	…	49_{-2}	…	…	45_{-2}	31_{-2}	IDN
…	Yes	Yes	Yes	Yes	Yes	…	…	…	…	…	…	JPN
Yes	Yes	Yes	Yes	…	…	83_{-3}	46_{-3}	…	…	…	…	LAO
…	…	…	…	Yes	Yes	…	…	…	…	88_{-2}	93_{-2}	MAC
Yes	Yes	Yes	Yes	Yes	Yes	86	71	88	47	73	42	MYS
…	…	Yes	Yes	…	…	…	…	…	…	…	…	MNG
Yes	Yes	Yes	Yes	…	…	…	…	…	…	…	…	MMR
Yes	Yes	Yes	Yes	…	…	…	…	…	…	…	…	PHL
…	Yes	Yes	Yes	Yes	Yes	…	100_{-2}	…	…	86_{-2}	85_{-2}	KOR
…	Yes	Yes	Yes	Yes	Yes	…	99_{-2}	…	…	89_{-2}	99_{-2}	SGP
Yes	Yes	Yes	Yes	Yes	Yes	…	…	…	…	50_{-2}	46_{-2}	THA
…	…	…	…	…	…	…	…	…	…	…	…	TLS
Yes	Yes	Yes	Yes	Yes	Yes	…	…	…	…	86_{-2}	81_{-2}	VNM

TABLE 2: Continued

	PARTICIPATION / COMPLETION																	
	A						B			C		D	E	F	G	H	I	J
	Out-of-school children (000,000)			Out-of-school rate (%)			Completion rate (%)			Over-age for grade (%)		GER primary (%)	NERA primary (%)	GIR last primary (%)	Transition from primary to lower secondary (%)	NERT lower secondary (%)	GIR last lower secondary grade (%)	NERT upper secondary (%)
	Primary	Lower secondary	Upper secondary	Primary	Lower secondary	Upper secondary	Primary	Lower secondary	Upper secondary	Primary	Lower secondary							
SDG indicator:				4.1.5			4.1.4			4.1.6				4.1.3			4.1.3	
Reference year:	2017											2017						
Oceania																		
Australia	0.1_{-1}	$-_{-1}$	$-_{-1}$	3_{-1}	1_{-1}	1_{-1}	…	…	…	0.2_{-1}	2_{-1}	101_{-1}	97_{-1}	…	…	99_{-1}	…	99_{-1}
Cook Islands	$-_{-2i}$	$-_{-1i}$	$-_{-1i}$	4_{-2i}	0.3_{-1i}	34_{-1i}	…	…	…	0.3_{-1}	0.2_{-1}	108_{-1i}	96_{-2i}	109_{-1i}	100_{-2}	100_{-1i}	94_{-1i}	66_{-1i}
Fiji	$-_{-1}$	…	…	0.1_{-1}	…	…	…	…	…	2_{-1}	4_{-1}	105_{-1}	100_{-1}	103_{-1}	98_{-2}	…	97_{-1}	…
Kiribati	-	…	…	3	…	…	…	…	…	2	10	100	97	100_{-1}	96_{-2}	…	93_{-1}	…
Marshall Islands	$-_{-1}$	$-_{-1i}$	$-_{-1i}$	21_{-1}	23_{-1i}	34_{-1i}	…	…	…	11_{-1}	23_{-1}	89_{-1}	79_{-1}	77_{-1}	…	77_{-1i}	…	66_{-1i}
Micronesia, F. S.	$-_{-2}$	$-_{-3}$	…	16_{-2}	18_{-3}	…	…	…	…	$-_{-2}$	$-_{-2}$	96_{-2}	84_{-2}	…	…	82_{-3}	…	…
Nauru	$-_{-1i}$	$-_{-1i}$	$-_{-1i}$	16_{-1i}	18_{-1i}	58_{-1i}	…	…	…	0.3_{-1}	$-_{-1}$	107_{-1i}	84_{-1i}	120_{-1i}	…	82_{-1i}	…	42_{-1i}
New Zealand	$-_{-1}$	$-_{-1}$	$-_{-1}$	1_{-1}	2_{-1}	4_{-1}	…	…	…	0.2_{-1}	0.3_{-1}	99_{-1}	99_{-1}	…	…	98_{-1}	…	96_{-1}
Niue	…	…	…	…	…	…	…	…	…	$-_{-1}$	2_{-2}	129_{-1i}	…	112_{-1i}	77_{-3}	…	112_{-2i}	…
Palau	$-_{-3i}$	…	$-_{-4i}$	1_{-3i}	…	2_{-4i}	…	…	…	14_{-3}	15_{-3}	115_{-3i}	99_{-3i}	96_{-3i}	97_{-4}	…	105_{-3i}	98_{-4i}
Papua New Guinea	0.3_{-1}	$-_{-1}$	0.3_{-1}	22_{-1}	12_{-1}	44_{-1}	…	…	…	47_{-1}	50_{-1}	112_{-1}	78_{-1}	79_{-1}	…	88_{-1}	64_{-1}	56_{-1}
Samoa	-	$-_{-1}$	$-_{-1}$	4	2_{-1}	19_{-1}	…	…	…	7	9	109	96	101	97_{-1}	98_{-1}	100	81_{-1}
Solomon Is	-	…	…	30	…	…	…	…	…	74	74	114	70	87	91_{-1}	…	71	…
Tokelau	$-_{-1i}$	$-_{-1i}$	$-_{-1i}$	8_{-1i}	1_{-1i}	70_{-1i}	…	…	…	2_{-1}	12_{-1}	102_{-1i}	92_{-1i}	…	…	99_{-1i}	…	30_{-1i}
Tonga	$-_{-2}$	$-_{-2}$	$-_{-2}$	0.1_{-2}	11_{-2}	43_{-2}	…	…	…	0.2_{-2}	2_{-2}	107_{-2}	100_{-2}	111_{-4}	…	89_{-2}	…	57_{-2}
Tuvalu	$-_{-1i}$	$-_{-1i}$	$-_{-1i}$	3_{-1i}	11_{-1i}	53_{-1i}	…	…	…	0.2_{-1}	1_{-1}	107_{-1i}	97_{-1i}	104_{-1i}	94_{-2}	89_{-1i}	75_{-1i}	47_{-1i}
Vanuatu	$-_{-2}$	$-_{-2}$	$-_{-2}$	13_{-2}	1_{-2}	44_{-2}	…	…	…	…	47_{-4}	120_{-2}	87_{-2}	94_{-4}	…	99_{-2}	53_{-4}	56_{-2}
Latin America and the Caribbean																		
Anguilla	…	…	…	…	…	…	…	…	…	…	…	…	…	…	…	…	…	…
Antigua and Barbuda	$-_{-2}$	$-_{-2}$	$-_{-2}$	19_{-2}	14_{-2}	30_{-2}	…	…	…	4_{-2}	18_{-2}	88_{-2}	81_{-2}	77_{-2}	…	86_{-2}	83_{-2}	70_{-2}
Argentina	$-_{-1}$	$-_{-1i}$	0.2_{-1i}	1_{-1}	1_{-1i}	9_{-1i}	…	…	…	3_{-1}	14_{-1}	109_{-1}	99_{-1}	102_{-1}	99_{-2}	99_{-1i}	88_{-1}	91_{-1i}
Aruba	$-_{-3i}$	…	…	1_{-3i}	…	…	…	…	…	9_{-3}	31_{-3}	117_{-3}	99_{-3i}	101_{-3}	…	…	99_{-3}	…
Bahamas	$-_{-1}$	$-_{-1}$	$-_{-1}$	12_{-1}	8_{-1}	13_{-1}	…	…	…	5_{-1}	…	95_{-1}	88_{-1}	99_{-1}	…	92_{-1}	…	87_{-1}
Barbados	-	-	-	10	2	4	…	…	…	0.1	2	92	90	…	…	98	…	96
Belize	-	-	-	1	11	36	96_{-1}	61_{-1}	49_{-1}	8	16	113	99	103	95_{-1}	89	67	64
Bolivia, P. S.	0.1	0.1	0.2	7	13	18	96_{-4}	92_{-4}	80_{-4}	5	14	99	93	93	97_{-1}	87	84	82
Brazil	0.4_{-1i}	0.5_{-1i}	2_{-1i}	3_{-1i}	4_{-1i}	17_{-1i}	85_{-2}	82_{-2}	63_{-2}	8_{-1}	18_{-1}	114_{-1i}	97_{-1i}	…	…	96_{-1i}	…	83_{-1i}
British Virgin Islands	…	…	…	…	…	…	…	…	…	4	18	96_{-1i}	…	81_{-1i}	98_{-2}	…	110_{-1i}	…
Cayman Islands	…	…	…	…	…	…	…	…	…	0.2_{+1}	0.4_{+1}	…	…	…	…	…	…	…
Chile	0.1_{-1}	$-_{-1}$	0.1_{-1}	7_{-1}	7_{-1}	7_{-1}	99_{-2}	98_{-2}	87_{-2}	5_{-1}	9_{-1}	100_{-1}	93_{-1}	93_{-1}	98_{-2}	93_{-1}	92_{-1}	93_{-1}
Colombia	0.2	0.2	0.3	6	6	16	92_{-2}	76_{-2}	73_{-2}	14	22	113	94	105	98_{-3}	94	76	84
Costa Rica	$-_{-1}$	$-_{-1}$	$-_{-1}$	3_{-1}	5_{-1}	11_{-1}	95_{-3}	67_{-3}	55_{-3}	6_{-1}	25_{-1}	110_{-1}	97_{-1}	96_{-1}	85_{-2}	95_{-1}	57_{-1}	89_{-1}
Cuba	-	-	0.1	3	0.2	19	100_{-3}	98_{-3}	86_{-3}	0.4	1	102	97	92	99_{-1}	100	96	81
Curaçao	…	…	…	…	…	…	…	…	…	…	…	173_{-4}	…	…	…	…	…	…
Dominica	$-_{-1}$	$-_{-2}$	$-_{-1}$	2_{-1}	1_{-2}	10_{-1}	…	…	…	5_{-1}	14_{-1}	112_{-1}	98_{-1}	118_{-1}	96_{-3}	99_{-2}	97_{-2}	90_{-1}
Dominican Republic	0.2_{-1}	$-_{-1}$	0.2_{-1}	12_{-1}	8_{-1}	24_{-1}	89_{-4}	82_{-4}	55_{-4}	17_{-1}	22_{-1}	102_{-1}	88_{-1}	93_{-1}	93_{-2}	92_{-1}	77_{-1}	76_{-1}
Ecuador	-	-	0.2	2	1	17	97_{-4}	86_{-4}	66_{-4}	4	9	104	98	105	99_{-1}	99	104	83
El Salvador	0.1	0.1	0.1	19	17	37	88_{-3}	72_{-3}	54_{-3}	15	20	97	81	91	92_{-1}	83	78	63
Grenada	$-_{-1}$	-	-	3_{-1}	14	14	…	…	…	2	8	102	97_{-1}	106	88_{-1}	86	90	86
Guatemala	0.3_{-1}	0.4_{-1}	0.4_{-1}	13_{-1}	31_{-1}	52_{-1}	78_{-2}	48_{-2}	35_{-2}	17_{-1}	27_{-1}	101_{-1}	87_{-1}	79_{-1}	89_{-2}	69_{-1}	63_{-1}	48_{-1}
Guyana	…	…	…	…	…	…	98_{-3}	84_{-3}	56_{-3}	…	…	…	…	…	…	…	…	…
Haiti	…	…	…	…	…	…	…	…	…	…	…	…	…	…	…	…	…	…
Honduras	0.2	0.2	0.3	16	36	51	83_{-4}	52_{-4}	42_{-4}	12	33_{-2}	95	84	85	71_{-2}	64	47_{-1}	49
Jamaica	…	-	-	…	19	22	…	…	…	1	4	…	…	…	95_{-1}	81	86	78
Mexico	0.1_{-1}	0.5_{-1}	2_{-1}	1_{-1}	7_{-1}	32_{-1}	96_{-1}	88_{-1}	53_{-1}	2_{-1}	3_{-1}	104_{-1}	99_{-1}	101_{-1}	96_{-2}	93_{-1}	92_{-1}	68_{-1}
Montserrat	…	…	…	…	…	…	…	…	…	-	1	…	…	…	…	…	…	…
Nicaragua	…	…	…	…	…	…	…	…	…	…	…	…	…	…	…	…	…	…
Panama	0.1_{-2}	$-_{-2}$	0.1_{-2}	12_{-2}	10_{-2}	33_{-2}	94_{-3}	78_{-3}	59_{-3}	10_{-2}	…	93_{-1}	88_{-2}	97_{-3}	100_{-4}	90_{-2}	…	67_{-2}
Paraguay	0.2_{-1}	0.1_{-1}	0.1_{-1}	21_{-1}	17_{-1}	31_{-1}	88_{-1}	78_{-1}	59_{-1}	14_{-1}	14_{-1}	91_{-1}	79_{-1}	89_{-1}	…	83_{-1}	64_{-1}	69_{-1}
Peru	-	…	…	1	…	…	96_{-3}	87_{-3}	82_{-3}	5	8	102	99	95	94_{-1}	96	87	74
Saint Kitts and Nevis	…	…	…	…	…	…	…	…	…	1_{-1}	2_{-1}	…	…	…	99_{-2}	…	…	…
Saint Lucia	…	-	-	…	12	21	…	…	…	1	2	…	…	…	97_{-1}	88	90	79
Saint Vincent/Grenadines	-	-	-	2	2	12	…	…	…	1	15	103	98	90	95_{-1}	98	102	88
Sint Maarten	…	…	…	…	…	…	…	…	…	15_{-3}	18_{-3}	…	…	…	…	…	…	…
Suriname	-	$-_{-2}$	$-_{-2}$	2	13_{-2}	38_{-2}	…	…	…	18	36	131	98	100	65_{-1}	87_{-2}	48	62_{-2}
Trinidad and Tobago	…	…	…	…	…	…	…	…	…	…	…	…	…	…	…	…	…	…
Turks and Caicos Islands	…	…	…	…	…	…	…	…	…	1_{-2}	3_{-2}	…	…	…	…	…	…	…
Uruguay	$-_{-1}$	$-_{-1}$	$-_{-1}$	2_{-1}	1_{-1}	20_{-1}	97_{-3}	69_{-3}	40_{-3}	4_{-1}	13_{-1}	105_{-1}	98_{-1}	102_{-1}	…	99_{-1}	…	80_{-1}
Venezuela, B. R.	0.5	0.3	0.3	14	18	28	95_{-4}	79_{-4}	71_{-4}	8	12	93	86	89	99_{-1}	82	72	72

LEARNING												
K: Administration of nationally representative learning assessment						L: Achieving minimum proficiency (%)						
Early grades		End of primary		End of lower secondary		Early grades		End of primary		End of lower secondary		
Reading	Mathematics	Reading	Mathematics	Reading	Mathematics	Reading	Mathematics	Reading	Mathematics	Reading	Mathematics	COUNTRY CODE
4.1.2						4.1.1						
2017												
Yes	Yes	Yes	Yes	Yes	Yes	95	96	94	95	82-2	78-2	AUS
Yes	Yes	Yes	Yes	No	No	...	...	...	...	...	...	COK
Yes	Yes	Yes	Yes	...	...	...	...	...	...	...	...	FJI
Yes	Yes	Yes	Yes	...	...	...	...	...	...	...	...	KIR
Yes	Yes	Yes	Yes	Yes	Yes	...	...	...	...	...	...	MHL
Yes	Yes	Yes	Yes	...	...	...	...	...	...	...	...	FSM
Yes	Yes	Yes	Yes	...	...	...	...	...	...	...	...	NRU
Yes	Yes	No	No	Yes	Yes	76-2	84-2	...	...	83-2	78-2	NZL
Yes	Yes	Yes	Yes	...	...	...	...	...	...	...	...	NIU
Yes	Yes	Yes	Yes	Yes	Yes	...	...	...	...	...	...	PLW
Yes	Yes	Yes	Yes	...	...	...	...	...	...	...	...	PNG
Yes	Yes	Yes	Yes	...	...	...	...	...	...	...	...	WSM
Yes	Yes	Yes	Yes	...	...	...	...	...	...	...	...	SLB
Yes	Yes	Yes	Yes	...	...	...	...	...	...	...	...	TKL
Yes	Yes	Yes	Yes	...	...	...	...	...	...	...	...	TON
Yes	Yes	Yes	Yes	...	...	...	...	...	...	...	...	TUV
Yes	Yes	Yes	Yes	...	...	...	...	...	...	...	...	VUT
Yes	Yes	Yes	Yes	No	No	59-2	38-2	76-2	67-2	...	...	AIA
Yes	Yes	Yes	Yes	No	No	38-2	46-2	50-2	78-2	...	...	ATG
Yes	Yes	Yes	Yes	Yes	Yes	62-1	63-1	67-1	59-1	62-1	38-1	ARG
No	No	No	No	No	No	...	...	...	...	...	...	ABW
Yes	Yes	Yes	Yes	Yes	Yes	...	...	...	...	...	...	BHS
Yes	Yes	Yes	Yes	No	No	...	...	87-1	60-1	...	...	BRB
No	No	Yes	Yes	No	No	...	...	...	...	...	...	BLZ
No	No	No	No	No	No	...	...	...	...	...	...	BOL
Yes	Yes	Yes	Yes	Yes	Yes	78-1	77-1	97-2	100-2	49-2	30-2	BRA
...	...	...	...	...	...	...	...	...	...	...	...	VGB
No	No	Yes	Yes	No	No	...	...	59-1	52-1	...	...	CYM
Yes	Yes	Yes	Yes	Yes	Yes	70	63	94-4	98-4	72-2	63-2	CHL
Yes	Yes	Yes	Yes	Yes	Yes	82	82	87	57	89	79	COL
Yes	Yes	Yes	Yes	Yes	Yes	89-4	84-4	94-4	95-4	60-2	38-2	CRI
Yes	Yes	Yes	Yes	Yes	Yes	...	...	...	...	...	...	CUB
...	...	...	...	...	...	...	...	...	...	...	...	CUW
Yes	Yes	Yes	Yes	[illegible]	[illegible]	[illegible]	[illegible]	[illegible]	[illegible]	[illegible]	[illegible]	[illegible]
Yes	Yes	Yes	Yes	Yes	Yes	46-4	28-4	65-4	63-4	28-2	9-2	DOM
Yes	Yes	Yes	Yes	Yes	Yes	75-1	78-1	68-1	61-1	72-1	11-1	ECU
Yes	Yes	Yes	Yes	Yes	Yes	...	...	...	...	...	...	SLV
Yes	Yes	Yes	Yes	No	No	54-2	43-2	66-2	57-2	...	...	GRD
Yes	Yes	Yes	Yes	Yes	Yes	50-3	40-3	40-3	44-3	15-4	18-4	GTM
Yes	Yes	Yes	Yes	Yes	Yes	...	...	...	...	...	...	GUY
No	No	Yes	Yes	Yes	Yes	...	...	...	...	...	...	HTI
Yes	Yes	Yes	Yes	Yes	Yes	93-1	92-1	84-1	77-1	89-1	61-1	HND
Yes	Yes	Yes	Yes	Yes	Yes	86-3	14-2	...	...	64-1	77-1	JAM
Yes	Yes	Yes	Yes	Yes	Yes	78-4	78-4	50-2	40-2	66	35	MEX
Yes	Yes	Yes	Yes	...	...	57-2	54-2	70-2	81-2	...	...	MSR
Yes	Yes	Yes	Yes	Yes	Yes	63-4	45-4	76-4	77-4	...	...	NIC
Yes	Yes	Yes	Yes	Yes	Yes	68-4	54-4	77-4	74-4	...	...	PAN
Yes	Yes	Yes	Yes	Yes	Yes	71-2	72-2	69-2	69-2	68-2	68-2	PRY
Yes	Yes	Yes	Yes	Yes	Yes	94-1	71-1	82-4	88-4	42-1	28-1	PER
Yes	Yes	Yes	Yes	Yes	Yes	...	...	...	...	...	...	KNA
Yes	Yes	Yes	Yes	...	...	68-2	62-2	62-2	46-2	...	...	LCA
Yes	Yes	Yes	Yes	Yes	Yes	...	...	...	...	...	...	VCT
...	...	...	...	...	...	...	...	...	...	...	...	SXM
...	...	...	...	...	...	...	...	...	...	...	...	SUR
...	Yes	Yes	Yes	Yes	Yes	...	...	76	63	58-2	48-2	TTO
No	No	Yes	Yes	No	No	...	...	70-2	...	...	...	TCA
Yes	Yes	Yes	Yes	Yes	Yes	81-4	75-4	90-4	94-4	61-2	48-2	URY
Yes	Yes	Yes	Yes	Yes	Yes	...	...	...	...	...	...	VEN

TABLE 2: Continued

	PARTICIPATION / COMPLETION																			
	A						B			C		D	E	F	G	H	I	J
	Out-of-school children (000,000)			Out-of-school rate (%)			Completion rate (%)			Over-age for grade (%)		GER primary (%)	NERA primary (%)	GIR last primary (%)	Transition from primary to lower secondary (%)	NERT lower secondary (%)	GIR last lower secondary grade (%)	NERT upper secondary (%)
	Primary	Lower secondary	Upper secondary	Primary	Lower secondary	Upper secondary	Primary	Lower secondary	Upper secondary	Primary	Lower secondary							
SDG indicator:				4.1.5			4.1.4			4.1.6				4.1.3			4.1.3	
Reference year:	2017											2017						
Europe and Northern America																		
Albania	-	-	-	3	1	17	...	...	...	2	3	110	97	107	98_{-1}	99	91	83
Andorra	...	...	...	...	...	...	...	...	...	2	8	...	...	...	...	...	...	...
Austria	...	$-_{-1}$	$-_{-1}$	...	0.3_{-1}	8_{-1}	...	99_{-3}	88_{-3}	...	7_{-1}	102_{-1}	...	100_{-1}	100_{-2}	100_{-1}	97_{-1}	92_{-1}
Belarus	-	-	-	4	1	1	...	...	...	1	1	102	96	101	98_{-1}	99	103	99
Belgium	$-_{-1}$	$-_{-1}$	$-_{-1}$	1_{-1}	3_{-1}	1_{-1}	...	92_{-3}	86_{-3}	1_{-1}	7_{-1}	103_{-1}	99_{-1}	...	...	97_{-1}	94_{-1}	99_{-1}
Bermuda	...	...	...	...	...	...	...	...	...	$-_{-2}$	$-_{-2}$	90_{-2}	...	81_{-2}	51_{-3}	...	80_{-2}	...
Bosnia and Herzegovina	...	...	...	...	...	...	...	...	...	1	1	...	...	...	99_{-1}	...	...	...
Bulgaria	$-_{-1}$	$-_{-1}$	$-_{-1}$	7_{-1}	7_{-1}	10_{-1}	...	93_{-3}	80_{-3}	1_{-1}	6_{-1}	95_{-1}	93_{-1}	95_{-1}	99_{-2}	93_{-1}	48_{-1}	90_{-1}
Canada	$-_{-1}$	$-_{-2}$	0.1_{-1i}	$-_{-1}$	0.1_{-2}	8_{-1i}	...	...	...	...	...	101_{-1}	100_{-1}	...	...	100_{-2}	...	92_{-1i}
Croatia	$-_{-1}$	$-_{-1}$	$-_{-1}$	2_{-1}	1_{-1}	14_{-1}	...	99_{-3}	95_{-3}	0.3_{-1}	2_{-1}	95_{-1}	98_{-1}	98_{-1}	99_{-2}	99_{-1}	92_{-1}	86_{-1}
Czechia	...	$-_{-1}$	$-_{-1}$	...	0.1_{-1}	2_{-1}	...	99_{-3}	94_{-3}	...	5_{-1}	100_{-1}	...	97_{-1}	100_{-2}	100_{-1}	97_{-1}	98_{-1}
Denmark	$-_{-1}$	$-_{-1}$	$-_{-1}$	1_{-1}	1_{-1}	12_{-1}	...	99_{-3}	82_{-3}	0.3_{-1}	1_{-1}	102_{-1}	99_{-1}	104_{-1}	100_{-2}	99_{-1}	99_{-1}	88_{-1}
Estonia	$-_{-1}$	$-_{-1}$	$-_{-1}$	6_{-1}	0.5_{-1}	4_{-1}	...	98_{-3}	83_{-3}	1_{-1}	4_{-1}	97_{-1}	94_{-1}	96_{-1}	100_{-2}	100_{-1}	108_{-1}	96_{-1}
Finland	$-_{-1}$	$-_{-1}$	$-_{-1}$	1_{-1}	1_{-1}	4_{-1}	...	100_{-3}	89_{-3}	...	...	100_{-1}	99_{-1}	101_{-1}	100_{-2}	99_{-1}	100_{-1}	96_{-1}
France	$-_{-1i}$	0.1_{-1i}	0.1_{-1i}	1_{-1i}	2_{-1i}	6_{-1i}	...	99_{-3}	86_{-3}	...	1_{-1}	102_{-1i}	99_{-1i}	...	...	98_{-1i}	98_{-1i}	94_{-1i}
Germany	$-_{-1i}$	...	...	0.2_{-1i}	...	...	...	92_{-3}	80_{-3}	...	...	103_{-1}	100_{-1i}	99_{-1}	100_{-2}	...	58_{-1}	...
Greece	$-_{-1}$	$-_{-1}$	$-_{-1}$	7_{-1}	7_{-1}	10_{-1}	...	99_{-3}	93_{-3}	1_{-1}	4_{-1}	94_{-1}	93_{-1}	94_{-1}	97_{-2}	93_{-1}	90_{-1}	90_{-1}
Hungary	$-_{-1}$	$-_{-1}$	$-_{-1}$	3_{-1}	4_{-1}	12_{-1}	...	99_{-3}	86_{-3}	1_{-1}	3_{-1}	102_{-1}	97_{-1}	99_{-1}	100_{-2}	96_{-1}	93_{-1}	88_{-1}
Iceland	$-_{-1}$	$-_{-1}$	$-_{-1}$	0.5_{-1}	0.1_{-1}	16_{-1}	...	100_{-3}	70_{-3}	$-_{-1}$	$-_{-1}$	100_{-1}	100_{-1}	...	...	100_{-1}	...	84_{-1}
Ireland	$-_{-1i}$	$-_{-1i}$	$-_{-1i}$	$-_{-1i}$	0.4_{-1i}	0.5_{-1i}	...	97_{-3}	94_{-3}	$-_{-1}$	0.2_{-1}	101_{-1i}	100_{-1i}	...	...	100_{-1i}	99_{-1i}	100_{-1i}
Italy	$-_{-1}$	$-_{-1}$	0.1_{-1}	1_{-1}	0.3_{-1}	5_{-1}	...	99_{-3}	83_{-3}	0.4_{-1}	2_{-1}	100_{-1}	99_{-1}	99_{-1}	100_{-2}	100_{-1}	100_{-1}	95_{-1}
Latvia	$-_{-1i}$	$-_{-1i}$	$-_{-1i}$	3_{-1i}	2_{-1i}	4_{-1i}	...	99_{-3}	84_{-3}	1_{-1}	4_{-1}	99_{-1i}	97_{-1i}	98_{-1i}	99_{-2}	98_{-1i}	96_{-1i}	96_{-1i}
Liechtenstein	$-_{-1i}$	$-_{-1i}$	$-_{-1i}$	1_{-1i}	5_{-1i}	13_{-1i}	...	...	...	0.1_{-1}	1_{-1}	105_{-1i}	99_{-1i}	100_{-1i}	93_{-2}	95_{-1i}	86_{-1i}	87_{-1i}
Lithuania	$-_{-1i}$	$-_{-1i}$	$-_{-1i}$	0.3_{-1i}	0.1_{-1i}	4_{-1i}	...	98_{-3}	89_{-3}	0.4_{-1}	3_{-1}	103_{-1i}	100_{-1i}	102_{-1i}	100_{-2}	100_{-1i}	101_{-1i}	96_{-1i}
Luxembourg	$-_{-1}$	$-_{-1}$	$-_{-1}$	1_{-1}	5_{-1}	18_{-1}	...	90_{-3}	69_{-3}	2_{-1}	8_{-1}	101_{-1}	99_{-1}	79_{-1}	...	95_{-1}	99_{-1}	82_{-1}
Malta	$-_{-1}$	$-_{-1}$	$-_{-1}$	2_{-1}	1_{-1}	13_{-1}	...	...	...	0.2_{-1}	1_{-1}	105_{-1}	98_{-1}	102_{-1}	99_{-2}	99_{-1}	100_{-1}	87_{-1}
Monaco	...	...	...	...	...	...	...	...	...	0.4	1	...	...	...	...	...	...	...
Montenegro	-	-	-	4	4	14	100_{-4}	99_{-4}	84_{-4}	2	1	98	96	90	100_{-1}	96	99	86
Netherlands	...	$-_{-1}$	$-_{-1}$	...	1_{-1}	0.1_{-1}	...	94_{-3}	79_{-3}	...	...	103_{-1}	...	...	...	99_{-1}	...	100_{-1}
Norway	$-_{-1}$	$-_{-1}$	$-_{-1}$	0.2_{-1}	0.5_{-1}	8_{-1}	...	99_{-3}	78_{-3}	$-_{-1}$	$-_{-1}$	100_{-1}	100_{-1}	101_{-1}	100_{-2}	100_{-1}	101_{-1}	92_{-1}
Poland	0.1_{-1}	0.1_{-1}	0.1_{-1}	4_{-1}	5_{-1}	8_{-1}	...	98_{-3}	92_{-3}	...	...	110_{-1}	96_{-1}	100_{-1}	100_{-2}	95_{-1}	95_{-1}	92_{-1}
Portugal	$-_{-1}$	$-_{-1}$	$-_{-1}$	4_{-1}	1_{-1}	2_{-1}	...	94_{-3}	65_{-3}	...	...	105_{-1}	96_{-1}	...	...	99_{-1}	...	98_{-1}
Republic of Moldova	$-_{i}$	$-_{i}$	$-_{i}$	10_{i}	15_{i}	35_{i}	...	...	...	0.4	1	91_{i}	90_{i}	90_{i}	98_{-1}	85_{i}	82_{i}	65_{i}
Romania	0.1_{-1}	0.1_{-1i}	0.2_{-1}	10_{-1}	9_{-1i}	23_{-1}	...	96_{-3}	81_{-3}	...	4_{-1}	89_{-1}	90_{-1}	92_{-1}	100_{-2}	91_{-1i}	86_{-1}	77_{-1}
Russian Federation	0.1_{-1i}	0.1_{-1i}	0.3_{-3i}	2_{-1i}	1_{-1i}	10_{-3i}	100_{-4}	99_{-4}	87_{-4}	...	...	102_{-1}	98_{-1i}	98_{-1}	100_{-2}	99_{-1i}	99_{-1}	90_{-3i}
San Marino	...	...	...	...	...	...	...	...	...	...	...	...	...	...	...	...	...	...
Serbia	$-_{i}$	$-_{i}$	$-_{i}$	1_{i}	2_{i}	11_{i}	99_{-3}	98_{-3}	76_{-3}	1	1	100_{i}	99_{i}	99_{i}	100_{-1}	98_{i}	95_{i}	89_{i}
Slovakia	...	$-_{-1}$	$-_{-1}$	...	5_{-1}	10_{-1}	...	100_{-3}	92_{-3}	...	...	98_{-1}	...	93_{-1}	99_{-3}	95_{-1}	87_{-2}	90_{-1}
Slovenia	$-_{-1}$	$-_{-1}$	$-_{-1}$	2_{-1}	2_{-1}	5_{-1}	...	100_{-3}	93_{-3}	1_{-1}	1_{-1}	99_{-1}	98_{-1}	97_{-1}	99_{-2}	98_{-1}	96_{-1}	95_{-1}
Spain	$-_{-1}$	$-_{-1}$	$-_{-1}$	1_{-1}	0.4_{-1}	1_{-1}	...	93_{-3}	67_{-3}	0.2_{-1}	9_{-1}	104_{-1}	99_{-1}	97_{-1}	99_{-2}	100_{-1}	92_{-1}	99_{-1}
Sweden	$-_{-1}$	$-_{-2}$	$-_{-1}$	0.4_{-1}	0.2_{-2}	1_{-1}	...	100_{-3}	93_{-3}	0.1_{-1}	0.3_{-1}	125_{-1}	100_{-1}	105_{-1}	100_{-2}	100_{-2}	108_{-1}	99_{-1}
Switzerland	$-_{-1}$	$-_{-1}$	0.1_{-1}	0.2_{-1}	0.4_{-1}	18_{-1}	...	99_{-3}	79_{-3}	0.2_{-1}	1_{-1}	104_{-1}	100_{-1}	97_{-1}	100_{-2}	100_{-1}	98_{-1}	82_{-1}
TFYR Macedonia	$-_{-2}$	...	...	8_{-2}	...	...	...	...	...	0.5_{-2}	...	94_{-2}	92_{-2}	91_{-2}	100_{-3i}	...	88_{-2i}	...
Ukraine	0.1_{-3}	0.1_{-3i}	$-_{-3i}$	7_{-3}	3_{-3i}	5_{-3i}	100_{-4}	99_{-4}	95_{-4}	1	1	100_{-3}	93_{-3}	103_{-3}	100_{-1}	97_{-3i}	95_{-3}	95_{-3i}
United Kingdom	$-_{-1}$	$-_{-1}$	0.1_{-1}	0.2_{-1}	0.1_{-1}	2_{-1}	...	100_{-3}	83_{-3}	$-_{-1}$	$-_{-1}$	101_{-1}	100_{-1}	101_{-1}	...	100_{-1}	...	98_{-1}
United States	1_{-1i}	0.3_{-3i}	1_{-3i}	4_{-1i}	2_{-3i}	7_{-3i}	99_{-4}	99_{-4}	92_{-4}	3_{-1}	4_{-1}	101_{-1i}	96_{-1i}	...	...	99_{-1i}	...	95_{-1i}

LEARNING												
K Administration of nationally representative learning assessment						L Achieving minimum proficiency (%)						
Early grades		End of primary		End of lower secondary		Early grades		End of primary		End of lower secondary		
Reading	Mathematics	Reading	Mathematics	Reading	Mathematics	Reading	Mathematics	Reading	Mathematics	Reading	Mathematics	COUNTRY CODE
4.1.2						4.1.1						
2017												
Yes	Yes	Yes	Yes	Yes	Yes	86-3	...	95-1	97-1	25-2	23-2	ALB
No	No	No	No	No	No	...	...	...	...	...	...	AND
...	...	Yes	Yes	Yes	Yes	...	...	...	...	77-2	78-2	AUT
...	...	Yes	Yes	Yes	...	...	...	...	...	...	...	BLR
Yes	Yes	Yes	Yes	Yes	Yes	...	...	...	...	80-2	80-2	BEL
No	No	Yes	Yes	Yes	Yes	...	...	...	...	...	...	BMU
...	...	...	...	...	...	...			...	...	...	BIH
Yes	Yes	Yes	Yes	Yes	Yes	...	...	...	92-2	59-2	58-2	BGR
...	Yes	...	...	Yes	Yes	...	...	...	...	89-2	86-2	CAN
...	...	Yes	Yes	Yes	Yes	...	...	...	93-2	80-2	68-2	HRV
...	Yes	...	...	Yes	Yes	...	96-2	...	...	78-2	78-2	CZE
Yes	Yes	Yes	Yes	Yes	Yes	...	96-2	...	...	85-2	86-2	DNK
Yes	Yes	Yes	Yes	Yes	Yes	...	...	...	...	89-2	89-2	EST
Yes	Yes	Yes	Yes	Yes	Yes		97-1	...	...	89-2	86-2	FIN
Yes	Yes	Yes	Yes	Yes	Yes	...	87-2	...	...	79-2	77-2	FRA
Yes	Yes	Yes	Yes	Yes	Yes	...	...	...	96-2	84-2	83-2	DEU
...	...	...	...	Yes	Yes	...	...	...	...	73-2	64-2	GRC
...	...	Yes	Yes	Yes	Yes	...	...	...	92-2	73-2	88-2	HUN
...	...	Yes	Yes	Yes	Yes	...	...	...	...	78-2	76-2	ISL
Yes	Yes	Yes	Yes	Yes	Yes	...	97-1	...	...	90-2	94-1	IRL
Yes	Yes	Yes	Yes	Yes	Yes	...	93-2	...	...	79-2	89-2	ITA
Yes	Yes	Yes	Yes	Yes	Yes	...	...	...	...	82-2	79-2	LVA
...	...	...	...	Yes	Yes	...	...	...	...	...	...	LIE
...	...	Yes	Yes	Yes	Yes	...	...	92	99	75-2	75-2	LTU
Yes	Yes	...	...	Yes	Yes	...	...	...	...	74-2	74-2	LUX
Yes	Yes	...	...	Yes	Yes	...	...	...	...	64-2	84-1	MLT
...	...	...	...	...	...	...	...	...	...	...	...	MCO
Yes	Yes	...	...	Yes	Yes	...	...	...	...	58-2	48-2	MNE
Yes	Yes	Yes	Yes	Yes	Yes	...	99-2	...	...	82-2	83-2	NLD
Yes	Yes	Yes	Yes	Yes	Yes	...	98-2	...	...	85-2	83-2	NOR
...	Yes	Yes	Yes	Yes	Yes	...	96-2			86-2	83-2	POL
...	Yes	Yes	Yes	Yes	Yes	...	97-2	...	...	83-2	76-2	PRT
...	...	...	...	Yes	Yes	...	...	...		54-2	50-2	MDA
...	...	...		Yes	Yes	...	...	...	...	61-2	60-2	ROU
...	...	Yes	Yes	Yes	Yes	...	...	...	98-2	84-2	81-2	RUS
...	...	...	...	...	...	...	...	...	...	...	...	SMR
Yes	Yes	Yes	Yes	Yes	Yes	...	...	...	91-2	...	...	SRB
...	...	Yes	Yes	Yes	Yes	...	...	...	88-2	68-2	72-2	SVK
Yes	Yes	Yes	Yes	Yes	Yes	...	95-2	...	...	85-2	84-2	SVN
...	Yes	Yes	Yes	Yes	Yes	...	93-2	...	...	84-2	78-2	ESP
Yes	Yes	Yes	Yes	Yes	Yes	...	95-2	...	...	82-2	79-2	SWE
...	...	...	...	Yes	Yes	...	...	...	...	80-2	84-2	CHE
...	...	...	...	Yes	Yes	...	...	...	...	29-2	30-2	MKD
...	...	...	...	...	...	...	...	...	...	...	...	UKR
Yes	Yes	Yes	Yes	Yes	Yes	...	...	...	...	82-2	78-2	GBR
Yes	Yes	No	No	Yes	Yes	69-2	95-2	...	...	81-2	71-2	USA

TABLE 3 : SDG 4, Target 4.2 – Early childhood

By 2030, ensure that all girls and boys have access to quality early childhood development, care and pre-primary education so that they are ready for primary education

	A Children under 5 developmentally on track (%)	B Under-5 stunting (%)	C Stimulating home environment (%)	D Children under 5 with 3+ children's books (%)	E GER pre-primary (%)	F NERA one year before primary entry (%)
SDG indicator:	4.2.1		4.2.3		4.2.4	4.2.2
Reference year:	2017					
Region	**Weighted average**					
World	…	22	…	…	50i	69i
Sub-Saharan Africa	61i	33	…	…	32i	42-1i
Northern Africa and Western Asia	…	16	…	…	32i	52i
Northern Africa	…	17	…	5i	41i	57i
Western Asia	…	15	…	…	25i	48i
Central and Southern Asia	…	32	…	…	25i	…
Central Asia	85i	12	84i	45i	35	56
Southern Asia	…	33	…	…	24i	…
Eastern and South-eastern Asia	…	13	…	…	81	87i
Eastern Asia	…	5	…	…	86	…
South-eastern Asia	…	26	67i	26i	68	91
Oceania	…	…	…	…	79i	83i
Latin America and the Caribbean	…	10	…	…	74i	95i
Caribbean	86i	8	69i	24i	68i	87i
Central America	82	14	75	34	65	94
South America	…	8	…	…	83i	94i
Europe and Northern America	…	…	…	…	85i	95i
Europe	…	…	…	…	92i	96i
Northern America	…	2	…	…	71i	93i
Low income	61i	35	…	…	22i	42i
Middle income	…	22	…	…	52i	…
Lower middle	…	32	…	…	36i	…
Upper middle	…	6	…	…	75	83i
High income	…	3	…	…	83i	93i

A Percentage of children aged 36 to 59 months who are developmentally on track in health, learning and psychosocial well-being (UNICEF Early Childhood Development Index [ECDI]) [*Source:* MICS country reports].

B Under-5 moderate or severe stunting rate (%) [*Source:* UNICEF, WHO, World Bank Joint Child Malnutrition Estimates (JME)]. (Regional aggregates are weighted averages of statistical JME estimates for the reference year, not of the observed country values in the country table.)

C Percentage of children aged 36 to 59 months experiencing positive and stimulating home learning environments [*Source:* MICS country reports].

D Percentage of children under age 5 living in households with three or more children's books [*Source:* MICS country reports].

E Gross enrolment ratio (GER) in pre-primary education.

F Adjusted net enrolment rate (NERA) one year before the official primary school entry age.

Notes:
Source: UIS unless noted otherwise. Data refer to school year ending in 2017 unless noted otherwise.
Aggregates represent countries listed in the table with available data and may include estimates for countries with no recent data.

(-) Magnitude nil or negligible.

(…) Data not available or category not applicable.

(± n) Reference year differs (e.g. -2: reference year 2015 instead of 2017).

(i) Estimate and/or partial coverage.

TABLE 3: Continued

	A	B	C	D	E	F	COUNTRY CODE
	Children under 5 developmentally on track (%)	Under-5 stunting (%)	Stimulating home environment (%)	Children under 5 with 3+ children's books (%)	GER pre-primary (%)	NERA one year before primary entry (%)	
SDG indicator:	4.2.1		4.2.3		4.2.4	4.2.2	
Reference year:				2017			
Sub-Saharan Africa							
Angola	...	38$_{-1}$	...	...	81$_{-1}$	66$_{-1i}$	AGO
Benin	61$_{-3}$	34$_{-3}$	28$_{-3}$	1$_{-3}$	25$_{-1}$	88$_{-1}$	BEN
Botswana	...	...	...	...	20$_{-3}$	34$_{-3i}$	BWA
Burkina Faso	...	27$_{-1}$	...	...	4	17	BFA
Burundi	...	56$_{-1}$	...	...	14	42	BDI
Cabo Verde	...	...	...	...	71	80	CPV
Cameroon	61$_{-3}$	32$_{-3}$	44$_{-3}$	4$_{-3}$	37	46$_{i}$	CMR
Central African Republic	...	...	...	...	3	...	CAF
Chad	33$_{-2}$	40$_{-2}$	47$_{-2}$	1$_{-2}$	1$_{-1}$	...	TCD
Comoros	...	...	...	...	20	39	COM
Congo	61$_{-2}$	21$_{-2}$	59$_{-2}$	3$_{-2}$	...	...	COG
Côte d'Ivoire	63$_{-1}$	22$_{-1}$	...	...	8	22	CIV
D. R. Congo	66$_{-3}$	43$_{-4}$	52$_{-3}$	1$_{-3}$	4$_{-2}$	...	COD
Djibouti	...	...	...	...	7	7	DJI
Equat. Guinea	...	...	...	...	43$_{-2}$	44$_{-2}$	GNQ
Eritrea	...	...	...	...	15	17	ERI
Eswatini	65$_{-3}$	26$_{-3}$	39$_{-3}$	6$_{-3}$	...	...	SWZ
Ethiopia	...	38$_{-1}$	...	...	30$_{-2}$	38$_{-2}$	ETH
Gabon	...	...	...	...	...	...	GAB
Gambia	...	25$_{-4}$	...	...	39	...	GMB
Ghana	...	19$_{-3}$	...	...	115	81	GHA
Guinea	49$_{-1}$	32$_{-1}$	...	...	...	41$_{-1}$	GIN
Guinea-Bissau	61$_{-3}$	28$_{-3}$	34$_{-3}$	[illegible]$_{-3}$	...	...	GNB
Kenya	...	26$_{-3}$	...	...	77$_{-1}$	...	KEN
Lesotho	...	33$_{-3}$	...	...	33$_{-1}$	36$_{-1}$	LSO
Liberia	...	32$_{-4}$	...	...	157$_{-1}$	88$_{-1}$	LBR
Madagascar	...	...	...	...	38	...	MDG
Malawi	60$_{-3}$	37$_{-2}$	29$_{-3}$	1$_{-3}$	81$_{-2}$	...	MWI
Mali	62$_{-2}$	30$_{-2}$	55$_{-2}$	0.3$_{-2}$	5	50	MLI
Mauritania	60$_{-2}$	28$_{-2}$	44$_{-2}$	1$_{-2}$	10$_{-2}$	...	MRT
Mauritius	...	...	...	...	101	91	MUS
Mozambique	...	...	...	...	...	...	MOZ
Namibia	...	23$_{-4}$	...	...	33	67	NAM
Niger	...	42$_{-1}$	...	...	8	22	NER
Nigeria	61	44$_{-1}$	...	...	...	...	NGA
Rwanda	63$_{-2}$	38$_{-2}$	48$_{-2}$	1$_{-2}$	21	42	RWA
Sao Tome and Principe	54$_{-3}$	17$_{-3}$	63$_{-3}$	6$_{-3}$	51$_{-1}$	54$_{-1}$	STP
Senegal	...	17$_{-1}$	...	...	16	10	SEN
Seychelles	...	...	...	...	103$_{-1}$	97$_{-1}$	SYC
Sierra Leone	...	38$_{-4}$	...	...	12	36	SLE
Somalia	...				...	...	SOM
South Africa	...	27$_{-1}$	...	...	25$_{-1}$	...	ZAF
South Sudan	...		...	...	10$_{-2}$	19$_{-2i}$	SSD
Togo	51$_{-3}$	28$_{-3}$	25$_{-3}$	1$_{-3}$	21	...	TGO
Uganda	65$_{-1}$	29$_{-1}$	...	...	14	...	UGA
United Republic of Tanzania	...	34$_{-2}$	...	...	42	52	TZA
Zambia	...	40$_{-4}$	...	...	...	...	ZMB
Zimbabwe	62$_{-3}$	27$_{-2}$	43$_{-3}$	3$_{-3}$	42$_{-4}$	36$_{-4}$	ZWE

TABLE 3: Continued

	A Children under 5 developmentally on track (%)	B Under-5 stunting (%)	C Stimulating home environment (%)	D Children under 5 with 3+ children's books (%)	E GER pre-primary (%)	F NERA one year before primary entry (%)	COUNTRY CODE
SDG indicator:	4.2.1		4.2.3		4.2.4	4.2.2	
Reference year:			2017				
Northern Africa and Western Asia							
Algeria	70_{-4}	...	78_{-4}	10_{-4}	...	...	DZA
Armenia	...	9_{-1}	...	...	52	...	ARM
Azerbaijan	...	18_{-4}	...	...	36_{i}	61_{i}	AZE
Bahrain	...	...	...	...	55	77	BHR
Cyprus	...	...	...	...	80_{-2i}	95_{-2i}	CYP
Egypt	...	22_{-3}	...	...	29	38	EGY
Georgia	88_{-2}	...	83_{-2}	58_{-2}	...	...	GEO
Iraq	...	...	...	...	...	...	IRQ
Israel	...	...	...	...	111_{-1}	100_{-1}	ISR
Jordan	...	...	...	...	...	...	JOR
Kuwait	...	5_{-2}	...	...	65	76	KWT
Lebanon	...	...	...	...	85	96	LBN
Libya	...	...	...	...	...	...	LBY
Morocco	...	...	...	...	54	54_{i}	MAR
Oman	68_{-3}	14_{-3}	81_{-3}	25_{-3}	54	83	OMN
Palestine	72_{-3}	7_{-3}	78_{-3}	20_{-3}	54	62	PSE
Qatar	...	...	...	...	61	93	QAT
Saudi Arabia	...	...	...	...	25_{-1}	50_{-1}	SAU
Sudan	...	38_{-3}	...	2_{-3}	45_{-1}	...	SDN
Syrian Arab Republic	...	...	...	...	6_{-4}	39_{-4}	SYR
Tunisia	...	...	...	...	44_{-1}	...	TUN
Turkey	...	10_{-4}	...	...	30_{-1}	66_{-1}	TUR
United Arab Emirates	...	...	...	...	82_{-1}	88_{-4i}	ARE
Yemen	...	46_{-4}	...	...	2_{-1}	4_{-4}	YEM
Central and Southern Asia							
Afghanistan	...	41_{-4}	...	...	...	...	AFG
Bangladesh	64_{-4}	36_{-3}	78_{-4}	9_{-4}	40	...	BGD
Bhutan	...	...	...	...	25	...	BTN
India	...	38_{-2}	...	...	13_{-1}	...	IND
Iran, Islamic Republic of	...	...	...	...	51_{-2}	47_{-2}	IRN
Kazakhstan	86_{-2}	8_{-2}	86_{-2}	51_{-2}	54	90_{-1}	KAZ
Kyrgyzstan	78_{-3}	13_{-3}	72_{-3}	27_{-3}	39	95	KGZ
Maldives	...	...	...	...	91	98	MDV
Nepal	64_{-3}	36_{-1}	67_{-3}	5_{-3}	86	85	NPL
Pakistan	...	...	...	...	80	...	PAK
Sri Lanka	...	17_{-1}	...	...	94_{-1}	...	LKA
Tajikistan	...	...	...	...	10	13	TJK
Turkmenistan	91_{-1}	12_{-2}	94_{-1}	48_{-1}	58_{-3}	...	TKM
Uzbekistan	...	...	...	...	27	37	UZB
Eastern and South-eastern Asia							
Brunei Darussalam	...	...	...	...	69	95	BRN
Cambodia	68_{-3}	32_{-3}	59_{-3}	4_{-3}	22	...	KHM
China	...	8_{-4}	...	...	86	...	CHN
DPR Korea	...	...	...	...	...	...	PRK
Hong Kong, China	...	...	...	...	107	100_{i}	HKG
Indonesia	...	36_{-4}	...	...	62	97	IDN
Japan	...	...	...	...	87_{-1}	...	JPN
Lao PDR	...	...	...	...	43	63	LAO
Macao, China	...	...	...	...	96	94	MAC
Malaysia	...	21_{-1}	25_{-1}	56_{-1}	97	99_{-2}	MYS
Mongolia	76_{-4}	11_{-4}	55_{-4}	33_{-4}	87	96	MNG
Myanmar	...	29_{-1}	54_{-1}	4_{-1}	10	...	MMR
Philippines	...	33_{-2}	...	...	96_{-1}	80_{-1}	PHL
Republic of Korea	...	...	...	...	98_{-1}	96_{-1}	KOR
Singapore	...	...	...	...	...	...	SGP
Thailand	91_{-1}	10_{-1}	93_{-1}	41_{-1}	74	97	THA
Timor-Leste	...	50_{-4}	...	...	18	33	TLS
Viet Nam	89_{-3}	25_{-2}	76_{-3}	26_{-3}	95	99	VNM

TABLE 3: Continued

	A	B	C	D	E	F	
	Children under 5 developmentally on track (%)	Under-5 stunting (%)	Stimulating home environment (%)	Children under 5 with 3+ children's books (%)	GER pre-primary (%)	NERA one year before primary entry (%)	COUNTRY CODE
SDG indicator:	4.2.1		4.2.3		4.2.4	4.2.2	
Reference year:	2017						
Oceania							
Australia	...	...	...	...	169-1	91-1	AUS
Cook Islands	...	...	...	...	106-1i	99-1i	COK
Fiji	...	...	...	...	...	...	FJI
Kiribati	...	...	...	...	...	...	KIR
Marshall Islands	...	...	...	...	40-1	66-1	MHL
Micronesia, F. S.	...	...	...	...	33-2	76-2	FSM
Nauru	...	...	...	...	69-1i	75-1i	NRU
New Zealand	...	...	...	...	92-1	92-1	NZL
Niue	...	...	...	...	172-1i	56-2i	NIU
Palau	...	...	...	...	75-3i	90-3i	PLW
Papua New Guinea	...	...	...	...	44-1	74-1	PNG
Samoa	...	5-3	...	...	51	37	WSM
Solomon Is	...	32-2	...	...	111	65-2	SLB
Tokelau	...	...	...	...	121-1i	88-1i	TKL
Tonga	...	...	...	...	42-2	...	TON
Tuvalu	...	...	...	...	107-1i	97-1i	TUV
Vanuatu	...	28-4	...	...	102-2	...	VUT
Latin America and the Caribbean							
Anguilla	...	...	...	...	...	...	AIA
Antigua and Barbuda	...	...	...	...	86-2	96-2	ATG
Argentina	...	...	...	...	75-1	99-1	ARG
Aruba	...	...		...	106-1	100-1	ABW
Bahamas	...	...	...	...	32-1	...	BHS
Barbados	...	...	...	...	79	90	BRB
Belize	82-2	15-2	88-2	44-2	48	84	BLZ
Bolivia, P. S.	...	16-1	...	...	75	92	BOL
Brazil	...	...	...	...	96-1i	97-1i	BRA
British Virgin Islands	...	...	...	...	77-1i	84-1i	VGB
Cayman Islands	...	...	...	...	...	...	CYM
Chile	...	2-3	...	...	85-1	97-1	CHL
Colombia	...	...	...	...	...	87	COL
Costa Rica	...	...	...	...	78-1	89-1	CRI
Cuba	89-3	...	89-3	48-3	101	100	CUB
Curaçao	...	...	...	...	...	...	CUW
Dominica	...	...	...	...	84-1	71-2	DMA
Dominican Republic	84-3	7-4	58-3	10-3	44-1	77-1	DOM
Ecuador	...	24-3	...	...	72	98	ECU
El Salvador	81-3	14-3	[illegible]	[illegible]	[illegible]	[illegible]	SLV
Grenada	...	...	...	...	[illegible]	84	GRD
Guatemala	...	46-[illegible]			[illegible]	[illegible]	GTM
Guyana	86-3	[illegible]	[illegible]	[illegible]	...	...	GUY
Haiti	...	...	...	...	...	...	HTI
Honduras	...	...	...	...	43	82	HND
Jamaica	...	6-3	...	...	82	96	JAM
Mexico	82-2	12-2	76-2	35-2	71-1	99-1	MEX
Montserrat	...	...	...	...	...	...	MSR
Nicaragua	...	...	...	...	...	...	NIC
Panama	80-4	...	74-4	26-4	61-1	73-1i	PAN
Paraguay	82-1	6-1	...	...	45-1	71-1	PRY
Peru	...	13-1	...	...	89	96	PER
Saint Kitts and Nevis	...	...	...	...	...	...	KNA
Saint Lucia	...	...	...	...	82	96	LCA
Saint Vincent/Grenadines	...	...	...	...	103	94	VCT
Sint Maarten	...	...	...	...	...	...	SXM
Suriname	...	...	...	...	101	97	SUR
Trinidad and Tobago	...	...	...	...	...	...	TTO
Turks and Caicos Islands	...	...	...	...	...	...	TCA
Uruguay	87-4	...	93-4	59-4	91-1	97-1	URY
Venezuela, B. R.	...	...	...	...	67	82	VEN

TABLE 3: Continued

	A	B	C	D	E	F	COUNTRY CODE
	Children under 5 developmentally on track (%)	Under-5 stunting (%)	Stimulating home environment (%)	Children under 5 with 3+ children's books (%)	GER pre-primary (%)	NERA one year before primary entry (%)	
SDG indicator:	4.2.1		4.2.3		4.2.4	4.2.2	
Reference year:				2017			
Europe and Northern America							
Albania	...	...	...	...	83	89$_{-2}$	ALB
Andorra	...	...	...	...	...	...	AND
Austria	...	...	...	...	104$_{-1}$	99$_{-1}$	AUT
Belarus	...	...	...	...	99	97	BLR
Belgium	...	...	...	...	116$_{-1}$	100$_{-1}$	BEL
Bermuda	...	...	...	...	62$_{-2}$	...	BMU
Bosnia and Herzegovina	...	...	...	...	...	...	BIH
Bulgaria	...	...	...	...	81$_{-1}$	95$_{-1}$	BGR
Canada	...	...	...	...	...	...	CAN
Croatia	...	...	...	...	63$_{-1}$	95$_{-1}$	HRV
Czechia	...	...	...	...	105$_{-1}$	92$_{-1}$	CZE
Denmark	...	...	...	...	96$_{-1}$	98$_{-1}$	DNK
Estonia	...	...	...	...	...	91$_{-1}$	EST
Finland	...	...	...	...	83$_{-1}$	99$_{-1}$	FIN
France	...	...	...	...	105$_{-1i}$	100$_{-1i}$	FRA
Germany	...	...	...	...	108$_{-1}$	...	DEU
Greece	...	...	...	...	46$_{-1}$	89$_{-1}$	GRC
Hungary	...	...	...	...	82$_{-1}$	91$_{-1}$	HUN
Iceland	...	...	...	...	95$_{-1}$	99$_{-1}$	ISL
Ireland	...	...	...	...	116$_{-1i}$	98$_{-1i}$	IRL
Italy	...	...	...	...	98$_{-1}$	98$_{-1}$	ITA
Latvia	...	...	...	...	95$_{-1i}$	97$_{-1i}$	LVA
Liechtenstein	...	...	...	...	103$_{-1i}$	100$_{-1i}$	LIE
Lithuania	...	...	...	...	87$_{-1i}$	99$_{-1i}$	LTU
Luxembourg	...	...	...	...	93$_{-1}$	99$_{-1}$	LUX
Malta	...	...	...	...	112$_{-1}$	98$_{-1}$	MLT
Monaco	...	...	...	...	...	...	MCO
Montenegro	94$_{-4}$	9$_{-4}$	98$_{-4}$	73$_{-4}$	62	69	MNE
Netherlands	...	...	...	...	95$_{-1}$	99$_{-1}$	NLD
Norway	...	...	...	...	96$_{-1}$	98$_{-1}$	NOR
Poland	...	...	...	...	70$_{-1}$	100$_{-1}$	POL
Portugal	...	...	...	...	93$_{-1}$	100$_{-1}$	PRT
Republic of Moldova	...	...	...	...	86$_{i}$	94$_{i}$	MDA
Romania	...	...	...	...	87$_{-1}$	88$_{-1}$	ROU
Russian Federation	...	...	...	...	89$_{-1}$	96$_{-1}$	RUS
San Marino	...	...	...	...	...	...	SMR
Serbia	95$_{-3}$	6$_{-3}$	96$_{-3}$	72$_{-3}$	61$_{i}$	97$_{i}$	SRB
Slovakia	...	...	...	...	93$_{-1}$	82$_{-1}$	SVK
Slovenia	...	...	...	...	92$_{-1}$	95$_{-1}$	SVN
Spain	...	...	...	...	95$_{-1}$	96$_{-1}$	ESP
Sweden	...	...	...	...	94$_{-1}$	99$_{-1}$	SWE
Switzerland	...	...	...	...	105$_{-1}$	100$_{-1}$	CHE
TFYR Macedonia	...	...	...	...	36$_{-2}$	44$_{-2}$	MKD
Ukraine	...	...	...	...	84$_{-4}$	...	UKR
United Kingdom	...	...	...	...	111$_{-1}$	100$_{-1}$	GBR
United States	...	...	...	...	72$_{-1i}$	91$_{-1i}$	USA

TABLE 4:

SDG 4, Target 4.3 – Technical, vocational, tertiary and adult education

By 2030, ensure equal access for all women and men to affordable and quality technical, vocational and tertiary education, including university

SDG 4, Target 4.4 – Skills for work

By 2030, substantially increase the number of youth and adults who have relevant skills, including technical and vocational skills, for employment, decent jobs and entrepreneurship

	A	B	C	D	E	F	G			H			
	Participation in adult education & training (%)	% of youth enrolled in TVET	TVET share of secondary enrolment (%)	Transition from upper secondary to tertiary (%)	Gross entry ratio into tertiary (%)	GER tertiary (%)	% of adults 15+ with ICT skills: Copy & paste within document	Use formula in spreadsheet	Write computer program	% of adults 25+ having attained at least: Primary	Lower secondary	Upper secondary	Post-secondary
SDG indicator:	4.3.1	4.3.3				4.3.2	4.4.1			4.4.3			
Reference year:	2017						2017						
Region	Weighted average						Weighted average						
World	...	4i	11i	93i	49i	38i	...	...	...	...	...	...	...
Sub-Saharan Africa	...	1i	6i	...	...	9i	...	...	...	...	...	...	...
Northern Africa and Western Asia	...	8i	14i	95i	53	44i	22i	14i	3i	82i	60i	45i	23i
Northern Africa	...	7i	14i	61	37	34i	16	6	2	...	...	...	...
Western Asia	24i	9i	14i	129i	72i	54i	...	26i	4i	83	61	45	24
Central and Southern Asia	...	1i	3i	118	42	25i	...	...	...	...	...	...	...
Central Asia	...	14	21	19	26	23	...	...	...	100i	99i	90i	54i
Southern Asia	...	1i	2i	121	42	25i	...	...	...	...	...	...	...
Eastern and South-eastern Asia	...	2i	16	74	60	46	...	...	...	...	...	...	...
Eastern Asia	...	1i	18	80	68	53	...	...	...	...	...	...	...
South-eastern Asia	...	5i	12	56i	39	34	...	...	5i	80	52	41	17i
Oceania	...	13i	29i	...	...	79i	...	...	...	100	94	75	46
Latin America and the Caribbean	...	6i	12i	88i	49i	51i	...	...	...	80	58	43	17
Caribbean	...	6i	15i	89i	...	45i	...	...	...	...	...	...	...
Central America	...	11	27	72	34	34	...	28	9	77	55	32	15
South America	...	5i	8	...	...	60i	26i	16i	3i	81	59	47	18
Europe and Northern America	43i	10i	18i	74i	62i	77i	53i	35i	...	...	...	...	...
Europe	43i	17i	26i	80i	70i	71i	53	35	...	...	...	...	...
Northern America	...	...	...	64	...	87i	...	...	...	99	96	89	44
Low income	...	1i	5i	...	11i	9i	...	...	...	...	...	...	...
Middle income	...	3i	10i	98	49	36i	...	...	...	...	...	...	...
Lower middle	...	2i	5i	105i	38	24i	...	...	...	...	...	...	...
Upper middle	...	4i	16i	86	64	52i	...	...	...	...	...	...	...
High income	46i	9i	16i	76i	66i	77i	...	...	...	...	...	...	...

A Participation rate of adults (25 to 64) in formal or non-formal education and training in the last 12 months (%) [*Source:* Eurostat].

B Percentage of youth (15 to 24) enrolled in technical and vocational education and training (TVET) programmes (ISCED levels 2 to 5) (%).

C Share of technical and vocational education and training (TVET) in total secondary enrolment (%).

D Gross transition ratio from secondary (all programmes) to tertiary education (ISCED levels 5 to 7).

E Gross entry ratio to first tertiary programmes (ISCED levels 5 to 7).

F Gross enrolment ratio (GER) in tertiary education.

G Percentage of adults (15 and over) with specific information and communications technology (ICT) skills [*Source:* International Telecommunication Union (ITU)].

H Percentage of adults (25 and over) who have attained at least a given level of education.

I Percentage of population of a given age group achieving at least a fixed level of proficiency in functional literacy and numeracy skills.

J Literacy rate, among youth (15 to 24) and adults (15 and above).

K Number of youth and adult illiterates, and percentage female.

Notes:
Source: UIS unless noted otherwise. Data refer to (school year ending in) year 2017 unless noted otherwise.
Aggregates include countries listed in the table with available data and may include estimations for countries with no recent data.

(-) Magnitude nil or negligible.

(...) Data not available or category not applicable.

(± n) Reference year differs (e.g. -2: reference year 2015 instead of 2017).

(i) Estimate and/or partial coverage.

SDG 4, Target 4.6 – Literacy and numeracy

By 2030, ensure that all youth and a substantial proportion of adults, both men and women, achieve literacy and numeracy

I				J		K			
% achieving proficiency in						Illiterates			
Literacy		Numeracy		Literacy rate (%)		% female		Number (000,000)	
Youth	Adults	Youth	Adults	Youth	Adults	Youth	Adults	Youth	Adults
4.6.1				4.6.2					
2017									
Weighted average								Sum	
...	...	...	...	91_{-1}	86_{-1}	57_{-1}	63_{-1}	102_{-1}	750_{-1}
...	...	...	...	75_{-1}	65_{-1}	57_{-1}	61_{-1}	48_{-1}	200_{-1}
...	...	...	...	90_{-1}	81_{-1}	58_{-1}	64_{-1}	9_{-1}	66_{-1}
...	...	...	...	90_{-1}	74_{-1}	53_{-1}	65_{-1}	4_{-1}	40_{-1}
...	56_{i}	...	51_{i}	89_{-1}	86_{-1}	62_{-1}	64_{-1}	5_{-1}	26_{-1}
...	...	...	...	89_{-1}	73_{-1}	57_{-1}	64_{-1}	39_{-1}	369_{-1}
...	...	...	...	100_{-1}	100_{-1}	49_{-1}	67_{-1}	$-_{-1}$	0.1_{-1}
...	...	...	...	89_{-1}	72_{-1}	57_{-1}	64_{-1}	39_{-1}	369_{-1}
...	...	...	...	99_{-1}	96_{-1}	49_{-1}	69_{-1}	4_{-1}	74_{-1}
...	...	...	...	100_{-1}	97_{-1}	50_{-1}	74_{-1}	1_{-1}	42_{-1}
...	...	...	...	97_{-1}	93_{-1}	49_{-1}	63_{-1}	3_{-1}	33_{-1}
...	...	...	...	...	...	...	...	...	...
...	...	...	...	98_{-1}	94_{-1}	43_{-1}	55_{-1}	2_{-1}	31_{-1}
...	...	...	...	...	...	...	...	...	...
...	...	...	...	98	93	49	61	0.5_{i}	8_{i}
...	...	...	...	99	94	36	53	1	19
...	...	...	...	100_{-2i}	99_{-1i}	50_{-2i}	58_{-1i}	0.4_{-2i}	7_{-1i}
...	...	...	...	100_{-1i}	99_{-1i}	46_{-1i}	63_{-1i}	0.2_{-1i}	4_{-1i}
...	...	...	...	...	...	...	...	...	...
...	...	...	...	73_{-1}	61_{-1}	57_{-1}	61_{-1}	36_{-1}	148_{-1}
...	...	...	...	93_{-1}	86_{-1}	57_{-1}	64_{-1}	66_{-1}	590_{-1}
...	...	...	...	89_{-1}	76_{-1}	57_{-1}	63_{-1}	59_{-1}	486_{-1}
...	...	...	...	98_{-1}	95_{-1}	52_{-1}	66_{-1}	7_{-1}	104_{-1}
...	...	...	...	...	...	44_{i}	61_{i}	...	...

TABLE 4: Continued

	A	B	C	D	E	F	G			H			
	Participation in adult education & training (%)	% of youth enrolled in TVET	TVET share of secondary enrolment (%)	Transition from upper secondary to tertiary (%)	Gross entry ratio into tertiary (%)	GER tertiary (%)	% of adults 15+ with ICT skills: Copy & paste within document	Use formula in spreadsheet	Write computer program	% of adults 25+ having attained at least: Primary	Lower secondary	Upper secondary	Post-secondary
SDG indicator:	4.3.1	4.3.3				4.3.2	4.4.1			4.4.3			
Reference year:	2017						2017						
Sub-Saharan Africa													
Angola	...	...	14_{-1}	...	10_{-2}	9_{-2}	...	...	...	44_{-3}	29_{-3}	16_{-3}	3_{-3}
Benin	...	1_{-1}	3_{-1}	...	...	13_{-1}	...	...	...	...	...	...	...
Botswana	...	...	...	...	42_{-3}	23	31_{-3}	20_{-3}	5_{-3}	...	...	...	...
Burkina Faso	...	1	3	46_{-1}	13	6	...	...	...	...	8_{-3}	3_{-3}	$-_{-3}$
Burundi	...	3	10	9	2	6	...	...	...	11_{-3}	6_{-3}	3_{-3}	1_{-3}
Cabo Verde	...	1	3	75	30	22	...	...	...	52_{-2}	29_{-2}	20_{-2}	12_{-2}
Cameroon	...	7_{-1}	22_{-1}	...	...	19_{-1}	...	...	...	...	...	...	...
Central African Republic	...	...	4	...	...	...	...	...	...	...	...	...	...
Chad	...	...	1_{-1}	...	...	3_{-3i}	...	...	...	...	...	...	...
Comoros	...	-	1	...	13_{-3}	9_{-3}	...	...	...	...	...	...	...
Congo	...	...	...	...	...	9_{-4}	...	...	...	...	...	...	...
Côte d'Ivoire	...	2	6	...	...	9_{-1}	...	...	...	35_{-3}	21_{-3}	11_{-3}	5_{-3}
D. R. Congo	...	...	19_{-2}	...	10_{-1}	7_{-1}	...	...	...	64_{-1}	51_{-1}	27_{-1}	9_{-1}
Djibouti	...	...	6	...	...	...	...	...	...	...	...	...	...
Equat. Guinea	...	...	...	...	...	...	...	...	...	...	...	...	...
Eritrea	...	0.3	1	18_{-1}	3_{-1}	2_{-1}	...	...	...	...	...	...	...
Eswatini	...	$-_{-2}$	4_{-1}	...	...	5_{-4}	...	...	...	...	...	...	...
Ethiopia	...	2_{-2i}	7_{-2}	...	...	8_{-3}	...	...	...	...	...	...	...
Gabon	...	...	...	...	...	...	...	...	...	...	...	...	...
Gambia	...	...	...	...	...	...	...	...	...	...	...	...	...
Ghana	...	1_{-1}	2	37	18	16	...	...	...	...	...	...	...
Guinea	...	1_{-3}	4_{-3}	...	18_{-3}	11_{-3}	...	...	...	...	...	...	...
Guinea-Bissau	...	...	...	...	...	...	...	...	...	...	...	...	...
Kenya	...	...	...	...	...	12_{-1}	...	...	...	...	...	...	...
Lesotho	...	1_{-2i}	2	...	12_{-3}	9_{-2}	...	...	...	...	...	...	...
Liberia	...	...	...	...	...	...	...	...	...	...	...	...	...
Madagascar	...	1	2	80_{-1}	8_{-1}	5_{-1}	...	...	...	...	...	...	...
Malawi	...	-	...	...	...	...	...	...	...	...	...	...	...
Mali	...	4	13	...	...	5_{-2}	...	...	...	13_{-1}	8_{-1}	6_{-1}	5_{-1}
Mauritania	...	0.3	1	...	6	5	...	...	...	...	...	...	...
Mauritius	...	1	12	...	...	39	...	...	...	...	...	...	...
Mozambique	...	1_{-2}	9	45_{-1}	9	7	...	...	...	36_{-2}	17_{-2}	9_{-2}	2_{-2}
Namibia	...	...	...	...	26_{-1}	21_{-1}	...	...	...	...	...	...	...
Niger	...	1	7	...	3	4	...	...	...	...	...	...	...
Nigeria	...	...	...	...	...	...	...	...	...	...	...	...	...
Rwanda	...	...	13	28	7	8	...	...	...	33_{-3}	12_{-3}	8_{-3}	3_{-3}
Sao Tome and Principe	...	4_{-2i}	6	...	...	13_{-2}	...	...	...	...	...	...	...
Senegal	...	-	3	...	...	11	...	...	...	22	18	11	10
Seychelles	...	2_{-1}	3_{-1}	16_{-1}	44_{-1}	21_{-1}	...	...	...	...	...	...	...
Sierra Leone	...	...	...	...	...	...	...	...	...	...	...	...	...
Somalia	...	...	...	...	...	...	...	...	...	...	...	...	...
South Africa	...	2_{-2}	7_{-1}	...	...	20_{-1}	...	...	...	82_{-2}	77_{-2}	65_{-2}	15_{-2}
South Sudan	...	...	...	...	...	...	...	...	...	...	...	...	...
Togo	...	3	6	...	...	13	...	...	...	...	...	...	...
Uganda	...	...	...	...	...	5_{-3}	...	...	...	...	...	...	...
United Republic of Tanzania	...	0.1	0.4	...	...	4_{-2}	...	...	...	...	...	...	...
Zambia	...	...	...	...	...	...	...	...	...	...	...	...	...
Zimbabwe	...	$-_{-4}$	...	...	8_{-4}	8_{-2}	4_{-3}	2_{-3}	1_{-3}	76_{-3}	59_{-3}	15_{-3}	13_{-3}

I: % achieving proficiency in – Literacy – Youth	I: Literacy – Adults	I: Numeracy – Youth	I: Numeracy – Adults	J: Literacy rate (%) – Youth	J: Literacy rate (%) – Adults	K: Illiterates – % female – Youth	K: % female – Adults	K: Number (000,000) – Youth	K: Number (000,000) – Adults	COUNTRY CODE
4.6.1				4.6.2						
2017										
...	...	...	...	77-3	66-3	67-3	71-3	1-3	5-3	AGO
...		...	...	...	...	...	...	...	...	BEN
...	...	...	...	98-3i	88-3i	13-3i	47-3i	--3i	0.2-3i	BWA
...	...	...	...	50-3	35-3	56-3	58-3	2-3	6-3	BFA
...	...	...	...	80-3	62-3	64-3	61-3	0.4-3	2-3	BDI
...	...	...	...	98-2	87-2	34-2	69-2	--2	--2	CPV
...	...	...	...	...	...	...	...	...	...	CMR
...	...	...	...	...	...	...	...	...	...	CAF
...	...	...	...	31-1	22-1	56-1	56-1	2-1	6-1	TCD
...	...	...	...	...	...	...	...	...	...	COM
...	...	...	...	...	...	...	...	...	...	COG
...	...	...	...	53-3	44-3	56-3	55-3	2-3	7-3	CIV
...	...	...	...	85-1	77-1	69-1	75-1	2-1	10-1	COD
...	...	...	...	...	...	...	...	...	...	DJI
...	...	...	...	98-3i	95-3i	32-3i	67-3i	--3i	--3i	GNQ
...	...	...	...	...	...	...	...	...	...	ERI
...	...	...	...	...	...	...	...	...	...	SWZ
...	...	...	...	...	...	...	...	...	...	ETH
...	...	...	...	...	...	...	...	...	...	GAB
...	...	...	...	61-4i	42-4i	57-4i	59-4i	0.1-4i	1-4i	GMB
...	...	...	...	...	...	...	...	...	...	GHA
...	...	...	...	46-3	32-3	59-3	58-3	1-3	5-3	GIN
...	...	...	...	60-3i	46-3i	64-3i	66-3i	0.1-3i	1-3i	GNB
...	...	...	...	87-3i	79-3i	51-3i	62-3i	1-3i	6-3i	KEN
...	...	...	...	87-3i	77-3i	23-3i	34-3i	0.1-3i	0.3-3i	LSO
...	...	...	...	...	...	...	...	...	...	LBR
...	...	...	...	...	...	...	...	...	...	MDG
...	...	...	...	73-2i	62-2i	49-2i	61-2i	1-2i	4-2i	MWI
...	...	...	...	49-2	33-2	60-2	59-2	2-2	6-2	MLI
...	...	...	...	...	...	...	...	...	...	MRT
...	...	...	...	...	93-1	...	67-1	...	0.1-1	MUS
...	...	...	...	71-2	56-2	64-2	68-2	2-2	7-2	MOZ
...	...	...	...	...	...	...	...	...	...	NAM
...	...	...	...	...	...	...	...	...	...	NER
...	...	...	...	...		...	...	...	...	NGA
...	...	...	...	85-3	71-3	47-3	60-3	0.3-3	2-3	RWA
	...	...	...	...	...	...	...	...	...	STP
...				69	[illegible]	60	65	1	4	SEN
...	...	...	...	...	...	...	...	...	...	SYC
...	...	...	...	57-4i	32-4i	59-4i	57-4i	1-4i	3-4i	SLE
...	...	...	...	...	...	...	...	...	...	SOM
...	...	...	...	99-2	94-2	37-2	60-2	0.1-2	2-2	ZAF
...	...	...	...	...	...	...	...	...	...	SSD
...	...	...	...	84-2	64-2	68-2	69-2	0.2-2	2-2	TGO
...	...	...	...	...	...	...	...	...	...	UGA
...	...	...	...	86-2	78-2	54-2	63-2	1-2	6-2	TZA
...	...	...	...	...	...	...	...	...	...	ZMB
...	...	...	...	90-3i	89-3i	36-3i	54-3i	0.3-3i	1-3i	ZWE

TABLE 4: Continued

	A	B	C	D	E	F	G			H			
	Participation in adult education & training (%)	% of youth enrolled in TVET	TVET share of secondary enrolment (%)	Transition from upper secondary to tertiary (%)	Gross entry ratio into tertiary (%)	GER tertiary (%)	% of adults 15+ with ICT skills: Copy & paste within document	Use formula in spreadsheet	Write computer program	% of adults 25+ having attained at least: Primary	Lower secondary	Upper secondary	Post-secondary
SDG indicator:	4.3.1	4.3.3				4.3.2	4.4.1			4.4.3			
Reference year:	2017						2017						
Northern Africa and Western Asia													
Algeria	…	…	…	34-3	32-3	48	…	…	…	…	…	…	…
Armenia	…	…	11-2	129	91	52	…	…	…	99-2	97-2	92-2	51-2
Azerbaijan	…	11i	18	…	33-2i	27i	57-1	19-1	1-1	98-1	96-1	89-1	30-1
Bahrain	…	3	7	74	61	46	56-1	49-1	14-1	63-1	53-1	42-1	18-1
Cyprus	48-1	6-2i	8-2	…	…	60-2i	43-1	21-1	3	95-1	80-1	71-1	38-1
Egypt	…	11	22	49-3	32-3	34-1	9-2	2-2	1-2	…	…	…	…
Georgia	…	2	4	…	…	58	22	7	1	99-1	98-1	93-1	51-1
Iraq	…	…	…	…	…	…	…	…	…	79-4	44-4	30-4	20-4
Israel	53-2	16-1	20-1	70-2	…	64-1	…	…	…	96-2	89-2	81-2	47-2
Jordan	…	1	3	…	…	32	…	…	…	…	…	…	…
Kuwait	…	--2	2-2	…	…	33-4	…	…	…	62	56	31	17
Lebanon	…	…	16	…	…	38	…	…	…	…	…	…	…
Libya	…	…	…	…	…	…	…	…	…	…	…	…	…
Morocco	…	3	8	124	53	34	44-1	19-1	5-1	…	…	…	…
Oman	…	-	-	81-1	61-1	45-1	…	…	…	84-2	66-2	50-2	21-2
Palestine	…	0.4	1	83	52	42	30-3	17-3	…	94-1	61-1	40-1	24-1
Qatar	…	0.2	1	48	27	16	34-2	32-2	6-2	87-1	67-1	41-1	24-1
Saudi Arabia	…	2-3i	5-3i	…	74-2	67-1	…	…	…	81-4	67-4	49-4	26-4
Sudan	…	…	1-1	…	…	17-2	4-1	2-1	2-1	…	…	…	…
Syrian Arab Republic	…	2-4	5-4	…	32-2	39-1	…	…	…	…	…	…	…
Tunisia	…	…	9-1	87-4	38	32	…	…	…	74-1	45-1	45-1	15-1
Turkey	21-1	26-1	25-1	138-3	92-3	104-1	…	26-1	3	81-1	54-1	34-1	17-1
United Arab Emirates	…	1-1	2-1	77-1	50-1	…	61-1	34-1	11-1	83-1	71-1	53-1	43-1
Yemen	…	--1	0.3-1	…	…	…	…	…	…	…	…	…	…
Central and Southern Asia													
Afghanistan	…	1	1	41-3	15-3	8-3	…	…	…	…	…	…	…
Bangladesh	…	1	4	…	…	18	…	…	…	56-1	42-1	29-1	14-1
Bhutan	…	-	2	…	…	11 4	…	…	…	…	…	…	…
India	…	…	1-1	125-1	42-1	27-1	…	…	…	…	…	…	…
Iran, Islamic Republic of	…	6-2	15-2	…	70-1	69-1	18-2	2-2	1-2	…	70-1	48-1	23-1
Kazakhstan	…	8	11	52	83	50	18	45	6	…	…	…	…
Kyrgyzstan	…	5	8	…	…	44	…	…	…	…	…	…	…
Maldives	…	…	…	…	…	14-3	…	…	…	…	…	…	…
Nepal	…	-	…	…	…	12	…	…	…	…	…	…	…
Pakistan	…	1	3	…	…	10	5-1	2-1	2-1	50-1	37-1	28-1	9-1
Sri Lanka	…	3	3	18	25	19	…	…	…	…	82-1	62-1	…
Tajikistan	…	…	1-4	-	-	31	…	…	…	100	95	81	23
Turkmenistan	…	…	8-3	…	…	8-3	…	…	…	…	…	…	…
Uzbekistan	…	23	35	12	10	9	…	…	…	100-1	100-1	93-1	63-1
Eastern and South-eastern Asia													
Brunei Darussalam	…	6	10	…	…	33	68-1	25-1	17-1	…	…	…	…
Cambodia	…	…	…	…	…	13	…	…	…	…	54-2	40-2	…
China	…	…	19	80	67	51	…	…	…	…	…	…	…
DPR Korea	…	--2	…	…	…	27+1	…	…	…	…	…	…	…
Hong Kong, China	…	1i	2	…	…	74	…	…	…	95-2	78-2	62-2	28-2
Indonesia	…	11	19	38	25	36	…	…	4+1	80-1	44-1	34-1	9-1
Japan	…	…	11-1	…	81-1	64-1	…	…	…	…	…	…	…
Lao PDR	…	0.4	1	60-1	27	16	…	…	…	…	…	…	…
Macao, China	…	1	4	…	…	85	…	…	…	90-1	73-1	52-1	26-1
Malaysia	…	6	13	…	38	42	79	36	11	94-1	74-1	58-1	21-1
Mongolia	…	6	…	131-2	91-2	65	…	…	…	…	…	…	…
Myanmar	…	0.1	0.1	…	…	16	…	…	…	…	…	…	…
Philippines	…	--2	…	…	…	35	…	…	…	84-4	70-4	58-4	33-4
Republic of Korea	…	15-1	10-1	…	…	94-1	…	61-1	4-1	96-2	86-2	76-2	40-2
Singapore	57-2	--1i	…	…	…	84-1i	73	55	9	86-1	80-1	71-1	53-1
Thailand	…	6-2	10	117-2	76-2	49-1	5-3	…	…	66-1	45-1	33-1	…
Timor-Leste	…	4	8	…	…	…	…	…	…	…	…	…	…
Viet Nam	…	…	…	111	58	28-1	…	…	…	…	…	…	…

	I				J		K				
	% achieving proficiency in				Literacy rate (%)		Illiterates				
	Literacy		Numeracy				% female		Number (000,000)		
	Youth	Adults	Youth	Adults	Youth	Adults	Youth	Adults	Youth	Adults	COUNTRY CODE
	4.6.1				4.6.2						
	2017										
	...	...	...	...	...	...	...	...	...	...	DZA
	...	...	...	...	...	...	...	...	...	...	ARM
	...	...	...	...	100_{-1}	100_{-1}	67_{-1}	69_{-1}	$-_{-1}$	$-_{-1}$	AZE
	...	...	...	...	...	...	...	...	...	...	BHR
	...	...	...	...	...	...	...	...	...	...	CYP
	...	...	...	...	94	81	58	65	1	12	EGY
	...	...	...	...	100_{-3}	100_{-3}	44_{-3}	63_{-3}	$-_{-3}$	$-_{-3}$	GEO
	...	...	...	...	52_{-4}	44_{-4}	53_{-4}	57_{-4}	3_{-4}	11_{-4}	IRQ
	78_{-2}	73_{-2}	70_{-2}	69_{-2}	...	...	...	...	...	...	ISR
	...	...	...	...	...	...	...	...	...	...	JOR
	...	...	...	...	99	96	30	52	-	0.1	KWT
	...	...	...	...	...	...	...	...	...	...	LBN
	...	...	...	...	...	...	...	...	...	...	LBY
	...	...	...	...	...	...	...	...	...	...	MAR
	...	...	...	...	99	96	30	52	-	0.1	OMN
	...	...	...	...	99_{-1}	97_{-1}	55_{-1}	77_{-1}	$-_{-1}$	0.1_{-1}	PSE
	...	...	...	...	...	...	...	...	...	...	QAT
	...	...	...	...	99_{-4}	94_{-4}	54_{-4}	64_{-4}	$-_{-4}$	1_{-4}	SAU
	...	...	...	...	...	...	...	...	...	...	SDN
	...	...	...	...	...	...	...	...	...	...	SYR
	...	...	...	...	96_{-3}	79_{-3}	55_{-3}	68_{-3}	0.1_{-3}	2_{-3}	TUN
	63_{-2}	54_{-2}	60_{-2}	50_{-2}	100_{-1}	96_{-1}	81_{-1}	85_{-1}	$-_{-1}$	2_{-1}	TUR
	...	...	...	...	...	...	...	...	...	...	ARE
	...	...	...	...	...	...	...	...	...	...	YEM
	...	...	...	...	...	...	...	...	...	...	AFG
	...	...	...	...	93	73	39	55	2	32	BGD
	...	...	...	...	...	...	...	...	...	...	BTN
	...	...	...	...	...	...	...	...	...	...	IND
	...	...	...	...	98_{-1}	86_{-1}	53_{-1}	66_{-1}	0.2_{-1}	9_{-1}	IRN
	...	...	...	...	...	...	...	...	...	...	KAZ
	...	...	...	...	...	...	...	...	...	...	KGZ
	...	...	...	...	99_{-3}	99_{-3}	32_{-3}	39_{-3}	$-_{-3}$	$-_{-3}$	MDV
	...	...	...	...	...	...	...	...	...	...	NPL
	...	...	...	...	73_{-3}	57_{-3}	62_{-3}	63_{-3}	10_{-3}	52_{-3}	PAK
	...	...	...	...	99	92	37	59	-	1	LKA
	...	...	...	...	100_{-3i}	100_{-3i}	41_{-3i}	63_{-3i}	$-_{-3i}$	$-_{-3i}$	TJK
	...	...	...	...	100_{-3i}	100_{-3i}	30_{-3i}	63_{-3i}	$-_{-3i}$	$-_{-3i}$	TKM
	...	...	...	...	100_{-1}	100_{-1}	49_{-1}	81_{-1}	$-_{-1}$	$-_{-1}$	UZB
	...	...	...	...	...	...	...	...	...	...	BRN
	...	...	...	...	92_{-2}	81_{-2}	47_{-2}	67_{-2}	0.2_{-2}	2_{-2}	KHM
	...	...	...	...	...	...	...	...	...	...	CHN
	...	...	...	...	...	...	...	...	...	...	PRK
	...	...	...	...	...	...	...	...	...	...	HKG
	...	...	...	...	100_{-1}	95_{-1}	51_{-1}	69_{-1}	0.1_{-1}	9_{-1}	IDN
	...	...	...	...	...	...	...	...	...	...	JPN
	...	...	...	...	92_{-2}	85_{-2}	67_{-2}	68_{-2}	0.1_{-2}	1_{-2}	LAO
	...	...	...	...	100_{-1}	97_{-1}	37_{-1}	75_{-1}	$-_{-1}$	$-_{-1}$	MAC
	...	...	...	...	...	...	...	...	...	...	MYS
	...	...	...	...	...	...	...	...	...	...	MNG
	...	...	...	...	85_{-1i}	76_{-1i}	51_{-1i}	60_{-1i}	1_{-1i}	9_{-1i}	MMR
	...	...	...	...	98_{-4}	96_{-4}	31_{-4}	45_{-4}	0.4_{-4}	2_{-4}	PHL
	...	...	...	...	...	...	...	...	...	...	KOR
	92_{-2}	74_{-2}	90_{-2}	72_{-2}	100_{-1}	97_{-1}	40_{-1}	79_{-1}	$-_{-1}$	0.1_{-1}	SGP
	...	...	...	...	98_{-2}	93_{-2}	45_{-2}	64_{-2}	0.2_{-2}	4_{-2}	THA
	...	...	...	...	...	...	...	...	...	...	TLS
	...	...	...	...	...	...	...	...	...	...	VNM

TABLE 4: Continued

	A	B	C	D	E	F	G			H			
	Participation in adult education & training (%)	% of youth enrolled in TVET	TVET share of secondary enrolment (%)	Transition from upper secondary to tertiary (%)	Gross entry ratio into tertiary (%)	GER tertiary (%)	% of adults 15+ with ICT skills			% of adults 25+ having attained at least			
							Copy & paste within document	Use formula in spreadsheet	Write computer program	Primary	Lower secondary	Upper secondary	Post-secondary
SDG indicator:	4.3.1	4.3.3				4.3.2	4.4.1			4.4.3			
Reference year:			2017							2017			
Oceania													
Australia	...	22_{-1}	37_{-1}	...	...	122_{-1}	...	...	...	100_{-2}	93_{-1}	76_{-1}	46_{-1}
Cook Islands	...	$-_{-1i}$	...	...	...	...	...	...	...	...	...	...	...
Fiji	...	...	...	...	...	...	...	...	...	...	...	...	...
Kiribati	...	...	...	...	...	...	...	...	...	...	...	...	...
Marshall Islands	...	1_{-1}	2_{-1}	...	...	...	...	...	...	...	...	...	...
Micronesia, F. S.	...	...	...	...	...	...	...	...	...	...	...	...	...
Nauru	...	$-_{-1i}$	...	...	...	...	...	...	...	...	...	...	...
New Zealand	67_{-2}	5_{-1}	15_{-1}	73_{-1}	93_{-1}	82_{-1}	...	...	...	100_{-1}	100_{-1}	70_{-1}	46_{-1}
Niue	...	$-_{-2i}$	...	...	...	...	...	...	...	...	...	...	...
Palau	...	$-_{-3i}$	...	...	...	64_{-4i}	...	...	...	99_{-4}	97_{-4}	88_{-4}	...
Papua New Guinea	...	2_{-1}	9_{-1}	...	...	...	...	...	...	...	...	...	...
Samoa	...	$-_{-1}$	...	...	...	...	...	...	...	...	...	...	...
Solomon Is	...	...	...	...	...	...	...	...	...	...	...	...	...
Tokelau	...	$-_{-1i}$	...	...	...	...	...	...	...	...	...	...	...
Tonga	...	2_{-2}	3_{-2}	...	...	...	...	...	...	...	...	...	...
Tuvalu	...	2_{-1i}	3_{-1}	...	...	...	...	...	...	...	...	...	...
Vanuatu	...	1_{-2}	2_{-2}	...	...	...	...	...	...	...	...	...	...
Latin America and the Caribbean													
Anguilla	...	...	...	...	...	...	...	...	...	...	...	...	...
Antigua and Barbuda	...	1_{-2}	3_{-2}	...	...	...	...	...	...	...	...	...	...
Argentina	...	$-_{-1}$	...	146_{-1}	95_{-1}	89_{-1}	...	...	...	92_{-1}	55_{-1}	...	19_{-1}
Aruba	...	...	...	...	11_{-2}	15_{-2}	54	45	5	...	...	...	...
Bahamas	...	$-_{-1}$	...	...	...	...	...	...	...	...	...	...	...
Barbados	...	-	...	...	...	...	...	...	...	...	...	...	...
Belize	...	3	8	44	22	25	...	...	...	...	...	...	...
Bolivia, P. S.	...	30	65	...	...	...	...	...	...	72_{-2}	59_{-2}	43_{-2}	24_{-2}
Brazil	...	4_{-1i}	4_{-1}	...	...	50_{-1i}	23_{-2}	13_{-2}	3_{-2}	78_{-2}	58_{-2}	44_{-2}	14_{-2}
British Virgin Islands	...	1_{-1i}	4	...	...	41_{-1i}	...	...	...	...	...	...	...
Cayman Islands	...	...	...	...	...	...	...	...	...	99_{-2}	95_{-2}	90_{-2}	55_{-2}
Chile	47_{-2}	18_{-1}	20_{-1}	101_{-3}	88_{-3}	90_{-1}	...	...	...	87_{-2}	79_{-2}	57_{-2}	20_{-2}
Colombia	...	4	8	65	...	60	38_{-1}	27_{-1}	...	77_{-1}	52_{-1}	47_{-1}	20_{-1}
Costa Rica	...	8_{-1}	24_{-1}	...	...	56	...	...	...	81_{-1}	53_{-1}	38_{-1}	21_{-1}
Cuba	...	12	25	43_{-1}	26_{-1}	34_{-1}	...	...	...	...	...	...	...
Curaçao	...	...	72_{-4}	...	...	21_{-4}	...	...	...	...	...	...	...
Dominica	...	$-_{-1}$	$-_{-2}$	...	...	...	...	...	...	...	...	...	...
Dominican Republic	...	2_{-1}	5_{-1}	140_{-1}	...	58	22_{-2}	11_{-2}	7_{-2}	67_{-2}	57_{-2}	35_{-2}	12_{-2}
Ecuador	...	9	15	...	...	46_{-2}	...	...	...	83_{-1}	52_{-1}	42_{-1}	13_{-1}
El Salvador	...	7	18	34_{-1}	20_{-1}	28_{-1}	...	...	...	56_{-4}	41_{-4}	27_{-4}	10_{-4}
Grenada	...	-	...	60_{-1}	45_{-1}	94	...	...	...	...	...	...	...
Guatemala	...	8_{-1}	24_{-1}	...	...	21_{-2}	...	...	...	62_{-3}	37_{-3}	27_{-3}	10_{-3}
Guyana	...	...	...	...	...	...	...	...	...	...	...	...	...
Haiti	...	...	...	...	...	...	...	...	...	...	...	...	...
Honduras	...	10	39	...	16_{-4}	21_{-2}	...	...	...	61_{-1}	34_{-1}	25_{-1}	11_{-1}
Jamaica	...	-	...	...	...	27_{-2}	16_{-2}	4_{-2}	1_{-2}	...	...	...	...
Mexico	...	12_{-1}	28_{-1}	73_{-3}	36_{-3}	37_{-1}	...	28	9	80_{-1}	60_{-1}	33_{-1}	15_{-1}
Montserrat	...	-	...	...	...	...	...	...	...	...	...	...	...
Nicaragua	...	...	...	...	...	...	...	...	...	...	...	...	...
Panama	...	...	16_{-1}	...	...	47_{-2}	...	...	...	...	...	...	...
Paraguay	...	5_{-1}	16_{-1}	...	...	...	...	...	...	75_{-1}	48_{-1}	37_{-1}	14_{-1}
Peru	...	1	2	...	...	70_{-1}	...	...	...	81_{-2}	62_{-2}	56_{-2}	21_{-2}
Saint Kitts and Nevis	...	$-_{-1}$	...	97_{-2}	...	...	...	...	...	...	...	...	...
Saint Lucia	...	0.4	1	...	...	20	...	...	...	...	46_{-4}	40_{-4}	15_{-4}
Saint Vincent/Grenadines	...	-	-	...	...	...	...	...	...	...	...	...	...
Sint Maarten	...	...	59_{-3}	8_{-3}	...	...	...	...	...	...	...	...	...
Suriname	...	19_{-2}	41_{-2}	...	...	...	...	...	...	...	...	...	...
Trinidad and Tobago	...	...	...	...	...	...	...	...	...	...	...	...	...
Turks and Caicos Islands	...	$-_{-2}$	...	...	...	...	...	...	...	...	...	...	...
Uruguay	...	10_{-1}	22_{-1}	...	...	56_{-2}	...	...	...	90_{-1}	55_{-1}	29_{-1}	12_{-1}
Venezuela, B. R.	...	2_{-2}	5	...	...	...	...	...	...	93_{-1}	74_{-1}	62_{-1}	35_{-1}

I % achieving proficiency in				J		K Illiterates				COUNTRY CODE
Literacy		Numeracy		Literacy rate (%)		% female		Number (000,000)		
Youth	Adults	Youth	Adults	Youth	Adults	Youth	Adults	Youth	Adults	
4.6.1				4.6.2						
2017										
…	…	…	…	…	…	…	…	…	…	AUS
…	…	…	…	…	…	…	…	…	…	COK
…	…	…	…	…	…	…	…	…	…	FJI
…	…	…	…	…	…	…	…	…	…	KIR
…	…	…	…	…	…	…	…	…	…	MHL
…	…	…	…	…	…	…	…	…	…	FSM
…	…	…	…		…	…	…	…	…	NRU
89_{-2}	88_{-2}	80_{-2}	81_{-2}	…	…	…	…	…	…	NZL
…	…	…	…	…	…	…	…	…	…	NIU
…	…	…	…	99_{-2}	97_{-2}	28_{-2i}	50_{-2i}	$-_{-2i}$	$-_{-2i}$	PLW
…	…	…	…	…	…	…	…	…	…	PNG
…	…	…	…	…	…	…	…	…	…	WSM
…	…	…	…	…	…	…	…	…	…	SLB
…	…	…	…	…	…	…	…	…	…	TKL
…	…	…	…	…	…	…	…	…	…	TON
…	…	…	…	…	…	…	…	…	…	TUV
…	…	…	…	95_{-3i}	85_{-3i}	47_{-3i}	55_{-3i}	$-_{-3i}$	$-_{-3i}$	VUT
…	…	…	…	…	…	…	…	…	…	AIA
…	…	…	…	…	99_{-2}	…	29_{-2}	…	$-_{-2}$	ATG
…	…	…	…	100_{-1i}	99_{-1i}	37_{-1i}	51_{-1i}	$-_{-1i}$	0.3_{-1i}	ARG
…	…	…	…	…	…	…	…	…	…	ABW
…	…	…	…	…	…	…	…	…	…	BHS
…	…	…	…	100_{-3i}	100_{-3i}	55_{-3i}	53_{-3i}	$-_{-3i}$	$-_{-3i}$	BRB
…	…	…	…	…	…	…	…	…	…	BLZ
…	…	…	…	99_{-2}	92_{-2}	49_{-2}	77_{-2}	$-_{-2}$	1_{-2}	BOL
…	…	…	…	99_{-2}	92_{-2}	31_{-2}	49_{-2}	0.4_{-2}	13_{-2}	BRA
…	…	…	…	…	…	…	…	$-_{+1}$	$-_{+1}$	VGB
…	…	…	…	…	…	…	…	…	…	CYM
61_{-2}	47_{-2}	47_{-2}	38_{-2}	99_{-2}	97_{-2}	42_{-2}	53_{-2}	$-_{-2}$	0.4_{-2}	CHL
…	…	…	…	99_{-1}	95_{-1}	36_{-1}	49_{-1}	0.1_{-1}	2_{-1}	COL
…	…	…	…	…	…	…	…	…	…	CRI
…	…				…	…	…	…	…	CUB
…	…	…	…	…	…	…				CUW
…	…	…	…	…	…	…	…	…	…	DMA
…	…	…	…	99_{-1}	94_{-1}	48_{-1}	51_{-1}	$-_{-1}$	0.5_{-1}	DOM
…	…	…	…	99_{-1}	94_{-1}	45_{-1}	60_{-1}	$-_{-1}$	1_{-1}	ECU
…	…	…		98_{-1}	88_{-1}	44_{-1}	63_{-1}	$-_{-1}$	1_{-1}	SLV
…	…	…	…	99_{-3i}	99_{-3i}	32_{-3i}	50_{-3i}	$-_{-3i}$	$-_{-3i}$	GRD
…	…	…	…	94_{-3}	81_{-3}	59_{-3}	66_{-3}	0.2_{-3}	2_{-3}	GTM
…	…	…	…	97_{-3i}	86_{-3i}	43_{-3i}	52_{-3i}	$-_{-3i}$	0.1_{-3i}	GUY
…	…	…	…	…	…	…	…	…	…	HTI
…	…	…	…	96_{-1}	89_{-1}	35_{-1}	51_{-1}	0.1_{-1}	1_{-1}	HND
	…	…	…	96_{-3i}	88_{-3i}	16_{-3i}	31_{-3i}	$-_{-3i}$	0.3_{-3i}	JAM
…	…	…	…	99_{-1}	95_{-1}	44_{-1}	60_{-1}	0.2_{-1}	5_{-1}	MEX
…	…	…	…	…	…	…	…	…	…	MSR
…	…	…	…	…	…	…	…	…	…	NIC
…	…	…	…	…	…	…	…	…	…	PAN
…	…	…	…	98_{-1}	95_{-1}	41_{-1}	57_{-1}	$-_{-1}$	0.3_{-1}	PRY
…	…	…	…	99_{-1}	94_{-1}	58_{-1}	76_{-1}	0.1_{-1}	1_{-1}	PER
…	…	…	…	…	…	…	…	…	…	KNA
…	…	…	…	…	…	…	…	…	…	LCA
…	…	…	…	…	…	…	…	…	…	VCT
…	…	…	…	…	…	…	…	…	…	SXM
…	…	…	…	…	…	…	…	…	…	SUR
…	…	…	…	…	…	…	…	…	…	TTO
…	…	…	…	…	…	…	…	…	…	TCA
…	…	…	…	99	99	31	39	-	-	URY
…	…	…	…	99_{-1}	97_{-1}	36_{-1}	49_{-1}	0.1_{-1}	1_{-1}	VEN

TABLE 4: Continued

	A	B	C	D	E	F	G			H			
	Participation in adult education & training (%)	% of youth enrolled in TVET	TVET share of secondary enrolment (%)	Transition from upper secondary to tertiary (%)	Gross entry ratio into tertiary (%)	GER tertiary (%)	% of adults 15+ with ICT skills: Copy & paste within document	Use formula in spreadsheet	Write computer program	% of adults 25+ having attained at least: Primary	Lower secondary	Upper secondary	Post-secondary
SDG indicator:	4.3.1	4.3.3				4.3.2	4.4.1			4.4.3			
Reference year:	2017						2017						
Europe and Northern America													
Albania	9_{-1}	5	9	65	46	57	...	...	...	...	...	...	...
Andorra	...	...	10	36	...	...	...	...	6	97_{-1}	72_{-1}	47_{-1}	32_{-1}
Austria	60_{-1}	28_{-1}	35_{-1}	77_{-1}	76_{-1}	83_{-1}	63_{-1}	45_{-1}	6_{-1}	...	99_{-3}	79_{-1}	29_{-1}
Belarus	...	8	13	77_{-4}	84_{-4}	87	...	...	...	...	...	...	...
Belgium	45_{-1}	25_{-1}	46_{-1}	71_{-2}	69_{-2}	76_{-1}	65_{-1}	44_{-1}	9_{-1}	96_{-1}	85_{-1}	67_{-1}	34_{-1}
Bermuda	...	$-_{-1}$	...	...	35	24_{-2}	...	...	...	...	...	...	...
Bosnia and Herzegovina	9_{-1}	...	38	61	...	...	...	...	...	84_{-1}	81_{-1}	62_{-1}	12_{-1}
Bulgaria	25_{-1}	15_{-1}	29_{-1}	108_{-2}	77_{-2}	71_{-1}	26_{-1}	14_{-1}	1	100_{-1}	95_{-1}	76_{-1}	...
Canada	...	...	5_{-1}	...	...	67_{-1i}	...	...	...	...	...	...	...
Croatia	32_{-1}	23_{-1}	40_{-1}	...	...	67_{-1}	42	32	5	...	...	...	...
Czechia	46_{-1}	25_{-1}	37_{-1}	86_{-2}	68_{-2}	64_{-1}	56	41	4	100_{-1}	100_{-1}	90_{-1}	20_{-1}
Denmark	50_{-1}	13_{-1}	23_{-1}	78_{-1}	85_{-3}	81_{-1}	68_{-1}	60_{-1}	14_{-1}	...	92_{-1}	78_{-1}	36_{-1}
Estonia	44_{-1}	12_{-1}	21_{-1}	...	...	71_{-1}	55_{-1}	44_{-1}	8	...	...	87_{-1}	...
Finland	54_{-1}	22_{-1}	48_{-1}	39_{-1}	60_{-1}	87_{-1}	69_{-1}	47_{-1}	8_{-1}	...	...	74_{-2}	35_{-2}
France	51_{-1}	19_{-1i}	18_{-1}	...	...	64_{-1i}	53_{-1}	40_{-1}	5_{-1}	98_{-1}	84_{-1}	70_{-1}	30_{-1}
Germany	52_{-1}	...	19_{-1}	74_{-1}	64_{-1}	68_{-1}	62_{-1}	38_{-1}	6_{-1}	100_{-1}	97_{-1}	83_{-1}	36_{-1}
Greece	17_{-1}	12_{-1}	16_{-1}	68_{-1}	...	126_{1}	52_{-1}	41_{-1}	9_{-1}	91_{-1}	65_{-1}	55_{-1}	27_{-1}
Hungary	56_{-1}	13_{-1}	12_{-1}	52_{-1i}	42_{-1i}	48_{-1}	51_{-1}	36_{-1}	3_{-1}	100_{-1}	97_{-1}	76_{-1}	29_{-1}
Iceland	...	10_{-1}	21_{-1}	...	73_{-2}	74_{-1}	80_{-3}	69_{-3}	18_{-3}	...	...	...	...
Ireland	...	8_{-1i}	...	...	...	78_{-1i}	42_{-1}	26_{-1}	4_{-1}	...	86	71	43
Italy	42_{-1}	23_{-1}	34_{-1}	73_{-2}	68_{-2}	63_{-1}	42_{-1}	31_{-1}	4_{-1}	95_{-2}	78_{-2}	49_{-2}	15_{-2}
Latvia	48_{-1}	16_{-1i}	20_{-1}	...	...	81_{-1i}	46_{-1}	31	2	100_{-2}	100_{-1}	89_{-1}	39_{-1}
Liechtenstein	...	25_{-1i}	35_{-1}	52_{-2}	59_{-2i}	35_{-1i}	...	...	...	...	...	...	...
Lithuania	28_{-1}	9_{-1i}	10_{-1}	97_{-1}	84_{-1i}	71_{-1i}	45_{-1}	41	4	99_{-1}	95_{-1}	86_{-1}	53_{-1}
Luxembourg	48_{-1}	23_{-1}	33_{-1}	42_{-1}	29_{-2}	20_{-1}	83_{-1}	68_{-1}	11_{-1}	...	100_{-2}	80_{-3}	69_{-2}
Malta	36_{-1}	11_{-1}	9_{-1}	46_{-1}	62_{-1}	49_{-1}	44_{-1}	82	7	99_{-1}	78_{-1}	38_{-1}	25_{-1}
Monaco	...	...	10	53	...	...	...	...	...	...	...	...	...
Montenegro	...	22	33	...	...	58	...	32	2_{-1}	...	...	...	...
Netherlands	64_{-1}	22_{-1}	36_{-1}	57_{-1}	65_{-1}	80_{-1}	70_{-1}	51_{-1}	8_{-1}	99_{-1}	90_{-1}	70_{-1}	32_{-1}
Norway	60_{-1}	18_{-1}	29_{-1}	71_{-1}	76_{-1}	81_{-1}	68_{-1}	85_{+1}	10_{-1}	100_{-1}	99_{-1}	78_{-1}	39_{-1}
Poland	26_{-1}	19_{-1}	28_{-1}	90_{-1}	76_{-2}	67_{-1}	41_{-1}	28_{-1}	3	99_{-1}	85_{-1}	85_{-1}	28_{-1}
Portugal	46_{-1}	17_{-1}	26_{-1}	76_{-1}	62_{-1}	63_{-1}	48_{-1}	36_{-1}	6_{-1}	91_{-1}	54_{-1}	37_{-1}	20_{-1}
Republic of Moldova	...	7_{i}	14	...	...	41_{i}	...	...	...	99_{-2}	96_{-2}	75_{-2}	...
Romania	7_{-1}	...	28_{-1}	114_{-1}	82_{-1}	48_{-1}	21_{-1}	13_{-1}	2	99_{-1}	90_{-1}	66_{-1}	18_{-1}
Russian Federation	...	14_{-3i}	16_{-1}	...	...	82_{-1}	...	23_{-1}	1_{-1}	...	...	...	...
San Marino	...	...	...	...	...	...	...	...	...	...	...	...	...
Serbia	20_{-1}	24_{i}	35	113_{-1}	97_{-1i}	66_{i}	...	34	6	97_{-1}	89_{-1}	71_{-1}	23_{-1}
Slovakia	46_{-1}	22_{-1}	32_{-1}	77_{-2}	57_{-2}	48_{-1}	51_{-1}	50	5	100_{-1}	99_{-1}	87_{-1}	21_{-1}
Slovenia	46_{-1}	34_{-1}	45_{-1}	71_{-1}	74_{-1}	78_{-1}	54_{-1}	42_{-1}	5_{-1}	100_{-1}	98_{-1}	82_{-1}	27_{-1}
Spain	43_{-1}	15_{-1}	18_{-1}	82_{-1}	81_{-1}	91_{-1}	52_{-1}	37_{-1}	7	91_{-1}	76_{-1}	49_{-1}	30_{-1}
Sweden	64_{-1}	12_{-1}	22_{-1}	105_{-1}	67_{-1}	64_{-1}	66_{-1}	51	12	100_{-1}	91_{-1}	76_{-1}	38_{-1}
Switzerland	69_{-1}	23_{-1}	37_{-1}	77_{-1}	87_{-2}	58_{-1}	...	...	9	...	97_{-1}	85_{-1}	...
TFYR Macedonia	13_{-1}	...	30_{-2}	88_{-3}	70_{-3}	41_{-2}	32_{-1}	21_{-1}	3_{-1}	...	...	...	...
Ukraine	...	4_{-3}	8	146_{i}	...	83_{-3}	...	...	...	...	...	...	...
United Kingdom	...	22_{-1}	46_{-1}	...	63_{-3}	59_{-1}	62_{-1}	47_{-1}	8_{-1}	100_{-3}	100_{-3}	75_{-3}	39_{-3}
United States	...	...	...	64_{-2}	53_{-2i}	89_{-1i}	...	...	...	99_{-1}	96_{-1}	89_{-1}	44_{-1}

I % achieving proficiency in				J		K Illiterates				COUNTRY CODE
Literacy		Numeracy		Literacy rate (%)		% female		Number (000,000)		
Youth	Adults	Youth	Adults	Youth	Adults	Youth	Adults	Youth	Adults	
4.6.1				4.6.2						
2017										
...	...	...	...	...	...	...	...	...	...	ALB
...	...	...	...	...	...	...	...	...	...	AND
...	...	...	...	...	...	...	...	...	...	AUT
...	...	...	...	...	...	...	...	...	...	BLR
...	...			...	...	...	...	...	...	BEL
...	...	...	...	...	...	...	...	...	...	BMU
...	...	...	...	100_{-4}	97_{-4}	48_{-4}	87_{-4}	$-_{-4}$	0.1_{-4}	BIH
...	...	...		...	...	...	...	...	...	BGR
...	...	...	...	...		...	...	...	...	CAN
...	...	...	...	...	...	...	...	...	...	HRV
...	...	...	...	...	...	...	...	...	...	CZE
...	...	...	...	...	...	...	...	...	...	DNK
...	...	...	...	...	...	...	...	...	...	EST
...	...	...	...	...	...	...	...	...	...	FIN
...	...	...	...	...	...	...	...	...	...	FRA
...	...	...	...	...	...	...	...	...	...	DEU
77_{-2}	73_{-2}	73_{-2}	71_{-2}	...	...	...	...	...	...	GRC
...	...	...	...	99_{-3i}	99_{-3i}	42_{-3i}	55_{-3i}	$-_{-3i}$	0.1_{-3i}	HUN
...	...	...	...	...	...	...	...	...	...	ISL
...	...	...	...	...	...	...	...	...	...	IRL
...	...	...	...	...	...	...	...	...	...	ITA
...	...	...	...	...	...	...	...	...	...	LVA
...	...	...	...	...	...	...	...	$-_{+1}$	$-_{+1}$	LIE
92_{-2}	85_{-2}	90_{-2}	83_{-2}	...	...	...	...	...	...	LTU
...	...	...	...	...	...	...	...	...	...	LUX
...	...	...	...	...	...	...	...	...	...	MLT
...	...	...	...	...	...	...	...	...	...	MCO
...	...	...	...	...	...	...	...	...	...	MNE
...	...	...	...	...	...	...	...	...	...	NLD
...	...	...	...	...	...	...	...	...	...	NOR
...	...	...	...	...	...	...	...	...	...	POL
...	...	...	...	...	...	...	...	...	...	PRT
...	...	...	...	...	...	...	...			MDA
...	...	...	...	...		...	...	...	...	ROU
...	...		...	...	...	...	...			RUS
...	...	...	...		...	...	...	$-_{+1}$	$-_{+1}$	SMR
...	...	...	...	100_{-1}	99_{-1}	48_{-1}	79_{-1}	$-_{-1}$	0.1_{-1}	SRB
...	...	...	...	...	...	...	...		...	SVK
88_{-2}	75_{-2}	86_{-2}	74_{-2}	100_{-3i}	100_{-3i}	31_{-3i}	57_{-3i}	$-_{-3i}$	$-_{-3i}$	SVN
...	...	...	...	100_{-1}	98_{-1}	51_{-1}	68_{-1}	$-_{-1}$	1_{-1}	ESP
...	...	...	...	...	...	...	...	...	...	SWE
...	...	...	...	...	...	...	...	...	...	CHE
...	...	...	...	...	...	...	...	...	...	MKD
...	...	...	...	...	...	...	...	...	...	UKR
...	...	...	...	...	...	...	...	...	...	GBR
...	...	...	...	...	...	...	...	...	...	USA

TABLE 5: SDG 4, Target 4.5 – Equity

By 2030, eliminate gender disparities in education and ensure equal access at all levels of education and vocational training for the vulnerable, including persons with disabilities, indigenous peoples and children in vulnerable situations

	GENDER															
	A			B				C		D		E				
	GPIA in completion			GPIA in minimum proficiency				GPIA in literacy rate		GPIA in adult proficiency		GPIA in gross enrolment ratio				
				End of primary		End of lower secondary										
	Primary	Lower secondary	Upper secondary	Reading	Mathematics	Reading	Mathematics	Youth	Adults	Literacy	Numeracy	Pre-primary	Primary	Secondary	Tertiary	
SDG indicator:	4.5.1															
Reference year:	2017															
Region	Median															
World	1.01i	1.00i	1.03i	…	…	1.12i	1.01i	1.00i	0.96i	…	…	1.00	0.99	1.01	1.16	
Sub-Saharan Africa	1.02i	0.86i	0.77i	…	…	…	…	0.88i	0.75i	…	…	1.02	0.96	0.95	0.75	
Northern Africa and Western Asia	…	1.02i	1.05i	…	…	1.30i	1.08i	1.00i	0.95i	…	…	1.00	0.99	1.00	1.19	
Northern Africa	1.01i	1.02i	0.96i	…	…	1.37i	1.04	0.98i	0.85i	…	…	0.99	0.95	0.98	1.02	
Western Asia	…	0.99i	1.07i	…	…	1.30i	1.10i	1.00i	0.96i	…	…	1.00	1.00	1.01	1.22	
Central and Southern Asia	1.00i	1.00i	0.94i	…	…	…	…	1.00i	0.99i	…	…	0.97	1.00	1.00	0.89	
Central Asia	1.00i	1.00i	1.03i	…	…	…	…	1.00i	1.00i	…	…	0.97	0.99	0.99	0.75	
Southern Asia	1.00i	0.96i	0.82i	…	…	…	…	1.00i	0.93i	…	…	0.98	1.00	1.03	0.91	
Eastern and South-eastern Asia	1.02i	1.08i	1.15i	…	…	1.12i	1.04i	1.00i	0.96i	…	…	1.00	0.99	1.01	1.15	
Eastern Asia	…	…	…	…	…	1.09i	1.02i	…	…	…	…	1.00	1.00	1.00	1.10	
South-eastern Asia	1.07i	1.08i	1.15i	…	…	1.24i	1.05i	1.00i	0.96i	…	…	1.02	0.98	1.03	1.17	
Oceania	…	…	…	…	…	…	…	…	…	…	…	1.01	0.99	1.05	…	
Latin America and the Caribbean	1.01i	1.09i	1.11i	1.06i	0.99i	…	…	1.01i	1.00i	…	…	1.02	0.97	1.04	1.27i	
Caribbean	…	…	…	…	…	…	…	…	…	…	…	1.03i	0.97i	1.05i	…	
Central America	1.01	1.06	1.10	1.07	0.97	…	…	1.00i	0.97i	…	…	1.02	0.99	1.04	1.18	
South America	1.02	1.10	1.12	1.04	0.99	1.10i	0.88i	1.01	1.00	…	…	1.01	0.97	1.04	1.14i	
Europe and Northern America	…	1.00	1.04	…	…	1.11	1.00	…	…	…	…	0.99	1.00	0.99	1.23	
Europe	…	1.00	1.04	…	…	1.11	1.00	…	…	…	…	0.99	1.00	0.99	1.22	
Northern America	1.00i	1.00i	1.03i	…	…	1.08	0.99	…	…	…	…	0.92	1.00	1.01	1.26	
Low income	0.97i	0.80i	0.69i	…	…	…	…	0.85i	0.65i	…	…	1.02	0.97	0.91	0.54	
Middle income	1.01i	1.02i	1.03i	…	…	…	…	1.00i	0.97i	…	…	1.01	0.99	1.01	1.17	
Lower middle	1.01i	1.02i	1.00i	…	…	…	…	1.00i	0.92i	…	…	1.00	0.98	0.99	1.04	
Upper middle	1.01i	1.04i	1.06i	…	…	1.17i	1.01i	1.00i	0.98i	…	…	1.01	0.99	1.03	1.20	
High income	…	1.00i	1.05i	…	…	1.11i	1.00	…	…	…	…	1.00	1.00	1.01	1.27	

A Adjusted gender parity index (GPIA) in school completion rate by level.

B Adjusted gender parity index (GPIA) in percentage of students with minimum level of proficiency at the end of given level.

C Adjusted gender parity index (GPIA) in youth and adult literacy rate.

D Adjusted gender parity index (GPIA) in percentage of adults aged 16 and over achieving at least a fixed level of proficiency in functional literacy and numeracy skills.

E Adjusted gender parity index (GPIA) in gross enrolment ratio by level.

F Adjusted parity index for location (rural-urban) and wealth (poorest to richest quintile) in school completion by level.

G Adjusted parity index for wealth (poorest to richest quintile) in achievement of minimum proficiency.

Notes:

Source: UIS and GEM Report analysis of household surveys. Data refer to school year ending in 2017 unless noted otherwise.
Aggregates represent countries listed in the table with available data and may include estimates for countries with no recent data.

(-) Magnitude nil or negligible.

(…) Data not available or category not applicable.

(± n) Reference year differs (e.g. -2: reference year 2015 instead of 2017).

(i) Estimate and/or partial coverage.

LOCATION/WEALTH															
F												G			
Disparity in primary completion				Disparity in lower secondary completion				Disparity in upper secondary completion				Wealth disparity in minimum proficiency			
Adjusted parity index		% of poorest completing		Adjusted parity index		% of poorest completing		Adjusted parity index		% of poorest completing		End of primary		End of lower secondary	
Location	Wealth	M	F	Location	Wealth	M	F	Location	Wealth	M	F	Reading	Mathematics	Reading	Mathematics
4.5.1															
2017															
Median															
0.88i	0.76i	67i	76i	0.86i	0.72i	63i	72i	0.68i	0.37i	27i	33i	...	...	0.67i	0.65i
0.67i	0.45i	33i	34i	0.42i	0.15i	11i	5i	0.20i	0.03i	2i	1i			...	...
...	...	...	...	0.95i	0.81i	70i	75i	0.68i	0.37i	27i	27i	...	...	0.60i	0.55i
0.96i	0.87i	87i	86i	0.76i	0.49i	30i	47i	0.60i	0.33i	14i	22i	...	...	0.47i	0.52
...	...	...	...	0.97i	0.88i	86i	88i	0.83i	0.63i	41i	58i	...	...	0.61i	0.55i
0.99i	0.82i	81i	80i	0.94i	0.62i	62i	56i	0.81i	0.58i	48i	47i	...	...	...	...
1.00i	1.00i	100i	100i	1.00i	0.99i	99i	99i	0.96i	0.91i	86i	89i	...	...	...	...
0.90i	0.75i	65i	68i	0.84i	0.50i	44i	38i	0.61i	0.18i	18i	4i	...	...	...	...
0.96i	0.81i	77i	86i	0.81i	0.52i	45i	60i	0.58i	0.24i	17i	29i	...	...	0.79i	0.78i
...	...	...	...	...	...	...	...	...	...	...	...	...	...	0.87i	0.85i
0.93i	0.69i	61i	73i	0.74i	0.40i	31i	45i	0.58i	0.23i	17i	22i	...	...	0.58i	0.72i
...	...	...	...	...	...	...	...	...	...	...	...	...	...	...	
0.95i	0.92i	88i	92i	0.81i	0.62i	55i	63i	0.66i	0.35i	30i	30i	0.82i	0.90i	...	...
...	...	...	...	...	...	...	...	...	...	...	...	...	...	...	...
0.92	0.86	83	86	0.76	0.56	51	51	0.55	0.30	24	25	0.86	0.91	...	...
0.97	0.92	90	94	0.83	0.73	61	75	0.68	0.44	36	43	0.88	0.86	0.56i	0.39i
...	...	...	...	1.00	0.99	98	98	0.96	0.83	75	81	...	...	0.76	0.70
...	...	...	...	1.00	0.99	98	99	0.96	0.83	75	81	...	...	0.74	0.70
...	0.98i	98i	98i	...	0.98i	98i	98i	...	0.88i	84i	87i	...	...	0.82	0.72
0.67i	0.44i	33i	30i	0.39i	0.17i	12i	5i	0.23i	0.05i	2i	1i	...	...	...	...
0.95i	0.84i	80i	85i	0.86i	0.62i	53i	56i	0.63i	0.32i	19i	25i	...	...	...	...
0.88i	0.69i	58i	65i	0.70i	0.37i	29i	30i	0.50i	0.17i	14i	9i	...	...	...	...
0.99i	0.92i	91i	94i	0.91i	0.79i	74i	76i	0.71i	0.43i	38i	41i	...	...	0.56i	0.53i
...	...	...	...	1.00i	0.99i	98i	98i	0.97i	0.83i	75i	82i	...	...	0.76i	0.70

TABLE 5: Continued

	GENDER															
	A			B				C		D		E			
				GPIA in minimum proficiency											
	GPIA in completion			End of primary		End of lower secondary		GPIA in literacy rate		GPIA in adult proficiency		GPIA in gross enrolment ratio			
	Primary	Lower secondary	Upper secondary	Reading	Mathematics	Reading	Mathematics	Youth	Adults	Literacy	Numeracy	Pre-primary	Primary	Secondary	Tertiary
SDG indicator:	4.5.1														
Reference year:	2017														
Sub-Saharan Africa															
Angola	0.89$_{-2}$	0.76$_{-2}$	0.64$_{-2}$	...	...	...	...	0.83$_{-3}$	0.67$_{-3}$	...	...	0.88$_{-1}$	0.86$_{-2}$	0.63$_{-1}$	0.77$_{-2}$
Benin	0.83$_{-3}$	0.51$_{-3}$	0.46$_{-3}$	0.97$_{-3}$	1.00$_{-3}$	...	...	...	...	...	...	1.04$_{-1}$	0.94	0.76$_{-1}$	0.43$_{-1}$
Botswana	...	...	...	...	...	1.19	1.11	1.03$_{-3i}$	1.02$_{-3i}$	...	...	1.03$_{-3}$	0.97$_{-3}$	...	1.29
Burkina Faso	...	...	...	0.96$_{-3}$	0.90$_{-3}$	...	...	0.77$_{-3}$	0.59$_{-3}$	...	...	0.99	0.98	0.97	0.52
Burundi	1.16	0.80	0.84	1.18$_{-3}$	1.11$_{-3}$	...	...	0.88$_{-3}$	0.78$_{-3}$	...	...	1.02	1.00	1.02	0.43
Cabo Verde	...	...	...	...	...	...	...	1.01$_{-2}$	0.89$_{-2}$	...	...	1.02	0.93	1.09	1.31
Cameroon	0.97$_{-3}$	0.90$_{-3}$	0.78$_{-3}$	1.15$_{-3}$	1.06$_{-3}$	...	...	...	...	...	...	1.02	0.90	0.86$_{-1}$	0.79$_{-1}$
Central African Republic	...	...	...	...	...	...	...	...	...	...	...	1.03	0.76$_{-1}$	0.66	...
Chad	0.78$_{-2}$	0.55$_{-2}$	0.37$_{-2}$	0.78$_{-3}$	0.64$_{-3}$	...	...	0.55$_{-1}$	0.45$_{-1}$	...	...	0.93$_{-1}$	0.78$_{-1}$	0.46$_{-1}$	0.20$_{-3i}$
Comoros	...	...	...	...	...	...	...	...	...	...	...	1.03	0.96	1.06	0.81$_{-3}$
Congo	...	...	...	1.10$_{-3}$	0.90$_{-3}$	...	...	...	...	...	...	...	...	...	0.75$_{-4}$
Côte d'Ivoire	0.88$_{-1}$	0.62$_{-1}$	0.82$_{-1}$	1.05$_{-3}$	0.79$_{-3}$	...	...	0.80$_{-3}$	0.73$_{-3}$	...	...	1.01	0.91	0.75	0.70$_{-1}$
D. R. Congo	0.93$_{-4}$	0.84$_{-4}$	0.70$_{-4}$	...	...	...	...	0.88$_{-1}$	0.75$_{-1}$	...	...	1.07$_{-2}$	0.99$_{-2}$	0.64$_{-2}$	0.56$_{-1}$
Djibouti	...	...	...	...	...	...	...	...	...	...	...	0.99	0.89	0.83	...
Equat. Guinea	...	...	...	...	...	...	...	1.01$_{-3i}$	0.95$_{-3i}$	...	...	1.02$_{-2}$	0.99$_{-2}$	...	...
Eritrea	...	...	...	...	...	...	...	...	...	...	...	0.98	0.86	0.90	0.71$_{-1}$
Eswatini	1.17$_{-3}$	1.13$_{-3}$	1.07$_{-3}$	...	...	...	...	...	...	...	...	...	0.92$_{-1}$	0.98$_{-1}$	1.04$_{-4}$
Ethiopia	1.01$_{-1}$	0.96$_{-1}$	1.11$_{-1}$	...	...	...	...	...	...	...	...	0.95$_{-2}$	0.91$_{-2}$	0.96$_{-2}$	0.48$_{-3}$
Gabon	...	...	...	...	...	...	...	...	...	...	...	...	...	...	...
Gambia	0.94$_{-4}$	0.96$_{-4}$	0.85$_{-4}$	...	...	...	...	0.85$_{-4i}$	0.65$_{-4i}$	...	...	1.07	1.08	...	...
Ghana	1.05$_{-3}$	1.00$_{-3}$	1.02$_{-3}$	1.00$_{-1}$	0.94$_{-4}$	...	...	...	...	...	...	1.02	1.01	0.97	0.72
Guinea	...	...	...	...	...	...	...	0.65$_{-3}$	0.50$_{-3}$	...	...	...	0.82$_{-1}$	0.66$_{-3}$	0.45$_{-3}$
Guinea-Bissau	0.80$_{-3}$	0.69$_{-3}$	0.52$_{-3}$	...	...	...	...	0.70$_{-3i}$	0.50$_{-3i}$	...	...	...	...	...	...
Kenya	1.06$_{-3}$	1.12$_{-3}$	0.85$_{-3}$	1.06$_{-2}$	1.03$_{-2}$	...	...	0.99$_{-3i}$	0.88$_{-3i}$	...	...	0.98$_{-1}$	1.00$_{-1}$	...	0.70$_{-1}$
Lesotho	1.33$_{-3}$	1.46$_{-3}$	1.32$_{-3}$	...	...	...	...	1.15$_{-3i}$	1.20$_{-3i}$	...	...	1.05$_{-1}$	0.97	1.26	1.34$_{-2}$
Liberia	0.90$_{-4}$	0.80$_{-4}$	0.53$_{-4}$	...	...	...	...	...	...	...	...	1.01$_{-1}$	0.92$_{-1}$	0.78$_{-1}$	...
Madagascar	...	...	...	...	...	...	...	...	...	...	...	1.09	1.00$_{-1}$	1.01	0.92$_{-1}$
Malawi	1.18$_{-2}$	0.92$_{-2}$	0.84$_{-2}$	...	...	...	...	1.01$_{-2i}$	0.79$_{-2i}$	...	...	1.01$_{-2}$	1.03	0.94	...
Mali	0.84$_{-2}$	0.75$_{-2}$	0.60$_{-2}$	0.93$_{-1}$	1.02$_{-1}$	...	...	0.65$_{-2}$	0.49$_{-2}$	...	...	1.06	0.89	0.81	0.42$_{-2}$
Mauritania	0.86$_{-2}$	0.73$_{-2}$	0.57$_{-2}$	...	...	...	...	...	...	...	...	1.21$_{-2}$	1.05	0.96	0.50
Mauritius	...	...	...	...	...	...	...	...	0.95$_{-1}$	...	...	1.00	1.02	1.07	1.22
Mozambique	...	...	...	...	...	...	...	0.79$_{-2}$	0.61$_{-2}$	...	...	...	0.93	0.91	0.81
Namibia	1.11$_{-4}$	1.23$_{-4}$	1.10$_{-4}$	...	...	...	...	...	...	...	...	1.05	0.97	...	1.43$_{-1}$
Niger	...	...	...	0.85$_{-3}$	0.67$_{-3}$	...	...	...	...	...	...	1.05	0.87	0.73	0.43
Nigeria	0.93$_{-4}$	0.75$_{-4}$	0.75$_{-4}$	...	...	...	...	...	...	...	...	...	0.94$_{-1}$	0.90$_{-1}$	...
Rwanda	1.22$_{-2}$	1.16$_{-2}$	0.84$_{-2}$	...	...	...	...	1.03$_{-3}$	0.87$_{-3}$	...	...	1.03	0.99	1.11	0.88
Sao Tome and Principe	1.07$_{-3}$	1.08$_{-3}$	1.43$_{-3}$	...	...	...	...	...	...	...	...	1.08$_{-1}$	0.96	1.13	1.03$_{-2}$
Senegal	1.02$_{-2}$	0.65$_{-2}$	0.67$_{-2}$	0.97$_{-1}$	1.02$_{-1}$	...	...	0.84	0.61	...	...	1.11	1.14	1.08	0.61
Seychelles	...	...	...	...	...	...	...	...	...	...	...	1.04$_{-1}$	0.99$_{-1}$	1.06$_{-1}$	1.46$_{-1}$
Sierra Leone	1.05$_{-4}$	0.66$_{-4}$	0.74$_{-4}$	...	...	...	...	0.79$_{-4i}$	0.60$_{-4i}$	...	...	1.09	1.01	0.95	...
Somalia	...	...	...	...	...	...	...	...	...	...	...	...	...	...	...
South Africa	...	...	...	...	...	...	1.08$_{-2}$	1.01$_{-2}$	0.98$_{-2}$	...	...	1.00$_{-1}$	0.96$_{-1}$	1.08$_{-1}$	1.29$_{-1}$
South Sudan	...	...	...	...	...	...	...	...	...	...	...	0.95$_{-2}$	0.71$_{-2}$	0.54$_{-2}$	...
Togo	0.89$_{-3}$	0.64$_{-3}$	0.49$_{-3}$	1.10$_{-3}$	0.95$_{-3}$	...	...	0.87$_{-2}$	0.66$_{-2}$	...	...	1.04	0.95	0.73	0.45
Uganda	1.07$_{-1}$	0.87$_{-1}$	0.79$_{-1}$	1.01$_{-2}$	0.85$_{-2}$	...	...	...	...	...	...	1.04	1.03	...	0.78$_{-3}$
United Republic of Tanzania	1.10$_{-2}$	0.86$_{-2}$	0.69$_{-2}$	...	...	...	...	0.97$_{-2}$	0.88$_{-2}$	...	...	1.01	1.02	1.01	0.51$_{-2}$
Zambia	1.03$_{-4}$	0.88$_{-4}$	0.68$_{-4}$	...	...	...	...	...	...	...	...	...	1.01$_{-4}$	...	...
Zimbabwe	1.03$_{-2}$	1.01$_{-2}$	0.77$_{-2}$	...	...	...	...	1.06$_{-3i}$	0.99$_{-3i}$	...	...	1.02$_{-4}$	0.98$_{-4}$	0.98$_{-4}$	0.90$_{-2}$

	LOCATION/WEALTH																
	F												G				
	Disparity in primary completion				Disparity in lower secondary completion				Disparity in upper secondary completion				Wealth disparity in minimum proficiency				
	Adjusted parity index		% of poorest completing		Adjusted parity index		% of poorest completing		Adjusted parity index		% of poorest completing		End of primary		End of lower secondary		
	Location	Wealth	M	F	Location	Wealth	M	F	Location	Wealth	M	F	Reading	Mathematics	Reading	Mathematics	COUNTRY CODE
	4.5.1																
	2017																
	0.37$_{-2}$	0.21$_{-2}$	21$_{-2}$	16$_{-2}$	0.20$_{-2}$	0.06$_{-2}$	5$_{-2}$	3$_{-2}$	0.15$_{-2}$	0.03$_{-2}$	2$_{-2}$	1$_{-2}$	...	...	...	...	AGO
	0.68$_{-3}$	0.35$_{-3}$	33$_{-3}$	20$_{-3}$	0.47$_{-3}$	0.15$_{-3}$	14$_{-3}$	1$_{-3}$	0.12$_{-3}$	0.02$_{-3}$	2$_{-3}$	-$_{-3}$	0.48$_{-3}$	0.51$_{-3}$	...	...	BEN
	...	...	...	...	...	...	...	...	...	...	...	...	...	...	...	0.64$_{-2}$	BWA
	...	...	...	...	...	...	...	...	...	...	...	...	0.70$_{-3}$	0.78$_{-3}$	...	...	BFA
	0.69	0.45	24	37	0.49	0.20	14	4	0.23	0.05	3	-	0.82$_{-3}$	0.99$_{-3}$	...	...	BDI
	...	...	...	...	...	...	...	...	...	...	...	...	...	...	...	...	CPV
	0.70$_{-3}$	0.37$_{-3}$	46$_{-3}$	27$_{-3}$	0.36$_{-3}$	0.15$_{-3}$	19$_{-3}$	4$_{-3}$	0.13$_{-3}$	0.01$_{-3}$	1$_{-3}$	-$_{-3}$	0.28$_{-3}$	0.22$_{-3}$	...		CMR
	...	...	...	...	...	...	...	...	...	...	...	...	...	...	...	...	CAF
	0.35$_{-2}$	0.27$_{-2}$	19$_{-2}$	12$_{-2}$	0.15$_{-2}$	0.12$_{-2}$	8$_{-2}$	2$_{-2}$	0.08$_{-2}$	0.02$_{-2}$	2$_{-2}$	-$_{-2}$	0.49$_{-3}$	0.60$_{-3}$	...	...	TCD
	...	...	...	...	...	...	...	...	...	...	...	...	...	...	...	...	COM
	...	...	...	...	...	...	...	...	...	...	...	...	0.23$_{-3}$	0.35$_{-3}$	...	...	COG
	0.56$_{-1}$	0.32$_{-1}$	30$_{-1}$	16$_{-1}$	0.27$_{-1}$	0.08$_{-1}$	8$_{-1}$	2$_{-1}$	0.13$_{-1}$	0.04$_{-1}$	4$_{-1}$	-$_{-1}$	0.45$_{-3}$	0.46$_{-3}$	...	...	CIV
	0.67$_{-4}$	0.53$_{-4}$	55$_{-4}$	42$_{-4}$	0.50$_{-4}$	0.32$_{-4}$	34$_{-4}$	21$_{-4}$	0.29$_{-4}$	0.12$_{-4}$	10$_{-4}$	4$_{-4}$	...	...	...	...	COD
	...	...	...	...	...	...	...			...	...	...	...	...	...	...	DJI
	...	...	...	...	...	...	...	...	...	[illegible]	...	...	...	...	...	...	GNQ
	...	...	...	...	...	...	...	...	...	[illegible]	...	...	...	...	...	...	ERI
	0.77$_{-3}$	0.59$_{-3}$	50$_{-3}$	56$_{-3}$	0.66$_{-3}$	0.32$_{-3}$	26$_{-3}$	24$_{-3}$	0.63$_{-3}$	0.21$_{-3}$	11$_{-3}$	13$_{-3}$	...	...	...	...	SWZ
	0.52$_{-1}$	0.35$_{-1}$	28$_{-1}$	28$_{-1}$	0.20$_{-1}$	0.08$_{-1}$	3$_{-1}$	5$_{-1}$	0.13$_{-1}$	0.04$_{-1}$	1$_{-1}$	2$_{-1}$	...	...	...	...	ETH
	...	...	...	...	...	...	...	...	...	...	...	...	...	...	...	...	GAB
	0.61$_{-4}$	0.57$_{-4}$	54$_{-4}$	44$_{-4}$	0.42$_{-4}$	0.36$_{-4}$	29$_{-4}$	25$_{-4}$	0.33$_{-4}$	0.24$_{-4}$	15$_{-4}$	8$_{-4}$	...	...	...	...	GMB
	0.75$_{-3}$	0.51$_{-3}$	42$_{-3}$	43$_{-3}$	0.61$_{-3}$	0.36$_{-3}$	28$_{-3}$	26$_{-3}$	0.42$_{-3}$	0.10$_{-3}$	7$_{-3}$	2$_{-3}$	...	...	...	...	GHA
	...	...	...	...	...	...	...	...	...	...	...	...	...	...	...	...	GIN
	0.23$_{-3}$	0.13$_{-3}$	8$_{-3}$	7$_{-3}$	0.22$_{-3}$	0.09$_{-3}$	5$_{-3}$	1$_{-3}$	0.14$_{-3}$	0.12$_{-3}$	4$_{-3}$	-$_{-3}$	...	...	...	...	GNB
	0.88$_{-3}$	0.65$_{-3}$	61$_{-3}$	65$_{-3}$	0.78$_{-3}$	0.45$_{-3}$	41$_{-3}$	43$_{-3}$	0.52$_{-3}$	0.16$_{-3}$	17$_{-3}$	7$_{-3}$	0.80$_{-2}$	0.79$_{-2}$	...	...	KEN
	0.73$_{-3}$	0.54$_{-3}$	28$_{-3}$	62$_{-3}$	0.49$_{-3}$	0.14$_{-3}$	5$_{-3}$	10$_{-3}$	0.26$_{-3}$	0.01$_{-3}$	-$_{-3}$	1$_{-3}$	...	...	...	...	LSO
	0.35$_{-4}$	0.19$_{-4}$	11$_{-4}$	11$_{-4}$	0.19$_{-4}$	0.07$_{-4}$	5$_{-4}$	2$_{-4}$	0.20$_{-4}$	0.05$_{-4}$	2$_{-4}$	1$_{-4}$	...	...	...	...	LBR
	...	...	...	...	...	...	...	...	...	...	...	...	...	...	...	...	MDG
	0.58$_{-2}$	0.35$_{-2}$	22$_{-2}$	29$_{-2}$	0.31$_{-2}$	0.11$_{-2}$	7$_{-2}$	5$_{-2}$	0.28$_{-2}$	0.07$_{-2}$	4$_{-2}$	2$_{-2}$	...	...	...	...	MWI
	0.54$_{-2}$	0.25$_{-2}$	23$_{-2}$	15$_{-2}$	0.36$_{-2}$	0.09$_{-2}$	8$_{-2}$	2$_{-2}$	0.23$_{-2}$	0.03$_{-2}$	2$_{-2}$	0.2$_{-2}$	0.47$_{-1}$	0.88$_{-1}$	...	...	MLI
	0.58$_{-2}$	0.32$_{-2}$	34$_{-2}$	21$_{-2}$	0.52$_{-2}$	0.26$_{-2}$	16$_{-2}$	15$_{-2}$	0.35$_{-2}$	0.13$_{-2}$	6$_{-2}$	3$_{-2}$	...	...	...	...	MRT
	...	...	...	...	...	...	...	...	...	...	...	...	...	...	...	...	MUS
	...	...	...	...	...	...	...	...	...	...	...	...	...	...	...	...	MOZ
	0.84$_{-4}$	0.72$_{-4}$	59$_{-4}$	80$_{-4}$	0.45$_{-4}$	0.27$_{-4}$	22$_{-4}$	24$_{-4}$	0.41$_{-4}$	0.11$_{-4}$	8$_{-4}$	7$_{-4}$	...	...	...	...	NAM
	...	...	...	...	...	...	...	...	...	...	...	...	0.09$_{-3}$	0.14$_{-3}$	...	...	NER
	0.62$_{-4}$	0.22$_{-4}$	27$_{-4}$	14$_{-4}$	0.49$_{-4}$	0.12$_{-4}$	18$_{-4}$	4$_{-4}$	0.48$_{-4}$	0.09$_{-4}$	14$_{-4}$	2$_{-4}$	...	...	...	...	NGA
	0.76$_{-2}$	0.48$_{-2}$	26$_{-2}$	38$_{-2}$	0.49$_{-2}$	0.24$_{-2}$	11$_{-2}$	12$_{-2}$	0.30$_{-2}$	0.08$_{-2}$	2$_{-2}$	4$_{-2}$	...	...	...	...	RWA
	0.90$_{-3}$	0.75$_{-3}$	70$_{-3}$	73$_{-3}$	0.86$_{-3}$	0.17$_{-3}$	9$_{-3}$	10$_{-3}$	0.63$_{-3}$	0.07$_{-3}$	-$_{-3}$	5$_{-3}$	...	...	...	...	STP
	0.60$_{-2}$	0.44$_{-2}$	33$_{-2}$	28$_{-2}$	0.40$_{-2}$	0.21$_{-2}$	14$_{-2}$	5$_{-2}$	0.13$_{-2}$	0.03$_{-2}$	1$_{-2}$	-$_{-2}$	0.46$_{-1}$	0.74$_{-1}$	...	...	SEN
	...	...	...	...	...	...	...	...	...	...	...	...	...	...	...	...	SYC
	0.66$_{-4}$	0.50$_{-4}$	41$_{-4}$	47$_{-4}$	0.37$_{-4}$	0.21$_{-4}$	21$_{-4}$	10$_{-4}$	0.13$_{-4}$	0.04$_{-4}$	2$_{-4}$	1$_{-4}$	...	...	...	...	SLE
	...	...	...	...	...	...	...	...	...	...	...	...	...	...	...	...	SOM
	...	...	...	...	...	...	...	...	...	...	...	...	...	...	...	0.39$_{-2}$	ZAF
	...	...	...	...	...	...	...	...	...	...	...	...	...	...	...	...	SSD
	0.67$_{-3}$	0.48$_{-3}$	46$_{-3}$	34$_{-3}$	0.29$_{-3}$	0.11$_{-3}$	7$_{-3}$	2$_{-3}$	0.14$_{-3}$	0.03$_{-3}$	2$_{-3}$	-$_{-3}$	0.31$_{-3}$	0.48$_{-3}$	...	...	TGO
	0.59$_{-1}$	0.26$_{-1}$	20$_{-1}$	17$_{-1}$	0.38$_{-1}$	0.12$_{-1}$	10$_{-1}$	4$_{-1}$	0.34$_{-1}$	0.07$_{-1}$	3$_{-1}$	3$_{-1}$	...	...	...	...	UGA
	0.83$_{-2}$	0.64$_{-2}$	54$_{-2}$	67$_{-2}$	0.35$_{-2}$	0.12$_{-2}$	9$_{-2}$	5$_{-2}$	0.26$_{-2}$	0.01$_{-2}$	0.4$_{-2}$	-$_{-2}$	...	...	...	...	TZA
	0.72$_{-4}$	0.47$_{-4}$	43$_{-4}$	45$_{-4}$	0.45$_{-4}$	0.22$_{-4}$	23$_{-4}$	15$_{-4}$	0.27$_{-4}$	0.02$_{-4}$	3$_{-4}$	0.4$_{-4}$	...	...	...	...	ZMB
	0.88$_{-2}$	0.76$_{-2}$	73$_{-2}$	76$_{-2}$	0.68$_{-2}$	0.42$_{-2}$	40$_{-2}$	39$_{-2}$	0.16$_{-2}$	0.02$_{-2}$	2$_{-2}$	-$_{-2}$	...	...	...	...	ZWE

TABLE 5: Continued

	GENDER														
	A			B				C		D		E			
	GPIA in completion			GPIA in minimum proficiency				GPIA in literacy rate		GPIA in adult proficiency		GPIA in gross enrolment ratio			
				End of primary		End of lower secondary									
	Primary	Lower secondary	Upper secondary	Reading	Mathematics	Reading	Mathematics	Youth	Adults	Literacy	Numeracy	Pre-primary	Primary	Secondary	Tertiary
SDG indicator:	4.5.1														
Reference year:	2017														
Northern Africa and Western Asia															
Algeria	1.01$_{-4}$	1.25$_{-4}$	1.41$_{-4}$	…	…	1.46$_{-2}$	1.16$_{-2}$	…	…	…	…	…	0.95	…	1.33
Armenia	1.00$_{-1}$	1.05$_{-1}$	1.25$_{-1}$	…	1.01	…	…	…	…	…	…	1.09	1.00	1.05$_{-2}$	1.22
Azerbaijan	…	…	…	…	…	…	…	1.00$_{-1}$	1.00$_{-1}$	…	…	1.00$_{i}$	1.02$_{i}$	1.01$_{i}$	1.13$_{i}$
Bahrain	…	…	…	…	…	…	1.13$_{-2}$	…	…	…	…	0.99	1.00	1.01	1.49
Cyprus	…	0.99$_{-3}$	1.10$_{-3}$	…	…	1.29$_{-2}$	…	…	…	…	…	0.99$_{-2i}$	1.00$_{-2i}$	0.99$_{-2i}$	1.26$_{-2i}$
Egypt	1.01$_{-3}$	1.02$_{-3}$	0.96$_{-3}$	…	…	…	1.08$_{-2}$	0.98	0.87	…	…	0.99	1.00	0.98	1.02$_{-1}$
Georgia	…	1.00$_{-4}$	1.00$_{-4}$	…	…	1.39$_{-2}$	1.13$_{-2}$	1.00$_{-3}$	1.00$_{-3}$	…	…	…	1.01	1.02	1.12
Iraq	…	…	…	…	…	…	…	0.85$_{-4}$	0.72$_{-4}$	…	…	…	…	…	…
Israel	…	…	…	…	…	1.13$_{-2}$	1.00$_{-2}$	…	…	1.01$_{-2}$	0.92$_{-2}$	1.00$_{-1}$	1.01$_{-1}$	1.02$_{-1}$	1.29$_{-1}$
Jordan	…	…	…	…	…	1.47$_{-2}$	1.16$_{-2}$	…	…	…	…	…	…	1.03	1.13
Kuwait	…	…	…	…	…	…	1.07$_{-2}$	1.00	0.98	…	…	1.00	1.00	1.07$_{-2}$	1.46$_{-4}$
Lebanon	…	…	…	…	…	1.11$_{-2}$	0.97$_{-2}$	…	…	…	…	0.96	0.92	0.99	1.14$_{-3}$
Libya	…	…	…	…	…	…	…	…	…	…	…	…	…	…	…
Morocco	…	…	…	…	…	…	1.00$_{-2}$	…	…	…	…	0.83	0.95	0.89	0.97
Oman	…	…	…	…	…	…	1.23$_{-2}$	1.00	0.96	…	…	1.05	1.03	0.97	1.45$_{-1}$
Palestine	1.01$_{-3}$	1.14$_{-3}$	1.28$_{-3}$	…	…	…	…	1.00$_{-1}$	0.97$_{-1}$	…	…	1.00	1.00	1.09	1.38
Qatar	…	…	…	…	…	1.33$_{-2}$	1.06$_{-2}$	…	…	…	…	1.03	0.99	1.20	1.87
Saudi Arabia	…	…	…	…	…	…	1.15$_{-2}$	1.00$_{-4}$	0.95$_{-4}$	…	…	0.99$_{-1}$	0.98$_{-1}$	0.77$_{-3i}$	1.00$_{-1}$
Sudan	0.97$_{-3}$	1.02$_{-3}$	0.83$_{-3}$	…	…	…	…	…	…	…	…	1.05$_{-1}$	0.94$_{-1}$	0.98$_{-1}$	1.02$_{-2}$
Syrian Arab Republic	…	…	…	…	…	…	…	…	…	…	…	0.96$_{-4}$	0.97$_{-4}$	1.00$_{-4}$	1.16$_{-1}$
Tunisia	…	…	…	…	…	1.28$_{-2}$	0.87$_{-2}$	0.99$_{-3}$	0.84$_{-3}$	…	…	1.00$_{-1}$	0.97$_{-1}$	1.10$_{-1}$	1.44
Turkey	…	…	…	…	1.01$_{-2}$	1.18$_{-2}$	1.03$_{-2}$	1.00$_{-1}$	0.95$_{-1}$	0.87$_{-2}$	0.71$_{-2}$	0.95$_{-1}$	0.99$_{-1}$	0.98$_{-1}$	0.87$_{-1}$
United Arab Emirates	…	…	…	…	…	1.31$_{-2}$	1.10$_{-2}$	…	…	…	…	1.07$_{-1}$	0.97$_{-1}$	0.94$_{-1}$	…
Yemen	0.78$_{-4}$	0.73$_{-4}$	0.64$_{-4}$	…	…	…	…	…	…	…	…	0.90$_{-1}$	0.87$_{-1}$	0.73$_{-1}$	…
Central and Southern Asia															
Afghanistan	0.56$_{-2}$	0.49$_{-2}$	0.46$_{-2}$	…	…	…	…	…	…	…	…	…	0.69	0.57	0.28$_{-3}$
Bangladesh	1.11$_{-3}$	1.02$_{-3}$	0.82$_{-3}$	…	…	…	…	1.03	0.93	…	…	1.03	1.07	1.15	0.70
Bhutan	…	…	…	…	…	…	…	…	…	…	…	1.06	1.00	1.09	0.74$_{-4}$
India	1.00$_{-2}$	0.96$_{-2}$	0.85$_{-2}$	1.03$_{-1}$	0.91$_{-1}$	…	…	…	…	…	…	0.94$_{-1}$	1.14$_{-1}$	1.02$_{-1}$	1.00$_{-1}$
Iran, Islamic Republic of	…	…	…	…	…	…	1.05$_{-2}$	1.00$_{-1}$	0.89$_{-1}$	…	…	0.97$_{-2}$	1.05$_{-2}$	1.00$_{-2}$	0.91$_{-1}$
Kazakhstan	1.00$_{-2}$	1.00$_{-2}$	1.02$_{-2}$	…	1.00$_{-2}$	1.13$_{-2}$	1.02$_{-2}$	…	…	…	…	1.01	1.02	1.01	1.21
Kyrgyzstan	1.00$_{-3}$	1.02$_{-3}$	1.03$_{-3}$	…	…	…	…	…	…	…	…	1.01	0.99	1.00	1.20
Maldives	…	…	…	…	…	…	…	1.00$_{-3}$	1.00$_{-3}$	…	…	1.00	1.00	…	1.51$_{-3}$
Nepal	0.99$_{-1}$	0.97$_{-1}$	…	…	…	…	…	…	…	…	…	0.94	1.06	1.10$_{i}$	1.10
Pakistan	…	…	…	1.04$_{-1}$	1.03$_{-1}$	…	…	0.82$_{-3}$	0.64$_{-3}$	…	…	0.87	0.86	0.81	0.87
Sri Lanka	…	…	…	…	…	…	…	1.01	0.98	…	…	0.99$_{-1}$	0.99	1.05	1.34
Tajikistan	…	…	…	…	…	…	…	1.00$_{-3i}$	1.00$_{-3i}$	…	…	0.86	0.99	0.90$_{-4}$	0.75
Turkmenistan	1.00$_{-1}$	1.00$_{-1}$	1.03$_{-1}$	…	…	…	…	1.00$_{-3i}$	1.00$_{-3i}$	…	…	0.97$_{-3}$	0.98$_{-3}$	0.96$_{-3}$	0.64$_{-3}$
Uzbekistan	…	…	…	…	…	…	…	1.00$_{-1}$	1.00$_{-1}$	…	…	0.96	0.98	0.99	0.61
Eastern and South-eastern Asia															
Brunei Darussalam	…	…	…	…	…	…	…	…	…	…	…	1.03	0.99	1.02	1.36
Cambodia	1.12$_{-3}$	0.96$_{-3}$	0.97$_{-3}$	…	…	1.30	1.22	1.01$_{-2}$	0.87$_{-2}$	…	…	1.04	0.98	…	0.87
China	1.02$_{-3}$	1.13$_{-3}$	1.02$_{-3}$	…	…	1.06$_{-2}$	1.00$_{-2}$	…	…	…	…	1.01	1.01	1.02$_{-4}$	1.17
DPR Korea	…	…	…	…	…	…	…	…	…	…	…	…	1.00$_{+1}$	1.01$_{-2}$	0.51$_{+1}$
Hong Kong, China	…	…	…	…	…	1.07$_{-2}$	1.02$_{-2}$	…	…	…	…	0.99	…	0.96	1.10
Indonesia	…	…	…	…	…	1.26$_{-2}$	1.06$_{-2}$	1.00$_{-1}$	0.96$_{-1}$	…	…	0.89	0.96	1.03	1.11
Japan	…	…	…	…	…	…	…	…	…	…	…	…	1.00$_{-1}$	1.01$_{-1}$	0.95$_{-1}$
Lao PDR	…	…	…	…	…	…	…	0.96$_{-2}$	0.88$_{-2}$	…	…	1.03	0.97	0.93	1.05
Macao, China	…	…	…	…	…	1.10$_{-2}$	1.03$_{-2}$	1.00$_{-1}$	0.97$_{-1}$	…	…	0.98	0.99	1.00	1.23
Malaysia	…	…	…	…	…	1.22$_{-2}$	1.06$_{-2}$	…	…	…	…	1.04	1.01	1.05	1.15
Mongolia	1.01$_{-3}$	1.05$_{-3}$	1.26$_{-3}$	…	…	…	…	…	…	…	…	1.00	0.98	…	1.30
Myanmar	1.03$_{-1}$	1.03$_{-1}$	1.33$_{-1}$	…	…	…	…	0.99$_{-1i}$	0.90$_{-1i}$	…	…	1.01	0.95	1.09	1.32
Philippines	1.12$_{-4}$	1.25$_{-4}$	1.22$_{-4}$	…	…	…	…	1.01$_{-4}$	1.01$_{-4}$	…	…	0.99$_{-1}$	0.97$_{-1}$	1.09$_{-1}$	1.24
Republic of Korea	…	…	…	…	…	1.12$_{-2}$	1.06$_{-2}$	…	…	…	…	1.00$_{-1}$	1.00$_{-1}$	1.00$_{-1}$	0.78$_{-1}$
Singapore	…	…	…	…	…	1.06$_{-2}$	1.01$_{-2}$	1.00$_{-1}$	0.97$_{-1}$	0.96$_{-2}$	0.93$_{-2}$	…	1.00$_{-1i}$	0.99$_{-1i}$	1.14$_{-1i}$
Thailand	1.01$_{-4}$	1.10$_{-4}$	1.13$_{-4}$	…	…	1.28$_{-2}$	1.03$_{-2}$	1.00$_{-2}$	0.96$_{-2}$	…	…	0.99	1.00	0.96	1.29$_{-1}$
Timor-Leste	1.10$_{-1}$	1.10$_{-1}$	1.10$_{-1}$	…	…	…	…	…	…	…	…	1.02	0.97	1.08	…
Viet Nam	1.01$_{-3}$	1.06$_{-3}$	1.17$_{-3}$	…	…	1.11$_{-2}$	1.04$_{-2}$	…	…	…	…	0.98	1.00	…	1.19$_{-1}$

LOCATION/WEALTH																
F												G				
Disparity in primary completion				Disparity in lower secondary completion				Disparity in upper secondary completion				Wealth disparity in minimum proficiency				
Adjusted parity index		% of poorest completing		Adjusted parity index		% of poorest completing		Adjusted parity index		% of poorest completing		End of primary		End of lower secondary		
Location	Wealth	M	F	Location	Wealth	M	F	Location	Wealth	M	F	Reading	Mathematics	Reading	Mathematics	COUNTRY CODE
4.5.1																
2017																
0.96$_{-4}$	0.87$_{-4}$	87$_{-4}$	86$_{-4}$	0.76$_{-4}$	0.49$_{-4}$	30$_{-4}$	47$_{-4}$	0.68$_{-4}$	0.33$_{-4}$	12$_{-4}$	22$_{-4}$	…	…	0.61$_{-2}$	0.49$_{-2}$	DZA
1.00$_{-1}$	0.99$_{-1}$	99$_{-1}$	99$_{-1}$	0.96$_{-1}$	0.93$_{-1}$	85$_{-1}$	99$_{-1}$	0.68$_{-1}$	0.64$_{-1}$	45$_{-1}$	55$_{-1}$	…	…	…	…	ARM
…	…	…	…	…	…	…	…	…	…	…	…	…	…	…	…	AZE
…	…	…	…	…	…	…	…	…	…	…	…	…	…	…	0.76$_{-2}$	BHR
	…	…	…	1.01$_{-3}$	0.96$_{-3}$	100$_{-3}$	92$_{-3}$	1.02$_{-3}$	0.93$_{-3}$	78$_{-3}$	99$_{-3}$	…	…	0.67$_{-2}$	…	CYP
0.97$_{-3}$	0.89$_{-3}$	87$_{-3}$	87$_{-3}$	0.89$_{-3}$	0.74$_{-3}$	70$_{-3}$	71$_{-3}$	0.60$_{-3}$	0.37$_{-3}$	77$_{-3}$	77$_{-3}$	…	…	…	0.55$_{-2}$	EGY
…	…	…	…	0.99$_{-4}$	0.99$_{-4}$	100$_{-4}$	96$_{-4}$	0.98$_{-4}$	0.89$_{-4}$	85$_{-4}$	92$_{-4}$	…	…	0.45$_{-2}$	0.37$_{-2}$	GEO
…	…	…	…	…	…	…	…	…	…	…	…	…	…	…	…	IRQ
…	…	…	…	…	…	…	…	…	…	…	…	…	…	0.68$_{-2}$	0.60$_{-2}$	ISR
…	…	…	…	…	…	…	…	…	…	…	…	…	…	0.59$_{-2}$	0.48$_{-2}$	JOR
…	…	…	…	…	…	…	…	…	…	…	…	…	…	…	0.54$_{-2}$	KWT
…	…	…	…	…	…	…	…	…	…	…	…	…	…	0.24$_{-2}$	0.72$_{-2}$	LBN
…	…	…	…	…	…	…	…	…	…	…	…	…	…	…	…	LBY
…	…	…	…	…	…	…	…	…	…	…	…	…	…	…	0.60$_{-2}$	MAR
…	…	…	…	…	…	…	…	…	…	…	…	…	…	…	0.64$_{-2}$	OMN
1.00$_{-3}$	0.99$_{-3}$	98$_{-3}$	100$_{-3}$	1.03$_{-3}$	0.82$_{-3}$	69$_{-3}$	84$_{-3}$	1.04$_{-3}$	0.63$_{-3}$	37$_{-3}$	62$_{-3}$	…	…	…	…	PSE
…	…	…	…	…	…	…	…	…	…	…	…	…	…	0.59$_{-2}$	0.46$_{-2}$	QAT
…	…	…	…	…	…	…	…	…	…	…	…	…	…	…	0.47$_{-2}$	SAU
0.71$_{-3}$	0.45$_{-3}$	45$_{-3}$	41$_{-3}$	0.61$_{-3}$	0.30$_{-3}$	29$_{-3}$	23$_{-3}$	0.45$_{-3}$	0.16$_{-3}$	14$_{-3}$	8$_{-3}$	…	…	…	…	SDN
…	…	…	…	…	…	…	…	…	…	…	…	…	…	…	…	SYR
…	…	…	…	…	…	…	…	…	…	…	…	…	…	0.34$_{-2}$	0.31$_{-2}$	TUN
…	…	…	…	…	…	…	…	…	…	…	…	…	0.62$_{-2}$	0.62$_{-2}$	0.55$_{-2}$	TUR
…	…	…	…	…	…	…	…	…	…	…	…	…	…	0.66$_{-2}$	0.65$_{-2}$	ARE
0.72$_{-4}$	0.39$_{-4}$	47$_{-4}$	20$_{-4}$	0.60$_{-4}$	0.29$_{-4}$	31$_{-4}$	9$_{-4}$	0.50$_{-4}$	0.18$_{-4}$	17$_{-4}$	4$_{-4}$	…	…	…	…	YEM
0.67$_{-2}$	0.58$_{-2}$	57$_{-2}$	31$_{-2}$	0.54$_{-2}$	0.42$_{-2}$	38$_{-2}$	13$_{-2}$	0.42$_{-2}$	0.26$_{-2}$	20$_{-2}$	4$_{-2}$	…	…	…	…	AFG
0.99$_{-3}$	0.70$_{-3}$	57$_{-3}$	68$_{-3}$	0.94$_{-3}$	0.40$_{-3}$	30$_{-3}$	27$_{-3}$	0.61$_{-3}$	0.10$_{-3}$	4$_{-3}$	3$_{-3}$	…	…	…	…	BGD
…	…	…	…	…	…	…	…	…	…	…	…	…	…	…	…	BTN
0.97$_{-2}$	0.82$_{-2}$	81$_{-2}$	80$_{-2}$	0.92$_{-2}$	0.62$_{-2}$	62$_{-2}$	56$_{-2}$	0.65$_{-2}$	0.18$_{-2}$	18$_{-2}$	9$_{-2}$	0.51$_{-1}$	0.50$_{-1}$	…	…	IND
…	…	…	…	…	…	…	…	…	…	…	…	…	…	…	0.53$_{-2}$	IRN
1.00$_{-2}$	1.00$_{-2}$	100$_{-2}$	100$_{-2}$	1.00$_{-2}$	0.99$_{-2}$	100$_{-2}$	99$_{-2}$	0.96$_{-2}$	0.90$_{-2}$	88$_{-2}$	89$_{-2}$	…	0.95$_{-2}$	0.67$_{-2}$	0.90$_{-2}$	KAZ
1.00$_{-3}$	0.98$_{-3}$	98$_{-3}$	98$_{-3}$	0.95$_{-3}$	0.92$_{-3}$	91$_{-3}$	92$_{-3}$	0.96$_{-3}$	0.91$_{-3}$	77$_{-3}$	85$_{-3}$	…	…	…	…	KGZ
…	…	…	…	…	…	…	…	…	…	…	…	…	…	…	…	MDV
0.83$_{-1}$	0.80$_{-1}$	73$_{-1}$	69$_{-1}$	0.77$_{-1}$	0.57$_{-1}$	50$_{-1}$	50$_{-1}$	…	…	…	…	…	…	…		NPL
…	…	…	…	…	…	…	…	…	…	…	…	0.72$_{-1}$	0.72$_{-1}$	…	…	PAK
…	…	…	…				…	…	…	…	…	…	…			LKA
…	…	…	…				…	…	…	…	…	…	…	…	…	TJK
1.00$_{-1}$	1.00$_{-1}$	100$_{-1}$	100$_{-1}$	1.00$_{-1}$	1.00$_{-1}$	99$_{-1}$	100$_{-1}$	1.01$_{-1}$	0.94$_{-1}$	86$_{-1}$	95$_{-1}$	…	…	…	…	TKM
…	…	…	…	…	…	…	…	…	…	…	…	…	…	…	…	UZB
…		…	…	…	…	…	…	…	…	…	…	…	…	…	…	BRN
0.83$_{-3}$	0.52$_{-3}$	42$_{-3}$	54$_{-3}$	0.53$_{-3}$	0.26$_{-3}$	15$_{-3}$	19$_{-3}$	0.31$_{-3}$	0.09$_{-3}$	5$_{-3}$	4$_{-3}$	…	…	…	…	KHM
0.99$_{-3}$	0.97$_{-3}$	94$_{-3}$	98$_{-3}$	0.88$_{-3}$	0.93$_{-3}$	74$_{-3}$	85$_{-3}$	0.70$_{-3}$	0.79$_{-3}$	59$_{-3}$	63$_{-3}$	…	…	0.61$_{-2}$	0.71$_{-2}$	CHN
…	…	…	…	…	…	…	…	…	…	…	…	…	…	…	…	PRK
…	…	…	…	…	…	…	…	…	…	…	…	…	…	0.91$_{-2}$	0.91$_{-2}$	HKG
…	…	…	…	…	…	…	…	…	…	…	…	…	…	0.44$_{-2}$	0.29$_{-2}$	IDN
…	…	…	…	…	…	…	…	…	…	…	…	…	…	…	…	JPN
…	…	…	…	…	…	…	…	…	…	…	…	…	…	…	…	LAO
…	…	…	…	…	…	…	…	…	…	…	…	…	…	0.93$_{-2}$	0.96$_{-2}$	MAC
…	…	…	…	…	…	…	…	…	…	…	…	…	…	0.53$_{-2}$	0.72$_{-2}$	MYS
0.98$_{-3}$	0.96$_{-3}$	94$_{-3}$	96$_{-3}$	0.77$_{-3}$	0.67$_{-3}$	63$_{-3}$	72$_{-3}$	0.45$_{-3}$	0.24$_{-3}$	13$_{-3}$	33$_{-3}$	…	…	…	…	MNG
0.91$_{-1}$	0.70$_{-1}$	64$_{-1}$	65$_{-1}$	0.47$_{-1}$	0.18$_{-1}$	18$_{-1}$	9$_{-1}$	0.31$_{-1}$	0.04$_{-1}$	1$_{-1}$	2$_{-1}$	…	…	…	…	MMR
0.95$_{-4}$	0.69$_{-4}$	58$_{-4}$	80$_{-4}$	0.86$_{-4}$	0.43$_{-4}$	29$_{-4}$	55$_{-4}$	0.81$_{-4}$	0.32$_{-4}$	23$_{-4}$	38$_{-4}$	…	…	…	…	PHL
…	…	…	…	…	…	…	…	…	…	…	…	…	…	0.83$_{-2}$	0.79$_{-2}$	KOR
…	…	…	…	…	…	…	…	…	…	…	…	…	…	0.79$_{-2}$	0.97$_{-2}$	SGP
1.00$_{-4}$	0.99$_{-4}$	97$_{-4}$	99$_{-4}$	0.98$_{-4}$	0.80$_{-4}$	69$_{-4}$	85$_{-4}$	0.78$_{-4}$	0.37$_{-4}$	23$_{-4}$	41$_{-4}$	…	…	0.58$_{-2}$	0.60$_{-2}$	THA
0.82$_{-1}$	0.62$_{-1}$	57$_{-1}$	63$_{-1}$	0.63$_{-1}$	0.37$_{-1}$	33$_{-1}$	35$_{-1}$	0.48$_{-1}$	0.23$_{-1}$	18$_{-1}$	20$_{-1}$	…	…	…	…	TLS
0.98$_{-3}$	0.92$_{-3}$	89$_{-3}$	91$_{-3}$	0.91$_{-3}$	0.62$_{-3}$	57$_{-3}$	64$_{-3}$	0.68$_{-3}$	0.22$_{-3}$	16$_{-3}$	25$_{-3}$	…	…	0.84$_{-2}$	0.78$_{-2}$	VNM

TABLE 5: Continued

	GENDER															
	A			B				C		D		E				
	GPIA in completion			GPIA in minimum proficiency				GPIA in literacy rate		GPIA in adult proficiency		GPIA in gross enrolment ratio				
				End of primary		End of lower secondary										
	Primary	Lower secondary	Upper secondary	Reading	Mathematics	Reading	Mathematics	Youth	Adults	Literacy	Numeracy	Pre-primary	Primary	Secondary	Tertiary	
SDG indicator:	4.5.1															
Reference year:	2017															
Oceania																
Australia	...	...	...	1.04	1.02	1.11_{-2}	1.00_{-2}	...	...	...	...	0.96_{-1}	1.00_{-1}	0.87_{-1}	1.30_{-1}	
Cook Islands	...	...	...	...	...	...	...	...	...	...	...	1.04_{-1i}	0.94_{-1i}	1.06_{-1i}	...	
Fiji	...	...	...	...	...	...	...	...	...	...	...	...	0.99_{-1}	...	...	
Kiribati	...	...	...	...	...	...	...	...	...	...	...	...	1.06	...	...	
Marshall Islands	...	...	...	...	...	...	...	...	...	...	...	0.93_{-1}	1.02_{-1}	1.09_{-1}	...	
Micronesia, F. S.	...	...	...	...	...	...	...	...	...	...	...	0.92_{-2}	1.00_{-2}	...	...	
Nauru	...	...	...	...	...	...	...	...	...	...	...	1.04_{-1i}	1.03_{-1i}	1.03_{-1i}	...	
New Zealand	...	...	...	...	...	1.11_{-2}	1.00_{-2}	...	...	1.01_{-2}	0.95_{-2}	1.01_{-1}	1.01_{-1}	1.06_{-1}	1.29_{-1}	
Niue	...	...	...	...	...	...	...	...	...	...	...	1.06_{-1i}	0.95_{-1i}	1.09_{-2i}	...	
Palau	...	...	...	...	...	...	...	1.01_{-2}	1.00_{-2}	...	...	1.08_{-3i}	0.96_{-3i}	1.05_{-3i}	1.35_{-4i}	
Papua New Guinea	...	...	...	...	...	...	...	...	...	...	...	0.99_{-1}	0.91_{-1}	0.73_{-1}	...	
Samoa	...	...	...	...	...	...	...	...	...	...	...	1.11	1.00	1.09_{-1}	...	
Solomon Is	...	...	...	...	...	...	...	...	...	...	...	1.02	0.99	...	...	
Tokelau	...	...	...	...	...	...	...	...	...	...	...	0.90_{-1i}	0.88_{-1i}	1.02_{-1i}	...	
Tonga	...	...	...	...	...	...	...	...	...	...	...	1.01_{-2}	0.97_{-2}	1.05_{-2}	...	
Tuvalu	...	...	...	...	...	...	...	...	...	...	...	1.04_{-1i}	0.97_{-1i}	1.20_{-1i}	...	
Vanuatu	...	...	...	...	...	...	...	1.01_{-3i}	0.97_{-3i}	...	...	0.97_{-2}	0.98_{-2}	1.05_{-2}	...	
Latin America and the Caribbean																
Anguilla	...	...	...	1.22_{-2}	1.23_{-2}	...	...	...	...	...	...	...	...	...	...	
Antigua and Barbuda	...	...	...	1.33_{-2}	1.14_{-2}	...	...	...	1.01_{-2}	...	...	0.98_{-2}	0.94_{-2}	1.02_{-2}	...	
Argentina	...	...	...	1.10_{-1}	0.95_{-1}	1.10_{-1}	0.86_{-1}	1.00_{-1i}	1.00_{-1i}	...	...	1.01_{-1}	1.00_{-1}	1.04_{-1}	1.40_{-1}	
Aruba	...	...	...	...	...	...	...	...	...	...	...	0.98_{-3}	0.97_{-3}	...	1.56_{-2}	
Bahamas	...	...	...	...	...	...	...	...	...	...	...	1.07_{-1}	1.05_{-1}	1.06_{-1}	...	
Barbados	...	...	...	...	...	...	...	1.00_{-3i}	1.00_{-3i}	...	...	1.04	0.98	1.04	...	
Belize	1.01_{-1}	1.15_{-1}	1.06_{-1}	...	...	...	...	...	...	...	...	1.05	0.95	1.05	1.38	
Bolivia, P. S.	1.00_{-4}	1.01_{-4}	0.98_{-4}	...	...	...	...	1.00_{-2}	0.92_{-2}	...	...	1.00	0.98	0.97	...	
Brazil	1.09_{-2}	1.10_{-2}	1.19_{-2}	1.04_{-4}	0.99_{-4}	1.17_{-2}	0.79_{-2}	1.01_{-2}	1.01_{-2}	...	...	1.05_{-1i}	0.97_{-1i}	1.05_{-1i}	1.28_{-1i}	
British Virgin Islands	...	...	...	...	...	...	...	...	...	...	...	...	...	...	...	
Cayman Islands	...	...	...	...	...	...	...	...	...	...	...	...	...	...	...	
Chile	1.00_{-2}	1.01_{-2}	1.05_{-2}	1.03_{-4}	1.00_{-4}	1.07_{-2}	0.88_{-2}	1.00_{-2}	1.00_{-2}	0.90_{-2}	0.70_{-2}	0.98_{-1}	0.97_{-1}	1.01_{-1}	1.12_{-1}	
Colombia	1.04_{-2}	1.10_{-2}	1.12_{-2}	1.02	0.98	1.02	0.96	1.01_{-1}	1.01_{-1}	...	...	...	0.97	1.05	1.14	
Costa Rica	1.01_{-3}	1.12_{-3}	1.19_{-3}	1.02_{-4}	1.01_{-4}	1.12_{-2}	0.76_{-2}	...	...	...	...	1.00_{-1}	1.01_{-1}	1.05_{-1}	1.21	
Cuba	1.00_{-3}	1.01_{-3}	1.01_{-3}	...	...	...	...	...	...	...	...	1.00	0.95	1.02	1.29_{-1}	
Curaçao	...	...	...	...	...	...	...	...	...	...	...	...	0.96_{-4}	1.08_{-4}	1.56_{-4}	
Dominica	...	...	...	...	...	...	...	...	...	...	...	1.03_{-1}	0.97_{-1}	0.99_{-2}	...	
Dominican Republic	1.09_{-4}	1.11_{-4}	1.26_{-4}	1.12_{-4}	0.99_{-4}	1.31_{-2}	0.95_{-2}	1.00_{-1}	1.00_{-1}	...	...	1.04_{-1}	0.92_{-1}	1.09_{-1}	1.44	
Ecuador	1.00_{-4}	1.03_{-4}	1.06_{-4}	1.05_{-1}	1.00_{-1}	1.06_{-1}	0.93_{-1}	1.00_{-1}	0.98_{-1}	...	...	1.05	1.01	1.03	1.14_{-2}	
El Salvador	1.04_{-3}	1.02_{-3}	1.09_{-3}	...	...	...	...	1.01_{-1}	0.96_{-1}	...	...	1.01	0.97	0.99	1.11_{-1}	
Grenada	...	...	...	...	...	...	...	1.01_{-3i}	1.00_{-3i}	...	...	1.06	0.95	1.05	1.19	
Guatemala	0.95_{-2}	0.87_{-2}	0.91_{-2}	1.12_{-3}	0.91_{-3}	...	...	0.98_{-3}	0.88_{-3}	...	...	1.02_{-1}	0.97_{-1}	0.95_{-1}	1.15_{-2}	
Guyana	1.03_{-3}	1.11_{-3}	1.24_{-3}	...	...	...	...	1.01_{-3i}	0.99_{-3i}	...	...	...	...	...	...	
Haiti	...	...	...	...	...	...	...	...	...	...	...	...	...	...	...	
Honduras	1.06_{-4}	1.25_{-4}	1.38_{-4}	1.06_{-4}	0.94_{-4}	...	...	1.02_{-1}	1.00_{-1}	...	...	1.01	1.00	1.12	1.27_{-2}	
Jamaica	...	...	...	...	...	...	...	1.05_{-3i}	1.10_{-3i}	...	...	1.01	...	1.06	1.42_{-2}	
Mexico	1.00_{-1}	0.99_{-1}	0.98_{-1}	1.22_{-2}	1.06_{-2}	1.15_{-2}	0.90_{-2}	1.00_{-1}	0.98_{-1}	...	...	1.02_{-1}	1.01_{-1}	1.08_{-1}	1.02_{-1}	
Montserrat	...	...	...	1.00_{-2}	1.36_{-2}	...	...	...	...	...	...	...	...	...	...	
Nicaragua	...	...	...	1.04_{-4}	0.95_{-4}	...	...	...	...	...	...	...	...	...	...	
Panama	1.01_{-3}	1.09_{-3}	1.11_{-3}	1.08_{-4}	0.98_{-4}	...	...	...	...	...	...	1.03_{-1}	0.98_{-1}	1.03_{-1}	1.36_{-2}	
Paraguay	1.09_{-1}	1.09_{-1}	1.12_{-1}	1.08_{-4}	1.02_{-4}	...	...	1.01_{-1}	0.98_{-1}	...	...	1.01_{-1}	0.96_{-1}	1.05_{-1}	...	
Peru	1.01_{-3}	1.02_{-3}	1.01_{-3}	0.98_{-4}	0.94_{-4}	1.10_{-1}	0.88_{-1}	1.00_{-1}	0.94_{-1}	...	...	1.01	1.00	1.00	1.11_{-1}	
Saint Kitts and Nevis	...	...	...	...	...	...	...	...	...	...	...	...	...	...	...	
Saint Lucia	...	...	...	1.15_{-2}	1.04_{-2}	...	...	...	...	...	...	1.07	...	1.01	1.50	
Saint Vincent/Grenadines	...	...	...	...	...	...	...	...	...	...	...	1.04	0.98	0.96	...	
Sint Maarten	...	...	...	...	...	...	...	...	...	...	...	...	...	...	...	
Suriname	...	...	...	...	...	...	...	...	...	...	...	1.01	1.01	1.24_{-2}	...	
Trinidad and Tobago	...	...	...	...	...	1.28_{-2}	1.16_{-2}	...	...	...	...	...	...	...	...	
Turks and Caicos Islands	...	...	...	...	...	...	...	...	...	...	...	...	...	...	...	
Uruguay	1.02_{-3}	1.16_{-3}	1.28_{-3}	1.05_{-4}	0.96_{-4}	1.16_{-2}	0.89_{-2}	1.01	1.01	...	...	1.02_{-1}	0.98_{-1}	...	...	
Venezuela, B. R.	1.03_{-4}	1.12_{-4}	1.13_{-4}	...	...	...	...	1.01_{-1}	1.00_{-1}	...	...	1.01	0.97	1.07	...	

LOCATION/WEALTH																
F												G				
Disparity in primary completion				Disparity in lower secondary completion				Disparity in upper secondary completion				Wealth disparity in minimum proficiency				
Adjusted parity index		% of poorest completing		Adjusted parity index		% of poorest completing		Adjusted parity index		% of poorest completing		End of primary		End of lower secondary		
Location	Wealth	M	F	Location	Wealth	M	F	Location	Wealth	M	F	Reading	Mathematics	Reading	Mathematics	COUNTRY CODE
4.5.1																
2017																
…	…	…	…	…	…	…	…	…	…	…	…	…	…	0.76_{-2}	0.71_{-2}	AUS
…	…	…	…	…	…	…	…	…	…	…	…	…	…	…	…	COK
…	…	…	…	…	…	…	…	…	…	…	…	…	…	…	…	FJI
…	…	…	…	…	…	…	…	…	…	…	…	…	…	…	…	KIR
…	…	…	…	…	…	…	…	…	…	…	…	…	…	…	…	MHL
…	…	…	…	…	…	…	…	…	…	…	…	…	…	…	…	FSM
…	…	…	…	…	…	…	…	…	…	…	…	…	…	…	…	NRU
…	…	…	…	…	…	…	…	…	…	…	…	…	…	0.77_{-2}	0.70_{-2}	NZL
…	…	…	…	…	…	…	…	…	…	…	…	…	…	…	…	NIU
…	…	…	…	…	…	…	…	…	…	…	…	…	…	…	…	PLW
…	…	…	…	…	…	…	…	…	…	…	…	…	…	…	…	PNG
…	…	…	…	…	…	…	…	…	…	…	…	…	…	…	…	WSM
…	…	…	…	…	…	…	…	…	…	…	…	…	…	…	…	SLB
…	…	…	…	…	…	…	…	…	…	…	…	…	…	…	…	TKL
…	…	…	…	…	…	…	…	…	…	…	…	…	…	…	…	TON
…	…	…	…	…	…	…	…	…	…	…	…	…	…	…	…	TUV
…	…	…	…	…	…	…	…	…	…	…	…	…	…	…	…	VUT
…	…	…	…	…	…	…	…	…	…	…	…	…	…	…	…	AIA
…	…	…	…	…	…	…	…	…	…	…	…	…	…	…	…	ATG
…	…	…	…	…	…	…	…	…	…	…	…	0.64_{-1}	0.59_{-1}	0.56_{-1}	0.31_{-1}	ARG
…	…	…	…	…	…	…	…	…	…	…	…	…	…	…	…	ABW
…	…	…	…	…	…	…	…	…	…	…	…	…	…	…	…	BHS
…	…	…	…	…	…	…	…	…	…	…	…	…	…	…	…	BRB
0.99_{-1}	0.92_{-1}	88_{-1}	94_{-1}	0.68_{-1}	0.38_{-1}	23_{-1}	44_{-1}	0.69_{-1}	0.25_{-1}	16_{-1}	21_{-1}	…	…	…	…	BLZ
0.96_{-4}	0.95_{-4}	90_{-4}	94_{-4}	0.87_{-4}	0.84_{-4}	79_{-4}	82_{-4}	0.59_{-4}	0.63_{-4}	55_{-4}	58_{-4}	…	…	…	…	BOL
0.88_{-2}	0.78_{-2}	69_{-2}	82_{-2}	0.81_{-2}	0.70_{-2}	61_{-2}	75_{-2}	0.66_{-2}	0.44_{-2}	33_{-2}	43_{-2}	1.09_{-4}	1.07_{-4}	0.51_{-2}	0.27_{-2}	BRA
…	…	…	…	…	…	…	…	…	…	…	…	…	…	…	…	VGB
…	…	…	…	…	…	…	…	…	…	…	…	…	…	…	…	CYM
1.00_{-2}	0.99_{-2}	98_{-2}	99_{-2}	1.00_{-2}	0.97_{-2}	97_{-2}	98_{-2}	0.90_{-2}	0.76_{-2}	70_{-2}	77_{-2}	0.95_{-4}	0.97_{-4}	0.62_{-2}	0.53_{-2}	CHL
0.90_{-2}	0.84_{-2}	79_{-2}	85_{-2}	0.69_{-2}	0.54_{-2}	47_{-2}	55_{-2}	0.58_{-2}	0.41_{-2}	36_{-2}	41_{-2}	0.81	0.50	1.36	0.68	COL
0.97_{-3}	0.92_{-3}	90_{-3}	91_{-3}	0.80_{-3}	0.55_{-3}	49_{-3}	52_{-3}	0.65_{-3}	0.43_{-3}	34_{-3}	39_{-3}	0.90_{-4}	0.90_{-4}	0.51_{-2}	0.36_{-2}	CRI
1.01_{-3}	…	…	…	1.00_{-1}	…			0.94_{-1}				…	…	…	…	CUB
…	…	…	…	…	…	…	…	…	…	…	…	…	…	…	…	CUW
…	…	…	…	…	…	…	…	…	…	…	…	…	…	…	…	DMA
0.92_{-4}	0.76_{-4}	69_{-4}	81_{-4}	0.92_{-4}	0.64_{-4}	53_{-4}	69_{-4}	0.73_{-4}	0.24_{-4}	19_{-4}	22_{-4}	0.60_{-4}	0.69_{-4}	0.26_{-2}	0.13_{-2}	DOM
0.98_{-4}	0.98_{-4}	95_{-4}	98_{-4}	0.86_{-4}	0.87_{-4}	81_{-4}	80_{-4}	0.63_{-4}	0.60_{-4}	47_{-4}	50_{-4}	0.61_{-1}	0.76_{-1}	0.70_{-1}	0.81_{-1}	ECU
0.92_{-3}	0.84_{-3}	78_{-3}	82_{-3}	0.74_{-3}	0.56_{-3}	53_{-3}	49_{-3}	0.55_{-3}	0.34_{-3}	27_{-3}	29_{-3}	…	…	…	…	SLV
…	…	…	…	…	…	…	…	…	…	…	…	…	…	…	…	GRD
0.83_{-2}	0.58_{-2}	58_{-2}	54_{-2}	0.55_{-2}	0.17_{-2}	21_{-2}	10_{-2}	0.43_{-2}	0.06_{-2}	7_{-2}	3_{-2}	0.73_{-4}	0.83_{-4}	…	…	GTM
1.01_{-3}	0.95_{-3}	91_{-3}	97_{-3}	0.90_{-3}	0.73_{-3}	58_{-3}	77_{-3}	0.80_{-3}	0.33_{-3}	20_{-3}	31_{-3}	…	…	…	…	GUY
…	…	…	…	…	…	…	…	…	…	…	…	…	…	…	…	HTI
0.85_{-4}	0.77_{-4}	70_{-4}	75_{-4}	0.60_{-4}	0.37_{-4}	26_{-4}	32_{-4}	0.43_{-4}	0.21_{-4}	13_{-4}	16_{-4}	1.32_{-4}	1.05_{-4}	…	…	HND
…	…	…	…	…	…	…	…	…	…	…	…	…	…	…	…	JAM
1.00_{-1}	0.92_{-1}	89_{-1}	94_{-1}	0.91_{-1}	0.76_{-1}	75_{-1}	76_{-1}	0.71_{-1}	0.36_{-1}	38_{-1}	25_{-1}	0.82_{-4}	0.93_{-4}	0.53_{-2}	0.48_{-2}	MEX
…	…	…	…	…	…	…	…	…	…	…	…	…	…	…	…	MSR
…	…	…	…	…	…	…	…	…	…	…	…	1.65_{-4}	1.49_{-4}	…	…	NIC
0.93_{-3}	0.88_{-3}	87_{-3}	89_{-3}	0.77_{-3}	0.61_{-3}	57_{-3}	57_{-3}	0.55_{-3}	0.26_{-3}	20_{-3}	25_{-3}	0.60_{-4}	0.63_{-4}	…	…	PAN
0.92_{-1}	0.76_{-1}	66_{-1}	86_{-1}	0.76_{-1}	0.48_{-1}	45_{-1}	49_{-1}	0.56_{-1}	0.20_{-1}	17_{-1}	20_{-1}	0.59_{-4}	0.65_{-4}	…	…	PRY
0.94_{-3}	0.92_{-3}	91_{-3}	92_{-3}	0.81_{-3}	0.76_{-3}	74_{-3}	73_{-3}	0.75_{-3}	0.63_{-3}	61_{-3}	59_{-3}	1.46_{-4}	1.23_{-4}	0.20_{-2}	0.19_{-2}	PER
…	…	…	…	…	…	…	…	…	…	…	…	…	…	…	…	KNA
…	…	…	…	…	…	…	…	…	…	…	…	…	…	…	…	LCA
…	…	…	…	…	…	…	…	…	…	…	…	…	…	…	…	VCT
…	…	…	…	…	…	…	…	…	…	…	…	…	…	…	…	SXM
…	…	…	…	…	…	…	…	…	…	…	…	…	…	…	…	SUR
…	…	…	…	…	…	…	…	…	…	…	…	…	…	0.60_{-2}	0.51_{-2}	TTO
…	…	…	…	…	…	…	…	…	…	…	…	…	…	…	…	TCA
1.01_{-3}	0.96_{-3}	93_{-3}	97_{-3}	0.84_{-3}	0.50_{-3}	39_{-3}	54_{-3}	0.71_{-3}	0.21_{-3}	11_{-3}	20_{-3}	1.04_{-4}	1.04_{-4}	0.53_{-2}	0.39_{-2}	URY
…	0.92_{-4}	89_{-4}	93_{-4}	…	0.80_{-4}	64_{-4}	76_{-4}	…	0.69_{-4}	54_{-4}	62_{-4}	…	…	…	…	VEN

TABLE 5: Continued

	GENDER															
	A			B				C		D		E				
	GPIA in completion			GPIA in minimum proficiency				GPIA in literacy rate		GPIA in adult proficiency		GPIA in gross enrolment ratio				
				End of primary		End of lower secondary										
	Primary	Lower secondary	Upper secondary	Reading	Mathematics	Reading	Mathematics	Youth	Adults	Literacy	Numeracy	Pre-primary	Primary	Secondary	Tertiary
SDG indicator:	4.5.1															
Reference year:	2017															
Europe and Northern America																
Albania	…	…	…	…	…	…	1.09_{-2}	…	…	…	…	0.99	0.97	0.94	1.37
Andorra	…	…	…	…	…	…	…	…	…	…	…	…	…	…	…
Austria	…	0.98_{-3}	1.01_{-3}	…	…	1.08_{-2}	0.93_{-2}	…	…	…	…	1.00_{-1}	0.99_{-1}	0.96_{-1}	1.16_{-1}
Belarus	…	…	…	…	…	…	…	…	…	…	…	0.96	1.00	0.98	1.20
Belgium	…	1.03_{-3}	0.99_{-3}	…	…	1.06_{-2}	0.97_{-2}	…	…	…	…	1.00_{-1}	1.00_{-1}	1.11_{-1}	1.23_{-1}
Bermuda	…	…	…	…	…	…	…	…	…	…	…	0.84_{-2}	0.98_{-2}	1.10_{-2}	1.57_{-2}
Bosnia and Herzegovina	…	…	…	…	…	…	…	1.00_{-4}	0.96_{-4}	…	…	…	…	…	…
Bulgaria	…	1.01_{-3}	0.90_{-3}	…	1.01_{-2}	1.26_{-2}	1.05_{-2}	…	…	…	…	0.99_{-1}	0.99_{-1}	0.97_{-1}	1.20_{-1}
Canada	…	…	…	…	…	1.07_{-2}	0.99_{-2}	…	…	…	…	…	1.00_{-1}	1.01_{-1}	1.25_{-1i}
Croatia	…	1.02_{-3}	0.98_{-3}	…	0.99_{-2}	1.12_{-2}	0.94_{-2}	…	…	…	…	0.96_{-1}	1.01_{-1}	1.04_{-1}	1.27_{-1}
Czechia	…	1.00_{-3}	1.00_{-3}	…	…	1.12_{-2}	1.01_{-2}	…	…	…	…	0.97_{-1}	1.01_{-1}	1.01_{-1}	1.29_{-1}
Denmark	…	1.01_{-3}	1.08_{-3}	…	…	1.07_{-2}	0.98_{-2}	…	…	…	…	0.99_{-1}	0.99_{-1}	1.03_{-1}	1.27_{-1}
Estonia	…	1.01_{-3}	1.10_{-3}	…	…	1.08_{-2}	1.02_{-2}	…	…	…	…	…	1.00_{-1}	1.01_{-1}	1.34_{-1}
Finland	…	1.00_{-3}	1.08_{-3}	…	…	1.11_{-2}	1.05_{-2}	…	…	…	…	1.00_{-1}	1.00_{-1}	1.09_{-1}	1.16_{-1}
France	…	1.01_{-3}	1.12_{-3}	…	…	1.11_{-2}	1.01_{-2}	…	…	…	…	1.00_{-1i}	0.99_{-1i}	1.01_{-1i}	1.19_{-1i}
Germany	…	0.99_{-3}	1.03_{-3}	…	1.00_{-2}	1.06_{-2}	0.95_{-2}	…	…	…	…	0.99_{-1}	0.99_{-1}	0.95_{-1}	1.00_{-1}
Greece	…	0.98_{-3}	0.99_{-3}	…	…	1.19_{-2}	1.03_{-2}	…	…	1.05_{-2}	0.94_{-2}	1.01_{-1}	1.00_{-1}	0.94_{-1}	0.98_{-1}
Hungary	…	1.00_{-3}	0.95_{-3}	…	1.00_{-2}	1.11_{-2}	0.97_{-2}	1.00_{-3i}	1.00_{-3i}	…	…	0.96_{-1}	1.00_{-1}	0.99_{-1}	1.20_{-1}
Iceland	…	1.00_{-3}	1.29_{-3}	…	…	1.16_{-2}	1.02_{-2}	…	…	…	…	1.02_{-1}	1.00_{-1}	1.00_{-1}	1.47_{-1}
Ireland	…	1.03_{-3}	1.03_{-3}	…	…	1.05_{-2}	1.00_{-1}	…	…	…	…	0.98_{-1i}	0.99_{-1i}	1.03_{-1i}	1.10_{-1i}
Italy	…	1.00_{-3}	1.09_{-3}	…	…	1.07_{-2}	0.99_{-2}	…	…	…	…	0.97_{-1}	1.00_{-1}	0.98_{-1}	1.25_{-1}
Latvia	…	1.02_{-3}	1.05_{-3}	…	…	1.15_{-2}	1.04_{-2}	…	…	…	…	0.99_{-1i}	1.00_{-1i}	0.98_{-1i}	1.35_{-1i}
Liechtenstein	…	…	…	…	…	…	…	…	…	…	…	1.05_{-1i}	0.96_{-1i}	0.78_{-1i}	0.55_{-1i}
Lithuania	…	0.99_{-3}	1.05_{-3}	…	1.01_{-2}	1.17_{-2}	1.03_{-2}	…	…	1.01_{-2}	0.99_{-2}	1.00_{-1i}	1.00_{-1i}	0.96_{-1i}	1.27_{-1i}
Luxembourg	…	1.04_{-3}	1.07_{-3}	…	…	1.09_{-2}	0.98_{-2}	…	…	…	…	0.97_{-1}	1.00_{-1}	1.03_{-1}	1.10_{-1}
Malta	…	1.02_{-3}	1.05_{-3}	…	…	1.21_{-2}	1.03_{-1}	…	…	…	…	1.03_{-1}	1.04_{-1}	1.04_{-1}	1.27_{-1}
Monaco	…	…	…	…	…	…	…	…	…	…	…	…	…	…	…
Montenegro	1.00_{-4}	1.01_{-4}	1.04_{-4}	…	…	1.22_{-2}	0.99_{-2}	…	…	…	…	0.98	0.99	1.00	1.22
Netherlands	…	0.98_{-3}	1.21_{-3}	…	…	1.08_{-2}	1.01_{-2}	…	…	…	…	1.00_{-1}	1.00_{-1}	1.02_{-1}	1.11_{-1}
Norway	…	0.99_{-3}	1.11_{-3}	…	…	1.12_{-2}	1.04_{-2}	…	…	…	…	1.00_{-1}	1.00_{-1}	0.97_{-1}	1.32_{-1}
Poland	…	1.03_{-3}	1.04_{-3}	…	…	1.11_{-2}	0.97_{-2}	…	…	…	…	0.97_{-1}	1.01_{-1}	0.97_{-1}	1.34_{-1}
Portugal	…	0.98_{-3}	1.21_{-3}	…	…	1.07_{-2}	0.99_{-2}	…	…	…	…	0.98_{-1}	0.96_{-1}	0.97_{-1}	1.10_{-1}
Republic of Moldova	…	…	…	…	…	1.33_{-2}	1.02_{-2}	…	…	…	…	0.99_{i}	1.00_{i}	0.99_{i}	1.23_{i}
Romania	…	1.02_{-3}	1.01_{-3}	…	…	1.10_{-2}	1.00_{-2}	…	…	…	…	1.00_{-1}	0.99_{-1}	0.99_{-1}	1.19_{-1}
Russian Federation	1.00_{-4}	1.00_{-4}	1.00_{-4}	…	1.00_{-2}	1.10_{-2}	0.99_{-2}	…	…	…	…	0.98_{-1}	1.00_{-1}	0.99_{-1}	1.16_{-1}
San Marino	…	…	…	…	…	…	…	…	…	…	…	…	…	…	…
Serbia	1.00_{-3}	1.00_{-3}	1.15_{-3}	…	1.04_{-2}	…	…	1.00_{-1}	0.99_{-1}	…	…	1.00_{i}	1.00_{i}	1.01_{i}	1.26_{i}
Slovakia	…	1.00_{-3}	1.01_{-3}	…	0.97_{-2}	1.18_{-2}	1.00_{-2}	…	…	…	…	0.98_{-1}	0.99_{-1}	1.01_{-1}	1.34_{-1}
Slovenia	…	1.00_{-3}	1.04_{-3}	…	…	1.13_{-2}	1.00_{-2}	1.00_{-3i}	1.00_{-3i}	1.02_{-2}	0.98_{-2}	0.97_{-1}	1.00_{-1}	1.02_{-1}	1.30_{-1}
Spain	…	1.00_{-3}	1.19_{-3}	…	…	1.08_{-2}	0.96_{-2}	1.00_{-1}	0.99_{-1}	…	…	1.00_{-1}	1.01_{-1}	1.01_{-1}	1.16_{-1}
Sweden	…	0.99_{-3}	1.02_{-3}	…	…	1.14_{-2}	1.03_{-2}	…	…	…	…	1.00_{-1}	1.03_{-1}	1.11_{-1}	1.35_{-1}
Switzerland	…	0.99_{-3}	0.94_{-3}	…	…	1.11_{-2}	0.99_{-2}	…	…	…	…	0.99_{-1}	0.99_{-1}	0.96_{-1}	1.02_{-1}
TFYR Macedonia	…	…	…	…	…	1.42_{-2}	1.06_{-2}	…	…	…	…	0.99_{-2}	1.00_{-2}	0.98_{-2}	1.20_{-2}
Ukraine	0.99_{-4}	1.00_{-4}	0.99_{-4}	…	…	…	…	…	…	…	…	0.97_{-4}	1.02_{-3}	0.98_{-3}	1.13_{-3}
United Kingdom	…	1.00_{-3}	1.06_{-3}	…	…	1.07_{-2}	0.97_{-2}	…	…	…	…	1.00_{-1}	1.00_{-1}	1.10_{-1}	1.26_{-1}
United States	1.00_{-4}	1.00_{-4}	1.03_{-4}	…	…	1.09_{-2}	0.98_{-2}	…	…	…	…	1.00_{-1i}	1.00_{-1i}	0.99_{-1i}	1.26_{-1i}

	LOCATION/WEALTH																
	F												G				
	Disparity in primary completion				Disparity in lower secondary completion				Disparity in upper secondary completion				Wealth disparity in minimum proficiency				
	Adjusted parity index		% of poorest completing		Adjusted parity index		% of poorest completing		Adjusted parity index		% of poorest completing		End of primary		End of lower secondary		
	Location	Wealth	M	F	Location	Wealth	M	F	Location	Wealth	M	F	Reading	Mathematics	Reading	Mathematics	COUNTRY CODE
	4.5.1																
	2017																
	…	…	…	…	…	…	…	…	…	…	…	…	…	…	…	…	ALB
	…	…	…	…	…	…	…	…	…	…	…	…	…	…	…	…	AND
	…	…	…	…	1.02$_{-3}$	0.94$_{-3}$	98$_{-3}$	90$_{-3}$	1.06$_{-3}$	0.79$_{-3}$	64$_{-3}$	80$_{-3}$	…	…	0.70$_{-2}$	0.70$_{-2}$	AUT
	…	…	…	…	…	…	…	…	…	…	…	…	…	…	…	…	BLR
	…	…	…	…	1.03$_{-3}$	0.84$_{-3}$	76$_{-3}$	89$_{-3}$	0.99$_{-3}$	0.78$_{-3}$	74$_{-3}$	77$_{-3}$	…	…	0.71$_{-2}$	0.69$_{-2}$	BEL
	…	…	…	…	…	…	…	…	…	…	…	…	…	…	…	…	BMU
	…	…	…	…	…	…	…	…	…	…	…	…	…	…			BIH
	…	…	…	…	0.93$_{-3}$	0.79$_{-3}$	79$_{-3}$	79$_{-3}$	0.78$_{-3}$	0.41$_{-3}$	50$_{-3}$	33$_{-3}$	…	0.81$_{-2}$	0.43$_{-2}$	0.47$_{-2}$	BGR
	…	…	…	…	…	…	…	…	…	…	…	…	…	…	0.86$_{-2}$	0.82$_{-2}$	CAN
	…	…	…	…	1.03$_{-3}$	0.99$_{-3}$	98$_{-3}$	100$_{-3}$	0.97$_{-3}$	0.94$_{-3}$	93$_{-3}$	89$_{-3}$	…	0.84$_{-2}$	0.77$_{-2}$	0.66$_{-2}$	HRV
	…	…	…	…	1.00$_{-3}$	1.00$_{-3}$	100$_{-3}$	100$_{-3}$	1.03$_{-3}$	0.90$_{-3}$	91$_{-3}$	85$_{-3}$	…	…	0.66$_{-2}$	0.64$_{-2}$	CZE
	…	…	…	…	1.00$_{-3}$	1.00$_{-3}$	99$_{-3}$	100$_{-3}$	0.77$_{-3}$	0.94$_{-3}$	78$_{-3}$	86$_{-3}$	…	…	0.81$_{-2}$	0.82$_{-2}$	DNK
	…	…	…	…	1.01$_{-3}$	1.00$_{-3}$	97$_{-3}$	97$_{-3}$	0.88$_{-3}$	0.76$_{-3}$	63$_{-3}$	80$_{-3}$	…	…	0.89$_{-2}$	0.84$_{-2}$	EST
	…	…	…	…	1.00$_{-3}$	1.00$_{-3}$	100$_{-3}$	100$_{-3}$	1.02$_{-3}$	0.98$_{-3}$	84$_{-3}$	88$_{-3}$	…	…	0.85$_{-2}$	0.81$_{-2}$	FIN
	…	…	…		0.99$_{-3}$	0.97$_{-3}$	96$_{-3}$	98$_{-3}$	1.02$_{-3}$	0.83$_{-3}$	72$_{-3}$	85$_{-3}$	…	…	0.66$_{-2}$	0.62$_{-2}$	FRA
	…	…	…	…	1.00$_{-3}$	0.96$_{-3}$	89$_{-3}$	94$_{-3}$	1.03$_{-3}$	0.83$_{-3}$	75$_{-3}$	77$_{-3}$	…	0.94$_{-2}$	0.80$_{-2}$	0.76$_{-2}$	DEU
	…	…	…	…	0.99$_{-3}$	0.99$_{-3}$	100$_{-3}$	97$_{-3}$	0.94$_{-3}$	0.83$_{-3}$	85$_{-3}$	81$_{-3}$	…	…	0.64$_{-2}$	0.60$_{-2}$	GRC
	…	…	…	…	0.99$_{-3}$	0.96$_{-3}$	97$_{-3}$	95$_{-3}$	0.96$_{-3}$	0.70$_{-3}$	68$_{-3}$	65$_{-3}$	…	0.72$_{-2}$	0.55$_{-2}$	0.63$_{-2}$	HUN
	…	…	…	…	1.00$_{-3}$	1.00$_{-3}$	100$_{-3}$	100$_{-3}$	0.89$_{-3}$	1.04$_{-3}$	54$_{-3}$	88$_{-3}$	…	…	0.82$_{-2}$	0.78$_{-2}$	ISL
	…	…	…	…	0.98$_{-3}$	1.00$_{-3}$	94$_{-3}$	98$_{-3}$	0.97$_{-3}$	0.93$_{-3}$	92$_{-3}$	95$_{-3}$	…	…	0.85$_{-2}$	0.83$_{-1}$	IRL
	…	…	…	…	1.00$_{-3}$	0.99$_{-3}$	98$_{-3}$	98$_{-3}$	0.96$_{-3}$	0.83$_{-3}$	68$_{-3}$	83$_{-3}$	…	…	0.70$_{-2}$	0.76$_{-2}$	ITA
	…	…	…	…	0.98$_{-3}$	0.95$_{-3}$	91$_{-3}$	99$_{-3}$	0.87$_{-3}$	0.73$_{-3}$	75$_{-3}$	80$_{-4}$	…	…	0.80$_{-2}$	0.74$_{-2}$	LVA
	…	…	…	…	…	…	…	…	…	…	…	…	…	…	…	…	LIE
	…	…	…	…	1.00$_{-3}$	1.03$_{-3}$	98$_{-3}$	100$_{-3}$	0.92$_{-3}$	0.95$_{-3}$	89$_{-3}$	…	…	0.90$_{-2}$	0.70$_{-2}$	0.68$_{-2}$	LTU
	…	…	…	…	1.06$_{-3}$	0.85$_{-3}$	78$_{-3}$	88$_{-3}$	1.11$_{-3}$	0.59$_{-3}$	54$_{-3}$	47$_{-3}$	…	…	0.60$_{-2}$	0.61$_{-2}$	LUX
	…	…	…	…	…	0.99$_{-3}$	97$_{-3}$	100$_{-3}$	…	0.73$_{-3}$	…	…	…	…	0.60$_{-2}$	0.70$_{-1}$	MLT
	…	…	…	…	…	…	…	…	…	…	…	…	…	…	…	…	MCO
	1.00$_{-4}$	0.99$_{-4}$	100$_{-4}$	99$_{-4}$	1.01$_{-4}$	0.96$_{-4}$	94$_{-4}$	98$_{-4}$	0.86$_{-4}$	0.66$_{-4}$	58$_{-4}$	63$_{-4}$	…	…	0.65$_{-2}$	0.60$_{-2}$	MNE
	…	…	…	…	…	0.95$_{-3}$	94$_{-3}$	92$_{-3}$	…	0.94$_{-3}$	76$_{-3}$	88$_{-3}$	…	…	0.77$_{-2}$	0.77$_{-2}$	NLD
	…	…	…	…	1.00$_{-3}$	0.99$_{-3}$	99$_{-3}$	99$_{-3}$	1.14$_{-3}$	0.93$_{-3}$	75$_{-3}$	82$_{-3}$	…	…	0.85$_{-2}$	0.80$_{-2}$	NOR
	…	…	…	…	1.00$_{-3}$	0.97$_{-3}$	92$_{-3}$	99$_{-3}$	0.97$_{-3}$	0.85$_{-3}$	78$_{-3}$	91$_{-3}$		…	0.79$_{-2}$	0.76$_{-2}$	POL
	…	…	…	…	1.00$_{-3}$	0.87$_{-3}$	87$_{-3}$	88$_{-3}$	0.98$_{-3}$	0.49$_{-3}$	40$_{-3}$	46$_{-3}$	…	…	0.76$_{-2}$	0.67$_{-2}$	PRT
	…	…	…	…	…	…	…	…	…	…	…	…	…	…	0.48$_{-2}$	0.48$_{-2}$	MDA
	…	…	…	…	0.95$_{-3}$	0.91$_{-3}$	90$_{-3}$	92$_{-3}$	0.84$_{-3}$	0.62$_{-3}$	62$_{-3}$	60$_{-3}$	…	…	0.54$_{-2}$	0.51$_{-2}$	ROU
	0.99$_{-4}$	1.00$_{-4}$	100$_{-4}$	100$_{-4}$	1.01$_{-4}$	1.01$_{-4}$	100$_{-4}$	100$_{-4}$	0.89$_{-4}$	0.92$_{-4}$	90$_{-4}$	80$_{-4}$	…	0.96$_{-2}$	0.85$_{-2}$	0.84$_{-2}$	RUS
	…	…	…	…	…	…	…	…	…	…	…	…	…	…	…	…	SMR
	0.99$_{-3}$	0.96$_{-3}$	95$_{-3}$	97$_{-3}$	1.00$_{-3}$	0.91$_{-3}$	94$_{-3}$	86$_{-3}$	0.86$_{-3}$	0.49$_{-3}$	44$_{-3}$	47$_{-3}$	…	0.76$_{-2}$	…	…	SRB
	…	…	…	…	1.00$_{-3}$	1.00$_{-3}$	100$_{-3}$	99$_{-3}$	1.02$_{-3}$	0.80$_{-3}$	74$_{-3}$	78$_{-3}$	…	0.64$_{-2}$	0.57$_{-2}$	0.61$_{-2}$	SVK
	…	…	…	…	…	1.00$_{-3}$	100$_{-3}$	100$_{-3}$	…	0.90$_{-3}$	85$_{-3}$	87$_{-3}$	…	…	0.81$_{-2}$	0.80$_{-2}$	SVN
	…	…	…	…	1.02$_{-3}$	0.91$_{-3}$	89$_{-3}$	87$_{-3}$	0.91$_{-3}$	0.48$_{-3}$	46$_{-3}$	47$_{-3}$	…	…	0.77$_{-2}$	0.68$_{-2}$	ESP
	…	…	…	…	1.00$_{-3}$	1.02$_{-3}$	100$_{-3}$	99$_{-3}$	0.96$_{-3}$	0.93$_{-3}$	89$_{-3}$	93$_{-3}$	…	…	0.78$_{-2}$	0.73$_{-2}$	SWE
	…	…	…	…	1.00$_{-3}$	1.00$_{-3}$	100$_{-3}$	100$_{-3}$	1.19$_{-3}$	0.64$_{-3}$	62$_{-3}$	57$_{-3}$	…	…	0.73$_{-2}$	0.78$_{-2}$	CHE
	…	…	…	…	…	…	…	…	…	…	…	…	…	…	0.46$_{-2}$	0.40$_{-2}$	MKD
	1.00$_{-4}$	1.00$_{-4}$	100$_{-4}$	100$_{-4}$	1.00$_{-4}$	0.99$_{-4}$	99$_{-4}$	100$_{-4}$	0.93$_{-4}$	0.85$_{-4}$	84$_{-4}$	85$_{-4}$	…	…	…	…	UKR
	…	…	…	…	1.00$_{-3}$	1.00$_{-3}$	100$_{-3}$	100$_{-3}$	0.96$_{-3}$	0.95$_{-3}$	80$_{-3}$	85$_{-3}$	…	…	0.81$_{-2}$	0.75$_{-2}$	GBR
	…	0.98$_{-4}$	98$_{-4}$	98$_{-4}$	…	0.98$_{-4}$	98$_{-4}$	98$_{-4}$	…	0.88$_{-4}$	84$_{-4}$	87$_{-4}$	…	…	0.78$_{-2}$	0.62$_{-2}$	USA

TABLE 6:

SDG 4, Target 4.7 – Education for sustainable development and global citizenship

By 2030, ensure that all learners acquire the knowledge and skills needed to promote sustainable development, including, among others, through education for sustainable development and sustainable lifestyles, human rights, gender equality, promotion of a culture of peace and non-violence, global citizenship and appreciation of cultural diversity and of culture's contribution to sustainable development

	A				B	C	
	Inclusion in national curricula				% of schools providing life skills-based HIV/AIDS education	% of students and youth with understanding of	
	Gender equality	Human rights	Sustainable development	Global citizenship		Scientific literacy	HIV/AIDS and sexuality
SDG indicator:	4.7.1				4.7.2	4.7.5	4.7.4
Reference year:	2015				2017		
Region	% of countries				Median		
World	14i	60i	43i	9i	...	...	...
Sub-Saharan Africa	...	...	...	...	...	...	29i
Northern Africa and Western Asia	...	...	...	...	...	...	...
Northern Africa	...	...	...	...	-i	...	...
Western Asia	...	...	...	...	...	...	...
Central and Southern Asia	33i	67i	50i	33i	...	...	...
Central Asia	...	...	...	...	...	...	...
Southern Asia	33	67	50	33	100i	...	...
Eastern and South-eastern Asia	-i	29i	29i	-i	...	...	...
Eastern Asia	...	...	...	...	...	...	...
South-eastern Asia	-i	20i	20i	-i	...	...	28i
Oceania	9i	36i	64i	18i	...	...	...
Latin America and the Caribbean	17i	78i	44i	11i	...	...	...
Caribbean	...	...	...	...	...	...	...
Central America	33	100	83	17	...	...	...
South America	12	75	25	-	...	...	...
Europe and Northern America	7i	67i	40i	7i	...	...	...
Europe	7i	67i	40i	7i	...	...	...
Northern America	...	...	...	...	100i	...	...
Low income	...	...	...	...	...	...	26i
Middle income	17i	66i	44i	12i	...	...	...
Lower middle	22i	44i	39i	6i	...	...	...
Upper middle	13i	83i	48i	17i	...	...	...
High income	4i	64i	48i	4i	...	...	...

A Inclusion in national curricula frameworks of issues relating to global citizenship and sustainable development [*Source:* UNESCO-IBE, 2016].

B Percentage of schools providing life skills-based HIV/AIDS education [*Source:* UNAIDS].

C Percentage of students and youth with adequate understanding of issues relating to global citizenship and sustainable development [*Sources:* OECD (PISA 2015 Annex B1); TIMMS; UNAIDS].

D Percentage of schools with basic drinking water, water, sanitation and hygiene (WASH) facilities (basic drinking water, basic [single-sex] sanitation or toilets, and basic handwashing facilities) [*Source:* WHO and UNICEF Joint Monitoring Programme].

E Percentage of primary schools with Information and Communications Technology (ICT) (electricity, computers or internet) used for pedagogical purposes.

F Percentage of public primary schools with access to adapted infrastructure and materials for students with disabilities.

G Level of bullying [*Source:* UNICEF].

H Level of attacks on students, teachers or institutions [*Source:* Global Coalition to Protect Education from Attack].

I Internationally mobile students, inbound and outbound numbers enrolled (thousand) and inbound and outbound mobility rates (as a percentage of total tertiary enrolment in the country).

J Volume of official development assistance flows (all sectors) for scholarships (all levels) and imputed student costs, total gross disbursements (million constant 2016 US$). Region totals include flows unallocated to specific countries. World total includes flows unallocated to specific countries or regions.

Notes:
Source: UIS unless noted otherwise. Data refer to school year ending in 2017 unless noted otherwise.
Aggregates represent countries listed in the table with available data and may include estimates for countries with no recent data.

(-) Magnitude nil or negligible.

(...) Data not available or category not applicable.

(± n) Reference year differs (e.g. -2: reference year 2015 instead of 2017).

(i) Estimate and/or partial coverage.

SDG 4, Means of implementation 4.a – Education facilities and learning environments

By 2030, build and upgrade education facilities that are child, disability and gender sensitive and provide safe, non-violent, inclusive and effective learning environments

SDG 4, Means of implementation 4.b – Scholarships

By 2020, substantially expand globally the number of scholarships available to developing countries

	D			E			F	G	H	I				J	
	% of schools with WASH facilities			% of schools with ICT for pedagogical purposes			% of schools with adapted infrastructure and materials for students with disabilities	Level of bullying	Level of attacks on education	Internationally mobile tertiary students: Mobility rate (%)		Internationally mobile tertiary students: Number (000)		Official development assistance, in US$ (000,000)	
	Basic drinking water	Basic sanitation or toilets	Basic handwashing	Electricity	Internet	Computers				Inbound	Outbound	Inbound	Outbound	Scholarships	Imputed student costs
SDG indicator:	4.a.1							4.a.2	4.a.3					4.b.1	
Reference year:	2017									2017				2016	
Region	Median								—	Median		Sum			
World	88i	85i	99i	100i	85i	94i	…	…	…	4i	6	5,085i	5,085i	1,231	1,940
Sub-Saharan Africa	53i	48i	…	28	…	14i	…	…	…	2i	6	137i	374	121	282
Northern Africa and Western Asia	92i	99i	99i	100i	73i	91i	…	…	…	4	7	468i	598	138	529
Northern Africa	82i	99	99i	100i	58i	88i	…	…	…	2	2	86i	147	74	310
Western Asia	93i	96i	100i	100i	85i	94i	…	…	…	5	8	382i	451	64	219
Central and Southern Asia	69i	74i	…	92i	45i	35i	…	…	…	0.4i	8	98i	769	80	267
Central Asia	84i	68i	58i	100i	66i	93i	9i	…	…	1	12	32	200	17	22
Southern Asia	59i	74i	…	67	45i	18i	…	…	…	0.3i	7	67i	569	63	246
Eastern and South-eastern Asia	100i	100i	100i	100i	99i	99i	…	…	…	2	3	613	1,346	178	410
Eastern Asia	100i	100i	100i	100i	99	99i	…	…	…	3	3	414	1,059	26	305
South-eastern Asia	71i	39i	46i	93i	…	…	…	…	…	1i	3	199	288	152	105
Oceania	88i	81i	61i	99i	26i	33i	2i	…	…	…	…	397i	31	56	2
Latin America and the Caribbean	83i	82i	…	99i	39i	81i	…	…	…	2i	2i	176i	310	63	171
Caribbean	…	…	…	100i	100i	100i	…	…	…	…	13i	…	36	6	8
Central America	82i	75	…	97i	22	30i	28i	…	…	1i	2	18i	56	8	38
South America	72i	77	…	96i	38i	70i	…	…	…	0.4i	2	110i	218	48	125
Europe and Northern America	100i	100i	100i	100i	100i	100i	…	…	…	7	6	3,196i	1,071	74	161
Europe	100i	100i	100i	100i	100i	100i	…	…	…	7	6	2,034i	946	74	161
Northern America	100i	100i	100i	100	100	100	100i	…	…	12	3	1,161i	125	…	…
Low income	43i	47i	21i	19i	…	…	…	…	…	1i	6	82-2i	326	95	210
Middle income	76i	76i	61i	95i	43i	67i	…	…	…	2i	6	1,212i	2,950	539	1,593
Lower middle	70i	68i	43i	87i	45i	41i	…	…	…	1i	5	250i	1,140	373	734
Upper middle	86i	83i	83i	99i	39i	93i	…	…	…	3i	6	962i	1,009	165	859
High income	100i	100i	100i	100i	100i	100i	…	…	…	8	5	3,800i	1,224	7	18

TABLE 6: Continued

	A				B	C	
	Inclusion in national curricula					% of students and youth with understanding of	
	Gender equality	Human rights	Sustainable development	Global citizenship	% of schools providing life skills-based HIV/AIDS education	Scientific literacy	HIV/AIDS and sexuality
SDG indicator:	4.7.1				4.7.2	4.7.5	4.7.4
Reference year:	2015				2017		
Sub-Saharan Africa							
Angola	...	...	...	...	...	...	...
Benin	...	...	...	...	...	...	...
Botswana	...	...	...	...	...	...	...
Burkina Faso	...	...	...	...	$-_{-1}$	...	...
Burundi	...	...	...	...	100	...	...
Cabo Verde	...	...	...	...	100	...	...
Cameroon	...	...	...	...	...	...	...
Central African Republic	...	...	...	...	...	...	...
Chad	...	...	...	...	...	...	13_{-2}
Comoros	...	...	...	...	...	...	...
Congo	...	...	...	...	...	...	...
Côte d'Ivoire	Low	High	Low	Low	...	...	...
D. R. Congo	None	Low	Low	Low	$-_{-2}$	...	20_{-3}
Djibouti	Low	None	Low	Low	...	...	...
Equat. Guinea	...	...	...	...	...	...	...
Eritrea	...	...	...	...	...	...	...
Eswatini	...	...	...	...	97_{-1}	...	...
Ethiopia	...	...	...	...	...	...	...
Gabon	...	...	...	...	...	...	...
Gambia	Low	High	Medium	Low	...	...	29_{-4}
Ghana	Low	Low	Low	Low	...	...	22_{-3}
Guinea	...	...	...	...	...	...	...
Guinea-Bissau	...	...	...	...	...	...	22_{-4}
Kenya	...	...	...	...	...	...	60_{-3}
Lesotho	Medium	High	Low	Low	...	...	36_{-3}
Liberia	...	...	...	...	...	...	34_{-4}
Madagascar	...	...	...	...	...	...	24_{-2}
Malawi	...	...	...	...	...	...	79_{-2}
Mali	...	...	...	...	...	...	26_{-4}
Mauritania	...	...	...	...	...	...	58_{-1}
Mauritius	Low	High	High	Low	...	...	32_{-3}
Mozambique	...	...	...	...	...	...	...
Namibia	Low	Medium	Medium	Low	...	...	58_{-4}
Niger	Low	None	Low	None	100_{-1}	...	22_{-1}
Nigeria	...	...	...	...	...	...	24_{-4}
Rwanda	Medium	None	Medium	Low	100_{-1i}	...	...
Sao Tome and Principe	...	...	...	...	100	...	...
Senegal	...	...	...	...	62	...	28_{-1}
Seychelles	Low	High	Low	Low	79_{-1}	...	...
Sierra Leone	...	...	...	...	43	...	29_{-4}
Somalia	...	...	...	...	...	...	...
South Africa	None	High	Low	None	...	...	...
South Sudan	Medium	High	Low	None	...	...	...
Togo	...	...	...	...	...	...	26_{-3}
Uganda	...	...	...	...	...	...	...
United Republic of Tanzania	Low	Low	None	Low	...	...	...
Zambia	Medium	Low	Medium	Low	...	...	44_{-3}
Zimbabwe	...	...	...	...	...	...	46_{-2}

	D: % of schools with WASH facilities			E: % of schools with ICT for pedagogical purposes			F	G	H	I: Internationally mobile tertiary students				J: Official development assistance, in US$ (000,000)		
										Mobility rate (%)		Number (000)				
	Basic drinking water	Basic sanitation or toilets	Basic handwashing	Electricity	Internet	Computers	% of schools with adapted infrastructure and materials for students with disabilities	Level of bullying	Level of attacks on education	Inbound	Outbound	Inbound	Outbound	Scholarships	Imputed student costs	COUNTRY CODE
SDG indicator:	4.a.1							4.a.2	4.a.3					4.b.1		
Reference year:	2017									2017				2016		
Sub-Saharan Africa																
Angola	…	…	…	22_{-1}	3_{-1}	7_{-1}	…	…	Affected$_{-1}$	…	5_{-2i}	…	13_{i}	2	2	AGO
Benin	…	…	…	21_{-1}	…	…	…	…	…	8_{-1}	5_{-1}	11_{-1}	6_{i}	3	10	BEN
Botswana	…	…	…	…	…	…	…	…	…	3	6_{i}	1	3_{i}	1	0.1	BWA
Burkina Faso	53_{-1i}	70_{-1i}	18_{-1i}	18	$-_{-1}$	$-_{-1}$	2	…	Affected	3_{-4}	5_{i}	…	6_{i}	1	6	BFA
Burundi	42_{-1i}	48_{-1i}	19_{-1i}	9	-		…	…	Sporadic	3	4_{i}	2	3_{i}	1	2	BDI
Cabo Verde	…			76	9	41	…	…	…	1	20_{i}	0.1	3_{i}	1	7	CPV
Cameroon	34_{-1i}	…	…	25	…	…	…	…	Affected	…	6_{-1}	…	25_{i}	8	65	CMR
Central African Republic	10_{-1i}	…	…	4_{-1}	…	…	…	…	Affected	…	…	…	2_{i}	1	2	CAF
Chad	23_{-1i}	…	…	…	…	…	…	…	None$_{-1}$	…	14_{-3i}	…	7_{i}	1	3	TCD
Comoros	…	…	…	41	8	31	…	…	…	$-_{-3}$	79_{-3i}	$-_{-3}$	6_{i}	5	5	COM
Congo	…	…	…	…	…	…	…	…	…	1_{-4}	24_{-4i}	0.3_{-4}	10_{i}	4	9	COG
Côte d'Ivoire	…	…	…	30	…	…	…	…	Sporadic	2_{-1}	6_{-1}	4_{-1}	12_{i}	4	18	CIV
D. R. Congo	…	…	…	9_{-2}	$-_{-2}$	$-_{-2}$	$-_{-2}$	…	Very heavy	0.4_{-1}	2_{-1}	2_{-1}	10_{i}	4	4	COD
Djibouti	…	…	…	95	…	…	…	…	…	…	…	…	2_{i}	1	4	DJI
Equat. Guinea	…	…	…	…	…	…	…	…	…	…	…	…	1_{i}	0.1	0.2	GNQ
Eritrea	…	…	…	29	…	…	…	…	…	…	19_{-1}	…	2_{i}	2	1	ERI
Eswatini	…	…	…	100_{-1}	16_{-1}	15_{-1}	12_{-1}	…	None	1_{-4}	35_{-4i}	$-_{-4}$	3_{i}	1	0.1	SWZ
Ethiopia	…	…	6_{-1i}	…	…	…	…	Medium$_{-4}$	Sporadic	…	1_{-3i}	…	7_{i}	6	5	ETH
Gabon	…	…	…	…	…	…	…	…	…	…	…	…	7_{i}	2	13	GAB
Gambia	…	82_{-1i}	…	36	…	100	…	…	…	…	…	…	2_{i}	1	0.2	GMB
Ghana	…	…	…	74	…	…	…	…	…	3	3_{i}	13	13_{i}	6	6	GHA
Guinea	10_{-1i}	…	…	14_{-1}	$-_{-1}$	$-_{-1}$	…	…	…	…	6_{-3i}	…	9_{i}	3	15	GIN
Guinea-Bissau	…	…	…	…	…	…	…	…	…	…	…	…	3_{i}	1	2	GNB
Kenya	…	…	…	83_{-1}	…	…	…	…	Heavy	1_{-1}	3_{-1}	5_{-1}	14_{i}	5	6	KEN
Lesotho	…	…	…	12_{-4}	…	…	…	…	…	0.3_{-2}	13_{-2i}	0.1_{-2}	3_{i}	0.4	0.1	LSO
Liberia	42_{-1i}	43_{-1i}	50_{-1i}	2_{-1}	…	0.3_{-1}	0.4_{-1}	…	Sporadic$_{-1}$	…	…	…	1_{i}	0.4	0.1	LBR
Madagascar	…	…	…	9	…	…	…	…	…	2_{-1}	4_{-1}	2_{-1}	5_{i}	3	9	MDG
Malawi	…	70_{-1i}	…	24	…	…	…	…	Affected$_{-1}$	…	…	…	2_{i}	1	0.3	MWI
Mali	…	20_{-1i}	…	16	…	…	…	…	Affected	1_{-2}	10_{-2i}	1_{-2}	9_{i}	3	10	MLI
Mauritania	…	27_{-1i}	…	28	…	14	…	…	…	1	24_{i}	0.3	5_{i}	1	4	MRT
Mauritius	100_{-1i}	100_{-1i}	…	100	35	100	31	…	…	5	19_{i}	2	7_{i}	1	5	MUS
Mozambique	…	48_{-1i}	15_{-1i}	…	…	…	…	…	None$_{-1}$	0.3	1_{i}	1	3_{i}	3	2	MOZ
Namibia	76_{-1i}	46_{-1i}	20_{-1i}	71	…	…	…	High$_{-4}$	…	7_{-1}	9_{-1}	4_{-1}	5_{i}	1	1	NAM
Niger	…	21_{-1i}	14_{-1i}	5	$-_{-1}$	2	$-_{-1}$	…	Sporadic	4	7_{i}	3	4_{i}	1	3	NER
Nigeria	…	…	…	…	…	…	…	…	Affected	…	…	…	89_{i}	4	12	NGA
Rwanda	44_{-1i}	88_{-1i}	48_{-1i}	56	75	69	18	…	…	2	6_{i}	1	5_{i}	3	1	RWA
Sao Tome and Principe	…	76_{-1i}	…	87	…	59	…	…	…	…	32_{-2i}	…	1_{i}	0.5	1	STP
Senegal	32_{-1i}	…	22_{-1i}	37	17	28	…	…	None$_{-1}$	8	8_{i}	14	12_{i}	4	31	SEN
Seychelles	100_{-1i}	100_{-1i}	100_{-1i}	100_{-1}	96_{-1}	100_{-1}	7_{-1}	…	…	$-_{-1}$	41_{-1}	$-_{-1}$	1_{i}	0.4	0.2	SYC
Sierra Leone	62_{-1i}	12_{-1i}	…	4	0.3	3	5	…	Sporadic	…	…	…	1_{i}	0.3	0.3	SLE
Somalia	…	…	…	…	…	…	…	…	Heavy	…	…	…	5_{i}	0.2	0.4	SOM
South Africa	78_{-1i}	…	…	…	…	…	…	High$_{-4}$	Sporadic$_{-1}$	4_{-1}	1_{-1}	45_{-1}	8_{i}	8	2	ZAF
South Sudan	…	…	…	…	…	…	…	…	Very heavy	…	…	…	1_{i}	0.4	0.1	SSD
Togo	…	23_{-1i}	…	24	…	…	…	…	Affected$_{-1}$	…	6_{i}	…	6_{i}	1	7	TGO
Uganda	69_{-1i}	79_{-1i}	37_{-1i}	…	…	…	…	…	Sporadic$_{-1}$	…	3_{-3i}	…	5_{i}	4	1	UGA
United Republic of Tanzania	…	47_{-1i}	22_{-1i}	85_{-1}	…	…	…	…	Affected$_{-1}$	…	4_{-1}	…	7_{i}	5	2	TZA
Zambia	79_{-1i}	66_{-1i}	54_{-1i}	…	…	…	…	…	…	…	…	…	5_{i}	2	0.3	ZMB
Zimbabwe	64_{-1i}	…	…	…	…	…	…	…	Affected$_{-1}$	0.5_{-2}	13_{-2i}	1_{-2}	18_{i}	1	1	ZWE

TABLE 6: Continued

	A				B	C	
	Inclusion in national curricula				% of schools providing life skills-based HIV/AIDS education	% of students and youth with understanding of	
	Gender equality	Human rights	Sustainable development	Global citizenship		Scientific literacy	HIV/AIDS and sexuality
SDG indicator:	4.7.1				4.7.2	4.7.5	4.7.4
Reference year:	2015				2017		
Northern Africa and Western Asia							
Algeria	…	…	…	…	-	29_{-2}	…
Armenia	None	Medium	Low	Low	…	…	39_{-1}
Azerbaijan	None	Medium	None	Low	…	…	…
Bahrain	…	…	…	…	…	73_{-2}	…
Cyprus	…	…	…	…	…	58_{-2}	…
Egypt	…	…	…	…	$-_{-1}$	42_{-2}	…
Georgia	…	…	…	…	…	49_{-2}	…
Iraq	Low	High	Medium	Low	…	…	…
Israel	…	…	…	…	…	69_{-2}	…
Jordan	…	…	…	…	…	50_{-2}	…
Kuwait	…	…	…	…	…	49_{-2}	…
Lebanon	…	…	…	…	…	37_{-2}	…
Libya	…	…	…	…	…	…	…
Morocco	…	…	…	…	…	47_{-2}	22_{-4}
Oman	…	…	…	…	…	72_{-2}	…
Palestine	None	Low	Low	Low	…	…	…
Qatar	Low	Medium	Medium	Low	100	50_{-2}	…
Saudi Arabia	…	…	…	…	…	49_{-2}	…
Sudan	…	…	…	…	…	…	…
Syrian Arab Republic	…	…	…	…	…	…	…
Tunisia	…	…	…	…	…	34_{-2}	…
Turkey	…	…	…	…	…	56_{-2}	…
United Arab Emirates	…	…	…	…	…	58_{-2}	…
Yemen	…	…	…	…	…	…	…
Central and Southern Asia							
Afghanistan	None	Low	Low	Low	…	…	12_{-2}
Bangladesh	…	…	…	…	-	…	…
Bhutan	Medium	Low	Medium	Medium	…	…	…
India	Low	High	High	Low	…	…	…
Iran, Islamic Republic of	…	…	…	…	…	73_{-2}	…
Kazakhstan	…	…	…	…	…	72_{-2}	…
Kyrgyzstan	…	…	…	…	100	…	…
Maldives	None	Medium	Medium	Low	100	…	…
Nepal	Medium	Medium	Low	Medium	…	…	…
Pakistan	Low	High	Low	Low	…	…	4_{-4}
Sri Lanka	…	…	…	…	100	…	…
Tajikistan	…	…	…	…	…	…	…
Turkmenistan	…	…	…	…	…	…	…
Uzbekistan	…	…	…	…	…	…	…
Eastern and South-eastern Asia							
Brunei Darussalam	None	Low	None	Low	…	…	…
Cambodia	…	…	…	…	…	…	40_{-3}
China	…	…	…	…	…	84_{-2}	…
DPR Korea	…	…	…	…	…	…	…
Hong Kong, China	Low	Medium	Medium	Low	95_{i}	91_{-2}	…
Indonesia	Low	Low	None	None	…	44_{-2}	…
Japan	…	…	…	…	…	90_{-2}	…
Lao PDR	…	…	…	…	…	…	…
Macao, China	…	…	…	…	…	92_{-2}	…
Malaysia	…	…	…	…	100	66_{-2}	41_{-2}
Mongolia	…	…	…	…	…	…	…
Myanmar	None	Low	Low	Low	…	…	17_{-2}
Philippines	None	None	None	None	…	…	15_{-4}
Republic of Korea	Low	Low	Low	Low	…	86_{-2}	…
Singapore	…	…	…	…	…	90_{-2}	…
Thailand	Low	Medium	Medium	Low	…	53_{-2}	…
Timor-Leste	…	…	…	…	…	…	…
Viet Nam	…	…	…	…	…	94_{-2}	…

	D: % of schools with WASH facilities			E: % of schools with ICT for pedagogical purposes			F	G	H	I: Internationally mobile tertiary students				J: Official development assistance, in US$ (000,000)		
	Basic drinking water	Basic sanitation or toilets	Basic handwashing	Electricity	Internet	Computers	% of schools with adapted infrastructure and materials for students with disabilities	Level of bullying	Level of attacks on education	Mobility rate (%): Inbound	Mobility rate (%): Outbound	Number (000): Inbound	Number (000): Outbound	Scholarships	Imputed student costs	COUNTRY CODE
SDG indicator:	4.a.1							4.a.2	4.a.3					4.b.1		
Reference year:	2017									2017				2016		
Northern Africa and Western Asia																
Algeria	93-1i	99-1i	99-1i	…	…	…	…	Low-4	None-1	1	1i	9	22i	15	77	DZA
Armenia	…	…	…	…	…	…	…	…	Sporadic-1	4	8i	5	8i	3	7	ARM
Azerbaijan	100-1i	100-1i	100-1i	100	53	94	…	…	Sporadic-1	2	21i	4	43i	2	7	AZE
Bahrain	100-1i	100-1i	100-1i	100	100	100	100	…	Sporadic-1	13	13i	6	6i	…	…	BHR
Cyprus	…	…	…	…	…	…	…	…	…	18-2	69-2i	7-2	16i	…	…	CYP
Egypt	…	100-1i	100-1i	100-1	48-1	88	…	…	Affected	2-1	1-1	51-1	32i	14	33	EGY
Georgia	74-1i	60-1i	12-1i	100	100	100	…	…	None-1	6	7i	8	11i	3	15	GEO
Iraq	…	…	…	…	…	…	…	…	Heavy	…	…	…	31i	4	8	IRQ
Israel	100-1i	100-1i	100-1i	100-1	85-1i	85-1i	…	Medium-4	Sporadic	3-3	4-1	…	14i	…	…	ISR
Jordan	93-1i	33-1i	…	100	67	67	…	…	None-1	14	8i	40	24i	5	12	JOR
Kuwait	100-1i	100-1i	100-1i	…	…	…	…	…	…	…	20-4i	…	22i	…	…	KWT
Lebanon	59-1i	93-1i	36-1i	…	…	…	…	…	Sporadic	9	7i	20	16i	3	25	LBN
Libya	…	95-1i	13-1i	…	…	…	…	…	Affected	…	…	…	12i	0.4	5	LBY
Morocco	82-1i	70-1i	…	95	79	77	17	…	…	2	5i	20	48i	19	126	MAR
Oman	92-1i	…	…	…	…	…	…	…	…	3-1	13-1	4-1	16i	…	…	OMN
Palestine	80-1i	81-1i	23-1i	100	57	76	31	…	Very heavy	-	11i	-	75i	5	14	PSE
Qatar	100-1i	100-1i	100-1i	100	100	100	100	…	…	35	20i	11	6i	…	…	QAT
Saudi Arabia	…	…	…	…	…	…	…	…	Sporadic	5-1	6-1	80-1	89i	…	…	SAU
Sudan	…	…	…	…	…	…	…	…	Affected	…	2-2i	…	13i	2	3	SDN
Syrian Arab Republic	…	…	…	…	…	…	…	…	Heavy	…	7-1	…	45i	15	47	SYR
Tunisia	70-1i	100-1i	…	100-1	58-1	96-1	…	…	…	2	7i	6	20i	13	67	TUN
Turkey	…	…	…	…	…	…	…	High-4	Very heavy	1-1	1-1	88-1	44i	16	69	TUR
United Arab Emirates	…	…	…	…	…	…	…	…	None-1	49-1	7-1	77-1	12i	…	…	ARE
Yemen	36-1i	25-1i	8-1i	…	…	…	…	…	Very heavy	…	…	…	24i	3	14	YEM
Central and Southern Asia																
Afghanistan	…	…	…	21	…	…	…	…	Very heavy	-‑3	7-3i	-‑3	29i	9	5	AFG
Bangladesh	74-1i	59-1i	44-1i	43-1	4-1	18-1	…	…	Sporadic	…	2i	…	56i	9	18	BGD
Bhutan	59-1i	76-1i	…	87-2	45-2	14-2	…	…	…	…	42-4i	…	4i	3	0.2	BTN
India	69-1i	73-1i	54-1i	47-1	…	10-1	64-1	…	Very heavy	0.1-1	1-1	45-1	306i	11	112	IND
Iran, Islamic Republic of	…	…	…	…	…	…	…	…	Sporadic-1	0.4-1	1-1	19-1	50i	6	67	IRN
Kazakhstan	…	…	…	…	…	…	4	…	…	2	14i	14	90i	4	10	KAZ
Kyrgyzstan	…	…	…	100	41	89	…	…		6	5i	15	12i	4	4	KGZ
Maldives	…	…	…	100	100	100	100	…	…	…	39-1i	…	3i	3	0.1	MDV
Nepal	47-1i	…	…	…	…	…	…	High-4	Sporadic	…	13i	…	49i	4	12	NPL
Pakistan	58-1i	…	…	…	…	…	…	…	Heavy	…	3i	…	57i	12	31	PAK
Sri Lanka	…	100-1i	…	97	…	35	…	…	None-1	0.5	7i	1	19i	7	2	LKA
Tajikistan	79-1i	44-1i	26-1i	…	…	…	…	…	…	1	8i	2	21i	2	1	TJK
Turkmenistan	…	…	…	…	…	…	…	…	…	0.2-3	107-3i	0.1-3	45i	1	1	TKM
Uzbekistan	90-1i	92-1i	90-1i	100	91	97	13	…	…	0.2	12i	1	33i	4	6	UZB
Eastern and South-eastern Asia																
Brunei Darussalam	…	…	…	…	…	…	…	Medium-3	…	4	31i	0.4	4i	…	…	BRN
Cambodia	…	39-1i	41-1i	…	…	…	…	Medium-4	…	…	3i	…	5i	12	3	KHM
China	…	…	…	…	93	94	…	…	None	0.4	2i	157	869i	17	299	CHN
DPR Korea	…	…	…	…	…	…	…	…	…	…	0.3-2i	…	2i	0.1	0.4	PRK
Hong Kong, China	100-1i	100-1i	100-1i	100	99i	99i	96i	…	…	11	12i	34	37i	…	…	HKG
Indonesia	66-1i	34-1i	42-1i	93	…	32	…	…	Affected-1	0.1	1i	6	45i	55	34	IDN
Japan	…	…	…	…	…	…	…	…	…	4-1	1-1	143-1	32i	…	…	JPN
Lao PDR	…	…	…	37-1	…	…	…	…	…	0.4	4i	0.5	5i	11	0.5	LAO
Macao, China	100-1i	100-1i	100-1i	100	100	100	60	…	…	45	8i	15	3i	…	…	MAC
Malaysia	100-1i	100-1i	100-1i	100	100	100	98-1	…	None-1	8	5i	101	64i	1	11	MYS
Mongolia	74-1i	63-1i	41-1i	…	71-1	…	…	Medium-4	…	1	6i	2	10i	8	5	MNG
Myanmar	71-1i	…	…	27	0.2	1	…	…	Affected	…	1i	…	8i	12	1	MMR
Philippines	50-1i	39-1i	46-1i	…	…	…	…	…	Very heavy	…	0.5i	…	17i	13	2	PHL
Republic of Korea	100-1i	100-1i	100-1i	100-1	100-1	100-1	…	Low-4	…	2-1	3-1	62-1	105i	…	…	KOR
Singapore	100-1i	100-1i	100-1i	100-1	…	…	…	…	…	27-1	13-1	53-1	25i	…	…	SGP
Thailand	…	…	…	…	…	…	…	…	Affected	1-1	1-1	32-1	30i	3	8	THA
Timor-Leste	…	…	…	…	…	…	…	…	…	…	…	…	2i	7	2	TLS
Viet Nam	…	…	…	…	…	…	…	Medium-4	None-1	0.2-1	4-1	6-1	82i	37	44	VNM

TABLE 6: Continued

	A				B	C	
	Inclusion in national curricula					% of students and youth with understanding of	
	Gender equality	Human rights	Sustainable development	Global citizenship	% of schools providing life skills-based HIV/AIDS education	Scientific literacy	HIV/AIDS and sexuality
SDG indicator:	4.7.1				4.7.2	4.7.5	4.7.4
Reference year:	2015				2017		
Oceania							
Australia	Low	High	Medium	Medium	...	82_{-2}	...
Cook Islands	None	Low	Low	Low	32_{-1}	...	...
Fiji	None	Medium	Medium	Low	...	...	...
Kiribati	Low	None	Low	None	...	...	...
Marshall Islands	...	...	...	...	...	...	...
Micronesia, F. S.	None	Low	Low	Low	...	...	...
Nauru	None	None	Low	Low	50_{-1}	...	...
New Zealand	None	Low	Medium	Low	...	83_{-2}	...
Niue	...	...	...	...	100_{-1}	...	...
Palau	...	...	...	...	...	...	...
Papua New Guinea	Low	Medium	Medium	Low	...	...	...
Samoa	None	Low	Medium	None	-	...	...
Solomon Is	...	...	...	...	-	...	...
Tokelau	Low	Low	Medium	None	...	...	...
Tonga	...	...	...	...	...	...	...
Tuvalu	Medium	Medium	High	Medium	...	...	...
Vanuatu	...	...	...	...	...	...	...
Latin America and the Caribbean							
Anguilla	...	...	...	...	...	...	...
Antigua and Barbuda	...	...	...	...	...	...	...
Argentina	None	Low	None	Low	...	60_{-2}	...
Aruba	...	...	...	...	...	...	...
Bahamas	...	...	...	...	...	...	4_{-3}
Barbados	...	...	...	...	...	...	46_{-3}
Belize	Low	Low	Low	None	...	...	76_{-3}
Bolivia, P. S.	...	...	...	...	...	...	...
Brazil	None	High	Low	Low	...	43_{-2}	...
British Virgin Islands	...	...	...	...	...	...	...
Cayman Islands	...	...	...	...	100_{+1}	...	...
Chile	Low	High	Medium	Low	...	65_{-2}	...
Colombia	...	...	...	...	...	51_{-2}	30_{-2}
Costa Rica	...	...	...	...	74_{-1}	54_{-2}	...
Cuba	...	...	...	...	...	...	...
Curaçao	...	...	...	...	...	...	...
Dominica	Low	Medium	Low	Low	100_{-1}	...	...
Dominican Republic	Low	Medium	Medium	Medium	...	14_{-2}	43_{-4}
Ecuador	...	...	...	...	...	...	...
El Salvador	Low	High	Medium	Low	...	...	36_{-3}
Grenada	Low	Low	Low	Low	100	...	...
Guatemala	Medium	High	Medium	Medium	...	...	22_{-2}
Guyana	...	...	...	...	...	...	...
Haiti	None	Low	None	Low	...	...	...
Honduras	Low	High	Medium	Low	...	...	...
Jamaica	...	...	...	...	...	...	...
Mexico	Low	High	Low	Low	...	52_{-2}	...
Montserrat	...	...	...	...	...	...	...
Nicaragua	Medium	High	Medium	Low	...	...	...
Panama	Low	Medium	Medium	Low	...	...	...
Paraguay	High	Medium	Low	Low	...	...	...
Peru	Low	High	Medium	Low	...	42_{-2}	75_{-1}
Saint Kitts and Nevis	...	...	...	...	...	...	...
Saint Lucia	...	...	...	...	...	...	...
Saint Vincent/Grenadines	...	...	...	...	100	...	...
Sint Maarten	...	...	...	...	...	...	...
Suriname	...	...	...	...	...	...	...
Trinidad and Tobago	...	...	...	...	...	54_{-2}	...
Turks and Caicos Islands	...	...	...	...	...	...	...
Uruguay	Low	High	Low	Low	100_{-1}	59_{-2}	...
Venezuela, B. R.	None	High	Low	Low	...	...	...

	D			E			F	G	H	I				J		
	% of schools with WASH facilities			% of schools with ICT for pedagogical purposes			% of schools with adapted infrastructure and materials for students with disabilities	Level of bullying	Level of attacks on education	Internationally mobile tertiary students: Mobility rate (%)		Number (000)		Official development assistance, in US$ (000,000)		
	Basic drinking water	Basic sanitation or toilets	Basic handwashing	Electricity	Internet	Computers				Inbound	Outbound	Inbound	Outbound	Scholarships	Imputed student costs	COUNTRY CODE
SDG indicator:	4.a.1							4.a.2	4.a.3					4.b.1		
Reference year:	2017									2017				2016		
Oceania																
Australia	100-1i	100-1i	100-1i	100-1	100-1	100-1	...	...	...	17-1	1-1	336-1	13i	...	...	AUS
Cook Islands	100-1i	100-1i	100-1i	100-1	100-1	100-1	4-1	...	...	...	...	...	0.2i	0.5	...	COK
Fiji	88-1i	76-1i	61-1i	98-1	...	...	...	...	...	...	...	...	1i	5	0.1	FJI
Kiribati	...	...	...	...	...	...	...	...	...	...	...	...	1i	3	-	KIR
Marshall Islands	3-1i	27-1i	36-1i	54-1	26-1	22-1	21-1	...	...	...	...	...	0.2i	0.1	...	MHL
Micronesia, F. S.	...	...	...	...	...	...	...	...	...	...	...	...	0.2i	0.2	-	FSM
Nauru	...	86-1i	...	67-1	-1	33-1	-1	...	...	...	...	...	0.2i	1	...	NRU
New Zealand	...	...	...	...	...	...	...	...	...	20-1	2-1	54-1	6i	...	...	NZL
Niue	100-1i	100-1i	100-1i	100-1	100-1	100-1	100-1	...	...	...	...	...	-i	0.3	...	NIU
Palau	...	...	...	...	...	...	...	...	...	...	4-4i	...	-i	0.1	-	PLW
Papua New Guinea	47-1i	45-1i	10-1i	...	...	...	...	...	Affected-1	...	...	...	2i	27	-	PNG
Samoa	...	...	...	100	14	14	-	...	...	...	...	...	1i	6	-	WSM
Solomon Is	17-1i	27-1i	17-1i	50	-	-	-	...	...	...	...	...	3i	5	-	SLB
Tokelau	...	...	...	...	...	...	...	...	...	...	...	...	0.1i	0.1	...	TKL
Tonga	...	...	...	...	...	...	...	...	...	...	...	...	1i	2	...	TON
Tuvalu	...	...	...	...	...	...	...	Medium-4	...	...	...	...	0.5i	2	...	TUV
Vanuatu	...	...	...	...	...	...	...	...	...	...	...	...	2i	3	2	VUT
Latin America and the Caribbean																
Anguilla	...	...	...	...	...	...	...	...	...	...	...	...	0.1i	...	...	AIA
Antigua and Barbuda	...	...	...	...	...	...	...	...	...	...	...	...	1i	-	-	ATG
Argentina	...	77-1i	...	96-1	38-1	62-1	...	High-4	...	2-1	0.3-1	76-1	8i	2	7	ARG
Aruba	...	...	...	...	...	...	...	...	...	28-2	14-2i	0.3-2	0.2i	...	...	ABW
Bahamas	...	...	...	...	...	...	...	Medium-4	...	...	...	...	3i	...	...	BHS
Barbados	100-1i	100-1i	100-1i	100	...	...	...	...	...	...	...	...	1i	...	...	BRB
Belize	76-1i	49-1i	66-1i	...	...	...	...	...	...	...	9i	...	1i	-	-	BLZ
Bolivia, P. S.	...	...	...	...	...	...	...	...	...	...	...	...	19i	2	3	BOL
Brazil	...	84-1i	61-1i	...	...	...	...	Medium-4	Sporadic-1	0.2-1	1-1	20-1	53i	12	50	BRA
British Virgin Islands	...	...	...	100	100	89	63	...	...	17-1	43-1	0.1-1	0.3i	...	...	VGB
Cayman Islands	...	...	...	100+1	100+1	100+1	100+1	...	...	...	...	...	0.5i	...	...	CYM
Chile	...	96-1i	...	...	...	...	...	Low-4	Affected-1	0.4-1	1-1	5-1	14i	3	9	CHL
Colombia	55-1i	61-1i	...	96	39	93	...	High-4	Affected	0.2	1i	5	37i	5	30	COL
Costa Rica	82-1i	70-1i	70-1i	97-1	22-1	45-1	60-1	Low-4	...	1	1i	3	3i	1	3	CRI
Cuba	...	...	...	...	...	...	...	...	...	...	1-1	...	2i	1	1	CUB
Curaçao				...	...	...	...	...	...	...	2-4i	...	0.2i	...	...	CUW
Dominica	100-1i	100-1i	100-1i	100-1	100-1	100-1	2-1	...	...	...	...		1i	0.2	0.2	DMA
Dominican Republic	...	90-1i	...	...	23-1	...	...	High-4	...	2	1i	10	4i	0.4	1	DOM
Ecuador	50-1i	83-1i	87-1i	75	37	73	...	High-4	None	1-2	3-2i	3-2	19i	2	7	ECU
El Salvador	[illegible]			[illegible]	[illegible]	[illegible]	[illegible]	Medium-4	...	[illegible]	1-1	1-1	4i	0.5	2	SLV
Grenada	100-1i	...	100-1i	100	100	100				72	5i	7	1i	0.1	-	GRD
Guatemala	...	76-1i	...	...	9-1	12-1	...	Low-4	...	...	1-2i	...	3i	1	2	GTM
Guyana	71-1i	17-1i	...	...	...	...	...	...	...	...	...	...	2i	0.4	0.1	GUY
Haiti	...	...	...	...	...	...	...	...	None-1	...	...	...	10i	3	5	HTI
Honduras	59-1i	82-1i	12-1i	48-1	16-1	16-1	5-1	Medium-4	...	1-2	2-2i	1-2	5i	0.5	1	HND
Jamaica	83-1i	83-1i	83-1i	94	84	33	12	...	...	...	6-2i	...	5i	0.4	0.4	JAM
Mexico	...	75-1i	...	...	39-1	...	...	Low-4	...	0.3-1	1-1	13-1	34i	4	30	MEX
Montserrat	...	...	...	100-1	100-1	100-1	...	...	...	...	...	...	-i	...	...	MSR
Nicaragua	...	43-1i	...	...	...	...	...	Medium-4	...	...	...	...	4i	1	1	NIC
Panama	...	82-1i	...	...	...	...	...	Medium-4	...	...	2-2i	...	3i	0.3	1	PAN
Paraguay	...	77-1i	...	94-1	5-1	5-1	...	Medium-4	...	...	...	...	12i	1	1	PRY
Peru	73-1i	68-1i	...	76	38	67	19	High-4	...	...	2-1	...	31i	2	11	PER
Saint Kitts and Nevis	84-1i	...	84-1i	100-1	...	...	...	...	...	73-3	13-2i	...	1i	...	...	KNA
Saint Lucia	99-1i	99-1i	99-1i	99	99	99	...	...	...	15	31i	0.5	1i	0.2	0.1	LCA
Saint Vincent/Grenadines	100-1i	100-1i	100-1i	100	100	100	100	...	...	...	...	...	1i	0.1	-	VCT
Sint Maarten	...	...	...	...	...	...	...	...	...	36-2	48-2i	0.1-2	0.1i	...	...	SXM
Suriname	...	...	...	...	...	...	...	...	...	...	...	...	1i	1	0.1	SUR
Trinidad and Tobago	...	...	...	...	...	...	...	...	...	...	...	...	4i	...	...	TTO
Turks and Caicos Islands	...	...	...	...	...	...	...	...	...	...	53-2i	...	0.2i	...	...	TCA
Uruguay	...	83-1i	...	100-1	100-1	100-1	100-1	Low-4	...	...	3-2i	...	5i	0.4	1	URY
Venezuela, B. R.	98-1i	90-1i	...	99-1	...	...	...	...	Very heavy	...	...	...	18i	1	7	VEN

TABLE 6: Continued

	A				B	C	
	Inclusion in national curricula				% of schools providing life skills-based HIV/AIDS education	% of students and youth with understanding of	
	Gender equality	Human rights	Sustainable development	Global citizenship		Scientific literacy	HIV/AIDS and sexuality
SDG indicator:	4.7.1				4.7.2	4.7.5	4.7.4
Reference year:	2015				2017		
Europe and Northern America							
Albania	...	...	...	...	...	58_{-2}	...
Andorra	...	...	...	...	100	...	...
Austria	...	...	...	...	...	79_{-2}	...
Belarus	...	...	...	...	...	...	...
Belgium	None	Medium	Low	Low	...	80_{-2}	...
Bermuda	...	...	...	...	100_{-1}	...	...
Bosnia and Herzegovina	...	...	...	...	...	...	...
Bulgaria	...	...	...	...	...	62_{-2}	19_{-1}
Canada	...	...	...	...	...	89_{-2}	...
Croatia	Low	Medium	Medium	Low	...	75_{-2}	...
Czechia	...	...	...	...	...	79_{-2}	...
Denmark	...	...	...	...	...	84_{-2}	...
Estonia	Low	High	Medium	Low	...	91_{-2}	...
Finland	...	...	...	...	100_{-1}	89_{-2}	...
France	Low	Medium	Medium	Low	...	78_{-2}	...
Germany	...	...	...	...	...	83_{-2}	...
Greece	...	...	...	...	...	67_{-2}	...
Hungary	Low	Low	Low	Low	...	74_{-2}	...
Iceland	Low	High	Medium	Low	...	75_{-2}	...
Ireland	Low	Low	Low	Low	...	85_{-2}	...
Italy	...	...	...	...	...	77_{-2}	...
Latvia	...	...	...	...	...	83_{-2}	...
Liechtenstein	...	...	...	...	...	...	...
Lithuania	Low	Low	Low	Low	...	75_{-2}	71_{-3}
Luxembourg	High	Low	None	Low	...	74_{-2}	...
Malta	None	High	Low	Low	...	67_{-2}	...
Monaco	...	...	...	...	100	...	...
Montenegro	...	...	...	...	...	49_{-2}	...
Netherlands	...	...	...	...	...	81_{-2}	...
Norway	None	Medium	Low	Low	...	81_{-2}	...
Poland	...	...	...	...	...	84_{-2}	...
Portugal	None	Medium	Medium	Low	...	83_{-2}	...
Republic of Moldova	...	...	...	...	100	58_{-2}	...
Romania	...	...	...	...	...	61_{-2}	...
Russian Federation	...	...	...	...	...	82_{-2}	...
San Marino	...	...	...	...	...	...	...
Serbia	Low	High	Low	Medium	...	...	...
Slovakia	...	...	...	...	...	69_{-2}	...
Slovenia	...	...	...	...	...	85_{-2}	...
Spain	...	...	...	...	...	82_{-2}	...
Sweden	Low	High	High	Low	...	78_{-2}	...
Switzerland	...	...	...	...	...	82_{-2}	...
TFYR Macedonia	...	...	...	...	...	37_{-2}	...
Ukraine	...	...	...	...	...	...	23_{-3}
United Kingdom	None	Low	Low	None	...	83_{-2}	...
United States	...	...	...	...	...	80_{-2}	...

	D			E			F	G	H	I				J		
	% of schools with WASH facilities			% of schools with ICT for pedagogical purposes						Internationally mobile tertiary students				Official development assistance, in US$ (000,000)		
										Mobility rate (%)		Number (000)				
	Basic drinking water	Basic sanitation or toilets	Basic handwashing	Electricity	Internet	Computers	% of schools with adapted infrastructure and materials for students with disabilities	Level of bullying	Level of attacks on education	Inbound	Outbound	Inbound	Outbound	Scholarships	Imputed student costs	COUNTRY CODE
SDG indicator:	4.a.1							4.a.2	4.a.3					4.b.1		
Reference year:	2017									2017				2016		
Europe and Northern America																
Albania	…	…	…	…	…	…	…	…	…	2	12i	2	17i	3	17	ALB
Andorra	100-1i	100-1i	100-1i	100	100	100	100	…	…	31	239i	0.2	1i	…	…	AND
Austria	…	…	…	…	…	…	…	…	…	16-1	4-1	70-1	18i	…	…	AUT
Belarus	100-1i	100-1i	100-1i	100	100	100	…	…	None-1	4	6i	18	26i	7	16	BLR
Belgium	100-1i	…	100-1i	100-1	100-1	100-1	…	…	…	12-1	3-1	61-1	14i	…	…	BEL
Bermuda	…	…		100-1	100-1	100-1	100-1	…	…	18-2	176-2i	0.2-2	2i	…	…	BMU
Bosnia and Herzegovina	…	…	…	…	…	…	…	…	…	7	12i	7	12i	2	26	BIH
Bulgaria	…	…	…	…	…	…	…	…	…	5-1	9-1	12-1	24i	…	…	BGR
Canada	…	…	…	…	…	…	…	…	…	12-1i	3-1i	189-1i	50i	…	…	CAN
Croatia	51-1i	34-1i	26-1i	…	…	…	…	…	…	0.4-1	6-1	1-1	9i	…	…	HRV
Czechia	…	…	…	…	…	…	…	…	…	12-1	3-1	43-1	13i	…	…	CZE
Denmark	100-1i	100-1i	100-1i	100-1	100-1	100-1	…	…	…	11-1	2-1	34-1	5i	…	…	DNK
Estonia	100-1i	100-1i	100-1i	100-1	100-1	100-1	…	Medium-4	…	7-1	8-1	3-1	4i	…	…	EST
Finland	100-1i	100-1i	100-1i	100-1	100-1	100-1	100-1	…	…	8-1	3-1	23-1	10i	…	…	FIN
France	100-1i	100-1i	100-1i	100-1	100-1	100-1	100-1	…	…	10-1	4-1	245-1	91i	…		FRA
Germany	100-1i	100-1i	100-1i	100-1	…	…	…	Low-4	…	8-1	4-1	245-1	119i	…	…	DEU
Greece	…	…	…	…	…	…	…	…	Sporadic	3-1	5-1	24-1	36i	…	…	GRC
Hungary	100-1i	92-1i	99-1i	100-1	100-1	100-1	…	…	…	9-1	4-1	26-1	12i	…	…	HUN
Iceland	…	…	…	…	…	…	…	…	…	7-1	14-1	1-1	3i	…	…	ISL
Ireland	…	…	…	…	…	…	…	…	None-1	8-1	7-1	18-1	15i	…	…	IRL
Italy	100-1i	100-1i	100-1i	100-1	70-1i	…	…	…	…	5-1	4-1	93-1	65i	…	…	ITA
Latvia	100-1i	100-1i	100-1i	100-1	100-1	100-1	18-1	…	…	8-1	7-1	6-1	6i	…	…	LVA
Liechtenstein	…	…	…	…	…	…	…	…	…	89-1	132-1	1-1	1i	…	…	LIE
Lithuania	…	…	…	…	…	…	…	…	…	4-1	8-1	5-1	11i	…	…	LTU
Luxembourg	…	…	…	…	…	…	…	…	…	47-1	147-1	3-1	10i	…	…	LUX
Malta	…	…	…	…	…	…	…	High-4	…	8-1	8-1	1-1	1i	…	…	MLT
Monaco	100-1i	100-1i	100-1i	100	100	100	100	…	…	0.3	44i	-	0.4i	…	…	MCO
Montenegro	…	…	…	…	…	…	…	…	…	…	20i	…	5i	0.3	2	MNE
Netherlands	100-1i	100-1i	100-1i	100-1	100-1	100-1	…	…	…	11-1	2-1	90-1	17i	…	…	NLD
Norway	100-1i	100-1i	100-1i	100-1	100-1	100-1	…	Medium-4	…	4-1	7-1	11-1	19i	…	…	NOR
Poland	…	…	…	100-1	100-1	100-1	…	Medium-4	…	3-1	2-1	55-1	25i	…	…	POL
Portugal	100-1i	100-1i	100-1i	100-1	100-1	100-1	…	…	…	5-2	4-1	…	13i	…	…	PRT
Republic of Moldova	100-1i	94-1i	100-1i	100	85	100	100	…	…	4	21i	4	20i	20	7	MDA
Romania	…	…	…	…	…	…	…	High-4	…	5-1	6-1	26-1	34i	…	…	ROU
Russian Federation	…	…	…	…	…	…	…	…	Affected	4-1	1-1	244-1	57i	…	…	RUS
San Marino	…	…	…	…	…	…	…	…	…				1i	…	…	SMR
Serbia	72-1i	74-1i	73-1i	…	…	…	…	…	…	4	6i	12	15i	8	20	SRB
Slovakia	100-1i	100-1i	100-1i	100-1	100-1i	100-1i	14-1i	…	…	6-1	19-1	10-1	32i	…	…	SVK
Slovenia	100-1i	100-1i	100-1i	100-1	100-1	100-1	…	…	…	3-1	3-1	3-1	3i	…	…	SVN
Spain	100-1i	100-1i	100-1i	100-1	100-1i	100-1	…	Medium-4	None-1	3-1	2-1	53-1	38i	…	…	ESP
Sweden	…	…	…	…	…	…	…	…	Sporadic-1	7-1	4-1	28-1	17i	…	…	SWE
Switzerland	100-1i	100-1i	100-1i	100-1	100-1	100-1	…	…	…	18-1	4-1	52-1	13i	…	…	CHE
TFYR Macedonia	…	…	…	…	…	…	…	…	…	3-2	8-2i	2-2	5i	1	8	MKD
Ukraine	…	…	83-1i	100	48	78	63	…	Heavy	3	5i	53	77i	11	65	UKR
United Kingdom	…	…	…	…	…	…	…	…	Sporadic	18-1	1-1	432-1	34i	…	…	GBR
United States	100-1i	100-1i	100-1i	100-2i	100-2i	100-2i	…	…	…	5-1	0.4-1	971-1	73i	…	…	USA

TABLE 7: SDG 4, Means of implementation 4.c – Teachers

By 2030, substantially increase the supply of qualified teachers, including through international cooperation for teacher training in developing countries, especially least developed countries and small island developing States

	Pre-primary						Primary						Secondary					
	A	B	C	D	E	F	A	B	C	D	E	F	A	B	C	D	E	F
	Classroom teachers (000)	Pupil/teacher ratio	% of trained classroom teachers	% of qualified classroom teachers	Teacher attrition rate (%)	Relative teacher salary level	Classroom teachers (000)	Pupil/teacher ratio	% of trained classroom teachers	% of qualified classroom teachers	Teacher attrition rate (%)	Relative teacher salary level	Classroom teachers (000)	Pupil/teacher ratio	% of trained classroom teachers	% of qualified classroom teachers	Teacher attrition rate (%)	Relative teacher salary level
SDG indicator:			4.c.1	4.c.3	4.c.6	4.c.5			4.c.1	4.c.3	4.c.6	4.c.5			4.c.1	4.c.3	4.c.6	4.c.5
Reference year:	2017						2017						2017					
Region	Sum	Median					Sum	Median					Sum	Median				
World	10,020i	16	84i	95i	…	…	31,573i	19	92i	99i	…	…	34,555i	13	87i	96i	…	…
Sub-Saharan Africa	720i	23	54i	72	…	…	4,280i	39	82	94	9i	…	2,731i	22	73i	80i	…	…
Northern Africa and Western Asia	413i	16	94i	98i	…	…	2,798i	15	100i	100i	…	…	3,068i	10i	100i	100i	…	…
Northern Africa	174i	25i	88i	100i	…	…	1,197	24	100	100	…	…	1,218	18i	84i	100i	…	…
Western Asia	239i	16	94i	94i	…	…	1,601i	12	100i	100i	…	…	1,832-1i	10	100i	100i	…	…
Central and Southern Asia	1,276-1i	12i	99i	96i	…	…	6,170i	25	96	97	2i	…	7,278i	17	98i	100i	…	…
Central Asia	179i	11i	100i	100i	…	…	252	22	99	98	4i	…	840	10i	98i	100i	…	…
Southern Asia	1,097-1i	18i	89i	92i	…	…	5,919i	30	88	95	2	…	6,438i	24	94i	96i	…	…
Eastern and South-eastern Asia	3,649	18	99i	99i	…	…	10,386	16	99	100	2i	…	10,165	14	97i	100	3i	…
Eastern Asia	2,687	18	…	96i	…	…	6,740	16	98i	100	2i	…	7,309	12	97i	100	3i	…
South-eastern Asia	962	18	98i	99	…	…	3,646	18	99	100	2i	…	2,856	17	96i	99	…	…
Oceania	57i	14	83i	100i	…	…	203i	20	90i	100i	…	…	55i	16i	…	84i	…	…
Latin America and the Caribbean	1,035i	16i	76i	95i	…	…	3,010i	17	90i	100i	…	…	3,887i	14	77i	98i	…	…
Caribbean	17i	11i	71i	97i	…	…	177	14	89	100i	…	…	153	11	73	98	…	…
Central America	229	19	89	98i	…	…	769	24	96i	97i	4i	…	1,059	15	90i	99i	…	…
South America	505i	20i	88i	…	…	…	1,437	19	88i	…	…	…	2,022i	19i	74i	…	…	…
Europe and Northern America	2,794i	12	…	…	…	0.68i	4,725i	13	…	…	…	0.80i	7,213i	10	…	…	…	0.93i
Europe	2,144i	12	…	…	…	0.69i	2,827i	13	…	…	…	0.81i	5,387i	10	…	…	…	0.93i
Northern America	642-1i	11	100i	100i	…	0.62i	1,864-1i	12	100i	100i	…	0.63i	1,822-1i	11	100i	99i	…	0.67i
Low income	371	25	47i	69	…	…	3,000i	40	80	95	…	…	1,929i	22	66i	84i	…	…
Middle income	7,340i	17	90i	94i	…	…	22,688i	22	95i	99i	…	…	25,058i	16	93i	96i	…	…
Lower middle	2,735i	20	93i	96i	…	…	11,582i	27	94	96	4i	…	11,414i	20	93i	92i	…	…
Upper middle	4,606	15	88i	94i	…	…	11,106	18	97i	100i	…	…	13,644i	13	89i	97i	…	…
High income	2,309i	13	…	…	…	…	5,884i	12	…	…	…	0.82i	7,567i	10	…	…	…	…

A Number of classroom teachers.

B Pupil/teacher ratio, headcount basis.

C Percentage of teachers who have received at least the minimum organized and recognized pre-service and in-service pedagogical training required to teach at a given level of education.

D Percentage of teachers qualified according to national standards.

E Teacher attrition rate (%).

F Ratio of actual teacher salaries to comparable workers [*Sources:* OECD; for secondary: GEM Report weighted average of OECD lower secondary and upper secondary data].

Notes:

Source: UIS unless noted otherwise. Data refer to school year ending in 2017 unless noted otherwise.

Aggregates represent countries listed in the table with available data and may include estimates for countries with no recent data.

(-) Magnitude nil or negligible.

(...) Data not available or category not applicable.

(± n) Reference year differs (e.g. -2: reference year 2015 instead of 2017).

(i) Estimate and/or partial coverage.

TABLE 7: Continued

	Pre-primary						Primary						Secondary						
	A	B	C	D	E	F	A	B	C	D	E	F	A	B	C	D	E	F	
	Classroom teachers (000)	Pupil/teacher ratio	% of trained classroom teachers	% of qualified classroom teachers	Teacher attrition rate (%)	Relative teacher salary level	Classroom teachers (000)	Pupil/teacher ratio	% of trained classroom teachers	% of qualified classroom teachers	Teacher attrition rate (%)	Relative teacher salary level	Classroom teachers (000)	Pupil/teacher ratio	% of trained classroom teachers	% of qualified classroom teachers	Teacher attrition rate (%)	Relative teacher salary level	COUNTRY CODE
SDG indicator:			4.c.1	4.c.3	4.c.6	4.c.5			4.c.1	4.c.3	4.c.6	4.c.5			4.c.1	4.c.3	4.c.6	4.c.5	
Reference year:	2017						2017						2017						
Sub-Saharan Africa																			
Angola	12$_{-1}$	...	...	72$_{-1}$	...	...	96$_{-1}$	50$_{-2}$	...	63$_{-1}$	15$_{-1}$	...	76$_{-1}$	27$_{-1}$	51$_{-2}$	52$_{-1}$	...	...	AGO
Benin	8$_{-1}$	19$_{-1}$	26$_{-1}$	100$_{-1}$	...	...	52	44	68	100	13	...	90$_{-1}$	11$_{-1}$	18$_{-1}$	69$_{-1}$	...	...	BEN
Botswana	2$_{-4i}$	12$_{-4i}$	55$_{-4i}$	55$_{-4i}$	...	...	15$_{-4}$	23$_{-4}$	99$_{-4}$	99$_{-4}$	...	...	...	...	...	...	...	...	BWA
Burkina Faso	4	18	34	71	4$_{-1}$	...	75	41	86	96	6	...	50	23	58	99	8	...	BFA
Burundi	3	32	100	69$_{-3}$	18$_{-1}$	...	43	50	100	100	11$_{-1}$	...	24	28	100	57	-$_{-1}$	...	BDI
Cabo Verde	1	18	29	29	...	...	3	21	93	99	2	...	4	16	94	91	4	...	CPV
Cameroon	76	21	67	61	...	...	98	45	81	73	9	...	115$_{-1}$	19$_{-1}$	54$_{-1}$	54$_{-1i}$	...	...	CMR
Central African Republic	0.3$_{-1}$	...	...	100$_{-1}$	...	...	10$_{-1}$	83$_{-1}$	...	100$_{-1}$	...	...	4	32	45$_{-1}$	55$_{-1}$	...	...	CAF
Chad	0.4$_{-4}$	...	52$_{-4}$	...	...	...	39$_{-1}$	57$_{-1}$	65$_{-4}$	...	...	...	19$_{-1}$	28$_{-1}$	53$_{-4}$	...	...	...	TCD
Comoros	1	20	56	44	...	...	6	19	51	49	...	...	13	5	86	...	...	...	COM
Congo	...	...	...	...	...	...	...	...	...	...	...	...	...	...	...	...	...	...	COG
Côte d'Ivoire	8	23	100	100	...	...	89	42	100	100	3	...	72	26	100$_{-1}$	100	...	...	CIV
D. R. Congo	15$_{-2}$	23$_{-2}$	21$_{-2}$	100$_{-3}$	...	...	415$_{-2}$	33$_{-2}$	95$_{-3}$	95$_{-2}$	...	...	324$_{-2}$	14$_{-2}$	24$_{-3}$	100$_{-3}$	...	...	COD
Djibouti	0.1$_{-1}$	29$_{-1}$	...	100$_{-1}$	...	...	2	30	100$_{-2}$	100	3	...	3	23	100$_{-2}$	100	...	...	DJI
Equat. Guinea	2$_{-2}$	17$_{-2}$	89$_{-2}$	8$_{-2}$	...	...	4$_{-2}$	23$_{-2}$	37$_{-2}$	61$_{-2}$	...	...	...	...	...	...	...	...	GNQ
Eritrea	2	29	40	50$_{-4}$	4	...	9	39	41	89	...	...	7	37	83$_{-4}$	84	...	...	ERI
Eswatini	...	...	...	...	...	...	9$_{-1}$	27$_{-1}$	70$_{-1}$	71$_{-1}$	...	...	7$_{-1}$	16$_{-1}$	73$_{-2}$	73$_{-1}$	...	...	SWZ
Ethiopia	23	...	...	100	...	...	...	...	...	...	...	...	...	...	...	...	...	...	ETH
Gabon	...	...	...	...	...	...	...	...	...	...	...	...	...	...	...	...	...	...	GAB
Gambia	3	35	69	69	...	...	9	39	88	88	...	...	7	...	95	95	...	...	GMB
Ghana	61	29	46$_{-2}$	46$_{-2}$	...	...	161	27	55	55	...	...	163	16	76	76	...	...	GHA
Guinea					...	...	30$_{-1}$	47$_{-1}$	75$_{-1}$	92$_{-1}$	22$_{-1}$	...	...	...	...	...	...	...	GIN
Guinea-Bissau	...	...	...	...	...	...	...	...	...	...	...	...	...	...	...	...	...	...	GNB
Kenya	111$_{-1}$	29$_{-1}$	82$_{-3}$	82$_{-3}$	...	...	267$_{-2i}$	31$_{-2i}$	...	...	...	...	199$_{-2i}$	...	...	...	...	...	KEN
Lesotho	3$_{-1}$	18$_{-1}$	100$_{-2}$	100$_{-2}$	...	...	11	33	87$_{-1}$	83$_{-1}$	...	...	5	25	89$_{-1}$	91$_{-1}$	...	...	LSO
Liberia	13$_{-1}$	48$_{-1}$	...	47$_{-1}$	...	...	26$_{-1}$	27$_{-1}$	47$_{-2}$	56$_{-1}$	...	...	15$_{-1}$	15$_{-1}$	62$_{-2}$	55$_{-1}$	...	...	LBR
Madagascar	36	23	10$_{-1}$	100	...	...	120	41$_{-1}$	15	100	...	...	77	20	21	86	...	...	MDG
Malawi	32$_{-2}$	42$_{-2}$	...	100$_{-2}$	...	...	71	62	91$_{-4i}$	94	...	...	14	70	66$_{-4i}$	57	...	...	MWI
Mali	6	20	...	...	...	...	66	38	...	...	...	...	58	17	...	...	...	...	MLI
Mauritania	2$_{-2}$	19$_{-2}$	...	...	...	...	17$_{-1}$	36$_{-1}$	85$_{-1}$	...	11$_{-1}$	...	9	24	97	...	...	...	MRT
Mauritius	...	13$_{-1}$	100$_{-1}$	100$_{-1}$	8$_{-2i}$	...	5	18	100	100	8	...	10	13	55	100	5	...	MUS
Mozambique	...	...	...	...	...	...	117	52	97	100	...	...	33	37	85$_{-2i}$	91$_{-2i}$		...	MOZ
Namibia	1	30	...	100			...	...	...	...	...		11		...	...	...	...	NAM
Niger	6	28	95	95	23		76	36	66	95		...	26	30	11	100	12	...	NER
Nigeria	...	...	...	...	...	...	...	...	...	...	...	...	...	...	...	...	...	...	NGA
Rwanda	7	32	43	85	1	...	44	58	93	98	2	...	30	20	58	80	5	...	RWA
Sao Tome and Principe	...	13$_{-2}$	28$_{-2}$	-$_{-2}$	...	...	1	31	27	...	...	...	1$_{-1}$	25$_{-1}$	36$_{-2}$	26$_{-2}$	...	...	STP
Senegal	11	22	37	100	...	...	65	33	75	100	-$_{-2}$	...	57	19	77$_{-1i}$	76$_{-2}$	...	...	SEN
Seychelles	0.2$_{-1}$	17$_{-1}$	86$_{-1}$	91$_{-1}$	...	...	1$_{-1}$	14$_{-1}$	83$_{-1}$	98$_{-1}$	9$_{-1}$	...	1$_{-1}$	12$_{-1}$	89$_{-1}$	99$_{-1}$	3$_{-1}$	...	SYC
Sierra Leone	6	14	37	21	...	...	38	39	54$_{-2}$	52$_{-4}$	11	...	...	22$_{-1}$	70$_{-2}$	37$_{-1}$	...	...	SLE
Somalia	...	...	...	...	...	...	...	...	...	...	...	...	...	...	...	...	...	...	SOM
South Africa	...	30$_{-3i}$	...	...	...	...	249$_{-2}$	30$_{-2}$	...	...	...	...	192$_{-1}$	27$_{-1}$	100$_{-1}$	80$_{-2}$	...	...	ZAF
South Sudan	3$_{-2}$	35$_{-2}$	...	87$_{-2}$	...	...	27$_{-2i}$	47$_{-2i}$	...	84$_{-2i}$	...	...	6$_{-2i}$	27$_{-2i}$	...	64$_{-2i}$	...	...	SSD
Togo	5	29	63$_{-2}$	28$_{-2}$	...	...	38	40	73$_{-2}$	33$_{-2}$	14$_{-3}$	...	...	...	...	...	...	...	TGO
Uganda	28	22	60	40	...	...	207	43	80	20	...	...	64$_{-3}$	...	...	85$_{-3}$	...	...	UGA
United Republic of Tanzania	13	114	50$_{-1}$	52	...	...	198	47	99$_{-1}$	97	...	...	112	17	...	93	...	...	TZA
Zambia	...	...	...	...	...	...	64$_{-4i}$	48$_{-4i}$	...	66$_{-4i}$	...	...	...	...	...	...	...	...	ZMB
Zimbabwe	10$_{-4}$	37$_{-4}$	27$_{-4}$	25$_{-4}$	...	...	73$_{-4}$	36$_{-4}$	86$_{-4}$	74$_{-4}$	...	...	43$_{-4}$	22$_{-4}$	73$_{-4}$	49$_{-4}$	...	...	ZWE

TABLE 7: Continued

	Pre-primary						Primary						Secondary						
	A	B	C	D	E	F	A	B	C	D	E	F	A	B	C	D	E	F	
	Classroom teachers (000)	Pupil/teacher ratio	% of trained classroom teachers	% of qualified classroom teachers	Teacher attrition rate (%)	Relative teacher salary level	Classroom teachers (000)	Pupil/teacher ratio	% of trained classroom teachers	% of qualified classroom teachers	Teacher attrition rate (%)	Relative teacher salary level	Classroom teachers (000)	Pupil/teacher ratio	% of trained classroom teachers	% of qualified classroom teachers	Teacher attrition rate (%)	Relative teacher salary level	COUNTRY CODE
SDG indicator:			4.c.1	4.c.3	4.c.6	4.c.5			4.c.1	4.c.3	4.c.6	4.c.5			4.c.1	4.c.3	4.c.6	4.c.5	
Reference year:	2017						2017						2017						
Northern Africa and Western Asia																			
Algeria	…	…	…	…	…	…	177	24	100_{-2}	100	…	…	…	…	…	…	…	…	DZA
Armenia	8	8	82	…	…	…	…	…	…	…	…	…	…	…	…	…	…	…	ARM
Azerbaijan	12	15	88	94	…	…	39	15	98	100	…	…	127	7	…	100	…	…	AZE
Bahrain	2	14	52	63	…	…	9	12	84	96	…	…	10	10	85	97	…	…	BHR
Cyprus	2_{-1}	13_{-2}	…	…	…	…	5_{-1}	12_{-2}	…	…	…	…	7_{-1}	10_{-2}	…	…	…	…	CYP
Egypt	50	26	77_{-1}	100_{-1}	…	…	511	24	74_{-1}	100_{-1}	…	…	588	15	67_{-1}	100_{-1}	…	…	EGY
Georgia	…	…	…	…	…	…	33	9	…	…	…	…	37	7	…	…	…	…	GEO
Iraq	…	…	…	…	…	…	…	…	…	…	…	…	…	…	…	…	…	…	IRQ
Israel	…	…	…	…	…	0.84_{-1}	74_{-1}	12_{-1}	…	…	…	0.88_{-1}	…	…	…	…	…	…	ISR
Jordan	7	18	100	100	3	…	53	21	100	100	11	…	67	11	100	100	…	…	JOR
Kuwait	9	9	75_{-2}	74_{-2}	…	…	31	9	79_{-2}	77_{-2}	…	…	44	8_{-2}	…	…	…	…	KWT
Lebanon	15	16	…	…	…	…	40	12	…	…	…	…	51	8	…	…	…	…	LBN
Libya	…	…	…	…	…	…	…	…	…	…	…	…	…	…	…	…	…	…	LBY
Morocco	…	…	…	…	…	…	150	28	100	100	4	…	140	20	100	100	…	…	MAR
Oman	3	23	100	100	…	…	38	10	100	100	…	…	30	10	100	100	…	…	OMN
Palestine	9	17	100	-	6_{-1}	…	19	25	100	63	6	…	37	20	100	50	5	…	PSE
Qatar	3	14	…	100	10	…	12	12	…	100	7	…	10	10	…	100	6	…	QAT
Saudi Arabia	40_{-1}	11_{-1}	100_{-1}	100_{-1}	…	…	320_{-1}	12_{-1}	100_{-1}	100_{-1}	…	…	312_{-3}	11_{-3i}	100_{-3}	100_{-3}	…	…	SAU
Sudan	40_{-1}	25_{-1}	…	96_{-3}	…	…	…	…	…	…	…	…	…	…	…	…	…	…	SDN
Syrian Arab Republic	5_{-4}	16_{-4}	35_{-4}	47_{-4}	…	…	…	…	…	…	…	…	…	…	…	…	…	…	SYR
Tunisia	16_{-1}	15_{-1}	100_{-1}	100_{-2}	…	…	70_{-1}	16_{-1}	100_{-1}	97_{-2}	…	…	…	…	…	…	…	…	TUN
Turkey	68_{-2}	17_{-2}	…	…	…	0.80_{-1}	295_{-2}	18_{-2}	…	…	…	0.80_{-1}	594_{-2}	18_{-2}	…	…	…	0.80_{-1i}	TUR
United Arab Emirates	5_{-1}	29_{-1}	100_{-1}	100_{-1}	…	…	19_{-1}	25_{-1}	100_{-1}	100_{-1}	…	…	46_{-1}	10_{-1}	100_{-1}	100_{-1}	…	…	ARE
Yemen	1_{-1}	26_{-1}	…	54_{-1}	…	…	145_{-1}	27_{-1}	…	59_{-1}	…	…	…	…	…	…	…	…	YEM
Central and Southern Asia																			
Afghanistan	…	…	…	…	…	…	144	44	…	…	…	…	75	39	…	…	…	…	AFG
Bangladesh	…	…	…	…	…	…	574	30	50_{i}	100	5_{-1}	…	451	34	66	100	1	…	BGD
Bhutan	1	11	100	100	…	…	3	35	100	100	2	…	7	11	100	100	…	…	BTN
India	461_{-2}	20_{-2}	…	…	…	…	$4,140_{-1}$	35_{-1}	70_{-1}	88_{-1}	12_{-1}	…	$4,639_{-1}$	28_{-1}	…	…	…	…	IND
Iran, Islamic Republic of	…	…	…	…	…	…	286_{-2}	27_{-2}	100_{-2}	100_{-2}	…	…	336_{-2}	17_{-2}	100_{-2}	96_{-2}	…	…	IRN
Kazakhstan	…	9_{-3}	100_{-3}	100_{-3}	…	…	65	21	100	100	7	…	268	7	100	100	…	…	KAZ
Kyrgyzstan	…	…	…	…	…	…	20	25	95	74	…	…	63	10	85	…	…	…	KGZ
Maldives	1	16	88	81_{-2}	8	…	4	10	90	83_{-2}	0.4	…	…	…	…	…	…	…	MDV
Nepal	48	20	89	92	-	…	198	21	97	95	-	…	116_{i}	29_{i}	89_{i}	88_{i}	…	…	NPL
Pakistan	…	…	…	…	…	…	484	45	82_{-2}	…	…	…	646_{i}	19_{i}	…	…	…	…	PAK
Sri Lanka	…	…	…	…	…	…	76	23	85	86	1	…	150_{-1}	17_{-1}	…	83_{-1}	…	…	LKA
Tajikistan	8	11	100_{-1}	57	…	…	35	22	100	97	…	…	…	…	…	…	…	…	TJK
Turkmenistan	…	…	…	…	…	…	…	…	…	…	…	…	…	…	…	…	…	…	TKM
Uzbekistan	60	12	98	100	1_{-1}	…	113	21	99	100	2_{-1}	…	377	10	98	100	3_{-1}	…	UZB
Eastern and South-eastern Asia																			
Brunei Darussalam	1	16	59	100	9	…	4	10	85	100	4	…	5	9	90	91	7	…	BRN
Cambodia	7	34	100	100	…	…	51	42	100	100	…	…	…	…	…	…	…	…	KHM
China	2,444	18	…	90	…	…	6,046	17	…	96	1	…	6,267	13	…	93	2	…	CHN
DPR Korea	…	…	…	…	…	…	74_{+1}	20_{+1}	…	100_{+1}	…	…	124_{+1}	17_{-2}	…	100_{+1}	…	…	PRK
Hong Kong, China	…	…	…	…	…	…	26	14	97	100	2	…	31	12	97	100	3_{-1i}	…	HKG
Indonesia	464	13	…	60	…	…	1,827	16	…	83	7_{-3}	…	1,586	15	…	93	…	…	IDN
Japan	105_{-1}	27_{-1}	…	…	…	…	415_{-1}	16_{-1}	…	…	…	…	638_{-1}	11_{-1}	…	…	…	…	JPN
Lao PDR	11	18	90	42	1	…	36	22	97	90	2	…	37_{i}	18_{i}	96_{i}	81_{i}	…	…	LAO
Macao, China	1	15	99	100	…	…	2	14	98	100	1_{-2}	…	3	10	91	100	3	…	MAC
Malaysia	65	15	91	100	…	…	265	12	99	100	2	…	231	12	95	100	…	…	MYS
Mongolia	7	33	100	96	…	…	10	30	100_{-1}	99	2	…	22	…	98	98	6	…	MNG
Myanmar	9	19	98	100	…	…	234	23	98_{-1}	96	…	…	150	26	93	97	…	…	MMR
Philippines	63_{-1}	34_{-1}	100_{-1}	96_{-1}	19_{-1}	…	493_{-1}	29_{-1}	100_{-1}	100_{-1}	1_{-1}	…	314_{-1}	24_{-1}	100_{-1}	100_{-1}	2_{-2}	…	PHL
Republic of Korea	99_{-1}	13_{-1}	…	…	…	…	164_{-1}	16_{-1}	…	…	…	…	233_{-1}	14_{-1}	…	…	…	…	KOR
Singapore	…	…	…	…	…	…	16_{-1}	15_{-1}	99_{-1i}	100_{-1}	…	…	15_{-1}	12_{-1}	99_{-1i}	100_{-1}	…	…	SGP
Thailand	…	…	…	…	…	…	305	16	100	100	…	…	262	24	100	100	…	…	THA
Timor-Leste	1	33	…	…	…	…	…	…	…	…	…	…	…	…	…	…	…	…	TLS
Viet Nam	251	18	99	99	…	…	397	20	100	100	…	…	…	…	…	…	…	…	VNM

TABLE 7: Continued

	Pre-primary						Primary						Secondary						
	A	B	C	D	E	F	A	B	C	D	E	F	A	B	C	D	E	F	
	Classroom teachers (000)	Pupil/teacher ratio	% of trained classroom teachers	% of qualified classroom teachers	Teacher attrition rate (%)	Relative teacher salary level	Classroom teachers (000)	Pupil/teacher ratio	% of trained classroom teachers	% of qualified classroom teachers	Teacher attrition rate (%)	Relative teacher salary level	Classroom teachers (000)	Pupil/teacher ratio	% of trained classroom teachers	% of qualified classroom teachers	Teacher attrition rate (%)	Relative teacher salary level	COUNTRY CODE
SDG indicator:			4.c.1	4.c.3	4.c.6	4.c.5			4.c.1	4.c.3	4.c.6	4.c.5			4.c.1	4.c.3	4.c.6	4.c.5	
Reference year:	2017						2017						2017						
Oceania																			
Australia	...	...	...	...	...	0.92$_{-1}$	...	...	...	...	...	0.93$_{-1}$	...	...	...	...	...	...	AUS
Cook Islands	-$_{-1}$	16$_{-1}$	78$_{-1}$	84$_{-2}$	...	...	0.1$_{-1}$	17$_{-1}$	95$_{-1}$	100$_{-2}$	...	...	0.1$_{-1}$	16$_{-1}$	98$_{-2}$	98$_{-2}$	...	...	COK
Fiji	...	...	...	...	...	...	6$_{-1}$	20$_{-1}$	90$_{-1}$	100$_{-1}$	...	...	...	...	...	...	...	...	FJI
Kiribati	...	...	...	...	...	...	1	25	73$_{-1}$	100	...	...	...	...	...	...	...	...	KIR
Marshall Islands	...	...	...	...	...	...	...	...	...	...	...	...	...	...	...	...	...	...	MHL
Micronesia, F. S.	...	...	...	...	...	...	1$_{-2i}$	20$_{-2i}$	...	...	...	...	...	...	...	...	...	...	FSM
Nauru	-$_{-1}$	22$_{-1}$	100$_{-1}$	100$_{-1}$	...	...	-$_{-1}$	40$_{-1}$	100$_{-1}$	100$_{-1}$	...	...	-$_{-1}$	25$_{-1}$	...	89$_{-3}$	...	...	NRU
New Zealand	14$_{-2}$	8$_{-2}$	...	...	...	...	26$_{-1}$	15$_{-1}$	...	...	...	0.85$_{-1}$	35$_{-1}$	14$_{-1}$	...	...	...	0.90$_{-1i}$	NZL
Niue	-$_{-1}$	6$_{-1}$	100$_{-1}$	100$_{-1}$	-$_{-1}$	...	-$_{-1}$	15$_{-1}$	92$_{-1}$	100$_{-1}$	...		-$_{-1}$	0$_{-1}$	100$_{-1}$	100$_{-1}$	...	...	NIU
Palau	-$_{-3}$	18$_{-3}$	...	100$_{-3}$	...	...	...	...	...	...	...	...	...	...	...	...	...	...	PLW
Papua New Guinea	9$_{-1}$	42$_{-1}$	...	...	...	...	36$_{-1}$	36$_{-1}$	...	...	...	...	15$_{-1}$	34$_{-1}$	...	...	...	...	PNG
Samoa	0.4	13	100	100$_{-1}$	...	...	...	...	...	...	...	...	1$_{-1}$	28$_{-1}$	...	...	...	...	WSM
Solomon Is	2	26	59$_{-3}$	26	...	...	4	26	74	78	2	...	2$_{-2}$	...	76$_{-2}$	84$_{-2}$	...	...	SLB
Tokelau	-$_{-1}$	4$_{-1}$	42$_{-1}$	...	...	...	-$_{-1}$	12$_{-1}$	67$_{-1}$	...	...	...	...	...	...	...	...	...	TKL
Tonga	0.2$_{-2}$	11$_{-2}$	...	...	...	...	1$_{-2}$	22$_{-2}$	92$_{-2}$	92$_{-2}$	...	...	1$_{-2}$	15$_{-2}$	59$_{-2}$	80$_{-2}$	...	...	TON
Tuvalu	0.1$_{-1}$	11$_{-1}$	88$_{-1}$	100$_{-3}$	...	...	0.1$_{-1}$	17$_{-1}$	77$_{-1}$	62$_{-2}$	...	...	0.1$_{-1}$	8$_{-1}$	46$_{-1}$	60$_{-2}$	...	...	TUV
Vanuatu	1$_{-2}$	16$_{-2}$	46$_{-2}$	52$_{-2}$	...		2$_{-2}$	27$_{-2}$	...	72$_{-2}$	...	...	1$_{-2}$	21$_{-2}$	...	79$_{-2}$	...	...	VUT
Latin America and the Caribbean																			
Anguilla	...	...	...	...	...	...	...	...	...	...	...	...	...	...	...	...	...	...	AIA
Antigua and Barbuda	0.4$_{-2}$	8$_{-2}$	65$_{-2}$	100$_{-2}$	...	...	1$_{-2}$	14$_{-2}$	65$_{-2}$	100$_{-2}$	...	...	1$_{-2}$	11$_{-2}$	73$_{-2}$	94$_{-2}$	...	...	ATG
Argentina	...	...	...	...	...	...	...	...	...	...	...	...	...	...	...	...	...	...	ARG
Aruba	...	...	...	...	...	...	...	...	...	...	...	...	...	...	...	...	...	...	ABW
Bahamas	0.2$_{-1}$	23$_{-1}$	76$_{-1}$	100$_{-1}$	...	...	2$_{-1}$	19$_{-1}$	90$_{-1}$	100$_{-1}$	...	...	2$_{-1}$	12$_{-1}$	85$_{-1}$	98$_{-1}$	...	...	BHS
Barbados	0.3	16	73	100	...	...	1	14	80	100	...	...	1	18	47	100	...	...	BRB
Belize	0.5	16	45$_{-1}$	55$_{-1}$	...	...	3	20	73$_{-1}$	...	...	...	2	17	54$_{-1}$	46$_{-1}$	...	...	BLZ
Bolivia, P. S.	11	33	92	...	...	...	73	19	58	...	...	...	60	21	57	...	...	...	BOL
Brazil	304$_{-1}$	17$_{-1}$	...	...	...	...	793$_{-1}$	20$_{-1}$	...	...	...	...	1,418$_{-1}$	17$_{-1}$	...	...	...	...	BRA
British Virgin Islands	...	8$_{-1}$	...	...	...	...	0.3	12	92	92	...	...	0.3	9	86	86	...	...	VGB
Cayman Islands	...	...	...	...	...	...	0.3$_{+1}$	16$_{+1}$	100$_{+1}$	100$_{+1}$	...	...	0.3$_{+1}$	11$_{+1}$	100$_{+1}$	100$_{+1}$	...	...	CYM
Chile	23$_{-2}$	27$_{-2}$	...	...	...	0.84$_{-2}$	80$_{-2}$	18$_{-2}$	...	...	...	0.80$_{-2}$	80$_{-2}$	19$_{-2}$	...	...	...	0.86$_{-2i}$	CHL
Colombia	51$_{-3}$	...	97$_{-3}$	94$_{-3}$	...	...	184	24	95	100	...	...	184	26	98	100	...	...	COL
Costa Rica	9$_{-1}$	12$_{-1}$	89$_{-1}$	97$_{-1}$	2$_{-1}$	...	40$_{-1}$	12$_{-1}$	94$_{-1}$	97$_{-1}$	1$_{-1}$	...	36$_{-1}$	13$_{-1}$	96$_{-1}$	99$_{-1}$	...	...	CRI
Cuba	...	...	...	...	...	...	83	9	100	76	...	...	86	9	100	77	...	...	CUB
Curaçao	...	...	...	...	...	...	...	...	...	...	...	...	...	...	...	...	...	...	CUW
Dominica	0.1$_{-1}$	11$_{-1}$	19$_{-1}$	39$_{-1}$	...	...	1$_{-1}$	13$_{-1}$	66$_{-1}$	100$_{-1}$	...	...	1$_{-1}$	11$_{-2}$	49$_{-1}$	57$_{-1}$			DMA
Dominican Republic	15$_{-1}$	14$_{-1}$	...	82$_{-1}$	...	...	69$_{-1}$	19$_{-1}$	[illegible]	87$_{-1}$	...	...	42$_{-2}$	22$_{-2}$	...	83$_{-2}$	...	...	DOM
Ecuador	32	21	83	...	12	...	78	25	82	...	13	...	88	22	74	...	11		ECU
El Salvador	8	27	94	100	7$_{-1}$	...	24	28	95	100	9	...	19	28	93	100	7	...	SLV
Grenada	0.3	12	37	36$_{-1}$	2	...	1	16	64	100	5	...	1	12	45	100	5$_{-1}$	...	GRD
Guatemala	...	...	...	...	...	...	108$_{-1}$	22$_{-1}$	...	...	...	...	98$_{-1}$	12$_{-1}$	...	...	...	...	GTM
Guyana	...	...	...	...	...	...	...	...	...	...	...	...	...	...	...	...	...	...	GUY
Haiti	...	...	...	...	...	...	...	...	...	...	...	...	...	...	...	...	...	...	HTI
Honduras	12$_{-1}$	19$_{-1}$	51$_{-4}$	51$_{-4}$	...	...	44	26	...	...	4$_{-1}$	...	39	17	...	...	...	...	HND
Jamaica	...	11$_{-1}$	75$_{-2}$	94$_{-1}$	...	...	11	22	96$_{-1}$	100$_{-1}$	3	...	13	15	100	100	16$_{-1}$	...	JAM
Mexico	193$_{-1}$	25$_{-1}$	85$_{-1}$	...	...	...	535$_{-1}$	27$_{-1}$	97$_{-1}$	...	...	...	842$_{-1}$	16$_{-1}$	87$_{-1}$	...	...	...	MEX
Montserrat	-	8	82	...	-	...	-	15	77$_{-1}$	43	-	...	-	9	72	100	9	...	MSR
Nicaragua	...	...	...	...	...	...	...	...	...	...	...	...	...	...	...	...	...	...	NIC
Panama	6$_{-1}$	15$_{-1}$	100$_{-1}$	100$_{-1}$	...	...	19$_{-1}$	21$_{-1}$	99$_{-1}$	90$_{-1}$	...	...	24$_{-1}$	15$_{-1}$	60$_{-1}$	84$_{-1}$	...	...	PAN
Paraguay	...	...	...	...	...	...	...	...	...	...	...	...	...	...	...	...	...	...	PRY
Peru	84	19	...	...	...	...	198	18	97	87	18$_{-2}$	...	190	15	89$_{-1i}$	80	20$_{-2}$	...	PER
Saint Kitts and Nevis	...	11$_{-2}$	...	100$_{-2}$	...	...	0.4$_{-1}$	14$_{-1}$	72$_{-1}$	99$_{-1}$	14$_{-2}$	...	1$_{-1}$	8$_{-1}$	62$_{-1}$	100$_{-1}$	5$_{-2}$	...	KNA
Saint Lucia	...	6$_{-1}$	70$_{-3}$	...	...	...	1	15	89	100	...	...	1	11	71	100	...	...	LCA
Saint Vincent/Grenadines	0.5	8	14$_{-4}$	...	...	...	1	14	84$_{-2}$	22	...	...	1	14	58$_{-2}$	51	...	...	VCT
Sint Maarten	...	...	...	...	...	...	...	...	...	...	...	...	0.4$_{-3}$	8$_{-3}$	...	93$_{-3}$	...	...	SXM
Suriname	1	29	99	...	...	...	5	15	98	...	...	...	3	12$_{-2}$	81$_{-1}$	57	...	...	SUR
Trinidad and Tobago	...	...	...	...	...	...	...	...	...	...	...	...	...	...	...	...	...	...	TTO
Turks and Caicos Islands	...	...	...	...	...	...	0.3$_{-3}$	9$_{-3}$	89$_{-3}$	...	...	...	0.2$_{-2}$	10$_{-2}$	98$_{-2}$	98$_{-2}$	...	...	TCA
Uruguay	...	...	...	...	...	...	28$_{-1}$	11$_{-1}$	100$_{-1}$	100$_{-1}$	...	...	...	...	...	...	...	...	URY
Venezuela, B. R.	...	...	...	...	...	...	...	...	...	...	...	...	...	...	...	...	...	...	VEN

TABLE 7: Continued

	Pre-primary						Primary						Secondary						
	A	B	C	D	E	F	A	B	C	D	E	F	A	B	C	D	E	F	
	Classroom teachers (000)	Pupil/teacher ratio	% of trained classroom teachers	% of qualified classroom teachers	Teacher attrition rate (%)	Relative teacher salary level	Classroom teachers (000)	Pupil/teacher ratio	% of trained classroom teachers	% of qualified classroom teachers	Teacher attrition rate (%)	Relative teacher salary level	Classroom teachers (000)	Pupil/teacher ratio	% of trained classroom teachers	% of qualified classroom teachers	Teacher attrition rate (%)	Relative teacher salary level	COUNTRY CODE
SDG indicator:			4.c.1	4.c.3	4.c.6	4.c.5			4.c.1	4.c.3	4.c.6	4.c.5			4.c.1	4.c.3	4.c.6	4.c.5	
Reference year:	2017						2017						2017						
Europe and Northern America																			
Albania	5	17	...	84	...	...	10	18	...	84	...	...	24	12	...	97	...	...	ALB
Andorra	0.2	14	100	100	6	...	0.4	10	100	100	7	...	1	8	100	100	8	...	AND
Austria	23_{-1}	11_{-1}	...	...	...	...	32_{-1}	10_{-1}	...	...	...	0.76_{-1}	73_{-1}	9_{-1}	...	...	...	0.93_{-1i}	AUT
Belarus	44	8	92	44	2	...	22	19	100	100	4	...	79	8	94	100	...	...	BLR
Belgium	36_{-1}	13_{-1}	...	...	...	...	71_{-1}	11_{-1}	...	...	...	...	131_{-1}	9_{-1}	...	...	...	...	BEL
Bermuda	0.1_{-1}	9_{-3}	100_{-1}	100_{-1}	...	...	0.4_{-1}	10_{-2}	100_{-1}	100_{-1}	...	...	1_{-1}	6_{-2}	100_{-1}	99_{-1}	...	...	BMU
Bosnia and Herzegovina	1	14	...	...	...	...	9	17	...	...	...	...	27	9	...	...	...	...	BIH
Bulgaria	19_{-1}	12_{-1}	...	...	...	...	15_{-1}	18_{-1}	...	...	...	...	39_{-1}	13_{-1}	...	...	...	...	BGR
Canada	...	...	...	...	...	...	...	...	...	...	...	...	...	...	...	...	...	...	CAN
Croatia	9_{-1}	13_{-1}	...	...	...	...	12_{-1}	14_{-1}	...	...	...	...	52_{-1}	7_{-1}	...	...	...	...	HRV
Czechia	...	14_{-4}	...	...	...	0.52_{-2}	...	19_{-4}	...	...	...	0.61_{-2}	...	12_{-4}	...	...	...	...	CZE
Denmark	...	...	...	...	...	0.68_{-1}	44_{-3}	11_{-3}	...	...	...	0.82_{-1}	49_{-3}	11_{-3}	...	...	...	...	DNK
Estonia	...	...	...	...	...	0.62_{-1}	7_{-1}	11_{-1}	...	...	...	0.91_{-1}	9_{-1}	9_{-1}	...	...	...	0.91_{-1i}	EST
Finland	18_{-1}	12_{-1}	...	...	...	0.66_{-2}	27_{-1}	13_{-1}	...	...	...	0.89_{-2}	41_{-1}	13_{-1}	...	...	...	1.05_{-2i}	FIN
France	126_{-4}	20_{-4}	...	...	...	0.78_{-3}	229_{-4}	18_{-4}	...	...	...	0.76_{-3}	457_{-4}	13_{-4}	...	...	...	0.94_{-3i}	FRA
Germany	316_{-1}	7_{-1}	...	...	...	...	238_{-1}	12_{-1}	...	...	...	0.90_{-1}	589_{-1}	12_{-1}	...	...	...	1.01_{-1i}	DEU
Greece	15_{-1}	11_{-1}	...	...	...	1.06_{-1}	70_{-1}	9_{-1}	...	...	...	1.06_{-1}	79_{-1}	8_{-1}	...	...	...	1.15_{-1i}	GRC
Hungary	26_{-1}	12_{-1}	...	...	...	0.66_{-1}	37_{-1}	11_{-1}	...	...	...	0.70_{-1}	81_{-1}	10_{-1}	...	...	...	0.72_{-1i}	HUN
Iceland	3_{-2}	5_{-2}	...	...	...	...	3_{-2}	10_{-2}	...	...	...	...	...	...	...	...	...	...	ISL
Ireland	...	...	...	...	...	...	...	...	...	...	...	...	...	...	...	...	...	...	IRL
Italy	133_{-1}	12_{-1}	...	...	...	0.68_{-3}	255_{-1}	11_{-1}	...	...	...	0.68_{-3}	457_{-1}	10_{-1}	...	...	...	0.71_{-3i}	ITA
Latvia	8_{-1}	10_{-1}	...	...	...	0.79_{-1}	11_{-1}	11_{-1}	...	...	...	0.80_{-1}	14_{-1}	8_{-1}	...	...	...	1.04_{-1i}	LVA
Liechtenstein	0.1_{-1}	8_{-1}	...	...	...	...	0.3_{-1}	8_{-1}	...	...	...	...	0.3_{-1}	10_{-1}	...	...	...	...	LIE
Lithuania	11_{-1}	9_{-1}	...	...	...	0.95_{-3}	8_{-1}	13_{-1}	...	...	...	0.95_{-3}	33_{-1}	8_{-1}	...	...	...	0.95_{-3i}	LTU
Luxembourg	2_{-1}	10_{-1}	...	...	...	1.80_{-1}	4_{-1}	8_{-1}	...	...	...	1.80_{-1}	5_{-1}	9_{-1}	...	...	...	2.02_{-1i}	LUX
Malta	1_{-1}	12_{-1}	...	...	...	...	2_{-1}	13_{-1}	...	...	...	...	4_{-1}	7_{-1}	...	...	...	...	MLT
Monaco	0.1	19	...	...	7	...	0.2	10	...	...	...	...	0.4_{i}	9_{i}	...	...	...	...	MCO
Montenegro	...	...	...	...	...	...	...	...	...	...	...	...	...	...	...	...	...	...	MNE
Netherlands	32_{-1}	16_{-1}	...	...	...	0.73_{-3}	102_{-1}	12_{-1}	...	...	...	0.73_{-3}	112_{-1}	14_{-1}	...	...	...	...	NLD
Norway	18_{-1}	10_{-1}	...	...	...	0.67_{-1}	49_{-1}	9_{-1}	...	...	...	0.75_{-1}	51_{-1}	9_{-1}	...	...	...	...	NOR
Poland	92_{-1}	12_{-1}	...	...	...	0.68_{-1}	229_{-1}	11_{-1}	...	...	...	0.79_{-1}	268_{-1}	9_{-1}	...	...	...	0.81_{-1i}	POL
Portugal	15_{-1}	17_{-1}	...	...	...	1.50_{-1}	50_{-1}	13_{-1}	...	...	...	1.38_{-1}	79_{-1}	10_{-1}	...	...	...	1.41_{-1i}	PRT
Republic of Moldova	10	13	90	...	...	...	8	18	99	...	...	...	23	10	98	...	...	...	MDA
Romania	35_{-1}	15_{-1}	...	...	...	...	49_{-1}	19_{-1}	...	...	...	...	125_{-1}	12_{-1}	...	...	...	...	ROU
Russian Federation	...	...	...	...	...	...	301_{-1}	21_{-1}	...	...	...	...	...	...	...	...	...	...	RUS
San Marino	...	...	...	...	...	...	...	...	...	...	...	...	...	...	...	...	...	...	SMR
Serbia	14	12	...	100	...	...	19	14	...	100	...	...	67	8	...	100	...	...	SRB
Slovakia	13_{-2}	12_{-2}	...	...	...	0.48_{-1}	14_{-2}	15_{-2}	...	...	...	0.64_{-1}	41_{-2}	11_{-2}	...	...	...	0.64_{-1i}	SVK
Slovenia	7_{-1}	9_{-1}	...	...	...	0.69_{-1}	9_{-1}	14_{-1}	...	...	...	0.87_{-1}	15_{-1}	10_{-1}	...	...	...	0.91_{-1i}	SVN
Spain	100_{-1}	14_{-1}	...	...	...	...	233_{-1}	13_{-1}	...	...	...	...	287_{-1}	12_{-1}	...	...	...	...	ESP
Sweden	81_{-1}	6_{-1}	...	...	...	0.76_{-1}	67_{-1}	12_{-1}	...	...	...	0.86_{-1}	66_{-1}	13_{-1}	...	...	...	0.90_{-1i}	SWE
Switzerland	15_{-1}	12_{-1}	...	...	...	...	49_{-1}	10_{-1}	...	...	...	...	62_{-1}	10_{-1}	...	...	...	...	CHE
TFYR Macedonia	...	...	...	...	...	...	8_{-2}	14_{-2}	...	...	...	...	18_{-2}	9_{-2}	...	...	...	...	MKD
Ukraine	...	...	...	...	...	...	127	13	87	84_{-4}	...	...	324	7	...	...	...	...	UKR
United Kingdom	25_{-1}	13_{-1}	...	...	...	...	314_{-1}	15_{-1}	...	...	...	...	393_{-1}	19_{-1}	...	...	...	...	GBR
United States	629_{-2}	14_{-2}	...	...	...	0.62_{-1}	$1,714_{-2}$	14_{-2}	...	...	...	0.63_{-1}	$1,661_{-2}$	15_{-2}	...	...	...	0.67_{-1i}	USA

Naika, 7 years old, takes part in the Healing and Education Through the Arts (HEART) programme in Haiti, which provides psychosocial support to children who survived Hurricane Matthew. The school where the programme is run was rebuilt by Save the Children.

CREDIT: Ray-ginald Louissaint Jr./Save the Children

Aid tables

INTRODUCTION

Two types of aid are presented in the following three tables.

First, data on **official development assistance** (ODA) are derived from the International Development Statistics (IDS) database of the Organisation for Economic Co-operation and Development (OECD). The IDS database records information provided annually by all members of the OECD Development Assistance Committee (DAC), as well as a growing number of non-DAC donors. Figures for net ODA come from the DAC database, while those for gross ODA and aid to education come from the Creditor Reporting System (CRS), a database of individual projects. Figures in the DAC and CRS databases are expressed in constant 2016 US dollars. The DAC and CRS databases are available at www.oecd.org/dac/stats/idsonline.htm.

ODA includes grants and loans that (a) are undertaken by the official sector, (b) have promotion of economic development and welfare as their main objective and (c) are at concessional financial terms (if a loan, having a grant element of at least 25%). In addition to financial flows, technical cooperation is included in aid; see www.oecd.org/dac/financing-sustainable-development/development-finance-data/dac-glossary.htm#ODA.

Second, data on **humanitarian assistance** come from the Financial Tracking Service (FTS) of the UN Office for the Coordination of Humanitarian Affairs (OCHA). The FTS aims to present a complete picture of all international humanitarian funding flows and collects financial contributions from government donors, UN-administered funds, UN agencies, non-government organizations (NGOs) and other humanitarian actors and partners, including in the private sector. The database is continuously updated to monitor whether the requirements of humanitarian response plans are fulfilled. Figures in the FTS database are expressed in current US dollars. The FTS is available at fts.unocha.org.

AID RECIPIENTS AND DONORS

The DAC list of *ODA recipients* consists of all low and middle income countries, based on the World Bank income classification, other than members of the G8 or European Union (EU). For further information, see www.oecd.org/development/financing-sustainable-development/development-finance-standards/historyofdaclistsofaidrecipientcountries.htm.

Bilateral donors are countries that provide development assistance directly to recipient countries. Most are DAC members. Bilateral donors also contribute substantially to the financing of multilateral donors through contributions recorded as multilateral ODA.

Multilateral donors are international institutions with government membership that conduct many or all of their activities supporting development and aid recipient countries. They include multilateral development banks (e.g. World Bank, regional development banks), UN agencies and regional groupings (e.g. certain EU and Arab agencies). When a bilateral donor contracts a multilateral donor to deliver a programme, this is recorded as a bilateral flow. A contribution by a DAC member to an agency is deemed a multilateral flow if it is pooled with other contributions and disbursed at the discretion of the agency to fund its own programmes and running costs.

For a list of bilateral and multilateral donors, see the 'Donors' worksheet at www.oecd.org/dac/financing-sustainable-development/development-finance-standards/DAC-CRS-CODES.xls.

TABLE 1: DEVELOPMENT AND HUMANITARIAN ASSISTANCE

Total ODA: Includes bilateral and multilateral aid for all sectors, as well as aid that is not allocated by sector, such as general budget support and debt relief.

Total ODA from bilateral donors is bilateral aid only, while aid as a percentage of gross national income (GNI) is bilateral and multilateral ODA.

Total humanitarian assistance: Everything reported to the FTS by public and private donors, UN agencies, UN funds, NGOs and others.

UN-coordinated appeals: A subset of international humanitarian assistance, which refers to all humanitarian response plans and appeals coordinated by OCHA or the office of the UN High Commissioner for Refugees, including strategic response plans, humanitarian response plans, flash appeals and regional refugee response plans. For definitions, see Chapter 5 of the *Global Humanitarian Assistance Report 2018*, devinit.org/wp-content/uploads/2018/06/GHA-Report-2018.pdf.

TABLES 2 AND 3: DEVELOPMENT ASSISTANCE TO EDUCATION BY DONOR AND BY RECIPIENT

Total aid to education: Direct aid to education plus 20% of general budget support (aid provided to governments without being earmarked for specific projects or sectors) to represent the estimated 15% to 25% of budget support that typically benefits the education sector.

Total aid to basic education: Direct aid to basic education plus 10% of general budget support, plus 50% of 'education, level unspecified'.

Total aid to secondary education: Direct aid to secondary education plus 5% of general budget support, plus 25% of 'education, level unspecified'.

Total aid to post-secondary education: Direct aid to post-secondary education plus 5% of general budget support, plus 25% of 'education, level unspecified'.

Direct aid to education: Aid to education reported in the CRS database as direct allocations to the education sector. It is the total of direct aid, as defined by DAC, to:

- Basic education, defined by DAC as covering primary education, basic life skills for youth and adults, and early childhood education
- Secondary education, both general secondary education and vocational training
- Post-secondary education, including advanced technical and managerial training
- Education, level unspecified, which refers to any activity that cannot be attributed solely to the development of a particular level of education, such as education research and teacher training. General education programme support is often reported within this subcategory.

Total aid per capita: It is calculated dividing the total aid (i) to basic education by the number of primary school age children and (ii) to secondary education by the number of secondary school age adolescents.

TABLE 1: Development and humanitarian assistance

	OFFICIAL DEVELOPMENT ASSISTANCE (ODA)								HUMANITARIAN ASSISTANCE	
	Total ODA net disbursements								US$ millions	
	Constant 2016 US$ millions				% of gross national income (GNI)				Total humanitarian assistance	UN-coordinated appeals
	2005	2015	2016	2017*	2005	2015	2016	2017*	2017**	2017**
Australia	1,855	2,758	2,290	2,209	0.25	0.29	0.27	0.23	252	112
Austria	1,333	789	986	564	0.52	0.35	0.42	0.30	47	19
Belgium	1,381	1,126	1,425	1,223	0.53	0.42	0.50	0.45	189	104
Canada	3,099	2,884	2,661	2,960	0.34	0.28	0.26	0.26	634	401
Czechia	73	71	71	75	0.11	0.12	0.14	0.13	7	4
Denmark	1,444	1,878	1,654	1,613	0.81	0.85	0.75	0.72	419	187
Estonia***	3	15	19	19	0.08	0.15	0.19	0.17	5	2
Finland	658	702	638	505	0.46	0.55	0.44	0.41	98	40
France	7,343	5,161	5,642	6,362	0.47	0.37	0.38	0.43	234	117
Germany	7,694	14,257	19,636	18,783	0.36	0.52	0.70	0.66	2,649	1,814
Greece	200	71	159	86	0.17	0.12	0.19	0.16	0	0
Hungary***	40	47	55	37	0.11	0.13	0.17	0.11	1	1
Iceland	19	35	48	52	0.18	0.24	0.28	0.29	4	2
Ireland	448	426	427	449	0.42	0.32	0.32	0.30	130	61
Italy	2,360	1,838	2,420	2,825	0.29	0.22	0.27	0.29	190	65
Japan	10,111	6,876	7,048	8,354	0.28	0.20	0.20	0.23	672	447
Kazakhstan***	...	34	13	...	...	0.02	0.02	...	0	...
Kuwait***	233	303	1,048	...	...	...	...	...	0	55
Lithuania***	2	10	14	13	0.06	0.12	0.14	0.13	0	0
Luxembourg	219	258	275	298	0.79	0.95	1.00	1.00	28	14
Netherlands	3,720	4,175	3,158	3,438	0.82	0.75	0.65	0.60	272	91
New Zealand	281	364	361	342	0.27	0.27	0.25	0.23	24	3
Norway	2,122	3,139	3,451	2,988	0.94	1.05	1.12	0.99	506	310
Poland	49	96	149	204	0.07	0.10	0.15	0.13	21	14
Portugal	226	140	125	109	0.21	0.16	0.17	0.18	0	...
Republic of Korea	499	1,458	1,548	1,541	0.10	0.14	0.16	0.14	62	49
Romania***	...	33	109	...	...	0.09	0.15	...	0	0
Slovakia	39	17	26	29	...	0.10	0.12	0.12	1	1
Slovenia	15	25	28	24	0.11	0.15	0.19	0.16	1	0
Spain	1,848	354	2,597	791	0.27	0.12	0.35	0.19	55	22
Sweden	2,403	4,832	3,452	3,673	0.94	1.40	0.94	1.01	565	303
Switzerland	1,878	2,649	2,773	2,279	0.42	0.51	0.53	0.46	452	129
United Arab Emirates***	545	4,334	4,171	4,364	...	1.18	1.21	1.31	291	2
United Kingdom	7,477	10,557	11,517	11,502	0.47	0.70	0.70	0.70	1,850	1,326
United States	30,985	26,994	28,535	29,757	0.23	0.17	0.19	0.18	6,515	4,868
TOTAL bilaterals****	**92,809**	**110,543**	**116,192**	**117,304**	**0.32**	**0.30**	**0.32**	**0.31**	**17,041**	**10,866**
African Development Bank	178	123	160						84	3
African Development Fund	913	2,050	2,029						...	...
Arab Fund for Economic and Social Development	...	54	48						...	...
Asian Development Bank Special Funds	920	1,440	1,375						...	...
EU Institutions	8,922	13,610	16,832						3,069	1,914
Arab Bank for Economic Development in Africa (BADEA)	58	71	...						...	
Climate Investment Funds	...	409	51						...	...
World Bank (International Development Association)	7,292	10,011	8,105						174	102
Inter-American Development Bank Special Fund	248	1,897	746						...	...
International Monetary Fund (Concessional Trust Funds)	202	301	129						...	...
OPEC Fund for International Development	63	169	236						2	1
UN Development Programme	427	419	377						1	1
UNICEF	761	1,389	1,440						111	85
UN Peacebuilding Fund	...	70	47						...	1
UN Relief and Works Agency for Palestine Refugees	375	768	717						...	14
World Food Programme	594	285	306						...	1
Global Fund	1,078	3,159	3,547						9	7
GAVI	...	1,718	1,339						...	...
Global Environment Facility	509	810	851						...	...
World Health Organization	...	661	534						...	...
TOTAL multilaterals****	**23,869**	**41,766**	**40,819**						**3,638**	**2,725**
TOTAL	**116,678**	**152,228**	**157,011**						**21,475**	**14,220**

Sources: OECD-DAC, DAC and CRS databases (2018) for total ODA and ODA as % of GNI; UN Office for the Coordination of Humanitarian Affairs Financial Tracking Service (FTS) (2018) for international humanitarian assistance and UN-coordinated appeals.

* Preliminary data
** FTS data are based on the US dollar exchange rate at the time of the donor country decision.
*** Estonia, Hungary, Kazakhstan, Kuwait, Lithuania, Romania and the United Arab Emirates are not members of the Development Assistance Committee (DAC) but are included in its Creditor Reporting System (CRS) database.
**** Total ODA includes ODA from other bilaterals and multilaterals not listed above. Total humanitarian assistance includes humanitarian assistance from other bilaterals, multilaterals and private foundations not listed above.
(...) indicates that data are not available.
Total ODA from DAC donors is bilateral ODA only (from both DAC and non-DAC members) while ODA as % of GNI includes multilateral ODA.
ODA as a share of GNI among bilateral donors refers to DAC members only.

TABLE 2: Development assistance to education by donor

	TOTAL AID Constant 2016 US$ millions								DIRECT AID Constant 2016 US$ millions							
	Education		Basic education		Secondary education		Post-secondary education		Education		Basic education		Secondary education		Post-secondary education	
	2005	2016	2005	2016	2005	2016	2005	2016	2005	2016	2005	2016	2005	2016	2005	2016
Australia	108	218	61	139	25	30	22	48	107	217	40	93	14	7	12	25
Austria	101	144	4	9	4	9	93	127	101	144	2	0	3	4	92	122
Belgium	103	86	24	25	15	40	65	21	102	86	15	15	11	35	60	16
Canada	182	209	128	116	29	50	25	43	172	207	101	73	16	29	12	21
Czechia	...	8	...	1	...	1	...	6	...	8	...	0	...	1	...	5
Denmark	50	58	32	34	9	9	10	15	40	56	16	17	1	0	2	6
Estonia*	...	2	...	0	...	0	...	1	...	2	...	...	...	0	...	1
Finland	...	46	...	33	...	8	...	5	...	46	...	27	...	5	...	2
France	1,183	1,168	70	98	22	217	1,091	852	1,171	1,133	45	50	10	193	1,078	828
Germany	1,277	1,987	101	344	134	326	1,042	1,316	1,265	1,986	73	205	119	257	1,028	1,247
Greece	37	1	6	1	3	0	28	0	37	1	0	...	0	...	26	0
Hungary*	...	24	...	0	...	0	...	24	...	24	...	...	...	...	...	24
Iceland	...	1	...	1	...	0	...	0	...	1	...	1	...	...	...	...
Ireland	58	34	36	15	11	9	11	9	54	34	20	7	3	5	4	5
Italy	73	98	31	41	16	21	26	35	68	98	1	24	1	13	12	26
Japan	832	710	195	233	102	127	535	351	795	559	109	59	59	40	492	264
Kazakhstan*	...	...	...	...	...	...	...	...	...	...	...	...	...	...	...	...
Kuwait*	...	44	...	22	...	11	...	11	...	44	...	...	...	...	...	...
Lithuania*	...	2	...	0	...	0	...	1	...	2	...	...	...	0	...	1
Luxembourg	34	51	15	13	13	36	6	2	34	51	3	12	7	35	0	1
Netherlands	339	110	198	15	34	20	107	75	306	110	139	13	4	19	77	74
New Zealand	49	72	19	18	6	7	24	47	42	67	15	14	4	5	22	45
Norway	217	384	141	298	26	29	50	57	200	379	104	261	8	10	31	39
Poland	...	38	...	5	...	2	...	31	...	38	...	1	...	0	...	29
Portugal	68	48	11	11	9	10	48	26	66	48	4	0	6	5	44	21
Republic of Korea	...	241	...	56	...	81	...	104	...	241	...	32	...	69	...	92
Romania*	...	28	...	2	...	2	...	24	...	28	...	0	...	1	...	23
Slovakia	...	5	...	1	...	1	...	2	...	5	...	0	...	1	...	2
Slovenia	...	7	...	0	...	0	...	7	...	7	...	...	...	0	...	7
Spain	216	50	82	21	55	17	79	13	214	50	56	8	41	11	66	6
Sweden	142	120	69	67	27	14	46	39	121	120	22	43	3	2	23	28
Switzerland	59	123	17	50	22	57	20	16	59	119	5	41	16	53	14	11
United Arab Emirates*	...	641	...	298	...	154	...	190	...	152	...	11	...	10	...	46
United Kingdom	359	1,322	283	825	38	241	37	256	261	1,306	211	615	2	136	1	152
United States	709	1,489	522	1,218	99	26	88	245	598	1,488	396	1,175	35	5	25	224
TOTAL bilaterals**	**6,195**	**9,571**	**2,043**	**4,012**	**696**	**1,559**	**3,455**	**4,000**	**5,814**	**8,857**	**1,377**	**2,800**	**363**	**952**	**3,122**	**3,394**
African Development Bank	...	2	...	0	...	0	...	1	...	2	...	...	...	...	...	1
African Development Fund	92	154	49	24	22	50	21	81	62	128	7	...	1	38	0	69
Arab Fund for Economic and Social Development	...	5	...	0	...	0	...	5	...	5	...	...	...	0	...	4
Asian Development Bank Special Funds	...	322	...	71	...	204	...	47	...	322	...	20	...	179	...	22
EU Institutions	731	1,134	379	493	143	246	209	396	536	1,003	246	235	77	117	142	267
Arab Bank for Economic Development in Africa	...	...	...	...	...	...	...	...	...	...	...	...	...	...	...	...
Climate Investment Funds	...	...	...	...	...	...	...	...	...	...	...	...	...	...	...	...
World Bank (International Development Association)	1,194	1,413	794	729	176	427	225	256	1,194	1,411	627	507	92	316	141	145
Inter-American Development Bank Special Fund	...	52	...	31	...	4	...	17	...	52	...	25	...	1	...	14
International Monetary Fund (Concessional Trust Funds)	128	188	64	94	32	47	32	47	...	...	...	...	...	...	...	...
OPEC Fund for International Development	...	19	...	8	...	6	...	5	...	19	...	1	...	3	...	2
UN Development Programme	4	2	1	1	2	0	1	0	4	...	0	...	1	...	0	...
UNICEF	73	87	72	54	1	18	0	16	73	87	72	21	1	1	0	...
UN Peacebuilding Fund	...	0	...	0	...	...	...	...	...	0	...	0	...	...	...	...
UN Relief and Works Agency for Palestine Refugees	234	453	234	453	...	...	...	...	234	453	234	453	...	...	...	...
World Food Programme	...	21	...	21	...	0	...	0	...	21	...	21	...	...	...	...
TOTAL multilaterals**	**2,456**	**3,865**	**1,593**	**1,985**	**376**	**1,006**	**487**	**874**	**2,103**	**3,515**	**1,186**	**1,290**	**173**	**658**	**283**	**527**
TOTAL	**8,651**	**13,435**	**3,636**	**5,997**	**1,072**	**2,564**	**3,942**	**4,874**	**7,917**	**12,373**	**2,563**	**4,089**	**536**	**1,611**	**3,406**	**3,921**

Source: OECD-DAC, CRS database (2018).

* Estonia, Hungary, Kazakhstan, Kuwait, Lithuania, Romania and the United Arab Emirates are not part of the Development Assistance Committee (DAC) but are included in its Creditor Reporting System (CRS) database.
** The total includes official development assistance (ODA) from other bilaterals and multilaterals not listed above.
(...) indicates that data are not available.
All data represent gross disbursements. The share of ODA disbursed to the education sector is a percentage of gross ODA disbursements as reported in the CRS statistical tables. Total ODA figures in Table 1 represent net disbursements as reported in the DAC statistical tables.
Aid from France, New Zealand and the United Kingdom includes funds disbursed to overseas territories.

SHARE IN TOTAL ODA					
%					
Education		Basic education		Secondary education	
2005	2016	2005	2016	2005	2016
6	10	57	64	23	14
8	15	4	6	4	6
7	6	23	29	14	46
6	8	70	55	16	24
…	11	…	9	…	17
3	4	63	59	18	15
…	11	…	21	…	12
…	7	…	72	…	17
16	21	6	8	2	19
17	10	8	17	10	16
18	1	15	50	8	25
…	44	…	1	…	0
…	3	…	94	…	3
13	8	62	45	18	27
3	4	43	42	21	22
8	10	23	33	12	18
…	…	…	…	…	…
…	4	…	50	…	25
…	14	…	22	…	13
16	19	44	26	38	70
9	3	58	13	10	18
17	20	39	25	12	10
10	11	65	78	12	8
…	26		14		6
30	38	16	23	14	21
…	16	…	23	…	34
…	26	…	7	…	7
…	19	…	21	…	29
…	25	…	2	…	5
12	2	38	41	25	34
6	3	49	56	19	12
3	4	29	41	38	47
…	15	…	46	…	24
5	11	79	62	11	18
2	5	74	82	14	2
7	**8**	**33**	**42**	**11**	**16**
…	1	…	17	…	9
10	8	53	15	24	32
…	11	…	6	…	4
…	23	…	22	…	63
8	7	52	43	20	22
…	…	…	…	…	…
16	17	66	52	15	30
…	7	…	60	…	8
-45	-145	50	50	25	25
…	8	…	41	…	33
1	0	32	50	50	25
10	6	99	61	1	20
…	0	…	100	…	…
62	63	100	100	…	…
…	7	…	100	…	0
10	**9**	**65**	**51**	**15**	**26**
7	**9**	**42**	**45**	**12**	**19**

TABLE 3: Development assistance to education by recipient

	TOTAL AID								TOTAL AID PER CAPITA			
	Constant 2016 US$ millions								Constant 2016 US$			
	Education		Basic education		Secondary education		Post-secondary education		Basic education		Secondary education	
	2005	2016	2005	2016	2005	2016	2005	2016	2005	2016	2005	2016
Sub-Saharan Africa	**2,413**	**3,046**	**1,153**	**1,423**	**367**	**763**	**894**	**859**	**10**	**9**	**4**	**6**
Unallocated within the region	*30*	*92*	*9*	*37*	*5*	*16*	*16*	*40*	...	...	...	...
Angola	36	21	20	9	4	6	11	7	9	2	1	1
Benin	57	40	24	15	7	11	26	15	18	9	6	6
Botswana	6	3	1	2	1	1	4	1	3	5	4	3
Burkina Faso	84	91	46	42	14	28	24	20	21	13	7	9
Burundi	33	15	17	5	7	5	10	5	13	3	6	3
Cabo Verde	47	17	10	3	6	5	31	10	132	42	80	70
Cameroon	118	100	15	12	5	12	99	77	5	3	2	3
Central African Republic	10	20	3	8	0	5	6	7	5	11	1	7
Chad	31	41	17	20	5	10	9	11	10	8	3	4
Comoros	8	15	0	2	0	2	7	11	5	17	2	18
Congo	29	17	5	2	3	2	21	13	10	3	6	3
Côte d'Ivoire	35	55	5	19	1	7	29	29	2	5	0	2
D. R. Congo	63	97	28	47	12	32	22	19	3	4	2	3
Djibouti	30	20	13	5	0	5	17	10	115	53	3	34
Equat. Guinea	8	1	5	0	1	1	2	1	58	2	13	4
Eritrea	19	6	12	1	4	0	3	4	25	1	6	1
Eswatini	1	6	0	4	0	1	0	0	2	19	1	5
Ethiopia	93	314	42	194	19	71	33	48	3	12	2	5
Gabon	25	19	2	1	0	3	22	15	11	3	1	12
Gambia	6	9	5	4	0	1	1	3	22	12	2	5
Ghana	129	178	81	58	12	86	36	35	25	14	4	21
Guinea	51	55	33	23	4	8	13	24	22	12	3	4
Guinea-Bissau	7	17	3	10	1	2	4	5	12	36	4	7
Kenya	80	100	42	48	16	16	21	37	7	6	3	2
Lesotho	15	8	12	5	2	2	1	1	32	14	10	7
Liberia	3	83	3	59	0	11	0	13	5	80	1	17
Madagascar	81	55	35	22	10	14	37	20	13	7	3	3
Malawi	66	106	33	64	23	17	11	26	14	21	12	7
Mali	112	112	65	64	18	22	29	26	32	21	11	9
Mauritania	26	19	9	3	2	9	16	7	18	5	4	14
Mauritius	15	15	0	3	0	4	15	8	2	34	1	33
Mozambique	169	170	99	105	25	38	45	26	24	18	11	11
Namibia	11	16	9	4	1	7	1	5	25	10	3	27
Niger	56	97	37	50	7	32	11	15	17	14	4	10
Nigeria	70	155	45	68	11	40	13	47	2	2	1	2
Rwanda	58	89	28	48	12	18	18	22	21	26	9	12
Sao Tome and Principe	6	4	1	1	1	1	4	2	61	32	28	52
Senegal	119	140	33	52	18	27	68	61	18	21	10	12
Seychelles	1	3	0	1	0	1	0	1	22	156	10	66
Sierra Leone	32	52	18	21	8	25	6	6	21	17	10	21
Somalia	5	62	3	34	1	16	1	12	2	14	1	8
South Africa	85	63	43	22	14	15	28	26	6	3	3	3
South Sudan	-	81	-	63	-	8	-	9	-	32	-	5
United Republic of Tanzania	162	179	89	85	32	70	40	24	12	8	6	10
Togo	17	22	2	4	0	7	14	10	3	3	0	6
Uganda	146	98	81	33	29	30	36	35	13	4	7	5
Zambia	113	43	67	26	22	10	25	7	28	8	16	5
Zimbabwe	10	25	3	15	1	6	5	4	1	5	1	3

DIRECT AID								SHARE					
Constant 2016 US$ millions								%							
Education		Basic education		Secondary education		Post-secondary education		Education in total ODA		Basic education in total aid to education		Secondary education in total aid to education			
2005	2016	2005	2016	2005	2016	2005	2016	2005	2016	2005	2016	2005	2016		
2,007	**2,727**	**679**	**926**	**130**	**515**	**656**	**611**	**8**	**7**	**48**	**47**	**15**	**25**		
29	88	0	25	1	10	12	34	2	4	29	40	18	17		
35	21	13	4	0	3	7	4	8	10	58	42	12	27		
47	37	13	12	2	9	21	14	15	8	42	37	13	26		
6	3	0	1	1	0	4	1	11	4	13	49	16	17		
61	68	24	23	3	19	13	11	11	9	55	47	16	31		
19	14	4	3	1	4	3	3	9	2	50	36	22	33		
44	15	1	1	2	4	27	8	27	15	21	16	13	28		
115	100	11	10	3	10	97	76	27	13	12	12	4	11		
8	6	2	1	0	1	6	3	10	4	32	41	5	26		
25	15	9	5	1	3	5	4	7	7	55	49	15	24		
8	15	0	1	-	2	7	11	34	28	6	13	2	14		
27	17	3	7	2	2	20	13	2	20	18	13	10	11		
35	44	4	4	1	2	29	24	37	9	14	34	3	13		
52	97	7	35	2	26	12	12	3	5	45	48	20	33		
30	14	13	1	-	3	16	8	39	11	44	25	1	23		
8	1	3	0	0	0	1	0	22	21	58	24	15	35		
14	6	9	0	3	0	1	4	5	9	63	17	22	8		
1	6	0	4	0	1	0	0	2	4	53	79	19	14		
81	314	21	139	8	44	22	21	4	8	45	62	20	23		
24	19	2	0	0	3	22	15	48	45	9	3	1	17		
6	9	4	1	0	0	0	2	10	9	82	46	6	15		
100	131	65	25	4	69	28	19	11	14	63	32	10	48		
51	41	32	13	4	3	13	19	24	10	65	42	9	15		
7	15	2	7	1	0	4	4	10	8	36	60	8	9		
47	100	23	43	7	13	12	34	10	5	53	48	20	16		
15	7	10	3	2	1	1	0	22	7	76	62	16	23		
3	71	2	41	0	2	0	4	1	10	83	71	8	13		
72	42	16	8	0	7	27	12	8	9	43	40	12	25		
48	91	17	47	15	9	3	17	11	9	50	60	34	16		
94	86	38	43	5	12	15	16	15	9	58	57	16	20		
26	19	8	1	1	8	16	6	13	7	33	18	6	46		
15	10	0	1	0	3	15	6	43	36	1	21	1	28		
129	165	58	75	5	23	25	12	12	11	58	62	15	23		
11	16	9	3	1	7	1	4	9	10	84	25	6	45		
42	78	25	29	1	21	5	4	10	10	66	52	13	33		
69	155	41	38	9	24	11	32	1	6	65	44	16	26		
37	69	13	35	4	12	11	16	10	8	48	54	20	21		
5	4	1	1	0	1	4	2	17	9	26	24	9	32		
114	128	20	37	12	19	61	54	16	19	28	37	15	19		
1	3	-	0	0	0	0	0	4	45	29	48	17	20		
11	33	[illegible]	[illegible]	[illegible]	10	1	1	0	0	50	41	24	47		
5	50	1	12	0	3	0	1	2	5	65	55	18	26		
85	51	27	8	7	8	20	19	12	5	50	25	17	24		
-	81	-	49	-	1	-	2	...	5	...	78	...	11		
88	179	38	63	6	59	15	14	10	8	55	47	20	39		
17	18	2	1	0	6	14	9	19	13	14	19	1	33		
131	98	43	26	10	26	18	31	11	6	55	34	20	31		
95	43	32	17	5	5	7	3	9	4	59	61	19	22		
10	25	1	13	0	6	5	3	2	4	33	59	11	26		

TABLE 3: Continued

	TOTAL AID								TOTAL AID PER CAPITA			
	Constant 2016 US$ millions								Constant 2016 US$			
	Education		Basic education		Secondary education		Post-secondary education		Basic education		Secondary education	
	2005	2016	2005	2016	2005	2016	2005	2016	2005	2016	2005	2016
Northern Africa and Western Asia	**1,680**	**2,835**	**582**	**1,391**	**191**	**420**	**908**	**1,024**	**12**	**35**	**4**	**9**
Unallocated within the region	*6*	*90*	*2*	*71*	*2*	*1*	*1*	*22*				
Algeria	164	106	4	1	4	3	156	101	1	0	1	1
Armenia	17	26	5	6	3	5	8	15	37	35	9	19
Azerbaijan	11	13	3	1	2	1	7	11	5	2	1	1
Bahrain	-	-	-	-	-	-	-	-	-	-	-	-
Cyprus	-	-	-	-	-	-	-	-	-	-	-	-
Egypt	93	495	43	230	13	103	37	163	4	20	1	10
Georgia	47	50	11	13	6	6	30	31	28	45	15	23
Iraq	131	82	88	37	32	17	11	28	21	-	9	-
Israel	-	-	-	-	-	-	-	-	-	-	-	-
Jordan	152	370	102	265	16	24	34	81	-	-	22	21
Kuwait	-	-	-	-	-	-	-	-	-	-	-	-
Lebanon	96	235	35	145	6	44	54	45	76	266	13	69
Libya	7	11	0	5	0	0	7	6	0	-	0	-
Morocco	291	280	22	43	18	74	251	163	6	11	5	21
Oman	1	-	0	-	0	-	0	-	0	-	1	-
Palestine	-	-	-	-	-	-	-	-	-	-	-	-
Qatar	5	-	1	-	2	-	2	-	0	-	1	-
Saudi Arabia	43	18	20	6	8	4	16	8	4	-	2	-
Sudan	67	118	19	52	2	5	45	61	10	18	1	2
Syrian Arab Republic	124	141	7	24	20	24	97	93	7	24	14	21
Tunisia	169	240	25	69	29	56	114	115	4	13	4	5
Turkey	-	-	-	-	-	-	-	-	...	-	-	-
United Arab Emirates	205	400	159	338	22	24	23	38	363	691	30	27
Yemen	53	153	35	81	5	28	13	44	10	19	1	7
Central and Southern Asia	**1,663**	**2,561**	**1,126**	**1,218**	**173**	**640**	**364**	**704**	**6**	**6**	**1**	**3**
Unallocated within the region	*4*	*13*	*0*	*2*	*1*	*2*	*4*	*8*	...	...	...	...
Afghanistan	212	245	181	107	13	44	18	94	43	18	4	8
Bangladesh	242	599	167	367	38	161	37	71	10	23	2	7
Bhutan	12	1	4	0	4	0	4	1	38	5	39	2
India	724	621	575	288	31	146	118	187	5	2	0	1
Iran, Islamic Republic of	54	76	1	1	2	0	52	74	0	0	0	0
Kazakhstan	10	30	2	5	1	3	8	22	2	5	0	2
Kyrgyzstan	12	47	4	20	2	15	7	12	8	45	3	22
Maldives	7	3	3	1	3	1	1	1	52	29	65	22
Nepal	46	139	29	72	4	35	13	31	8	23	1	8
Pakistan	241	644	135	305	44	177	62	162	7	14	2	6
Sri Lanka	52	103	13	37	12	43	27	23	8	22	5	16
Tajikistan	16	15	10	7	3	4	3	4	14	10	2	3
Turkmenistan	2	3	0	0	0	1	2	2	1	1	0	2
Uzbekistan	29	23	2	4	16	8	11	11	1	2	3	2
Eastern and South-eastern Asia	**1,297**	**1,427**	**199**	**360**	**100**	**309**	**999**	**758**	**1**	**2**	**0**	**2**
Unallocated within the region	*1*	*6*	*1*	*3*	*0*	*0*	*1*	*3*	...	...	...	...
Brunei Darussalam	-	-	-	-	-	-	-	-	-	-	-	-
Cambodia	39	108	18	46	4	31	17	31	9	24	2	17
China	727	476	27	32	14	89	686	355	0	0	0	1
DPR Korea	1	1	0	0	0	0	1	1	0	0	0	0
Hong Kong, China	-	-	-	-	-	-	-	-	...	-	-	-
Indonesia	136	198	44	71	23	34	70	93	2	3	1	1
Republic of Korea	-	-	-	-	-	-	-	-	-	-	-	-
Lao PDR	28	80	13	46	4	21	11	13	16	61	4	21
Macao, China	-	-	-	-	-	-	-	-	-	-	-	-
Malaysia	20	32	2	2	2	1	16	29	1	1	1	0
Mongolia	34	44	8	11	1	11	25	22	30	41	3	37
Myanmar	12	135	4	60	0	36	8	39	1	12	0	6
Philippines	66	65	25	36	22	6	18	23	2	3	3	1
Singapore	-	-	-	-	-	-	-	-	...	-	...	-
Thailand	44	32	3	10	2	5	39	18	1	2	0	1
Timor-Leste	24	30	11	10	5	11	8	8	55	49	38	60
Viet Nam	165	219	43	33	21	63	101	123	5	5	2	7

DIRECT AID								SHARE					
Constant 2016 US$ millions								%					
Education		Basic education		Secondary education		Post-secondary education		Education in total ODA		Basic education in total aid to education		Secondary education in total aid to education	
2005	2016	2005	2016	2005	2016	2005	2016	2005	2016	2005	2016	2005	2016
1,551	**2,311**	**459**	**933**	**130**	**191**	**846**	**795**	**5**	**9**	**35**	**49**	**11**	**15**
6	98	2	73	2	1	1	21	0	10	43	76	37	1
164	106	3	0	4	3	155	101	46	67	3	1	3	3
13	26	2	4	2	5	7	15	9	8	29	21	21	20
7	13	1	0	0	0	5	11	5	17	28	8	14	5
-	-	-	-	-	-	-	-	…	…	…	…	…	…
-	-	-	-	-	-	-	-	…	…	…	…	…	…
93	162	35	42	9	9	33	68	8	23	46	46	14	21
37	50	4	4	3	2	27	27	15	11	23	26	13	12
131	34	87	8	32	3	10	13	1	4	67	45	25	21
-	-	-	-	-	-	-	-	…	…	…	…	…	…
95	352	73	228	1	6	19	62	19	14	67	77	11	7
-	-	-	-	-	-	-	-	…	…	…	…	…	…
96	235	32	137	5	40	52	41	39	21	37	62	7	19
7	11	-	5	-	-	7	6	29	6	1	44	0	0
291	277	17	30	16	68	249	157	38	14	7	15	6	27
1	-	-	-	0	-	0	-	4	…	3	…	35	…
-	-	-	-	-	-	-	-	…	…	…	…	…	…
5	-	0	-	1	-	2	-	19	…	12	…	37	…
30	18	6	4	1	3	9	7	2	2	46	34	17	22
67	118	19	47	2	2	45	58	88	1	29	44	4	4
114	136	1	5	17	14	94	83	34	22	6	17	16	17
169	240	15	3	24	23	109	82	41	7	15	29	17	23
-	-	-	-	-	-	-	-	…	…	…	…	…	…
172	390	128	314	7	12	8	26	19	17	78	85	11	6
53	47	34	27	4	1	13	17	17	8	67	53	9	18
1,568	**2,509**	**964**	**890**	**92**	**476**	**283**	**540**	**14**	**16**	**68**	**48**	**10**	**25**
5	13	0	2	1	2	4	8	1	3	2	15	26	19
203	244	165	90	5	35	9	86	7	6	86	44	6	18
221	599	133	305	21	130	20	40	17	24	69	61	16	27
12	1	3	0	3	0	3	0	12	2	36	39	32	14
724	621	568	239	28	122	114	163	38	23	79	46	4	24
54	76	1	0	1	0	51	74	51	65	1	1	3	0
10	30	1	0	0	0	8	19	4	49	16	18	5	9
8	42	1	10	1	10	5	7	4	9	30	42	17	32
7	3	1	0	2	0	0	1	8	12	38	39	41	19
43	128	25	49	2	24	11	20	10	13	63	52	9	25
192	627	52	167	2	108	20	93	14	22	56	47	18	27
61	85	0	21	10	34	24	13	4	28	26	36	23	41
8	15	5	5	0	2	1	3	6	5	62	48	17	24
2	3	0	0	-	1	2	2	6	10	14	12	0	36
29	23	1	1	16	6	11	10	16	5	8	10	55	33
1,252	**1,477**	**177**	**180**	**64**	**219**	**963**	**668**	**15**	**24**	**15**	**25**	**8**	**22**
1	6	1	3	-	0	1	3	0	3	52	42	0	4
-	-	-	-	-	-	-	-	…	…	…	…	…	…
39	107	13	26	2	21	15	20	7	15	46	43	11	29
727	476	20	4	11	75	682	341	40	-60	4	7	2	19
1	1	0	0	-	-	1	1	2	1	4	31	0	4
-	-	-	-	-	-	-	-	…	…	…	…	…	…
117	198	24	25	13	11	60	70	5	-179	32	36	17	17
-	-	-	-	-	-	-	-	…	…	…	…	…	…
28	80	10	41	3	18	9	11	9	20	47	58	15	26
-	-	-	-	-	-	-	-	…	…	…	…	…	…
20	32	0	0	1	0	15	29	65	-62	9	5	10	3
33	44	6	7	0	10	24	20	15	13	23	24	3	26
12	135	4	24	0	18	7	21	8	9	34	45	3	77
66	65	22	28	21	2	16	19	11	23	39	55	34	9
-	-	-	-	-	-	-	-	…	…	…	…	…	…
44	32	1	5	1	3	37	15	-30	14	7	30	5	16
22	30	8	3	4	8	6	5	12	13	46	35	23	38
141	215	19	13	9	53	89	113	8	8	26	15	13	29

TABLE 3: Continued

	TOTAL AID Constant 2016 US$ millions								TOTAL AID PER CAPITA Constant 2016 US$			
	Education		Basic education		Secondary education		Post-secondary education		Basic education		Secondary education	
	2005	2016	2005	2016	2005	2016	2005	2016	2005	2016	2005	2016
Oceania	**203**	**235**	**92**	**100**	**49**	**49**	**62**	**86**	**27**	**24**	**15**	**14**
Unallocated within the region	7	57	3	21	2	14	3	22	...	...	...	
Cook Islands	4	6	0	1	2	4	1	1	231	490	938	1,913
Fiji	22	17	10	5	5	2	8	9	101	52	46	19
Kiribati	6	10	1	5	3	0	2	5	51	321	230	25
Marshall Islands	15	3	8	2	4	1	4	1	1,090	200	585	101
Micronesia, F. S.	34	9	17	6	8	2	9	2	-	-	...	...
Nauru	0	3	0	0	0	3	0	0	34	212	19	2,078
Niue	4	1	2	1	1	0	1	1	10,950	3,894	3,458	2,237
Palau	3	1	2	0	1	0	1	0	1,041	260	336	66
Papua New Guinea	51	61	29	29	8	13	14	19	31	21	10	13
Samoa	14	14	1	5	7	2	6	8	52	156	231	60
Solomon Is	15	18	11	8	1	3	3	8	144	81	15	30
Tokelau	4	3	2	2	1	1	1	1	10,354	10,713	3,959	3,989
Tonga	8	7	4	4	1	0	3	3	270	261	91	17
Tuvalu	4	2	1	0	1	1	2	1	854	231	390	562
Vanuatu	12	22	2	12	5	3	5	6	63	-	159	-
Latin America and the Caribbean	**577**	**757**	**217**	**286**	**111**	**138**	**250**	**333**	**4**	**6**	**2**	**3**
Unallocated within the region	9	37	5	6	1	5	3	26	...	...	...	...
Anguilla	0	-	0	-	0	-	0	-	-	...	-	...
Antigua and Barbuda	-	0	-	0	0	0	0	0	-	4	28	3
Argentina	20	24	2	4	3	6	15	14	0	1	1	1
Aruba	-	-	-	-	-	-	-	-	-	-	-	-
Bahamas	-	-	-	-	-	-	-	-	-	-	-	-
Barbados	0	-	0	-	0	-	0	-	1	-	8	-
Belize	1	1	0	1	0	0	0	0	8	14	2	4
Bolivia, P. S.	53	36	25	6	13	9	15	21	19	4	11	7
Brazil	52	99	8	15	5	11	40	73	1	-	0	-
British Virgin Islands	-	-	-	-	-	-	-	-	-	-	-	-
Cayman Islands	-	-	-	-	-	-	-	-	...	...	...	...
Chile	16	25	1	4	1	5	13	16	1	3	1	3
Colombia	36	61	4	10	6	11	27	40	1	3	1	2
Costa Rica	4	12	1	3	0	4	3	5	1	8	1	10
Cuba	5	4	0	1	1	1	4	3	0	1	1	1
Dominica	1	2	0	1	0	0	1	1	49	99	39	61
Dominican Republic	13	21	5	13	6	2	2	5	5	11	5	2
Ecuador	19	23	3	8	6	5	9	10	2	4	4	3
El Salvador	12	24	6	8	3	5	4	10	7	12	4	7
Grenada	14	1	12	1	1	0	0	0	814	43	111	30
Guatemala	27	39	16	27	3	6	8	6	7	12	2	3
Guyana	13	7	7	1	4	1	3	5	58	16	47	6
Haiti	29	113	14	76	4	19	11	19	10	53	2	12
Honduras	60	44	39	36	11	6	10	2	34	30	12	6
Jamaica	13	7	12	3	0	3	1	1	-	-	1	13
Mexico	32	50	2	5	2	6	28	39	0	0	0	0
Montserrat	4	0	2	0	1	0	1	0	4,012	-	3,424	-
Nicaragua	60	50	27	30	18	16	15	4	35	41	28	26
Panama	5	5	1	2	1	0	3	2	2	5	4	1
Paraguay	9	8	4	3	2	3	2	2	5	4	3	4
Peru	46	44	15	17	12	9	19	17	4	5	4	3
Saint Kitts and Nevis	0	-	0	-	0	-	0	-	-	...	-	...
Saint Lucia	2	1	1	0	1	0	0	0	26	-	52	9
Saint Vincent/Grenadines	1	0	0	0	0	0	0	0	22	7	43	4
Suriname	4	3	1	1	0	0	2	2	18	14	6	4
Trinidad and Tobago	1	-	0	-	0	-	1	-	0	-	0	-
Turks and Caicos Islands	-	-	0	-	-	-	-	-	-	...	...	...
Uruguay	5	5	0	1	2	2	2	2	1	5	7	7
Venezuela, B. R.	13	11	3	1	2	2	8	8	1	0	1	1

DIRECT AID								SHARE					
Constant 2016 US$ millions								%							
Education		Basic education		Secondary education		Post-secondary education		Education in total ODA		Basic education in total aid to education		Secondary education in total aid to education			
2005	2016	2005	2016	2005	2016	2005	2016	2005	2016	2005	2016	2005	2016		
190	**226**	**34**	**43**	**20**	**20**	**33**	**58**	**15**	**14**	**45**	**43**	**24**	**21**		
7	*57*	*3*	*13*	*1*	*10*	*2*	*18*	*3*	*18*	*42*	*37*	*23*	*24*		
4	5	0	-	2	3	1	1	42	32	11	15	55	67		
22	17	0	1	0	0	3	7	30	14	44	32	22	12		
6	10	0	5	3	0	2	5	19	17	13	49	52	4		
15	3	0	0	0	-	0	0	23	27	49	53	26	22		
34	8	0	2	0	-	0	0	27	18	50	61	25	19		
0	3	-	0	-	2	0	0	2	15	28	10	14	77		
1	0	0	0	-	0	0	0	14	11	48	41	22	25		
1	1	0	0	0	-	0	0	13	4	53	54	23	13		
51	61	17	3	2	1	9	7	15	11	56	47	15	22		
14	14	0	2	6	0	5	6	29	16	11	33	48	13		
11	18	9	2	0	0	2	5	6	10	72	42	7	16		
0	1		0	-	0	0	-	19	24	46	56	23	24		
8	7	2	4	0	0	2	2	23	9	50	59	15	4		
3	2	0	0	-	1	1	1	35	10	34	12	16	31		
12	19	1	10	5	3	4	6	25	17	17	54	44	16		
551	**740**	**126**	**204**	**66**	**97**	**204**	**291**	**9**	**7**	**38**	**38**	**19**	**18**		
9	*37*	*3*	*4*	*0*	*4*	*2*	*24*	*5*	*7*	*53*	*18*	*12*	*13*		
0	-	-	-	0	-	-	-	1	...	11	...	84	...		
0	0	-	-	0	-	0	0	-	197	...	39	...	19		
20	74	1	0	3	4	14	12	20	902	9	17	16	24		
-	-	-	-	-	-	-	-	...	...	...	...	...	...		
-	-	-	-	-	-	-	-	...	...	...	...	...	...		
0	-	-	-	0	-	0	-	-11	...	7	...	62	...		
1	1	0	0	0	0	0	0	5	3	61	60	15	16		
53	36	8	3	5	7	7	19	8	5	47	17	25	26		
52	99	3	2	3	5	38	66	27	15	14	15	9	11		
-	-	-	-	-	-	-	-	...	...	...	...	...	...		
-	-	-	-	-	-	-	-	...	...	...	...	...	...		
16	25	0	0	1	3	13	14	9	14	7	16	8	20		
36	61	3	6	5	9	26	38	5	6	10	16	16	18		
4	12	0	2	0	3	3	4	15	12	18	29	9	32		
5	4	0	0	1	0	4	3	6	0	8	12	13	13		
1	1	-	0	0	-	0	0	6	20	33	38	19	19		
13	21	5	12	5	2	1	5	16	12	43	64	43	10		
19	23	2	5	6	3	9	9	7	9	17	34	33	20		
12	24	3	7	1	5	2	9	6	18	49	35	23	23		
13	0	12	-	1	-	0	0	25	14	87	48	10	24		
27	39	14	24	2	4	7	5	10	15	58	69	13	15		
5	7	2	1	2	0	0	5	8	11	50	19	29	7		
29	98	7	56	0	4	7	9	6	11	50	67	12	16		
56	44	25	33	4	5	3	1	8	11	66	81	18	14		
13	7	11	3	0	3	0	1	30	28	92	44	2	44		
32	50	2	1	1	1	27	37	14	6	7	11	5	12		
0	0	-	-	-	-	-	-	14	0	50	50	25	25		
55	50	10	27	9	14	6	2	7	12	45	61	30	32		
5	5	0	2	1	0	2	2	21	20	14	47	30	8		
9	8	3	2	1	3	2	1	16	9	50	40	24	39		
43	44	8	12	9	7	16	14	9	14	32	40	27	21		
0	-	-	-	-	-	0	-	10	...	45	...	23	...		
2	1	0	-	1	-	0	0	17	6	30	31	47	16		
1	0	0	-	0	-	0	0	13	2	32	38	46	19		
4	3	0	0	-	0	2	1	8	16	31	31	11	10		
1	-	-	-	0	-	1	-	-43	...	2	...	6	...		
0	-	0	-	-	-	-	-	-	...	...	...	...	...		
5	5	0	0	2	1	2	1	26	28	8	26	47	39		
13	11	3	0	1	2	8	8	24	26	23	10	13	19		

TABLE 3: Continued

	TOTAL AID								TOTAL AID PER CAPITA			
	Constant 2016 US$ millions								Constant 2016 US$			
	Education		Basic education		Secondary education		Post-secondary education		Basic education		Secondary education	
	2005	2016	2005	2016	2005	2016	2005	2016	2005	2016	2005	2016
Europe and Northern America	**266**	**470**	**33**	**104**	**28**	**68**	**207**	**298**	**1**	**2**	**0**	**1**
Unallocated within the region	*7*	*37*	*1*	*2*	*4*	*2*	*1*	*34*	...	...	...	...
Albania	33	30	7	5	4	4	22	21	29	28	8	12
Belarus	17	31	0	4	0	1	17	26	1	9	0	2
Bermuda	-	-	-	-	-	-	-	-	-	-	-	-
Bosnia and Herzegovina	37	35	5	4	3	2	30	30	-	-	...	...
Croatia	16	-	1	-	0	-	15	-	3	-	1	-
Malta	-	-	-	-	-	-	-	-	-	-	-	-
Republic of Moldova	10	56	1	8	0	18	9	30	4	-	0	-
Montenegro	-	4	1	1	0	0	-	3	30	15	6	5
Serbia	56	89	11	30	10	18	35	41	36	109	13	32
Slovenia	-	-	-	-	-	-	-	-	-	-	-	-
TFYR Macedonia	22	13	5	3	4	0	13	10	45	26	13	2
Ukraine	68	175	1	49	2	22	65	103	0	-	0	-
Unallocated by region or country	*549*	*2,104*	*235*	*1,115*	*53*	*177*	*260*	*812*	...	...	...	...
Low income countries	1,920	2,873	1,047	1,486	289	651	584	735	13	14	4	7
Lower middle income countries	3,701	5,540	1,795	2,441	465	1,295	1,442	1,804	6	8	1	3
Upper middle income countries	2,294	2,499	508	787	226	382	1,562	1,330	2	4	1	2
High income countries	72	62	7	13	12	14	53	35	0	0	0	0
Unallocated by income	*661*	*2,462*	*278*	*1,269*	*81*	*223*	*301*	*970*	...	...	...	...
Least developed countries	2,442	3,833	1,365	2,016	379	932	698	885	12	14	4	8
Sub-Saharan Africa	2,413	3,046	1,153	1,423	367	763	894	859	10	9	4	6
Northern Africa and Western Asia	1,680	2,835	582	1,391	191	420	908	1,024	12	35	4	9
Central and Southern Asia	1,663	2,561	1,126	1,218	173	640	364	704	6	6	1	3
Eastern and South-eastern Asia	1,297	1,427	199	360	100	309	999	758	1	2	0	2
Oceania	203	235	92	100	49	49	62	86	27	24	15	14
Latin America and the Caribbean	577	757	217	286	111	138	250	333	4	6	2	3
Europe and Northern America	266	470	33	104	28	68	207	298	1	2	0	1
Unallocated by region or country	*549*	*2,104*	*235*	*1,115*	*53*	*177*	*260*	*812*	...	...	...	...
TOTAL	**8,648**	**13,435**	**3,636**	**5,997**	**1,072**	**2,564**	**3,942**	**4,874**	**6**	**9**	**1**	**4**

Source: OECD-DAC, CRS database (2018).

(...) indicates that data are not available. (-) represents a nil value.
The country groupings by level of income are as defined by the World Bank but include only countries shown in the table. They are based on the list of countries by income group as revised in July 2018.
All data represent gross disbursements.

DIRECT AID								SHARE					
Constant 2016 US$ millions								%					
Education		Basic education		Secondary education		Post-secondary education		Education in total ODA		Basic education in total aid to education		Secondary education in total aid to education	
2005	2016	2005	2016	2005	2016	2005	2016	2005	2016	2005	2016	2005	2016
251	**347**	**11**	**18**	**17**	**25**	**196**	**255**	**7**	**11**	**12**	**22**	**11**	**15**
7	37	-	0	4	1	1	33	1	4	18	5	63	4
30	29	2	2	2	2	19	20	10	18	21	16	13	12
17	31	0	1	0	0	16	24	27	-138	2	12	1	5
-	-	-	-	-	-	-	-	...	...	...	...	...	...
33	35	1	1	1	1	28	28	6	8	12	10	8	6
16	-	-	-	0	-	15	-	12	...	4	...	2	...
-	-	-	-	-	-	-	-	...	...	...	...	...	...
10	53	0	2	0	16	9	27	6	17	7	14	2	33
1	4	1	0	0	0	-	3	-	4	...	16	...	8
50	49	3	2	6	4	31	28	5	14	20	33	17	20
-	-	-	-	-	-	-	-	...	...	...	...	...	...
19	13	3	2	2	0	12	10	9	8	24	22	16	3
68	95	0	6	2	1	65	82	15	11	1	28	3	13
547	2,091	163	896	17	67	224	702	3	4	43	53	10	8
1,587	2,508	669	1,006	100	411	395	495	10	9	55	52	15	23
3,411	4,991	1,361	1,566	248	857	1,225	1,366	12	13	48	44	13	23
2,201	2,371	359	497	151	237	1,487	1,185	7	14	22	31	10	15
70	62	2	3	9	9	50	30	24	28	10	21	16	22
649	2,440	172	1,018	28	97	248	845	2	4	42	52	12	9
2,070	3,452	896	1,383	145	615	463	568	10	11	56	53	16	24
2,007	2,727	679	926	130	515	656	611	8	7	48	47	15	25
1,551	2,311	459	933	130	191	846	795	5	9	35	49	11	15
1,568	2,509	964	890	92	476	283	540	14	16	68	48	10	25
1,252	1,422	127	180	64	219	963	668	15	24	15	25	8	22
190	226	34	43	20	20	33	58	15	14	45	43	24	21
551	740	126	204	66	97	204	291	9	7	38	38	19	18
251	347	11	18	17	25	196	255	7	11	12	22	11	15
547	2,091	163	896	17	67	224	702	3	4	43	53	10	8
7,917	**12,373**	**2,563**	**4,089**	**536**	**1,611**	**3,406**	**3,921**	**7**	**9**	**42**	**45**	**12**	**19**

Glossary

Adjusted net enrolment ratio (ANER). Enrolment of the official age group for a given level of education either at that level or the levels above, expressed as a percentage of the population in that age group.

Adult educational attainment rate. Number of persons aged 25 and above by the highest level of education attained, expressed as a percentage of the total population in that age group.

Adult literacy rate. Number of literate persons aged 15 and above, expressed as a percentage of the total population in that age group.

Child or under-5 mortality rate. Probability of dying between birth and the fifth birthday, expressed per 1,000 live births.

Completion rate by level. Percentage of children aged three to five years older than the official age of entry into the last grade of an education level who have reached the last grade of that level. For example, the primary attainment rate in a country with a 6-year cycle where the official age of entry into the last grade is 11 years is the percentage of 14- to 16-year-olds who have reached grade 6.

Conflict-affected country. For a given year, any country with 1,000 or more battle-related deaths (including fatalities among civilians and military actors) over the preceding 10-year period and/or more than 200 battle-related deaths in any one year over the preceding 3-year period, according to the Uppsala Conflict Data Program Battle-Related Deaths Dataset.

Constant price. Price of a particular item adjusted to remove the overall effect of general price changes (inflation) since a given baseline year.

Early childhood education and care (ECEC). Services and programmes that support children's survival, growth, development and learning – including health, nutrition and hygiene, and cognitive, social, emotional and physical development – from birth to entry into primary school.

Early Childhood Development Index (ECDI). Index of fulfilment of developmental potential that assesses children aged 36 to 59 months in four domains: literacy-numeracy, and physical, social-emotional, and cognitive development. The information is collected through the UNICEF Multiple Indicator Cluster Surveys. A child is 'on track' overall if they are 'on track' in at least three of the four domains.

Education levels according to the International Standard Classification of Education (ISCED), which is the classification system designed to serve as an instrument for assembling, compiling and presenting comparable indicators and statistics of education both within countries and internationally. The system, introduced in 1976, was revised in 1997 and 2011.

- **Pre-primary education (ISCED level 0).** Programmes at the initial stage of organized instruction, primarily designed to introduce very young children, aged at least 3 years, to a school-type environment and provide a bridge between home and school. Variously referred to as infant education, nursery education, pre-school education, kindergarten or early childhood education, such programmes are the more formal component of ECEC. Upon completion of these programmes, children continue their education at ISCED 1 (primary education).

- **Primary education (ISCED level 1).** Programmes generally designed to give pupils a sound basic education in reading, writing and mathematics, and an elementary understanding of subjects such as history, geography, natural sciences, social sciences, art and music.

- **Secondary education (ISCED levels 2 and 3).** Programmes made up of two stages: lower and upper secondary. Lower secondary education (ISCED 2) is generally designed to continue the basic programmes of the primary level but the teaching is typically more subject-focused, requiring more specialized teachers for each subject area. The end of this level often coincides with the end of compulsory education. In upper secondary education (ISCED 3), the final stage of secondary education in most countries, instruction is often organized even more along subject lines and teachers typically need a higher or more subject-specific qualification than at ISCED level 2.

- **Post-secondary non-tertiary education (ISCED level 4).** It provides learning experiences building on secondary education, preparing for labour market entry as well as tertiary education.

- **Tertiary education (ISCED levels 5–8).** It builds on secondary education, providing learning activities in specialized fields of education. It aims at learning at a high level of complexity and specialization. It comprises:

  - Level 5: Short-cycle tertiary education, often designed to provide participants with professional knowledge, skills and competences. It is practically based, occupationally specific and prepares students to enter the labour market.

  - Level 6: Bachelor's, often designed to provide participants with intermediate academic and/or professional knowledge, skills and competences, leading to a first degree or equivalent qualification.

  - Level 7: Master's or equivalent level, often designed to provide participants with advanced academic and/or professional knowledge, skills and competences, leading to a second degree or equivalent qualification.

  - Level 8: Doctoral or equivalent level, designed primarily to lead to an advanced research qualification.

Education for Sustainable Development (ESD). A type of education that aims to enable learners to constructively and creatively address present and future global challenges and create more sustainable and resilient societies.

Global Citizenship Education (GCED). A type of education that aims to empower learners to assume active roles to face and resolve global challenges and to become proactive contributors to a more peaceful, tolerant, inclusive and secure world.

Gross domestic product (GDP). The value of all final goods and services produced in a country in one year.

Gross enrolment ratio (GER). Total enrolment in a specific level of education, regardless of age, expressed as a percentage of the population in the official age group corresponding to this level of education. The GER can exceed 100% because of early or late entry and/or grade repetition.

Gross intake rate (GIR). Total number of new entrants to a given grade of primary education, regardless of age, expressed as a percentage of the population at the official school entrance age for that grade.

Gross national income (GNI). The value of all final goods and services produced in a country in one year (gross domestic product) plus income that residents have received from abroad, minus income claimed by non-residents.

Information and communications technology (ICT) skills. Individuals are considered to have such skills if they have undertaken certain computer-related activities in the last three months: copying or moving a file or folder; using copy and paste tools to duplicate or move information within a document; sending emails with attached files (e.g. document, picture, video); using basic arithmetic formulas in a spreadsheet; connecting and installing new devices (e.g. a modem, camera, printer); finding, downloading, installing and configuring software; creating electronic presentations with presentation software (including text, images, sound, video or charts); transferring files between a computer and other devices; and writing a computer program using a specialized programming language.

Literacy. According to UNESCO's 1958 definition, the term refers to the ability of an individual to read and write with understanding a simple short statement related to his/her everyday life. The concept of literacy has since evolved to embrace several skill domains, each conceived on a scale of different mastery levels and serving different purposes.

Net attendance rate (NAR). Number of pupils in the official age group for a given level of education who attend school at that level, expressed as a percentage of the population in that age group.

Net enrolment rate (NER). Enrolment of the official age group for a given level of education, expressed as a percentage of the population in that age group.

New entrants. Pupils entering a given level of education for the first time; the difference between enrolment and repeaters in the first grade of the level.

Never been to school rate. Percentage of children aged three to five years older than the official entrance age into primary education who have never been to school. For example, in a country where the official entrance age is 6 years, the indicator is calculated over the age group 9 to 11 years.

Out-of-school adolescents and youth. Those of lower or upper secondary school age who are not enrolled in primary, secondary, post-secondary non-tertiary or tertiary education.

Out-of-school children. Children in the official primary school age range who are not enrolled in either primary or secondary school.

Over-age for grade rate. The percentage of pupils in each level of education (primary, lower secondary and upper secondary) who are two years or more above the intended age for their grade.

Parity index. It is a measure of inequality defined as the ratio of the values of an education indicator of two population groups. Typically, the numerator is the value of the disadvantaged group and the denominator is the value of the advantaged group. An index value between 0.97 and 1.03 indicates parity. A value below 0.97 indicates disparity in favour of the advantaged group. A GPI above 1.03 indicates disparity in favour of the disadvantaged group. An adjusted parity index is symmetrical around 1 and limited to a range between 0 and 2. Groups can be defined by:

- Gender. Ratio of female to male values of a given indicator.
- Location. Ratio of rural to urban values of a given indicator.
- Wealth/income. Ratio of the poorest 20% to the richest 20% of a given indicator.

Private institutions. Institutions that are not operated by public authorities but are controlled and managed, whether for profit or not, by private bodies such as non-government organizations, religious bodies, special interest groups, foundations or business enterprises.

Public expenditure on education. Total current and capital expenditure on education by local, regional and national governments, including municipalities. Household contributions are excluded. The term covers public expenditure for both public and private institutions.

Pupil/teacher ratio (PTR). Average number of pupils per teacher at a specific level of education.

Pupil/qualified teacher ratio. Average number of pupils per qualified teacher at a specific level of education.

Pupil/trained teacher ratio (PTTR). Average number of pupils per trained teacher at a specific level of education.

Purchasing power parity (PPP). An exchange rate adjustment that accounts for price differences between countries, allowing international comparisons of real output and income.

Qualified teacher. Teacher who has the minimum academic qualification necessary to teach at a specific level of education in a given country.

School age population. Population of the age group officially corresponding to a given level of education, whether enrolled in school or not.

Skills. Non-innate capabilities that can be learned and transmitted, and have economic or social benefits to both individuals and their societies.

Stunting rate. Proportion of children in a given age group whose height for their age is between two and three standard deviations below the reference median established by the National Center for Health Statistics and the World Health Organization.

Teacher attrition rate. Number of teachers at a given level of education leaving the profession in a given school year, expressed as a percentage of teachers at that level and in that school year.

Technical and vocational education and training (TVET). Programmes designed mainly to prepare students for direct entry into a particular occupation or trade (or class of occupations or trades).

Total net enrolment rate. Number of pupils of the official school age group for a given level of education who are enrolled in any level of education (primary, secondary, post-secondary or tertiary education), expressed as a percentage of the corresponding school age population.

Trained teacher. Teacher who has fulfilled at least the minimum organized teacher-training requirements (pre-service or in-service) to teach a specific level of education according to the relevant national policy or law.

Transition rate to secondary education. Number of new entrants to the first grade of secondary education in a given year, expressed as a percentage of the number of pupils who were enrolled in the final grade of primary education in the previous year and who do not repeat that grade the following year. The indicator measures transition to secondary general education only.

Youth literacy rate. Number of literate persons aged 15 to 24, expressed as a percentage of the total population in that age group.

MIGRATION AND DISPLACEMENT TERMS

Accreditation. Process by which an officially approved body, on the basis of assessment of learning outcomes and/or competences according to specified purposes and methods, awards qualifications (certificates, diplomas or titles), or grants equivalences, credit units or exemptions, or issues documents such as portfolios of competences.

Assimilation. Adaptation of one ethnic or social group – usually a minority – to the culture of another. Assimilation involves the subsuming of language, traditions, values, mores, behaviour or even fundamental vital interests.

Asylum-seeker. A person who seeks safety from persecution or serious harm in a country other than his or her own and awaits a decision on the application for refugee status under relevant international and national instruments.

Brain drain. Emigration of (highly) skilled individuals from the country of origin.

Brain gain. Immigration of (highly) skilled individuals to a destination country. Also called reverse brain drain.

Certification. The formal acknowledgement of successful achievement of a defined set of outcomes.

Citizenship. The status of being a citizen of the country in which one was born or naturalized, to which one owes allegiance and by which one is entitled to be protected, assuming one has not renounced or lost this status.

Deportation. The action by a state, in the exercise of its sovereignty, of removing a non-national from its territory after refusal of admission or termination of permission to remain.

Detention. Restriction on freedom of movement, usually through enforced confinement, by government authorities.

Discrimination. A failure to treat persons equally when no reasonable distinction can be found between those favoured and those not favoured.

Displacement. Forced removal/flight of a person from his/her home or country, often as a result of armed conflict or natural disaster.

Emigration. The act of leaving one country with a view to settling in another.

First-generation immigrant. A foreign-born person who has relocated in a new country.

Foreign-born. Someone born abroad, including naturalized citizens and children born abroad to nationals.

High-skilled migration. Migration of people having a university degree or extensive/equivalent experience in a given field.

Immigration. A process by which non-nationals move to a country for the purpose of settlement.

Immigration status. Status a migrant is accorded under the immigration law of the host country.

Influx. A continuous arrival of large numbers of non-nationals in a country.

Interculturalism. Existence and equitable interaction of diverse cultures and possibility of generating shared cultural expressions through dialogue and mutual respect.

Internal migration. Movement of people to a new area within a country to establish residence.

Internally displaced people. People forced/obliged to flee or leave their homes or places of habitual residence, in particular as a result, or in order to avoid the effects, of armed conflict, generalized violence, human rights violations or natural or human-made disasters, who have not crossed an internationally recognized national border.

International migrant. A person who changes his/her country of usual residence. Short-term migrants are those who have done so for at least 3 but fewer than 12 months; long-term migrants are those who have done so for at least one year. (Not all countries use this definition in practice.)

International migration. Movement of people across one or more national borders to settle in another country.

Irregular migration. Migration outside the regulatory norms of the sending, transit and receiving countries.

Migrant. At the international level, no universally accepted definition exists. The term is usually understood to cover all cases where a person has taken freely a decision to migrate without an external compelling factor; it therefore applies to persons, and family members, moving to another country or region to better their material or social conditions and improve their or their family's prospects. The United Nations defines migrant as an individual who has resided abroad for more than one year irrespective of the causes and the means of migration.

Migration. The movement of a person or group of persons across a national border or within a country.

Mixed heritage. Used to describe a native-born person with one foreign-born and one native-born parent.

Multiculturalism. Culturally diverse nature of human society referring not only to elements of ethnic or national culture, but also linguistic, religious and socio-economic diversity.

National. Person who is a citizen of a given country.

Nationality. Legal bond between an individual and a nation, acquired by birth, adoption, marriage or descent.

Native. Belonging to a particular place or country by birth.

Nomads. People who travel from place to place to find fresh pasture for their animals or other means of livelihood and have no permanent home.

Pastoralists. People whose primary occupation is the raising of livestock.

People with a migrant background. People who are either immigrants or foreign born or have at least one parent who is an immigrant or a foreigner.

Reception centre. A facility lodging asylum-seekers or migrants in an irregular situation, upon arrival in a receiving country, while their status is determined.

Recognition. Official acknowledgement of skills and competences by awarding qualifications (certificate, diploma, title); granting equivalence, credit units or waivers; or validating gained skills and/or competences.

Recognition of prior learning. Identifying, documenting, assessing and certifying (mainly) non-formal and informal learning outcomes according to standards used in formal education and training.

Refugee. One who, owing to a well-founded fear of persecution for reasons of race, religion, nationality, political opinion or membership of a particular group, is outside the country of one's nationality and cannot or, owing to such fear, will not seek the protection of that country.

Remittances. Money earned or acquired by migrants transferred back to their country or community of origin.

Return. The act or process of going back to a country or place of departure.

Returning foreign-born student. Foreign-born student with at least one native-born parent

Seasonal worker. A migrant whose work is dependent on seasonal conditions and performed only part of the year.

Second-generation immigrant. Person whose parents are immigrants

Stateless person. Person who is not considered a national by any country under its laws.

Unaccompanied minor. Person under the age of legal responsibility without a parent, guardian or other adult responsible for them.

Undocumented migrant. See Irregular migration.

Validation. Process involving structured assessment, evaluation, documentation and recognition of a person's knowledge and competences, independently of how it is acquired.

Abbreviations

AIDS	Acquired immunodeficiency syndrome
ASEAN	Association of Southeast Asian Nations
ASER	Annual Status of Education Report (India)
CCT	Conditional cash transfer
CRRF	Comprehensive Refugee Response Framework
CRS	Creditor Reporting System (OECD)
CSO	Civil society organization
CTRP	Commonwealth Teacher Recruitment Protocol
DAC	Development Assistance Committee (OECD)
DACA	Deferred Action for Childhood Arrivals (US)
DHS	Demographic and Health Survey
DigComp	Digital Competence Framework for Citizens
DPO	Disabled people's organization
DIOC	Database on Immigrants in OECD and non-OECD Countries
ECDI	Early Childhood Development Index
ECEC	Early childhood education and care
ECW	Education Cannot Wait
EFA	Education for All
EHEA	European Higher Education Area
EI	Education International
EMIS	Education management information system
EU	European Union
Eurostat	Statistical office of the European Union
FAO	Food and Agriculture Organization of the United Nations
FTS	Financial Tracking Service (OCHA)
GAML	Global Alliance to Monitor Learning
GCC	Gulf Cooperation Council
GCPEA	Global Coalition to Protect Education from Attack
GDP	Gross domestic product
GEM Report	*Global Education Monitoring Report*
GER	Gross enrolment ratio
GNI	Gross national income

GPE	Global Partnership for Education
GPI	Gender parity index
HIV	Human immunodeficiency virus
HLPF	High-level Political Forum on Sustainable Development
HRP	Humanitarian response plan
HSK	Heimatliche Sprache und Kulture ('home language and culture', Zurich)
IAEG-SDGs	Inter-agency and Expert Group on SDG Indicators
IALS	International Adult Literacy Survey
IBE	International Bureau of Education (UNESCO)
IBRD	International Bank for Reconstruction and Development (World Bank)
ICCS	International Civics and Citizen Survey
ICT	Information and communications technology
IDA	International Development Association (World Bank)
IDMC	Internal Displacement Monitoring Centre (Norwegian Refugee Council)
IDP	Internally displaced person
IEA	International Association for the Evaluation of Educational Achievement
IFAD	International Fund for Agricultural Development
IFFEd	International Finance Facility for Education (proposed)
IIEP	International Institute for Educational Planning (UNESCO)
ILO	International Labour Office/Organization
IMF	International Monetary Fund
IOM	International Organization for Migration
IRC	International Rescue Committee
ISCED	International Standard Classification of Education
ITU	International Telecommunication Union
JMP	Joint Monitoring Programme (WHO/UNICEF)
JRC	Joint Research Centre (EU)
LAMP	Literacy Assessment and Monitoring Programme (UIS)
LMHE2020	Learning Mobility in Higher Education 2020
MDG	Millennium Development Goal
MICS	Multiple Indicator Cluster Survey
MOOC	Massive open online course
NER	Net enrolment rate
NGO	Non-government organization
OCHA	Office for the Coordination of Humanitarian Affairs (UN)
ODA	Official development assistance
OECD	Organisation for Economic Co-operation and Development
OHCHR	Office of the United Nations High Commissioner for Human Rights
PIAAC	Programme for the International Assessment of Adult Competencies (OECD)

PIRLS	Progress in International Reading Literacy Study
PISA	Programme for International Student Assessment (OECD)
PPP	Purchasing power parity
RACHEL	Remote Area Community Hotspot for Education and Learning
R&D	Research and development
RRP	Refugee response plan
SABER	Systems Approach for Better Education Results (World Bank)
SAR	Scholars at Risk
SDG	Sustainable Development Goal
SHARE	Support to Higher Education in the ASEAN Region (EU)
SRP	Student Refugee Program (Canada)
STEP	Skills toward Employment and Productivity (World Bank)
TALIS	Teaching and Learning International Survey (OECD)
TCG	Technical Cooperation Group
TEC	Temporary education centre (Turkey)
TEP	Transitional education plan
TIMSS	Trends in International Mathematics and Science Study
TVET	Technical and vocational education and training
UIL	UNESCO Institute for Lifelong Learning
UIS	UNESCO Institute for Statistics
UK	United Kingdom
UN	United Nations
UNAIDS	Joint United Nations Programme on HIV/AIDS
UNDP	United Nations Development Programme
UNESCO	United Nations Educational, Scientific and Cultural Organization
UNGEI	United Nations Girls' Education Initiative
UNHCR	United Nations High Commissioner for Refugees
UNICEF	United Nations Children's Fund
UNODC	United Nations Office on Drugs and Crime
UNPD	United Nations Population Division
UNRWA	United Nations Relief and Works Agency for Palestine Refugees in the Near East
UNSC	United Nations Statistical Commission
UOE	UIS/OECD/Eurostat
US	United States
WASH	Water, sanitation and hygiene
WEF	World Education Forum
WFP	World Food Programme (United Nations)
WHO	World Health Organization (United Nations)
WUSC	World University Service of Canada

References

THEMATIC SECTION

CHAPTER 1

Fargues, P. 2017. *International Migration and Education: A Web of Mutual Causation*. (Background paper for *Global Education Monitoring Report 2019*.)

Sanz, R. 2018. *Education and Migration: An Assessment of the Types and Range of IOM's Education and Vocational Training Projects*. Geneva, Switzerland, International Organization for Migration.

Türk, V. and Garlick, M. 2016. From burdens and responsibilities to opportunities: The comprehensive refugee response framework and a global compact on refugees. *International Journal of Refugee Law*, Vol. 28, No. 4, pp. 656–78.

United Nations. 2013. *Secretary-General's Remarks to High-Level Dialogue on International Migration and Development*. New York, United Nations Secretary-General. www.un.org/sg/en/content/sg/statement/2013-10-03/secretary-generals-remarks-high-level-dialogue-international. (Accessed 15 September 2018.)

___. 2016. *New York Declaration for Refugees and Migrants*, New York, United Nations General Assembly.

___. 2017. *Making Migration Work For All: Report of the Secretary-General*, United Nations General Assembly.

___. 2018a. *Global Compact for Safe, Orderly and Regular Migration*. Geneva, Switzerland, The United Nations, International Organization for Migration.

___. 2018b. *Global Compact on Refugees*, Geneva, Switzerland, United Nations High Commissioner for Refugees.

CHAPTER 2

Abuya, B. 2018. *The Movement of Families, Households, and Individuals within Countries and Its Relationship with Education: Challenges and Opportunities in a Shifting World*. (Background paper for *Global Education Monitoring Report 2019*.)

Africa Education Trust. 2017. *Pastoralist Teachers*. London, Africa Education Trust. https://africaeducationaltrust.org/pastoralist-teachers. (Accessed 13 February 2018.)

Agarwal, S. 2014. *Making the Invisible Visible*. Pune, India, Info Change India. (Issue 28.)

Ahlin, L., Andersson, M. and Thulin, P. 2017. *Human Capital Sorting: The 'When'and 'Who'of Sorting of Talents to Urban Regions*. Stockholm, Research Institute of Industrial Economics. (IFN Working Paper 1155.)

Aide et Action, Bernard van Leer Foundation and UNESCO. 2015. *National Consultation on "Children and Internal Migration in India"*. New Delhi, Aide et Action/Bernard van Leer Foundation/UNESCO.

Aina, C., Casalone, G. and Ghinetti, P. 2015. Internal migration and educational outcomes in Italy: Evidence from a cohort of youths. *Papers in Regional Science*, Vol. 94, No. 2, pp. 295–316.

Alaluusua, S. 2017. *Rural to urban migration and young female domestic workers in the 21st century Lima, Peru*. Conference paper for Migrating out of Poverty: From Evidence to Policy, London, March 28–29.

All China Women's Federation and National Bureau of Statistics of China. 2016. Number of migrant worker children growing up away from their parents in China in 2005 and 2010, by age group (in millions). www.statista.com/statistics/258437/number-of-left-behind-children-in-china-by-age-group. (Accessed 15 September 2018.)

Álvarez, C., Santelices, C., Bertachini, H., Chong, J. C., Cossens, S., Cruz-Aguayo, Y., Di Maro, V., Díaz, L., Linares, A. M. and Maffioli, A. 2011. *Development Effectiveness Overview 2010*. Washington, DC, Inter-American Development Bank.

Ananga, E. D. 2013. Child migration and dropping out of basic school in Ghana: The case of children in a fishing community. *Creative Education*, Vol. 4, No. 06, pp. 405–110.

Anti-Slavery International. 2013. *Small Grants, Big Change: Influencing Policy and Practice for Child Domestic Workers*. London, Anti-Slavery International.

Anti-Slavery International and Volunteers for Social Justice. 2017. *Slavery in India's Brick Kilns and the Payment System: Way Forward in the Fight for Fair Wages, Decent Work and Eradication of Slavery*. London, Anti-Slavery International/Volunteers for Social Justice.

Antoninis, M. 2014. Tackling the largest global education challenge? Secular and religious education in northern Nigeria. *World Development*, Vol. 59, pp. 82–92.

Ares Abalde, M. 2014. *School Size Policies: A Literature Review*. Paris, Organisation for Economic Co-operation and Development. (OECD Education Working Papers 106.)

Autti, O. and Hyry-Beihammer, E. K. 2014. School closures in rural Finnish communities. *Journal of Research in Rural Education (Online)*, Vol. 29, No. 1, p. 1.

Bai, Y., Zhang, L., Liu, C., Shi, Y., Mo, D. and Rozelle, S. 2018. Effect of parental migration on the academic performance of left behind children in North Western China. *Journal of Development Studies*, Vol. 54, No. 7, pp. 1154–70.

Bajaj, M. and Gupta, M. 2013. *Meeting Migrant Families' Needs Through On-site Crèches*. The Hague, Netherlands, Bernard van Leer Foundation. (Early Childhood Matters, 121.)

Baker, J. L., Watanabe, M., Soriano, B. A. V., Limkin, J. L. C., Shi, T., Hooton, C. A., Piatkowski, M. M., Sivaev, D., Lasida Adji, F., Toborowicz, J. J., Tang, L., Nebrija, J. C., Eleazar, F., Martinez, M. T. and Cuttaree, V. 2017. *Philippines Urbanization Review: Fostering Competitive, Sustainable and Inclusive Cities*. Washington, DC, World Bank.

Batkhuyag, B. and Dondogdulam, T. 2018. *Mongolia Case Study: The Evolving Education Needs and Realities of Nomads and Pastoralists*. (Background paper for *Global Education Monitoring Report 2019*.)

Baxter, L. P. and Meyers, N. M. 2016. Increasing urban Indigenous students' attendance: Mitigating the influence of poverty through community partnership. *Australian Journal of Education*, Vol. 60, No. 3, pp. 211–28.

Beaton, W. and McDonell, L. 2014. *Kindergarten Transitions II: A Scan of Existing Supportive Programs for Aboriginal Children and Families in British Columbia*. Ottawa, Urban Aboriginal Knowledge Network Western Regional Research Center.

Becerra-Lubies, R. and Fones, A. 2016. The needs of educators in intercultural and bilingual preschools in Chile: A case study. *International Journal of Multicultural Education*, Vol. 18, No. 2, pp. 58–84.

Beck, S., Vreyer, P. D., Lambert, S., Marazyan, K. and Safir, A. 2015. Child Fostering in Senegal. *Journal of Comparative Family Studies*, Vol. 46, No. 1, pp. 57–73.

Beijing Normal University. 2009. *Impact Assessment of Basic Education in Western Areas Project: Final Report*. Beijing, Institute of Education Economics, Beijing Normal University.

Bengtsson, S. and Dyer, C. 2017. *Ensuring High Quality Primary Education for Children from Mobile Populations: A Desk Study*. Doha/Berlin, Educate a Child/German Federal Ministry for Economic Cooperation and Development.

Berker, A. 2009. The impact of internal migration on educational outcomes: Evidence from Turkey. *Economics of Education Review*, Vol. 28, No. 6, pp. 739–49.

Bernard, A., Bell, M. and Cooper, J. 2018. *Internal Migration and Education: A Cross-National Comparison*. (Background paper for *Global Education Monitoring Report 2019*.)

Blumenstock, J. E. 2012. Inferring patterns of internal migration from mobile phone call records: Evidence from Rwanda. *Information Technology for Development*, Vol. 18, No. 2, pp. 107–25.

BRAC. 2017. *2017 Annual Report*. Dhaka, BRAC.

Brand, E., Bond, C. and Shannon, C. 2016. *Indigenous in the City: Urban Indigenous Populations in Local and Global Contexts*. Brisbane, Australia, Poche Centre for Indigenous Health, University of Queensland.

Buaraphan, K. 2013. Educational quality of small schools in Thailand. *European Journal of Social Science*, Vol. 41, No. 1, pp. 130–47.

Cameron, S. 2012. *Education, Urban Poverty and Migration: Evidence from Bangladesh and Vietnam*. Florence, Italy, UNICEF Office of Research (Working Paper 2012-15).

CARE International. 2016. *Somali Girls' Education Promotion Project (SOMGEP): Transition – Proposal*. Geneva, Switzerland, CARE International.

Champion, T., Cooke, T. and Shuttleworth, I. 2017. *Internal Migration in the Developed World: Are We Becoming Less Mobile?* New York, Routledge.

Chandrasekhar, S. and Bhattacharya, L. 2018. *Understanding the Scope of the Challenge, and Moving towards a Coherent Policy Framework for Education for Seasonal Migrants at the State Level in India*. (Background paper for *Global Education Monitoring Report 2019*.)

Cherng, H. S. 2018. *Who Teaches and How do they View Different Groups of Students and Parents? The Case of China.* (Background paper for *Global Education Monitoring Report 2019.*)

China Daily. 2016. Incentives needed to boost urbanization's full benefits. *China Daily*, 30 January. www.chinadaily.com.cn/china/2016-01/30/content_23318879.htm. (Accessed March 5 2018.)

Coffey, D. 2013. Children's welfare and short-term migration from rural India. *Journal of Development Studies*, Vol. 49, No. 8, pp. 1101–17.

De Brauw, A., Mueller, V. and Lee, H. L. 2014. The role of rural–urban migration in the structural transformation of Sub-Saharan Africa. *World Development*, Vol. 63, pp. 33–42.

Del Popolo, F., Oyarce, A. M., Ribotta, B. and Rodríguez, J. 2007. *Indigenous Peoples and Urban Settlements: Spatial Distribution, Internal Migration and Living Conditions*. Santiago, United Nations Economic Commission for Latin America and the Caribbean.

Development Workshop. 2012. *Baseline Study Concerning Children of the 6–14 Age Group Affected by Seasonal Agricultural Migration*. Ankara, Development Workshop.

ECOSOC. 2010. *Indigenous Peoples and Boarding Schools: A Comparative Study*. Paper presented at the Permanent Forum on Indigenous Issues. New York, United Nations Economic and Social Council.

Education Scotland. 2015. *Schools (Consultation) (Scotland) Act 2010 as Amended: Overview and Guidance for Education Authorities*. Livingston, UK, Education Scotland.

Erulkar, A., Medhin, G. and Negeri, L. 2017. *The Journey of Out-of-School Girls in Ethiopia: Examining Migration, Livelihoods, and HIV*. Addis Ababa, Population Council.

ESSPIN. 2014. *Introducing Modern Education into Islamic Schools in Northern Nigeria: A Report on ESSPIN's 1st Phase Experience 2008–2014 – Practice Paper*. Abuja, Nigeria, Education Sector Support Programme in Nigeria.

European Commission, EACEA and Eurydice. 2013. *Funding of Education in Europe 2000–2012: The Impact of the Economic Crisis*. Luxembourg, Publications Office of the European Union.

Faggian, A., Rajbhandari, I. and Dotzel, K. R. 2017. The interregional migration of human capital and its regional consequences: A review. *Regional Studies*, Vol. 51, No. 1, pp. 128–43.

FAO. 2013. *Pastoralist Field Schools Training of Facilitators Manual 2013*. Nairobi, Food and Agriculture Organization of the United Nations/Farmer Field Schools Promotion Services.

___. 2018. *Saving Livelihoods Saves Lives*. Rome, Food and Agriculture Organization of the United Nations.

Findlay, I., Garcea, J., Hansen, J., Antsanen, R., Cheng, J. and Holden, B. 2014. *Comparing the Lived Experience of Urban Aboriginal Peoples with Canadian Rights to Quality of Life*. Ottawa, Urban Aboriginal Knowledge Network Prairie Regional Research Centre.

Forcier Consulting. 2016. *Pastoral Education Program Study Report*. Juba, Forcier Consulting/South Sudan Ministry of Education, Science and Technology/Winrock International/FHI 360.

France Ministry of Education. 2017. *L'état de l'école 2017 : coûts, activités, résultats – 34 indicateurs sur le système éducatif français [The state of school 2017: Costs, Activities, Results – 34 indicators on the French education system]*. Paris, Ministry of National Education. (In French.)

Fratesi, U. and Percoco, M. 2014. Selective migration, regional growth and convergence: Evidence from Italy. *Regional Studies*, Vol. 48, No. 10, pp. 1650–68.

Friedman, E. 2017. Teachers' work in China's migrant schools. *Modern China*, Vol. 43, No. 6, pp. 559–89.

Galiani, S. and Schargrodsky, E. 2010. Property rights for the poor: Effects of land titling. *Journal of Public Economics*, Vol. 94, No. 9, pp. 700–29.

Gavonel, M. F. 2017. *Patterns and Drivers of Internal Migration among Youth in Ethiopia, India, Peru and Vietnam*. Oxford, UK, Young Lives, Oxford Department of International Development, University of Oxford. (Working Paper 169.)

Gentilini, U. 2015. *Entering the City: Emerging Evidence and Practices with Safety Nets in Urban Areas*. Washington, DC, World Bank. (Social Protection and Labor Discussion Paper 1504.)

Goble, P. 2017. *Two-thirds of Russia's Villages Have Disappeared or Soon Will, Statistics Show*. Staunton, Va., Window on Eurasia. http://windowoneurasia2.blogspot.fr/2017/11/two-thirds-of-russias-villages-have.html. (Accessed 11 April 2018.)

Goodburn, C. 2015. Migrant girls in Shenzhen: gender, education and the urbanization of aspiration. *China Quarterly*, Vol. 222, pp. 320–38.

Granato, N., Haas, A., Hamann, S. and Niebuhr, A. 2015. The impact of skill-specific migration on regional unemployment disparities in Germany. *Journal of Regional Science*, Vol. 55, No. 4, pp. 513–39.

Han, J. 2004. Survey report on the state of compulsory education among migrant children in Beijing. *Chinese Education and Society*, Vol. 37, No. 5, pp. 29–55.

Han, J., Liang, Y. and Chen, A. 2018. *China's Small Rural Schools: Challenges and Responses*. (Background paper for *Global Education Monitoring Report 2019*.)

Hannum, E., Hu, L.-C. and Shen, W. 2018. *Being Left Behind in China: The Short- and Long-Term Consequences on Education, Well-Being and Life Opportunities*. (Background paper for *Global Education Monitoring Report 2019*.)

Härmä, J., Pikholz, L. and Hinton, P. 2017. *Low Fee Private Schools in Low-income Districts of Kampala, Uganda*. Chicago, Ill., CapitalPlus Exchange.

Hedges, S., Mulder, M. B., James, S. and Lawson, D. W. 2016. Sending children to school: rural livelihoods and parental investment in education in northern Tanzania. *Evolution and Human Behavior*, Vol. 37, No. 2, pp. 142–51.

Hoechner, H. 2018. *Qur'anic Schools in Northern Nigeria: Everyday Experiences of Youth, Faith and Poverty*. Cambridge, UK, Cambridge University Press.

Hofleitner, A., Chiraphadhanakul, T. V. and State, B. 2013. Coordinated migration. Berkeley, Calif., Facebook Data Science Team. www.facebook.com/notes/10151930946453859. (Accessed 1 November 2017.)

Hong'e, M. 2015. *10 mln Left-behind Children Go Without Parents for Whole Year*. Beijing, China News Service. www.ecns.cn/cns-wire/2015/06-19/169896.shtml. (Accessed 8 June 2018.)

Hopkins, E., Bastagli, F. and Hagen-Zanker, J. 2016. *Internal Migrants and Social Protection: A Review of Eligibility and Take-Up*. London, Overseas Development Institute. (ODI Working Paper 436.)

Hu, S. 2017. "It's for Our Education": Perception of Parental Migration and Resilience Among Left-behind Children in Rural China. *Social Indicators Research*, pp. 1–21.

Huy, Q. 2017. Household registration books to be scrapped by 2020. Cau Giay District, Vietman. www.vneconomictimes.com/article/vietnam-today/household-registration-books-to-be-scrapped-by-2020. (Accessed 15 September 2018).

ILO. 2013. *Domestic Workers Across the World: Global and Regional Statistics and the Extent of Legal Protection*. Geneva, Switzerland, International Labour Organization.

___. 2015. *World Report on Child Labour 2015: Paving the Way to Decent Work for Young People*. Geneva, Switzerland, International Labour Organization.

___. 2017a. *Global Estimates of Child Labour: Results and Trends, 2012–2016*. Geneva, Switzerland, International Labour Organization.

___. 2017b. *Tackling Child Labour in Domestic Work: A Handbook for Action for Domestic Workers and their Organisations*. Geneva, Switzerland, International Labour Organisation.

India Ministry of Finance. 2017. *Labour Migration in India Increasing at an Accelerating Rate, Reveals New Study: Economic Survey 2016–17*. New Delhi, Ministry of Finance, http://pib.nic.in/newsite/PrintRelease.aspx?relid=157799 (Accessed 15 September 2018.)

India Ministry of Housing and Urban Poverty Alleviation. 2016. *India Habitat III National Report 2016*. New Delhi, Ministry of Housing and Urban Poverty Alleviation.

Isiugo-Abanihe, U. C. and IOM Nigeria. 2016. *Migration in Nigeria: A Country Profile 2014*. Geneva, Switzerland, International Organization for Migration.

Jagannathan, S. 2001. *The Role of Nongovernmental Organizations in Primary Education: A Study of Six NGOs in India*. Washington, DC, World Bank. (World Bank Policy Research Working Paper 2530.)

JBS International. 2017. *Somali Girls' Education Promotion Programme Endline Evaluation Report*. Geneva, Switzerland, CARE International.

Jingzhong, Y. and Lu, P. 2011. Differentiated childhoods: impacts of rural labor migration on left-behind children in China. *Journal of Peasant Studies*, Vol. 38, No. 2, pp. 355–77.

Kukutai, T. 2011. Maori demography in Aotearoa New Zealand: Fifty years on. *New Zealand Population Review*, Vol. 37, p. 45.

Lanyasunya, A. R., Ogogo, C. O. and Waweru, S. N. 2012. An empirical investigation of viability of alternative approaches to basic education among the Samburu nomadic pastoralists of northern Kenya. *Journal of Education and Practice*, Vol. 3, No. 15, pp. 56–64.

Ling, M. 2015. "Bad Students Go to Vocational Schools!": Education, Social Reproduction and Migrant Youth in Urban China. *China Journal*, No. 73, pp. 108–31.

Liu, Z., Yu, L. and Zheng, X. 2018. No longer left-behind: The impact of return migrant parents on children's performance. *China Economic Review*, Vol. 49, pp. 184–96.

Marazyan, K. 2015. Foster children's educational outcomes when child fostering is motivated by norms: The case of Cameroon. *Journal of Comparative Family Studies*, Vol. 46, No. 1, pp. 85–103.

Mberu, B., Béguy, D. and Ezeh, A. C. 2017. Internal migration, urbanization and slums in sub-Saharan Africa. Groth, H. and May, J. F. (eds), *Africa's Population: In Search of a Demographic Dividend*. Cham, Springer, pp. 315–32.

Muhidin, S. 2018. *Internal Migration and Education in Indonesia*. (Background paper for *Global Education Monitoring Report 2019*.)

New Zealand Ministry of Social Development. 2016. *The Social Report 2016: Te Pūrongo Oranga Tangata*. Wellington, Ministry of Social Development.

Ngugi, M. 2016. Challenges facing mobile schools among nomadic pastoralists: A case study of Turkana county, Kenya. *American Journal of Educational Research*, Vol. 4, No. 1, pp. 22–32.

Nguyen, C. V. 2016. Does parental migration really benefit left-behind children? Comparative evidence from Ethiopia, India, Peru and Vietnam. *Social Science and Medicine*, Vol. 153, pp. 230–39.

No, F., Chin, S. A. and Khut, S. 2018. *An Evaluation Report on the National Literacy Campaign 2015 in Cambodia*. Phnom Penh, UNESCO.

Nusche, D., Radinger, T., Busemeyer, M. R. and Theisens, H. 2016. *OECD Reviews of School Resources: Austria*. Paris, Organisation for Economic Co-operation and Development.

OECD. 2015. *Improving Schools in Sweden: An OECD Perspective*. Paris, Organisation for Economic Co-operation and Development.

___. 2016a. *Education in China: A Snapshot*. Paris, Organisation for Economic Co-operation and Development.

___. 2016b. *PISA 2015 Results (Volume II): Policies and Practices for Successful Schools*. Paris, Organisation for Economic Co-operation and Development.

OECD and UNESCO. 2016. *Education in Thailand: An OECD-UNESCO Perspective - Reviews of National Policies for Education*. Paris, Organisation for Economic Co-operation and Development/UNESCO.

Okonkwo, H. I. and Ibrahim, M. 2014. Contemporary issues in nomadic minority & Almajiri education: Problems and prospects. *Journal of Education and Practice*, Vol. 5, No. 24, pp. 19–27.

Olaniran, S. O. 2018. Almajiri education: policy and practice to meet the learning needs of the nomadic population in Nigeria. *International Review of Education*, Vol. 64, No. 1, pp. 111–26.

Ontario Ministry of Education. 2017. *Supporting Students and Communities: A Discussion Paper to Strengthen Education in Ontario's Rural and Remote Communities*. Toronto, Canada, Ontario Ministry of Education.

Patunru, A. A. and Kusumaningrum, S. 2013. *Child Domestic Workers (CDW) in Indonesia: Case Studies of Jakarta and Greater Areas*. Jakarta, International Labour Organization/Pusat Kajian Perlindungan Anak.

Perlman, J. 2010. *Favela: Four Decades of Living on the Edge in Rio de Janeiro*. Oxford, UK, Oxford University Press.

Piper, B. and Zuilkowski, S. S. 2015. Teacher coaching in Kenya: Examining instructional support in public and nonformal schools. *Teaching and Teacher Education*, Vol. 47, pp. 173–83.

Pons, A., Amoroso, J., Herczynski, J., Kheyfets, I., Lockheed, M. and Santiago, P. 2015. *OECD Reviews of School Resources: Kazakhstan*. Paris, Organisation for Economic Co-operation and Development.

Quattri, M. and Watkins, K. 2016. *Child Labour and Education: A Survey of Slum Settlements in Dhaka*. London, Overseas Development Institute.

Raggl, A. 2015. Teaching and learning in small rural primary schools in Austria and Switzerland: Opportunities and challenges from teachers' and students' perspectives. *International Journal of Educational Research*, Vol. 74, pp. 127–35.

Randall, S. 2015. Where have all the nomads gone? Fifty years of statistical and demographic invisibilities of African mobile pastoralists. *Pastoralism*, Vol. 5, No. 1, p. 22.

Rao, J. and Jingzhong, Y. 2016. From a virtuous cycle of rural-urban education to urban-oriented rural basic education in China: An explanation of the failure of China's Rural School Mapping Adjustment policy. *Journal of Rural Studies*, No. 47, pp. 601–11.

Reed, M. N. 2012. Meeting the educational needs of seasonal migrant children: An analysis of educational programs at brick kilns in India. PhD thesis, International Studies. Tucson, Aris., University of Arizona.

Resosudarmo, B. P. and Suryadarma, D. 2014. The impact of childhood migration on educational attainment: Evidence from rural-urban migrants in Indonesia. *Asian Population Studies*, Vol. 10, No. 3, pp. 319–33.

Reza, S. 2016. Hyper-individualized recruitment: Rural-urban labour migration and precarious construction work in Bangladesh. *Migration, Mobility, and Displacement*, Vol. 2, No. 2, pp. 40–61.

Rigotti, J. I. R. and Hadad, R. M. 2018. *An analysis of the relationship between internal migration and education in Brazil.* (Background paper for *Global Education Monitoring Report 2019.*)

Ryks, J., Howden-Chapman, P., Robson, B., Stuart, K. and Waa, A. 2014. Maori participation in urban development: Challenges and opportunities for indigenous people in Aotearoa New Zealand. *Lincoln Planning Review,* Vol. 6, No. 1–2, pp. 4–17.

Sahoo, N. 2016. *A Tale of Three Cities: India's Exclusionary Urbanisation.* New Delhi, Observer Research Foundation. (Issue Brief 156.)

Santiago, P., Fiszbein, A., Jaramillo, S. G. and Radinger, T. 2017. *OECD Reviews of School Resources: Chile.* Paris, Organisation for Economic Co-operation and Development.

Santiago, P., Levitas, A., Rado, P. and Shewbridge, C. 2016. *OECD Reviews of School Resources: Estonia.* Paris, Organisation for Economic Co-operation and Development.

Scott-Villiers, P., Wilson, S., Kabala, N., Kullu, M., Ndung'u, D. and Scott-Villiers, A. 2015. *A Study of Education and Advocacy in Kenya's Arid and Semi-Arid Lands.* New York, UNICEF.

Shack/Slum Dwellers International. 2018. *Know Your City: Slum Dwellers Count.* Cape Town, Shack/Slum Dwellers International.

Shewbridge, C., Godfrey, K., Hermann, Z. and Nusche, D. 2016. *OECD Reviews of School Resources: Lithuania.* Paris, Organisation for Economic Co-operation and Development.

Siddhu, G., Jha, S. and Lewin, K. 2015. *Universalising Secondary Education in India: Seeking Efficiency, Effectiveness, and Equity in Planning Enhanced Access and Improving Quality.* Conference paper for UKFIET, The Education and Development Forum, Oxford, UK, University of Oxford, 15–17 September.

Somalia Ministry of Education, Culture and Higher Education. 2017a. *Education Sector Analysis 2012–2016.* Mogadishu, Ministry of Education, Culture and Higher Education.

___. 2017b. *Education Sector Strategic Plan 2018–2020.* Mogadishu, Ministry of Education, Culture and Higher Education.

Somaliland Ministry of Education and Higher Studies. 2017. *Education Sector Strategic Plan 2017–2021.* Hargeisa, Somaliland Ministry of Education and Higher Studies.

South African Cities Network. 2016. *State of South African Cities Report 2016.* Cape Town, South African Cities Network.

Statistics Finland. 2017. *Official Statistics of Finland: Providers of Education and Educational Institutions – Releases.* Helsinki, Statistics Finland. www.stat.fi/til/kjarj/tie_en.html. (Accessed 13 April 2018.)

Statistics Norway. 2018. *Pupils in Primary and Lower Secondary School.* Oslo, Statistics Norway. www.ssb.no/en/utgrs. (Accessed 13 April 2018.)

Steiner-Khamsi, G. and Stolpe, I. 2005. Non-traveling 'best practices' for a traveling population: The case of nomadic education in Mongolia. *European Educational Research Journal,* Vol. 4, No. 1, pp. 22–35.

Strayer, N. 2016. The great out-of-state migration: where students go. *New York Times,* 26 August. www.nytimes.com/interactive/2016/08/26/us/college-student-migration.html. (Accessed 5 March 2018.)

Subbaraman, R., O'Brien, J., Shitole, T., Shitole, S., Sawant, K., Bloom, D. E. and Patil-Deshmukh, A. 2012. Off the map: The health and social implications of being a non-notified slum in India. *Environment and Urbanization,* Vol. 24, No. 2, pp. 643–63.

Swedish National Agency for Education. 2018. *Number of comprehensive schools and small schools.* Stockholm, Swedish National Agency for Education. (Accessed 17 April 2018.)

TADAMUN. 2015. *Inequality and Underserved Areas: A Spatial Analysis of Access to Public Schools in the Greater Cairo Region.* Cairo, TADAMUN, The Cairo Urban Solidarity Initiative. www.tadamun.co/2015/09/08/inequality-underserved-areas-spatial-analysis-access-public-schools-greater-cairo-region. (Accessed 5 February 2018.)

Taiwo, F. J. 2013. Transforming the Almajiri education for the benefit of the Nigerian society. *Journal of Educational and Social Research,* Vol. 3, No. 9, pp. 67–72.

The Economist. 2015. China's left behind: little match children. 17 October. www.economist.com/briefing/2015/10/17/little-match-children. (Accessed 15 September 2018.)

Tsang, B. 2018. Migrant education: family strategies and public policies. Kong, P., Postiglione, G. and Hannum, E. (eds), *China's Rural Education in Transition.* Abingdon-on-Thames, UK, Routledge.

UN Habitat. 2003. *Slums of the World: The Face of Urban Poverty in the New Millennium?* Nairobi, UN Habitat.

___. 2016a. *Participatory Slum Upgrading Programme.* Nairobi, UN Habitat.

___. 2016b. *Slum Almanac 2015/2016: Tracking Improvement in the Lives of Slum Dwellers.* Nairobi, UN Habitat.

___. 2016c. *Urbanization and Development: Emerging Futures – World Cities Report 2016*. Nairobi, UN Habitat.

UNDESA. 2014. *World Urbanization Prospects 2014*. New York, United Nations Department of Economic and Social Affairs.

___. 2017. *World Population Policies Database, 1976–2015*. New York, Population Division, United Nations Department of Economic and Social Affairs. https://esa.un.org/PopPolicy/dataquery_report.aspx. (Accessed 1 September 2018.)

UNDP. 2009. *Human Development Report 2009: Overcoming Barriers – Human Mobility and Development*. New York, United Nations Development Programme.

UNESCO. 2013. *Social Inclusion of Internal Migrants in India*. New Delhi, UNESCO.

___. 2015. *EFA Global Monitoring Report 2015: Education for All 2000–2015 – Achievements and Challenges*. Paris, UNESCO.

___. 2016a. *From a Single Slum Classroom to Winning the UNESCO King Hamad Prize*. Paris, UNESCO. www.unesco.org/new/en/culture/themes/dynamic-content-single-view/news/from_a_single_slum_classroom_to_winning_the_unesco_king_hama. (Accessed 30 January 2018.)

___. 2016b. *Global Education Monitoring Report 2016: Education for People and Planet – Creating Sustainable Futures for All*. Paris, UNESCO.

___. 2018. *An Evaluation Report on the National Literacy Campaign 2015 in Cambodia*. Phnom Penh, UNESCO.

UNICEF. 2012. *The State of the World's Children 2012: Children in an Urban World*. New York, UNICEF.

UNICEF and Baan Dek Foundation. 2017. *Building Futures in Thailand: Support to Children Living in Construction Site Camps*. Bangkok, UNICEF.

United Kingdom Department of Education. 2018. *Schools, Pupils and their Characteristics: January 2018 – National Tables*. London, Department of Education. www.gov.uk/government/statistics/schools-pupils-and-their-characteristics-january-2018. (Accessed 15 September 2018.)

United Kingdom Education and Skills Funding Agency. 2017. *Table A1: School Capacity in State-funded Primary and Secondary Schools*. London, United Kingdom Education and Skills Funding Agency. www.gov.uk/government/statistics/school-capacity-academic-year-2016-to-2017. (Accessed 15 September 2018.)

United Nations Task Team. 2015. *Habitat III Issues Papers: 1 – Inclusive Cities*. New York, United Nations Department of Economic and Social Affairs/United Nations Development Programme/United Nations High Commissioner for Human Rights.

United States DOE. 2015. *Integrated Postsecondary Education Data System (IPEDS), Spring 2015, Fall Enrollment Component Table 309.30*. Washington, DC, National Center for Education Statistics, United States Department of Education.

Van de Glind, H. 2010. *Migration and Child Labour: Exploring Child Migrant Vulnerabilities and Those of Children Left-Behind*. Geneva, Switzerland, International Labour Organization.

Van Luot, N. and Dat, N. B. 2017. The psychological well-being among left-behind children of labor migrant parents in rural northern Vietnam. *Open Journal of Social Sciences*, Vol. 5, No. 06, p. 188.

Vutha, H., Pide, L. and Dalis, P. 2014. *The Impacts of Adult Migration on Children's Well-being: The Case of Cambodia*. Phnom Penh, Cambodia Development Resource Institute.

Wang, A., Medina, A., Luo, R., Shi, Y. and Yue, A. 2016. To board or not to board: Evidence from nutrition, health and education outcomes of students in rural China. *China and World Economy*, Vol. 24, No. 3, pp. 52–66.

Wang, X., Ling, L., Su, H., Cheng, J., Jin, L. and Sun, Y. H. 2015. Self-concept of left-behind children in China: A systematic review of the literature. *Child: Care, Health and Development*, Vol. 41, No. 3, pp. 346–55.

Webb, A. and Radcliffe, S. 2013. Mapuche demands during educational reform, the Penguin Revolution and the Chilean Winter of Discontent. *Studies in Ethnicity and Nationalism*, Vol. 13, No. 3, pp. 319–41.

World Bank. 2009. *World Development Report: Reshaping Economic Geography*. Washington, DC, World Bank.

___. 2016. *Indigenous Latin America in the Twenty-First Century*. Washington DC, World Bank.

World Bank and Viet Nam Academy of Social Sciences. 2016. *Viet Nam's Household Registration System*. Ha Noi, Hong Duc Publishing House.

Wu, X. and Zhang, Z. 2015. Population migration and children's school enrollments in China, 1990–2005. *Social Science Research*, Vol. 53, pp. 177–90.

Yan, W. 2015. Report: Chinese families become smaller. *China Daily*, 13 May. www.chinadaily.com.cn/china/2015-05/13/content_20708152.htm. (Accessed 5 March 2018.)

Ye, W. 2016. Internal migration and citizenship education in China's Shenzhen city. *Education and Urban Society*, Vol. 48, No. 1, pp. 77–97.

Yiu, L. 2014. Social change and school integration in urban China: The state, politics of migration, and citizenship. Hong Kong, University of Hong Kong. (Unpublished.)

Yiu, L. 2018. Access and equity for rural migrants in Shanghai. Kong, P., Postiglione, G. and Hannum, E. (eds), *China's Rural Education in Transition*. Abingdon-on-Thames, UK, Routledge.

Zhou, S. and Cheung, M. 2017. Hukou system effects on migrant children's education in China: Learning from past disparities. *International Social Work*, Vol. 60, No. 6, pp. 1327–42.

CHAPTER 3

Ahrenholz, B., Fuchs, I., Birnbaum, T. 2016. Modelle der Beschulung von Seiteneinsteigerinnen und Seiteneinsteigern in der Praxis [Models of Schooling of Lateral Entrants in Practice]. *BiSS-Journal*, No. 5., pp. 14–17. (In German.)

Al-deen, T. J. and Windle, J. 2017. 'I feel sometimes I am a bad mother': The affective dimension of immigrant mothers' involvement in their children's schooling. *Journal of Sociology*, Vol. 53, No. 1, pp. 110–26.

Alba Soular, D. 2017. LCPS board aims to protect immigrants with new policy. *Las Cruces Sun News*, 19 April. https://eu.lcsun-news.com/story/news/education/lcps/2017/04/19/lcps-board-aims-protect-immigrants-new-policy/100606972. (Accessed 6 April 2018.)

American Immigration Council. 2018. *The Dream Act, DACA, and other Policies Designed to Protect Dreamers*. www.americanimmigrationcouncil.org/sites/default/files/research/the_dream_act_daca_and_other_policies_designed_to_protect_dreamers.pdf. (Accessed 15 September 2018.)

Antman, F. M. 2012. Gender, educational attainment, and the impact of parental migration on children left behind. *Journal of Population Economics*. Vol. 25, No. 4, pp. 1187–214.

Audren, G., Baby-Collin, V. and Dorier, E. 2016. Quelles mixités dans une ville fragmentée ? Dynamiques locales de l'espace scolaire marseillais [What diversity in a fragmented city? Local dynamics in Marseille's schools]. *Lien social et politiques*, No. 77, p. 38. (In French.)

Ballatore, R. M., Fort, M. and Ichino, A. 2015. *The Tower of Babel in the Classroom: Immigrants and Natives in Italian Schools*. London, Centre for Economic Policy Research. (Discussion Paper 10341.)

Basteck, C., Huesmann, K. and Nax, H. 2015. *Matching practices for secondary schools: Germany*. www.matching-in-practice.eu/wp-content/uploads/2015/01/MiP_-Profile_No.21.pdf. (Accessed 15 September 2018).

Beck, A., Corak, M. and Tienda, M. 2012. Age at immigration and the adult attainments of child migrants to the United States. *The Annals of the American Academy of Political and Social Science*, Vol. 643, No. 1, pp. 134–59.

Betts, J. R. and Fairlie, R. W. 2003. Does immigration induce 'native flight' from public schools into private schools? *Journal of Public Economics*, Vol. 87, No. 5–6, pp. 987–1012.

Bossavie, L. 2017a. *Immigrant Concentration at School and Natives' Achievement: Does Length of Stay in the Host Country Matter?* Munich, University of Munich. (Archive Paper 82401.)

___. 2017b. *Immigrant Concentration at School and Natives' Achievement: Does the Type of Migrants and Natives Matter?* Munich, University of Munich. (Archive Paper 80308.)

Brunello, G. and De Paola, M. 2017. *School Segregation of Immigrants and Its Effects on Educational Outcomes in Europe*. Luxembourg, European Expert Network on Economics of Education. (Analytical Report 30.)

Bunar, N. 2017. *Migration and Education in Sweden: Integration of Migrants in the Swedish School Education and Higher Education Systems*. Stockholm, NESET II.

Capps, R., Fix, M. and Zong, J. 2016. *A Profile of U.S. Children with Unauthorized Immigrant Parents*. Washington, DC, Migration Policy Institute.

Caritas Maroc. 2015. *L'integration scolaire des élèves primo-arrivants allophones dans le système scolaire public marocain: Observations et recommendations de Caritas* [School Integration of Newcomer Foreign Students in the Moroccan Public School System: Caritas Observations and Recommendations]. Rabat, Caritas Maroc. (In French.)

Charles, J. 2018a. As Chile prepares for new president, Haitians warned they won't find 'paradise' there. *Miami Herald*, 1 March. www.miamiherald.com/news/nation-world/world/americas/haiti/article202590229.html (Accessed 15 September 2018.)

___. 2018b. Haitians gamble on a better life in Chile. But the odds aren't always in their favour. *Miami Herald*, 1 March. (Accessed 15 September 2018.)

Cohen Goldner, S. and Epstein, G. S. 2014. Age at immigration and high school dropouts. *IZA Journal of Migration*, Vol. 3, No. 1.

Cortes, P. 2015. The feminization of international migration and its effects on the children left behind: Evidence from the Philippines. *World Development*, Vol. 65, pp. 62–78.

Crul, M. 2013. Snakes and ladders in educational systems: Access to higher education for second-generation Turks in Europe. *Journal of Ethnic and Migration Studies*, Vol. 39, No. 9, pp. 1383–401.

Crul, M., Schnell, P., Herzog-Punzenberger, B., Wilmes, M., Slootman, M. and Aparicio Gómez, R. 2012. School careers of second-generation youth in Europe: Which education systems provide the best chances for success? Crul, M., Schneider, J. and Lelie, F. (eds), *The European Second Generation Compared: Does the Integration Context Matter?*, Amsterdam, Amsterdam University Press, pp. 101–64.

Crush, J., Chikanda, A. and Tawodzera, G. 2015. The third wave: Mixed migration from Zimbabwe to South Africa. *Canadian Journal of African Studies*, Vol. 49, No. 2, pp. 363–82.

Davis, J. and Brazil, N. 2016. Disentangling fathers' absences from household remittances in international migration: The case of educational attainment in Guatemala. *International Journal of Educational Development*, Vol. 50, pp. 1–11.

Davoli, M. and Entorf, H. 2018. *The PISA Shock, Socioeconomic Inequality, and School Reforms in Germany*. Bonn, Germany, Institute of Labor Economics.

Dietz, B., Gatskova, K. and Ivlevs, A. 2015. *Emigration, Remittances and the Education of Children Staying Behind: Evidence from Tajikistan*. Bonn, Germany, Institute of Labor Economics. (Discussion Paper 9515.)

Dillon, M. and Walsh, C. A. 2012. Left behind: the experiences of children of the Caribbean whose parents have migrated. *Journal of Comparative Family Studies*, Vol. 43, No. 6, pp. 871–902.

Docquier, F. and Deuster, C. 2018. *International Migration and Human Capital Inequality: A Dyadic Approach*. (Background paper for *Global Education Monitoring Report 2019*.)

Docquier, F. and Marfouk, A. 2006. International migration by educational attainment (1990–2000). Ozden, C. and Schiff, M. (eds), *International Migration, Remittances and the Brain Drain*. Washington, DC, World Bank, pp. 151–99.

Dominican Republic National Statistical Office. 2013. *Primera Encuesta Nacional de Inmigrantes en la República Dominicana (ENI-2012) [First National Immigrants Survey in the Dominican Republic]*. Santo Domingo, Oficina Nacional de Estadística. (In Spanish.)

___. 2018. *Segunda Encuesta Nacional de Inmigrantes en la República Dominicana [Second National Survey on Immigrants in the Dominican Republic]*. Santo Domingo, Oficina Nacional de Estadística. (In Spanish.)

Duncan, B., Grogger, J., Leon, A. S. and Trejo, S. J. 2017. *New Evidence of Generational Progress for Mexican Americans*. New York, National Bureau of Economic Research.

Endo, I., De Luna-Martínez, J. and De Smet, D. 2017. *Three things to know about migrant workers and remittances in Malaysia*. Washington, DC, World Bank. http://blogs.worldbank.org/eastasiapacific/three-things-to-know-about-migrant-workers-and-remittances-in-malaysia. (Accessed 15 September 2018.)

Entorf, H. and Lauk, M. 2008. Peer effects, social multipliers and migration at school: An international comparison. *Journal of Ethnic and Migration Studies*, Vol. 34, No. 4, pp. 634–54.

European Commission/EACEA/Eurydice. 2017. *Key Data on Teaching Languages at School in Europe: Eurydice Report*. Luxembourg, Publications Office of the European Union.

Eurostat. 2017. *Early Leavers from Education and Training*. Luxembourg, Eurostat. https://ec.europa.eu/eurostat/statistics-explained/index.php/Early_leavers_from_education_and_training. (Accessed 14 September 2018).

Fauvelle-Aymar, C. 2014. *Migration and employment in South Africa: An econometric analysis of domestic and international migrants*. Johannesburg, African Centre for Migration and Society, University of the Witwatersrand.

Feliciano, C. 2005. Educational selectivity in U.S. immigration: How do immigrants compare to those left behind? *Demography*, Vol. 42, No. 1, pp. 131–52.

FIDH. 2016. *Women and Children from Kyrgyzstan Affected by Migration: An Exacerbated Vulnerability*. Paris, International Federation for Human Rights.

Fincke, G. and Lange, S. 2012. *Segregation an Grundschulen: Der Einfluss der elterlichen Schulwahl [Segregation in Elementary Schools: The Influence of Parental School Choice]*. Berlin, Expert Council of German Foundations on Integration and Migration. (In German.)

Fougère, D., Kiefer, N., Monso, O. and Pirus, C. 2017. *La concentration des enfants étrangers dans les classes de collèges : Quels effets sur les résultats scolaires ? [The Concentration of Foreign Children at College: What Effects on School Results?]* Paris, Ministère de l'Éducation Nationale. (In French.)

FRA. 2017. *Current Migration Situation in the EU: Education*. Vienna, European Union Agency for Fundamental Rights.

France Human Rights Defender. *Droit fondamental à l'éducation : une école pour tous, un droit pour chacun – Rapport droits de l'enfant 2016. [Basic Right to Education: A School for All, a Right for Everyone – Child Rights Report 2016]*. Paris, Défenseur des droits. (In French).

Gambino, C. P., Trevelyan, E. N. and Fitzwater, J. T. 2014. *The Foreign-Born Population from Africa: 2008–2012*. Washington, DC, United States Census Bureau.

Geay, C., McNally, S. and Telhaj, S. 2013. Non-native speakers of English in the classroom: What are the effects on pupil performance? *The Economic Journal*, Vol. 123, No. 570, pp. F281–F307.

Georgetown Law Human Rights Institute. 2014. *Left Behind: How Statelessness in the Dominican Republic Limits Children's Access to Education*. Washington, DC, Georgetown Law.

Glenn, C. L. and de Jong, E. J. 1996. *Educating Immigrant Children: Schools and Language Minorities in Twelve Nations*. New York, Routledge.

Golash-Boza, T. and Merlin, B. 2016. Here's how undocumented students are able to enroll at American universities. *The Conversation*, 24 November. https://theconversation.com/heres-how-undocumented-students-are-able-to-enroll-at-american-universities-69269. (Accessed 15 September 2018.)

Gönsch, I., Kleinegees, U., Krüger-Hemmer, C., Malecki, A., Schmidt, A. and Vollmar, M. 2016. Bildung: Auszug aus dem Datenreport 2016 [Education: Excerpt from the Data Report 2016]. Federal Agency for Civic Education (ed.), *Datenreport 2016 Ein Sozialbericht für die Bundesrepublik Deutschland*. Bonn, Germany, Statistisches Bundesamt (Destatis) and Wissenschaftszentrum Berlin für Sozialforschung in Zusammenarbeit mit Das Sozio-oekonomische Panel/Deutschen Institut für Wirtschaftsforschung. (In German.)

Gonzalez-Betancor, S. M. and Lopez-Puig, A. J. 2016. Grade retention in primary education is associated with quarter of birth and socioeconomic status. *PLOS ONE*, Vol. 11, No. 11, p. e0166431.

Gould, E. D., Lavy, V. and Paserman, M. D. 2009. Does immigration affect the long-term educational outcomes of natives? Quasi-experimental evidence. *Economic Journal*, Vol. 119, No. 540.

Grigt, S. 2017. *Il viaggio della speranza: L'istruzione dei minori rifugiati e non accompagnati in Italia* [The Journey of Hope: Education for Refugee and Unaccompanied Children in Italy]. Rome, Coordinamento Nazionale Comunità di Accoglienza. (In Italian.)

Hardoy, I. and Schøne, P. 2013. Does the clustering of immigrant peers affect the school performance of natives? *Journal of Human Capital*, Vol. 7, No. 1, pp. 1–25.

Hessen Ministry of Justice for Integration and Europe. 2013. *Statistical Report on the Education of Children with an Immigration Background in Hessen: Pre-School, Primary, and Secondary Education 2011–2012*. Hessen, Germany, State Ministry of Justice for Integration and Europe.

HRW. 2016. *Closed Doors: Mexico's Failure to Protect Central American Refugee and Migrant Children*, Human Rights Watch. www.hrw.org/report/2016/03/31/closed-doors/mexicos-failure-protect-central-american-refugee-and-migrant-children. (Accessed 15 September 2018).

Hsin, A. and Ortega, F. 2018. The effects of deferred action for childhood arrivals on the educational outcomes of undocumented students. *Demography*, Vol. 55, No. 4, pp. 1487–506.

Huddleston, T., Bilgili, Ö., Joki, A.-L. and Vankova, Z. 2015. *Migrant Integration Policy Index*. Barcelona, Spain/Brussels, Barcelona Centre for International Affairs/Migration Policy Group.

IACHR. 2015. *Situation of Human Rights in the Dominican Republic*, Washington, DC, Inter-American Commission on Human Rights.

Ichou, M. 2018. *The Forms and Determinants of Children of Immigrants' Academic Trajectories in French Primary and Secondary Schools*. (Background paper for *Global Education Monitoring Report 2019*.)

IIASA. 2018 *Global migration and educational expansion: Scenarios and projections of population-level interactions*. (Background paper for *Global Education Monitoring Report 2019*.)

INDH. 2018. *Manifestaciones de Discriminación Racial en Chile: un Estudio de Percepciones [Manifestations of Racial Discrimination in Chile: A Study of Perceptions]*. Santiago, National Human Development Initiative. (In Spanish.)

Institute on Statelessness and Inclusion. 2017. *The World's Stateless Children*. Oisterwijk, Netherlands, Institute on Statelessness and Inclusion.

IOM. 2017. *World Migration Report 2018*. Geneva, Switzerland, International Organization for Migration.

___. 2018. *Libya's Migrant Report Round 17 January-February 2018: Flow Monitoring*. Geneva, Switzerland, International Organization for Migration.

Italy MIUR. 2017a. *"Distribuzione degli alunni con cittadinanza non italiana tra le scuole e formazione delle classi" in riferimento alla Circolare Ministeriale 8 gennaio 2010, n.2. [Distribution of Pupils with Non-Italian Citizenship among the Schools and Training in Classes]*, Rome, Ministero dell'Istruzione, dell'Università e della Ricerca. (In Italian.)

___. 2017b. *Gli Alunni Stranieri nel Sistema Scolastico Italiano, A.S. 2015/2016 [Foreign Students in the Italian School System]*, Rome, Ministero dell'Istruzione, dell'Università e della Ricerca. (In Italian.)

___. 2018. *Gli Alunni Stranieri nel Sistema Scolastico Italiano, A.S. 2016/2017. [Foreign Students in the Italian School System]*, Rome, Ministero dell'Istruzione, dell'Università e della Ricerca. (In Italian.)

Jensen, P. and Rasmussen, A. W. 2011. The effect of immigrant concentration in schools on native and immigrant children's reading and math skills. *Economics of Education Review*, Vol. 30, No. 6, pp. 1503–15.

Junta de Andalucìa. 2018. *Enseñanza de español e integración [Teaching of Spanish and integration]*. www.juntadeandalucia.es/temas/estudiar/primaria-eso/integracion.html. (Accessed 15 September 2018.) (In Spanish.)

Keller, K. and Grob, A. 2010. Mehr Qualität und breiterer Zugang [More Quality and Wider Access]. *Psychoscope*, Vol. 6, pp. 8–11. (In German.)

Kuka, E., Shenhav, N. and Shih, K. 2018. *Do Human Capital Decisions Respond to the Returns to Education? Evidence from DACA*. New York, National Bureau of Economic Research. (Working Paper 24315.)

Las Cruces Public Schools. 2017. *Superintendent testifies on immigration impact*. Las Cruces, NM, Las Cruces Public Schools. http://lcps.k12.nm.us/2017/12/08/superintendent-testifies-on-immigration-impact. (Accessed 20 September 2018.)

Le Matin. 2015. *L'intégration des migrants passe aussi par l'école [Integration of Migrants also Goes Through School]*. https://lematin.ma/journal/2015/l-integration-des-migrants-passe-aussi-par-l-ecole/234414.html. (Accessed 15 September 2018.)

Le Pichon, E., Baauw, S., Van Erning, R. (2016). Country Report: The Netherlands. Utrecht, Netherlands, EDINA and European Commission.

Linton, J. M., Griffin, M. and Shapiro, A. J. 2017. Detention of immigrant children. *American Academy of Pediatrics*. Vol. 139, No. 5, pp. 1–11.

Lüdemann, E. and Schwerdt, G. 2013. Migration background and educational tracking. *Journal of Population Economics*, Vol. 26, No. 2, pp. 455–81.

Lynch, M. 2008. *Futures Denied: Statelessness among Infants, Children, and Youth*. Washington, DC, Refugees International.

Mahlke, H. and Yamamoto, L. 2017. Venezuelan displacement: A challenge to Brazil. *Forced Migration Review*, Vol. 56.

Minello, A. and Barban, N. 2012. The educational expectations of children of immigrants in Italy. *The Annals of the American Academy of Political and Social Science*, Vol. 643, No. 1, pp. 78–103.

Miranda, A. 2011. Migrant networks, migrant selection, and high school graduation in Mexico. Polachek, S. W. and Tatsiramos, K. (eds), *Research in Labor Economics*, Vol. 33, pp. 263–306.

MMP. 2017. *Mexican Migration Project (MMP): Data Overview*. Princeton, NJ. https://mmp.opr.princeton.edu/databases/dataoverview-en.aspx. (Accessed 15 September 2018.)

Mordecai, K., Gonzalez Diaz, J. C. and Martine, I. 2017. *Dreams Deferred: The Struggle of Dominicans of Haitian Descent to Get their Nationality Back*. Washington, Robert F. Kennedy Human Rights/American Jewish World Service/Centro de Desarrollo Sostenible/United Nations Democracy Fund.

Morris-Lange, S., Wendt, H. and Wohlfarth, C. 2013. *Segregation an deutschen Schulen: Ausmaß, Folgen und Handlungsempfehlungen für bessere Bildungschancen [Segregation in German schools: Extent, Consequences and Recommendations for Better Educational Opportunities]*. Berlin, Sachverständigenrat deutscher Stiftungen fur Integration und Migration GmbH. (In German.)

Mourji, F., Ferrié, J.-N., Radi, S. and Alioua, M. 2016. *Les migrants subsahariens au Maroc : Enjeux d'une migration de résidence [Sub-Saharan migrants in Morocco: Stakes of a residential migration]*. Konrad Adenauer Stiftung. Rabat, Morocco. (In French.)

MPI. 2018. *Deferred Action for Childhood Arrivals (DACA) Data Tools*. Washington, DC, Migration Policy Institute. www.migrationpolicy.org/programs/data-hub/deferred-action-childhood-arrivals-daca-profiles. (Accessed 16 August 2018.)

Nakhid, R. and Welch, A. 2017. Protection in the absence of legislation in Trinidad and Tobago. *Forced Migration Review*, Vol. 56, pp. 42–44.

Nawarat, N. 2017. Discourse on migrant education policy: Patterns of words and outcomes in Thailand. *Kasetsart Journal of Social Sciences*, pp. 1–8.

Nonnenmacher, S. and Yonemura, A. 2018. *Migration and Education in West Africa*. (Background paper for *Global Education Monitoring Report 2019*.)

Oberdabernig, D. and Schneebaum, A. 2017. Catching up? The educational mobility of migrants' and natives' children in Europe. *Applied Economics*, Vol. 49, No. 37, pp. 3701–28.

OECD. 2015. *Immigrant Students at School: Easing the Journey Towards Integration*. Paris, Organisation for Economic Co-operation and Development.

___. 2016. *PISA 2015 Results (Volume I): Excellence and Equity in Education*. Paris, Organisation for Economic Co-operation and Development.

___. 2017. *Catching Up? Intergenerational Mobility and Children of Immigrants*. Paris, Organisation for Economic Co-operation and Development.

___. 2018. *The Resilience of Students with an Immigrant Background: Factors that Shape Well-being*. Paris, Organisation for Economic Co-operation and Development.

OHCHR. 2018. *Status of Ratification Interactive Dashboard*. Geneva, Switzerland, Office of the United Nations High Commissioner for Human Rights. http://indicators.ohchr.org. (Accessed 15 September 2018.)

Ohinata, A. and van Ours, J. C. 2013. How immigrant children affect the academic achievement of native Dutch children. *The Economic Journal*, Vol. 123, No. 570, pp. F308–F31.

Open Society Justice Initiative. 2013. *Discrimination in German schools*. Open Society Foundations. www.opensocietyfoundations.org/fact-sheets/discrimination-german-schools. (Accessed 15 September 2018.)

Pavez-Soto, I. and Chan, C. 2018. The second generation in Chile: Negotiating identities, rights, and public policy. *International Migration*, Vol. 56, No. 2, pp. 82–96.

Qassemy, H., Barré, C., Cruanes, J., Ezzarouały, J., Meric, B., Msaddeq, M., Regragui, M. and Tournecuillert, V. 2014. *Les enfants migrants et l'école marocaine : État des lieux sur l'accès à l'éducation des enfants migrants subsahariens au Maroc [Migrant Children and the Moroccan School: State of Access to Education for Sub-Saharan Migrant Children in Morocco]*. Agadir, Moroco, Oum El Banine. (In French.)

Rangvid, B. S. 2007. School composition effects in Denmark: quantile regression evidence from PISA 2000. *Empirical Economics*, Vol. 33, No. 2, pp. 359–88.

Reveco, C. D. 2018. *Amid record numbers of arrivals, Chile turns rightward on immigration*. www.migrationpolicy.org/article/amid-record-numbers-arrivals-chile-turns-rightward-immigration. (Accessed 30 May 2018.)

Right to Education Initiative. 2018. *The Right to Education of Migrants, Refugees and Forcibly Displaced People: International Legal Framework, Remaining Challenges and Identification of States' Best Practices*. (Background paper for *Global Education Monitoring Report 2019*.)

Rodríguez-Izquierdo, R. M. and Darmody, M. 2017. Policy and practice in language support for newly arrived migrant children in Ireland and Spain. *British Journal of Educational Studies*, pp. 1–17.

Ruffini, B. and D'Addio, A. C. 2018. *Unaccompanied and Separated Children in Italy*. (Background paper for *Global Education Monitoring Report 2019*.)

Ryelandt, N. 2013. Les décrets « inscriptions » et « mixité sociale » de la Communauté française [The 'Registration' and 'Diversity' Decrees of the French Community]. *Courrier hebdomadaire du CRISP*,

Schneeweis, N. 2015. Immigrant concentration in schools: Consequences for native and migrant students. *Labour Economics*, Vol. 35, pp. 63–76.

Scown, C. 2018. *Countering the Effects of Trump's Immigration Policies In schools*. Washington, DC, Center for American Progress. www.americanprogress.org/issues/education-k-12/news/2018/05/03/450274/countering-effects-trumps-immigration-policies-schools. (Accessed 15 September 2018.)

Sekundarschulen Berlin. 2018. *Schüler mit Migrationshintergrund [Immigrant Students]*. Berlin, ISS Berlin. www.sekundarschulen-berlin.de/migrationshintergrund. (Accessed 16 July.)

Silió, E. 2015. La caída de inmigrantes reduce un 13% los extranjeros en las aulas [The decreasing number of immigrants reduces the number of foreigners at school by 13%], *El País*, 10 September. https://elpais.com/ccaa/2015/09/09/madrid/1441822071_744781.html. (Accessed 15 September 2018.)

Skolverket. 2018. *Rätt till modersmålsundervisning* [Right to mother tongue education]. www.skolverket.se/regler-och-ansvar/ansvar-i-skolfragor/ratt-till-modersmalsundervisning. (Accessed 15 September 2018.) (In Swedish.)

Skoverket. 2016. *Språkintroduktion Report 436 [Language Introduction Report 436]*. Stockolm, Skolverket.

Tangermann, J. and Hoffmeyer-Zlotnik, P. 2018. *Unaccompanied Minors in Germany: Challenges and Measures after the Clarification of Residence Status*. Nuremberg, German National Contact Point for the European Migration Network.

Tani, M. 2018. *Migration and Education*. (Background paper for *Global Education Monitoring Report 2019*.)

Teye, J. K., Awumbila, M. and Benneh, Y. 2015. Intraregional migration in the ECOWAS region: Trends and emerging challenges. Akoutou, A. B., Sohn, R., Vogl, M. and Yeboah, D. (eds), *Migration and Civil Society as Development Drivers: A Regional Perspective*. Bonn, Germany, West Africa Institute/Center for European Integration Studies, pp. 185–196.

The Economist. 2018. Chile gives immigrants a wary welcome. 4 December. www.economist.com/the-americas/2018/04/12/chile-gives-immigrants-a-wary-welcome. (Accessed 15 September 2018.)

The Nation. 2017. Schools for migrant workers' children close along Myanmar-Thai border. Bangkok, Nation News Network.

Tokunaga, T. 2018. *Possibilities and Constraints of Immigrant Students in the Japanese Educational System*. (Background paper for *Global Education Monitoring Report 2019*.)

UNHCR. 2015. *I Am Here, I Belong: The Urgent Need to End Childhood Statelessness*. Copenhagen, United Nations High Commissioner for Refugees.

UNICEF. 2017. *Five-fold increase in number of refugee and migrant children traveling alone since 2010*. New York, UNICEF.

United Nations Department for Economic and Social Affairs. 2017a. *International Migrant Stock by Age*. New York, United Nations.

___. 2017b. *International Migration Report 2017*. New York, United Nations.

United States Customs and Border Protection. 2018. *U.S. Border Patrol Southwest Border Apprehensions by Sector FY2017*. www.cbp.gov/newsroom/stats/usbp-sw-border-apprehensions-fy2017. (Accessed 15 September 2018.)

van de Werfhorst, H. G. and Heath, A. 2018. Selectivity of migration and the educational disadvantages of second-generation immigrants in ten host societies. *European Journal of Population*, pp. 1–32.

Van Houtte, M. and Stevens, P. A. 2010. School ethnic composition and aspirations of immigrant students in Belgium. *British Educational Research Journal*, Vol. 36, No. 2, pp. 209–37.

van Ours, J. C. and Veenman, J. 2006. Age at immigration and educational attainment of young immigrants. *Economics Letters*, Vol. 90, No. 3, pp. 310–16.

World Bank. 2018. *Moving for Prosperity: Global Migration and Labor Markets*. Washington, DC, World Bank.

Yang, D. 2008. International migration, remittances and household investment: evidence from Philippine migrants' exchange rate shocks. *The Economic Journal*, Vol. 118, No. 528, pp. 591–630.

Zagheni, E., Weber, I. and Gummadi, K. 2017. Leveraging Facebook's advertising platform to monitor stocks of migrants. *Population and Development Review*, Vol. 43, No. 4, pp. 721–34.

CHAPTER 4

Abdul-Hamid, H., Patrinos, H. A., Reyes, J., Kelcey, J. and Diaz Varela, A. 2016. *Learning in the Face of Adversity: The UNRWA Education Program for Palestinian Refugees*. Washington, DC, World Bank.

ACU. 2017. *Schools in Syria: Thematic Report*. Gaziantep, Turkey, Assistance Coordination Unit.

AEWG. 2018. *When is accelerated education a relevant response?* Geneva, Switzerland, Accelerated Education Working Group. https://eccnetwork.net/wp-content/uploads/AEWG-Accelerated-Education-decision-tree.pdf. (Accessed 16 August 2018.)

AFAD. 2013. Syrian Refugees in Turkey, 2013. Ankara, Republic of Turkey, Prime Ministry, Disaster and Emergency Management Presidency.

African Union. 2012. *African Union Convention for the Protection and Assistance of Internally Displaced Persons in Africa (Kampala Convention)*. Kampala, African Union.

___. 2017. *List of Countries which have Signed, Ratified/Acceded to the African Union Convention for the Protection and Assistance of Internally Displaced Persons in Africa (Kampala Convention)*. Addis Ababa, African Union.

Al-Sabahi, M. and Motahar, G. 2017. Using public schools as shelter for IDPs in Yemen. *Forced Migration Review*, No. 55, p. 1.

Anagnostou, D. and Nikolova, M. 2017. Η ενσωμάτωση των προσφύγων στο εκπαιδευτικό σύστημα στην Ελλάδα: Πολιτική και διαχείριση σε «κινούμενη άμμο» *[The Inclusion of Refugees in the Greek Education System]*. Athens, Hellenic Foundation for European and Foreign Policy. (In Greek.)

Arik Akyuz, B. M. 2018. *Evolution of National Policy in Turkey on Integration of Syrian Children into the National Education System*. (Background paper for *Global Education Monitoring Report 2019*.)

Baal, N. and Ronkainen, L. 2017. *Obtaining Representative Data on IDPs: Challenges and Recommendations*. Geneva, Switzerland, United Nations High Commissioner for Refugees.

Bakonyi, A., Léderer, A. and Szerekes, Z. 2017. *Best Interest out of Sight: The Treatment of Asylum Seeking Children in Hungary*. Budapest, Hungarian Helsinki Committee.

Bangladesh Ministry of Primary and Mass Education. 2015. *Third Primary Education Development Program (PEDP-3)*. Dhaka, Directorate of Primary Education.

Baumann, B. 2017. Sprachförderung und Deutsch als Zweitsprache in der Lehrerbildung: ein Deutschlandweiter Überblick [Language Support and German as a Second language in Teacher Education: A Germany-Wide Overview]. Becker-Mrotzek, M., Rosenberg, P., Schroeder, C. and Witte, A. (eds), *Deutsch als Zweitsprache in der Lehrerbildung [German as a Second Language in Teacher Education]*. Münster, Germany, Waxmann. (In German.)

BBC. 2018. US Ends Aid to Palestinian Refugee Agency Unrwa. 1 September. www.bbc.com/news/world-us-canada-45377336. (Accessed 4 September 2018.)

Behrman, S. and Kent, A. 2018. *Climate Refugees: Beyond the Legal Impasse?* Abingdon-on-Thames, UK, Routledge.

Betts, A. 2018. Don't make African nations borrow money to support refugees. *Foreign Policy*, 21 February. https://foreignpolicy.com/2018/02/21/dont-make-african-nations-borrow-money-to-support-refugees. (Accessed 2 July 2018.)

Bunar, N., Vogel, D., Stock, E., Grigt, S. and López Cuesta, B. 2018. *Education: Hope for Newcomers in Europe*. Brussels, Education International.

Bundeszentrale für Politische Bildung. 2018. *Integration and Integration Policies in Germany*. Bonn, Germany, Bundeszentrale für Politische Bildung. www.bpb.de/gesellschaft/migration/laenderprofile/262812/integration-and-integration-policies-in-germany. (Accessed 15 September 2018.)

Burde, D., Guven, O., Kelcey, J., Lahmann, H. and Al-Abbadi, K. 2015. *What Works to Promote Children's Educational Access, Quality of Learning, and Wellbeing in Crisis-Affected Contexts: Education Rigorous Literature Review*. London, Department for International Development.

Cas, A. G. 2016. Typhoon aid and development: The effects of typhoon-resistant schools and instructional resources on educational attainment in the Philippines. *Asian Development Review*, Vol. 33, No. 1, pp. 183–201.

CCCM Cluster and REACH. 2017. *Comparative Multi-Cluster Assessment of Internally Displaced Persons Living in Camps: Iraq Assessment Report – July 2017*. Geneva, Switzerland, REACH Initiative.

COE. 2016. *Enhancing the Legal Framework in Ukraine for Protecting the Human Rights of Internally Displaced Persons*. Strasbourg, France, Council of Europe.

Colombia Ministry of Health and Social Protection and Profamilia. 2017. *Encuesta Nacional de Demografía y Salud, Tomo 1: Componente Demográfico [National Demographic and Health Survey, Volume 1: Demographic Component]*. Bogota, Profamilia. (In Spanish.)

Coşkun, İ. and Emin, M. N. 2016. *A Road Map for the Education of Syrians in Turkey: Opportunities and Challenges*. Ankara, Foundation for Political, Economic and Social Research.

CRRF. 2018a. *108 schools located in refugee camps and settlements now declared official Chadian schools*. Geneva, Switzerland, United Nations High Commissioner for Refugees, Comprehensive Refugee Response Framework. www.globalcrrf.org/crrf_highlight/108-schools-located-in-refugee-camps-and-settlements-now-declared-official-chadian-schools. (Accessed 16 August 2018.)

___. 2018b. *Comprehensive Refugee Response Framework Global Digital Portal: Rwanda*, Geneva, United Nations High Commissioner for Refugees, Comprehensive Refugee Response Framework. www.globalcrrf.org/crrf_country/rwanda. (Accessed 16 August 2018.)

Culbertson, S. and Constant, L. 2015. *Education of Syrian Refugee Children: Managing the Crisis in Turkey, Lebanon and Jordan*. Santa Monica, CA, RAND Corporation.

Dallal, Y. M. 2016. Saving Syria's lost generation through education. *Turkish Policy Quarterly*, Vol. 15, No. 3, pp. 107–14.

Dalrymple, K. A. 2018. *Education in Support of Burundian Refugees in Tanzania*. (Background paper for *Global Education Monitoring Report 2019*.)

Dare, A. 2015. *Beyond Access: Refugee Students' Experiences of Myanmar State Education*. Bangkok, Save the Children.

de Hoop, J., Morey, M. and Seidenfeld, D. 2018. *No Lost Generation: Supporting the School Participation of Displaced Syrian Children in Lebanon*. New York, UNICEF.

Delegation of the European Union in Turkey. 2017. *EU and Turkish Ministry of National Education Launch €300 Million Project to Improve Syrian Children's Access to Education*. Ankara, European Union. www.avrupa.info.tr/en/pr/eu-and-turkish-ministry-national-education-launch-eu300-million-project-improve-syrian-childrens. (Accessed 27 August 2018.)

Dolan, J., Golden, A., Ndaruhutse, S. and Winthrop, R. 2012. *Building Effective Teacher Salary Systems in Fragile and Conflict-Affected States*. Reading, UK, CfBT Education Trust/Center for Universal Education at Brookings.

Dorcas. 2016. *Education Needs Assessment: Iraq, KRI, Dohuk Governorate, Amedi District*. Andijk, Iraq, Dorcas Relief and Development.

Dryden-Peterson, S. 2006. Livelihoods in the region: the present is local, the future is global? Reconciling current and future livelihood strategies in the education of Congolese refugees in Uganda. *Refugee Survey Quarterly*, Vol. 25, No. 2, pp. 81–92.

___. 2015. *The Educational Experiences of Refugee Children in Countries of First Asylum*. Washington, DC, Migration Policy Institute.

Dryden-Peterson, S. and Adelman, E. 2016. *Inside Syrian Refugee Schools: Teachers Struggle to Create Conditions for Learning*. Washington, DC, Brookings Institution. www.brookings.edu/blog/education-plus-development/2016/02/10/inside-syrian-refugee-schools-teachers-struggle-to-create-conditions-for-learning. (Accessed 15 September 2018.)

Dryden-Peterson, S., Adelman, E., Alvarado, S., Anderson, K., Bellino, M. J., Brooks, R., Bukhari, S. U. S., Cao, E., Chopra, V., Faizi, Z., Gulla, B., Maarouf, D., Reddick, C., Scherrer, B., Smoake, E. and Suzuki, E. 2018. *Inclusion in National Education Systems*. (Background paper for *Global Education Monitoring Report 2019*.)

ECW. 2018. *Results Report: April 2017–March 2018*. New York, Education Cannot Wait.

Education Cluster. 2014. *Response to Typhoon Haiyan (Yolanda)*. Geneva, Switzerland, Education Cluster.

___. 2018. *Iraq Education Cluster Dashboard (as of December 2017)*. Baghdad, Education Cluster.

EI. 2017. *Situation Analysis of Education in Lebanon*. Brussels, Education International.

Espinosa, M. J. C. 2009. The constitutional protection of IDPs in Colombia. Rivadeneira, R. A. (ed.), *Judicial Protection of Internally Displaced Persons. The Colombian Experience*. Washington, DC, Project on Internal Displacement.

Eurocities. 2017. *Cities' Actions for the Education of Refugees and Asylum Seekers*. Brussels, Eurocities.

Fazel, M. 2018. Psychological and psychosocial interventions for refugee children resettled in high-income countries. *Epidemiology and Psychiatric Sciences*, Vol. 27, pp. 117–23.

Ferris, E. and Winthrop, R. 2011. *Education and Displacement: Assessing Conditions for Refugees and Internally Displaced Persons Affected by Conflict*. (Background paper for *Global Education Monitoring Report 2019*.)

FMRP. 2005. *Bangladesh Social Sector Performance Surveys: Secondary Education in Bangladesh*. Dhaka, Financial Management Reform Programme.

FRA. 2017. *Current Migration Situation in the EU: Education*. Vienna, European Union Agency for Fundamental Rights.

GCPEA. 2018. *Education Under Attack 2018*. New York, Global Coalition to Protect Education from Attack.

Ghaffar-Kucher, A. 2018. *Uncertain Prospects and Ambiguous Futures: The Challenges and Opportunities of Educating the Forcibly Displaced*. (Background paper for *Global Education Monitoring Report 2019*.)

GPE. 2016. *GPE's Work in Conflict-affected and Fragile Countries*. Washington, DC, Global Partnership for Education.

GPE and UNESCO IIEP. 2016. *Guidelines for Transitional Education Plan Preparation*. Washington, DC/Paris, Global Partnership for Education/UNESCO International Institute for Educational Planning.

Graham, H. R., Minhas, R. S. and Paxton, G. 2016. Learning problems in children of refugee background: A systematic review. *Pediatrics*, Vol. 137, No. 6.

Greece Government Official Gazette. 2018. Αναδιοργάνωση των δομών υποστήριξης της πρωτοβάθμιας και δευτεροβάθμιας εκπαίδευσης και άλλες διατάξεις [*Reorganisation of the Primary and Secondary Education Support Structures and other Provisions*. Athens. (In Greek.)

Greece Ministry of Education, Research and Religious Affairs. 2017. *Refugee Education Project. A. Assessment Report on the Integration Project of Refugee Children in Education (March 2016-April 2017). B. Proposals for the Education of Refugee Children during the 2017–2018 School Year*. Athens, Ministry of Education, Research and Religious Affairs.

Hoodfar, H. 2007. Women, religion and the 'Afghan Education Movement' in Iran. *Journal of Development Studies*, Vol. 43, No. 2, pp. 265–93.

___. 2010. Refusing the Margins: Afghan Refugee Youth in Iran. Chatty, D. (ed.), *Deterritorialized Youth: Sahrawi and Afghan Refugees at the Margins of the Middle East*. New York, Berghahan Books.

Human Rights Watch. 2013. *Unwelcome Guests: Iran's Violation of Afghan Refugee and Migrant Rights*. New York, Human Rights Watch.

___. 2016 *"We're Afraid for Their Future": Barriers to Education for Syrian Refugee Children in Jordan*. New York, Human Rights Watch.

___. 2017. *World Report 2018*. New York, Human Rights Watch.

___. 2018. *"Without Education They Lose Their Future": Denial of Education to Child Asylum Seekers on the Greek Islands*. New York, Human Rights Watch.

IASC. 2007. *IASC Guidelines on Mental Health and Psychosocial Support in Emergency Settings*. Geneva, Switzerland, Inter-Agency Standing Committee.

ICRC. 2016. *Translating the Kampala Convention into Practice: A Stocktaking Exercise*. Geneva, Switzerland, International Committee of the Red Cross.

IDMC. 2015. *Global Overview 2015: People Internally Displaced by Conflict and Violence*. Geneva, Switzerland, Internal Displacement Monitoring Centre.

___. 2018a. *Global International Displacement Database*. Geneva, Switzerland, Internal Displacement Monitoring Centre.

___. 2018b. *Global International Displacement Database: Displacement Data*. Geneva, Switzerland, Internal Displacement Monitoring Centre.

___. 2018c. *Global Report on Internal Displacement 2018*. Geneva, Switzerland, Internal Displacement Monitoring Centre.

___. 2018d. *Monitoring Platform: How IDMC Monitors*. Geneva, Switzerland, Internal Displacement Monitoring Centre. www.internal-displacement.org/monitoring-tools/monitoring-platform. (Accessed 27 August 2018.)

IGAD. 2017a. *Annex to the Djibouti Declaration on Regional Refugee Education: Djibouti Plan of Action on Refugee Education in IGAD Member States*. Djibouti, Intergovernmental Authority on Development.

___. 2017b. *Djibouti Declaration on Regional Conference on Refugee Education in IGAD Member States*. Djibouti, Intergovernmental Authority on Development.

Igbinedion, S., Newby, L. and Sparkes, J. 2017. *Joint Education Needs Assessment: Northeast Nigeria*. Geneva, Switzerland, ACAPS/Education in Emergencies Working Group Nigeria.

INEE. 2009. *INEE Guidance Notes on Teacher Compensation in Fragile States, Situations of Displacement and Post-Crisis Recovery*. New York, Inter-Agency Network for Education in Emergencies.

___. 2017. *Introduction to Training for Primary School Teachers in Crisis Contexts*. New York, Inter-Agency Network for Education in Emergencies.

IOM. 2017. *National Monitoring System Report on the Situation of Internally Displaced Persons*. Kiev, International Organization for Migration.

Ionesco, D., Mokhnacheva, D. and Gemenne, F. 2016. *The Atlas of Environmental Migration*. Abingdon-on-Thames, UK, Routledge.

Janmyr, M. 2018. UNHCR and the Syrian refugee response: Negotiating status and registration in Lebanon. *The International Journal of Human Rights*, Vol. 22, No. 3, pp. 393–419.

Jordan Ministry of Planning and International Cooperation. 2018. *The Jordan Response Plan for the Syria Crisis: 2018–2020*. Amman, Ministry of Planning and International Cooperation.

Karasapan, O. 2015. *The Impact of Libyan Middle-class Refugees in Tunisia*. Washington, DC, Brookings Institution. www.brookings.edu/blog/future-development/2015/03/17/the-impact-of-libyan-middle-class-refugees-in-tunisia. (Accessed 15 September 2018.)

Karen News. 2018. *Karen language teaching moves up to grade 4 in Pago region schools*. 12 April. http://karennews.org/2018/04/karen-language-teaching-moves-up-to-grade-4-in-pago-region-schools. (Accessed 16 August 2018.)

Khalain, N. B. 2018. Over 100,000 students study Karen literature in Ayeyarwady region, *Burma News International*, 12 August. www.bnionline.net/en/news/over-100000-students-study-karen-literature-ayeyarwady-region. (Accessed 16 August 2018.)

Kirk, J. and Winthrop, R. 2013. Teaching in contexts of emergency and state fragility. Kirk, J., Dembele, M. and Baxter, S. (eds), *More and Better Teachers for Quality Education for All*, Collaborative Works.

Kompani, K. 2018. *Getting Syrian Refugee Students to School Safely*. San Francisco, CA, Medium. https://medium.com/@UNmigration/meet-the-syrian-parents-getting-their-kids-to-school-safely-8fee528d786e. (Accessed 15 September 2018.)

Marshall, D. 2015. *Building a New Life in Australia: The Longitudinal Study of Humanitarian Migrants*. Greenway, Australia, Australian Government Department of Social Services.

Mendenhall, M., Gomez, S. and Varni, E. 2018. *Teaching Amidst Conflict and Displacement: Persistent Challenges and Promising Practices for Refugee, Internally Displaced and National Teachers*. (Background paper for *Global Education Monitoring Report 2019*.)

Nicolle, H. 2018. *Inclusion of Afghan Refugees in the National Education Systems of Iran and Pakistan*. (Background paper for *Global Education Monitoring Report 2019*.)

Norwegian Refugee Council. 2018. *Attacks on schools deny access to education*. Oslo, Norwegian Refugee Council. www.nrc.no/news/2018/july/attacks-on-schools-deny-access-to-education. (Accessed 4 September 2018.)

NRC and UNHCR. 2015. *Breaking the Cycle: Education for the Future of Afghan Refugees*. Oslo/Geneva, Switzerland, Norwegian Refugee Council/United Nations High Commissioner for Refugees.

Phyu, E. S. 2018. *Govt to promote ethnic language teaching assistants*, *The Myanmar Times*, 2 August. www.mmtimes.com/news/govt-promote-ethnic-language-teaching-assistants.html. (Accessed 16 August 2018.)

Potsdam University. 2017. *Refugee Teachers Program*. Potsdam, Germany, Potsdam University. www.uni-potsdam.de/unterrichtsinterventionsforsch/refugee.html. (Accessed 12 November 2017.)

REACH and UNICEF. 2017. *Access to Education of Refugee and Migrant Children outside Accommodation (Open) Sites, Athens and Thessaloniki, Greece*, UNICEF/REACH Initiative.

Reeves Ring, H. and West, A. R. 2015. Teacher retention in refugee and emergency settings: The state of the literature. *The International Education Journal: Comparative Perspectives*, Vol. 14, No. 3, pp. 106–21.

ReliefWeb. 2018. *Tanzania: Comprehensive Refugee Response Framework Withdrawal (ECHO Daily Flash of 24 January 2018)*. https://reliefweb.int/report/united-republic-tanzania/tanzania-comprehensive-refugee-response-framework-withdrawal-eeas-dg. (Accessed 2 July 2018.)

Right to Protection with Coalition of Non-Governmental Organizations. 2017. *Current State of the Rights and Freedoms of Internally Displaced Persons in Ukraine: Stakeholders' Report*. Kiev, Ukraine.

Save the Children. 2015. *Education Safe from Disasters: Country Briefs in Asia and the Pacific in 2015*. Singapore, Save the Children.

___. 2017a. *Restoring Hope, Rebuilding Futures: A Plan of Action for Delivering Universal Education for South Sudanese Refugees in Uganda*. London, Save the Children.

___. 2017b. *Unlocking Childhood: Current Immigration Detention Practices and Alternatives for Child Asylum Seekers and Refugees in Asia and the Pacific*. London, Save the Children.

Save the Children, UNHCR and Pearson. 2017. *Promising Practices in Refugee Education: Synthesis Report*. London/Geneva, Save the Children/United Nations High Commissioner for Refugees/Pearson.

Shah, R. 2015. *Norwegian Refugee Council's Accelerated Education Responses: A Meta-Evaluation*. Oslo, Norwegian Refugee Council.

Shah, R., Flemming, J. and Boisvert, K. 2017. *Synthesis Report Accelerated Education Working Group: Accelerated Education Principles Field Studies*. Washington, DC, Accelerated Education Working Group.

Shaw, L., Edwards, M. and Rimon, A. 2014. *KANI Independent Review: Review Report*. Brisbane, Australia, Griffith University.

Shiohata, M. 2018. *Education for Displaced Populations in Karen State, Myanmar*. (Background paper for *Global Education Monitoring Report 2019*.)

Sirkeci, I. 2017. Turkey's refugees, Syrians and refugees from Turkey: A country of insecurity. *Migration Letters*, Vol. 14, No. 1, pp. 124–44.

Solomon Islands Ministry of Education and Human Resources Division. 2011. *Policy Statement and Guidelines for Disaster Preparedness and Education in Emergency Situations in Solomon Islands*. Honiara, Ministry of Education and Human Resources Division.

___. 2016. *Education Strategic Framework 2016–2030*. Honiara, Ministry of Education and Human Resources Division.

Squire, C. 2000. *Education of Afghan Refugees in the Islamic Republic of Iran*. Tehran, UNESCO.

Strauss, N. 2016. *Teachers organizing for quality education provision for refugees*. Bremen, Germany, Gewerkschaft Erziehung und Wissenschaft. www.gew-hb.de/aktuelles/detailseite/neuigkeiten/teachers-organizing-for-quality-education-provision-for-refugees. (Accessed 28 May 2018.)

Sullivan, A. L. and Simonson, G. R. 2016. A systematic review of school-based social-emotional interventions for refugee and war-traumatized youth. *Review of Educational Research*, Vol. 86, No. 2, pp. 503–30.

Tousi, M. D. and Kiamanesh, A. 2010. Basic Education Status of Afghan Refugees in Iran. Elliott, G., Fourali, C. and Issler, S. (eds), *Education and Social Change: Connecting Local and Global Perspectives*. New York, Continuum.

Turkey Ministry of National Education. 2014. *Genelge 2014/21 [Circular 2014/21]*. Ankara, General Directorate of Basic Education. (In Turkish.)

Tyrer, R. A. and Fazel, M. 2014. School and community-based interventions for refugee and asylum seeking children: A systematic review. *PLOS ONE*, Vol. 9, No. 2, p. e89359.

UBOS and ICF. 2018. *Uganda: Demographic and Health Survey 2016*. Kampala/Rockville, MD, Uganda Bureau of Statistics/ICF International.

Uganda Ministry of Education and Sports. 2018. *Education Response Plan for Refugees and Host Communities in Uganda*. Kampala, Ministry of Education and Sports.

UNESCO. 2015. *Education 2030: Incheon Declaration and Framework for Action – Towards Inclusive and Equitable Quality Education and Lifelong Learning for All*. Paris, UNESCO.

___. 2016. *No More Excuses: Provide Education to All Forcibly Displaced People*. Paris, UNESCO. (Global Education Monitoring Report Policy Paper 26.)

UNHCR. 1998. *Guiding Principles on Internal Displacement*. Geneva, Switzerland, United Nations High Commissioner for Refugees.

___. 2012. *2012–2016 UNHCR Global Education Strategy*. Geneva, Switzerland, United Nations High Commissioner for Refugees.

___. 2015a. *Chad: Curriculum Transition Overview*. Geneva, Switzerland, United Nations High Commissioner for Refugees.

___. 2015b. *Education Issue Brief 3: Curriculum Choices in Refugee Settings*. Geneva, Switzerland, United Nations High Commissioner for Refugees.

___. 2015c. *Ethiopia Refugee Education Strategy 2015–2018*. Geneva, Switzerland, United Nations High Commissioner for Refugees.

___. 2016a. *2015 Year-End Report*. Tunis, United Nations High Commissioner for Refugees.

___. 2016b. *Ethiopia: Education Factsheet – May 2016*. Geneva, Switzerland, United Nations High Commissioner for Refugees.

___. 2016c. *Missing Out: Refugee Education in Crisis*. Geneva, Switzerland, United Nations High Commissioner for Refugees.

___. 2017a. *Practical Application of the Comprehensive Refugee Response Framework: Preliminary Progress Update*. Geneva, Switzerland, United Nations High Commissioner for Refugees.

___. 2017b. *Somalia Situation 2017: Supplementary Appeal January–December 2017*. Geneva, Switzerland, United Nations High Commissioner for Refugees.

___. 2017c. *South Sudan Regional Refugee Response Plan: January–December 2018*. Geneva, Switzerland, United Nations High Commissioner for Refugees.

___. 2017d. *Working towards Inclusion: Refugees within the National Systems of Ethiopia*. Geneva, Switzerland, United Nations High Commissioner for Refugees.

___. 2018a. *Access to Formal Education for Refugee and Migrant Children*. Greece Education Sector Working Group/ United Nations High Commissioner for Refugees.

___. 2018b. *Bangladesh Refugee Emergency Population Factsheet*. Geneva, Switzerland, United Nations High Commissioner for Refugees.

___. 2018c. *Dadaab Refugee Complex*. Geneva, Switzerland, United Nations High Commissioner for Refugees. www.unhcr.org/ke/dadaab-refugee-complex. (Accessed 29 June 2018.)

___. 2018d. *Global Trends 2017: Annex Tables*. UNHCR (ed.). Geneva, Switzerland, United Nations High Commissioner for Refugees.

___. 2018e. *Global Trends: Forced Displacement in 2017*. Geneva, Switzerland, United Nations High Commissioner for Refugees.

___. 2018f. *Kakuma Camp Population Statistics by Country of Origin, Sex and Age Group*. Kakuma, Kenya, United Nations High Commissioner for Refugees.

___. 2018g. *Population Statistics*. Geneva, Switzerland, United Nations High Commissioner for Refugees.

___. 2018h. *Uganda Refugee Response: Monthly Snapshot – June 2018*. Kampala, United Nations High Commissioner for Refugees.

___. 2018i. *UNHCR Pakistan: No Changes to Afghan Refugee School Textbooks*. Islamabad, United Nations High Commissioner for Refugees. http://unhcrpk.org/unhcr-pakistan-no-changes-to-afghan-refugee-school-textbooks. (Accessed 27 August 2018.)

UNHCR and WFP. 2017. *Chad: Socioeconomic and Vocational Profiling of Sudanese, Central African and Nigerian Refugees*. Geneva, Switzerland/Rome, Italy, United Nations High Commissioner for Refugees/World Food Programme.

UNICEF. 2015. *Rwanda CO Situation Report*. New York, UNICEF.

___. 2016. *Out of School Children in Ukraine: A Study on the Scope and Dimensions of the Problem with Recommendations for Action*. New York, UNICEF.

UNISDR and GADRRRES. 2017. *Comprehensive School Safety: A Global Framework in Support of the Global Alliance for Disaster Risk Reduction and Resilience in the Education Sector and The Worldwide Initiative for Safe Schools*. Geneva, Switzerland, United Nations International Strategy for Disaster Reduction/Global Alliance for Disaster Risk Reduction and Resilience in the Education Sector.

United Nations. 2016. *Summary Overview Document: Leaders' Summit on Refugees*. New York, United Nations.

UNOCHA. 2017a. *Children are #NotATarget*. New York, United Nations Office for the Coordination of Humanitarian Affairs. www.unocha.org/story/children-are-notatarget. (Accessed 15 September 2018.)

___. 2017b. *Nigeria Humanitarian Response Plan 2018: January–December 2018*. New York, United Nations Office for the Coordination of Humanitarian Affairs. https://reliefweb.int/sites/reliefweb.int/files/resources/2018_hrp_v5.4.pdf. (Accessed 15 September 2018.)

___. 2017c. *Ukraine: Humanitarian Response Plan 2018*. Kiev, United Nations Office for the Coordination of Humanitarian Affairs.

UNRWA. 2016. *Schools on the Front Line: The Impact of Armed Conflict and Violence on UNRWA Schools and Education Services*. Amman, United Nations Relief and Works Agency.

___. 2017a. *Education in Emergencies: Ensuring Quality Education in Times of Crisis*. Amman, United Nations Relief and Works Agency.

___. 2017b. *UNRWA in Figures*. Jerusalem, United Nations Relief and Works Agency.

___. 2018a. *2017 Pledges to UNRWA's Programmes (Cash and In-kind): Overall Donor Ranking at 31 December 2017*. Amman, United Nations Relief and Works Agency.

___. 2018b. *UNRWA Schools to Start on Time*. Amman, United Nations Relief and Works Agency.

Uwezo. 2018. *Are Our Children Learning? Uwezo Learning Assessment in Refugee Contexts in Uganda*. Kampala, Twaweza.

Vogel, D. and Stock, E. 2017. *Opportunities and Hope Through Education: How German Schools Include Refugees*. Brussels, Education International.

Wachiaya, C. 2017. *Rwandan School Bridges Language Gulf for Burundian Students*. Mahama Refugee Camp, United Nations High Commissioner for Refugees. www.unhcr.org/news/stories/2017/9/59bf8ebd4/rwandan-school-bridges-language-gulf-burundian-students.html. (Accessed 15 September 2018.)

WFP, UNHCR and Bafia. 2016. *WFP, UNHCR Joint Assessment Mission: Islamic Republic of Iran*. Rome/Geneva, Switzerland, World Food Programme/United Nations High Commissioner for Refugees.

Women Educational Researchers of Kenya. 2017. *Out of School Children Assessment; Dadaab Refugee Camp*. Nairobi, United Nations High Commissioner for Refugees.

Yavcan, B. and El-Ghali, H. A. 2017. *Higher Education and Syrian Refugee Students: The Case of Turkey (Policies, Practices, and Perspectives)*. Beirut, United Nations High Commissioner for Refugees.

Zaw, J. 2018. Second batch of Myanmar refugees in thailand repatriated. *UCA News*, 8 May. www.ucanews.com/news/second-batch-of-myanmar-refugees-in-thailand-repatriated/82243. (Accessed 16 August 2018.)

Zolfaghari, H. 2016. *Statement by H. E. Dr. Hossein Zolfaghari, Deputy Minister of Interior of the Islamic Republic of Iran, in the 67th Session of the Executive Committee*. Geneva, Switzerland, United Nations High Commissioner for Refugees.

CHAPTER 5

Adair, J. K. 2015. *The Impact of Discrimination on the Early Schooling Experiences of Children from Immigrant Families*. Washington, DC, Migration Policy Institute.

Adair, J. K., Tobin, J. and Arzubiaga, A. E. 2012. The dilemma of cultural responsiveness and professionalization: listening closer to immigrant teachers who teach children of recent immigrants. *Teachers College Record*, Vol. 114, No. 12, pp. 1–37.

All Together Now. 2018. *Everyday Racism*. Sydney, Australia, All Together Now. http://alltogethernow.org.au/everyday-racism. (Accessed 30 May 2018.)

Amnesty International. 2016. *Refugees Welcome Survey 2016: Views of Citizens Across 27 Countries*. London, Amnesty International.

April, D., D'Addio, A. C., Kubacka, K. and Smith, W. C. 2018. *Issues of Cultural Diversity, Migration, and Displacement in Teacher Education Programmes*. (Background paper for *Global Education Monitoring Report 2019*.)

Askins, K. 2015. Being together: Everyday geographies and the quiet politics of belonging. *ACME: An International E-Journal for Critical Geographies*, Vol. 14, No. 2, pp. 470–78.

Barrett, M., Byram, M., Lázár, I., Mompoint-Gaillard, P. and Philippou, S. 2013. *Developing Intercultural Competence Through Education*. Strasbourg, France, Council of Europe.

Brader, T., Valentino, N. A. and Suhay, E. 2008. What triggers public opposition to immigration? Anxiety, group cues, and immigration threat. *American Journal of Political Science*, Vol. 52, pp. 959–78.

Brezicha, K. and Hopkins, M. 2016. Shifting the zone of mediation in a suburban new immigrant destination: Community boundary spanners and school district policymaking. *Peabody Journal of Education*, Vol. 91, pp. 366–82.

Bunar, N., Vogel, D., Stock, E., Grigt, S. and López Cuesta, B. 2018. *Education: Hope for Newcomers in Europe*. Brussels, Education International.

Busse, V. and Krause, U.-M. 2015. Addressing cultural diversity: Effects of a problem-based intercultural learning unit. *Learning Environment Research*, Vol. 18, pp. 425–52.

Canadian Multicultural Education Foundation/Alberta Teachers' Association. 2016. *Promoting Success with Arab Immigrant Students: Teacher Resources*. Edmonton, Alta, Canadian Multicultural Education Foundation/Alberta Teachers' Association.

Cavaille, C. and Marshall, J. 2018. *Education and Anti-Immigration Attitudes: Evidence from Compulsory Schooling Reforms Across Western Europe*. (Unpublished.)

César, M. and Oliveira, I. 2005. The curriculum as a tool for inclusive participation: Student's voices in a case study in a Portuguese multicultural school. *European Journal of Psychology in Education*, Vol. 20, No. 1, pp. 29–43.

City Council of Vallodolid. 2017. *"You Also Count!": The Fourteenth Edition of the Intercultural Week of Valladolid Turns Its Eyes to Zorrilla*. City Council of Valladolid. www.valladolid.es/es/actualidad/noticias/cuentas-decimocuarta-edicion-semana-intercultural-valladoli. (Accessed 1 March 2018.)

Crush, J. and Tawodzera, G. 2014. Exclusion and discrimination: Zimbabwean migrant children and South African schools. *Journal of International Migration and Integration*, Vol. 15, No. 4, pp. 677–93.

Cunningham, W. A., Nezlek, J. B. and Banaji, M. R. 2004. Implicit and explicit ethnocentrism: revisiting the ideologies of prejudice. *Personality and Social Psychology Bulletin*, Vol. 30, No. 10, pp. 1332–46.

d'Hombres, B. and Nunziata, L. 2016. Wish you were here? Quasi-experimental evidence on the effect of education on self-reported attitude toward immigrants. *European Economic Review*, Vol. 90, pp. 201–24.

De Leon, N. 2014. Developing intercultural competence by participating in intensive intercultural service-learning. *Michigan Journal of Community Service Learning*, Fall 2014, pp. 17–30.

Dempster, H. and Hargrave, K. 2017. *Understanding Public Attitudes Towards Refugees and Migrants*. London, Overseas Development Institute/Chatham House. (Working Paper 512.)

Doney, J. and Wegerif, R. 2017. *Measuring Open-Mindedness: An Evaluation of the Impact of Our School Dialogue Programme on Students' Open-Mindedness and Attitudes to Others*. London, Tony Blair Institute for Global Change.

Donlevy, V., Meierkord, A. and Rajania, A. 2016. *Study on the Diversity within the Teaching Profession with Particular Focus on Migrant and/or Minority Background*. Brussels, European Commission.

EI. 2017a. *Sweden: Fast Track Training for Migrant Teachers*. Brussels, Education International. www.ei-ie.org/en/detail/15468/sweden-fast-track-training-for-migrant-teachers. (Accessed 28 February 2018.)

___. 2017b. *Teachers for Migrants' and Refugees' Rights: Teaching Resources to Support Immigrant and Refugee Students in Canada*. Brussels, Education International. www.education4refugees.org/updates/293-teaching-resources-to-support-immigrant-and-refugee-students-in-canada. (Accessed 25 May 2018.)

Epstein, G. S. and Heizler, O. 2015. Ethnic identity: A theoretical framework. *IZA Journal of Migration*, Vol. 4, No. 1, p. 9.

Erdal, M. B. and Oeppen, C. 2013. Migrant balancing acts: understanding the interactions between integration and transnationalism. *Journal of Ethnic and Migration Studies*, Vol. 39, No. 6, pp. 867–84.

Esipova, N., Ray, J., Pugliese, A., Tsabutashvili, D., Laczko, F. and Rango, M. 2015. *How the World Views Migrants*. Geneva, Switzerland, International Organization for Migration.

Esses, V., Hamilton, L. K. and Gaucher, D. 2017. The global refugee crisis: empirical evidence and policy implications for improving public attitudes and facilitating refugee resettlement. *Social Issues and Policy Review*, Vol. 11, No. 1, pp. 78–123.

Esses, V. M., Medianu, S. and Lawson, A. S. 2013. Uncertainty, threat, and the role of the media in promoting the dehumanization of immigrants and refugees. *Journal of Social Issues*, Vol. 69, No. 3, pp. 518–36.

Essomba, M. A., Tarrés, A. and Franco-Guillén, N. 2017. *Research for CULT Committee: Migrant Education – Monitoring and Assessment*. Brussels, European Parliament.

Faas, D. 2011. The nation, Europe and migration: A comparison of geography, history and citizenship education curricula in Greece, Germany and England. *Journal of Curriculum Studies*, Vol. 43, No. 4, pp. 471–92.

Faas, D., Hajisoteriou, C. and Angelides, P. 2014. Intercultural education in Europe: Policies, practices and trends. *British Education Research Journal*, Vol. 40, No. 2, pp. 300–18.

Fazel, M. 2015. A moment of change: Facilitating refugee children's mental health in UK schools. *International Journal of Educational Development*, Vol. 41, pp. 255–61.

Fine-Davis, M. and Faas, D. 2014. Equality and diversity in the classroom: A comparison of students' and teachers' attitudes in six European countries. *Social Indicators Research*, Vol. 119, No. 3, pp. 1319–34.

Ford, R. 2012. *Parochial and Cosmopolitan Britain: Examining the Social Divide in Reactions to Immigration*. Washington, DC, German Marshall Fund of the United States.

Geschke, D., Sassenberg, K., Ruhrmann, G. and Sommer, D. 2010. Effects of linguistic abstractness in the mass media: how newspaper articles shape readers' attitudes toward migrants. *Journal of Media Psychology*, Vol. 22, No. 3, pp. 99–104.

Gholami, R. 2017. The 'sweet spot' between submission and subversion: Diaspora, education and the cosmopolitan project. D. Carment and A. Sadjed (eds), *Diaspora as Cultures of Cooperation*, Cham, Switzerland, Palgrave Macmillan, pp. 49–68.

Gichuru, M., Riley, J. G., Robertson, J. and Park, M.-H. 2015. Perceptions of head start teachers about culturally relevant practice. *Multicultural Education*, Winter 2015, pp. 46–50.

Gorski, P. C. 2009. What we're teaching teachers: An analysis of multicultural teacher education coursework syllabi. *Teaching and Teacher Education*, Vol. 25, pp. 309–18.

Gropas, R. and Triandafyllidou, A. 2011. Greek education policy and the challenge of migration: An 'intercultural' view of assimilation. *Race Ethnicity and Education*, Vol. 14, No. 3, pp. 399–419.

Gross, D. 2015. Latvian school in Australia: Comparison of two immigration waves. Lulle, A. and Kļave, A. L. (eds), *Radot iespējas attīstībai: diasporas bērnu un jauniešu izglītība [Creating Opportunities for Development: Education for Children and Youth in the Diaspora]*. Riga, University of Latvia Academic Publishing. (In Latvian.)

Gundelach, B. 2014. In diversity we trust: The positive effect of ethnic diversity on outgroup trust. *Political Behavior*, Vol. 36, pp. 125–42.

Hainmueller, J. and Hopkins, D. J. 2014. Public attitudes toward immigration. *Annual Review of Political Science*, Vol. 17, pp. 225–49.

Hanemann, U. 2018. *Language and Literacy Programmes for Migrants and Refugees: Challenges and Ways Forward*. (Background paper for *Global Education Monitoring Report 2019*.)

Harte, E., Herrera, F. and Stepanek, M. 2016. *Education of EU Migrant Children in EU Member States*. Cambridge, UK, RAND Europe.

Heath, A. and Richards, L. 2016. *Attitudes Towards Immigration and Their Antecedents: Topline Results from Round 7 of the European Social Survey*. London, European Social Survey.

Hintermann, C., Markom, C., Weinhäupl, H. and Üllen, S. 2014. Debating migration in textbooks and classrooms in Austria. *Journal of Educational Media, Memory, and Society*, Vol. 6, No. 1, pp. 79–106.

Howden, D. 2016. *The Manufacture of Hatred: Scapegoating Refugees in Central Europe*. New York, News Deeply, Refugees Deeply. www.newsdeeply.com/refugees/articles/2016/12/14/the-manufacture-of-hatred-scapegoating-refugees-in-central-europe. (Accessed 20 February 2018.)

Huddleston, T., Bilgili, O., Joki, A.-L. and Vankova, Z. 2015. *Migrant Integration Policy Index 2015*. Barcelona/Brussels, Barcelona Centre for International Affairs/Migration Policy Group.

Ireland DOES. 2010. *Intercultural Education Strategy: 2010–2015*. Dublin, Department of Education and Skills.

____. 2014. *2014–16: DICE Project Strategic Plan*. Dublin, Department of Education and Skills.

____. 2016. *New Law Will Make Process of School Admissions Easier for Children and Parents*. Dublin, Department of Education and Skills.

Ireland DOJE. 2017. *The Migrant Integration Strategy*. Dublin, Department of Justice and Equality.

Ireland State Examinations Commission. 2018. *Non-Curricular EU Language Subjects*. www.examinations.ie/?l=en&mc=ex&sc=eu. (Accessed 30 May 2018.)

Islam in Europe. 2010. *Norway: Immigrants, Muslims Portrayed Negatively in the Media*. Islam in Europe. http://islamineurope.blogspot.fr/2010/02/norway-immigrants-muslims-portrayed.html. (Accessed 20 February 2018.)

Johnson, J. D. and Lecci, L. 2003. Assessing anti-white attitudes and predicting perceived racism: The Johnson-Lecci scale. *Personality and Social Psychology Bulletin*, Vol. 29, No. 3, pp. 299–312.

Kaizer Chiefs. 2017. *KC Anti-Xenophobia Campaign Known as Africa4Life*. Johannesburg, South Africa, Kaizer Chiefs Football Club. www.kaizerchiefs.com/press-releases/kc-anti-xenophobia-campaign-known-africa4life. (Accessed 1 March 2018.)

Kawakami, K., Amodio, D. M. and Hugenberg, K. 2017. Intergroup perception and cognition: An integrative framework for understanding the causes and consequences of social categorization. Olson, J. M. (ed.), *Advances in Experimental Social Psychology*, Vol. 55. Cambridge, Mass., Academic Press, pp. 1–80.

Kerry, P. 2017. Migrant film fest explores 'Remapping the Borders'. *The Korea Herald*, 26 October. www.koreaherald.com/view.php?ud=20171024000654. (Accessed 1 March 2018.)

Khalifa, M. A., Gooden, M. A. and Davis, J. E. 2016. Culturally responsive school leadership: A synthesis of the literature. *Review of Educational Research*, Vol. 86, No. 4, pp. 1272–311.

Kim, S. and Slapac, A. 2015. Culturally responsive, transformative pedagogy in the transnational era: Critical perspectives. *Educational Studies*, Vol. 51, No. 1, pp. 17–27.

Kincheloe, J. L. 2011. Critical ontology: Visions of selfhood and curriculum. Kincheloe, J. L., Hayes, K., Steinberg, S. R. and Tobin, K. (eds), *Key Works in Critical Pedagogy*. Rotterdam, Netherlands, Sense Publishing, pp. 201–18.

King, R. and Lulle, A. 2016. *Research on Migration: Facing Realities and Maximising Opportunities – A Policy Review*. Brussels, European Commission.

Klimenko, E. 2014. *Fostering Tolerance towards Migrants: Efforts of the State – The Polish Experience and the Case of Russia*. Warsaw, Institute of Public Affairs.

La Barbera, MC. 2015. Identity and migration: An introduction. La Barbera, MC. (ed.), *Identity and Migration in Europe: Multidisciplinary Perspectives*. Cham, Switzerland, Springer International, pp. 1–11.

Lashley, L. 2018. A reflection on the professional and cultural experience of migrant teachers: The case of postcolonial Guyanese teachers in British mainstream primary schools. *International Journal of Educational Policy Research and Review*, Vol. 5, No. 2, pp. 31–9.

Leeman, Y. and Saharso, S. 2013. Coming of age in Dutch schools: Issues of schooling and identity. *Education Inquiry*, Vol. 4, No. 1, pp. 11–30.

Lin, M. H., Kwan, V. S. Y., Cheung, A. and Fiske, S. T. 2005. Stereotype content model explains prejudice for an envied outgroup: Scale of anti-Asian American stereotypes. *Personality and Social Psychology Bulletin*, Vol. 31, No. 1, pp. 34–47.

Lindahl, E. 2007. *Gender and Ethnic Interactions among Teachers and Students: Evidence from Sweden*. Uppsala, Sweden. Institute for Evaluation of Labour Market and Education Policy. (Working Paper 25.)

Lipińska, E. and Seretny, A. 2011. *Doświadczenia nauczania w skupiskach polonijnych na obczyźnie [Teaching Experiences in Polish Communities Abroad]*. Paper for the 3rd Conference of Polish Scientific Associations Abroad: Polish Youth Abroad – Educational Tasks. Krakow, Poland. (In Polish.)

Maguire, M. H. 2010. Lessons in understanding Montreal heritage language contexts: Whose literacies and voices are privileged? *Cahiers de L'ILOB/OLBI Working Papers*, Vol. 1, pp. 25–50.

Major, B., Gramzow, R. H., McCoy, S., Levin, S., Schmader, T. and Sidanius, J. 2002. Perceiving personal discrimination: the role of group status and legitimizing ideology. *Journal of Personality and Social Psychology*, Vol. 82, No. 3, pp. 269–282.

Malakolunthu, S. 2010. Culturally responsive leadership for multicultural education: The case of 'Vision School' in Malaysia. *Procedia: Social and Behavioral Sciences*, Vol. 9, pp. 1162–69.

Manik, S. 2014. South African migrant teachers' decision-making: Levels of influence and 'relative deprivation'. *Journal of Southern African Studies*, Vol. 40, No. 1, pp. 151–65.

Marino Institute of Education. 2018. *Migrant Teacher Project*. Dublin, Marino Institute of Education. www.mie.ie/en/Research/Migrant_Teacher_Project. (Accessed 28 February 2018.)

Maytree Foundation. 2012. *Good Ideas from Successful Cities: Municipal Leadership on Immigrant Integration*. Toronto, Ont., Maytree Foundation.

Murray, K. E. and Marx, D. M. 2013. Attitudes toward unauthorized immigrants, authorized immigrants, and refugees. *Cultural Diversity and Ethnic Minority Psychology*, Vol. 19, No. 3, pp. 332–41.

NASUWT and Runnymede Trust. 2017. *Visible Minorities, Invisible Teachers: BME Teachers in the Education System in England*. London, NASUWT/Runnymede Trust.

O'Dowd, R. and Lewis, T. (eds). 2016. *Online Intercultural Exchange: Policy, Pedagogy, Practice*. Oxford, UK, Routledge.

OECD. 2014. *TALIS 2013 Results: An International Perspective on Teaching and Learning*. Paris, Organisation for Economic Co-Operation and Development.

___. 2017. *People on the Move*. Paris, Organisation for Economic Co-operation and Development. (Trends Shaping Education, Spotlight 11.)

Opertti, R., Scherz, H., Magni, G., Kang, H. and Abuhamdieh, S. 2018. *Migration Concepts and Themes in Education Documents*. (Background paper for *Global Education Monitoring Report 2019*.)

ORPEG. 2017. *Ośrodek Rozwoju Polskiej Edukacji za Granicą [Centre for the Development of Polish Education Abroad]*. Website. Warsaw, Ośrodek Rozwoju Polskiej Edukacji za Granicą. www.orpeg.pl/index.php/about-us. (Accessed 19 May 2018.) (In Polish.)

Oslo Council. 2018. *OXLO: Oslo Extra Large, a City for All*, Oslo Council. www.oslo.kommune.no/politikk-og-administrasjon/prosjekter/oxlo-oslo-extra-large-en-by-for-alle/#gref. (Accessed 1 March 2018.)

Palaiologu, N. and Faas, D. 2012. How 'intercultural' is education in Greece? Insights from policymakers and educators. *Compare: A Journal of Comparative and International Education*, Vol. 42, No. 4, pp. 563–84.

Pica-Smith, C. and Poynton, T. 2014. Supporting interethnic and interracial friendships among youth to reduce prejudice and racism in schools: The role of the school counselor. *Professional School Counseling*, Vol. 18, No. 1, pp. 82–89.

Poland Ministry of Education. 2017. *Edukacja polskich dzieci za granicą [Polish Children Education Abroad]*. Warsaw, Ministry of Education. https://men.gov.pl/ministerstwo/informacje/edukacja-polskich-dzieci-za-granica.html. (Accessed 19 May 2018.) (In Polish.)

PPMI. 2017. *Preparing Teachers for Diversity: The Role of Initial Teacher Education*. Luxembourg, European Commission.

Reitz, A. K., Asendorpf, J. B. and Motti-Stefanidi, F. 2015. When do immigrant adolescents feel personally discriminated against? Longitudinal effects of peer preference. *International Journal of Behavioral Development*, Vol. 39, No. 3, pp. 197–209.

RET International. 2018a. *Casa en Tierra Ajena (Cine-Foro) [House in a Foreign Land (Cinema-Forum)]*. Geneva, Switzerland, RET International. https://loquenosune.org/category/campana-en-accion/costa-rica/. (Accessed 1 March 2018.) (In Spanish.)

___. 2018b. *What Unites Us: About this Campaign*, Geneva, Switzerland, RET International. https://loquenosune.org/sobre-esta-campana/. (Accessed 1 March 2018.)

Sandoval-Hernández, A. and Miranda, D. 2018. *Exploring ICCS 2016 to Measure Progress toward Target 4.7*. (Background paper for *Global Education Monitoring Report 2019*.)

Santerini, M. 2010. *La qualità della scuola interculturale [The Quality of Intercultural Schools]*. Trento, Erickson. (In Italian.)

Schmitt, M. T., Branscombe, N. R., Postmes, T. and Garcia, A. 2014. The consequences of perceived discrimination for psychological well-being: A meta-analytic review. *Psychological Bulletin*, Vol. 140, No. 4.

Schüller, S. 2012. *The Effects of 9/11 on Attitudes toward Immigration and the Moderating Role of Education*. Bonn, Germany, Institute for the Study of Labor. (Discussion Paper 7052.)

Smith, W. C. and Persson, A. 2018. Supporting teachers for culturally and linguistically diverse pedagogy. Population Research Institute, Pennsylvania State University. (Unpublished.)

Smyth, E. 2015. *Wellbeing and School Experiences Among 9- and 13-Year-Olds: Insights from the Growing Up in Ireland Study*. Dublin, Economic and Social Research Institute.

SOM. 2012. *Mapping the Politicisation of Immigration*. Brussels, European Commission, Support and Opposition to Migration. (Policy Brief, September.)

Stark, L., Plosky, W. D., Horn, R. and Canavera, M. 2015. 'He always thinks he is nothing': The psychosocial impact of discrimination on adolescent refugees in urban Uganda. *Social Science and Medicine*, Vol. 146, pp. 173–81.

Stöhr, T. and Wichardt, P. C. 2016. *Conflicting Identities: Cosmopolitan or Anxious? Appreciating Concerns of Host Country Population Improves Attitudes Towards Immigrants*. Kiel, Germany, Kiel Institute for the World Economy. (Working Paper 2045.)

Strabac, Z., Aalberg, T. and Valenta, M. 2014. Attitudes towards Muslim immigrants: Evidence from survey experiments across four countries. *Journal of Ethnic and Migration Studies*, Vol. 40, No. 1, pp. 100–18.

Swim, J. K., Hyers, L. L., Cohen, L. L., Fitzgerald, D. C. and Bylsma, W. H. 2003. African American college students' experiences with everyday racism: Characteristics of and responses to these incidents. *Journal of Black Psychology*, Vol. 29, No. 1, pp. 38–67.

TENT. 2016. *Public Perceptions of the Refugee Crisis*. New York, TENT Foundation.

Thomé-Williams, A. C. 2016. Developing intercultural communicative competence in Portuguese through Skype and Facebook. *Intercultural Communication Studies*, Vol. 25, No. 1, pp. 213–33.

Toulouse, P. R. 2018. *Truth and Reconciliation in Canadian Schools*. Winnipeg, Portage and Main Press.

UNESCO. 2006. *UNESCO Guidelines on Intercultural Education*. Paris, UNESCO.

Van Briel, B., Darmody, M. and Kerzil, J. 2016. *Education Policies and Practices to Foster Tolerance, Respect for Diversity and Civic Responsibility in Children and Young People in the EU*. Luxembourg, European Union.

van den Berg, D., van Dijk, M. and Grootscholte, M. 2011. *Diversiteitsmonitor 2011: Cijfers en Feiten over Diversiteit in het PO, VO, MBO en op Lerarenopleidingen – Een Update van de Diversiteitmonitor 2010. [Diversity Monitor 2011: Facts and Figures*

Concerning Diversity in Primary, Secondary, Vocational and Teacher Education: An Update to the Diversity Monitor 2010]. The Hague, Sectorbestuur Onderwijsarbeidsmarkt [Education Sector Employment]. (In Dutch.)

Watanabe, T. 2010. Education for Brazilian pupils and students in Japan: Towards a multicultural symbiotic society. *Procedia: Social and Behavioral Sciences*, Vol. 7, pp. 164–70.

WEF. 2017. *Migration and Its Impact on Cities*. Geneva, Switzerland, World Economic Forum.

Weiner, M. F. 2018. Curricular alienation: multiculturalism, tolerance, and immigrants in Dutch primary school history textbooks. *Humanity and Society*, Vol. 42, No. 2, pp. 147–70.

Wells, A. S., Fox, L. and Cordova-Cobo, D. 2016. *How Racially Diverse Schools and Classrooms Can Benefit All Students*. New York, Century Foundation.

Westlake, D. 2011. *Multiculturalism Policies for Immigrant Minorities: Scores for Each Indicator from 1980, 1990, 2000, and 2010*. Kingston, Queen's University. www.queensu.ca/mcp/immigrant-minorities/results. (Accessed 15 October 2017.)

Winkler, H. 2015. *Why do Elderly People Oppose Immigration When They're Most Likely to Benefit?* Washington, DC, Brookings Institution. www.brookings.edu/blog/future-development/2015/07/22/why-do-elderly-people-oppose-immigration-when-theyre-most-likely-to-benefit.(Accessed 2 March 2018.)

WVS. 2016. *WVS Wave 6 (2010–2014) [data]*, Vienna, World Values Survey. www.worldvaluessurvey.org/WVSDocumentationWV6.jsp. (Accessed 1 November 2017.)

Yohani, S. 2013. Educational cultural brokers and the school adaptation of refugee children and families: Challenges and opportunities. *International Migration and Integration*, Vol. 14, pp. 61–79.

Zakharia, Z. 2016. Bilingual education in the Middle East and North Africa. O. García et al. (eds), *Bilingual and Multilingual Education*. Cham, Switzerland, Springer, pp. 1–13.

CHAPTER 6

Agunias, D. R. and Newland, K. 2012. *Developing a Road Map for Engaging Diasporas in Development: A Handbook for Policymakers and Practitioners in Home and Host Countries*. Geneva, Switzerland/Washington, International Organization for Migration/Migration Policy Institute.

Albania Government. 2010. *Strategy on Reintegration of Returned Albanian Citizens 2010–2015*. Tirana, Government of Albania.

Albania Ministry of Social Welfare and Youth. 2014. *Employment and Skills Strategy 2014–2020*. Tirana, Ministria e Punës dhe Çështjeve Sociale.

Aleksynska, M. and Tritah, A. 2013. Occupation–education mismatch of immigrant workers in Europe: Context and policies. *Economics of Education Review*, Vol. 36, pp. 229–44.

Altbach, P. G. and Knight, J. 2007. The internationalization of higher education: Motivations and realities. *Journal of Studies in International Education*, Vol. 11, No. 3–4, pp. 290–305.

Bardak, U. 2014. *Migration and Skills Development Agenda in ETF Partner Countries*. Turin, Italy, European Training Foundation.

Barjaba, K. and Barjaba, J. 2015. *Embracing Emigration: The Migration-Development Nexus in Albania*. Washington, DC, Migration Policy Institute. www.migrationpolicy.org/article/embracing-emigration-migration-development-nexus-albania. (Accessed 18 September 2018.)

Batalova, J., Fix, M. and Bachmeier, J. D. 2016. *The Costs of Brain Waste among Highly Skilled Immigrants in the United States*. Washington, DC, Migration Policy Institute/New American Economy/World Education Services.

Benabdallah, L. and Robertson, W. 2018. Xi Jinping pledged $60 billion for Africa. Where will the money go? *Washington Post*, 17 September. www.washingtonpost.com/news/monkey-cage/wp/2018/09/17/xi-jinping-pledged-60-billion-for-africa-where-will-the-money-go. (Accessed 17 September 2018.)

Bettie, M. 2015. Ambassadors unaware: the Fulbright Program and American public diplomacy. *Journal of Transatlantic Studies*, Vol. 13, No. 4, pp. 358–72.

Bhagwati, J. and Hamada, K. 1974. The brain drain, international integration of markets for professionals and unemployment: A theoretical analysis. *Journal of Development Economics*, Vol. 1, No. 1, pp. 19–42.

Bhandari, R. and Belyavina, R. 2012. Trends and directions in global student mobility. *International Higher Education*, No. 66, pp. 14–15.

Bhandari, R. and Robles, C. 2018. *International Higher Education: Shifting Mobilities, Policy Challenges, and New Initiatives*. (Background paper for *Global Education Monitoring Report 2019*.)

Bonfati, S., Matos, A. D. d., Liebig, T. and Xenogiani, T. 2014. *Migrants' Qualifications and Skills and Their Links with Labour Market Outcomes*. Paris, Organisation for Economic Co-operation and Development.

Brenn-White, M. and van Rest, E. 2012. *English-Taught Master's Programs in Europe: New Findings on Supply and Demand*. New York, Institute of International Education.

British Council. 2014. *Exploring the Impacts of Transnational Education on Host Countries: A Pilot Study*. London, British Council.

Brücker, H., Glitz, A., Lerche, A. and Romiti, A. 2015. *Occupational Recognition and Immigrant Labor Market Outcomes*. Chicago, IL, Society of Labor Economists. (Unpublished.)

Cangiano, A. 2015. Migration policies and migrant employment outcomes. *Comparative Migration Studies*, Vol. 2, No. 4, pp. 417–43.

CARICOM. 2017. *CSME – A Journey not a Destination: CARICOM Heads*. www.caricom.org/media-center/communications/press-releases/csme-a-journey-not-a-destination-caricom-heads. (Accessed 17 September 2018.)

Castagnone, E., Nazio, T., Bartolini, L. and Schoumaker, B. 2015. Understanding transnational labour market trajectories of African-European migrants: Evidence from the MAFE survey. *International Migration Review*, Vol. 49, No. 1, pp. 200–31.

CEDEFOP. 2016. *How to Make Visible and Value Refugees' Skills and Competences*. Thessaloniki, European Centre for the Development of Vocational Training.

___. 2018. *What Is the European Skills Passport?* Thessaloniki, European Centre for the Development of Vocational Training. https://europass.cedefop.europa.eu/europass-support-centre/general-questions-europass/what-european-skills-passport. (Accessed 17 September 2018.)

Chuang, I. and Ho, A. 2016. *HarvardX and MITx: Four Years of Open Online Courses – Fall 2012–Summer 2016*. Cambridge, MA, Massachusetts Institute of Technology/Harvard University.

Council of Europe. 2018. *Chart of signatures and ratifications of Treaty 165*. Strasbourg, France, Council of Europe. www.coe.int/en/web/conventions/full-list/-/conventions/treaty/165/signatures. (Accessed 17 September 2018.)

Desiderio, M. V. and Hooper, K. 2015. *Improving Migrants' Labour Market Integration in Europe from the Outset: a Cooperative Approach to Predeparture Measures*. Brussels, Migration Policy Institute/Migration Policy Centre/INTERACT.

Dessoff, A. 2012. Asia's burgeoning higher education hubs. *International Educator*, Vol. 21, No. 4, p. 16.

Deuster, C. and Docquier, F. 2018. *International Migration and Human Capital Inequality: A Dyadic Approach*. (Background paper for Global Education Monitoring Report2019.)

European Commission. 2017. *Integration: New Skills Profile Tool to Help Non-EU Nationals Enter the Labour Market*. Brussels, European Commission.

___. 2018. *Intra-Africa: Supporting Academic Mobility in Africa*. Brussels, European Commission, Education, Audiovisual and Culture Executive Agency. https://eacea.ec.europa.eu/intra-africa. (Accessed 17 September 2018.)

European Commission, Eurostudent and Eurydice. 2018. *The European Higher Education Area in 2018: Bologna Process Implementation Report*. Luxembourg: Publications Office of the European Union.

Eurostat. 2014. *Obstacles to Getting a Suitable Job by Migration Status, Labour Status and Educational Attainment Level*. Luxembourg, Eurostat.

___. 2016. *Key Figures on Europe: 2016 Edition*. Luxembourg, Publications Office of the European Union.

Farrugia, C. 2014. *Charting New Pathways to Higher Education: International Secondary Students in the United States*. New York, Center for Academic Mobility Research/Institute of International Education.

___. 2017. *Globally Mobile Youth: Trends in International Secondary Students in the United States, 2013–2016*. New York, Institute of International Education.

Farrugia, C. and Bhandari, R. 2016. *Open Doors 2015: Report on International Educational Exchange*. New York, Institute of International Education.

Farrugia, C. and Mahmoud, O. 2016. *Beyond Borders: Measuring Academic Mobility between the United States and Mexico*. New York, Institute of International Education Center for Academic Mobility Research and Impact.

Gëdeshi, I. and Xhaferaj, E. 2016. *Social and Economic Profile of the Return Migrants in Albania*. Tirana, International Organization for Migration.

GFMD. 2013. *Enhancing the Development Impacts of Labour Migration and Circular Mobility through More Systematic Labour Market and Skills Matching*. Geneva, Switzerland, Global Forum on Migration and Development.

Girard, M. and Smith, M. 2012. Working in a regulated occupation in Canada: an immigrant–native born comparison. *Journal of International Migration and Integration*, Vol. 14, No. 2, p. 219–244.

Global Affairs Canada. 2017. *Economic Impact of International Education in Canada: 2017 Update*. Ottawa, Global Affairs Canada. www.international.gc.ca/education/assets/pdfs/Economic_Impact_International_Education_in_Canada_2017.pdf. (Accessed 15 September 2018.)

Hanson, G. H. and Slaughter, M. J. 2016. *High-Skilled Immigration and the Rise of STEM Occupations in U.S. Employment*. Washington, DC, National Bureau of Economic Research.

Hausmann, R. and Nedelkoska, L. 2017. *Welcome Home in a Crisis: Effects of Return Migration on the Non-migrants' Wages and Employment*. Cambridge, MA, Harvard University. (HKS Working Paper RWP17-015.)

Hawthorne, L. 2013. *Recognizing Foreign Qualifications*. Washington, DC, Migration Policy Institute.

Hazelkorn, E. 2015. *Rankings and the Reshaping of Higher Education: the battle for World-Class Excellence*. Basingstoke, UK, Palgrave Macmillan.

HEGlobal. 2016. *The Scale and Scope of UK Higher Education Transnational Education*. Birmingham, UK, Higher Education International Unit.

IAU. 2008. *Affirming Academic Values in Internationalization of Higher Education: A Call for Action*. Paris, International Association of Universities.

ICEF Monitor. 2017. What rankings are most important to students? 6 September. http://monitor.icef.com/2017/09/what-rankings-are-most-important-to-students. (Accessed 21 September 2018.)

___. 2018. South Korea: record growth in international student enrolment. 21 February. http://monitor.icef.com/2018/02/south-korea-record-growth-international-student-enrolment. (Accessed 17 September 17 2018.)

IEduChina. 2016. *IEduChina: About us*. Shenzen, China, IEduChin, Shenzhen Huliangangwan Net Technology. www.ieduchina.com/service/aboutus_en.html. (Accessed 17 September 2018.)

IIE. 2015. *What International Students Think about U.S. Higher Education: Attitudes and Perceptions of Prospective Students from Around the World*. New York, Institute of International Education.

ILO. 2010. *Guidelines for Recognizing the Skills of Returning Migrant Workers*. Bangkok, International Labour Organization.

IOM. 2013. *Recognition of Qualifications and Competences of Migrants*. Brussels, International Organization for Migration.

IOM and INSTAT. 2013. *Return Migration and Reintegration in Albania 2013*. International Organization for Migration/Republic of Albania Institute of Statistics.

Kago, C. and Masinde, W. 2017. Free movement of workers. Ugirashebuja, E., Ruhangisa, J. E., Ottervanger, T. and Cuyvers, A. (eds), *East African Community Law: Institutional, Substantive and Comparative EU Aspects*. Leiden, Netherlands, Brill.

Karugaba, M. 2009. *Doctors to Be Bonded*. Kampala, New Vision. www.newvision.co.ug/new_vision/news/1245025/doctors-bonded. (Accessed 17 September 2018.)

Kennedy, K. 2017. Germany surpasses international student target three years early. *The PIE News*, 30 November. https://thepienews.com/news/germany-surpasses-international-student-target-three-years-early. (Accessed 21 September 2018.)

Kerr, S. P., Kerr, W., Özden, Ç. and Parsons, C. 2016. Global talent flows. *Journal of Economic Perspectives*, Vol. 30, No. 4, pp. 83–106.

Knight, J. 2012. Student mobility and internationalization: trends and tribulations. *Research in Comparative and International Education*, Vol. 7, No. 1, pp. 20–33.

___. 2016. Transnational education remodeled: toward a common TNE framework and definitions. *Journal of Studies in International Education*, Vol. 20, No. 1, pp. 34–47.

Kottasova, I. 2016. Saudi Arabia cuts funding for students abroad. *CNN Money*, 9 February. https://money.cnn.com/2016/02/09/news/saudi-arabia-students-overseas. (Accessed 18 September 2018.)

Kovacheva, V. and Grewe, M. 2015. *Migrant Workers in the German Healthcare Sector*. Hamburg, Germany, Hamburg Institute of International Economics.

Kuroda, K., Sugimura, M., Kitamura, Y. and Asada, S. 2018. *Internationalization of Higher Education and Student Mobility in Japan and Asia*. (Background paper for *Global Education Monitoring Report 2019*.)

Ligami, C. 2017. Heads of state declare common higher education area. *University World News*, 19 May. www.universityworldnews.com/article.php?story=20170519145012846. (Accessed 18 September 2018.)

Lodigiani, R. and Sarli, A. 2017. Migrants' competence recognition systems: controversial links between social inclusion aims and unexpected discrimination effects. *European Journal for Research on the Education and Learning of Adults*, Vol. 8, No. 1, pp. 127–44.

Maslen, G. 2018. Foreign students' economic contribution soars by 22%. *University World News*, 10 April. www.universityworldnews.com/article.php?story=20180410110537639. (Accessed 18 September 2018.)

McManus, C. and Nobre, C. A. 2017. Brazilian scientific mobility program: science without borders – preliminary results and perspectives. *Anais da Academia Brasileira de Ciências*, Vol. 89, No. 1, pp. 773–86.

Mori, R. 2018. *Higher Education Possibilities for and Constraints on International Students in Japan*. (Background paper for *Global Education Monitoring Report 2019*.)

Nafie, R. 2017. What Germany is doing right to edge past the competition. The PIE News, 7 April. https://thepienews.com/analysis/germany-edge-past-competition-international-students. (Accessed 18 September 2018.)

Nikolovska, M. 2010. *Education and Business: Albania*. Turin, European Training Foundation.

NOKUT. 2017. *NOKUT's Qualifications Passport for Refugees*. Oslo, Norwegian Agency for Quality Assurance in Education. www.nokut.no/en/nyheter-2016/NOKUTs-Qualifications-Passport-for-Refugees. (Accessed 15 March 2018.)

NSF. 2018. 2016. *Doctorate Recipients from U.S. Universities*. Alexandria, VA, National Science Foundation.

OECD. 2014. *International Migration Outlook 2014*. Paris, Organisation for Economic Co-operation and Development.

___. 2017. *International Migration Outlook 2017*. Paris, Organisation for Economic Co-operation and Development.

OECD/European Union. 2015. *Indicators of Immigrant Integration 2015: Settling In*. Paris, Organisation for Economic Co-operation and Development/European Union.

Owen, T. and Lowe, S. J. 2008. *Labour Market Integration of Skilled Immigrants: Good Practices for the Recognition of International Credentials*. Paris, UNICEF.

Piracha, M. and Vadean, F. 2010. Return migration and occupational choice: evidence from Albania. *World Development*, Vol. 38, No. 8, pp. 1141–55.

Project Atlas. 2016. *Infographics and Data*. New York, Institute of International Education. www.iie.org/Research-and-Insights/Project-Atlas/Explore-Data. (Accessed 15 April 2018.)

___. 2017. *Infographics and Data*. New York, Institute of International Education. www.iie.org/Research-and-Insights/Project-Atlas/Explore-Data. (Accessed 15 April 2018.)

Rauhvargers, A. 2004. Improving the recognition of qualifications in the framework of the Bologna process. *European Journal of Education*, Vol. 39, No. 3, pp. 331–47.

Redden, E. 2016. A big world out there. *Inside Higher Ed*, 24 February. www.insidehighered.com/news/2016/02/24/researchers-survey-landscape-internationalization-higher-education. (Accessed 15 September 2018.)

Republic of Moldova Government. 2017. *Moldovan national framework of qualifications to upgrade*. Kishinev, Government of Republic of Moldova. https://gov.md/en/content/moldovan-national-framework-qualifications-upgrade. (Accessed 21 September 2018.)

Rietig, V. 2016. *Moving Beyond Crisis: Germany's New Approaches to Integrating Refugees into the Labour Market*. Washington, DC, Migration Policy Institute.

Rumbley, L. E. and de Wit, H. 2017. International faculty mobility: crucial and understudied. *International Higher Education*, No. 88, pp. 6–8.

Sawahl, W. 2009. Algeria: study abroad cuts to tackle brain drain. *University World News*, 3 May. www.universityworldnews.com/article.php?story=20090430201022419. (Accessed 18 September 2018.)

Shah, D. 2018. *By the Numbers: MOOCs in 2017*. Class Central. www.class-central.com/report/mooc-stats-2017. (Accessed 18 September 2018.)

Sharma, Y. 2017. Talent drive looks to bring in international students. *University World News*, 16 March. www.universityworldnews.com/article.php?story=20170316161911243. (Accessed 18 September 2018.)

Souto-Otero, M. and Villalba-Garcia, E. 2015. Migration and validation of non-formal and informal learning in Europe: inclusion, exclusion or polarisation in the recognition of skills? *International Review of Education*, Vol. 61, No. 5, pp. 585–607.

Sumption, M., Papademetriou, D. G. and Flamm, S. 2013. *Skilled Immigrants in the Global Economy: Prospects for International Cooperation on Recognition of Foreign Qualifications*. Washington, DC, Migration Policy Institute.

Teichler, U., Ferencz, I. and Wächter, B. 2011. *Mapping Mobility in European Higher Education. Vols I and II*. Brussels, European Commission, Directorate General for Education and Culture.

UNDESA. 2015. *Trends in International Migrant Stock: Migrants by Destination and Origin (Table 16)*. New York, United Nations Department of Economic and Social Affairs, Population Division. www.un.org/en/development/desa/population/migration/data/estimates2/estimates15.shtml. (Accessed 18 September 2018.)

___. 2017. *Total population (both sexes combined) by region, subregion and country, annually for 1950–2100 (thousands)*. United Nations Department of Economic and Social Affairs, Population Division. https://population.un.org/wpp/DVD/Files/1_Indicators%20(Standard)/EXCEL_FILES/1_Population/WPP2017_POP_F01_1_TOTAL_POPULATION_BOTH_SEXES.xlsx. (Accessed 18 September 2018.)

UNESCO. 2015. *Draft Preliminary Report Concerning the Preparation of a Global Convention on the Recognition of Higher Education Qualifications*. Paris, UNESCO.

___. 2017a. *Global Education Monitoring Report 2017/8: Accountability in Education – Meeting Our Commitments*. Paris, UNESCO.

___. 2017b. *Progress Report on the Preparation of the Draft Global Convention on the Recognition of Higher Education Qualifications*. Paris, UNESCO.

UNESCO IESALC. 2018. Declaration, Third Regional Conference on Higher Education for Latin America and the Caribbean. Córdoba, Argentina, 11–15 June.

United Nations. 2018. *Global Compact for Safe, Orderly and Regular Migration*. New York, United Nations.

Universities UK. 2017. *International Students Now Worth £25 billion to UK Economy: New Research*. London, Universities UK. www.universitiesuk.ac.uk/news/Pages/International-students-now-worth-25-billion-to-UK-economy---new-research.aspx. (Accessed 18 September 2018.)

Van Bouwel, L. and Veugelers, R. 2009. *Does University Quality Drive International Student Flows?* Leuven, Catholic University of Leuven, Faculty of Business and Economics.

___. 2013. The determinants of student mobility in Europe: the quality dimension. *European Journal of Higher Education*, Vol. 3, No. 2, pp. 172–90.

Vathi, Z. and Zajmi, I. 2017. *Children and Migration in Albania: Latest Trends and Protection Measures Available*. Tirana, Terre des hommes.

Walcutt, L. 2016. The scholarship struggle Saudi Arabian students are facing. *Forbes*, 28 September. www.forbes.com/sites/leifwalcutt/2016/09/28/the-scholarship-struggle-saudi-arabian-students-are-facing. (Accessed 18 September 2018.)

Waruru, M. 2017. Hurdles ahead for East Africa's Common Higher Education Area. *The Pie News*, 18 July. https://thepienews.com/news/hurdles-ahead-east-african-community-common-higher-education-area/. (Accessed 18 September 2018.)

Woldegiorgis, E. T. and Knight, J. 2017. *Achieving African higher education regionalization*. Knight, J. and Woldegiorgis, E. T. (eds), *Regionalization of African Higher Education*. Rotterdam, Springer, pp. 209–20.

World Bank. 2009. *The Nurse Labor & Education Markets in the English-speaking CARICOM: Issues and Options for Reform*. Washington, DC, World Bank.

___. 2010. *Financing Higher Education in Africa*. Washington, DC, World Bank. (Africa Regional Educational Publications.)

MONITORING SECTION

CHAPTER 7

Arp-Nisen, J. D. and Massey, D. S. 2006. *Latin American Migration Project*. Princeton, NJ, https://lamp.opr.princeton.edu/. (Accessed 18 September 2018.)

Beauchemin, C. 2012. *Migrations between Africa and Europe: Rationale for a survey design*. Paris, French Institute for Demographic Studies.

Buber-Ennser, I., Kohlenberger, J., Rengs, B., Al Zalak, Z., Goujon, A., Striessnig, E., Potančoková, M., Gisser, R., Testa, M. R. and Lutz, W. 2016. Human capital, values, and attitudes of persons seeking refuge in Austria in 2015. *PLOS ONE*, Vol. 11, No. 9.

Carletto, G. 2018. *Scaling up the Collection of Microdata on Migrants, Refugees and IDPs*. Washington, DC, World Bank, Development Data Group.

DIW. 2017. *IAB-BAMF-SOEP Survey of Refugees in Germany*. Berlin, Deutsches Institut für Wirtschaftsforschung [German Institute for Economic Research]. www.diw.de/de/diw_02.c.244287.de/ueber_uns/menschen_am_diw_berlin/mitarbeiter/innen.html?id=diw_01.c.538695.en. (Accessed 18 September 2018.) (In German.)

Englund, G. 2018. *Estimating the Number of Forcibly Displaced School-Age Children not Accessing Education*. (Background Paper for *Global Education Monitoring Report 2019*.)

Freier, L. F. and Parent, N. 2018. *A South American Migration Crisis: Venezuelan Outflows Test Neighbors' Hospitality*. Washington, DC, Migration Policy Institute. www.migrationpolicy.org/article/south-american-migration-crisis-venezuelan-outflows-test-neighbors-hospitality. (Accessed 15 September 2018.)

IAEG-SDGs. 2017. *Tier Classification for Global SDG Indicators*. New York, Inter-agency and Expert Group on SDG Indicators, United Nations Statistical Commission.

LIfBI. 2016. *Das Projekt: ReGES – Refugees in the German Educational System*. Bamberg, Germany, Leibniz Institute for Educational Trajectories. (In German.)

Mexican Migration Project. 2018. *Database version 161*. Princeton, NJ/Guadalajara, Mexico, Princeton University/ University of Guadalajara. http://mmp.opr.princeton.edu. (Accessed 15 September 2018.)

OECD and GEMR. 2018. *Learning from Data*. Paris, Organisation for Economic Co-operation and Development/ Global Education Monitoring Report.

ReliefWeb. 2018. *UNHCR and IOM chiefs call for more support as the outflow of Venezuelans rises across the region*. Geneva, Switzerland, International Organization for Migration. https://reliefweb.int/report/venezuela-bolivarian-republic/ unhcr-and-iom-chiefs-call-more-support-outflow-venezuelans. (Accessed 15 September 2018.)

Richardson, D. and Ali, N. 2014. *An Evaluation of International Surveys of Children*. Paris, Organisation for Economic Cooperation and Development.

SERISS. 2018. *Survey Codings*. Synergies for Europe's Research Infrastructures in the Social Sciences. www.surveycodings.org. (Accessed 15 September 2018.)

UIS. 2001. *Education for All Indicators Expert Group Meeting: Report on the Meeting and Proposals for the Future Development of EFA Indicators*. Montreal, Que., UNESCO Institute for Statistics.

UN Statistical Commission. 2018. *International Recommendations on Refugees Statistics*. New York, United Nations, Statistical Commission, Expert Group on Refugee and Internally Displaced Persons Statistics.

UNHCR. 2018. *Global Trends: Forced Displacement in 2017*. Geneva, Switzerland, United Nations High Commissioner for Refugees.

UNICEF, IOM, UNHCR, Eurostat and OECD. 2018. *A Call to Action*. New York, UNICEF.

United Nations. 2015. *Transforming our World: the 2030 Agenda for Sustainable Development*. New York, United Nations.

World Bank. 2018a. *Asylum Seekers in the European Union*. Washington, DC, World Bank.

___. 2018b. *Central Microdata Catalogue*, Washington, DC, World Bank. http://microdata.worldbank.org/index.php/catalog/ central (Accessed 17 September 2018.)

CHAPTER 8

Administrative Tribunal of Lille. 2016. *Ordonnance du 6 septembre 2016 [Ordinance of 6 September 2016]*. Lille, France, Tribunal administratif. (No. 1606500.) (In French.)

Administrative Tribunal of Versailles. 2016. *Ordonnance du 19 octobre 2006 [Ordinance of 19 October 2006]*. Versailles, France, Tribunal administratif. (No. 1306559.) (In French.)

Alexander, M. and Alkema, L. 2018. Global estimation of neonatal mortality using a Bayesian hierarchical splines regression model. *Demographic Research*, Vol. 38, pp. 335–72.

Alkema, L., Chou, D., Hogan, D., Zhang, S., Moller, A.-B., Gemmill, A., Fat, D. M., Boerma, T., Temmerman, M., Mathers, C. and Say, L. 2016. Global, regional, and national levels and trends in maternal mortality between 1990 and 2015, with scenario-based projections to 2030: a systematic analysis by the UN Maternal Mortality Estimation Inter-Agency Group. *The Lancet*, Vol. 387, No. 10017, pp. 462–74.

Alkema, L. and New, J. R. 2012. Progress toward global reduction in under-five mortality: a bootstrap analysis of uncertainty in Millennium Development Goal 4 estimates. *PLOS Medicine*, Vol. 9, No. 12.

ASER. 2018. *Annual Status of Education Report 2017: 'Beyond Basics' (Rural)*. New Delhi, Pratham Education Foundation.

CBS and UNICEF. 2018. *Democratic People's Republic of Korea: Multiple Indicator Cluster Survey*. Pyongyang, Central Bureau of Statistics of the DPR Korea/UNICEF.

CESCR. 1999. *Implementation of the International Covenant on Economic, Social and Cultural Rights: General Comment No. 13*. New York, United Nations Economic and Social Council, Committee on Economic, Social and Cultural Rights.

___. 2009. *Non-discrimination in Economic, Social and Cultural Rights: General Comment No. 20*. New York, United Nations Economic and Social Council, Committee on Economic, Social and Cultural Rights.

___. 2017. *Concluding Observations on the Sixth Periodic Report of the Netherlands*. New York, United Nations Economic and Social Council, Committee on Economic, Social and Cultural Rights.

CMW. 2013. *General Comment No. 2 on the Rights of Migrant Workers in an Irregular Situation and Members of their Families*. New York, United Nations, Office of the High Commissioner for Human Rights, Committee on Migrant Workers.

CMW and CRC. 2017. *Joint General Comment No. 4 (2017) of the Committee on the Protection of the Rights of all Migrant Workers and Member of their Families and No. 23 (2017) of the Committee on the Rights of the Child on State Obligations Regarding the Human Rights of Children in the Context of International Migration in Countries of Origin, Transit, Destination, and Return*. New York, United Nations, Office of the High Commissioner for Human Rights, Committee on Migrant Workers and Committee on the Rights of the Child.

Cortes, R. 2017. *Human Rights of Migrants and Their Families in Argentina as Evidence for Development of Human Rights Indicators: a Case Study*. Global Knowledge Partnership on Migration and Development. Washington, DC, World Bank.

Delvino, N. and Spencer, S. 2014. *Irregular Migrants in Italy: Law and Policy on Entitlements to Services*. Oxford, UK, University of Oxford.

Equal Rights Trust. 2017. *Learning InEquality: Using Equality Law to Tackle Barriers to Primary Education for Out-of-School Children*. London, Equal Rights Trust.

FIDH. 2016. *Women and Children from Kyrgyzstan Affected by Migration: An Exacerbated Vulnerability*. Paris, International Federation for Human Rights.

France Human Rights Defender. 2017. *Décision 2017-023 du 30 janvier 2017 relative au refus d'inscription en classe de maternelle d'un enfant, constitutif d'une discrimination fondée sur la résidence et l'origine [Decision ... on the refusal to enroll a child in kindergarten, which constitutes discrimination based on residence and origin]*. Paris, Défenseur des droits. (In French.)

IEA. 2017. *PIRLS 2016 International Results in Reading*. Boston, TIMSS & PIRLS International Study Center. https://timssandpirls.bc.edu/pirls2016/index-pirls.html. (Accessed 15 September 2018)

___. 2018. *IEA's Rosetta Stone: Measuring Global Progress Toward the UN Sustainable Development Goal for Quality Education by Linking Regional Assessment Results to TIMSS and PIRLS International Benchmarks of Achievement*. Amsterdam, International Association for the Evaluation of Educational Achievement.

IEA and UNESCO. 2017. *Measuring SDG 4: How PIRLS Can Help?* Amsterdam/Paris, IEA/UNESCO.

Italy Council of State. 2014. *Council Judgement of 27 February*. Rome, Consiglio di Stato. (No. 1734.)

Leech, G. 2017. *Migrant children turned away from schools in Russia*. New York, Human Rights Watch. www.hrw.org/news/2017/02/09/migrant-children-turned-away-schools-russia. (Accessed 1 May 2018.)

PAL Network. 2018. *ASER Afghanistan joins the Citizen Led Assessment folds*. Nairobi, PAL Network http://palnetwork.org/aser-afghanistan-joins-the-citizen-led-assessment-folds. (Accessed September 2018.)

Ramanujan, P. and Deshpande, A. 2018. *A Study of Access, Transition and Learning in Secondary Schools*. New Delhi, ASER Centre.

RTE Project. 2017. *Accountability from a Human Rights Perspective: the Incorporation and Enforcement of the Right to Education in the Domestic Legal Order*. (Background paper for *Global Education Monitoring Report 2017/8*.)

RTEI. 2018. *The Status of the Right to Education of Migrants: International Legal Framework, Remaining Barriers at National Level and Good Examples of States' Implementation*. (Background paper for *Global Education Monitoring Report 2019*.)

Spencer, S. and Hughes, V. 2015. *Outside and In: Legal Entitlements to Health Care and Education for Migrants with Irregular Status in Europe*. Oxford, UK, Centre on Migration Policy and Society.

Spreen, C. A. and Vally, S. 2012. Monitoring the right to education for refugees, migrants and asylum seekers. *Southern African Review of Education*, Vol. 18, No. 2, pp. 71–89.

Statistics Sierra Leone. 2018. *Sierra Leone Multiple Indicator Cluster Survey 2017: Survey Findings Report*. Freetown, Statistics Sierra Leone.

UIS. 2017a. *Counting the Number of Children Not Learning: Methodology for a Global Composite Indicator for Education*. Montreal, Que., UNESCO Institute for Statistics.

___. 2017b. *More than One-Half of Children and Adolescents Are Not Learning Worldwide*. Montreal, Que., UNESCO Institute for Statistics.

___. 2018. *SDG 4 Data Digest 2018*. Montreal, Que., UNESCO Institute for Statistics.

UN General Assembly. 1951. *Convention Relating to the Status of Refugees*. New York, United Nations.

___. 1954. *Convention Relating to the Status of Stateless Persons*. New York, United Nations.

UNESCO. 2016. *Global Education Monitoring Report 2016: Education for People and Planet – Creating Sustainable Futures for All*. Paris, UNESCO.

___. 2018. *Combining School Completion Rate Estimates from Multiple Sources: the Adjusted Bayesian Completion Rates (ABC) Model*. Paris, UNESCO.

UNICEF. 2017. *Collecting Data on Foundational Learning Skills & Parental Involvement in Education*. New York, UNICEF. (Methodological Paper 5.)

CHAPTER 9

Adams, L. and Denboba, A. 2017. *Iraq Early Childhood Development*. Washington, DC, World Bank. (SABER Country Reports 2014.)

Anderson, K., Raikes, A., Kosaraju, S. and Solano, A. 2017. *National Early Childhood Care and Education Quality Monitoring Systems*. New York, Center for Universal Education/Brookings Institution/UNICEF.

Bertram, T. and Pascal, C. (2016). *Early Childhood Policies and Systems in Eight Countries: Findings from IEA's Early Childhood Education Study*. Hamburg, Germany, International Association for the Evaluation of Educational Achievement.

Bouchane, K., Yoshikawa, H., Murphy, K. M. and Lombardi, J. 2018. *Early Childhood Development and Early Learning for Children in Crisis and Conflict*. (Background paper for *Global Education Monitoring Report 2019*.)

Britto, P. R., Lye, S. J., Proulx, K., Yousafzai, A. K., Matthews, S. G., Vaivada, T., Perez-Escamilla, R., Rao, N., Ip, P., Fernald, L. C. H., MacMillan, H., Hanson, M., Wachs, T. D., Yao, H., Yoshikawa, H., Cerezo, A., Leckman, J. F. and Bhutta, Z. A. 2017. Nurturing care: promoting early childhood development. *The Lancet*, Vol. 389, No. 10064, pp. 91–102.

Center on the Developing Child. 2007. *The Science of Early Childhood Development*. Cambridge, MA, Harvard University, Center on the Developing Child. (Accessed 19 September 2018.)

Children on the Edge. 2015. *Far from the Beaten Track: Reaching Displaced Children in the Outlying Mountains of Kachin State, Myanmar*. Chichester, UK, Children on the Edge. www.childrenontheedge.org/latest-stories/-far-from-the-beaten-track-reaching-displaced-children-in-the-outlying-mountains-of-kachin-state-burma. (Accessed 16 August 2018.)

Consultative Group on Early Childhood Care and Development. 2016. *Global Report on Equity and Early Childhood*. Leiden, Netherlands, International Step by Step Association.

Dallain, S.-C. and Scott, K.-J. 2017. *Little Ripples: Refugee-Led Early Childhood Education*. New Delhi, Institute for Advanced Computer Technology.

IAEG-SDGs. 2018. *Work Plan for Tier III SDG Global Indicators: Goal 4 – Target Number 4.2*. New York, Inter-agency and Expert Group on SDG Indicators, United Nations Statistical Commission.

International Rescue Committee. 2016. *Bekaa and Akkra*. London, Save the Children International/IDELA Network.

___. 2017. *Impact of War on Syrian Children's Learning: Testing Shows Gaps in Literacy and Math Skills*. New York, International Rescue Committee.

MacArthur Foundation. 2017. *Sesame Workshop & International Rescue Committee Awarded $100 Million for Early Childhood Education of Syrian Refugees*. Chicago, IL, MacArthur Foundation. www.macfound.org/press/press-releases/sesame-workshop-and-international-rescue-committee-awarded-100-million-early-childhood-education-syrian-refugees (Accessed 16 August 2018.)

Ministry of Women and Child Development. 2013. *National Early Childhood Care and Education Policy (ECCE) Policy*. New Delhi, Ministry of Women and Child Development.

National Research Council of the National Academies. 2008. *Early Childhood Assessment*. Washington, DC, National Academies Press.

OECD. 2018. *Early Learning Matters*. Paris, Organisation for Economic Co-operation and Development.

Park, M., Katsiaficas, C. and McHugh, M. 2018. *Responding to the ECEC Needs of Children of Refugees and Asylum Seekers in Europe and North America*. Washington, DC, Migration Policy Institute.

Paul, S. 2017. Quality standards for early childhood services: examples from South and South East Asia. *Early Childhood Matters*, Vol. 2017, pp. 70–73.

Raikes, A. 2017. Measuring child development and learning. *European Journal of Education*, Vol. 52, No. 4, pp. 511–22.

South Africa Department of Basic Education. 2015. *The South African National Curriculum Framework for Children from Birth to Four*. Pretoria, Department of Basic Education.

Steinberg, R. 2018. *Bringing Hope to Children in Kenya's Kalobeyei Refugee Settlement*. New York, UNICEF.

The Early Childhood Commission. 2018. *Report for the 2017 Economic and Social Survey of Jamaica: 'Social Development, Social Protection and Culture'*. Kingston, The Early Childhood Commission.

The Lancet. 2016. Advancing early childhood development: from science to scale. 4 October.

Uganda Ministry of Education and Sports. 2018. *Education Response Plan for Refugees and Host Communities in Uganda*. Kampala, Ministry of Education and Sports.

UIS. 2018. *SDG 4 Data Digest 2018*. Montreal, Que., UNESCO Institute for Statistics.

UNHCR. 2018a. *Population Statistics*. Geneva, Switzerland, United Nations High Commissioner for Refugees.

___. 2018b. *Uganda: July 2018*. Geneva, Switzerland, United Nations High Commissioner for Refugees.

___. 2018c. *Uganda Country Refugee Response Plan: the integrated Response Plan for Refugees from South Sudan, Burundi and the Democratic Republic of the Congo*. Nairobi, United Nations High Commissioner for Refugees.

UNICEF. 2012. *School Readiness*. New York, UNICEF.

___. 2017. *Development of the Early Childgood Development index in MICS Surveys*. New York, UNICEF. (MICS Methodological Paper.)

___. 2018. *Early Childhood Development*. New York, UNICEF.

United Nations. 2016. *New York Declaration for Refugees and Migrants*. New York, United Nations.

___. 2018. *Secretary-General's Remarks at Education Above All Event*. New York, United Nations Secretary-General. www.un.org/sg/en/content/sg/statement/2018-04-27/secretary-generals-remarks-education-above-all-event-prepared (Accessed 19 September 2018.)

Verdisco, A., Cueto, S., Thompson, J. and Neuschmidt, O. 2015. *Urgency and Possibility: First Initiative of Comparative Data on Child Development in Latin America*. Washington, DC, Inter-American Development Bank.

World Bank. 2013a. Bulgaria. *SABER Country Report*. Washington, DC, World Bank.

___. 2013b. *What Matters Most for Early Childhood Development?* Washington, DC, World Bank.

___. 2015. *Former Yugoslav Republic of Macedonia Early Childhood Development*. Washington, DC, World Bank. (SABER Country Reports 2015.)

WHO, UNICEF and World Bank Group. 2018. *Nurturing Care for Early Childhood Development: a Framework for Helping Children Survive and Thrive to Transform Health and Human Potential*. Geneva, Switzerland/New York/Washington, DC, World Health Organization/UNICEF /World Bank.

Wortham, S. C. 2012. *Assessment in Early Childhood Education*, 6th ed. London, Pearson.

CHAPTER 10

Al-Hawamdeh, A. and El-Ghali, H. A. 2017. *Higher Education and Syrian Refugee Students: the Case of Jordan*. Beirut, UNESCO Regional Bureau for Education in the Arab States/United Nations High Commissioner for Refugees.

Amer, M. 2018. *Youth and Adult Participation in Formal and Non-formal Education and Training in Egypt, Jordan and Tunisia*. (Background paper for *Global Education Monitoring Report 2019*.)

Andersson, P. and Fejes, A. 2010. Mobility of knowledge as a recognition challenge: experiences from Sweden. *International Journal of Lifelong Education*, Vol. 29, No. 2, pp. 201–18.

Better Work Jordan. 2016a. *Better Work Jordan: Influence and Action*. Amman, Better Work Jordan. https://betterwork.org/blog/2016/12/15/better-work-jordan-influence-and-action. (Accessed 16 August 2018.)

___. 2016b. *UNHCR Work Permit Pilot Project to Support Syrian Refugee Employment in Jordan's Apparel Industry*. Amman, Better Work Jordan. https://betterwork.org/jordan/wp-content/uploads/UNHCR-4.pdf (Accessed 16 August 2018.)

CEDEFOP. 2011. *Employment-Related Mobility and Migration, and Vocational Education and Training*. Luxembourg, European Center for the Development of Vocational Training.

Charpin, A. and Aiolfi, L. 2011. *Evaluation of the Concrete Results Obtained through Projects Financed under AENEAS and Thematic Programme for Migration and Asylum*. Brussels, IBF International Consulting.

Clement, U. 2014. *Improving the Image of Technical and Vocational Education and Training*. Bonn, Germany, Federal Ministry for Economic Cooperation and Development.

Council of Europe. 2018. *European Qualifications Passport for Refugees*. Strasbourg, France, Council of Europe. www.coe.int/en/web/education/recognition-of-refugees-qualifications (Accessed 17 September 2018.)

de la Rama, S. 2018. *Recognition of Prior Learning for Migrant Workers: the Philippine Experience*. Paper for UNESCO-UNEVOC TVET Learning Forum, Bonn, Germany, 24–25 May.

Desiderio, M. V. 2016. *Integrating Refugees into Host Country Labor Markets: Challenges and Policy Options*. Washington, DC, Migration Policy Institute.

Dryden-Peterson, S. and Giles, W. 2010. Introduction: higher education for refugees. *Refuge*, Vol. 27, No. 2, pp. 3–10.

ERN+. 2017. *Student Scholarships for Refugees: Expanding Complementary Pathways of Admission to Europe*. Geneva, Switzerland, European Resettlement Network.

ETF. 2014. *Migration and Skills Development Agenda in ETF Partner Countries: ETF Position Paper*. Turin, Italy, European Training Foundation.

___. 2015. *Migrant Support Measures from an Employment and Skills Perspective (MISMES): Global Inventory with a Focus on Countries of Origin*. Turin, Italy, European Training Foundation.

___. 2017a. *Migrant Support Measures from an Employment and Skills Perspective (MISMES): Jordan*. Turin, Italy, European Training Foundation.

___. 2017b. *Migrant Support Measures from an Employment and Skills Perspective (MISMES): Lebanon*. Turin, Italy, European Training Foundation.

European Commission. 2016. *EU Regional Trust Fund in Response to the Syrian Crisis: Action Document for Vocational Education and Training & Higher Education Programme for Vulnerable Syrian Youth*. Brussels, European Commission.

European Employment Policy Observatory. 2016. *Challenges in the Labour Market Integration of Asylum Seekers and Refugees*. Luxembourg, European Employment Policy Observatory.

Eurostat. 2017. *Adult Learning Statistics*. Luxembourg, Eurostat. https://ec.europa.eu/eurostat/statistics-explained/index.php/Adult_learning_statistics. (Accessed 17 September 2018.)

___. 2018. *Participation Rate in Education and Training (Last 4 Weeks) by Sex and Age*. Luxembourg, Eurostat. http://appsso.eurostat.ec.europa.eu/nui/show.do?dataset=trng_lfs_01&lang=en. (Accessed 17 September 2018.)

Ferede, M. K. 2018. *Higher Education for Refugees*. (Background paper for *Global Education Monitoring Report 2019*.)

Ferreyra, M. M., Avitabile, C., Álvarez, J. B. and Paz, F. H. 2017. *At a Crossroads: Higher Education in Latin America and the Caribbean*. Washington DC, World Bank.

Germany Federal Ministry of Education and Research. 2017a. *Report on the Recognition Act 2017*. Berlin, Federal Ministry of Education and Research.

___. 2017b. *Report on Vocational Education and Training 2017*. Berlin, Federal Ministry of Education and Research.

ILO. 2018. *ILO, UNHCR Strengthen Partnership to Promote Employment for Refugees and Jordanian Host Communities in Jordan*. Geneva, Switzerland, International Labour Organization. www.ilo.org/pardev/news/WCMS_634696/lang--en/index.htm. (Accessed 16 August 2018.)

Johnstone, D. B. and Marcucci, P. N. 2010. *Financing Higher Education Worldwide: Who Pays? Who Should Pay?* Baltimore, MD, Johns Hopkins University Press.

Karasapan, O. 2017. *Syrian Refugees and the Slow March to "Acceptance"*. Washington, DC, Brookings Institution. www.brookings.edu/blog/future-development/2017/09/07/syrian-refugees-and-the-slow-march-to-acceptance. (Accessed 16 August 2018.)

Kirişci, K., Brandt, J. and Erdoğan, M. M. 2018. *Syrian Refugees in Turkey: Beyond the Numbers*, Brookings Institution. www.brookings.edu/blog/order-from-chaos/2018/06/19/syrian-refugees-in-turkey-beyond-the-numbers. (Accessed 20 September 2018.)

Kirkegaard, A. M. Ø. and Nat-George, S. M.-L. W. 2016. Fleeing through the globalised education system: the role of violence and conflict in international student migration. *Globalisation, Societies and Education*, Vol. 14, No. 3, pp. 390–402.

Lifeline Syria. 2018. *Lifeline Syria*. Toronto, Ont., Lifeline Syria. www.lifelinesyria.ca. (Accessed 16 August 2018.)

Milton, S. and Barakat, S. 2016. Higher education as the catalyst of recovery in conflict-affected societies. *Globalisation, Societies and Education*, Vol. 14, No. 3, pp. 403–21.

Murakami, Y. and Blom, A. 2008. *Accessibility and Affordability of Tertiary Education in Brazil, Colombia, Mexico and Peru within a Global Context*. Washington, DC, World Bank. (Working Paper 4517.)

OECD. 2016a. *Making Integration Work: Refugees and Others in Need of Protection*. Paris, Organisation for Economic Co-operation and Development

___. 2016b. *Working Together: Skills and Labour Market Integration of Immigrants and their Children in Sweden*. Paris, Organisation for Economic Co-operation and Development

OECD and UNHCR. 2018. *Engaging with Employers in the Hiring of Refugees: A 10-Point Multi-stakeholder Action Plan for Employers, Refugees, Governments and Civil Society*. Paris/Geneva, Switzerland, Organisation for Economic Co-operation and Development/United Nations High Commissioner for Refugees.

Safi, M. 2014. *Shifting Focus: Policies to Support the Labor Market Integration of New Immigrants in France*. Washington, DC/Geneva, Switzerland, Migration Policy Institute/International Labour Organization.

Singh, M. 2018. *Pathways to Empowerment: Recognizing the Competences of Syrian Refugees in Egypt, Iraq, Jordan, Lebanon and Turkey*. Hamburg, Germany, UNESCO Institute for Lifelong Learning.

UNESCO. 2017. *Global Education Monitoring Report 2017/8: Accountability in Education – Meeting Our Commitments*. Paris, UNESCO.

___. 2018. *Recognition, Validation and Accreditation of Youth and Adult Basic Education as a Foundation of Lifelong Learning*. Hamburg, Germany, UNESCO Institute for Lifelong Learning.

UNESCO and Council of Europe. 2016. *Monitoring the Implementation of the Lisbon Recognition Convention*. Paris/Strasbourg, France, UNESCO/Council of Europe.

UNESCO-UNEVOC and University of Nottingham. 2018. *Human Migration and TVET: a Concept Paper for the UNEVOC Network*. Bonn, Germany, UNESCO-UNEVOC/University of Nottingham (Unpublished.)

UNHCR. 2015a. *DAFI 2014 Annual Report*. Geneva, Switzerland, United Nations High Commissioner for Refugees.

___. 2015b. *Higher Education Considerations for Refugees in Countries Affected by the Syria and Iraq Crises*. Geneva, Switzerland, United Nations High Commissioner for Refugees.

___. 2017. *DAFI 2016 Annual Report*. Geneva, Switzerland, United Nations High Commissioner for Refugees.

___. 2018. *Turn the Tide: Refugee Education in Crisis*. Geneva, Switzerland, United Nations High Commissioner for Refugees.

UNICEF. 2015. *Curriculum, Accreditation and Certification for Syrian Children in Syria, Turkey, Lebanon, Jordan, Iraq and Egypt*. Amman, UNICEF Middle East and North Africa Regional Office.

___. 2018. *Youth Economic Engagement*. Amman, UNICEF Middle East and North Africa Regional Office.

UNRWA. 2016. *UNRWA Technical and Vocational Education and Training Programme*. Amman, UNRWA Education Department.

Usher, A. and Medow, J. 2010. *Global Higher Education Rankings 2010: Affordability and Accessibility in Comparative Perspective*. Toronto, Ont., Higher Education Strategy Associates.

World Bank. 2012. *Putting Higher Education to Work*. Washington, DC, World Bank.

___. 2014. *World Bank Support to Education: a Systems Approach to Achieve Learning for All*. Washington, DC, World Bank. www.worldbank.org/en/results/2014/04/28/world-bank-support-to-education-a-systems-approach-to-achieve-learning-for-all. (Accessed 15 September 2018.)

WUSC. 2007. *Fostering Tomorrow's Global Leaders*. Ottawa, World University Service of Canada.

Zetter, R. and Ruaudel, H. 2016. *Refugees' Right to Work and Access to Labor Markets: an Assessment – Part I: Synthesis*. Washington, DC, Global Knowledge Partnership on Migration and Development.

CHAPTER 11

Atkinson, A. and Messy, F. 2013. *Promoting Financial Inclusion through Financial Education: OECD/INFE Evidence, Policies and Practice*. Paris, Organisation for Economic Co-operation and Development. (Working Paper 34 on Finance, Insurance and Private Pensions.)

___. 2015. *Financial Education for Migrants and Their Families*. Paris, Organisation for Economic Co-operation and Development. (Working Paper 38 on Finance, Insurance and Private Pensions.)

Attia, H. and Engelhardt, H. 2016. *Financial Education Initiatives in the Arab Region: a Stocktaking Report*. Eschborn, Germany, Deutsche Gesellschaft für Internationale Zusammenarbeit.

Bacigalupo, M., Kampylis, P., Punie, Y. and Van den Brande, G. 2016. *EntreComp: the Entrepreneurship Competence Framework*. Luxembourg, European Commission.

Brown, R. P., Connell, J. and Jimenez-Soto, E. V. 2014. Migrants' remittances, poverty and social protection in the South Pacific: Fiji and Tonga. *Population, Space and Place*, Vol. 20, No. 5, pp. 434–54.

Carretero, S., Vuorikari, R. and Punie, Y. 2017. *The Digital Competence Framework for Citizens, With Eight Proficiency Levels and Examples of Use*. Luxembourg, Joint Research Centre/European Commission.

Chernyshenko, O., Kankaraš, M. and Drasgow, F. 2018. *Social and Emotional Skills for Student Success and Wellbeing: Conceptual Framework for the OECD Study on Social and Emotional Skills*. Paris, Organisation for Economic Co-operation and Development. (Education Working Paper 173.)

Doi, Y., McKenzie, D. and Zia, B. 2012. *Who You Train Matters: Identifying Complementary Effects of Financial Education on Migrant Households*. Washington, DC, World Bank.

Entorf, H. and Hou, J. 2018. *Financial Education for the Disadvantaged? A Review*. Bonn, Germany, Institute of Labor Economics.

European Commission. 2018a. *Boosting Children's Digital Literacy: an Urgent Task for Schools*. Brussels, EU Science Hub. https://ec.europa.eu/jrc/en/news/boosting-children-s-digital-literacy-urgent-task-schools. (Accessed 19 September 2018.)

European Commission. 2018b. *Communication from the Commission to the European Parliament, the Council, the European Economic and Social Committee and the Committee of the Regions on the Digital Education Action Plan*. Brussels, European Commission. https://eur-lex.europa.eu/legal-content/EN/TXT/PDF/?uri=CELEX:52018DC0022&from=EN. (Accessed 19 September 2018.)

Fatehkia, M., Kashyap, R. and Weber, I. 2018. Using Facebook ad data to track the global digital gender gap. *World Development*, Vol. 107, pp. 189–209.

Fau, S. and Moreau, Y. 2018. *Building Tomorrow's Digital Skills: What Conclusions Can We Draw from International Comparative Indicators?* Paris, UNESCO.

Fernandes, D., Lynch Jr, J. G. and Netemeyer, R. G. 2014. Financial literacy, financial education, and downstream financial behaviors. *Management Science*, Vol. 60, No. 8, pp. 1861–83.

Gibson, J., McKenzie, D. and Zia, B. 2012. *The Impact of Financial Literacy Training for Migrants*. Washington, DC, World Bank.

Global Entrepreneurship Monitor. 2018. *Global Report 2017/18*. London, Global Entrepreneurship Research Association.

GMG. 2017. *Migration, Remittances and Financial Inclusion: Challenges and Opportunities for Women's Economic Empowerment*. New York, UN Women/Global Migration Group.

GPFI. 2015. *Financial Education for Migrants and their Families: OECD/INFE Policy Analysis and Practical Tools*. Paris, Global Partnership for Financial Inclusion/Organisation for Economic Co-operation and Development.

Haenssgen, M. J. 2018. Manifestations, drivers, and frictions of mobile phone use in low- and middle-income settings: a mixed methods analysis of rural India and China. *Journal of Development Studies*.

IEA. 2017. *The IEA'S International Computer and Information Literacy Study (ICILS) 2018: What's Next for IEA's ICILS in 2018?* Amsterdam, International Association for the Evaluation of Educational Achievement.

IOM. 2018. *Mastercard, UN Migration Agency Team Up to Help Vulnerable Migrants, Refugees in Romania*. Geneva, International Organization for Migration. www.iom.int/news/mastercard-un-migration-agency-team-help-vulnerable-migrants-refugees-romania. (Accessed 19 September 2018.)

Kaiser, T. and Menkhoff, L. 2017. *Does Financial Education Impact Financial Literacy and Financial Behavior, and If So, When?* Washington, DC, World Bank.

Klapper, L., Lusardi, A. and Van Oudheusden, P. 2015. *Financial Literacy around the World: Insights from the Standard & Poor's Ratings Services Global Financial Literacy Survey*. Washington, DC, World Bank.

Laajaj, R., Arias, O., Macours, K., Rubio-Codina, M. and Vakis, R. 2018. *How Well Do We Measure Non-cognitive Skills in Developing Countries? Initial Lessons from STEP Skills Measurement Program*. Washington, DC, World Bank. (Poverty and Equity Note 3.)

Lusardi, A. and Mitchell, O. S. 2014. The economic importance of financial literacy: theory and evidence. *Journal of Economic Literature*, Vol. 52, No. 1, pp. 5–44.

Michaud, P.-C. 2017. *The Value of Financial Literacy and Financial Education for Workers: a Financially Literate Workforce Helps the Economy, but Acquiring the Needed Skills Can Be Costly*. Montreal, Que., IZA World of Labor. https://wol.iza.org/articles/the-value-of-financial-literacy-and-financial-education-for-workers/long. (Accessed 20 September 2018.)

ODI. 2012. *How to Maximise the Impact of Youth Entrepreneurship Support in Different Contexts: a Consultation*. London, Overseas Development Institute.

OECD. 2016a. *Entrepreneurship 360 Guidance Note for Teachers and School Managers*. Paris, Organisation for Economic Co-operation and Development.

___. 2016b. *Responses to the Refugee Crisis: Financial Education and the Long Term Integration of Refugees and Migrants*. Paris, Organisation for Economic Co-operation and Development.

___. 2017a. *PISA 2015 Results (Volume V): Collaborative Problem Solving*. Paris, Organisation for Economic Co-operation and Development.

___. 2017b. *Social and Emotional Skills: Well-being, Connectedness and Success*. Paris, Organisation for Economic Co-operation and Development.

___. 2018. *Financial Inclusion Programme for Migrants: Mexico*. Paris, Organisation for Economic Co-operation and Development.

Pix. 2018. *Cultivez vos expériences numériques [Cultivate your Digital Experiences]*. Paris, Ministry of Higher Education, Research and Innovation. www.pix.fr. (Accessed 6 November 2018.)

Rosenberg, K. 2017. *Financial Literacy for Migrant Workers and Their Families in Sri Lanka*. Colombo, HELVETAS Swiss Intercooperation.

Seshan, G. and Yang, D. 2014. Motivating migrants: a field experiment on financial decision-making in transnational households. *Journal of Development Economics*, Vol. 108, pp. 119–27.

UIS. 2018. *A Global Framework of Reference on Digital Literacy Skills for Indicator 4.4.2*. Montreal, Que., UNESCO Institute for Statistics.

UNESCO. 2018. *Digital Inclusion for Low-skilled and Low-literate People*. Paris, UNESCO.

UNODC. 2015. *The Role of Recruitment Fees and Abusive and Fraudulent Recruitment Practices of Recruitment Agencies in Trafficking in Persons*. Vienna, United Nations Office on Drugs and Crime.

Vie, J.-J., Marteau, B., Denos, N. and Tort, F. 2017. *PIX: A Platform for Certification of Digital Competencies*. (Unpublished).

World Bank. 2017a. *Financial Education in the Arab World: Strategies, Implementation and Impact*. Rabat, World Bank.

___. 2017b. *Redesigning Financial Education to Engage and Entertain Audiences Is Delivering Results*. Washington, DC, World Bank. www.worldbank.org/en/news/feature/2017/08/02/redesigning-financial-education-to-engage-audiences-is-delivering-results. (Accessed 23 September 2018.)

___. 2018. *Migration and Remittances Data*. Washington, DC, World Bank. www.worldbank.org/en/topic/migrationremittancesdiasporaissues/brief/migration-remittances-data. (Accessed 20 September 2018.)

CHAPTER 12

Abuya, B. 2018. *The Movement of Families, Households, and Individuals within Countries and Its Relationship with Education: Challenges and Opportunities in a Shifting World*. (Background paper for *Global Education Monitoring Report 2019*.)

APHRC. 2014. *Population and Health Dynamics in Nairobi's Informal Settlements: Report of the Nairobi Cross-sectional Slums Survey (NCSS) 2012*. Nairobi, African Population and Health Research Center.

Bangladesh Bureau of Statistics. 2015. *Census of Slum Areas and Floating Population 2014*. Dhaka, Ministry of Planning, Bangladesh Bureau of Statistics, Statistics and Informatics Division.

Bangladesh Bureau of Statistics and UNICEF Bangladesh. 2017. *Child Well-Being Survey in Urban Areas of Bangladesh 2016: Final Report*. Dhaka, Bangladesh Bureau of Statistics/UNICEF Bangladesh.

Ben-Moshe, L. and Magaña, S. 2014. An introduction to race, gender, and disability: intersectionality, disability studies, and families of color. *Women, Gender, and Families of Color*, Vol. 2, No. 2, pp. 105–14.

Beukes, A. 2015. *Making the Invisible Visible: Generating Data on 'Slums' at Local, City and Global Scales*. London, International Institute for Environment and Development.

Bhatkal, T., Avis, W. and Nicolai, S. 2015. *Towards a Better Life? A Cautionary Tale of Progress in Ahmedabad*. London, Overseas Development Institute.

Community Organisation Resource Centre. 2016. *Close Out Report: Rapid Appraisal of Informal Settlements in the Western Cape*. Cape Town, South Africa, SA SDI Alliance/Community Organisation Resource Centre/Western Cape Government.

Crock, M., Smith-Khan, L., McCallum, R. and Saul, B. 2017. *The Legal Protection of Refugees with Disabilities: Forgotten and Invisible?* Cheltenham, UK, Edward Elgar Publishing Ltd.

Hagen, E. 2017. *Open Mapping from the Ground Up: Learning from Map Kibera*. Brighton, UK, University of Sussex, Institute of Development Studies.

HelpAge International and Handicap International. 2014. *Hidden Victims of the Syrian Crisis: Disabled, Injured and Older Refugees*. London, HelpAge International/Handicap International.

Hendriks, B. 2008. *Jordanian Sign Language: Aspects of Grammar from a Cross-Linguistic Perspective*. Utrecht, Netherlands, Netherlands National Graduate School of Linguistics.

Humanity and Inclusion. 2018. *Disability Statistics in Humanitarian Action*. Lyon, Humanity and Inclusion. https://humanity-inclusion.org.uk/en/disability-statistics-in-humanitarian-action. (Accessed 21 September 2018.)

HRW. 2016. *We're Afraid for Their Future: Barriers to Education for Syrian Refugee Children in Jordan*. Human Rights Watch. www.hrw.org/report/2016/08/16/were-afraid-their-future/barriers-education-syrian-refugee-children-jordan. (Accessed 21 September 2018.)

IIED. 2017. *Community-driven Data Collection in Informal Settlements*. London, International Institute for Environment and Development.

JRC. 2018. *Global Definition of Cities and Settlements*. Luxembourg, European Commission, EU Science Hub, Joint Research Centre, Global Human Settlement Layer. https://ghsl.jrc.ec.europa.eu/degurba.php. (Accessed 21 September 2018.)

Lucci, P., Bhatkal, T. and Khan, A. 2018. Are we underestimating urban poverty? *World Development*, Vol. 103, pp. 297–310.

McCallum, R. and Martin, H. M. 2013. Comment: the CRPD and children with disabilities. *Australian International Law Journal*, Vol. 20, pp. 17–31.

Ngware, M., Abuya, B. A., Kassahun, Mutisya, M. M., Peter and Oketch, M. 2013. *Quality and Access to Education in Urban Informal Settlements in Kenya*. Nairobi, African Population and Health Research Center.

NUDIPU. 2018. *Refugees: Advocacy for Inclusion of Refugee Persons with Disabilities in Development Process*. Kampala, National Union of Disabled Persons of Uganda. http://nudipu.org/refugees/. (Accessed 15 September 2018.)

Refugee Law Project. 2014. *From the Frying Pan into the Fire: Psychosocial Challenges Faced by Vulnerable Refugee Women and Girls in Kampala*. Kampala, Refugee Law Project.

Shack/Slum Dwellers International. 2018. *Know Your City: Slum Dwellers Count*. Cape Town, South Africa, Shack/Slum Dwellers International.

Smith-Khan, L. and Crock, M. 2018. *Making Rights to Education Real for Refugees with Disabilities*. (Background paper for *Global Education Monitoring Report 2019*.)

Statistics Sierra Leone. 2018. *Sierra Leone Multiple Indicator Cluster Survey 2017: Survey Findings Report*. Freetown, Statistics Sierra Leone.

UIS. 2018. *Handbook on Measuring Equity in Education*. Montreal, Que., UNESCO Institute for Statistics.

UN Habitat. 2016. *Urbanization and Development: Emerging Futures – World Cities Report 2016*. Nairobi, UN Habitat.

UNICEF. 2016. *Module on Child Functionning: Questionnaires*. New York, UNICEF. https://data.unicef.org/resources/module-child-functioning/. (Accessed 9 September 2018).

. 2017. *Washington Group on Disability Statistics Module on Child Functioning*. New York, UNICEF.

UNICEF Bangladesh. 2010. *Understanding Urban Inequalities in Bangladesh: a Prerequisite for Achieving Vision 2021 – A Study Based on the Results of the 2009 Multiple Indicator Cluster Survey*. Dhaka, UNICEF Bangladesh.

Women's Refugee Commission. 2017. *Vulnerability- and Resilience-based Approaches in Response to the Syrian Crisis: Implications for Women, Children and Youth with Disabilities*. New York, Women's Refugee Commission.

CHAPTER 13

ACTA. 2017. *Inquiry into Migrant Settlement Outcomes: Submission to the Joint Standing Committee on Migration*. Melbourne, Australia, Australian Council of TESOL Associations.

Andrade, P. C. L. 2018. *Boa Prática: Promoção e Reforço de Alfabetização e Formação de Imigrantes das Comunidades Africanas em Cabo Verde [Good Practice: Promotion and Reinforcement of Literacy and Training of Immigrants from African Communities in Cabo Verde]*. Brasília, National Directorate of Education, Literacy Service and Adult Education. (Unpublished.)

Bacishoga, K. B. and Johnston, K. A. 2013. Impact of mobile phones on integration: the case of refugees in South Africa. *The Journal of Community Informatics*, Vol. 9, No. 4.

Basu, K., Navayon, M. and Ravallion, M. 2001. *Is Knowledge Shared within Households?* Washington, DC, World Bank. (Working Paper 2261.)

Benigno, V., de Jong, J. and Van Moere, A. 2017. *How Long Does it Take to Learn a Language? Insights from Research on Language Learning*. London, Pearson.

Benseman, J. 2014. Adult refugee learners with limited literacy: needs and effective responses. *Refuge*, Vol. 30, No. 1, pp. 93–103.

Capps, R., Newland, K., Fratzke, S., Groves, S., Auclair, G., Fix, M. and McHugh, M. 2015. *The Integration Outcomes of U.S. Refugees: Successes and Challenges*. Washington, DC, Migration Policy Institute.

Centre for Multicultural Youth. 2013. *Education and Training in Victoria: a Guide for Newly Arrived Young People and Their Families*. Carlton, Centre for Multicultural Youth.

Choi, J. and Ziegler, G. 2015. Literacy education for low-educated second language learning adults in multilingual contexts: the case of Luxembourg. *Multilingual Education*, Vol. 5, No. 4.

Council of Europe. 2017. *A Council of Europe Toolkit*. Strasbourg, France, Council of Europe. www.coe.int/en/web/language-support-for-adult-refugees/home. (Accessed 5 June 2018.)

Demie, F. 2013. English as an additional language pupils: how long does it take to acquire English fluency? *Language and Education*, Vol. 1, pp. 59–69.

Greenberg, D., Ginsburg, L. and Wrigley, H. S. 2017. Research updates: reading, numeracy, and language education. *New Directions for Adult and Continuing Education*, Vol. 155, pp. 83–94.

Grotlüschen, A., Buddeberg, K., Koch, S. and Hollander, I. D. 2016. *Literacy in the Netherlands: Country Report Adult*. Cologne, Germany, European Literacy Policy Network.

Hakuta, K., Butler, Y. G. and Witt, D. 2000. *How Long Does it Take English Learners to Attain Proficiency?* Oakland, CA, University of California Linguistic Minority Research Institute. (Policy Report 2000-1.)

Hanemann, U. 2018. *Language and Literacy Programmes for Migrants and Refugees: Challenges and Ways Forward.* (Background paper for *Global Education Monitoring Report 2019*.)

Isphording, I. E. 2015. *What Drives the Language Proficiency of Immigrants?* Bonn, Germany, IZA World of Labor. https://wol.iza.org/articles/what-drives-language-proficiency-of-immigrants/long. (Accessed 15 September 2018.)

Iversen, V. and Palmer-Jones, R. 2008. Literacy sharing, assortative mating, or what? Labour market advantages and proximate illiteracy revisited. *Journal of Development Studies*, Vol. 44, No. 6, pp. 797–838.

King, R. and Lulle, A. 2016. *Research on Migration: Facing Realities and Maximising Opportunities: a Policy Review.* Brussels, European Commission.

Maddox, B. 2007. Worlds apart? Ethnographic reflections on "effective literacy" and intrahousehold externalities. *World Development*, Vol. 35, No. 3, pp. 532–41.

Malessa, E. 2018. Learning to read for the first time as adult immigrants in Finland: reviewing pertinent research of low-literate or non-literate learners' literacy acquisition and computer-assistaed literacy training. *Apples – Journal of Applied Language Studies*, Vol. 12, No. 1, pp. 25–54.

McIntyre, N. 2017. Migrants told to learn English upon entering UK face three-year wait for lessons. *The Independent*, 9 January. www.independent.co.uk/news/uk/home-news/migrants-wait-years-english-classes-government-lessons-esol-a7517221.html. (Accessed 5 June 2018.)

Naeb, R. and Young-Scholten, M. 2017. International training of teachers of low-educated adult migrants. Beacco, J.-C., Krumm, H.-J., Little, D. and Thalgott, P. (eds), *The Linguistic Integration of Adult Migrants: Some Lessons from Research.* Berlin, De Gruyter, pp. 419–24.

New Zealand Ministry of Business. 2017a. *New Zealand Migrant Settlement and Integration Strategy: Outcomes Indicators 2016.* Wellington, Ministry of Business, Innovation and Employment.

___. 2017b. *New Zealand Refugee Resettlement Strategy.* Wellington, Ministry of Business, Innovation and Employment.

Ng, E., Pottie, K. and Spitzer, D. 2011. Official language proficiency and self-reported health among immigrants to Canada. *Health Reports*, Vol. 22, No. 4.

Permanyer, I., Garcia, J. and Esteve, A. 2013. The impact of educational homogamy on isolated illiteracy levels. *Demography*, Vol. 50, No. 6, pp. 2209–25.

Plutzar, V. and Ritter, M. 2008. *Language Learning in the Context of Migration and Integration: Challenges and Options for Adult Learners.* Strasbourg, France, Council of Europe. (Case Study 3.)

Refugee Action. 2016. *Let Refugees Learn: Challenges and Opportunities to Improve Language Provision to Refugees in England.* London, Refugee Action.

Riekmann, W., Buddeberg, K. and Grotlüschen, A. 2016. *Das mitwissende Umfeld von Erwachsenen mit geringen Lese-und Schreibkompetenzen: Ergebnisse aus der Umfeldstudie [The Informative Environment of Adults with Low Literacy Skills: Results from the Environmental Study].* Münster, Germany, Waxmann.

Sbertoli, G. and Arnesen, H. 2014. Language and initial literacy training for immigrants: the Norwegian approach. Mallows, D. (ed.), *Language Issues in Migration and Integration: Perspectives from Teachers and Learners.* London, British Council, pp. 123–34.

Scheible, J. A. 2018. *Alphabetisierung und Deutscherwerb von Geflüchteten: Deutschkenntnisse und Förderbedarfe von Erst- und Zweitschriftlernenden in Integrationskursen. [Literacy and German Acquisition of Refugees: Knowledge of German and the Needs of First- and Second-Language Learners in Integration Courses].* Nuremberg, Germany, Federal Office for Migration and Refugees/Research Center Migration, Integration and Asylum.

Schellekens, P. 2011. *Teaching and Testing the Language Skills of First and Second Language Speakers.* Cambridge, UK, Cambridge ESOL.

Scottish Government. 2017. *New Scots: Integrating Refugees in Scotland's Communities: 2014-2017 Final Report.* Edinburgh, Local Government and Communities Directorate.

Tammelin-Laine, T. 2014. *Aletaan alusta: Luku- ja kirjoitustaidottomat aikuiset uutta kieltä oppimassa [Let's Start from the Beginning: Non-literate Adults Learning a New Language].* Jyväskylä, Finland, Jyväskylä University Printing House. (In Finnish.)

UIS. 2018. *Mini-LAMP for Monitoring Progress towards SDG 4.6.1.* Montreal, Que., UNESCO Institute for Statistics/ Global Alliance to Monitoring Learning.

UNESCO. 2016. *Global Education Monitoring Report 2016: Education for People and Planet – Creating Sustainable Futures for All.* Paris, UNESCO.

UNESCO and UIL. 2016. *Recommendation on Adult Learning and Education.* Paris, UNESCO.

Wierth, A. 2017. Berlin spricht Arabisch *[Berlin Speaks Arabic].* Berlin, Taz. www.taz.de/!5373447/. (Accessed 17 September 2018.)

CHAPTER 14

Bhatia, K. and Ghanem, H. 2017. *How Do Education and Unemployment Affect Support for Violent Extremism? Evidence from Eight Arab Countries*. Washington, DC, Brookings Institution.

Briggs, R. and Feve, S. 2013. *Review of Programs to Counter Narratives of Violent Extremism: What Works and What Are the Implication for Government?* London, Institute for Strategic Dialogue.

Bromley, P., Lerch, J. and Jimenez, J. D. 2016. *Education for Global Citizenship and Sustainable Development: Content in Social Science Textbooks*. (Background paper for *Global Education Monitoring Report 2016*.)

Crabtree, S. and Kluch. 2017. *Terrorism, Migration Trouble Many in Europe*. Washington, DC, Gallup. https://news.gallup.com/poll/212405/terrorism-migration-trouble-europe.aspx. (Accessed 1 October 2018.)

Davies, L. 2009. Educating against extremism: towards a critical politicisation of young people. *International Review of Education*, Vol. 55, No. 2–3, pp. 183–203.

Dreher, A., Gassebner, M. and Schaudt, P. 2017. *The Effect of Migration on Terror: Made at Home or Imported from Abroad?* Munich, Germany, CESifo. (Working Paper 6441.)

European Commission. 2016. *Strengthening Media Literacy and Critical Thinking to Prevent Violent Radicalisation*. Luxemburg, European Commission.

Europol. 2018. *European Union Terrorism Situation and Trend Report 2018*. The Hague, European Union Agency for Law Enforcement Cooperation.

ENAR. 2017. *Racism and Discrimination in the Context of Migration in Europe: ENAR Shadow Report 2015–2016*. Brussels, European Network Against Racism.

Gambetta, D. and Hertog, S. 2016. *Engineers of Jihad: the Curious Connection between Violent Extremism and Education*. Princeton, NJ, Princeton University Press.

GCTF. 2014. *Good Practices on Women and Countering Violent Extremism*. New York, Global Counterterrorism Forum.

Giscard d'Estaing, S. 2017. Engaging women in countering violent extremism: avoiding instrumentalisation and furthering agency. *Gender and Development*, Vol. 25, No. 1, pp. 103–18.

ICCT. 2018. *Victims' Voices Indonesia*. Jakarta, International Centre for Counter-Terrorism.

INEE. 2017. *Preventing Violent Extremism: An Introduction to Education and Preventing Violent Extremism*. New York, Inter-Agency Network for Education in Emergencies.

International Alert. 2016. *Why Young Syrians Choose to Fight: Vulnerability and Resilience to Recruiment by Violent Extremist Groups in Syria*. London, International Alert.

International Alert Philippines/Mindanao Business Council. 2018. *Equality and Political Leadership: Building Inclusive and Safe Spaces for the Moro Youth in the Philippines*. Manila, International Alert Philippines/Mindanao Business Council.

Kellner, D. and Share, J. 2007. Critical media literacy, democracy, and the reconstruction of education. Macedo, D. and Steinberg, S. R. (eds), *Media Literacy: A Reader*. New York, Peter Lang, pp. 3–23.

Krueger, A. B. and Maleckova, J. 2003. Education, poverty and terrorism: is there a causal connection? *Journal of Economic Perspectives*, Vol. 17, No. 4, pp. 119–44.

Lelo, S. M. 2011. Countering Terrorism through Education of Populations: The Case of African Countries. *Counter Terrorism in Diverse Communities*, pp. 249–60. (NATO Science for Peace and Security Series - E: Human and Societal Dynamics.)

Losito, B., Agrusti, G., Damiani, V. and Schulz, W. 2016. *Young People's Perceptions of Europe in a Time of Change: IEA International Civic and Citizenship Education Study 2016 European Report*. Amsterdam, International Association for the Evaluation of Educational Achievement.

Mirahmadi, H., Ziad, W., Farooq, M. and Lamb, R. D. 2015. *Empowering Pakistan's Civil Society to Counter Global Violent Extremism*. Washington, DC, Brookings Institution.

UN MGCY. 2015. *UN Major Group for Children and Youth's Vision & Priorities for Delivery of the Sustainable Development Goals and the Post-2015 Development Agenda: an Updated Position Paper for the SD 2015 Programme – "Post 2 Post: Enhancing Stakeholder Engagement in the Post-Rio+20/Post-2015 Process"*. New York, UN Major Group for Children and Youth. https://sustainabledevelopment.un.org/content/documents/7031MGCYUpdatedPost2015PositionPaper-March2015.pdf. (Accessed 12 September 2018).

OECD. 2018. *Prepating Our Youth for an Inclusive and Sustainable World: the OECD PISA Global Competence Framework*. Paris, Organization for Economic Co-operation and Development.

Patel, F. and Koushik, M. 2017. *Countering Violent Extremism*. New York, Brennan Center for Justice, New York University School of Law.

RAN. 2018. *Preventing Radicalisation to Terrorism and Violent Extremism: Approaches and Practices*. Brussels, Radicalisation Awareness Network.

Sandoval-Hernández, A. and Miranda, D. 2018. *Exploring ICCS 2016 to measure progress toward target 4.7*. (Background paper for *Global Education Monitoring Report 2019*.)

Schulz, W., Ainley, J., Fraillon, J., Losito, B., Agrusti, G. and Friedman, T. 2017. *Becoming Citizens in a Changing World: IEA International Civic and Citizenship Education Study 2016 International Report*. Amsterdam, Springer.

Treviño, E., Béjares, C., Wyman, I. and Villalobos, C. 2018. Influence of teacher, student and school characteristics on students' attitudes toward diversity. Sandoval-Hernández, A., Isac, M. M. and Miranda, D. (eds), *Teaching Tolerance in a Globalized World*. Cham, Switzerland, International Association for the Evaluation of Educational Achievement/Springer.

UNESCO. 2016. *A Teachers' Guide on the Prevention of Violent Extremism*. Paris, UNESCO.

___. 2017a. *Preventing Violent Extremism through Education: A Guide for Policy-makers*. Paris, UNESCO.

___. 2017b. *Terrorism and the media. A Handbook for Journalists*. Paris, UNESCO.

___. 2018a. *Evidence of effectiveness of education activities in PVE-E: main considerations*. Paper presented at Preliminary Consultation on Inter-institutional Cooperation on the Prevention of Violent Extremism through Education, Paris, 18 April.

___. 2018b. *Results of the 6th Consultation on the implementation of the 1974 Recommendation*. Paris, UNESCO.

United Nations. 2015. *Plan of Action to Prevent Violent Extremism. Report of the Secretary-General*. New York, United Nations.

CHAPTER 15

Behaghel, L., De Chaisemartin, C. and Gurgand, M. 2017. Ready for boarding? The effects of a boarding school for disadvantaged students. *American Economic Journal: Applied Economics*, Vol. 9, No. 1, pp. 140–64.

Cox, J. W. and Rich, S. 2018. No, there haven't been 18 school shootings in 2018. That number is flat wrong. *Washington Post*, 15 February. www.washingtonpost.com/amphtml/local/no-there-havent-been-18-school-shooting-in-2018-that-number-is-flat-wrong/2018/02/15/65b6cf72-1264-11e8-8ea1-c1d91fcec3fe_story.html. (Accessed 1 August 2018.)

EPDC. 2009. *How (Well) is Education Measured in Household Surveys? A Comparative Analysis of the Education Modules in 30 Household Surveys from 1996–2005*. Washington, DC, Education Policy and Data Center/International Household Survey Network.

Fahed, N. and Albina, M. 2016. *Tabshoura Kindergarten: Using Digital Resources in Early Childhood Education – Final Narrative Report*. Beirut, Lebanese Alternative Learning/World Vision.

GBC. 2016. *Exploring the Potential of Technology to Deliver Education and Skills to Syrian Refugee Youth*. London, Global Business Coalition for Education/Theirworld.

GCPEA. 2018. *Education Under Attack 2018*. New York, Global Coalition to Protect Education from Attack.

Gershoff, E. T. 2017. School corporal punishment in global perspective: prevalence, outcomes, and efforts at intervention. *Psychology, Health and Medicine*, Vol. 22, No. sup1, pp. 224–39.

GIZ. 2016. *Education in Conflict and Crisis: How Can Technology Make a Difference? A Landscape Review*. Bonn, German Society for International Cooperation.

Global Initiative to End All Corporal Punishment of Children. 2018. *Working towards Universal Prohibition of Corporal Punishment: A Special Report for the High Level Global Conference held by H.E. the President of Malta, May-June 2018*. London, Global Initiative to End All Corporal Punishment of Children.

JMP. 2017. *Progress on Drinking Water, Sanitation and Hygiene: 2017 Update and SDG Baselines*. Geneva, Switzerland, World Health Organization/UNICEF Joint Monitoring Programme.

Lachal, C. 2015. *Ideas Box: An Innovating Psychosocial Tool for Emergency Situations – Impact Study in the Kavumu and Bwagirisa Camps, Burundi*. Washington, DC, Libraries Without Borders.

Menashy, F. and Zakharia, Z. 2017. *Investing in the Crisis: Private Participation in the Education of Syrian Refugees*. Brussels, Education International.

OHCHR. 2000. *Optional Protocol to the Convention on the Rights of the Child on the Involvement of Children in Armed Conflict*. Geneva, Switzerland, Office of the High Commissioner for Human Rights. www.ohchr.org/en/professionalinterest/pages/opaccrc.aspx. (Accessed 25 September 2018.)

Richardson, D. and Fen Hiu, C. 2018. *Developing a Global Indicator on Bullying of School-aged Children*. New York, UNICEF.

Rumie. 2018. *Frequently Asked Questions*. Toronto, Ont., Rumie Initiative www.rumie.org/learnsyria/faq.html (Accessed 25 September 2018.)

Safaricom. 2017. *Instant Network Schools (INS)*. Nairobi, Safaricom Twaweza. www.safaricom.co.ke/sustainabilityreport_2017/innovation/instant-network-schools-ins. (Accessed 25 September 2018.)

Tauson, M. and Stannard, L. 2018. *Edtech for Learning in Emergencies and Displaced Settings: a Rigorous Review and Narrative Synthesis*. London, Save the Children.

UNESCO. 2017. *School Violence and Bullying: Global Status Report*. Paris, UNESCO.

___. 2018a. *SDG Thematic Indicator 4.a.2: Safe, Non-violent, Inclusive and Effective Learning Environments – Percentage of Students Who Experienced Bullying during the Past 12 Months, by Sex*. Paris, UNESCO.

___. 2018b. *A Lifeline to Learning: Leveraging Technology to Support Education for Refugees*. Paris, UNESCO.

UNGEI. 2018. *A Whole School Approach to Prevent School-Related Gender-Based Violence: Minimum Standards and Monitoring Framework*. New York, United Nations Girls' Education Initiative.

UNICEF. 2015. *Advancing WASH in Schools Monitoring*. New York, UNICEF.

UNICEF and WHO. 2018. *Drinking Water, Sanitation and Hygiene in Schools: Global Baseline Report 2018*. New York, UNICEF/World Health Organization.

Vodafone Foundation. 2017. *Instant Network Schools: a Connected Education Programme*. Newbury, Vodafone Foundation.

Wang, A., Shi, Y., Yue, A., Lou, R. and Medina, A. 2016. *To Board or Not to Board? Comparing Nutrition, Health and Education Outcomes Between Boarding and Non-Boarding Students in Rural China*. Stanford, CA, Rural Education Action Program.

Wilton, K., Shioiri-Clark, M., Galanek, G. and Murphy, K. 2017. *Parenting in Displacement: Adapting Vroom for Displaced Syrian Families*. New York, International Rescue Committee.

Wimpenny, K., Merry, S. K., Tombs, G. and Villar–Onrubia, D. 2016. *Opening Up Education in South Mediterranean Countries: a Compendium of Case Studies and Interviews with Experts about Open Educational Practices and Resources*. Rome, UniMed.

CHAPTER 16

Baláž, V., Williams, A. and Chrančoková, M. 2018. Connectivity as the facilitator of intra-European student migration. *Population, Space and Place*, Vol. 24, No. 3, p. e2101.

Chao, R. Y. J. 2017. Mobility, mutual recognition and ASEAN Community building: the road to sustainable ASEAN integration. *Journal of International and Comparative Education (JICE)*, Vol. 6, No. 2, pp. 105–21.

Chun, J.-h. 2016. Can CAMPUS Asia program be a next ERASMUS? The possibilities and challenges of the CAMPUS Asia program. *Asia Europe Journal*, Vol. 14, No. 3, pp. 279–96.

European Commission. 2014. *The Erasmus Impact Study: Effects of Mobility on the Skills and Employability of Students and the Internationalisation of Higher Education Institutions*. Luxembourg, Publications Office of the European Union.

___. 2015. *ECTS Users' Guide*. Luxembourg, Publications Office of the European Union.

___. 2016. *The Erasmus Impact Study Regional Analysis*. Luxembourg, European Commission.

___. 2017. *Erasmus+ Annual Report 2016*. Brussels, European Commission.

___. 2018a. *Combined Evaluation of Erasmus+ and Predecessor Programmes: Final Report – Main Evaluation Report*, Vol. 1. Brussels, European Commission.

___. 2018b. *Erasmus+ Programme Guide*. Luxembourg, Publications Office of the European Union.

Flisi, S., Dinis da Costa, P. and Soto-Calvo, E. 2015. *Learning Mobility*. Ispra, Italy, Joint Research Centre.

Flisi, S. and Sánchez-Barrioluengo, M. 2018. *Learning Mobility Benchmark II: an Estimation of the Benchmark*. Luxembourg, Publications Office of the European Union.

Hauschildt, K., Mishra, S., Netz, N. and Gwosc, C. 2015. *Social and Economic Conditions of Student Life in Europe: Eurostudent V 2012-2015*. Bielefeld, Germany, Bertelsmann.

ICEF Monitor. 2018. *Funding for Erasmus+ should double to €30 billion, says European Commission*. Bonn, Germany, International Consultants for Education and Fairs. http://monitor.icef.com/2018/05/funding-erasmus-double-e30-billion-says-european-commission/. (Accessed 1 October 2018.)

Kuhn, T. 2012. Why educational exchange programmes miss their mark: cross-border mobility, education and European identity. *Journal of Common Market Studies*, Vol. 50, No. 6, pp. 994–1010.

Rasplus, J. 2018. ASEAN shares best practice on student mobility. *University World News*, 29 June. www.universityworldnews.com/article.php?story=20180629090604303. (Accessed 1 October 2018.)

Schnepf, S. and D'Hombres, B. 2018. *International Mobility of Italian and UK Students: Does it Pay Off and for Whom?* Ispra, Italy, European Commission.

Schnepf, S., Ghirelli, C. and Verzillo, S. 2017. *Feasibility Study on Measuring the Causal Impact of Erasmus+ Actions*. Ispra, Joint Research Centre.

Schnepf, S. V. 2018. *Unequal Uptake of Higher Education Mobility in the UK: the Importance of Social Segregation in Universities and Subject Areas*. Luxembourg, Publications Office of the European Union. (Working Paper in Economics and Finance 2018/6.)

SHARE. 2016. *Mapping Student Mobility and Credit Transfer Systems in ASEAN Region*. Jakarta, SHARE Project Management Office.

___. 2017. *Studying Abroad, Becoming ASEAN: Regional Student Mobility as a Driver of the ASEAN Community*. Jakarta, SHARE Project Management Office.

Sigalas, E. 2010. Cross-border mobility and European identity: the effectiveness of intergroup contact during the ERASMUS year abroad. *European Union Politics*, Vol. 11, No. 2, pp. 241–65.

Yavaprabhas, S. 2014. The harmonization of higher education in Southeast Asia. Yonezawa, A., Kitamura, Y., Meerman, A. and Kuroda, K. (eds), *Emerging International Dimensions in East Asian Higher Education*. Dordrecht, Netherlands, Springer, pp. 81–102.

Yonezawa, A., Kitamura, Y., Meerman, A. and Kuroda, K. 2014. The emergence of international dimensions in East Asian higher education: pursuing regional and global development. Yonezawa, A., Kitamura, Y., Meerman, A. and Kuroda, K. (eds), *Emerging International Dimensions in East Asian Higher Education*. Dordrecht, Netherlands, Springer, pp. 1–13.

CHAPTER 17

Arab Youth Survey. 2017. *The Middle East: a Region Divided*. Dubai, ASDA'A Burson-Marsteller.

Ávalos, B. and Valenzuela, J. P. 2016. Education for all and attrition/retention of new teachers: a trajectory study in Chile. *International Journal of Educational Development*, Vol. 49, pp. 279–90.

Bense, K. 2016. International teacher mobility and integration: a review and synthesis of the current empirical research and literature. *Educational Research Review*, Vol. 17, pp. 37–49.

Borman, G. D. and Dowling, N. M. 2008. Teacher attrition and retention: a meta-analytic and Narrative review of the research. *Review of Educational Research*, Vol. 78, No. 3, pp. 367–409.

Boyd, D., Grossman, P., Lankford, H., Loeb, S. and Wyckoff, J. 2008. *Who Leaves? Teacher Attrition and Student Achievement*. National Bureau of Economic Research. (Working Paper 14022.)

Cabezas, V. G., Gallego, F., Santelices, V. and Zarhi, M. 2011. *Factores Correlacionados con las Trayectorias Laborales de Docentes en Chile, con Especial Énfasis en sus Atributos Académicos [Factors Correlating with Labour Trajectories of Chilean Teachers, with Special Emphasis on their Academic Characteristics]*. Santiago, Fondo de Investigación y Desarrollo en Educación [Research and Development Fund in Education].

Commonwealth Consortium for Education. 2015. *Commonwealth teacher recruitment protocol*. London, Commonwealth Consortium for Education. http://commonwealtheducation.org/portfolio-items/commonwealth-teacher-recruitment-protocol/. (Accessed 15.11 2017.)

Crush, J., Chikanda, A. and Tawodzera, G. 2012. *The Third Wave: Mixed Migration from Zimbabwe to South Africa*. Cape Town, South Africa, Southern African Migration Programme.

de Villiers, J. J. R. 2017. Career plans of final-year South African student teachers: migration to 'greener pastures'? *Africa Education Review*, Vol. 14, No. 3–4, pp. 212–29.

de Villiers, R. and Books, S. 2009. Recruiting teachers online: marketing strategies and information dissemination practices of UK-based agencies. *Educational Review*, Vol. 61, No. 3, pp. 315–25.

de Villiers, R. and Weda, Z. 2017. Zimbabwean teachers in South Africa: a transient greener pasture. *South African Journal of Education*, Vol. 37, No. 3.

den Brok, P., Wubbels, T. and van Tartwijk, J. W. F. 2017. Exploring beginning teachers' attrition in the Netherlands. *Teachers and Teaching: Theory and Practice*, Vol. 23, No. 8.

EI. 2014. *Getting Teacher Migration & Mobility Right*. Brussels, Education International.

___. 2016. *Discriminatory Practices in the Gulf States*. Brussels, Education International. www.education4refugees.org/teachers-on-the-move/national-and-regional-examples/59-discriminatory-practices-in-the-gulf-states. (Accessed 22 January 2018.)

European Commission. 2017a. *Comparability Study of the Hong Kong Qualifications Framework (HKQF) and the European Qualifications Framework for Lifelong Learning (EQF): Joint Technical Report*. Brussels, European Commission.

___. 2017b. *Erasmus+. The EU programme for education, training, youth and sport (2014-2020)*. Luxembourg, European Commission.

Farah, S. 2011. *Private Tutoring Trends in the UAE*. Dubai, Dubai School of Government. (Policy Brief 26.)

Finster, M. 2015. *Identyfing, Monitoring, and Benchmarking Teacher Retention and Turnover: Guidelines for TIF Grantees*. Washington, DC, Teacher Incentive Fund/United States Department of Education.

Goldring, R., Taie, S. and Riddles, M. 2014. *Teacher Attrition and Mobility: Results From the 2012–13 Teacher Follow-up Survey (NCES 2014-077)*. Washington, DC, National Center for Education Statistics.

Hadley Dunn, A. 2013. *Teachers Without Borders? The Hidden Consequences of International Teachers in U.S. Schools*. New York, Teachers College Press.

INEP. 2018. *Sinopses Estatísticas da Educação Básica [Synopsis of Basic Education Statistics]*. Brasilia, Instituto Nacional de Estudos e Pesquisas Educacionais Anisio Teixeira http://portal.inep.gov.br/web/guest/sinopses-estatisticas-da-educacao-basica. (Accessed 6 July 2018.) (In Portuguese.)

IOM. 2013. *Recognition of Qualifications and Competences of Migrants*. Brussels, International Organization for Migration.

___. 2014. *Needs Assessment in the Nigerian Education System*. Abuja, International Organization for Migration.

Jha, N. and Ryan, C. 2017. *The Careers of Teachers in Australia: a Descriptive Study*. Melbourne, Australia, Melbourne Institute Applied Economic and Social Research.

Kapiszewski, A. 2006. *Arab versus Asian Migrant Workers in the GCC Countries*. Beirut, United Nations Secretariat Population Division.

Keevy, J., Green, W. and Manik, S. 2014. *The Status of Migrant Teachers in South Africa*. Waterkloof, South African Qualifications Authority.

Lindqvist, P., Nordänger, U. K. and Carlsson, R. 2014. Teacher attrition the first five years: a multifaceted image. *Teaching and Teacher Education*, Vol. 40, pp. 94–103.

Le Donné, N. 2018. *Diversity and Equity in TALIS 2018 3rd Policy Forum: Strength Through Diversity and GEMR*. Paris, Organisation for Economic Co-operation and Development.

Macdonald, D. 1999. Teacher attrition: a review of literature. *Teaching and Teacher Education*, Vol. 15, No. 8, pp. 835–48.

Manik, S. 2014. South African migrant teachers' decision-making: levels of influence and 'relative deprivation'. *Journal of Southern African Studies*, Vol. 40, No. 1, pp. 151–65.

McKenzie, P., Weldon, P., Rowley, G., Murphy, M. and McMillan, J. 2014. *Staff in Australia's Schools 2013: Main Report on the Survey*. Canberra, Australian Council for Educational Research.

Nicotera, A., Pepper, M., Springer, J. and Milanowski, A. 2017. *Analyzing Teacher Retention by Performance Level and School Need Examples From Maricopa County: Case Study*. Washington DC, Teacher Inventive Fund.

Niyubahwe, A., Mukamurera, J. and Jutras, F. 2013. Professional integration of immigrant teachers in the school system: a literature review. *McGill Journal of Education*, Vol. 48, No. 2, pp. 279–96.

OECD. 2005. *Teachers Matter: Attracting, Developing and Retaining Effective Teachers*. Paris, Organisation for Economic Co-operation and Development.

OFSTED and Wilshaw, M. 2016. *HMCI's Monthly Commentary: February 2016*. London, UK Government. http://dera.ioe.ac.uk/25655/1/HMCI%27s%20monthly%20commentary%20February%202016%20-%20Authored%20articles%20-%20GOV_UK.pdf. (Accessed 1 October 2018.)

Plecki, M. L., Elfers, A. M. and van Windekens, A. 2017. *Examining Beginning Teacher Retention and Mobility in Washington State*. Seattle, WA, Washingon State Office of Superintendent of Public Instruction.

Ridge, N., Shami, S. and Kippels, S. 2017. Arab migrant teachers in the United Arab Emirates and Qatar: challenges and opportunities. Babar, Z. (ed.), *Arab Migrant Communities in GCC*. New York, Oxford University Press.

Skolverket. 2018. *Apply for certification with a foreign diploma*. Stockolm, Skolverket. www.skolverket.se/regler-och-ansvar/larar--och-forskollararlegitimation/larar--och-forskollararlegitimation-med-utlandsk-examen/certification-of-teachers-with-a-foreign-dimploma. (Accessed 2 October 2018.)

Startz, D. 2017. *Immigrant teachers play a critical role in American schools*. Washington, DC, Brookings Institution. www.brookings.edu/blog/brown-center-chalkboard/2017/03/16/immigrant-teachers-play-a-critical-role-in-american-schools. (Accessed 15 September 2018.)

UIS. 2016. *Glossary: teacher attrition rate*. Montreal, Que., UNESCO Institute for Statistics. http://uis.unesco.org/node/334809. (Accessed 31 May 2018.)

UNESCO. 2009. *Secondary Teacher Policy Research in Asia: Teacher Numbers, Teacher Quality – Lessons from Secondary Educaiton in Asia*. Bangkok, UNESCO.

UNESCO. 2014. *Teacher Issues in Uganda: a Shared Vision for an Effective Teachers Policy*. Kampala/Dakar, Uganda Ministry of Education and Sport/UNESCO International Institute for Educational Planning (Pôlel de Dakar).

UNESCO/Commonwealth Secretariat. 2012. *Next Steps in Managing Teacher Migration: Papers of the Sixth Commonwealth Research Symposium on Teacher Mobility, Recruitment and Migration*. Paris/London, UNESCO/ Commonwealth Secretariat.

United Kingdom Government. 2016. *Immigration Rules*. London, UK Government. www.gov.uk/guidance/immigration-rules/immigration-rules-appendix-k-shortage-occupation-list. (Accessed 20 January 2018.)

Weldon, P. 2018. Early career teacher attrition in Australia: evidence, definition, classification and measurement. *Australian Journal of Education*, Vol. 62, No. 1, pp. 61–78.

CHAPTER 18

Aufseeser, D., Bourdillon, M., Carothers, R. and Lecoufle, O. 2018. Children's work and children's well-being: implications for policy. *Development Policy Review*, Vol. 36, No. 2, pp. 241–61.

Bouton, S., Cis, D., Mendonca, L., Pohl, H., Remes, J., Ritchie, H. and Woetzel, J. 2013. *How to Make a City Great: a Review of the Steps City Leaders Around the World Take to Transform their Cities into Great Places to Live and Work*. New York, McKinsey.

Canavera, M., Akesson, B. and Landis, D. 2014. *Social Service Workforce Training in the West and Central Africa Region*. Geneva, Switzerland, UNICEF/CPC Learning Network.

Cruz, I. G. L. 2017. Policing, schooling and human capital accumulation. *Journal of Economic Behavior and Organization*. pp. 1–26.

Dammert, A. C., de Hoop, J., Mvukiyehe, E. and Rosati, F. C. 2018. Effects of public policy on child labor: current knowledge, gaps, and implications for program design. *World Development*, Vol. 110, pp. 104–23.

Danby, N. 2017. *Lessons from Inspector Clouseau: what America's police can learn from Europe*. Boston, Harvard Political Review. http://harvardpolitics.com/online/lessons-inspector-clouseau-americas-police-can-learn-european-nations/ (Accessed May 24 2018.)

EUFRA. 2017. *Current Migration Situation in the EU: Community Policing*. Vienna, European Union Agency for Fundamental Rights.

Fielding, D. 2018. The Co-evolution of education and tolerance: evidence from England. *Social Forces*, Vol. 96, No. 4, pp. 1825–50.

Friedemann, B. 2016. *City to City: a Guide to the UCLG Learning Universe*. Barcelona, Spain, United Cities and Local Governments.

Ghignoni, E., Croce, G. and Ricci, A. 2018. Fixed term contracts and employers' human capital: the role of educational spillovers. *Papers in Regional Science*, Vol. 97, No. 2, pp. 301–22.

Global Social Service Workforce Alliance. 2015. *The State of the Social Service Workforce 2015 Report: a Multi-Country Review*. Washington, DC, Global Social Service Workforce Alliance.

___. 2016. *The State of the Social Service Workforce 2016 Report*. Washington, DC, Global Social Service Workforce Alliance.

IntraHealth International. 2013. *An Assessment of the Public Sector Social Service Workforce in Ethiopia*. Chapel Hill, N.C./ Washington, DC/Addis Ababa/New York, IntraHealth International/US Agency for International Development/ Ethiopia Ministry of Labour and Social Affairs/UNICEF.

IOM Indonesia. 2016. *National Police Chief Launches Two-year IOM Indonesia Training for 7,000 Female Officers*. Bandar Lampung, Indonesia, International Organization for Migration. https://indonesia.iom.int/national-police-chief-launches-two-year-iom-indonesia-training-7000-female-officers. (Accessed 15 September 2018.)

Jetter, M. and Parmeter, C. F. 2018. Sorting through global corruption determinants: institutions and education matter – not culture. *World Development*, Vol. 109, pp. 279–94.

Maru, V. 2009. *Access to Justice and Legal Empowerment: a Review of World Bank Practice*. Washington, DC, World Bank. (Justice and Development Working Paper 9/2009.)

Meshram, D. S. and Meshram, S. 2016. Energizing planning education in India. Kumar, A., Meshram, D. S. and Gowda, K. (eds), *Urban and Regional Planning Education: Learning for India*. New Delhi, Springer, pp. 17–32.

Mordechay, K. and Ayscue, J. B. 2018. Policies needed to build inclusive cities and schools. *Education Policy Analysis Archives*, Vol. 26, p. 98.

Namati. 2014. *Building a movement of grassroots legal advocates*. San Francisco, CA, Namati. https://namati.org/wp-content/uploads/2015/02/Namati-who-we-are-how-we-work-where-were-going.pdf. (Accessed 17 September 2018.)

New York State Commission on Judicial Conduct. 2017. *New York State Commission on Judicial Conduct: Annual Report 2017*. New York, New York State Commission on Judicial Conduct.

OECD and Open Society Foundations. 2016. *Leveraging the SDGs for Inclusive Growth: Delivering Access to Justice for All*. Paris, Organisation for Economic Co-operation and Development.

Orme, B. 2018. *School of Judges: Lessons in Freedom of Information and Expression from (and for) Latin America's Courtrooms*. Paris, UNESCO.

Paterson, C. 2011. Adding value? A review of the international literature on the role of higher education in police training and education. *Police Practice and Research*, Vol. 12, No. 4, pp. 286–97.

Pearman, F. A. and Swain, W. A. 2017. School choice, gentrification, and the variable significance of racial stratification in urban neighborhoods. *Sociology of Education*, Vol. 90, No. 3, pp. 213–35.

Pyman, M., Cohen, J., Boardman, M., Webster, B. and Seymour, N. 2012. *Arresting Corruption in the Police: the Global Experience of Police Corruption Reform Efforts*. London, Transparency International UK.

Roby, J. 2016. *The Evidence Base on the Social Service Workforce: Current Knowledge, Gaps and Future Research Direction*. Washington, DC, Global Service Workforce Alliance.

Rydberg, J. and Terrill, W. 2010. The effect of higher education on police behavior. *Police Quarterly*, Vol. 13, No. 1, pp. 92–120.

Sabet, D. 2010. Police reform in Mexico: Advances and persistent obstacles. Olson, E. L., Donnelly, R. A. and Shirk, D. A. (eds), *Shared Responsibility*. Washington, DC, Mexico Institute, pp. 247–69.

Thijs, P., Te Grotenhuis, M. and Scheepers, P. 2018. The paradox of rising ethnic prejudice in times of educational expansion and secularization in the Netherlands, 1985–2011. *Social Indicators Research*, pp. 1–26.

UCLG. 2010. *Policy Paper on Urban Strategic Planning: Local Leaders Preparing for the Future of Our Cities*. Barcelona, Spain, United Cities and Local Governments.

UCLG and Learning UCLG. 2018. *Monitoring the Global Agenda in Municipalities: the Mandala Tool*. Barcelona, Spain, United Cities and Local Governments/Learning UCLG/United Nations Development Programme.

UN Habitat. 2016a. *Capacity Building and Knowledge Form the Foundation of the New Urban Agenda: a Position Paper*. Nairobi, United Nations Human Settlements Programme.

___. 2016b. *Urbanization and Development: Emerging Futures – World Cities Report 2016*. Nairobi, United Nations Human Settlements Programme.

UNDESA. 2014. *World Urbanization Prospects 2014*. New York, United Nations Department of Economic and Social Affairs.

UNDP. 2017. *Global Programme on Strengthening the Rule of Law and Human Rights for Sustaining Peace and Fostering Development: 2016 Annual Report*. New York, United Nations Development Programme.

UNODC. 2011. *Resource Guide on Strengthening Judicial Integrity and Capacity*. Vienna, United Nations Office on Drugs and Crime.

___. 2013. *Training of trainers to enhance police response in addressing child sexual exploitation in the Mekong*. Bangkok, United Nations Office on Drugs and Crime. www.unodc.org/southeastasiaandpacific/en/2013/08/childhood-training/story.html. (Accessed May 24 2018.)

___. 2016. *Global Study on Legal Aid: Global Report*. New York, United Nations Office on Drugs and Crime.

UNODC Statistics. 2017. *Criminal Justice: Total Police Personnel and Total Professional Judges or Magistrates*. Vienna, United Nations Office on Drugs and Crime. https://data.unodc.org/. (Accessed 29 May 2018.)

Watson, V. and Agbola, B. 2013. *Who Will Plan Africa's Cities?* London, Africa Research Institute.

Wodtke, G. T. and Parbst, M. 2017. Neighborhoods, schools, and academic achievement: a formal mediation analysis of contextual effects on reading and mathematics abilities. *Demography*, Vol. 54, No. 5, pp. 1653–76.

World Bank. 2003. *Legal and Judicial Reform: Strategic Directions*. Washington, DC, World Bank.

Yan, H. 2016. States require more training time to become a barber than a police officer. *CNN*, 28 September. https://edition.cnn.com/2016/09/28/us/jobs-training-police-trnd/index.html. (Accessed May 24 2018.)

CHAPTER 19

Acerenza, S. and Gandelman, N. 2017. *Household Education Spending in Latin America and the Caribbean: Evidence from Income and Expenditure Surveys*. Washington, DC, Inter-American Development Bank. (Working Paper IDB-WP-773.)

Acosta, P. 2006. *Labor Supply, School Attendance, and Remittances from International Migration : the Case of El Salvador*. Washington, DC, World Bank. (Policy Research Working Paper 3903.)

Adams, R. H. and Cuecuecha, A. 2010. Remittances, household expenditure and investment in Guatemala. *World Development*, Vol. 38, No. 11, pp. 1626–41.

Amuedo-Dorantes, C. and Pozo, S. 2010. Accounting for remittance and migration effects on children's schooling. *World Development*, Vol. 38, No. 12, pp. 1747–59.

Angelucci, M. 2015. Migration and financial constraints: evidence from Mexico. *Review of Economics and Statistics*, Vol. 97, No. 1, pp. 224-28.

Antman, F. M. 2012. Gender, educational attainment, and the impact of parental migration on children left behind. *Journal of Population Economics*, Vol. 25, No. 4, pp. 1187–214.

Askarov, Z. and Doucouliagos, H. 2018. *A meta-analysis of the effects of remittances on on household education expenditure*. Paris, UNESCO.

Aviles, S. 2017. *Finance Outcomes, Not Fragmentation: Shift from Funding to Financing Analytical Paper on WHS Self-Reporting on Agenda for Humanity Transformation 5D*. New York, Agenda for Humanity.

Azam, J.-P. and Gubert, F. 2006. Migrants' remittances and the household in Africa: a review of evidence. *Journal of African Economies*, Vol. 15, No. suppl 2, pp. 426–62.

Bansak, C. and Chezum, B. 2009. How do remittances affect human capital formation of school-age boys and girls? *American Economic Review*, Vol. 99, No. 2, pp. 145–48.

Bazzi, S. 2017. Wealth heterogeneity and the income elasticity of migration. *American Economic Journal: Applied Economics*, Vol. 9, No. 2, pp. 219–55.

Bendavid-Hadar, I. and Ziderman, A. 2010. *A New Model for Equitable and Efficient Resource Allocation to Schools: the Israeli Case*. Bonn, Germany, UNESCO.

Bermeo, S. B. and Leblang, D. 2015. Migration and foreign aid. *International Organization*, Vol. 69, No. 3, pp. 627–57.

Berthélemy, J.-C., Beuran, M. and Maurel, M. 2009. Aid and migration: substitutes or complements? *World Development*, Vol. 37, No. 10, pp. 1589–99.

Boeri, T. 2010. Immigration to the land of redistribution. *Economica*, Vol. 77, No. 308, pp. 651–87.

Bouoiyour, J., Miftah, A. and Mouhoud, E. M. 2016. Education, male gender preference and migrants' remittances: interactions in rural Morocco. *Economic Modelling*, Vol. 57, pp. 324–31.

Bourenane, N., Bourjij, S. and Lheriau, L. 2011. *Reducing the Cost of Migrant Remittances to Optimize their Impact on Development: Financial Products and Tools for the Maghreb Region and the Franc Zone*. Paris, French Development Agency/African Development Bank.

Brown, R. P., Connell, J. and Jimenez-Soto, E. V. 2014. Migrants' remittances, poverty and social protection in the South Pacific: Fiji and Tonga. *Population, Space and Place*, Vol. 20, No. 5, pp. 434–54.

Calero, C., Bedi, A. S. and Sparrow, R. 2009. Remittances, liquidity constraints and human capital investments in Ecuador. *World Development*, Vol. 37, No. 6, pp. 1143–54.

California Department of Education. 2018. *Migrant Education Program Fundind*. Sacramento, CA, California Department of Education. www.cde.ca.gov/sp/me/mt/funding.asp. (Accessed 17 September 2018.)

Canada Office of the Prime Minister. 2018. *Canada and partners announce historic investment in education for women and girls in crisis and conflict situations*. Ottawa, Government of Canada. https://pm.gc.ca/eng/news/2018/06/09/canada-and-partners-announce-historic-investment-education-women-and-girls-crisis. (Accessed 3 October 2018.)

Castaldo, A., Deshingkar, P. and McKay, A. 2012. *Internal Migration, Remittances and Poverty: Evidence from Ghana and India*. Brighton, UK, Migrating out of Poverty Research Programme Consortium. (Working Paper 7.)

Clemens, M. A. and Postel, H. 2018. *Deterring Emigration with Foreign Aid: An Overview of Evidence from Low-Income Countries*. Washington, DC, Center for Global Development. (Policy Paper 119.)

Clemens, M. A., Radelet, S., Bhavnani, R. R. and Bazzi, S. 2012. Counting chickens when they hatch: timing and the effects of aid on growth. *Economic Journal*, Vol. 122, No. 561, pp. 590–617.

Clemens, M. A. and Tiongson, E. R. 2017. Split decisions: household finance when a policy discontinuity allocates overseas work. *Review of Economics and Statistics*, Vol. 99, No. 3, pp. 531–43.

Czaika, M. and Mayer, A. 2011. Refugee movements and aid responsiveness of bilateral donors. *Journal of Development Studies*, Vol. 47, No. 3, pp. 455–74.

Dao, T. H., Docquier, F., Parsons, C. and Peri, G. 2016. *Migration and Development: Dissecting the Anatomy of the Mobility Transition*. Louvain-la-Neuve, Institut de Recherches Économiques et Sociales de l'Université catholique de Louvain.

Davis, J. and Brazil, N. 2016. Disentangling fathers' absences from household remittances in international migration: the case of educational attainment in Guatemala. *International Journal of Educational Development*, Vol. 50, pp. 1–11.

de Haas, H. 2007. Turning the tide? Why development will not stop migration. *Development and Change*, Vol. 38, No. 5, pp. 819–41.

Démurger, S. and Wang, X. 2016. Remittances and expenditure patterns of the left behinds in rural China. *China Economic Review*, Vol. 37, pp. 177–90.

di Gropello, E. 2006. *Meeting the Challenges of Secondary Education in Latin America and East Asia: Improving Efficiency and Resource Mobilization*. Washington, DC, World Bank.

Dreher, A., Fuchs, A. and Langlotz, S. 2018. *The Effects of Foreign Aid on Refugee Flows*. Munich, Germany, CESifo Group Munich.

Dustmann, C. and Okatenko, A. 2014. Out-migration, wealth constraints, and the quality of local amenities. *Journal of Development Economics*,Vol. 110, pp. 52–63.

ECW. 2018a. *US$1.8 billion required for Education Cannot Wait to support 8.9 million children and youth by 2021*. Washington, DC, Education Cannot Wait. www.educationcannotwait.org/hlsg. (Accessed 3 October 2018.)

___. 2018b. *Results Report: April 2017–March 2018*. Washington, DC, Education Cannot Wait.

___.2018c. *Strategic Plan*. Education Cannot Wait. Washington, DC, Education Cannot Wait.

Education Commission. 2017. *Resilience building and humanitarian: development nexus*. Luxembourg, European Commission. https://ec.europa.eu/europeaid/policies/fragility-and-crisis-management/resilience-building-humanitarian-development-nexus_en. (Accessed 3 October 2018.)

___. 2018. *Principles for the Design of the International Financing Facility for Education*. New York, Education Commission.

Essomba, M. A., Tarrés, A. and Franco-Guillén, N. 2017. *Research for CULT Committee: Migrant Education – Monitoring and Assessment*. Brussels, European Parliament.

European Parliament. 2016. *At a Glance: Integrating Migrants and their Children through Education*. Brussels, European Parliament.

Fanjul, G. 2018. *The Externalisation of Europe's Responsibilities*. Madrid, Research Centre for Policy Coherence and Development.

Farrie, D., Luhm, T. and Johnson, E. M. 2015. *Understanding New Jersey's School Funding Formula: the Role of Adjustment Aid*. Pittsburgh, Pa., Education Law Center.

Fazekas, M. 2012. *School Funding Formulas: Review of Main Characteristics and Impacts*. Paris, Organisation for Economic Co-operation and Development.

Foko, B., Tiyab, B. K. and Husson, G. 2012. *An Analytical and Comparative Perspective for 15 African Countries Household Education Spending*. Dakar, Pôle de Dakar.

Fratzscher, V. M. and Junker, S. 2015. *Integration von Flüchtlingen: eine langfristig lohnende Investition [Integration of Refugees: a Long-Term Worthwhile Investment]*. Berlin, DIW Wochenbericht. (In German.)

Freund, C. and Spatafora, N. 2005. *Remittances: Transaction Costs, Determinants, and Informal Flows*. Washington, DC, World Bank. (Policy Research Working Paper 3704.)

Gamso, J. and Yuldashev, F. 2018a. Does rural development aid reduce international migration? *World Development*, Vol. 110, pp. 268–82.

___. 2018b. Targeted foreign aid and international migration: Is development promotion an effective immigration policy? *International Studies Quarterly*, No. 029.

Germany Federal Office for Migrants and Refugees (2011). *Lehrkräfte mit Migrationshintergrund: Handlungsempfehlungen zum Netzwerkaufbau [Teachers with a Migration Background: Recommendations for Network Building]*. Nuremberg, BAMF/ Hertie Fundation. (In German.)

Gibson, J., Boe-Gibson, G., Rohorua, H. T. a. S. and McKenzie, D. 2007. Efficient remittance services for development in the Pacific. *Asia-Pacific Development Journal*, Vol. 14, No. 2, pp. 55–74.

Global Education Cluster. 2010. *The Short Guide to Rapid Joint Education Needs Assessments*. Geneva, Switzerland, Global Education Cluster.

GPE. 2018. *Global Partnership for Education launches new public-private initiative to address the data challenge in global education*. Washington, DC, Global Partnership for Education. www.globalpartnership.org/news-and-media/news/global-partnership-education-launches-new-public-private-initiative-address-data-challenge-global-education. (Accessed 3 October 2018.)

Gubert, F. and Nordman, C. J. 2009. *Migration trends in North Africa: focus on Morocco, Tunisia and Algeria*. Paris, Organisation for Economic Co-operation and Development.

Ibourk, A. and Bensaïd, M. 2014. Impact des transferts de fonds des migrants marocains sur l'éducation de leurs enfants restés au Maroc [Impact of Moroccan migrants' remittances on the education of their children left behind in Morocco]. *Migrations Société*, No. 5, pp. 13–28.

Kandel, W. and Massey, D. S. 2002. The culture of Mexican migration: a theoretical and empirical analysis. *Social Forces*, Vol. 80, No. 3, pp. 981–1004.

Kandel, W. A. 2011. *Fiscal Impacts of the Foreign-Born Population*. Washington, D,C, Congressional Research Service.

Karamperidou, D., Richardson, D. Zapata, J. 2018. *Education in Multi-Sectoral Responses to Displacement Crises*. Florence, Italy, UNICEF Office of Research – Innocenti. (Background paper for *Global Education Monitoring Report 2019*.)

Klein, A. 2018. DeVos team considering reshuffling of Education Department's main K-12 office. *Education Week*, 13 May. https://blogs.edweek.org/edweek/campaign-k-12/2018/05/devos_department_budget_consolidate_OESE.html. (Accessed 5 October 2018.)

Lanati, M. and Thiele, R. 2017. *The Impact of Foreign Aid on Migration Revisited*. Fiesole, Italy, European University Institute.

Loveday, J. and Molina, O. 2006. *Remesas Internacionales y Bienestar: una Aproximación para el Caso Peruano – Informe Final [International Remittances and Welfare: an Approach for the Peruvian Case – Final Report]*. Lima, Consorcio de Investigación Económica y Social [Consortium of Economic and Social Research].

Lucas, R. E. 2005. *International Migration and Economic Development: Lessons from Low-income Countries*. Northampton, MA, Edward Elgar.

Mansour, W., Chaaban, J. and Litchfield, J. 2011. The impact of migrant remittances on school attendance and education attainment: evidence from Jordan. *International Migration Review*, Vol. 45, No. 4, pp. 812–51.

McKenzie, D. and Rapoport, H. 2006. *Can Migration Reduce Educational Attainment? Evidence from Mexico*. Washington, DC, World Bank. (Policy Research Working Paper 3952.)

Metcalfe-Hough, V. and Poole, L. 2018. *Grand Bargain Annual Independent Report 2018*. London, Humanitarian Policy Group.

National Academies of Sciences, Engineering and Medicine. 2017. Estimating the fiscal impacts of immigration: conceptual issues. Mackie, C. and Blau, F. D. (eds), *The Economic and Fiscal Consequences of Immigration*. Washington, DC, The National Academies Press.

Nguyen, C. V. and Nguyen, H. Q. 2015. Do internal and international remittances matter to health, education and labor of children and adolescents? The case of Vietnam. *Children and Youth Services Review*, Vol. 58, pp. 28–34.

NRC and Save the Children. 2015. *Walk the Talk: Review of Donors' Humanitarian Policies on Education*. Oslo, Norwegian Refugee Council/Save the Children Norway.

OCHA. 2017. *No time to retreat: First Annual Synthesis Report on Progress since the World Humanitarian Summit*. New York, United Nations Office for the Coordination of Humanitarian Affairs.

____. 2018. *New Way of Working*. New York, Agenda for Humanity. www.agendaforhumanity.org/initiatives/5358. (Accessed 15 September 2017).

OCHA and UNDP. 2018. *Transcend humanitarian-development divides and shift from funding to financing: Analytical Paper on WHS Self-Reporting on Agenda for Humanity Transformations 4C and 5D*. New York, Agenda for Humanity.

OECD. 2009. *International Migration and the Economic Criris: Understanding the Links and Shaping Policy Responses*. Paris, Organisation for Economic Co-operation and Development.

____. *Education at a Glance: OECD Indicators 2011 Annex 3 – Sources, Methods and Technical Notes, Chapter B: Financial Investment in Education*. Paris, Organisation for Economic Co-operation and Development.

____. 2012. *Equity and Quality in Education: Supporting Disadvantaged Students and Schools*. Paris, Organisation for Economic Co-operation and Development.

____. 2013. *International Migration Outlook 2013*. Paris, Organisation for Economic Co-operation and Development.

____. 2015. *Why Modernise Official Development Assistance?* Paris, Organisation for Economic Co-operation and Development.

____. 2017. *OECD Reviews of School Resources: The Funding of School Education Connecting Resources and Learning*. Paris, Organisation for Economic Co-operation and Development.

OECD CRS. 2018. *Creditor Reporting System*. Paris, Organisation for Economic Co-operation and Development. https://stats.oecd.org/Index.aspx?DataSetCode=CRS1. (Accessed 5 November 2019.)

ODI. 2016. *Education Cannot Wait Proposing a Fund for Education in Emergencies*. London, Overseas Development Institute.

Oregon Department of Education. 2018. *Title I-C Migrant Education*. Salem, OR, Department of Education.

Parida, J. K., Mohanty, S. K. and Raman, K. R. 2015. Remittances, household expenditure and investment in rural India: evidence from NSS data. *Indian Economic Review*, Vol. L, No. 1, pp. 79–104.

Powers, E. T. 2011. *The Impact of Economic Migration on Children's Cognitive Development: Evidence from the Mexican Family Life Survey*. Washington, DC, Inter-American Development Bank. (Working Paper 246.)

Ratha, D., Mohapatra, S., Özden, Ç., Plaza, S., Shaw, W. and Shimeles, A. 2011. *Leveraging Migration for Africa: Remittances, Skills, and Investments*. Washington, DC, World Bank.

Ravn, B. 2009. *Country Report Denmark: Parental involvement including ethnic minority parents in Denmark 2009*. Copenhagen, Danish School of Education. www.involve-migrants-improve-school.eu/fileadmin/user_upload/Country_Reports/Denmark.pdf. (Accessed 5 November 2019.)

Riddell, A. and Niño-Zarazua, M. 2016. The efectiveness of foreign aid to education: what can be learned? *International Journal of Educational Development*, Vol. 48, pp. 23–36.

Robles, V. F. and Oropesa, R. S. 2011. International migration and the education of children: evidence from Lima, Peru. *Population Research and Policy Review*, Vol. 30, No. 4, pp. 591–618.

Roos, M. 2017. *Entwicklungen von 2014 bis 2016 im Programm QUIMS mit Fokus auf den obligatorischen Schwerpunkten [Developments from 2014 to 2016 in the QUIMS Programme with a Focus on Compulsory Subjects]*. Baar, Switzerland Volksschulamts des Kantons/Spetrum3 GmbH.

Save the Children. 2018. *Time to Act*. London, Save the Children UK.

Scholten, P., Baggerman, F., Dellouche, L., Kampen, V., Wolf, J. and Ypma, R. 2017. *Policy Innovation in Refugee Integration? A Comparative Analysis of Innovative Policy Strategies toward Refugee Integration in Europe*. Rotterdam, Netherlands, Dutch Department of Social Affairs and Employment.

Semyonov, M. and Gorodzeisky, A. 2006. Labor migration, remittances and household income: a comparison between Filipino and Filipina overseas workers. *International Migration Review*, Vol. 39, No. 1, pp. 45–68.

Statistics Canada. 2015. *Chapter B Financial resources invested in education*. Ottawa, Statistics Canada. www150.statcan.gc.ca/n1/pub/81-604-x/2014001/ch/chb-eng.htm. (Accessed 16 September 2018).

____. 2017. *Chapter B Financial resources invested in education*. Ottawa, Statistics Canada. www150.statcan.gc.ca/n1/pub/81-604-x/2016001/ch/chb-eng.htm. (Accessed 16 September 2018).

Sugarman, J., Morris-Lange, S. and Margie, M. 2016. *Improving Education for Migrant-Background Students: a Transatlantic Comparison of School Funding*. Washington, DC., Migration Policy Institute.

Uganda Ministry of Education and Sports. 2018. *Education Response Plan for Refugees and Host Communities in Uganda*. Kampa, Ministry of Education and Sports.

United States Department of Education. 2018a. *Fiscal Year 2018 Budget Summary and Background Information*. Washington, DC, Department of Education.

____. 2018b. *U.S. Department of Education Budget News*. Washington, DC, Department of Education.

UNESCO. 2013. *Financing Secondary Education in the Asia-Pacific Region: Education Policy Research Series Discussion Document*. Bangkok, UNESCO Asia and Pacific Regional Bureau for Education.

____. 2015a. *Incheon Declaration and Framework for Action for the Implementation of Sustainable Development Goal 4*. Paris, UNESCO.

____. 2015b. *Pricing the Right to Education: the Cost of Reaching New Targets by 2030*. Paris, UNESCO.

____. 2015c. *Humanitarian Aid for Education: Why It Matters and Why More is Needed?* Paris, UNESCO (*Education for All Global Monitoring Report* Policy Paper 21).

UNHCR. 2016. UNHCR and GPE agree on closer collaboration to ensure children's education during crisis. Geneva, Switzerland, United Nations High Commissioner on Refugees. www.unhcr.org/news/press/2016/4/572a43b94/unhcr-and-gpe-agree-on-closer-collaboration-to-ensure-childrens-education.html. (Accessed 15 September 2018).

____. 2017. *East, Horn of Africa and the Great Lakes Region Refugees and Asylum Seekers by country of Asylum as of 30 September 2017*. Geneva, Switzerland, United Nations High Commissioner on Refugees. https://data2.unhcr.org/es/documents/download/60678. (Accessed 1 September 2018).

United Kingdom Department of Education. 2017. *The National Funding Formula for Schools and High Needs*. London, Department of Education.

United Nations. 2016. *One Humanity: Shared Responsibility*. New York, United Nations.

Vargas-Silva, C. 2017. *The Fiscal Impact of Immigration in the UK*. Oxford, Migration Observatory/Centre on Migration/Policy and Society.

Vázquez, S. T. and Sobrao, D. G. 2016. Reshaping geographical allocation of aid: the role of immigration in Spanish official development assistance. *Journal of International Relations and Development*, Vol. 19, No. 3, pp. 333–64.

Watkins, K. and Quattri, M. 2014. *Lost in Intermediation: How Excessive Charges Undermine the Benefits of Remittances for Africa*. London, Overseas Development Institute.

Whittaker, F. 2018. *Full National Funding Formula Roll-Out Delayed until 2021*. London, Schools Week. https://schoolsweek.co.uk/full-national-funding-formula-roll-out-delayed-until-2021/. (Accessed 5 October 2018.)

Winthrop, R. and Matsui, E. 2013. *A New Agenda for Education in Fragile States*. Washington, DC, Brookings Institution, Center for Universal Education. (Working Paper 10.)

World Bank. 2016. *World Bank Goup Global Crisis Response Platform*. Washington, DC, World Bank.

___. 2017a. *IDA18 Regional Sub-window for Refugees and Host Communities*. Washington, DC, World Bank. http://ida.worldbank.org/financing/replenishments/ida18-overview/ida18-regional-sub-window-for-refugees-host-communities. (Accessed 15 September 2018).

___. 2017 b. 2016-2017 *Annual Report*. Washington, DC, Global Concessional Financing Facility/World Bank.

___. 2018a. *Migration and Remittances: Recent Developments and Outlook*. Washington, DC, World Bank. (Migration and Development Brief 29.)

___. 2018b. *Remittance Prices Worldwide*. Washington, DC, World Bank. (Issue 25, March.)

Xuequan, M. 2018. *Factbox: China's rural workers in 2017*. Beijing, Xinhua. www.xinhuanet.com/english/2018-05/01/c_137149523.htm. (Accessed 1 August 2018.)

Yang, D. 2005. *International Migration, Human Capital, and Entrepreneurship: Evidence from Philippine Migrants' Exchange Rate Shocks*. Washington, DC, World Bank. (Policy Research Working Paper 3578.)

Yang, D. and Choi, H. 2007. Are remittances insurance? Evidence from rainfall shocks in the Philippines. *World Bank Economic Review*, Vol. 21, No. 2, pp. 219–48.

Zurich Education Department. 2011a. *Mehrsprachig und interkulturell: Beispiele gutter Zusammenarbeit zwischen Lehrpersonen der Heimatlichen Sprache und Kultur (HSK) und der Volksschule [Multilingual and Intercultural: Examples of Good Cooperation between Teachers of the Native Language and Culture (HSK) and Elementary Schools]*. Zurich Canton Education Directorate, Switzerland. (In German.)

___. 2011b. *Rahmenlehrplan für Heimatliche Sprache und Kultur (HSK) [Curriculum for Native Language and Culture]*. Zurich Canton Education Directorate, Switzerland. (In German.)

___. 2014. *Schwerpunkte von QUIMS 2014-2017 [Focus: QUIMS 2014-2017]*. Zurich Canton Education Directorate, Switzerland. (In German.)

___. 2016. *Heimatliche Sprache und Kultur (HSK) in der Zürcher Volksschule: Zusammenfassender Bericht 2016 [Native Language and Culture (HSK) in Zurich Elementary Schools: Summary Report 2016]*. Zurich Canton Education Directorate, Switzerland. (In German.)

Country index

This index covers the Executive Summary and Chapters 1 to 20. Page numbers in *italics* indicate infographics, figures and tables; those in **bold** refer to material in boxes; ***bold italics*** indicates a figure or table in a box. Definitions of terms can be found in the glossary, and additional information on countries can be found in the aid tables and statistical annex.

J

K

L

M

N

O

P

Q

R

S

T

U

V

Y

Z